ALEXANDER
POPE

*selected poetry
& prose*

The medallion of Pope, by his friend Jonathan Richardson the elder, is taken from the title page of the authorized edition of Pope's LETTERS, 1737.

ALEXANDER POPE

selected poetry
& prose

SECOND EDITION
Edited with an Introduction by
William K. Wimsatt

HOLT, RINEHART AND WINSTON, INC.
New York   Chicago   San Francisco   Atlanta
Dallas   Montreal   Toronto   London   Sydney

IN MEMORIAM
W.A.W.

CONTENTS

FOREWORD

The human learner, we are told, learns a half of all he ever knows by the age of two or three, and is half as tall as he will ever be. The image of an author transmitted by the earliest of his editors and biographers has a similar status. The letters of Pope edited and published by himself, the editorial labors of Pope and Warburton upon the poems, the anecdotes so assiduously put down by Spence, are the grounds of all that follows. Still, there is a sense in which the professor is more than twice the infant. The most recent twenty years in scholarship devoted to the life and works of Alexander Pope give us an impressive, even frightening, instance of the kind of growth that can occur in maturity. Three events of maximum import may be cited: the late George Sherburn's edition of the *Correspondence of Alexander Pope,* in five volumes, 1956; the completion of the Twickenham edition of the *Poems of Pope* (Vol. vi, *Minor Poems,* by Norman Ault and John Butt, 1954; Vol. i, *Pastoral Poetry and An Essay on Criticism,* by E. Audra and Aubrey L. Williams, 1961; Vols. vii–x, the *Iliad* and *Odyssey,* by Maynard Mack and associates, 1967); and the variorum edition in two volumes of the *Anecdotes* of Joseph Spence, by James M. Osborn, 1966. The same period has seen a concomitant tidal wave of bibliographical, biographical, and critical studies of Pope, both books and substantial shorter essays. It is risky to use numbers in an assertion of this sort, but surely the feeling of the scholar who busies himself with Pope today must be that the past twenty years have at least doubled the store of our precise and readily available information about Pope and our responsibility for coping with recently published materials. In a considerable expansion of the Bibliographical Note which I originally supplied for this anthology, I have tried to do justice to the new situation. Let me here confess my general and grateful debt not only to the master works just mentioned but to the conversation of the learned authors, especially that of my friends Maynard Mack, James Osborn, Aubrey Williams, and Douglas Knight. Let me acknowledge a special debt also to three who are now deceased: to George Sherburn, to the general editor of the Twickenham edition, John Butt, and to the editor of the Twickenham *Rape of the Lock,* Geoffrey Tillotson. My colleague Eugene Waith has given me good advice relating to the annotation of Pope's Preface to Shakespeare.

Such a flood of recent attention to the poetry and person of Alexander

Pope cannot but remind us of the uneven history of his reputation—his up-and-down *Nachleben*—during the two and a quarter centuries since his death. Throughout the second half of the eighteenth century, we understand that reputation was very high, not only in Britain but in Continental Europe. (He was well known in France, of course, and also in Spain, Italy, Germany, and Poland.) And we think we understand how with the rise of romantic "imagination" and "vision" and with the mellowing of these into Victorian dignities and splendors, Pope's status not only as an ethical poet and satiric teacher but as a moral person suffered a gradual decline. A minor romantic like W. L. Bowles would edit Pope (with misgivings and reservations). A major romantic like Wordsworth, in his youth, knew some thousands of Pope's verses by heart, and Byron, the exception to the age, would rebut Bowles and would legislate in spirited hyperbole: "Thou shalt believe in Milton, Dryden, Pope." But in the mature time of the great Victorians, Matthew Arnold felt assured in the pronouncement: "Dryden and Pope are classics of our prose." The early decades of our own century lapsed in quiet absentmindedness, awakened only somewhat feverishly by the imagination of the Bloomsbury era: Strachey's Cambridge-lecture image of a fiendish Twickenham monkey ladeling out hot oil on the heads of passersby, Edith Sitwell's contrary biography of a sweet little boy injured by a wild cow. The title and the contents of an American professor's book of 1929, Austin Warren's *Alexander Pope as Critic and Humanist,* may be read, at least in retrospect, as a signal of how the dormant prestige of Pope would soon respond to the current of neometaphysical thought which was then sharpening the atmosphere of university studies. Essays by F. R. Leavis in 1933 and W. H. Auden in 1937 were bold announcements of a trend which, amplified in recent years by the almost physical force of the general explosion in academic productions, has led to the bibliographical hyperdevelopment described in my opening paragraph.

But a literary reputation is not one single or simple continuum. During the ripest decades of Victorianism when Pope's moral reputation was at its palest, two of his most highly qualified judges, the Reverend Whitwell Elwin and Professor W. J. Courthope, labored to bring forth their truly great edition of Pope's *Works* in ten volumes (1871–1889), Vol. v being Courthope's biography. And running concurrently at levels connected with but different from the work of the scholars and litterateurs, we can trace what we may call, too simply, but for the sake of differentiation, the "popular" reputation of Pope. Popular reputations of literary figures are especially palpable in Britain. Witness Sir Walter Scott (the two-hundred-foot Gothic tower on Princes Street in Edinburgh), Burns (the cottages in Ayrshire, the monuments, the Brig, the Kirk), Dickens (the general upheaval in his honor in 1970), Shakespeare of course (the jubilees, the festivals, the theaters). And witness Pope in the year 1888, the two-hundredth anniversary of his birth. The *Loan Museum Catalogue* of books, manuscripts, pictures and personal relics exhibited in the Twickenham Town Hall during a week of that July and August may be consulted today in research libraries. Less readily available is a document upon which I shall draw for a few other details, a jumbo pictorial *Pope Commemoration Supplement to the Richmond and Twickenham Times,*[1] issued on Saturday, August 4, 1888, and containing, among other testimonials, the record of a "Water Fete" which had opened the celebration, on Monday evening:—the Cross Deep of the Thames ablaze with small boats; a string of lamps along the bend of Eel Pie Island creating the impression of a second flotilla; and a famous old pleasure barge, the *Maria Wood,* moored in midstream, its two decks crowded with ladies and gentlemen swaying to the music of a brass band. A horde of visitors entered Pope's grounds through the surviving grotto, which was decorated with Chinese lanterns flashing on what remained of his mirrors and crystals. They walked out onto his lawn under the initials "A.P." formed with Vauxhall Lamps, and they looked up to see the same initials on the tower of the house which years earlier had replaced Pope's villa. They were bathed in a flood of limelight, glaring white, or at moments turning to warm red or soft green. Other lanterns flashed their lights upon the cedars and out over the water and along the Surrey shore, revealing the presence of "one to two thousand" more persons on the towing path. Somewhere in the neighborhood rockets were going up.

The illuminated celebration of that night in 1888 is a moment in the history of homage to Alexander Pope which is not likely ever to be repeated—not even in the year 1988. The homogeneity and continuity of a people's consciousness represented in that moment will not, even in that borough by the Thames, have persisted so long. Possibly, even probably, no fireworks anywhere will mark the coming tricentennial. But a poet's afterlife can continue in many changed ways. Pope has in fact a very numerous audience today, in some senses a more serious and understanding audience of celebrators than ever before—if we consider only what centers in and goes out from the universities and colleges of Britain, the Commonwealth, and America. Beyond question, we can expect community celebrations to be held in honor of Alexander Pope in 1988. They

---

[1] It is a pleasure to acknowledge the kindness of Mr. T. V. Roberts, Borough Librarian of Twickenham.

will take the form of lecture series, voluble symposia, and elegant exhibitions. Casting my eye to the horizon of the scene immediately before me, I can think of a magnificent display of books, of manuscripts, and above all of icons—these exhibit best—engraved and painted riverscapes of Richmond and Twickenham, a lawn at the water's edge and a Palladian villa, portraits of the English Horace and Homer, mezzotint and line engravings, etchings, chalk and plumbago drawings, oil paintings—among them one of a sparkling seven-year-old boy—a noble profile on a large copper medal, a pastel inscribed for Martha Blount, a delicately chiseled marble bust.

The celebration of a classic is a cooperative work of the living. It gives me much pleasure to acknowledge that the present revision of my earlier memorial to Alexander Pope has been accomplished with the assistance of the following students of English literature: Randall Q. Au, Barbara Packer, John Crigler, Robert Young, and Albert Braunmüller.

W. K. Wimsatt

Silliman College
Yale University
1 June 1971

INTRODUCTION

I. CHRONOLOGICAL SUMMARY OF POPE'S CAREER

1688   Pope was born on May 21 in London. His father, Alexander Pope, son of a Hampshire Anglican clergyman, was a successful linen merchant who had become a Roman Catholic. A second wife, the poet's mother, Editha Turner, was also a Catholic, of a genteel Yorkshire family. At the Revolution of 1688 the merchant retired from business with a fortune of about £10,000.

c. 1700   The Pope family moved to Whitehill House, a small farm at Binfield in Windsor Forest, a neighborhood which was the retreat of other Catholic gentry. The poet grew up to be about four feet six inches in height, crookbacked, tubercular and sickly, the victim of chronic headaches—but of a countenance exceedingly delicate and animated. While yet a boy, he read English, Latin, and French poetry, and the great classical critics. With the encouragement of his father he wrote verses.

1705   Emerging from the pious influence of his home, Pope first visited Will's coffeehouse in London, formerly the headquarters of Dryden and still the resort of his circle—the dramatists Wycherley and Congreve, the actor Betterton, the poet Granville, the man about town Henry Cromwell, the deistic physician Samuel Garth, the fashionable gentleman and critic William Walsh. Pope's association with cultivated neighbors of the Forest and his poetic gift qualified him, despite a certain rustic awkwardness, for an easy transition to the intercourse of the Tory gentlemen and wits.

1709   In May, the *Pastorals,* Pope's first published work, appeared in Tonson's *Poetical Miscellanies.* Begun in 1704, these four graceful Virgilian poems had been shown to various friends and polished by Walsh, who gave Pope the reiterated and memorable advice that his aim as a poet should be "correctness."

1711   In May appeared the *Essay on Criticism,* Pope's precocious reenactment of Horace, Vida, and Boileau, his epitome of the orderly tradition which he had received from the litterateurs of the preceding generation. This poem elicited a furious attack from the veteran critic John Dennis (*Reflections Critical and Satirical upon a Late Rhapsody . . .*) and the judicious praise of Addison in *Spectator* No. 253. Pope became friendly with Addison, Steele, and other Whig wits, the "little Senate" of Addison, sitting in Button's coffeehouse when it opened in 1712.

1712 In May, the first version of *The Rape of the Lock,* two cantos, appeared in Lintot's *Miscellaneous Poems,* a high burlesque account of a prank and a tiff which had occurred among Pope's society friends of the Forest. In *Spectator* No. 378, for May 14, *Messiah, a Sacred Eclogue* (after Isaiah and Virgil).

1713 In March, *Windsor Forest,* a topographical poem enhanced by a celebration of the Tory Peace of Utrecht and dedicated to Granville, now Lord Lansdowne, Queen Anne's Secretary of War. In April, a Prologue for Addison's Whig tragedy *Cato.* During this year Pope contributed essays to Steele's *Guardian.* No. 40 (April 27) is his ironic eulogy of rival Theocritan *Pastorals* by the Buttonian Whig Ambrose Philips.

1714 In March, the second and expanded version of *The Rape of the Lock,* five cantos, with the epic machinery of the sylphs, the most brilliant of all Pope's poems, and the masterpiece of mock-heroical literature. During the spring of this year Pope was attending meetings of the Scriblerus Club with a new set of Tory friends: the Queen's physician Dr. John Arbuthnot, the poets John Gay and Thomas Parnell, and Jonathan Swift, party writer and confidant of the Lord Treasurer, Robert Harley, Earl of Oxford. Pope now formed his important friendship with another member of the ministry, Henry St. John, Viscount Bolingbroke. The Scriblerus Club, meeting in Arbuthnot's apartments at Kensington Palace, began *The Memoirs of Martinus Scriblerus,* universal pedant in the arts and sciences. From the activities of this club came also *Gulliver's Travels,* 1726, and Pope's *Dunciad,* 1728. The group was dispersed and the ascendancy of Pope's Tory friends ended when Arbuthnot's patient Queen Anne died on August 1. We may imagine Pope at this period as frequently in movement between his parents' home at Binfield and the London house of his Whig friend the painter Charles Jervas.

1715 Volume I of Pope's *Iliad,* the first four books, with critical Prefaces and notes, appeared on June 6, and two days later, the rival *First Book of Homer's Iliad,* by Addison's protégé the Oxford scholar Thomas Tickell. Pope's success was unqualified. The completion of the *Iliad* was his major task for the next five years (vol. II appeared in 1716, vol. III in 1717, vol. IV in 1718, vols. V and VI in 1720) and earned him the moderate fortune which religious adherence and a spirit of independence prevented his obtaining by the avenues of patronage. His receipts for the whole were more than £5,000.

1716 The Pope family sold their Binfield farm and settled near the Earl of Burlington's villa on the waterside at Chiswick outside London.

In March the disreputable bookseller Edmund Curll published *Court Poems,* an embarrassment to Pope's friend Lady Mary Wortley Montagu, which two days later Pope avenged by administering an emetic to Curll in a friendly glass of sack and publishing an account of the episode.

1717 In June, the first collected volume of Pope's *Works,* containing among other new poems the *Verses to the Memory of an Unfortunate Lady* and *Eloïsa to Abelard,* Pope's chief expressions in the pathetic and romantic mode. The latter especially might be taken as a personal message by Lady Mary, far away in Turkey. On October 23 of this year, Pope's father died.

1719 Pope and his mother moved to the villa at Twickenham on the Thames near Richmond, his most celebrated residence. For almost ten years now Pope's literary activities were to be chiefly editing and translating. His original writing was limited to epitaphs and other occasional verses for friends. His interest turned toward building and gardening. A taste for baroque landscaping indicated five years earlier in his *Guardian* No. 173 now expressed itself in the artful variegation of his small plot and the construction of his grotto. In this period flourished his friendships with the aristocratic builders and landscapers Burlington, Bathurst (owner of the park at Cirencester), Cobham (owner of Stowe), and the professionals William Kent and Charles Bridgeman. Pope became a recognized authority and an influence on English gardening. During the next twenty years we may imagine his spending the winter seasons and early summers at Twickenham and the late summers and autumns, so far as rheumatisms, influenzas, and the racking of his sickly body by coach travel would permit, in a series of prolonged visits to the great houses of his friends or to the waters at Bath.

1721 In September, Pope's *Epistle to Addison* (*Moral Essay* V), in Tickell's posthumous edition of Addison's works.

1725 In March, Pope's edition of Shakespeare, in six volumes, on which he had been actively at work, with the assistance of friends, since 1721. In April, vols. I–III of his *Odyssey.* Bolingbroke, back from exile, settled not far from Pope, in rustic retirement at Dawley Farm, Uxbridge.

1726 In March, Lewis Theobald's *Shakespeare Restored: or a Specimen of the Many Errors, as well Committed, as Unamended by Mr. Pope in his late Edition of This Poet.* In June, volumes IV–V of the *Odyssey,* a translation in which Pope had been much assisted by his friends the hack poets William Broome and Elijah Fenton. Pope's profit may have been more than £5,000.

1728 In March, Pope's prose *Peri Bathous: or of the Art of Sinking in Poetry* (a Scriblerus document), and following it in May, *The Dunciad.*

An Heroic Poem. In Three Books. The King of the Dunces was Lewis Theobald. Pope's period of cultivating his garden in patient retirement was over. Stimulated by Swift during visits from Ireland in the preceding two years, he now spoke back to the pedants, poetasters, journalists, and party writers who in one way or another had been his antagonists since his appearance on the literary scene. He had entered on the most important phase of his literary career.

1729 In April, *The Dunciad Variorum with the Prolegomena of Scriblerus,* a volume fortified with several sorts of burlesque critical apparatus. The names of the dunces, before indicated by initials, were now printed in full.

1731 In December, the *Epistle to the Earl of Burlington, of Taste* (*Moral Essay* IV, *of the Use of Riches*). The generally hostile response to this poem included (in January, 1732) the Grubstreet *Miscellany on Taste* with a pseudo-Hogarthian print "Burlington Gate" as frontispiece.

1733 In January, the *Epistle to Bathurst* (*Moral Essay* III, *of the Use of Riches*). In February, the *First Satire of the Second Book of Horace Imitated,* to Mr. Fortescue (the satirist's anxious conversation with his lawyer); and in the same month anonymously the First Epistle of the *Essay on Man.* In March, anonymously the Second Epistle of the *Essay;* and in May, anonymously the Third Epistle. The *Moral Essays* and the *Essay on Man* were parts of a projected "ethic work" on a far grander scale. With the deist Bolingbroke as "guide, philosopher, and friend," Pope had been hard at work for the past three or four years storing up the *Essay on Man.* His aim seems to have been that this example of "moralized song," published almost simultaneously with two of his acknowledged pieces, should be accepted by the public (as indeed it quickly was) before its authorship was known. Meanwhile, in the *Epistle to Fortescue,* one of his cutting satires, Pope had been characteristically successful. The lines on "Sappho" (his former friend Lady Mary Wortley Montagu) and "Fanny" (the court favorite Lord Hervey) provoked in March *Verses Addressed to the Imitator of Horace, by a Lady,* and later Lord Hervey's *Letter from a Nobleman at Hampton Court. . . .* In November Pope published anonymously under the title *The Impertinent* (with a probable aim at Hervey) his "versification" of Donne's Fourth Satire.

1734 In January, the *Epistle to Cobham* (*Moral Essay* I, *of the Knowledge and Characters of Men*), and anonymously the Fourth Epistle of the *Essay on Man,* concluding an *annus mirabilis,* Pope's most intensive year of publication in the ethical way. On June 7 Pope's mother died, at the age of ninety-one.

1735 In January, the *Epistle to Dr. Arbuthnot* (later the Prologue to the Satires), the satirist's flashing apologia for his embattled career. Here the finished portrait of Addison as "Atticus" appears and that of Lord Hervey as "Sporus." In February, *The Characters of Women, to a Lady* (*Moral Essay* II). The lady was Martha Blount, the friend of Windsor Forest days who remained to the end of his life, through slanders and imbroglios, the faithful center of Pope's affections. In May, the unauthorized edition of Pope's *Letters* by Edmund Curll was an event which Pope had tempted by a series of anonymous communications to Curll and by other stratagems during several years past. The *Letters,* like the *Epistle to Arbuthnot* a satirist's apology, an image of the "honest man" and loyal friend, brought Pope one of the most helpful admirers of his later years, the philanthropist Ralph Allen of Prior Park near Bath.

1737 In May, *The First Epistle of the Second Book of Horace, to Augustus* (George II), the subtlest of Pope's political and literary irony in the mode of classical imitation.

1738 In May, *One Thousand Seven Hundred and Thirty-Eight, Dialogue* I, and in July, *Dialogue* II, his final and fiercest political satire (the Epilogue to the Satires). During the past two years Pope had been in close touch with the Prince of Wales, his Secretary George Lyttelton, and other "Patriot" leaders like Wyndham and Chesterfield, mentioned in *Dialogue* II. In the following year Pope's villa was the scene of their meetings. He had become the Laureate of the Opposition, and not in vain. The Horatian satires kept pace with corruption, excise policy, and Spain, in preparing Sir Robert Walpole for the downfall of 1742.

1740 In April, in Lord Radnor's garden at Twickenham, Pope met the Reverend William Warburton, the last important prompter of his career, destined to be his literary executor and the editor of the posthumous edition of his *Works* in 1751. In 1738 and 1739 Warburton (a former ally of Theobald) had defended Pope's *Essay on Man* against the attacks of the Swiss theologian Crousaz, and Pope had sent warm thanks. The meeting of the two resulted at once in a glow of mutual admiration.

1741 In April, Pope's *Works,* vol. II, contained his correspondence with Swift, a publication contrived by Pope through several years of devious effort. Swift, aged and imbecile at Dublin, had not seen Pope since before the *Dunciad,* on his Twickenham visit of 1727. In the same volume Pope put *The Memoirs of Martinus Scriblerus,* begun by Swift, Arbuthnot, and Pope as members of the Scriblerus Club. From November until toward the end of January, 1742, Pope and Warburton were at Prior Park working on the text and notes of Pope's last poem—the massive climax of his satiric career:

1742 In March, *The New Dunciad: As it was Found in the Year*

1741—a fourth book, the "Accomplishment of the Prophecies" in the third concerning "the *Kingdom of the Dull* upon earth." Ths provoked (in July) from the aged Whig dramatist and Poet Laureate Colley Cibber *A Letter . . . to Mr. Pope, Inquiring into the Motives that might induce him in his Satyrical Works, to be so frequently fond of Mr. Cibber's Name.*

1743 In October, *The Dunciad in Four Books Printed according to the Complete Copy found in the Year 1742.* The original hero of the poem, Lewis Theobald, was dethroned in favor of Colley Cibber.

1744 During the last months of his life Pope labored with Warburton on a collected edition of the *Works.* The *Essay on Criticism* and the *Essay on Man* were published with Warburton's notes. The four main *Ethic Epistles* were printed and copies sent to friends. "Here I am like Socrates," said Pope to the anecdotist Joseph Spence, "distributing my morality among my friends as I am dying." He had long aggravated his chronic infirmities by efforts to keep pace with stronger men in the role of gentleman gourmet. "The death of Pope," says Johnson, "was imputed by some of his friends to a silver saucepan, in which it was his delight to eat potted lampreys." He was dying now of asthma and dropsy. A friend sent for a priest, and, though there would appear to have been something of the afterthought about the action, Pope received the last rites of the Roman Catholic Church with profound devotion. He died on May 30. Spence records that "his departure was so easy . . . that it was imperceptible even to the standers by."

*   *   *   *   *

The foregoing summary will perhaps be appropriately supplemented by the two following impressions of Pope in his late maturity, one constructed by Samuel Johnson from reports current during the latter half of the eighteenth century, and one remembered by friends from the conversation of Sir Joshua Reynolds.

His stature was so low that, to bring him to a level with common tables, it was necessary to raise his seat. But his face was not displeasing, and his eyes were animated and vivid. . . . His most frequent assailant was the headache, which he used to relieve by inhaling the steam of coffee, which he very frequently required. Most of what can be told concerning his petty peculiarities was communicated by a female domestic of the Earl of Oxford, who knew him perhaps after the middle of life. He was then so weak as to stand in perpetual need of female attendance; extremely sensible of cold, so that he wore a kind of fur doublet under a shirt of a very coarse warm linen with fine sleeves. When he rose, he was invested in [a] bodice made of stiff canvas, being scarcely able to hold himself erect till they were laced, and he then put on a flannel waistcoat. One side was contracted. His legs were so slender that he enlarged their bulk with three pair of stockings, which were drawn on and off by the maid; for he was not able to dress or undress himself, and neither went to bed nor rose without help. His weakness made it very difficult for him to be clean. His hair had fallen almost all away, and he used to dine sometimes with Lord Oxford, privately, in a velvet cap. His dress of ceremony was black with a tiewig and a little sword. . . . When he wanted to sleep he "nodded in company," and once slumbered at his own table while the Prince of Wales was talking of poetry. The reputation which his friendship gave procured him many invitations; but he was a very troublesome inmate. He brought no servant and had so many wants that a numerous attendance was scarcely able to supply them. Wherever he was he left no room for another, because he exacted the attention and employed the activity of the whole family. . . . One of his constant demands was of coffee in the night, and to the woman that waited on him in his chamber he was very burdensome; but he was careful to recompense her want of sleep, and Lord Oxford's servant declared that in a house where her business was to answer his call she would not ask for wages. He had another fault, easily incident to those who suffering much pain think themselves entitled to whatever pleasures they can snatch. He was too indulgent to his appetite; he loved meat highly seasoned and of strong taste, and at the intervals of the table amused himself with biscuits and dry conserves. If he sat down to a variety of dishes, he would oppress his stomach with repletion, and though he seemed angry when a dram was offered him, did not forbear to drink it. . . . Swift complains that he was never at leisure for conversation, because he "had always some poetical scheme in his head." It was punctually required that his writing-box should be set upon his bed before he rose; and Lord Oxford's domestic related that in the dreadful winter of Forty she was called from her bed by him four times in one night to supply him with paper, lest he should lose a thought.

—Samuel Johnson, *Life of Pope,* 1781, in *Lives,* ed. G. B. Hill, Oxford, 1905, vol. iii, pp. 196–199, 208–209 (paragraphs 255–261, 277).

Sir Joshua Reynolds once saw Pope. It was about the year 1740. . . . [He was sent, one day, to make a purchase for his master at a sale of pictures. The auction room was crowded, and he was at the upper end of it, close to the auctioneer. There was a bustle near the door, and he presently heard "Mr. Pope, Mr. Pope," whispered through the room. The crowd opened a passage for the poet, and the hands of all were held out to touch him as he passed along, bowing to the company on either side.

Reynolds, though not in the front row, put out his hand under the arm of a person who stood before him, and the hand that had penned the *Rape of the Lock* was shaken by that which was to immortalize on canvas the Belindas of the coming age. . . .] [Pope] was, according to Sir Joshua's account, about four feet six high; very humpbacked and deformed; he wore a black coat; and according to the fashion of that time, had on a little sword. . . . he had a large and very fine eye; and a long handsome nose; his mouth had those peculiar marks which always are found in the mouths of crooked persons; and the muscles which run across the cheek were so strongly marked as to appear like small cords. Roubiliac the statuary, who made a bust of him from life, observed that his countenance was that of a person who had been much afflicted with headache, and that he should have known the fact from the contracted appearance of the skin above the eyebrows, though he had not been otherwise apprised of it.

—James Prior, *Life of Edmond Malone,* London, 1860, pp. 428–429, "Maloniana"; and Charles R. Leslie and Tom Taylor, *Life and Times of Sir Joshua Reynolds,* London, 1865, i, 24. The passage inserted in brackets is from Leslie and Taylor.

* * * * *

II. INTRODUCTION TO THE POEMS

I

A salient feature of the literary man in the Augustan age is a certain amphibiousness—in political, religious, and, more broadly, in social relations. Before the rise of the great reading middle classes (during Pope's lifetime) the man of letters had been dependent on his patrons, and even in Pope's day he found it important to have aristocratic friends. His friendships had much to do with determining whether a poet wrote or did not write, wrote well or badly, starved in a garret or gave suppers in a villa.[1] This fact was not merely a social and economic cause of literature; it entered into the very mind of the writer and gave him a certain kind of matter and a cast of thought. At one period in the career of

---

[1] The classic study at the social, political, and economic level is Alexandre Beljame's *Men of Letters and the English Public in the Eighteenth Century 1660–1744, Dryden, Addison, Pope,* trans. E. O. Lorimer, London, 1948 (French editions, 1881, 1897).

Pope's great predecessor Dryden it was his critical doctrine that poets did best to copy the conversation of gentle folk, and especially that of the king. In Dryden's Dedication of his comedy *Marriage à la Mode* to the courtier and wit John Wilmot, Earl of Rochester, the most abject corollaries of the doctrine appear:

I am sure, if there be anything in this play, wherein I have raised myself beyond the ordinary lowness of my comedies, I ought wholly to acknowledge it to the favour of being admitted into your lordship's conversation. . . . Wit seems to have lodged itself more nobly in this age, than in any of the former; and people of my mean condition are only writers, because some of the nobility, and your lordship in the first place, are above the narrow praises which poesy could give you. . . . But . . . I have so much self-interest, as to be content with reading some papers of your verses, without desiring you should proceed to a scene, or play. . . . Your lordship has but another step to make, and from the patron of wit, you may become its tyrant.

Dryden was to repent of these flatteries, and partly (so the tradition runs) through cudgels wielded in fulfilment of the fear expressed in the last sentence quoted.[1] Where his heart was when he wrote this Epistle Dedicatory it might be difficult to say, but we can make a guess about his tongue. A situation of superiority in talent and inferiority of privilege had produced a special way of talking—and perhaps even of seeing—double. The mind that could write thus was hovering on the verge of something else, as sometimes became clear. In Dryden's *Defence of the Essay of Dramatic Poesy,* he argues the critical issue of rhymed plays with his noble brother-in-law Sir Robert Howard, author of *The Duke of Lerma.*

For my own concernment in the controversy, it is so small, that I can easily be contented to be driven from a few notions. . . ; especially by one, who has the reputation of understanding all things: and I might justly make that excuse for my yielding to him, which the philosopher made to the Emperor; why should I offer to contend with him, who is master of more than twenty legions of arts and sciences?

A dubious trend in this profession of humility becomes soon more overt.

As for the play of *The Duke of Lerma,* having so much altered and

---

[1] Rochester's responsibility for the Rose Alley ambuscade of 1679 has been questioned by recent scholarship but is perhaps still available for speculation.

beautified it as he has done, it can justly belong to none but him. Indeed they must be extreme ignorant, as well as envious, who would rob him of that honour; for you see him putting in his claim to it, even in the first two lines.

> Repulse upon repulse, like waves thrown back,
> That slide to hang upon obdurate rocks.

After this, let detraction do its worst; for if this be not his, it deserves to be.

In Pope's time, it is true, the author's position was no longer the same. After the Revolution of 1688 patronage was not merely aristocratic; it was political. The author had public party connections. Writing either for Whig or for Tory ministry or for both, he was more vendible and independent—except for the temporarily depressing effect of the Walpolean practicality and Hanoverian thickheadedness. A successful writer like Pope—and preeminently Pope himself, who found a fortune in literature—though he valued his aristocratic and politically important friends, was no less valued and courted by them. "Thanks to Homer," wrote Pope, "I live and thrive, Indebted to no Prince or Peer alive." He refused a handsome offer from Lord Halifax, preferring, as he later told Spence, "liberty without a coach." Yet along with much else that Pope inherited from the generation of Dryden, there was a distinctive idiom of irony—not the irony of Greek tragedy, for example, nor the romantic irony of sardonic introspection, nor that of metaphysical paradox, but just the irony, as we have seen, of a professional class which pays compliments for reward to men higher but duller. It was a peculiar blend of obsequiousness (toned down to politeness with Pope) and insult (tuned up to satire), a special product of an era and of a social and artistic consciousness. We may find it directly noted by Pope, transformed and embodied in his satiric material—"Damn with faint praise, assent with civil leer"—"And he himself one vile Antithesis." Or it may run more or less slyly in the lines of his own satire. *Guardian* No. 40, where as anonymous critic he compared his own Virgilian pastorals with the rustic ones of the Whig poet Ambrose Philips, afforded the opportunity to sound much like Dryden. "Mr. Pope hath fallen into the same error with Virgil. His clowns do not converse in all the simplicity proper to the country." But Philips!

How he still charms the ear with these artful repetitions of the epithets; and how significant is the last verse! I defy the most common reader to repeat them, without feeling some motions of compassion.

In the *Epistle to Augustus* (The First Epistle of the Second Book of Horace) the method appears at its most mature and most immune to redress.

> How shall the Muse, from such a Monarch, steal
> An hour, and not defraud the Public Weal? (5–6)

> Your Arms, your Actions, your Repose to sing! (395)

There were those in 1737 who read this poem as a panegyric on the King and the ministry.

The social relations which underlie such satire were in the case of Pope accentuated by the fact that he was among the country gentlemen of the Tory opposition. His friends, as he boasts in his satires, were the leaders who had fallen from grace, the Jacobite lords, Bolingbroke and Atterbury, in the tower or in exile, Cobham, a Whig soldier who had opposed the regime, poets like Gay, who lost favor at court, and Swift, disappointed of a bishopric, relegated to a deanery in Ireland. Later Pope took up with the recalcitrant Prince of Wales and the young Patriot politicians. One must, moreover, go on to name another circumstance which, in the special case of Pope as an outsider, swings the argument even further toward ambiguities and uncertainties: that is, the fact of his religious adherence, that he was a Roman Catholic under conditions of extreme embarrassment and a Catholic of a certain sort. Pope professed his religion steadfastly, rejecting the invitations of powerful friends, Oxford and Atterbury, that he come over with them and enjoy the political emoluments to which his genius entitled him. To Grubstreet he was "Pope Alexander." He wrote to a French correspondent that the *Essay on Man* derived not from Spinoza or Leibniz but from Pascal and Fénelon, the latter of whom he would "readily imitate in submitting" all his opinions "to the Decision of the Church." He died fortified by the sacraments. He was offering only a partial, diplomatic reason when he wrote to Atterbury that he would remain loyal for the sake of his mother. But one may wonder whether Pope would have angered the Allens—as his friend Martha Blount is conjectured to have done—by asking for their chariot to Mass in Bath. As a youngster, first loose in the London coffeehouses, he was capable of writing a parody of a Psalm, or at least of Sternhold and Hopkins. In his poems, from the *Essay on Criticism* to the *Dunciad,* his attitude toward the medieval Church is that of any English churchman or man of letters of his day: "And the Monks finished what the Goths begun." Whether through innocence or through lack of concern, he could drift, with the help of Bolingbroke, into the vague philosophy, something like deism, of the *Essay on Man*. His most serious standard was ethical. "Yet am I," he wrote to Swift, "of the religion of Erasmus, a catholic," and again in one of his self-portraits of the satirist:

Verse-man or Prose-man, term me which you will,
Papist or Protestant, or both between,
Like good Erasmus in an honest Mean,
In moderation placing all my glory,
While Tories call me Whig, and Whigs a Tory. (*Satire* II, i.)

The Horatian rule of swearing by the word of no master (*nullius in verba,* as the words were aptly condensed on the shield of the sceptical Royal Society) found its appropriate witty imitation in the verse of Pope:

Sworn to no Master, of no Sect am I:
As drives the storm, at any door I knock:
And house with Montaigne now, or now with Locke. (*Epistle* I, i)

One must beware of course the temptation to read a poet's character from his poems (especially from his "imitations") in order to read his character back into his poems. For Pope this caution is especially appropriate, as his poetry was not soul-searching autobiography but public utterance calculated for the society in which he lived. Whatever his inner state, if he were to write poetry, Pope had to use the idiom of exchange. A certain correlation, however, between Pope's politics and religion and his poetry (and no less between the age in which he lived and his poetry) may be argued. Pope was not to be the poet of a massive and culminating architecture, a *Divina Commedia* or a *King Lear*. His was not "Milton's strong pinion," which "not Heaven can bound," nor even the continuing, if circling and subterranean, river of a *Prelude*. The *Ode to Music,* Pope's attempt "to boldly follow Pindar's pathless way," is one of his least impressive performances. Only in a limited sense is he a successful poet in the organ tones of the *Messiah*. Pope's orientation was secular. At the same time religious claims were strong enough to keep the needle nervously vibrating. He had, as the critics have told us, the prime requisite of the satirist, the habit of tolerating where most he disapproved, an irony and hesitation with regard to all things. This was the quality of mind which generated the kindly, the pitying and tearful devastation of the "Atticus" portrait. Pope's poetry is the expression of one kind of experience, the equilibrium, the two-way vision, which in satire assumes the shape of the dubious compliment, the smiling insult.

II

But a poet is a man of letters, and this, especially when the poet is Alexander Pope, means a man who inherits and tries to push further a literary tradition. Other ages of English poetry have not been so certain about this. That of Wordsworth and Shelley a hundred years later was rather in the position of trying to discard a tradition which was considered bad; that of Spenser and Shakespeare acknowledged its tradition, but in a spirit of discovery, as translating a thing far back and unattainably heroic. By the time of Pope the tradition had become clearer and more demanding; it invited only perfection. In the third Part of his youthful *Essay on Criticism* Pope outlined the "Progress" of the tradition as he had received it, naming the critics doubtless that he had read as a boy at Binfield, the great ones of antiquity, Aristotle, Horace, Longinus, Quintilian (re-established by the Italian editions and commentaries of the sixteenth century), and the recent French critics, especially Boileau. Authorities like these and their ideas can affect the work of a poet in two main and rather different ways, either by furnishing the very materials and vocabulary of which he makes his poems, or by having something to do, in a strictly theoretical way, with the kind of poetry he writes. The first kind of influence is usually more obvious and easier to deal with. Especially is this so for Pope, because he wrote an *Essay on Criticism,* which is after all *about* the critical tradition. We hear mainly of Pope's respect for a certain kind of "nature" (the word occurs twenty-one times in the *Essay*), the universal and archetypal patterns of human reason and value which the critics derived from Stoic and Aristotelian philosophy and ultimately from Plato:[1] "Unerring NATURE, still divinely bright, One clear, unchanged, and universal light." As Dryden, quoting an Italian writer, explains in the Parallel of Painting and Poetry prefixed to his translation of the French painter Du Fresnoy's *De Arte Graphica:*

Nature always intends a consummate Beauty in her Productions, yet through the Inequality of the Matter, the Forms are altered. . . . For which Reason, the artful Painter, and the Sculptor, imitating the Divine Maker, form to themselves, as well as they are able, a Model of Superior Beauties.

[1] Consult L. I. Bredvold, "The Tendency toward Platonism in Neo-Classical Esthetics," *English Literary History,* I (September, 1934), 91–119; A. O. Lovejoy, "Nature as Aesthetic Norm," *Modern Language Notes,* XLII (November, 1927), 444–450.

Or, as Pope puts it, with an eye more on actuality:

> In some fair body thus th' informing soul
> With spirits feeds, with vigour fills the whole. (76–77)

Pope too, following Boileau, can harmonize the principle of Nature or Reason, reinforced by Cartesian rationalism and the independent spirit of the Moderns, with the principle of authority or reverence for the Ancient models. The reconciliation was not, as a matter of fact, so difficult, for both principles have in common the concept of an objective and universal truth. What is permanent will have been known to the ancients, and conversely: "Those Rules of old discovered, not devised, Are Nature still, but Nature methodized." And "Nature and Homer were, he found, the same." Again, a pronounced strain in Pope's theory is the antithetic concept of Taste, the intuitive and untrammeled principle of both creation and appreciation. Taste as it appeared in a poem was a "grace beyond the reach of art," something related to the ecstasy of the ancient romantic critic Longinus (not the rules of Aristotle and Horace). It was associated with what rises "out of nature's common order, . . . The shapeless rock, or hanging precipice." One of the prevailing implications of Pope's nicely blended *Essay* would seem to be that a poet needs not only taste (inspiration) but good sense (reason and rules), and the critic, not only good sense but taste.

But it is a different matter to show how these principles of universal Nature and Reason, of Authority, and of Taste, affected Pope's poetry in any deeper way, that is, influenced him to write poetry of any particular kind. The easiest case can be made for the authority of the classic models, for there is a clear sense in which Pope's burlesques, translations, and imitations are written in the classic spirit. On the other hand, one might hesitate to say that Pope followed nature more accurately than Shakespeare, or that he had better taste than Wordsworth. The sense in which the doctrine of Nature determined what kind of nature went into Pope's poems was an oblique one. Nature for Rousseau and Wordsworth was to be the spontaneous and primitive, the opposite of the artificial or the institutionally restricted—with the result that today nature tends to be that part of the primitive which we experience on a picnic. Almost in direct antithesis, nature for Pope was the regular and civilized, the opposite of the abnormal, eccentric, or barbarous (though there are hints of a primitivistic philosophy of nature in his *Essay on Man*). Though Pope liked gardens, and not the geometric French kind but the kind improved according to his own baroque taste in variegations, yet nature for him was not mainly the "thousand blended notes" which Wordsworth would hear in a grove nor even the mountains and chasms in the presence of which Addison and the critic John Dennis experienced a "delightful horror." It was rather the nature of the human being and the milieu created by him, cities and estates, politics, society, and business, poetry and conversation. This much appears from the subject matter of Pope's most characteristic poems. Yet, again, this is not a stated part of the literary theory, and it results not so much from a literary as from a social philosophy. The specifically literary theory of nature (that art imitates what is either ideally or in fact universally true, rather than what is particular) could scarcely have any more precise relation to Pope's poetry than to any other poetry of equal rank. In a note to the *Iliad* (VI, 595) Pope anticipated his posthumous critic Warton in praising particular circumstances (both Pope and Warton of course had classical precedents in Longinus and Quintilian), and Pope's own poems, with their filigree of coffee-service and card game or clutter of assorted Dunces, make the universal as brilliantly particular as it could well be. As for the *ideal* universal, Pope's poetry surely deals for the most part with "our Mortification . . . the Deformities, and Disproportions which are in us" (to quote again from Dryden's Parallel), and here it derives its theoretical justification less from the Platonic or Stoic universal than from Aristotelian ethical types, not of perfection but of aberration; from the concession which Aristotle had to make to the comic mask, ugly though not painful; or from the apology which Horace offered for the style of his satires, colloquial, realistic, scarcely poetic.

Another side of the tradition, however, remains to claim our notice —that of verbal rhetoric, or style, a thing which Pope inherited from earlier English and French poets and from Roman poets, but also, along with nature and reason, from Aristotle and the other critics. Here again we have what can be treated as a part of Pope's subject matter, with ingeniously chiming illustrations from the section, in Part II of the *Essay on Criticism,* on words, word music, and the sound seeming "an echo to the sense." Pope, refining on the ancient Dionysius of Halicarnassus and the Renaissance Italian Vida, gives the final touch, by simultaneous enunciation and demonstration, to a favorite neoclassic principle.

> When Ajax strives some rock's vast weight to throw,
> The line too labours, and the words move slow. (370–371)

Pope's interest in the word, however, is something more pervasive— something related to the fact that he and his friends were among the last men to be trained thoroughly in an antique kind of respect for the word. From the several small schools which he attended, from his "family priest," as he expressed it to Spence, and no doubt even more from his own reading of Aristotle and Quintilian, Pope had learned what a generation later Samuel Johnson seems still to have learned in the grammar school of Lichfield, and what toward the end of the century an exceptional boy like Coleridge at Christ's Hospital and under the exceptional master Bowyer, whom he celebrates in the first chapter of his *Biographia,* might still learn. But the era was one in which these things were being forgotten. In Pope's day vestiges of the ancient tradition might be seen in such a popular treatise on prose as William Smith's *Mysterie of Rhetorique Unveiled.* There was much less in Edward Bysshe's reigning *Art of Poetry.* We must go back to Puttenham's *Arte of English Poesie* in the time of Elizabeth to find an Englishman expounding any very elaborate system of verbal poetics. Recent feats of scholarship have shown that to know "small Latin and less Greek" in Shakespeare's or in Milton's grammar school was to know what in our century would be considered formidable. With the Latin and Greek, even at the schoolboy level, went a system of "grammatical" and rhetorical analysis which has now for several hundred years been below the intellectual horizon for all but antiquarian specialists.

It must be admitted that the repertoire of classical word figures, while it might be interpreted according to a sound philosophy of style, might also promote an unhappy division between sense and ornament in writing. The principle of "decorum" might assert that the figures (antithesis, metaphor, hyperbole) should be appropriate to the pith of what was being said (that Catiline was a traitor), but even this principle might leave the figures in the position rather of detachable veneer than of functional or deeply integrated forms of expression. A certain trend of Renaissance intellectual history, while it simplified and unified some kinds of writing (notably the scientific), at the level of rhetorical theory wedged the cleft between sense and ornament to the breaking point. At the end of the sixteenth century the French logician Peter Ramus, by a Platonic simplification, claimed the ancient rhetorical divisions of "invention" and "disposition" for dialectic or logic, leaving for "rhetoric" only eloquence or style. In the seventeenth century occurred the more momentous Cartesian sundering of matter and spirit, manifest for England in the determined scientific program of the Royal Society and the corollary mistrust of words, figures, and imagination by such writers as the Society's historian Sprat and the philosophers Bacon, Hobbes, and Locke. A scientist, said Sprat, will endeavor to say "so many things, almost in an equal

number of words."[1] (In the fresh dawn of empirical science, "Few words,"
as the poet Herrick almost put it, "are best when once we go-a-Maying.")
The tide against words had run so far in Pope's day that his fellow spirit
Swift, in Book III of *Gulliver's Travels,* the Voyage to Laputa, satirizing
the Royal Society as the Grand Academy of Lagado, found the oppor-
tunity for this telling irony:

The other project was a scheme for entirely abolishing all words what-
soever; and this was urged as a great advantage in point of health as well
as brevity. . . . An expedient was therefore offered, that since words are
only names for things, it would be more convenient for all men to carry
about them such things as were necessary to express the particular busi-
ness they are to discourse on.

At this crisis in the reputation of the word, two ways of vindication were
open to its champions. One was that taken by the Neapolitan Professor
Giambattista Vico, who, full of mistrust for the rational seventeenth-
century gentlemen, in 1725 published his *New Science,* signalling a move-
ment that in the course of two centuries has raised the word to the new
prestige with which students of poetry today are familiar—Coleridgean,
Crocean, romantic, idealistic, symbolic. The other way was that taken by
Pope and his friends (unaware of Vico, and less philosophers of the word
than master practitioners of it). It was the old way, the classical—none-
theless effective for looking backward—a way realistic enough to see a
difference between words and things, though subtle enough to see also a
manifold relationship. Without identifying words and things, Pope may
yet have read two senses in the famous advice of Quintilian: "Let care
in words be solicitude for things."[1] The phrase "to advantage" in Pope's
"nature to advantage dressed" bore a large burden of meaning. His view
of words could not be the simple one of Bacon, that words are but
"images of things."

The three great "tours" of poetry, Pope said to Spence, are the design,
the language, and the versification. The second of these, language, was
intimately connected with another important concept, that of "wit." The
term occurs forty-six times in the *Essay on Criticism,* with the variety of
meanings which it conveniently and "wittily" bore. "Nay wits had pen-

[1] Thomas Sprat, *The History of the Royal Society* (London, 1667), p. 42.
Cf. A. C. Howell, "Res et Verba," *English Literary History,* XIII (June,
1946), 131–142.
[1] *Curam ergo verborum rerum volo esse sollicitudinem* (*Institutio Ora-
toria,* VIII, Proem, 20).

sions, and young Lords had wit." "One glaring Chaos and wild heap of wit." A seventeenth-century English equivalent for imagination or fancy ("invention" in Pope's Preface to the *Iliad*), "wit" in its favorable connotation is a kind of mental alertness to resemblances (as Locke and Addison discussed it) and also (though neither Locke nor Addison approved thoroughly of this) a kind of verbal smartness, a meaning compressed and pointed in a juncture of words. "Wit" (*esprit*), wrote one of the French critics, Père Bouhours, "is a solid, radiant object" (*c'est un corps solide qui brille*). In a peculiar sense, a sense as peculiar as Pope's poetry is when compared to Elizabethan or Romantic, wit is the quality of Pope's poetry.

The whole matter has something to do with another Augustan concept, that of "correctness," what the respected critic William Walsh advised Pope to achieve. "Correctness" sometimes seems to have meant (as in Addison's *Spectators* on the Longinian sublime) a kind of low perfection which was the opposite of inspired genius, and in this sense the term is not helpful. We should not like to say that Pope is either more or less correct (perfect or imperfect in his own kind of technique) than Shakespeare, and certainly not that Pope's perfection is a kind of lowness. But the term as Walsh used it referred more specifically to the precise and tensile frame of words and meter which was the neo-classic couplet, a frame of words derived (with improvements) from the rhetorical tradition, and a necessary condition for the kind of verbal density and brilliance to which we have alluded.

To put the matter simply yet, I believe, essentially: the figures of speech found in classical prose and poetry and described by Aristotle and the Roman rhetoricians, though multiplied during the centuries and often confused, fell into a few classes of main importance: 1. logical patterns of parallel and contrast in syllable, word, and phrase; 2. metaphoric meanings (often and correctly taken as figures of thought); and 3. a series of non-logical phonetic auxiliaries of metaphor, variously graded as pun, "turn" (or *traductio*), and alliteration. To this third group it is important to add the medieval Latin and vernacular figure of rhyme, a figure which was capable of entering into very nice relations with the logical figures of the first group and which, as a step beyond the verbalism even of classical rhetoric, was a special opportunity for the compressions of wit.

The logical figures of parallel and contrast may at times have been somewhat too obvious and emphatic in the prose orations of a heavily inflected language. (Pope's poetry too was later to be called prose.) But in the tinier compass of Pope's couplet the metrical parallels of lines and

half lines both contain and offset the logical parallels, and the piquancy
of rhyme replaces the more logical thump of Latin and Greek parallel
endings. The basic structure is the modulated parallel, of two, occasionally
three, elements, more or less antithetical.

> Resolved to win, he meditates the way,
> By force to ravish, or by fraud betray.

> For fools admire, but men of sense approve.

> Ten censure wrong for one who writes amiss.

> Charms strike the sight, but merit wins the soul.

This structure often appears in the inverted order (*chiasmus*), with a
curious reinforcement of interest in rhyme.

> Works without show, and without pomp presides.

> Whatever Nature has in worth denied,
> She gives in large recruits of needful Pride.

> Whether the nymph shall break Diana's law,
> Or some frail China jar receive a flaw.

Such a tightened and exact economy of parallel is at every step on the
verge of shrinking into something tighter. Its inevitable tendency is
compression or ellipsis (what Geoffrey Tillotson calls a "prehensile activity
with syntax"), producing the figure known as *zeugma* (yoking). If
A,B,X and C,D,X, then more simply, and sufficiently, A,B and C,D,X.

> Where nature moves, and rapture warms the *mind*.

> 'Tis *what* the vicious fear, the virtuous shun.

> And now a bubble *burst,* and now a world.

> Where wigs with wigs, with sword-knots sword-knots *strive*.

It is as if this mind would streamline itself into perfect emphasis and
point; the rigors of its compression admit no syllable that may be taken
for granted. The pressure upon the focal word is intense. No wonder if
the word should spread and part somewhat—yielding two meanings:

> Or *stain* her honour, or her new brocade.

> Or *lose* her heart, or necklace, at a ball.[1]

> Dost sometimes counsel *take*—and sometimes Tea.

---

[1] Today we will not permit a word to do so much. It must be repeated.
"Gentlemen still *lose* their shirts in the stock market and ladies go right

Metaphor or pun or both? The logic of parellel has made a concentration point where the meaning explodes in witty duplicity. The precise metrical control and the close ordering of syntax enable a constant focus upon words in numerous other neat ways of varying or "turning" upon them. The word, or its sound, if not split into two meanings, is repeated, with sometimes a hint of another meaning.

> Yet graceful ease, and sweetness void of pride,
> Might hide her faults, if Belles had faults to hide.

> Jilts ruled the state, and statesmen farces writ;
> Nay wits had pensions, and young Lords had wit.

Finally, the metrical and logical structure of Pope's couplet is the ideal frame for the brilliancies of rhyme. The difference between the logically parallel ending (classical *homoioteleuton—retinēre-obtinēre, exstinguendam-infringendam*) and the non-logical parallel of rhyme (*maids-masquerades, Beau-glow, caprice-nice*)[1] is one of the most radical of stylistic differences, an epitome of the difference between prose rhetoric and poetical rhetoric, as well as of the difference between the running couplet of Chaucer and the epigrammatic closed couplet of Pope. Rhyme is the apex of the rhetorical phenomena which characterize Pope's verse, the non-logical element which chiefly complicates and gives weight to the merely abstract logic of parallel and antithesis. "Symphonie" or "cadence," said the Elizabethan theorist Puttenham, meaning rhyme, is "all the sweetnesse and cunning in our vulgar poesie." And Pope told his friend Spence:

I have nothing to say for rhyme but that I doubt whether a poem can support itself without it in our Language, unless it be stiffened with such strange words as are likely to destroy our language itself.[2]

Rhyme has often been recognized as a binding element in verse structure. But the opportunity for binding occurs most clearly where there is difference or separation.

> One speaks the glory of the British Queen,
> And one describes a charming Indian screen.

on *losing* their jewels in taxicabs" (Howard Brubaker, *The New Yorker,* March 23, 1946, p. 47).

[1] Cf. my essays "One Relation of Rhyme to Reason: Alexander Pope," *Modern Language Quarterly,* V (September, 1944), 323–338; "Rhetoric and Poems: The Example of Pope," *English Institute Essays,* 1948.

[2] *Anecdotes,* ed. Singer, p. 200.

It is a curious thing that "queen" should rhyme with "screen"; they are very unlike objects. But Pope has found a connection in classifying them as topics of social chatter, and has pointed this connection in the parallel of his couplet. Then the concord in sound comes to his aid as an amusing ratification. The music of the rhyme is mental. In such inverted structures as the couplets about "pride" and "Diana's law" which we have quoted above, an especially odd, almost magic, relation of phonetic likeness (*denied-pride, law-flaw*) encourages us to perceive the otherwise asserted affinity between ideas—the receptivity of the mental void to pride, the unfortunate readiness of lovely and whole things to be broken. As Addison hinted in his celebrated *Spectator* No. 62, on wit, false wit, and mixed wit, the truth is that the smartest rhymes are not very far from puns. They take advantage of phonetic likeness to insinuate a meaning. A few of Pope's proper-name rhymes are excellent examples—in a way that may be illuminated if we recall the formula for a certain old-fashioned kind of riddle to be found in *The Farmer's Almanac*. Why is A like B? Because it sounds like B or like something connected with B.[1] Why is a certain poet a dangerous influence upon married women? Because his name sounds like a certain verb.

> Poor Cornus sees his frantic wife elope,
> And curses Wit, and Poetry, and Pope.

Though Pope had nothing to do with the misfortune of Cornus, the rhyme at least is a *fait accompli*. Why is a certain scholar a graceless figure? Because his name shows it.

> Yet ne'er one sprig of laurel graced these ribalds,
> From slashing *Bentley* down to pidling *Tibalds*.

Here the words *sprig* and *pidling* play a part too in demonstrating what it means to have a name like that. The rhyming terminations of Pope's lines are the structural completions—the musical assertions, if one wishes a metaphor from another art—of the meanings which appear within the line in metaphoric zeugmas, puns, "turns," and alliterative intimations. The parallels of verse and logic are the contrived occasions of smart verbal events. There is a poetic value which in a special sense resides in words, or in words and the exact juncture at which they find themselves.

---

[1] "Why is a dog more warmly clad in summer than in winter? Because in winter he wears a fur coat; but in summer he wears a fur coat and pants."

III

In the period of his maturity the satirist pointed to the innocence of his early career.

Soft were my numbers; who could take offence
While pure Description held the place of Sense?
Like gentle *Fanny's* was my flowery theme,
A painted mistress, or a purling stream. (*Arbuthnot,* 147–150)

At the same time he boasted:

That not in Fancy's maze he wandered long,
But stooped to Truth, and moralized his song. (340–341)

There can be no question that if, as Professor Root likes to speculate, Pope had ended his career about 1717, the gallant, delicate and sensitive —perhaps pre-romantic—young poet of the frontispiece to the *Works* of that year, we should have had a different image for retrospect. Yet too much might be made of what the apologist in 1735 said about the poems of his first period, the "pure Description" (of the *Pastorals,* no doubt, and *Windsor Forest*) or "Fancy's maze" (*The Rape of the Lock*). In the great age of the Parallel between Poetry and Painting, when the supposed Horatian principle that poetry is verbal painting (*ut pictura poesis*) reigned without serious challenge, in the day of Newton's *Optics,* Addison's Lockean Pleasures of the visual imagination, and Thomson's often too thickly painted snowscape, thunderstorm, or sunshine, it is one of the marks of Pope's genius that he did not succumb to the princi- ple—at least not in any ambitious poem. Pope himself painted and had painter friends, he was a landscape gardener and architect, and we find such moments in his minor poetry as this in the lines *On His Grotto:*

where Thames' translucent wave
Shines a broad mirror through the shadowy cave;
Where lingering drops from mineral roofs distill,
And pointed crystals break the sparkling rill.

There may be too many sheer painterly epithets here (in a poem stem- ming from his architectural activity). The same tendency doubtless shows in the *Pastorals* and *Windsor Forest.* "My humble Muse, in unambitious strains, Paints the green forests and the flowery plains." In the Preface to the *Pastorals* he may cast suspicion upon himself when he argues that "the year has not that variety in it to furnish every month with a particular description, as it may every season." But then the reason for the description must be remembered—which was to correspond to human ages and passions. The cool, melodious, generalized and Virgilian symbols of Pope's *Pastorals* are not really nature description. It is an accepted (if far from complete, and perhaps not quite accurate) criticism of *Windsor Forest* to say that the landscape is a sylvan gallery for portraits of sportsman and statesman. Warburton was to put the principle bluntly in a note to the *Epistle to Augustus* (1. 319).

Descriptive poetry is the lowest work of a Genius. Therefore when Mr. Pope employs himself in it, he never fails, as here, to ennoble it with some moral stroke or other.

It would be easy enough to build up a case for Pope as a poet of quasi-romantic sensory acuteness. It is in his most mature poetry that one would find the best examples: "Die of a rose in aromatic pain," "Where slumber Abbots, purple as their wines," or the lines which he himself is said to have thought his most harmonious:

Lo! where Mæotis sleeps, and hardly flows
The freezing Tanais through a waste of snows. (*Dunciad* III, 87)

But such examples—like the best romantic descriptive poetry too—are not verbal odors, or verbal pictures, or verbal music; they are more like thoughts realized in the senses. It is the embodied concept which gives the *élan*.

The same kind of comments should be made about Pope's two poems in the pathetic mode, *Eloïsa* and the *Elegy to an Unfortunate Lady,* upon which the pre-romantic Warton believed Pope's reputation would largely depend. It is not as if the characteristic Pope did not reveal himself clearly—not as if he had made the plunge of *Epipsychidion* or *Adonais*. The complaint of *Eloïsa* is notable for its melancholy Miltonic landscape and its Ovidian tone, but no less for its complex psychology, its overlay of Christian upon pagan, its alternations of "grace and nature, virtue and passion," the casuistries of its rationale. The *Elegy* has its Elizabethan diction and metaphysical panegyric, its ghost, dagger and bleeding bosom borrowed from the "she" tragedies. But as in Gray's later and more celebrated *Elegy,* the sentiment for the neglected dead blends sweetly with observations on the end of pride. Through the Gothic and obscure atmosphere of Pope's *Elegy,* the sharp face of the satirist is distinctly visible.

Like Eastern Kings a lazy state they keep,
And close confined to their own palace, sleep.

>Thus unlamented pass the proud away,
>The gaze of fools, and pageant of a day!

In the end what was most remarkable about Pope was his capacity to assimilate almost any poetic vein to satire. Even the *Dunciad* contains its glimpse of Gothic moonlight—strangely shed.

>Silence, ye Wolves! while Ralph to Cynthia howls,
>And makes Night hideous—Answer him, ye Owls! (III, 165–166)

(In the next few lines, the Thames passage from Denham's *Cooper's Hill*, inspiration of *Windsor Forest*, makes an equally strange appearance: "Flow, Welsted, flow! like thine inspirer, Beer; Though stale, not ripe; though thin, yet never clear.") There was a way of writing verse, a "line of wit," toward which the genius of the age inclined. Pope, writing an elegiac lament, falls into his way, as before him Dryden, even in his forensic and bombastic drama, when he writes a notable line (if he is not echoing Shakespeare) may write something which sounds today like Pope.

>Youth should watch joys, and shoot 'em as they fly.

>Mean soul! and darest not gloriously offend.

>Cursed by your love, and blasted by your praise.[1]

Pope's career was to make the triumphant best of what was felt in the bones as the idiom of poetry.

    With that other of Pope's early poems, the most dramatic, continuously moving, and complete of his career, *The Rape of the Lock*, the critic's difficulty is to find words not too heavy to praise the intricacies of its radiant sense. The tone is that learned in the *Tatler* and *Spectator* school of didactic raillery at the morals and taste of the fair sex. The "pure wit" (*merum sal*) which was acknowledged by Addison, the "inexplicable beauties" of which Berkeley wrote to Pope, the "triumph of insignificance" celebrated a century later by Hazlitt, are ethical innuendo and "playing with fire." How far chimaeras might be indulged in poetry (as far as they seemed or deserved to be true, or as far as accepted by tradition, like fauns and fairies?) was one of the delicate critical issues of the seventeenth century, treated, for instance, in the verse *Essay upon Unnatural Flights in Poetry* by Pope's friend George Granville. *The Rape*

---

[1] *Aureng-Zebe* (1676), Acts III and IV. Cf. Pope, *Essay on Man*, I, 13; *Essay on Criticism*, 1. 159; *Satires* II, i, 84.

of the Lock is "Fancy's maze" in the sense that it is a brightly embroidered story, full of scenes, such as the Miltonic speech of Ariel to the other sylphs, the descent of Umbriel to the Spenserian Cave of Spleen, the Homeric battle of whalebone and bodkin, the Ariostan lunar limbo of vanity, in which literal plot, epic allegory, and fairy tale are irresolvably blended. The Rosicrucian sylphs and the battling belles and beaux are opposite parts of a spectrum, shaded from fabulous fancy to reality in so subtle a way that the latter survives the most aureate and airy liberties. The "mock-heroical" or high burlesque significance of the whole (whereby littleness is ironically exalted) depends less on fancy in any pictorial sense than on the sophisticated realities of the drawing room and on the echoes of an august and spacious tradition—Agamemnon's sceptre and Dido's funeral flames, "Thrones, Dominations, Princedoms, Virtues, Powers." The epic frame of reference is a way of criticism doubly successful because it is also a way of protecting the drawing room from that remainder of reality which looks in once, grimly, from a distance, when "wretches hang that jurymen may dine." The sophistication of the poem itself lies in its being no less affectionate than critical. A soft lustre falls upon the heroine and upon her surroundings. The raillery, like Pope's prefatory letter to the real-life heroine, Miss Arabella Fermor, is gallant. "If this Poem had as many Graces as there are in your Person, or in your Mind, yet I could never hope it should pass through the world half so Uncensured as You have done." The characteristic imagery is of silvery light (from lamp, vase, and token), Arabian perfume, the incense of coffee and chocolate. The characteristic rhetoric is the playful bathos—of husbands and lapdogs mentioned in the same breath, hearts and necklaces, chastity and shattered china. If the burlesque method of the poem is that of Boileau's *Lutrin* and Garth's grotesque *Dispensary,* the theme is one dear to the most refined spirit of Comedy, that of Molière's *Misanthrope,* Congreve's *Way of the World,* and Meredith's *Egoist*—the combat between the sexes, the finesses of premarital approach, as these are complicated and made perverse by the claims of social vanity.

At the inspirational level, it was one of the miracles of Pope's career that he could (against the advice of Addison) add the machinery of the sylphs, without wrecking the poem, and the highly colored and special incident of the game of Ombre. The latter succeeds and, aside from its internal interest, enhances the whole poem. Pope exploits the pictorial features of a pack of cards to make both a technically acceptable and imaginatively significant texture, "particolored" and "shining." His court cards meet the demands of realistic recognition and at the same time, like actual playing cards, especially the full-length cards of that day, are human and symbolic characters—the "warlike Amazon" of Spades, the "Club's black Tyrant," unwieldy and pompous, the "embroidered King" and "refulgent Queen" of Diamonds. "The Knave of Diamonds tries his wily arts, And wins (oh shameful chance!) the Queen of Hearts." Belinda pales and trembles at the threatened ruin. And the next moment she exults in her triumph—how precariously won! with what connivance of fate, for all her "skill"! And here is the prefiguration of actual downfall. For fate can take what it gives. The Baron has other weapons—"the glittering Forfex"—and if he loses the tour of Ombre, he wins the canto. The game of Ombre expands and reverberates delicately in the whole poem. The episode is a microcosm of the whole, a reflecting epitome of the combat which is its theme.

IV

The characteristic rhetoric of *The Rape of the Lock* is the bathos. To pass now to what may be supposed the extreme opposite among Pope's larger works, the *Essay on Man*—that is, from fancy to philosophy—we should note how the antithetic rhetorical frames have a different tilt or a different characteristic meaning, that of paradox.

> A hero perish, or a sparrow fall.
>
> And now a bubble burst, and now a world.
>
> The sot a hero, lunatic a king.
>
> And not a vanity is given in vain.

The difference is dramatic. The collocation of jewelry, china, and honor were imputed to the toyshop of Belinda's heart. But hero and sparrow, bubble and world, are compared in the speaker's own most earnest mind. Two basic paradoxes run through the *Essay,* especially through the first two *Epistles:* that humanity is both a very important and a very trivial thing; that we know a lot, but that we know very little. It is these which gleam variously in some of the most memorable passages, like the fourteen lines devoted to the Indian in Epistle I.

> Lo, the poor Indian! whose *untutored* mind   19
> Sees God in clouds, or hears him in the wind;
> His soul, proud Science *never* taught to *stray*
> Far as the solar walk, or milky way. (99–102)

The words which I have italicized point the paradox of knowledge, the obverse of which appears in Epistle II.

> Superior beings [i.e., angels], when of late they saw   20
> A mortal Man unfold all Nature's law,
> Admired such wisdom in an earthly shape,
> And showed a NEWTON as we show an Ape. (31–34)

The complementary paradox, that of being, runs through the links of the Great Chain in Epistle I and assumes toward the end of that Epistle a variety of theological forms. "All are but parts of one stupendous whole." "All Nature is but Art, unknown to thee." The fusion of the two paradoxes, that of knowledge and that of being, seen in the line just quoted, swells in the torrential opening of Epistle II.

> Placed on this isthmus of a middle state,   19
> A Being darkly wise, and rudely great:
>
> *   *   *   *   *
>
> Chaos of Thought and Passion, all confused;
> Still by himself abused, or disabused.
>
> *   *   *   *   *
>
> Sole judge of Truth, in endless Error hurled.
> The glory, jest, and riddle of the world!

There can be no question that a passage like this, echoing as it does through the whole poem, achieves a certain grandeur of direction and dramatizes something like a cosmic reverence before the veiled face of awful truths. Nevertheless, we may have difficulty when we try to take the poem as an entirety, rather than as a collection of eloquent moments. The matter is not really what a recent critic calls Pope's "inability to think and his ability to write as if he thought perfectly,"[1] or what Pope seems to confess in an Horatian Epistle to his "Guide, Philosopher, and Friend" Bolingbroke: ". . . no Prelate's Lawn with hair shirt lined Is half so incoherent as my Mind." We should be willing to let Crousaz and Warburton argue whether Pope was a deist or whether he had consistently any philosophic view at all. And the matter is not how much specific doctrine, rather than optimistic prompting, Pope derived from Bolingbroke, or how deeply Pope was immersed in classical, patristic, scholastic, and Renaissance traditions, what English divines, *esprits forts,* and fashionable heretics of his own day were his favorites. Criticism of the poem must inquire whether the inheritance of philosophy as Pope managed it generates any power. One trouble may be that the arguments of the last

[1] Yvor Winters, *The Anatomy of Nonsense* (Norfolk, 1943), p. 151.

two Epistles, "Of the Nature and State of Man with respect to Society," "Of the Nature and State of Man with respect to Happiness," too closely repeat, or merely expand, those of the first two; and another may be that the very paradoxical energy, so nervous and teetering, cannot soar or sweep to any climax. It may be too that Pope when under the control of his ideas loses some of the tactful wit which appears to be intuitive with him elsewhere.

> Not louder shrieks to pitying heaven are cast,   20.6
> When husbands, or when lap dogs breathe their last;
> (*Rape of the Lock,* III, 157–158)

> The lamb thy riot dooms to bleed today,   19
> Had he thy Reason, would he skip and play?
> (*Essay on Man,* I, 81–82)

The tender (almost vegetarian) sentiment which appears in these lines about the lamb—and again, at more length, in Epistle III ("No murder clothed him, and no murder fed")—suggests that Pope's ethical sense (illustrating Shaftesbury's theory) worked best in close connection with his sense of laughter.

Pope's *Moral Essays* also, intended as subdevelopments, in a master philosophic structure, of the fourth Epistle of the *Essay on Man,* may be read conveniently as anthologies or visited as galleries. The theory of the chameleon Ruling Passion, the contention that "Most Women have no Characters at all," and the Providential economics of the misuse of wealth, are less impressive than the dreadful portrait of a duchess, Atossa (inserted by Pope only on his deathbed), the bitter Juvenalian picture of the aged belles ("Still round and round the Ghosts of Beauty glide, And haunt the places where their Honour died"), the rise and fall of the parvenu Sir Balaam, or the most significant landscapes Pope ever painted, Timon's stupendous villa and the contrasted plantations where man's imperium is asserted by the Good Sense of Bathurst and Boyle.

An excellent essay on Pope bears the title "The Mask of Pope"[1] and argues that Pope wrote his most vital poetry when he forgot solemn theories and allowed himself to play. When he says that he "stooped to truth and moralized his song," there is an irony of which he may not be fully aware. Though the terms are genetic, referring to the poet rather than to his poetry, it may be they are the easiest way to a certain fact. The *Essay on Man* was written on a benevolent theory, expounded by both

---

[1] Austin Warren, "The Mask of Pope," *Sewanee Review,* LIV (Winter, 1946), 19–33.

Pope and Bolingbroke in their letters—it was "a book to make mankind look upon this life in comfort and pleasure, and put morality in good humour." Likewise Pope's Homeric translations proceeded from a theory of the grandeur of epic (a theory standardized by Le Bossu, applied to *Paradise Lost* by Addison in his *Spectators,* illustrated by the dunce Blackmore at monstrous length, and burlesqued by Pope himself in a *Guardian*). They proceeded too from a theory of translation, pleasantly set forth in the prefaces of Dryden. The assumptions would seem to have been something like this: Epic is the highest genre of poetry and the norm. The greatest epics are the Greek and Latin. There is nothing to match these in English. Translation is eminently possible. And so forth. We confront the fact that the translations and the *Essay on Man* made a large part of Pope's reputation in the eighteenth century and were the works through which he most largely exercised his influence upon English poetry. But judgments of value are not to be reached by the statistics of noses. Pope's *Iliad* is possibly the most spirited and readable verse translation of Homer in English—better than the flamboyance of Chapman or the weighty Miltonics of Cowper. But then it may be that Homer cannot be satisfactorily translated into English verse. Critics have considered the oratorical passages in Pope's *Iliad,* like the speech of Sarpedon to Glaucus in Book XII or the Grecian debates in Book IX, as the most successful, because giving most scope to Pope's heightened style. Their closest parallel in original literature, and a curiously close one, may be certain sequences in the drama of Racine. Pope's Homer is written in the terse rhetorical patterns of which he became a subconscious and automatic master, but they are something like blank patterns of the life in his other poems. To take one instance of fairly close parallel, in Book IX of the *Iliad:*

> Strong as they were, the bold Curetes failed,   20.6
> While Meleager's thundering arm prevailed. (665–666)

In the Horatian Epistle II, ii, published just twenty years later:

> Hopes after hopes of pious Papists failed,   21.6
> While mighty William's thundering arm prevailed. (62–63)

It is true that we may have here an element of self-parody, a mock-heroic joke which would be especially savored by Pope himself and his friends. Certain parallels between Pope's *Iliad* and his earlier *Rape of the Lock* are so piquant as to present a tricky problem of parody in reversed time.[1] But

[1] William Frost, "*The Rape of the Lock* and Pope's Homer," *Modern Language Quarterly,* VIII (September, 1947), 342–354.

in any case, the color and warmth is with the contemporary allusion. The style of Pope's Homer has a more remotely hectic and honorific glare.

> So many flames before proud Ilion blaze,   20
> And brighten glimmering Xanthus with their rays.
>   (*Iliad*, VIII, 560)

It was through his Homer that Pope (with an eye on Milton) did most to complete the development of English "poetic diction," the faithful coupling of nouns with a certain vocabulary of glossy epithets—*verdant, pendant, gelid, fleecy, finny, gilded, painted, dusky, shady.* "We acknowledge him [Homer] the Father of Poetical Diction," said Pope in the Preface to his *Iliad*. And Samuel Johnson would cite an earlier critic to the effect that "There is scarcely a happy combination of words or a phrase poetically elegant in the English language which Pope has not inserted in his version of Homer." "Poetic diction" was one curious fruit of Pope's great gift and concern for the word.

V

"Shut the door," writes Pope in his *Peri Bathous,* and then gives the equivalent of this in pseudo-poetic diction: "The wooden guardian of our privacy Quick on its axle turn." Pope is writing a prelude to the *Dunciad.* He is in the *Dunciad* mood.

> Shut, shut the door, good John! fatigued, I said,   19.6
> Tie up the knocker, say I'm sick, I'm dead.

These are the auspicious opening lines of the *Epistle to Arbuthnot* or Prologue to the Satires. Pope, like Horace, would have defended his low diction (*sermo pedestris*) in satires and didactic poems by saying that they were second grade, not lofty like the theme of Ilium. He was having fun; the mask was on. The saving grace of such a theory, or escape from theory, washed out poetic diction by letting in more kinds of diction and with them a fuller measure of life. "The word neither diffident nor ostentatious," says the modern poet,

> An easy commerce of the old and the new,   18
> The common word exact without vulgarity,
> The formal word precise but not pedantic.[1]

---

[1] "Little Gidding" from *Four Quartets,* copyright, 1943, by T. S. Eliot. By permission of Harcourt, Brace and Company, Inc.

Pope's satires are conspicuous for the variety of materials which they assimilate and for their toughness in naming things by their ordinary names—a virtue which Matthew Arnold was to find in Homer but not in Pope's Homeric translations (though Arnold was too lofty to approve the names *mutton* and *chicks* and *Hounslow Heath,* which he found in Pope's satires). This free use of vocabulary, joined with Pope's rhetorical nicety, constitutes what may be called his verbal marksmanship—the essential skill of the sportsman who would "shoot Folly as it flies."

Though satire moved with colloquial ease, its professed purpose was serious, that of holding up vice and folly to scornful ridicule—and sometimes too, as in the *Epistle to Arbuthnot,* of vindicating the ethos of the satirist himself. Arbuthnot and Pope made solemn professions to each other about the reforming and chastising power of satire. In the *Epistle to Augustus* Pope, following Horace rather loosely, wrote:

> Hence Satire rose, that just the medium hit,   20.6
> And heals with Morals what it hurts with Wit. (261–262)

But these lines should perhaps not be taken very seriously. Whether the satire healed or not, it must have hurt—and obviously it was fun to write, and to read if you were of the author's party or disinterested. In his 1717 Preface Pope had avowed that the chief advantage "accruing from a Genius to Poetry" was "the agreeable power of self-amusement." It is amusement we should seek in reading the satires, the bracing experience of wit. The characters both of dunces and vilifiers and of Pope himself (the fiendish monkey ladling out boiling oil) have become too much mixed up in the reading of his work. We are likely to be too much concerned with making interpretations which reveal mostly our own characters. There is perhaps no available answer to the question just how much more amiable Pope was than each of his enemies, or whether such feats as giving an emetic to Curll in a friendly glass of sack, or doctoring letters and tricking Curll into publishing them, or such traits as his elaborately pretended insensibility to criticism, are offset by Pope's filial piety, his forbearing to answer the attacks of the dunces for twenty years, his patience with his profligate protégé Savage, his charity in writing a Prologue for the aged blind Dennis. The more relevant thing for criticism is the *persona* of a satirist in a poem, the dramatic character of A. Pope feigned by himself in conversation with a virtuous friend, a masterpiece of fighting traits justified by benevolent intentions and milky innocence— or mock-innocence (it matters not; in either case, the victims must squirm, and the self-portrait remains in some degree inscrutable). The *Epistle to*

Arbuthnot is an exquisite vibration between mayhem and pious profes-
sions. After the ruthless "No creature smarts so little as a fool,"

> As yet a child, nor yet a fool to fame,   20
> I lisped in numbers, for the numbers came. (127–128)

After the ravaged portraits of the full-blown Bufo and amphibious Sporus
left hanging,

> Yet soft by nature, more a dupe than wit,   20
> *Sappho* can tell you how this man was bit. (368–369)

It is the skill and tact of the eviscerations which compel us in some
measure to accept the professions. We are coerced to the enjoyment of a
mixed view. The portrait of Addison as "Atticus" ends in laughter and
tears.

In the other of his satires which is deservedly best known, the *Epistle
to Augustus,* Pope gave the theory of translation and imitation of models
its ultimate and most rewarding twist. The imitated satires and epistles of
Horace were basically different from the translated Homer in that they
made a free use of Horace to score hits upon neo-Augustan London. One
of the freest uses of Horace that might have been conceived was to take
his panegyric submission to Octavius Augustus and reapply it to a monarch
(George Augustus) so grossly inferior that the irony was spontaneous.

> A vile Encomium doubly ridicules: 20.6
> There's nothing blackens like the ink of fools. (410–411)

This strategy frames the poem at beginning and end. The rest is Pope's
history of English literature ("Waller was smooth; but Dryden taught to
join The varying verse, the full-resounding line") or his view of one
quarrel between Ancients and Moderns—not that between the classics and
the late Renaissance (Boileau and Perrault), but one inside that, par-
alleling the case of Augustan literary Rome, between archaic and neo-
classic England. Here is the downright Augustan view, contested in
Temple's essays, transcended in Dryden's mellow Preface to his *Fables,*
complacently established in Addison's *Account of the Greatest English
Poets.* Again we ought to look to the fun of the thing:

> Chaucer's worst ribaldry is learned by rote,   19.6
> And beastly Skelton Heads of houses quote. (37–38)

At the same time the *Epistle* is an extraordinary instance, even for Pope,
of flickering shifts, or shimmers, of argument and tone. "Who now reads
Cowley? . . . But still I love the language of his heart."

Ward tried on Puppies, and the Poor, his Drop;   21
Even Radcliffe's Doctors travel first to France,
Nor dare to practise till they've learned to dance. (182–184)

The main point Pope is making is that only poets presume to practice before learning their craft (though this comes inside a general defence of poets). But the glancing, cursory satire is not content without hitting the doctors as it passes, two words being sufficient, *poor* and *dance*. The satire operates in all directions at once.

Of the other satires and epistles which Pope wrote in the Horatian way, *Satire* II, i, the mock-anxious dialogue with his counsel Fortescue, is perhaps the most amusing, a dress rehearsal for the *Epistle to Arbuthnot*. The friendly interlocutor urges restraint. The satirist plunges rashly on. "Fools rush into my head, and so I write." The second of the two *Dialogues* of 1738 (where the interlocutor only poses as a friend) contains the political satirist's surprisingly vehement statement of his conscious power and the high aim of his art. "Yes, I am proud; I must be proud to see Men not afraid of God, afraid of me." "O sacred weapon! left for Truth's defence, Sole Dread of Folly, Vice, and Insolence!" The other Epistles, to Murray, to Bolingbroke, to Colonel Anthony Browne, the Satire addressed to Bethel, and the two versifications of Donne, are less intense examples of the mode. Pope is to be read here as we listen to a rambling but accurate and cogent conversationalist, always pointed, occasionally breaking into brilliance. The *Epistle* to the Colonel (Horace, II, ii) contains the finely turned lyric complaint:

Years following years, steal something every day,   21
At last they steal us from ourselves away;
In one our Frolics, one Amusements end,
In one a Mistress drops, in one a Friend:
This subtle Thief of life, this paltry Time,
What will it leave me, if it snatch my rhyme?
If every wheel of that unwearied Mill
That turned ten thousand verses, now stands still? (72–79)

Reading Pope's tonic satire written in the decade 1730–1740, we may forget the infirmities and the fear of them which crowded so large on his horizon by reason both of the primitive medical age in which he lived and of his own specially wretched constitution. We may forget the constant proximity of death during the "long disease his life." These were the years when Pope's friends, Gay, Arbuthnot, Caryll, and others (many of his friends were older than he) were falling away, when Swift grew imbecile, when Pope himself was approaching the end.

After the Dialogues of 1738 one might have thought that Pope was played out. For about two years the wheels of the "unwearied mill" were actually at a stand. The unpromising event which seems to have reinspired motion was the alliance with Warburton. Lord Marchmont twitted Pope that he was trying to show how strong a poet he was by "what a quantity of dullness" he could carry on his back without sinking. In some strange way Warburton, a heavy annotator who by a slightly different turn of fate might have found himself among Pope's victims, afforded the support which enabled Pope to retire into the country and put together from his fragments a fourth *Dunciad* that was a climax to his life work. Few poets who have lived even to Pope's middle age have concluded their careers so strongly. The three-book *Dunciad* of 1728 and the larger *Dunciad* into which the first evolved differ from the Horatian satires in assuming the mock-heroic form and in being a more concentrated attack, not on vice and folly in general, but specifically on the abuses against knowledge—on "the diabolical power of stupidity." The *Dunciad* differs from *The Rape of the Lock* in that while both are mock-heroic, the latter, as Professor Tillotson has put it, is the "exquisitely diminished shadow" of a complete epic and hence of the epic form itself, the former is the "grotesque, life-size shadow" of an epic fragment. *Dunciad* I, where the Goddess of Dullness fixes on Bays (Theobald or Cibber) and anoints him King of her realm, is a magnified image of Dryden's *MacFlecknoe*. *Dunciad* II matches the funeral games of the *Aeneid* with the obscene, muddy, and sleepy contests of booksellers, poets, and critics. *Dunciad* III, close in structure to the prophetic visions of *Aeneid* VI and *Paradise Lost* XI and XII, is a Pisgah sight of the past, present, and future reign of Dullness. Whatever story struggles through the elaborate satire of these books is even more obstructed in the fourth (the accomplishment of the prophecies in III), which is unequalled in Pope's work for the density, intricacy, and wide heterogeneity of its materials (natural and artificial, social and philosophic, aristocratic and proletarian, pompous and frivolous) and for the pressure of wit under which they are amalgamated. *Dunciad* IV leaves story behind and becomes phantasmagoria or dream sequence. Certain details of Book I which applied first to the learned activities of Theobald become anomalous when we think of Cibber as hero. Under the dispensation of Book IV this scarcely seems to matter. Pope anticipates techniques by which at a later date his hero might have been a composite, a fluid transmogrification of pedant into laureate. The Cibberian forehead looms dimly enough through the Cimmerian gloom. The fantastic courtiers of Dullness—"bard and blockhead, side by side," "Dunce scorning Dunce," "Whore, Pupil, and laced Governor from France," fops, botanists, and sable pedants, spectres and harlot forms, all the "pert" and active as well as vacuous and torpid enemies of knowledge—throng on one another's heels in the kaleidoscopic twilight, the dusky Inferno, of such royal birthday drawing rooms as Fielding had shown on the stage in *Pasquin* and the *Author's Farce,* or, as the scene itself fades and transforms, of such an academic assembly for the conferring of degrees as Pope and Warburton had recently missed at Oxford. This is perhaps the place to remark, after both Pope and Warburton, that the identification of the dunces is not important. The notes supplied by Pope and his friends are part of the burlesque of pedantry—on a cruder level than the poem itself. "The context," as Professor Warren writes, "provides the categories, which are permanent, while the proper names are annually replaceable."

Like *The Rape of the Lock* and the *Essay on Man,* the *Dunciad* has its characteristic rhetoric, counterpart of the poem's satiric richness, a compression where metaphor, personification and paradoxical antithesis are inextricable:

> *Morality,* by her false Guardians drawn,
> *Chicane* in Furs, and *Casuistry* in Lawn. (IV, 27–28)

> There to her heart sad Tragedy addrest
> The dagger wont to pierce the Tyrant's breast. (IV, 37–38)

> And Alma Mater lie dissolved in Port! (III, 338)

As a treatise on knowledge (a comic expression of what might have been the second part of Pope's master philosophical development out of the *Essay on Man*) the *Dunciad* had been from the beginning implicitly also a treatise on language, whether in its philosophic or in its poetic and rhetorical abuses—"Major, Minor, and Conclusion quick," or "Figures ill paired, and Similes unlike." In *Dunciad* IV that preoccupation is developed even more distinctly out of the literary, educational, and metaphysical materials. Pope's last work is his most emphatic statement of the affinity between good sense and eloquence, nonsense and bombast.

> There foamed rebellious *Logic,* gagged and bound;
> There, stripped, fair *Rhetoric* languished on the ground;
> His blunted Arms by *Sophistry* are borne,
> And shameless *Billingsgate* her Robes adorn. (IV, 23–26)

Pope's career was devoted to the creative power of the word. *Dunciad* IV celebrates the word as destructive. "Since Man from beast by Words is known," says the pedant of the birchen garland, "Words are Man's province, Words we teach alone." And the *word* continues to resound:

". . . keep them in the pale of Words till death," "Give law to Words, or war with Words alone," ". . . on Words is still our whole debate," "First slave to Words, then vassal to a Name." These are preparations which are not lost sight of in the tremendous close of the poem.[1]

The opening of the book (like that of Pope's other mock-heroic *The Rape of the Lock,* and like that of *Dunciad* I) echoes an epic invocation, this time not daintily, nor even grotesquely, but with a negation which equals the solemnity of the Miltonic original. The power addressed by Pope must be implored to *refrain.*

> Yet, yet a moment, one dim Ray of Light
> Indulge, dread Chaos, and eternal Night!
> Of darkness visible so much be lent,
> As half to show, half veil, the deep Intent.
>
> * * * * *
>
> Suspend a while your Force inertly strong,
> Then take at once the Poet and the song.

The close of the poem raises burlesque to a stature that may well evoke the name of Longinus and carries the theme of negation to its limit. A yawn that spreads through fourteen lines, a vain invitation to the Muse to continue, and "the all-composing Hour" has arrived. . . . "The sable Throne . . . of *Night* primeval and of *Chaos* old!" "*Art* after *Art* goes out." With a final boldness, the poet reaches for the fullest metaphysical implications and theological mysteries attached to the word—the Logos:

> Lo! thy dread Empire, CHAOS! is restored;
> Light dies before thy uncreating word.

---

[1] The transfer of this close, or something like it, from the end of the original *Dunciad* III does not preclude special relations with details of *Dunciad* IV.

BIBLIOGRAPHICAL NOTE

The text of this edition is that of the large octavo edition of Pope's *Works* in nine volumes, 1751, by his literary executor William Warburton, except that: (1) elliptical spellings (e.g., *barb'rous, int'rest, sat'rist, vent'rous, pleas'd, thro'*) have been expanded or, in the case of most second-person singular verbs, simplified by omission of the apostrophe (e.g., *deignst, knowst*); (2) archaic spellings (e.g., *chear, dipt, plaister, prest, shew, syren, Cressi, Switz*) have been changed unless in rhyming positions; (3) a good many hyphens have been eliminated (in this I have tended to follow modern American rather than British usage); (4) commas, semicolons, other marks of punctuation, and quotation marks have occasionally been changed, omitted, or added where a conflict with modern usage was disturbing to sense; (5) a few clear mistakes have been corrected; (6) in the prose pieces titles of books have been italicized; (7) a few prose passages set in italic and one set largely in Gothic (the mock proclamation prefixed to the *Dunciad*) and the italicized verse quotations in the prose pieces have been changed to roman. I have for the most part followed Warburton's printer in the use of italics and capitals.

I have not been eager to load the pages of this volume with glosses of the kind which a reader can readily supply for himself from *Webster's Collegiate Dictionary* or *The Oxford Companion to English Literature*. The notes to the poems are mostly reproduced from Warburton's edition and are identified as Warburton's or as Pope's by the initials W. and P., either with or without brackets, as the initial does or does not actually appear in that edition. Where the initial does not appear, the authorship of the note has been determined so far as possible from the last editions seen by Pope. The standard of selection has been interest no less than information, and the notes of Pope and his literary executor have been preferred (even where less exact) to those of later editors, as having their own kind of dramatic relation to the poems. Unsigned notes or additions to Pope and Warburton notes are my own insertions. Some of these have been adapted and a few have been quoted verbatim from the edition of Pope's *Works* in ten volumes, 1871–1889, by Whitwell Elwin and W. J. Courthope. Others are derived from *The Twickenham Edition of the Poems of Alexander Pope,* eleven volumes, London, 1937–1969. Pope's prose essays in criticism were very slightly annotated by him;

these, especially the Preface to the *Iliad* and the Preface to *Shakespeare*, have therefore invited a larger array of my own annotations. I have indicated the sources of a number of these notes at appropriate places.

The now completed *Twickenham Edition of The Poems of Alexander Pope* includes the following: vol. i, *Pastoral Poetry and an Essay on Criticism*, ed. E. Audra and Aubrey Williams, 1961; vol. ii, *The Rape of the Lock and Other Poems*, ed. Geoffrey Tillotson, 1940 (rev. ed., 1954); vol. iii.1, *An Essay on Man*, ed. Maynard Mack, 1950; vol. iii.2, *Epistles to Several Persons*, ed. F. W. Bateson, 1951 (rev. ed., 1961); vol. iv, *Imitations of Horace*, ed. John Butt, 1939; vol. v, *The Dunciad*, ed. James Sutherland, 1943; vol. vi, *Minor Poems*, ed. Norman Ault and John Butt, 1954; vols. vii–viii, ix–x, *Translations of Homer, The Iliad, The Odyssey*, ed. Maynard Mack, Norman Callan, Robert Fagles, William Frost, and Douglas M. Knight, 1967; vol. xi, *Index*, ed. Maynard Mack, 1969. The *Twickenham* texts (with the exception of Homer) and selected annotations are available in a single volume, *The Poems of Alexander Pope*, ed. John Butt, London, 1963. Some of Pope's prose works may be read conveniently in modern editions: Norman Ault, ed., *The Prose Works of Alexander Pope*, vol. i, *The Earlier Works*, Oxford, 1963; Edna Leake Steeves (and R. H. Griffith), eds., *The Art of Sinking in Poetry: Martinus Scriblerus'* ΠΕΡΙ ΒΑΘΟΤΣ: *A Critical Edition* . . . , London, 1952; Charles Kerby-Miller, ed., *Memoirs of the Extraordinary Life, Works and Discoveries of Martinus Scriblerus* (by Pope and others), New Haven, 1950. Useful recent selected editions of Pope, with perceptive critical introductions are: Aubrey Williams, ed., *The Poetry and Prose of Alexander Pope*, Boston (Riverside), 1967; Martin Price, ed., *The Selected Poetry of Pope*, New York (Signet Classics), 1970.

The best of the early biographies of Pope and still the best short biography is that of Samuel Johnson, 1781 (see vol. iii of his *Lives of the Poets*, ed. G. B. Hill, Oxford, 1905). Another early biography that helped to set patterns for a tradition was that of Owen Ruffhead, London, 1761. Robert Carruthers' *Life of Pope*, London, 1853 (revised, 1857) is full of interest for the close student of Pope. W. J. Courthope's *Life of Pope* in vol. v of the Elwin-Courthope edition is still the most carefully comprehensive account for the years after 1727. George Sherburn, *The Early Career of Alexander Pope*, Oxford, 1934, puts the years up to 1727 under a special illumination. Edith Sitwell, *Alexander Pope*, London, 1930, is a sentimentally sympathetic tribute. Bonamy Dobrée's *Alexander Pope*, London, 1951, is picturesque literary biography. Norman Ault, *New Light on Pope*, London, 1949, gives reliable information in a number of special areas. And so does Robert Rogers, *The Major Satires of Alexander Pope*,

Urbana, 1955. Peter Quennell's *Alexander Pope: The Education of Genius 1688–1728*, London, 1968, is the first part of a book designed to bring the journalistic tradition in Pope biography up to date.

One of the manuscript sources available to Ruffhead and Johnson was the collection of notes made by Pope's friend, the Oxford Professor of Poetry, Joseph Spence, a selection of which was originally published as *Anecdotes . . . Collected from the Conversation of Mr. Pope,* by Samuel W. Singer, London, 1820. This basic biographical document is now available in a variorum text edited with meticulous and generous annotation by James M. Osborn, two volumes, Oxford, 1966. The most complete edition of Pope's *Letters* was for many years that in vols. vi–x of the Elwin–Courthope edition of the *Works.* Not only the number of letters but accuracy of texts, dating, identification of correspondents and general annotation were vastly improved and floods of new light thrown on Pope's life and literary career by the late George Sherburn's edition of *The Correspondence of Alexander Pope,* five volumes, Oxford, 1956. G. S. Rousseau, "A New Pope Letter," *PQ: Philological Quarterly,* XLV (1966), 409–418, adds one of Pope's best epistolary essays, about an outing by boat to the romantic ruins of Netley Abbey.

In 1957 John Butt published an essay ("Pope's Poetical Manuscripts," *Proceedings of the British Academy,* XL, 23–39) surveying the possibilities for study of Pope's habits of composition in the forty-eight surviving manuscripts in his hand (at the Bodleian Library, the British Museum, the Pierpont Morgan Library, the Huntington Library, and elsewhere). Four large manuscript poems of Pope are now available for study in handsome facsimile editions: Robert M. Schmitz, ed., *Pope's Windsor Forest 1712, A Study of the Washington University Holograph,* St. Louis, 1952; Earl R. Wasserman, *Pope's "Epistle to Bathurst," A Critical Reading with an Edition of the Manuscripts,* Baltimore, 1960; Maynard Mack, ed., *Alexander Pope, An Essay on Man, Reproductions of the Manuscripts in the Pierpont Morgan Library and the Houghton Library with the Printed Text of the Original Edition,* Oxford, 1962; Robert M. Schmitz, *Pope's Essay on Criticism 1709, A Study of the Bodleian Manuscript Text with Facsimiles, Transcripts, and Variants,* St. Louis, 1962.

One form of biographical record resides in the portraits of poets executed from life sittings. This record is especially ample and significant with Pope who, living in the high baroque era of the sisterhood of the fine arts and especially of painting and poetry, assiduously cultivated the friendship of the leading portraitists of his day and worked to project a visual public image of himself as the Homeric and Horatian man of virtue and genius. The present editor when selecting the profile vignette etching of Pope which has appeared on the title page of all printings of the first edition of this anthology, from 1951, began a study which led to *The Portraits of Alexander Pope,* New Haven, 1965, a book which presents more than two hundred pictures of Pope, arranged according to eighty-one life types.

Not only bibliographical studies but biographical and critical studies as well owe an immeasurable debt to R. H. Griffith's *Alexander Pope, a Bibliography,* vol. i, Austin, 1922, *Pope's Own Writings, 1709–1734;* vol. ii, Austin, 1927, *Pope's Own Writings, 1735–1751,* reprinted in two volumes, London, 1962.

Respectable criticism of Pope began with Joseph Warton's moderately progressive *Essay on the Genius and Writings of Pope,* vol. i, 1756; vol. ii, 1782. Hazlitt's lecture *On Dryden and Pope* in his *Lectures on the English Poets,* 1818, is a sparkling instance of romantic appreciation. Matthew Arnold's essay *The Study of Poetry* in T. H. Ward's *English Poets,* 1880, marks the low point of Pope's reputation as a "classic of our prose." The first three decades of the present century produced no marked change in critical attitudes toward Pope. But beginning about 1930, with the advent of a more "metaphysical" and hence soon of a more "classical" temper in literary studies, a new Pope is represented in a steadily lengthening series of scholarly critiques: Austin Warren's pioneer *Alexander Pope as Critic and Humanist,* Princeton, 1929; Emile Audra, *L'Influence Française dans L'Oeuvre de Pope,* Paris, 1931; R. K. Root, *The Poetical Career of Alexander Pope,* Princeton, 1938; Geoffrey Tillotson's penetrating study *The Poetry of Pope,* Oxford, 1938; Douglas M. Knight, *Pope and the Heroic Tradition,* New Haven, 1951 (on Pope's *Iliad,* a study leading toward the Twickenham *Homer* of 1967—see above); Ian Jack, *Pope,* London, 1954 (Pope's mastery in three main poetic genres—descriptive, didactic, satiric); Aubrey L. Williams, *Pope's Dunciad, A Study of Its Meaning,* Baton Rouge, 1955 (a landmark in the application of classical and Renaissance learning to the elucidation of Pope); Rebecca Price Parkin, *The Poetic Workmanship of Alexander Pope,* Minneapolis, 1955 (various *personae* or "implied dramatic speakers" in Pope's poems); G. Wilson Knight, *Laureate of Peace,* New York, 1955 (the inner flame of Pope's genius, a Nietzschean tension of Dionysian and Apollonian); Geoffrey Tillotson, *Pope and Human Nature,* 1958; Reuben Brower, *Alexander Pope, the Poetry of Allusion,* Oxford, 1959 (the Homeric, Virgilian, and Horatian Pope); Benjamin Boyce, *The Character Sketches in Pope's Poems,* Durham, N.C., 1962 (La Bruyère rather than Kneller—satire of type and individual); Thomas R. Edwards, Jr., *This Dark Estate: A Reading of Pope,* Berkeley and Los

Angeles, 1963 (emergent personal conflicts with the Augustan manner in Pope's later career); Thomas E. Maresca, *Pope's Horatian Poems,* Ohio State University, 1966 (elaborate application to Pope's poems of seventeenth–century Horatian moral commentary); Rachel Trickett, *The Honest Muse, A Study in Augustan Verse,* Oxford, 1967 (Pope as the Restoration simple, honest man in panegyric, satire, and elegy); Maynard Mack, *The Genius of the Place: Alexander Pope and the Theme of Retirement,* Toronto, 1969 (Pope as the retired philosopher king in his grotto, loosing his shafts of satire at the passing horsemen of the corrupt public world—a remarkably rounded vision of biographical and poetic elements in the focus of Pope's garden and grotto).

Among numerous shorter critical essays, the following are some that merit special attention: F. R. Leavis, "Pope," (from *Scrutiny,* 1933) in *Revaluation,* London, 1936 (Pope's metaphysical toughness); W. H. Auden, "Alexander Pope," in *From Anne to Victoria,* edited by Bonamy Dobrée, London, 1937 (Pope as the poet of the Augustan social reality); Geoffrey Tillotson, "Eighteenth-Century Poetic Diction" and "Alexander Pope" in *Essays in Criticism and Research,* Cambridge, 1942 (pioneer essays in the funded meanings of English "poetic diction"); Cleanth Brooks, "The Case of Miss Arabella Fermor: A Re-Examination," *Sewanee Review,* LI (1943), 505–524 (the saving graces of irony—also in *The Well-Wrought Urn,* New York, 1947); George Sherburn, "The *Dunciad,* Book IV," in *Studies in English . . . University of Texas,* Austin, 1944 (phantasmagoric images from the London theater of farce and burlesque); Austin Warren, "The Mask of Pope," *Sewanee Review,* LIV (1946), 19–33 (also in his *Rage for Order,* Chicago, 1948—see above p. liv); Maynard Mack, " 'Wit and Poetry and Pope': Some Observations on His Imagery," in *Pope and His Contemporaries,* ed. James L. Clifford and Louis A. Landa, Oxford, 1949 (the indirections of Pope's "poetry of statement"); Maynard Mack, "The Muse of Satire," *The Yale Review,* XLI (1951), 80–92 (three voices of Pope's satire, the *vir bonus,* the *ingénu,* the public defender); Samuel H. Monk, "A Grace Beyond the Reach of Art, *JHI: Journal of the History of Ideas,* V (1944), 131–150 (background of a key phrase in the *Essay on Criticism*); E. N. Hooker, "Pope on Wit: The 'Essay on Criticism'," in R. F. Jones *et al., The Seventeenth Century,* Stanford, 1951 (background of another key term in the *Essay on Criticism*); William Empson, "Wit in the 'Essay on Criticism'," *Hudson Review,* II (1950), 559–577 (wit as salon talk, criticism, poetry—also in his *Complex Words,* 1951); J. M. Cameron, "Doctrinal to an Age: Notes Toward a Revaluation of Pope's *Essay on Man," Dublin Review,* (1951), 54–69 (better than "versified philosophy"); Douglas M. Knight, "Pope as a Student of Homer," *Comparative Literature,* IV (1952), 75–82 (mediation between Homer and the English Augustan realities); Hugo M. Reichard, "Pope's Social Satire: Belles-Lettres and Business," *PMLA,* LXVII (1952), 420–434 (the *Dunciad* view of commercialized society, debased art); Henry Pettit, "Pope's *Eloïsa to Abelard:* An Interpretation," *University of Colorado Studies,* IV (1953), 67–74 (erotic emotionalism vs. Cartesian rationalism); Elias F. Mengel, Jr., "Patterns of Imagery in Pope's *Arbuthnot,*" *PMLA,* LXIX (1954), 189–197 (motifs of disease and animality); G. R. Hibbard, "The Country House Poem of the Seventeenth Century," *Journal of the Warburg and Courtauld Institutes,* XIX (1956), 159–174 (development of the genre from Jonson's "To Penshurst" through Pope's *Epistle to Burlington*); Brendan O'Hehir, "Virtue and Passion: The Dialectic of *Eloïsa to Abelard,*" *Texas Studies in Literature and Language,* II (1960), 219–232 (rhetorical violence, dialectic purpose); Frederick S. Troy, "Pope's Images of Man," *Massachusetts Review,* I (1960), 359–384 (classical morality in satire, rationalist sentiment in the *Essay on Man*); Aubrey Williams, "The 'Fall of China' and *The Rape of the Lock,*" *PQ: Philological Quarterly,* XLI (1962), 412–425 (human frailty imaged in the shattering of China vessels); John M. Aden, "Pope and the Satiric Adversary," *SEL: Studies in English Literature,* II (1962), 267–286 (interlocutors, friendly and hostile); Alvin B. Kernan, "The *Dunciad* and the Plot of Satire," *SEL: Studies in English Literature,* II (1962), 255–266 (geometry of the *Dunciad,* expansion into nothingness); Bertrand A. Goldgar, "Pope's Theory of the Passions: The Background of Epistle II of the *Essay on Man,*" *PQ: Philological Quarterly,* XLI (1962), 730–742 (French Pyrrhonism, English Latitudinarianism); Benjamin Boyce, "Baroque and Satire: Pope's Frontispiece for the 'Essay on Man'," *Criticism,* IV (1962), 14–27, eight plates (Italian capriccio background of the ruins of time, for Pope's best-known drawing); Giorgio Melchiori, "Pope in Arcady: The Theme of *Et in Arcadia Ego* in his Pastorals," *English Miscellany,* XIV (1963), 83–93 (Pope and Poussin—a shadow over the pastoral world); David Ridgley Clark, "Landscape Painting Effects in Pope's Homer," *JAAC: Journal of Aesthetics and Art Criticism,* XXII (1963), 25–28 (arrested action, Claudian perspectives); G. Thomas Fairclough, "Pope and Boileau: A Supplementary Note," *Neuphilologische Mitteilungen,* LXIV (1963), 232–243 (Jansenism and Augustan common sense); Peter Dixon, "Pope's Shakespeare," *JEGP: Journal of English and German Philology,* LXIII (1964), 191–203 (Shakespeare a kindred satiric spirit); F. E. L. Priestley, "Pope and the Great Chain of Being," in *Essays . . . Presented to A. S. P. Woodhouse,* ed. Millar McClure and F. W. Watt, Toronto, 1964 ("ALL subsists by elemental strife"); Tony Tanner, "Reason and the Grotesque: Pope's *Dunciad*," *Critical Quarterly*, VII (1965), 145–160 (pessimism of the Enlightenment dream); Martin C. Battestin, "The Transforming Power: Nature and Art in Pope's Pastorals," *Eighteenth Century Studies*, II (1969), 183–204 (lapsarian man—the gulf between art and nature).

A number of the articles listed above and some others relating to all main aspects of Pope's literary career have been usefully collected in *Essential Articles for the Study of Alexander Pope*, ed. Maynard Mack, Hamden, Connecticut: Archon Books, 1964, 2nd ed., revised and enlarged, 1968.

ALEXANDER POPE

selected poetry
& prose

PREFACE

I am inclined to think that both the writers of books, and the readers of them, are generally not a little unreasonable in their expectations. The first seem to fancy that the world must approve whatever they produce, and the latter to imagine that authors are obliged to please them at any rate. Methinks, as on the one hand, no single man is born with a right of controlling the opinions of all the rest; so on the other, the world has no title to demand, that the whole care and time of any particular person should be sacrificed to its entertainment. Therefore I cannot but believe that writers and readers are under equal obligations, for as much fame, or pleasure, as each affords the other.

Every one acknowledges, it would be a wild notion to expect perfection in any work of man: and yet one would think the contrary was taken for granted, by the judgment commonly passed upon Poems. A Critic supposes he has done his part, if he proves a writer to have failed in an expression, or erred in any particular point: and can it then be wondered at, if the Poets in general seem resolved not to own themselves in any error? For as long as one side will make no allowances, the other will be brought to no acknowledgments.

I am afraid this extreme zeal on both sides is ill-placed; Poetry and Criticism being by no means the universal concern of the world, but only the affair of idle men who write in their closets, and of idle men who read there.

Yet sure upon the whole, a bad Author deserves better usage than a bad Critic: for a Writer's endeavour, for the most part, is to please his Readers, and he fails merely through the misfortune of an ill judgment; but such a Critic's is to put them out of humour; a design he could never go upon without both that and an ill temper.

I think a good deal may be said to extenuate the fault of bad Poets. What we call a Genius, is hard to be distinguished

by a man himself, from a strong inclination: and if his genius
be ever so great, he cannot at first discover it any other way, than
by giving way to that prevalent propensity which renders him
the more liable to be mistaken. The only method he has, is to
make the experiment by writing, and appealing to the judgment
of others: now if he happens to write ill (which is certainly no
sin in itself) he is immediately made an object of ridicule. I
wish we had the humanity to reflect that even the worst authors
might, in their endeavour to please us, deserve something at our
hands. We have no cause to quarrel with them but for their
obstinacy in persisting to write; and this too may admit of alle-
viating circumstances. Their particular friends may be either
ignorant, or insincere; and the rest of the world in general is
too well bred to shock them with a truth, which generally their
Booksellers are the first that inform them of. This happens not
till they have spent too much of their time, to apply to any pro-
fession which might better fit their talents; and till such talents
as they have are so far discredited as to be but of small service
to them. For (what is the hardest case imaginable) the repu-
tation of a man generally depends upon the first steps he makes
in the world, and people will establish their opinion of us, from
what we do at that season when we have least judgment to di-
rect us.

On the other hand, a good Poet no sooner communicates his
works with the same desire of information, but it is imagined
he is a vain young creature given up to the ambition of fame;
when perhaps the poor man is all the while trembling with the
fear of being ridiculous. If he is made to hope he may please the
world, he falls under very unlucky circumstances: for, from the
moment he prints, he must expect to hear no more truth, than
if he were a Prince, or a Beauty. If he has not very good sense
(and indeed there are twenty men of wit, for one man of sense)
his living thus in a course of flattery may put him in no small
danger of becoming a Coxcomb: if he has, he will consequently
have so much diffidence as not to reap any great satisfaction from
his praise; since, if it be given to his face, it can scarce be distin-
guished from flattery, and if in his absence, it is hard to be cer-
tain of it. Were he sure to be commended by the best and most

knowing, he is as sure of being envied by the worst and most ignorant, which are the majority; for it is with a fine Genius as with a fine fashion, all those are displeased at it who are not able to follow it: and it is to be feared that esteem will seldom do any man so much good, as ill-will does him harm. Then there is a third class of people who make the largest part of mankind, those of ordinary or indifferent capacities; and these (to a man) will hate, or suspect him: a hundred honest Gentlemen will dread him as a Wit, and a hundred innocent Women as a Satirist. In a word, whatever be his fate in Poetry, it is ten to one but he must give up all the reasonable aims of life for it. There are indeed some advantages accruing from a Genius to Poetry, and they are all I can think of: the agreeable power of self-amusement when a man is idle or alone; the privilege of being admitted into the best company; and the freedom of saying as many careless things as other people, without being so severely remarked upon.

I believe, if any one, early in his life, should contemplate the dangerous fate of authors, he would scarce be of their number on any consideration. The life of a Wit is a warfare upon earth; and the present spirit of the learned world is such, that to attempt to serve it (any way) one must have the constancy of a martyr, and a resolution to suffer for its sake. I could wish people would believe what I am pretty certain they will not, that I have been much less concerned about Fame than I durst declare till this occasion, when methinks I should find more credit than I could heretofore: since my writings have had their fate already, and it is too late to think of prepossessing the reader in their favour. I would plead it as some merit in me, that the world has never been prepared for these Trifles by Prefaces, biased by recommendations, dazzled with the names of great Patrons, wheedled with fine reasons and pretences, or troubled with excuses. I confess it was want of consideration that made me an author; I writ because it amused me; I corrected because it was as pleasant to me to correct as to write; and I published because I was told I might please such as it was a credit to please. To what degree I have done this, I am really ignorant; I had too much fondness for my productions to judge of them at first, and too much judgment to be pleased with them at last. But I have reason to think they can have no reputation which will continue long, or which deserves to do so: for they have always fallen short not only of what I read of others, but even of my own Ideas of Poetry.

If any one should imagine I am not in earnest, I desire him to reflect, that the Ancients (to say the least of them) had as much Genius as we: and that to take more pains, and employ more time, cannot fail to produce more complete pieces. They constantly applied themselves not only to that art, but to that single branch of an art, to which their talent was most powerfully bent; and it was the business of their lives to correct and finish their works for posterity. If we can pretend to have used the same industry, let us expect the same immortality: Though if we took the same care, we should still lie under a further misfortune: they writ in languages that became universal and everlasting, while ours are extremely limited both in extent and in duration. A mighty foundation for our pride! when the utmost we can hope, is but to be read in one Island, and to be thrown aside at the end of one Age.

All that is left us is to recommend our productions by the imitation of the Ancients: and it will be found true, that, in every age, the highest character for sense and learning has been obtained by those who have been most indebted to them. For, to say truth, whatever is very good sense, must have been common sense in all times; and what we call Learning, is but the knowledge of the sense of our predecessors. Therefore they who say our thoughts are not our own, because they resemble the Ancients, may as well say our faces are not our own, because they are like our Fathers: And indeed it is very unreasonable, that people should expect us to be Scholars, and yet be angry to find us so.

I fairly confess that I have served myself all I could by reading; that I made use of the judgment of authors dead and living; that I omitted no means in my power to be informed of my errors, both by my friends and enemies: But the true reason these pieces are not more correct, is owing to the consideration how short a time they, and I, have to live: One may be ashamed to consume half one's days in bringing sense and rhyme together; and what Critic can be so unreasonable, as not to leave a man time enough for any more serious employment, or more agreeable amusement?

The only plea I shall use for the favour of the public, is, that I have as great a respect for it, as most authors have for themselves; and that I have sacrificed much of my own self-love for its sake, in preventing not only many mean things from seeing the light, but many which I thought tolerable. I would not be like those Authors, who forgive themselves some particular lines for the sake of a whole Poem, and *vice versa* a whole Poem for the sake of some particular lines. I believe no one qualification is so likely to make a good writer, as the power of rejecting his own thoughts; and it must be this (if any thing) that can give me a chance to be one. For what I have published, I can only hope to be pardoned; but for what I have burned, I deserve to be praised. On this account the world is under some obligation to me, and owes me the justice in return, to look upon no verses as mine that are not inserted in this collection. And perhaps nothing could make it worth my while to own what are really so, but to avoid the imputation of so many dull and immoral things, as partly by malice, and partly by ignorance, have been ascribed to me. I must further acquit myself of the presumption of having lent my name to recommend any Miscellanies, or Works of other men; a thing I never thought becoming a person who has hardly credit enough to answer for his own.

In this office of collecting my pieces, I am altogether uncertain, whether to look upon myself as a man building a monument, or burying the dead.

If Time shall make it the former, may these Poems (as long as they last) remain as a testimony, that their Author never made his talents subservient to the mean and unworthy ends of Party or Self-interest; the gratification of public prejudices, or private passions; the flattery of the undeserving, or the insult of the unfortunate. If I have written well, let it be considered that 'tis what no man can do without good sense, a quality that not only renders one capable of being a good writer, but a good man. And if I have made any acquisition in the opinion of any one under the notion of the former, let it be continued to me under no other title than that of the latter.

But if this publication be only a more solemn funeral of my Remains, I desire it may be known that I die in charity, and in my senses; without any murmurs against the justice of this age, or any mad appeals to posterity. I declare I shall think the world in the right, and quietly submit to every truth which time shall discover to the prejudice of these writings; not so much as wishing so irrational a thing, as that every body should be deceived merely for my credit. However, I desire it may then be considered, That there are very few things in this collection which were not written under the age of five and twenty: so that my youth may be made (as it never fails to be in Executions) a case of compassion. That I was never so concerned about my works as to vindicate them in print, believing, if any thing was good, it would defend itself, and what was bad could never be defended. That I used no artifice to raise or continue a reputation, depreciated no dead author I was obliged to, bribed no living one with unjust praise, insulted no adversary with ill language; or when I could not attack a Rival's works, encouraged reports against his Morals. To conclude, if this volume perish, let it serve as a warning to the Critics, not to take too much pains for the future to destroy such things as will die of themselves; and a *Memento mori* to some of my vain contemporaries the Poets, to teach them that, when real merit is wanting, it avails nothing to have been encouraged by the great, commended by the eminent, and favoured by the public in general.

November 10, 1716

PASTORALS
With a discourse on pastoral
WRITTEN IN THE YEAR MDCCIV

Rura mihi et rigui placeant in vallibus amnes,
Flumina amem, sylvasque, inglorius!
VIRGIL [Georgics ii. 485–486.]

A DISCOURSE ON
PASTORAL POETRY[1]

There are not, I believe, a greater number of any sort of verses than of those which are called Pastorals; nor a smaller, than of those which are truly so. It therefore seems necessary to give some account of this kind of Poem, and it is my design to comprise in this short paper the substance of those numerous dissertations the Critics have made on the subject, without omitting any of their rules in my own favour. You will also find some points reconciled, about which they seem to differ, and a few remarks, which, I think, have escaped their observation.

The original of Poetry is ascribed to that Age which succeeded the creation of the world: and as the keeping of flocks

---

[1] Written at sixteen years of age. P.

seems to have been the first employment of mankind, the most ancient sort of poetry was probably *pastoral*. It is natural to imagine, that the leisure of those ancient shepherds admitting and inviting some diversion, none was so proper to that solitary and sedentary life as singing; and that in their songs they took occasion to celebrate their own felicity. From hence a Poem was invented, and afterwards improved to a perfect image of that happy time; which by giving us an esteem for the virtues of a former age, might recommend them to the present. And since the life of shepherds was attended with more tranquility than any other rural employment, the Poets chose to introduce their Persons, from whom it received the name of Pastoral.

A Pastoral is an imitation of the action of a shepherd, or one considered under that character. The form of this imitation is dramatic, or narrative, or mixed of both; the fable simple, the manners not too polite nor too rustic: the thoughts are plain, yet admit a little quickness and passion, but that short and flowing: the expression humble, yet as pure as the language will afford; neat, but not florid; easy, and yet lively. In short, the fable, manners, thoughts, and expressions are full of the greatest simplicity in nature.

The complete character of this poem consists in simplicity, brevity, and delicacy; the two first of which render an eclogue natural, and the last delightful.

If we would copy Nature, it may be useful to take this Idea along with us, that Pastoral is an image of what they call the golden age. So that we are not to describe our shepherds as shepherds at this day really are, but as they may be conceived then to have been; when the best of men followed the employment. To carry this resemblance yet farther, it would not be amiss to give these shepherds some skill in astronomy, as far as it may be useful to that sort of life. And an air of piety to the Gods should shine through the Poem, which so visibly appears in all the works of antiquity: and it ought to preserve some relish of the old way of writing; the connection should be loose, the narrations and descriptions short, and the periods concise. Yet it is not sufficient, that the sentences only be brief, the whole Eclogue should be so too. For we cannot suppose Poetry in those days to have been the business of men, but their recreation at vacant hours.

But with a respect to the present age, nothing more conduces to make these composures natural, than when some Knowledge in rural affairs is discovered. This may be made to appear rather done by chance than on design, and sometimes is best shown by inference; lest by too much study to seem natural, we destroy that easy simplicity from whence arises the delight. For what is inviting in this sort of poetry proceeds not so much from the Idea of that business, as of the tranquility of a country life.

We must therefore use some illusion to render a Pastoral delightful; and this consists in exposing the best side only of a shepherd's life, and in concealing its miseries. Nor is it enough to introduce shepherds discoursing together in a natural way; but a regard must be had to the subject; that it contain some particular beauty in itself, and that it be different in every Eclogue. Besides, in each of them a designed scene or prospect is to be presented to our view, which should likewise have its variety. This variety is obtained in a great degree by frequent comparisons, drawn from the most agreeable objects of the country; by interrogations to things inanimate; by beautiful digressions, but those short; sometimes by insisting a little on circumstances; and lastly, by elegant turns on the words, which render the numbers extremely sweet and pleasing. As for the numbers themselves, though they are properly of the heroic measure, they should be the smoothest, the most easy and flowing imaginable.

It is by rules like these that we ought to judge of Pastoral. And since the instructions given for any art are to be delivered as that art is in perfection, they must of necessity be derived from those in whom it is acknowledged so to be. It is therefore from the practice of Theocritus and Virgil (the only undisputed authors of Pastoral) that the Critics have drawn the foregoing notions concerning it.

Theocritus excels all others in Nature and simplicity. The

subjects of his Idyllia are purely pastoral; but he is not so exact in his persons, having introduced reapers and fishermen as well as shepherds. He is apt to be too long in his descriptions, of which that of the Cup in the first pastoral is a remarkable instance. In the manners he seems a little defective, for his swains are sometimes abusive and immodest, and perhaps too much inclining to rusticity; for instance, in his fourth and fifth Idyllia. But 'tis enough that all others learnt their excellencies from him, and that his Dialect alone has a secret charm in it, which no other could ever attain.

Virgil, who copies Theocritus, refines upon his original: and in all points where judgment is principally concerned, he is much superior to his master. Though some of his subjects are not pastoral in themselves, but only seem to be such; they have a wonderful variety in them, which the Greek was a stranger to. He exceeds him in regularity and brevity, and falls short of him in nothing but simplicity and propriety of style; the first of which perhaps was the fault of his age, and the last of his language.

Among the moderns, their success has been greatest who have most endeavoured to make these ancients their pattern. The most considerable Genius appears in the famous Tasso, and our Spenser. Tasso in his *Aminta* has as far excelled all the Pastoral writers, as in his *Gierusalemme* he has outdone the Epic poets of his country. But as this piece seems to have been the original of a new sort of poem, the Pastoral Comedy, in Italy, it cannot so well be considered as a copy of the ancients. Spenser's *Calendar,* in Mr. Dryden's opinion, is the most complete work of this kind which any nation has produced ever since the time of Virgil. Not but that he may be thought imperfect in some few points. His Eclogues are somewhat too long, if we compare them with the ancients. He is sometimes too allegorical, and treats of matters of religion in a pastoral style, as Mantuan had done before him. He has employed the Lyric measure, which is contrary to the practice of the old Poets. His Stanza is not still the same, nor always well chosen. This last may be the reason his expression is sometimes not concise enough: for the Tetrastich has obliged him to extend his sense to the length of four lines, which would have been more closely confined in the Couplet.

In the manners, thoughts, and characters, he comes near to Theocritus himself; though, notwithstanding all the care he has taken, he is certainly inferior in his Dialect: For the Doric had its beauty and propriety in the time of Theocritus; it was used in part of Greece, and frequent in the mouths of many of the greatest persons: whereas the old English and country phrases of Spenser were either entirely obsolete, or spoken only by people of the lowest condition. As there is a difference betwixt simplicity and rusticity, so the expression of simple thoughts should be plain, but not clownish. The addition he has made of a Calendar to his Eclogues, is very beautiful; since by this, besides the general moral of innocence and simplicity, which is common to other authors of Pastoral, he has one peculiar to himself; he compares human Life to the several Seasons, and at once exposes to his readers a view of the great and little worlds, in their various changes and aspects. Yet the scrupulous division of his Pastorals into Months, has obliged him either to repeat the same description, in other words, for three months together; or, when it was exhausted before, entirely to omit it: whence it comes to pass that some of his Eclogues (as the sixth, eighth, and tenth for example) have nothing but their Titles to distinguish them. The reason is evident, because the year has not that variety in it to furnish every month with a particular description, as it may every season.

Of the following Eclogues I shall only say, that these four comprehend all the subjects which the Critics upon Theocritus and Virgil will allow to be fit for pastoral: That they have as much variety of description, in respect of the several seasons, as Spenser's: that in order to add to this variety, the several times of the day are observed, the rural employments in each season or time of day, and the rural scenes or places proper to such employments; not without some regard to the several ages of man, and the different passions proper to each age.

But after all, if they have any merit, it is to be attributed to some good old Authors, whose works as I had leisure to study, so I hope I have not wanted care to imitate.

SPRING[2]

The First Pastoral, or Damon

To Sir William Trumbull

FIRST in these fields I try the sylvan strains,
Nor blush to sport on Windsor's blissful plains:
Fair Thames, flow gently from thy sacred spring,
While on thy banks Sicilian Muses sing;
Let vernal airs through trembling osiers play,   5
And Albion's cliffs resound the rural lay.

    You, that too wise for pride, too good for power,
Enjoy the glory to be great no more,
And carrying with you all the world can boast,
To all the world illustriously are lost!   10
O let my Muse her slender reed inspire,
Till in your native shades you tune the lyre:[3]
So when the Nightingale to rest removes,
The Thrush may chant to the forsaken groves,
But, charmed to silence, listens while she sings,   15
And all th' aërial audience clap their wings.

    Soon as the flocks shook off the nightly dews,
Two Swains, whom Love kept wakeful, and the Muse,
Poured o'er the whitening vale their fleecy care,
Fresh as the morn, and as the season fair: 20
The dawn now blushing on the mountain's side,
Thus Daphnis spoke, and Strephon thus replied.

---

[2] These Pastorals were written at the age of sixteen . . . . the Author esteemed these as the most correct in the versification, and musical in the numbers, of all his works . . . . In a letter of his to Mr. *Walsh* about this time we find an enumeration of several Niceties in Versification, which perhaps have never been strictly observed in any *English* poem, except in these Pastorals. They were not printed till 1709. P.

[3] Sir W. Trumbull was born in Windsor Forest, to which he retreated, after he had resigned the post of Secretary of State to King William III. P.

12

Daphnis

Hear how the birds, on every gloomy spray,
With joyous music wake the dawning day!
Why sit we mute when early linnets sing,   25
When warbling Philomel salutes the spring?
Why sit we sad when Phosphor shines so clear,
And lavish Nature paints the purple year?

Strephon

Sing then, and Damon shall attend the strain,
While yon slow oxen turn the furrowed plain.   30
Here the bright crocus and blue violet glow;
Here western winds on breathing roses blow.
I'll stake yon lamb, that near the fountain plays,
And from the brink his dancing shade surveys.

Daphnis

And I this bowl, where wanton ivy twines,   35
And swelling clusters bend the curling vines:
Four figures rising from the work appear,
The various seasons of the rolling year;
And what is that, which binds the radiant sky,
Where twelve fair signs in beauteous order lie?   40

Damon

Then sing by turns, by turns the Muses sing,
Now hawthorns blossom, now the daisies spring,
Now leaves the trees, and flowers adorn the ground;
Begin, the vales shall every note rebound.

Strephon

Inspire me, Phœbus, in my Delia's praise   45
With Waller's strains, or Granville's moving lays![4]
A milk-white bull shall at your altars stand,
That threats a fight, and spurns the rising sand.

Daphnis

O Love! for Sylvia let me gain the prize,
And make my tongue victorious as her eyes;   50
No lambs or sheep for victims I'll impart,
Thy victim, Love, shall be the shepherd's heart.

Strephon

Me gentle Delia beckons from the plain,
Then hid in shades, eludes her eager swain;
But feigns a laugh, to see me search around,   55
And by that laugh the willing fair is found.

Daphnis

The sprightly Sylvia trips along the green,
She runs, but hopes she does not run unseen;
While a kind glance at her pursuer flies,
How much at variance are her feet and eyes!   60

Strephon

O'er golden sands let rich Pactolus flow,
And trees weep amber on the banks of Po;

---

[4] George Granville, afterwards Lord Lansdowne, known for his Poems, most of which he composed very young, and proposed Waller as his model. P.

Blest Thames's shores the brightest beauties yield,
Feed here my lambs, I'll seek no distant field.

Daphnis

    Celestial Venus haunts Idalia's groves;   65
Diana Cynthus, Ceres Hybla loves;
If Windsor shades delight the matchless maid,
Cynthus and Hybla yield to Windsor shade.

Strephon

    All nature mourns, the Skies relent in showers,
Hushed are the birds, and closed the drooping flowers;
If Delia smile, the flowers begin to spring,   71
The skies to brighten, and the birds to sing.

Daphnis

    All nature laughs, the groves are fresh and fair,
The Sun's mild lustre warms the vital air;
If Sylvia smiles, new glories gild the shore,   75
And vanquished nature seems to charm no more.

Strephon

    In spring the fields, in autumn hills I love,
At morn the plains, at noon the shady grove,
But Delia always; absent from her sight,
Nor plains at morn, nor groves at noon delight.   80

Daphnis

    Sylvia's like autumn ripe, yet mild as May,
More bright than noon, yet fresh as early day;

Even spring displeases, when she shines not here;
But blest with her, 'tis spring throughout the year.

Strephon

Say, Daphnis, say, in what glad soil appears,   85
A wondrous Tree that sacred Monarchs bear:[5]
Tell me but this, and I'll disclaim the prize,
And give the conquest to thy Sylvia's eyes.

Daphnis

Nay tell me first, in what more happy fields
The Thistle springs, to which the Lily yields:[6]   90
And then a nobler prize I will resign;
For Sylvia, charming Sylvia, shall be thine.

Damon

Cease to contend, for, Daphnis, I decree,
The bowl to Strephon, and the lamb to thee:
Blest Swains, whose Nymphs in every grace excel;   95
Blest Nymphs, whose Swains those graces sing so well!
Now rise, and haste to yonder woodbine bowers,
A soft retreat from sudden vernal showers;
The turf with rural dainties shall be crowned,
While opening blooms diffuse their sweets around.   100
For see! the gathering flocks to shelter tend,
And from the Pleiads fruitful showers descend.

[5] An allusion to the Royal Oak, in which Charles II had been hid from
the pursuit after the battle of Worcester. P.
[6] Alludes to the device of the Scots Monarchs, the Thistle, worn by Queen
Anne; and to the arms of France, the Fleur-de-lis. The two riddles are in
imitation of those in Virgil *Eclogue* iii.
    Dic quibus in terris inscripti nomina *Regum*
    Nascantur *Flores, et* Phyllida solus habeto. P.

SUMMER

The Second Pastoral, or Alexis

To Dr. Garth

A Shepherd's Boy (he seeks no better name)
Let forth his flocks along the silver Thame,
Where dancing sunbeams on the waters played,
And verdant alders formed a quivering shade.
Soft as he mourned, the streams forgot to flow,   5
The flocks around a dumb compassion show,
The Naiads wept in every watery bower,
And Jove consented in a silent shower.

    Accept, O GARTH,[7] the Muse's early lays,
That adds this wreath of Ivy to thy Bays;   10
Hear what from Love unpractised hearts endure,
From Love, the sole disease thou canst not cure.

    Ye shady beeches, and ye cooling streams,
Defence from Phœbus', not from Cupid's beams,
To you I mourn, nor to the deaf I sing,   15
The woods shall answer, and their echo ring.[8]
The hills and rocks attend my doleful lay,
Why art thou prouder and more hard than they?
The bleating sheep with my complaints agree,
They parched with heat, and I inflamed by thee.   20
The sultry Sirius burns the thirsty plains,
While in thy heart eternal winter reigns.

    Where stray ye, Muses, in what lawn or grove,
While your Alexis pines in hopeless love?
In those fair fields where sacred Isis glides,   25

---

[7] Dr. Samuel Garth, Author of *The Dispensary,* was one of the first friends of the Author, whose acquaintance with him began at fourteen or fifteen. Their friendship continued from the year 1703 to 1718, which was that of his death. P.

[8] A line out of Spenser's *Epithalamion.* P.

Or else where Cam his winding vales divides?
As in the crystal spring I view my face,
Fresh rising blushes paint the watery glass;
But since those graces please thy eyes no more,
I shun the fountains which I sought before.   30
Once I was skilled in every herb that grew,
And every plant that drinks the morning dew;
Ah, wretched shepherd, what avails thy art,
To cure thy lambs, but not to heal thy heart!

    Let other swains attend the rural care,   35
Feed fairer flocks, or richer fleeces shear:
But nigh yon mountain let me tune my lays,
Embrace my Love, and bind my brows with bays.
That flute is mine which Colin's[9] tuneful breath
Inspired when living, and bequeathed in death;   40
He said; Alexis, take this pipe, the same
That taught the groves my Rosalinda's name:
But now the reeds shall hang on yonder tree,
For ever silent since despised by thee.
Oh! were I made by some transforming power   45
The captive bird that sings within thy bower!
Then might my voice thy listening ears employ,
And I those kisses he receives, enjoy.

    And yet my numbers please the rural throng,
Rough Satyrs dance, and Pan applauds the song: 50
The Nymphs, forsaking every cave and spring,
Their early fruit, and milk-white turtles bring;
Each amorous nymph prefers her gifts in vain,
On you their gifts are all bestowed again.
For you the swains the fairest flowers design,   55
And in one garland all their beauties join;
Accept the wreath which you deserve alone,
In whom all beauties are comprised in one.

    See what delights in sylvan scenes appear!
Descending Gods have found Elysium here.   60

---

[9] The name taken by Spenser in his *Eclogues,* where his mistress is cele-
brated under that of Rosalinda. P.

In woods bright Venus with Adonis strayed,
And chaste Diana haunts the forest shade.
Come, lovely nymph, and bless the silent hours,
When swains from shearing seek their nightly bowers;
When weary reapers quit the sultry field,   65
And crowned with corn their thanks to Ceres yield.
This harmless grove no lurking viper hides,
But in my breast the serpent Love abides.
Here bees from blossoms sip the rosy dew,
But your Alexis knows no sweets but you.   70
Oh deign to visit our forsaken seats,
The mossy fountains, and the green retreats!
Where'er you walk, cool gales shall fan the glade,
Trees, where you sit, shall crowd into a shade:
Where'er you tread, the blushing flowers shall rise,   75
And all things flourish where you turn your eyes.
Oh! how I long with you to pass my days,
Invoke the Muses, and resound your praise!
Your praise the birds shall chant in every grove,
And winds shall waft it to the powers above.   80
But would you sing, and rival Orpheus' strain,
The wondering forests soon should dance again,
The moving mountains hear the powerful call,
And headlong streams hang listening in their fall!
    But see, the shepherds shun the noonday heat,   85
The lowing herds to murmuring brooks retreat,
To closer shades the panting flocks remove;
Ye Gods! and is there no relief for Love?
But soon the sun with milder rays descends
To the cool ocean, where his journey ends: 90
On me love's fiercer flames for ever prey,
By night he scorches, as he burns by day.

AUTUMN[10]

The Third Pastoral, or Hylus and Aegon

To Mr. Wycherley

BENEATH the shade a spreading Beech displays,
Hylas and Ægon sung their rural lays,
This mourned a faithless, that an absent Love,
And Delia's name and Doris' filled the Grove.
Ye Mantuan nymphs, your sacred succour bring;   5
Hylas and Ægon's 'rural lays I sing.

    Thou, whom the Nine with Plautus' wit inspire,[11]
The art of Terence, and Menander's fire;[12]
Whose sense instructs us, and whose humour charms,
Whose judgment sways us, and whose spirit warms!   10
Oh, skilled in Nature! see the hearts of Swains,
Their artless passions, and their tender pains.

    Now setting Phœbus shone serenely bright,
And fleecy clouds were streaked with purple light;
When tuneful Hylas with melodious moan,   15
Taught rocks to weep and made the mountains groan.

    Go, gentle gales, and bear my sighs away!
To Delia's ear, the tender notes convey.

---

[10] This Pastoral consists of two parts, like the viiith of Virgil: the Scene, a Hill; the Time at Sunset. P.

[11] Mr. Wycherley, a famous Author of Comedies; of which the most celebrated were the *Plain Dealer* and *Country Wife*. He was a writer of infinite spirit, satire, and wit. The only objection made to him was that he had too much. However, he was followed in the same way by Mr. Congreve; though with a little more correctness. P.

[12] This line evidently alludes to that famous Character given of Terence, by Cæsar:

> Tu quoque, tu in summis, *ó dimidiate Menander,*
> Poneris, et merito, puri sermonis amator;
> Lenibus atque utinam scriptis adjuncta foret *vis
> Comica.* [W.]

As some sad Turtle his lost love deplores,
And with deep murmurs fills the sounding shores; 20
Thus, far from *Delia,* to the winds I mourn,
Alike unheard, unpitied, and forlorn.
    Go, gentle gales, and bear my sighs along!
For her, the feathered quires neglect their song:
For her, the limes their pleasing shades deny; 25
For her, the lilies hang their heads and die.
Ye flowers that droop, forsaken by the spring,
Ye birds that, left by summer, cease to sing,
Ye trees that fade when autumn heats remove,
Say, is not absence death to those who love? 30
    Go, gentle gales, and bear my sighs away!
Cursed be the fields that cause my Delia's stay;
Fade every blossom, wither every tree,
Die every flower, and perish all, but she.
What have I said? where'er my Delia flies, 35
Let spring attend, and sudden flowers arise;
Let opening roses knotted oaks adorn,
And liquid amber drop from every thorn.
    Go, gentle gales, and bear my sighs along!
The birds shall cease to tune their evening song, 40
The winds to breathe, the waving woods to move,
And streams to murmur, ere I cease to love.
Not bubbling fountains to the thirsty swain,
Not balmy sleep to laborers faint with pain,
Not showers to larks, nor sunshine to the bee, 45
Are half so charming as thy sight to me.
    Go, gentle gales, and bear my sighs away!
Come, Delia, come; ah, why this long delay?
Through rocks and caves the name of Delia sounds,
Delia, each cave and echoing rock rebounds. 50
Ye powers, what pleasing frenzy soothes my mind!
Do lovers dream, or is my Delia kind?
She comes, my Delia comes!—Now cease my lay,
And cease, ye gales, to bear my sighs away!
    Next Ægon sung, while Windsor groves admired;
Rehearse, ye Muses, what yourselves inspired. 56

Resound, ye hills, resound my mournful strain!
Of perjured Doris, dying I complain:
Here where the mountains lessening as they rise
Lose the low vales, and steal into the skies: 60
While laboring oxen, spent with toil and heat,
In their loose traces from the field retreat:
While curling smokes from village tops are seen,
And the fleet shades glide o'er the dusky green.

Resound, ye hills, resound my mournful lay!   65
Beneath yon poplar oft we passed the day:
Oft on the rind I carved her amorous vows,
While she with garlands hung the bending boughs:
The garlands fade, the vows are worn away;
So dies her love, and so my hopes decay.   70

Resound, ye hills, resound my mournful strain!
Now bright Arcturus glads the teeming grain,
Now golden fruits on loaded branches shine,
And grateful clusters swell with floods of wine;
Now blushing berries paint the yellow grove;   75
Just Gods! shall all things yield returns but love?

Resound, ye hills, resound my mournful lay!
The shepherds cry, "Thy flocks are left a prey"—
Ah! what avails it me, the flocks to keep,
Who lost my heart while I preserved my sheep.   80
Pan came, and asked, what magic caused my smart,
Or what ill eyes malignant glances dart?
What eyes but hers, alas, have power to move!
And is there magic but what dwells in love?

Resound, ye hills, resound my mournful strains!   85
I'll fly from shepherds, flocks, and flowery plains.
From shepherds, flocks, and plains, I may remove,
Forsake mankind, and all the world—but love!
I know thee, Love! on foreign Mountains bred,
Wolves gave thee suck, and savage Tigers fed.   90
Thou wert from Etna's burning entrails torn,
Got by fierce whirlwinds, and in thunder born!

Resound, ye hills, resound my mournful lay!
Farewell, ye woods! adieu the light of day!

One leap from yonder cliff shall end my pains,   95
No more, ye hills, no more resound my strains!
    Thus sung the shepherds till th' approach of night,
The skies yet blushing with departing light,
When falling dews with spangles decked the glade,
And the low sun had lengthened every shade.   100

WINTER[13]

The Fourth Pastoral, or Daphne

To the Memory of Mrs. Tempest[14]

Lycidas

THYRSIS, the music of that murmuring spring,
Is not so mournful as the strains you sing.
Nor rivers winding through the vales below,
So sweetly warble, or so smoothly flow.
Now sleeping flocks on their soft fleeces lie,   5
The moon, serene in glory, mounts the sky,
While silent birds forget their tuneful lays,
Oh sing of Daphne's fate, and Daphne's praise!

[13] This was the Poet's favourite Pastoral.   [W.]
[14] This Lady was of an ancient family in Yorkshire, and particularly admired by the Author's friend Mr. Walsh, who, having celebrated her in a Pastoral Elegy, desired his friend to do the same, as appears from one of his Letters, dated September 9, 1706: "Your last Eclogue being on the same subject with mine on Mrs. Tempest's death, I should take it very kindly in you to give it a little turn as if it were to the memory of the same lady." Her death having happened on the night of the great storm in 1703, gave a propriety to this eclogue, which in its general turn alludes to it. The scene of the Pastoral lies in a grove, the time at midnight. P.

Thyrsis

Behold the groves that shine with silver frost,
Their beauty withered, and their verdure lost.   10
Here shall I try the sweet Alexis' strain,
That called the listening Dryads to the plain?
Thames heard the numbers as he flowed along,
And bade his willows learn the moving song.

Lycidas

So may kind rains their vital moisture yield,   15
And swell the future harvest of the field.
Begin; this charge the dying Daphne gave,
And said: "Ye shepherds, sing around my grave!
Sing, while beside the shaded tomb I mourn,
And with fresh bays her rural shrine adorn."   20

Thyrsis

Ye gentle Muses, leave your crystal spring,
Let Nymphs and Sylvans cypress garlands bring;
Ye weeping Loves, the stream with myrtles hide,
And break your bows, as when Adonis died;
And with your golden darts, now useless grown,   25
Inscribe a verse on this relenting stone:
"Let nature change, let heaven and earth deplore,
Fair Daphne's dead, and love is now no more!"
'Tis done, and nature's various charms decay,
See gloomy clouds obscure the cheerful day!   30
Now hung with pearls the dropping trees appear,
Their faded honours scattered on her bier.
See, where on earth the flowery glories lie,
With her they flourished, and with her they die.
Ah what avail the beauties nature wore?   35
Fair Daphne's dead, and beauty is no more!

For her the flocks refuse their verdant food,
Nor thirsty heifers seek the gliding flood.
The silver swans her hapless fate bemoan,
In notes more sad than when they sing their own;   40
In hollow caves sweet Echo silent lies,
Silent, or only to her name replies;
Her name with pleasure once she taught the shore,
Now Daphne's dead, and pleasure is no more!
    No grateful dews descend from evening skies,   45
Nor morning odours from the flowers arise;
No rich perfumes refresh the fruitful field,
Nor fragrant herbs their native incense yield.
The balmy Zephyrs, silent since her death,
Lament the ceasing of a sweeter breath;   50
Th' industrious bees neglect their golden store!
Fair Daphne's dead, and sweetness is no more!
    No more the mounting larks, while Daphne sings,
Shall listening in mid air suspend their wings;
No more the birds shall imitate her lays,   55
Or hushed with wonder, hearken from the sprays:
No more the streams their murmur shall forbear,
A sweeter music than their own to hear,
But tell the reeds, and tell the vocal shore,
Fair Daphne's dead, and music is no more!   60
    Her fate is whispered by the gentle breeze,
And told in sighs to all the trembling trees;
The trembling trees, in every plain and wood,
Her fate remurmur to the silver flood;
The silver flood, so lately calm, appears   65
Swelled with new passion, and o'erflows with tears;
The winds and trees and floods her death deplore,
Daphne, our grief! our glory now no more!
    But see! where Daphne wondering mounts on high
Above the clouds, above the starry sky   70
Eternal beauties grace the shining scene,
Fields ever fresh, and groves for ever green!
There while you rest in Amaranthine bowers,

Or from those meads select unfading flowers,
Behold us kindly, who your name implore,   75
Daphne, our Goddess, and our grief no more!

Lycidas

    How all things listen, while thy Muse complains!
Such silence waits on Philomela's strains,
In some still evening, when the whispering breeze
Pants on the leaves, and dies upon the trees.   80
To thee, bright goddess, oft a lamb shall bleed,
If teeming ewes increase my fleecy breed.
While plants their shade, or flowers their odours give,
Thy name, thy honour, and thy praise shall live!

Thyrsis

    But see, Orion sheds unwholesome dews,   85
Arise, the pines a noxious shade diffuse;
Sharp Boreas blows, and Nature feels decay,
Time conquers all, and we must Time obey.
Adieu, ye vales, ye mountains, streams and groves,[15]
Adieu, ye shepherd's rural lays and loves;   90
Adieu, my flocks, farewell ye sylvan crew,
Daphne, farewell, and all the world adieu!

[15] These four last lines allude to the several subjects of the four Pastorals,
and to the several scenes of them, particularized before in each. P.

THE GUARDIAN NO. 40

Monday, April 27, 1713

Being a Continuation of some former papers on the Subject of Pastorals

Compulerantque greges Corydon et Thyrsis in unum:
Ex illo Corydon, Corydon est tempore nobis.

[Virgil *Eclogue* vii. 2, 70.]

1. I designed to have troubled the reader with no further discourses of Pastoral; but being informed that I am taxed of partiality in not mentioning an Author whose Eclogues are published in the same volume with Mr. Philips's, I shall employ this paper in observations upon him, written in the free Spirit of Criticism, and without any apprehension of offending that Gentleman, whose character it is, that he takes the greatest care of his works before they are published, and has the least concern for them afterwards.

2. I have laid it down as the first rule of Pastoral, that its idea should be taken from the manners of the Golden Age, and the Moral formed upon the representation of Innocence; 'tis therefore plain that any deviations from that design degrade a Poem from being truly pastoral. In this view it will appear, that Virgil can only have two of his Eclogues allowed to be such: his first and ninth must be rejected, because they describe the ravages of armies, and oppressions of the innocent; Corydon's criminal

passion for Alexis throws out the second; the calumny and railing in the third are not proper to that state of concord; the eighth represents unlawful ways of procuring love by enchantments, and introduces a shepherd whom an inviting precipice tempts to self-murder: As to the fourth, sixth, and tenth, they are given up by Heinsius,[16] Salmasius, Rapin, and the critics in general. They likewise observe that but eleven of all the Idyllia of Theocritus are to be admitted as pastorals: and even out of that number the greater part will be excluded for one or other of the reasons above-mentioned. So that when I remarked in a former paper, that Virgil's eclogues, taken altogether are rather Select poems than Pastorals; I might have said the same thing with no less truth of Theocritus. The reason of this I take to be yet unobserved by the critics, viz. They never meant them all for pastorals.

Now it is plain Philips hath done this, and in that particular excelled both Theocritus and Virgil.

3. As Simplicity is the distinguishing characteristic of Pastoral, Virgil hath been thought guilty of too courtly a style; his language is perfectly pure, and he often forgets he is among peasants. I have frequently wondered, that since he was so conversant in the writings of Ennius, he had not imitated the rusticity of the Doric as well by the help of the old obsolete Roman language, as Philips hath by the antiquated English: For example, might he not have said *quoi* instead of *cui; quoijum* for *cujum; volt* for *vult,* etc. as well as our modern hath *welladay* for *alas, whileome* for *of old, make mock* for *deride,* and *witless younglings* for *simple lambs,* etc. by which means he had attained as much of the air of Theocritus, as Philips hath of Spenser?

4. Mr. Pope hath fallen into the same error with Virgil. His clowns do not converse in all the simplicity proper to the country: His names are borrowed from Theocritus and Virgil, which are improper to the scene of his pastorals. He introduces Daphnis, Alexis, and Thyrsis on British plains, as Virgil had done before him on the Mantuan: Whereas Philips, who hath the strictest regard to propriety, makes choice of names peculiar to the country, and more agreeable to a reader of delicacy; such as Hobbinol, Lobbin, Cuddy and Colin Clout.

[16] See Rapin *De Carmine Pastorali,* Part III. [P.]

5. So easy as pastoral writing may seem (in the simplicity we have described it) yet it requires great reading, both of the ancients and moderns, to be a master of it. Philips hath given us manifest proofs of his knowledge of books. It must be confessed his competitor hath imitated *some single thoughts* of the ancients well enough (if we consider he had not the happiness of an University education) but he hath dispersed them here and there, without that order and method which Mr. Philips observes, whose *whole* third pastoral is an instance how well he hath studied the fifth of Virgil, and how judiciously reduced Virgil's thoughts to the standard of Pastoral; as his contention of Colin Clout and the Nightingale shows with what exactness he hath imitated every line in Strada.

6. When I remarked it as a principal fault, to introduce fruits and flowers of a foreign growth, in descriptions where the scene lies in our own country, I did not design that observation should extend also to animals, or the sensitive life; for Mr. Philips hath with great judgment described Wolves in England in his first pastoral. Nor would I have a poet slavishly confine himself (as Mr. Pope hath done) to one particular Season of the year, one certain Time of the day, and one unbroken Scene in each eclogue. 'Tis plain Spenser neglected this pedantry, who in his pastoral of November mentions the mournful song of the Nightingale,

> Sad Philomel her song in tears doth steep.

And Mr. Philips, by a poetical creation, hath raised up finer beds of flowers than the most industrious gardener; his roses, endives, lilies, kingcups, and daffodils, blow all in the same season.

7. But the better to discover the merits of our two contemporary Pastoral writers, I shall endeavour to draw a parallel of them, by setting several of their particular thoughts in the same light, whereby it will be obvious how much Philips hath the advantage. With what simplicity he introduces two shepherds singing alternately?

HOBB. Come, Rosalind, O come, for without thee
What pleasure can the country have for me?
Come, Rosalind, O come; my brinded kine,
My snowy sheep, my farm and all, is thine.

LANQ. Come, Rosalind, O come; here shady bowers,
  Here are cool fountains, and here springing flowers.
  Come, Rosalind; here ever let us stay,
  And sweetly waste our livelong time away.

Our other pastoral writer, in expressing the same thought, deviates into downright Poetry:

STREPH. In Spring the fields, in Autumn hills I love,
  At morn the plains, at noon the shady grove,
  But Delia always; forced from Delia's sight,
  Nor plains at morn, nor groves at noon delight.

DAPH. Sylvia's like Autumn ripe, yet mild as May,
  More bright than noon, yet fresh as early day;
  Even Spring displeases, when she shines not here,
  But blest with her, 'tis Spring throughout the year.

In the first of these authors, two shepherds thus innocently describe the behaviour of their mistresses:

HOBB. As Marian bathed, by chance I passed by,
  She blushed, and at me cast a sidelong eye:
  Then swift beneath the crystal wave she tried
  Her beauteous form, but all in vain, to hide.

LANQ. As I to cool me bathed one sultry day,
  Fond Lydia lurking in the sedges lay.
  The wanton laughed, and seemed in haste to fly;
  Yet often stopped, and often turned her eye.

The other modern (who it must be confessed hath a knack of versifying) hath it as follows:

STREPH. Me gentle Delia beckons from the plain,
  Then, hid in shades, eludes her eager swain;
  But feigns a Laugh, to see me search around,
  And by that Laugh the willing fair is found.

DAPH. The sprightly Sylvia trips along the green,
  She runs, but hopes she does not run unseen;
  While a kind glance at her pursuer flies,
  How much at variance are her feet and eyes!

There is nothing the writers of this kind of poetry are fonder of than descriptions of pastoral Presents. Philips says thus of a Sheep hook,

> Of seasoned elm; where studs of brass appear,
> To speak the giver's name, the month and year;
> The hook of polished steel, the handle turned,
> And richly by the graver's skill adorned.

The other of a bowl embossed with figures:

> where wanton ivy twines,
> And swelling clusters bend the curling vines;
> Four figures rising from the work appear,
> The various seasons of the rolling year;
> And, what is that which binds the radiant sky,
> Where twelve bright signs in beauteous order lie?

The simplicity of the swain in this place, who forgets the name of the Zodiac, is no ill imitation of Virgil: but how much more plainly and unaffectedly would Philips have dressed this thought in his Doric?

> And what that hight, which girds the welkin sheen,
> Where twelve gay signs in meet array are seen?

If the reader would indulge his curiosity any further in the comparison of particulars, he may read the first pastoral of Philips with the second of his contemporary, and the fourth and sixth of the former with the fourth and first of the latter; where several parallel places will occur to every one.

Having now shown some parts, in which these two writers may be compared, it is a justice I owe to Mr. Philips to discover those in which no man can compare with him. First, That beautiful rusticity, of which I shall only produce two instances out of a hundred not yet quoted:

> O woful day! O day of woe! quoth he,
> And woful I, who live the day to see!

The simplicity of diction, the melancholy flowing of the numbers, the solemnity of the sound, and the easy turn of the words in this Dirge (to make use of our author's expression) are extremely elegant.

In another of his pastorals, a shepherd utters a Dirge not much inferior to the former, in the following lines:

Ah me the while! ah me! the luckless day,
Ah luckless lad! the rather might I say;
Ah silly I! more silly than my sheep,
Which on the flowery plains I once did keep.

How he still charms the ear with these artful repetitions of the epithets; and how significant is the last verse! I defy the most common reader to repeat them, without feeling some motions of compassion.

In the next place I shall rank his Proverbs, in which I formerly observed he excels: For example:

A rolling stone is ever bare of moss;
And, to their cost, green years old proverbs cross.
He that late lies down, as late will rise,
And sluggard-like, till noonday snoring lies.

Against Ill luck all cunning foresight fails;
Whether we sleep or wake, it nought avails.
. . .
. . . Nor fear, from upright sentence, wrong.

Lastly, his elegant Dialect, which alone might prove him the eldest born of Spenser, and our only true Arcadian. I should think it proper for the several writers of Pastoral, to confine themselves to their several Counties. Spenser seems to have been of this opinion: for he hath laid the scene of one of his Pastorals in Wales; where with all the simplicity natural to that part of our island, one shepherd bids the other good morrow, in an unusual and elegant manner:

Diggon Davy, I bid hur God-day:
Or Diggon hur is, or I missay.

Diggon answers:

Hur was hur, while it was daylight;
But now hur is a most wretched wight, etc.

But the most beautiful example of this kind that I ever met with, is in a very valuable piece which I chanced to find among some old manuscripts, entitled, *A Pastoral Ballad:* which I think, for its nature and simplicity, may (notwithstanding the modesty of the title) be allowed a perfect Pastoral. It is composed in the Somersetshire dialect, and the names such as are proper to the country people. It may be observed as a further beauty of this Pastoral, the words Nymph, Dryad, Naiad, Faun, Cupid, or Satyr, are not once mentioned throughout the whole. I shall make no apology for inserting some few lines of this excellent piece. Cicily breaks thus into the subject, as she is going a milking:

CICILY. Rager, go vetch tha Kee,[17] or else tha Zun
      Will quite be go, bevore c'have half a don.

ROGER. Thou shouldst not ax ma tweece, but I've a bee
      To dreve our bull to bull tha Parson's Kee.

It is to be observed, that this whole dialogue is formed upon the passion of *Jealousy;* and his mentioning the Parson's Kine naturally revives the jealousy of the shepherdess Cicily, which she expresses as follows:

CICILY. Ah Rager, Rager, ches was zore avraid,
      When in yon Vield you kissed the Parson's maid:
      Is this the love that once to me you zed,
      When from the Wake thou broughtst me gingerbread?

ROGER. Cicily, thou charg'st me valse,—I'll zwear to thee,
      Tha Parson's maid is still a maid for me.

In which answer of his, are expressed at once that Spirit of Religion, and that Innocence of the Golden age, so necessary to be observed by all writers of Pastoral.

At the conclusion of this piece, the author reconciles the Lovers, and ends the Eclogue the most simply in the world:

    So Rager parted vor to vetch tha Kee,
    And vor her bucket in went Cicily.

I am loth to show my fondness for antiquity so far as to prefer

[17] That is, the Kine or Cows. [P.]

this ancient British author to our present English Writers of Pastoral; but I cannot avoid making this obvious remark, that Philips hath hit into the same road with this old West Country Bard of ours.

After all that hath been said, I hope none can think it any injustice to Mr. Pope that I forebore to mention him as a Pastoral writer; since, upon the whole, he is of the same class with Moschus and Bion, whom we have excluded that rank; and of whose Eclogues, as well as some of Virgil's, it may be said, that (according to the description we have given of this sort of poetry) they are by no means Pastorals, but something better.

1713

THE GUARDIAN No. 173

[On Gardens]¹⁸

Tuesday, September 29, 1713

Nec sera comantem
Narcissum, aut flexi tacuissem vimen Acanthi,
Pallentesque hederas, et amantes littora myrtos.
[VIRGIL *Georgic* iv. 122–24.]

I lately took a particular friend of mine to my house in the
country, not without some apprehension, that it could afford little
entertainment to a man of his polite taste, particularly in archi-

---

¹⁸ *Guardian* No. 173 pursues a theme parallel to that of No. 40. Virgilian
pastoral (the poetry of Arcadian simplicity) and Virgilian georgic (the
poetry of the farming way of life) had close affinities for the Augustan
gentleman's preoccupation with the farming and gardening of his country
estate. In this *Guardian* citing classical precedents for a natural taste in
plantation and making fun of topiary extravagance, Pope anticipates his
own horticultural activities which would begin six years later at Twicken-
ham and would be a dominant motif of the last twenty-five years of his
life. He anticipates also his important poem on taste in landscaping and
architecture, the Fourth *Moral Essay,* or *Epistle to Burlington* (1731).
Windsor Forest is an early poem which makes interesting connections
in the same areas. Cf. above the Introduction and Bibliographical Note,
pp. xvii, xxviii, liv, lvi.

tecture and gardening, who had so long been conversant with all that is beautiful and great in either. But it was a pleasant surprise to me, to hear him often declare he had found in my little retirement that beauty which he always thought wanting in the most celebrated seats (or, if you will, Villas) of the nation. This he described to me in those verses with which Martial begins one of his epigrams:

> Baiana nostri villa, Basse, Faustini,
> Non otiosis ordinata myrtetis,
> Viduaque platano, tonsilique buxeto,
> Ingrata lati spatia detinet campi;
> Sed rure vero, barbaroque lætatur.[19]

There is certainly something in the amiable simplicity of unadorned Nature, that spreads over the mind a more noble sort of tranquility, and a loftier sensation of pleasure, than can be raised from the nicer scenes of art.

This was the taste of the Ancients in their gardens, as we may discover from the descriptions extant of them. The two most celebrated wits of the world have each of them left us a particular picture of a Garden; wherein those great masters being wholly unconfined, and painting at pleasure, may be thought to have given a full idea of what they esteemed most excellent in this way. These (one may observe) consist entirely of the useful part of horticulture, fruit trees, herbs, water, etc. The pieces I am speaking of are Virgil's account of the garden of the old Corycian,[20] and Homer's of that of Alcinous. [The first of these is already known to the English reader, by the excellent versions of Mr. Dryden and Mr. Addison. The other having never been attempted in our language with any elegance, and being the most beautiful plan of this sort that can be imagined, I shall here present the reader with a translation of it.

---

[19] "Bassus, the country seat of our friend Faustinus at Baia does not spread over the fields unfruitfully in rows of idle myrtle, vineless plane trees, plantations of fancy clipped boxwood. It rejoices in the true rustic, the untrimmed farm." Martial *Epigram* iii. 58. 1–5.
[20] *Georgic* iv. 126–46.

The Gardens of Alcinous
from Homer's Odyssey vii. [112-32].

Close to the Gates a spacious Garden lies,
From Storms defended and inclement Skies:
Four Acres was th' allotted Space of Ground,
Fenced with a green Enclosure all around.
Tall thriving Trees confessed the fruitful Mold;
The reddening Apple ripens here to Gold,
Here the blue Fig with luscious Juice o'erflows,
With deeper Red the full Pomegranate glows,
The Branch here bends beneath the weighty Pear,
And verdant Olives flourish round the Year.
The balmy Spirit of the Western Gale
Eternal breathes on Fruits untaught to fail:
Each dropping Pear a following Pear supplies,
On Apples Apples, Figs on Figs arise:
The same mild Season gives the Blooms to blow,
The Buds to harden, and the Fruits to grow.
Here ordered Vines in equal Ranks appear
With all th' United Labors of the Year,
Some to unload the fertile Branches run,
Some dry the blackening Clusters in the Sun,
Others to tread the liquid Harvest join,
The groaning Presses foam with Floods of Wine.
Here are the Vines in early Flower descried,
Here Grapes discolored on the sunny Side,
And there in Autumn's richest Purple dyed.
Beds of all various Herbs, forever green,
In beauteous Order terminate the Scene.
Two plenteous Fountains the whole Prospect crowned;
This through the Gardens leads its Streams around,
Visits each Plant, and waters all the Ground:
While that in Pipes beneath the Palace flows,
And thence its Current on the Town bestows;
To various Use their various Streams they bring,
The People one, and one supplies the King.][21]

[21] Pope's verse translation of *Odyssey* vii. 112–32 and the two immediately

Sir William Temple has remarked,[22] that this garden of Homer contains all the justest rules and provisions which can go toward composing the best gardens. Its extent was four Acres, which, in those times of simplicity, was looked upon as a large one, even for a Prince. It was enclosed all round for defence; and for conveniency joined close to the gates of the Palace.

He mentions next the Trees, which were standards, and suffered to grow to their full height. The fine description of the Fruits that never failed, and the eternal Zephyrs, is only a more noble and poetical way of expressing the continual succession of one fruit after another throughout the year.

The Vineyard seems to have been a plantation distinct from the Garden; as also the beds of Greens mentioned afterwards at the extremity of the enclosure, in the usual place of our Kitchen Gardens.

The two Fountains are disposed very remarkably. They rose within the enclosure, and were brought in by conduits or ducts; one of them to water all parts of the gardens, and the other underneath the Palace into the Town, for the service of the public.

How contrary to this simplicity is the modern practice of gardening? We seem to make it our study to recede from Nature, not only in the various tonsure of greens into the most regular and formal shapes, but even in monstrous attempts beyond the reach of the art itself: we run into sculpture, and are yet better pleased to have our Trees in the most awkward figures of men and animals, than in the most regular of their own.

> Hinc et nexilibus videas e frondibus hortos,
> Implexos late muros, et mœnia circum

preceding sentences are omitted from Warburton's text (1751) of *Guardian* 173. The passage is here restored from the *Guardian* text, but is normalized. Cf. Norman Ault, ed. *The Prose Works of Alexander Pope,* I (Oxford, 1936), 145–51. In 1725 the passage appears as part of Pope's *Odyssey* (vii. 142–75). Pope himself omits it from *Guardian* 173 in Volume ii of his *Works . . . in Prose* (1741).

[22] Sir William Temple's essay *Upon the Gardens of Epicurus, or of Gardening, in the Year 1685* appears in his *Miscellanea, the Second Part,* 1690.

Porrigere, et latas e ramis surgere turres;
Deflexam et myrtum in puppes, atque ærea rostra:
In buxisque undare fretum, atque e rore rudentes.
Parte alia frondere suis tentoria castris;
Scutaque, spiculaque, et jaculantia citria vallos.[23]

I believe it is no wrong observation, that persons of genius, and those who are most capable of art, are always most fond of nature; as such are chiefly sensible, that all art consists in the imitation and study of nature: On the contrary, people of the common level of understanding are principally delighted with the little niceties and fantastical operations of art, and constantly think that finest which is least natural. A Citizen is no sooner proprietor of a couple of Yews, but he entertains thoughts of erecting them into Giants, like those of Guildhall. I know an eminent Cook, who beautified his country seat with a Coronation-dinner in greens, where you see the Champion flourishing on horseback at one end of the table, and the Queen in perpetual youth at the other.

For the benefit of all my loving countrymen of this curious taste, I shall here publish a catalogue of Greens to be disposed of by an eminent Town Gardener, who has lately applied to me upon this head. He represents, that for the advancement of a politer sort of ornament in the Villas and Gardens adjacent to this great city, and in order to distinguish those places from the mere barbarous countries of gross nature, the world stands much in need of a virtuoso Gardener, who has a turn to sculpture, and is thereby capable of improving upon the ancients, in the imagery of Evergreens. I proceed to his catalogue.

> Adam and Eve in Yew; Adam a little shattered by the fall of
> the Tree of Knowledge in the great storm; Eve and the Serpent very flourishing.

[23] "Here you see a garden enclosed with plaited boughs, vast woven walls, battlements stretching all around, and big towers of greenery rising; myrtles tortured into ship shapes, poops and prows, waves billowing out of boxwood, and cordage formed of dew; elsewhere tented encampments of foliage, shields, javelins, and a palisade of darting cedars." I have not identified this passage.

Noah's ark in Holly, the ribs a little damaged for want of
water.

The Tower of Babel, not yet finished.

St. George in Box; his arm scarce long enough, but will be in
a condition to stick the Dragon by next April.

A green Dragon of the same, with a tail of Ground-Ivy for
the present.

      N.B. These two not to be sold separately.

Edward the Black Prince in Cypress.

A Laurustine Bear in Blossom, with a Juniper Hunter in
Berries.

A pair of Giants, stunted, to be sold cheap.

A Queen Elizabeth in Phillyrea, a little inclining to the green
sickness, but of full growth.

Another Queen Elizabeth in Myrtle, which was very forward,
but miscarried by being too near a Savine.

An old Maid of honor in Wormwood.

A topping Ben Jonson in Laurel.

Divers eminent modern Poets in Bays, somewhat blighted, to
be disposed of a pennyworth.

A quickset Hog shot up into a Porcupine, by being forgot a
week in rainy weather.

A Lavender Pig, with Sage growing in his belly.

A pair of Maidenheads in Fir, in great forwardness.

He also cutteth family pieces of men, women, and children,
so that any gentleman may have his lady's effigies in Myrtle,
or his own in Hornbeam.

*Thy Wife shall be as the fruitful Vine, and thy Children as
Olive branches round thy table.*[24]

---

[24] Cf. *Psalms* 128:3.

MESSIAH
A *Sacred Eclogue*

In Imitation of Virgil's Pollio

ADVERTISEMENT

In reading several passages of the Prophet Isaiah, which foretell the coming of Christ and the felicities attending it, I could not but observe a remarkable parity between many of the thoughts, and those in the *Pollio* of Virgil. This will not seem surprising, when we reflect, that the Eclogue was taken from a Sibylline prophecy on the same subject. One may judge that Virgil did not copy it line by line, but selected such ideas as best agreed with the nature of pastoral poetry, and disposed them in that manner which served most to beautify his piece. I have endeavoured the same in this imitation of him, though without admitting any thing of my own; since it was written with this particular view, that the reader, by comparing the several thoughts, might see how far the images and descriptions of the Prophet are superior to those of the Poet. But as I fear I have prejudiced them by my management, I shall subjoin the passages of Isaiah, and those of Virgil, under the same disadvantage of a literal translation. P.

> YE Nymphs of Solyma! begin the song:
> To heavenly themes sublimer strains belong.
> The mossy fountains, and the sylvan shades,
> The dreams of Pindus and th' Aonian maids,
> Delight no more—O thou my voice inspire   5
> Who touched Isaiah's hallowed lips with fire!

Rapt into future times, the Bard begun:
A Virgin shall conceive, a Virgin bear a Son![1]
From Jesse's root behold a branch arise,
Whose sacred flower with fragrance fills the skies: 10
Th' Æthereal spirit o'er its leaves shall move,
And on its top descends the mystic Dove.
Ye Heavens! from high the dewy nectar pour,
And in soft silence shed the kindly shower!
The sick and weak the healing plant shall aid,   15
From storms a shelter, and from heat a shade.
All crimes shall cease, and ancient fraud shall fail;
Returning Justice lift aloft her scale;
Peace o'er the world her olive wand extend,
And white-robed Innocence from heaven descend.   20
Swift fly the years, and rise th' expected morn!
Oh spring to light, auspicious Babe, be born!
See Nature hastes her earliest wreaths to bring,
With all the incense of the breathing spring:
See lofty Lebanon his head advance,   25
See nodding forests on the mountains dance:
See spicy clouds from lowly Saron rise,
And Carmel's flowery top perfumes the skies!
Hark! a glad voice the lonely desert cheers;
Prepare the way! a God, a God appears:[2]   30
A God, a God! the vocal hills reply,
The rocks proclaim th' approaching Deity.
Lo, earth receives him from the bending skies!
Sink down ye mountains, and ye valleys rise,
With heads declined, ye cedars homage pay;   35
Be smooth ye rocks, ye rapid floods give way!

---

[1] "Jam redit et Virgo, redeunt Saturnia regna . . . ." Virgil *Eclogue* iv.
6 ff. "Behold, a virgin shall conceive, and bear a son." *Isaiah* 7:14. For
further parallels, pointed out by Pope in various notes to this poem, see
Eclogue iv *passim* and *Isaiah*, especially 9:6-7; 35:1; 60:13; 44:23; 35:7;
55:13.
[2] "The voice of him that crieth in the wilderness, prepare ye the way of
the Lord! make straight in the desert a highway for our God!" *Isaiah*
40:3. P.

The Saviour comes! by ancient bards foretold:
Hear him, ye deaf, and all ye blind, behold!
He from thick films shall purge the visual ray,
And on the sightless eyeball pour the day: 40
'Tis he th' obstructed paths of sound shall clear,
And bid new music charm th' unfolding ear:
The dumb shall sing, the lame his crutch forego,
And leap exulting like the bounding roe.
No sigh, no murmur the wide world shall hear,   45
From every face he wipes off every tear.
In adamantine chains shall Death be bound,
And Hell's grim Tyrant feel th' eternal wound.
As the good shepherd tends his fleecy care,
Seeks freshest pasture and the purest air,   50
Explores the lost, the wandering sheep directs,
By day o'ersees them, and by night protects,
The tender lambs he raises in his arms,
Feeds from his hand, and in his bosom warms;
Thus shall mankind his guardian care engage,   55
The promised father of the future age.
No more shall nation against nation rise,
Nor ardent warriours meet with hateful eyes,
Nor fields with gleaming steel be covered o'er,
The brazen trumpets kindle rage no more;   60
But useless lances into scythes shall bend,
And the broad falchion in a ploughshare end.
Then palaces shall rise; the joyful Son
Shall finish what his short-lived Sire begun;
Their vines a shadow to their race shall yield,   65
And the same hand that sowed, shall reap the field.
The swain in barren deserts with surprise
See lilies spring, and sudden verdure rise;
And starts, amidst the thirsty wilds to hear
New falls of water murmuring in his ear.   70
On rifted rocks, the dragon's late abodes,
The green reed trembles, and the bulrush nods.
Waste sandy valleys, once perplexed with thorn,
The spiry fir and shapely box adorn:

To leafless shrubs the flowering palms succeed,   75
And odorous myrtle to the noisome weed.
The lambs with wolves shall graze the verdant mead,
And boys in flowery bands the tiger lead;[3]
The steer and lion at one crib shall meet,
And harmless serpents lick the pilgrim's feet.   80
The smiling infant in his hand shall take
The crested basilisk and speckled snake,
Pleased the green lustre of the scales survey,
And with their forky tongue shall innocently play.
Rise, crowned with light, imperial Salem, rise!   85
Exalt thy towery head, and lift thy eyes!
See, a long race thy spacious courts adorn;
See future sons, and daughters yet unborn,
In crowding ranks on every side arise,
Demanding life, impatient for the skies!   90
See barbarous nations at thy gates attend,
Walk in thy light, and in thy temple bend;
See thy bright altars thronged with prostrate kings
And heaped with products of Sabæan springs!
For thee Idume's spicy forests blow,   95
And seeds of gold in Ophir's mountains glow.
See heaven its sparkling portals wide display,
And break upon thee in a flood of day!
No more the rising Sun shall gild the morn,
Nor evening Cynthia fill her silver horn;   100
But lost, dissolved in thy superior rays,
One tide of glory, one unclouded blaze
O'erflow thy courts: the Light himself shall shine
Revealed, and God's eternal day be thine!
The seas shall waste, the skies in smoke decay,   105
Rocks fall to dust, and mountains melt away;
But fixed his word, his saving power remains;
Thy realm for ever lasts, thy own MESSIAH reigns!

---

[3] "The wolf also shall dwell with the lamb, and the leopard shall lie down with the kid, and the calf and the young lion and the fatling together: and a little child shall lead them." *Isaiah* 11:6. P.

WINDSOR FOREST

To The Right Honourable
George Lord Lansdowne

Non injussa cano: Te nostræ, *Vare,* myricæ.
Te *Nemus* omne canet; nec Phœbo gratior ulla est,
Quam sibi quæ *Vari* præscripsit pagina nomen.
                    Virgil [*Eclogue* vi. 10–12.]

THY forests, Windsor! and they green retreats,
At once the Monarch's and the Muse's seats,
Invite my lays. Be present, sylvan maids!
Unlock your springs, and open all your shades.
GRANVILLE commands; your aid, O Muses, bring!   5
What Muse for GRANVILLE can refuse to sing?
    The Groves of Eden, vanished now so long,
Live in description, and look green in song:
These, were my breast inspired with equal flame,
Like them in beauty, should be like in fame.   10

[4] This poem was written at two different times: the first part of it, which relates to the country, in the year 1704, at the same time with the Pastorals: the latter part was not added till the year 1713, in which it was published. P.

Here hills and vales, the woodland and the plain,
Here earth and water seem to strive again;
Not Chaos-like together crushed and bruised,
But, as the world, harmoniously confused:
Where order in variety we see,   15
And where, though all things differ, all agree.
Here waving groves a chequered scene display,
And part admit, and part exclude the day;
As some coy nymph her lover's warm address
Nor quite indulges, nor can quite repress.   20
There, interspersed in lawns and opening glades,
Thin trees arise that shun each other's shades.
Here in full light the russet plains extend:
There wrapped in clouds the bluish hills ascend.
Even the wild heath displays her purple dyes,   25
And midst the desert fruitful fields arise,
That crowned with tufted trees and springing corn,
Like verdant isles the sable waste adorn.
Let India boast her plants, nor envy we
The weeping amber or the balmy tree,   30
While by our oaks the precious loads are borne,
And realms commanded which those trees adorn.
Not proud Olympus yields a nobler sight,
Though gods assembled grace his towering height,
Than what more humble mountains offer here,   35
Where, in their blessings, all those Gods appear.
See Pan with flocks, with fruits Pomona crowned,
Here blushing Flora paints th' enamelled ground,
Here Ceres' gifts in waving prospect stand,
And nodding tempt the joyful reaper's hand;   40
Rich Industry sits smiling on the plains,
And peace and plenty tell, a STUART reigns.
        Not thus the land appeared in ages past,
A dreary desert, and a gloomy waste,
To savage beasts and savage laws a prey,   45
And kings more furious and severe than they;
Who claimed the skies, dispeopled air and floods,
The lonely lords of empty wilds and woods:

Cities laid waste, they stormed the dens and caves,
(For wiser brutes were backward to be slaves.)   50
What could be free, when lawless beasts obeyed,
And even the elements a Tyrant swayed?
In vain kind seasons swelled the teeming grain,
Soft showers distilled, and suns grew warm in vain;
The swain with tears his frustrate labour yields,   55
And famished dies amidst his ripened fields.
What wonder then, a beast or subject slain
Were equal crimes in a despotic reign?
Both doomed alike, for sportive Tyrants bled,
But while the subject starved, the beast was fed.   60
Proud Nimrod first the bloody chase began,
A mighty hunter, and his prey was man:
Our haughty Norman boasts that barbarous name,
And makes his trembling slaves the royal game.
The fields are ravished from th' industrious swains,[5] 65
From men their cities, and from Gods their fanes:
The levelled towns with weeds lie covered o'er;
The hollow winds through naked temples roar;
Round broken columns clasping ivy twined;
O'er heaps of ruin stalked the stately hind;   70
The fox obscene to gaping tombs retires,
And savage howlings fill the sacred quires.
Awed by his Nobles, by his Commons curst,
Th' Oppressor ruled tyrannic where he durst,
Stretched o'er the Poor and Church his iron rod,   75
And served alike his Vassals and his God.
Whom even the Saxon spared and bloody Dane,
The wanton victims of his sport remain.
But see, the man who spacious regions gave
A waste for beasts, himself denied a grave![6]   80

[5] Alluding to the destruction made in the New Forest, and the tyrannies exercised there by William I. P.
[6] The place of his interment at Caen in Normandy was claimed by a Gentleman as his inheritance, the moment his servants were going to put him in his tomb: so that they were obliged to compound with the owner before they could perform the King's obsequies. [W.]

Stretched on the lawn his second hope survey,
At once the chaser, and at once the prey:
Lo Rufus, tugging at the deadly dart,
Bleeds in the forest like a wounded hart.
Succeeding monarchs heard the subjects' cries,   85
Nor saw displeased the peaceful cottage rise.
Then gathering flocks on unknown mountains fed,
O'er sandy wilds were yellow harvests spread,
The forests wondered at th' unusual grain,
And secret transport touched the conscious swain.   90
Fair Liberty, Britannia's Goddess, rears
Her cheerful head, and leads the golden years.
        Ye vigorous swains! while youth ferments your
blood,
And purer spirits swell the sprightly flood,
Now range the hills, the gameful woods beset,   95
Wind the shrill horn, or spread the waving net.
When milder autumn summer's heat succeeds,
And in the new-shorn field the partridge feeds,
Before his lord the ready spaniel bounds,
Panting with hope, he tries the furrowed grounds;   100
But when the tainted gales the game betray,
Couched close he lies, and meditates the prey:
Secure they trust th' unfaithful field beset,
Till hovering o'er 'em sweeps the swelling net.
Thus (if small things we may with great compare)   105
When Albion sends her eager sons to war,
Some thoughtless Town, with ease and plenty blest,
Near, and more near, the closing lines invest;
Sudden they seize th' amazed, defenceless prize,
And high in air Britannia's standard flies.   110
        See! from the brake the whirring pheasant springs,
And mounts exulting on triumphant wings:
Short is his joy; he feels the fiery wound,
Flutters in blood, and panting beats the ground.
Ah! what avail his glossy, varying dyes,   115
His purple crest, and scarlet-circled eyes,
The vivid green his shining plumes unfold,

His painted wings, and breast that flames with gold?
    Nor yet, when moist Arcturus clouds the sky,
The woods and fields their pleasing toils deny.   120
To plains with well-breathed beagles we repair,
And trace the mazes of the circling hare:
(Beasts, urged by us, their fellow-beasts pursue,
And learn of man each other to undo.)
With slaughtering guns th' unwearied fowler roves,   125
When frosts have whitened all the naked groves;
Where doves in flocks the leafless trees o'ershade,
And lonely woodcocks haunt the watery glade.
He lifts the tube, and levels with his eye;
Straight a short thunder breaks the frozen sky: 130
Oft, as in airy rings they skim the heath,
The clamorous Lapwings feel the leaden death:
Oft, as the mounting larks their notes prepare,
They fall, and leave their little lives in air.
    In genial spring, beneath the quivering shade,   135
Where cooling vapours breathe along the mead,
The patient fisher takes his silent stand,
Intent, his angle trembling in his hand:
With looks unmoved, he hopes the scaly breed,
And eyes the dancing cork, and bending reed.   140
Our plenteous streams a various race supply,
The bright-eyed perch with fins of Tyrian dye,
The silver eel, in shining volumes rolled,
The yellow carp, in scales bedropped with gold,
Swift trouts, diversified with crimson stains,   145
And pikes, the tyrants of the watery plains.
    Now Cancer glows with Phœbus' fiery car:
The youth rush eager to the sylvan war,
Swarm o'er the lawns, the forest walks surround,
Rouse the fleet hart, and cheer the opening hound.   150
Th' impatient courser pants in every vein,
And, pawing, seems to beat the distant plain:
Hills, vales, and floods appear already crossed,
And ere he starts, a thousand steps are lost.
See the bold youth strain up the threatening steep,   155

Rush through the thickets, down the valleys sweep,
Hang o'er their coursers' heads with eager speed,
And earth rolls back beneath the flying steed.
Let old Arcadia boast her ample plain,
Th' immortal huntress, and her virgin train;   160
Nor envy, Windsor! since thy shades have seen
As bright a Goddess, and as chaste a Queen;[7]
Whose care, like hers, protects the sylvan reign,
The Earth's fair light, and Empress of the Main.
      Here too, 'tis sung, of old Diana strayed,   165
And Cynthus' top forsook for Windsor shade;
Here was she seen o'er airy wastes to rove,
Seek the clear spring, or haunt the pathless grove;
Here armed with silver bows, in early dawn,
Her buskined Virgins traced the dewy lawn.   170
      Above the rest a rural nymph was famed,
Thy offspring, Thames! the fair Lodona named;
(Lodona's fate, in long oblivion cast,
The Muse shall sing, and what she sings shall last.)
Scarce could the Goddess from her nymph be known,
But by the crescent and the golden zone.   176
She scorned the praise of beauty, and the care;
A belt her waist, a fillet binds her hair;
A painted quiver on her shoulder sounds,
And with her dart the flying deer she wounds.   180
It chanced, as eager of the chase, the maid
Beyond the forest's verdant limits strayed,
Pan saw and loved, and, burning with desire,
Pursued her flight; her flight increased his fire.
Not half so swift the trembling doves can fly,   185
When the fierce eagle cleaves the liquid sky;
Not half so swiftly the fierce eagle moves,
When through the clouds he drives the trembling doves;
As from the God she flew with furious pace,
Or as the God, more furious, urged the chase.   190
Now fainting, sinking, pale, the nymph appears;

[7] Queen Anne. [W.]

Now close behind, his sounding steps she hears;
And now his shadow reached her as she run,
His shadow lengthened by the setting sun;
And now his shorter breath, with sultry air,   195
Pants on her neck, and fans her parting hair.
In vain on father Thames she call for aid,
Nor could Diana help her injured maid.
Faint, breathless, thus she prayed, nor prayed in vain;
"Ah, Cynthia! ah—though banished from thy train,   200
Let me, O let me, to the shades repair,
My native shades—there weep, and murmur there."
She said, and melting as in tears she lay,
In a soft, silver stream dissolved away.
The silver stream her virgin coldness keeps,   205
For ever murmurs, and for ever weeps;
Still bears the name the hapless virgin bore,[8]
And bathes the forest where she ranged before.
In her chaste current oft the Goddess laves,
And with celestial tears augments the waves.   210
Oft in her glass the musing shepherd spies
The headlong mountains and the downward skies,
The watery landscape of the pendent woods,
And absent trees that tremble in the floods;
In the clear azure gleam the flocks are seen,   215
And floating forests paint the waves with green,
Through the fair scene roll slow the lingering streams,
Then foaming pour along, and rush into the Thames.
        Thou, too, great father of the British floods!
With joyful pride surveyst our lofty woods;   220
Where towering oaks their growing honours rear,
And future navies on thy shores appear.
Not Neptune's self from all his streams receives
A wealthier tribute than to thine he gives.
No seas so rich, so gay no banks appear,   225
No lake so gentle, and no spring so clear.
Nor Po so swells the fabling Poet's lays,

[8] The River Loddon. [P.]

While led along the skies his current strays,
As thine, which visits Windsor's famed abodes,
To grace the mansion of our earthly Gods: 230
Nor all his stars above a lustre show,
Like the bright Beauties on thy banks below;
Where Jove, subdued by mortal Passion still,
Might change Olympus for a nobler hill.
     Happy the man whom this bright Court
approves,   235
His Sovereign favours, and his Country loves:
Happy next him, who to these shades retires,
Whom Nature charms, and whom the Muse inspires:
Whom humbler joys of home-felt quiet please,
Successive study, exercise, and ease.   240
He gathers health from herbs the forest yields,
And of their fragrant physic spoils the fields:
With chymic art exalts the mineral powers,
And draws the aromatic souls of flowers:
Now marks the course of rolling orbs on high;   245
O'er figured worlds now travels with his eye;
Of ancient writ unlocks the learnèd store,
Consults the dead, and lives past ages o'er:
Or wandering thoughtful in the silent wood,
Attends the duties of the wise and good,   250
T' observe a mean, be to himself a friend,
To follow nature, and regard his end;
Or looks on heaven with more than mortal eyes,
Bids his free soul expatiate in the skies,
Amid her kindred stars familiar roam,   255
Survey the region, and confess her home!
Such was the life great Scipio once admired;
Thus Atticus, and TRUMBULL thus retired.
     Ye sacred Nine! that all my soul possess,
Whose raptures fire me, and whose visions bless,   260
Bear me, oh bear me to sequestered scenes,
The bowery mazes, and surrounding greens:
To Thames's banks, which fragrant breezes fill,
Or where ye Muses sport on COOPER'S HILL.

(On COOPER'S HILL eternal wreaths shall grow,   265
While lasts the mountain, or while Thames shall flow.)
I seem through consecrated walks to rove,
I hear soft music die along the grove:
Led by the sound, I roam from shade to shade,
By godlike Poets venerable made: 270
Here his first lays majestic DENHAM sung;
There the last numbers flowed from COWLEY'S tongue.[9]
O early lost! what tears the river shed,
When the sad pomp along his banks was led?
His drooping swans on every note expire,   275
And on his willows hung each Muse's lyre.
    Since fate relentless stopped their heavenly voice,
No more the forests ring, or groves rejoice;
Who now shall charm the shades, where COWLEY strung
His living harp, and lofty DENHAM sung?   280
But hark! the groves rejoice, the forest rings!
Are these revived? or is it GRANVILLE sings?
'Tis yours, my Lord, to bless our soft retreats,
And call the Muses to their ancient seats;
To paint anew the flowery sylvan scenes,   285
To crown the forests with immortal greens,
Make Windsor hills in lofty numbers rise,
And lift her turrets nearer to the skies;
To sing those honours you deserve to wear,
And add new lustre to her silver star.   290
    Here noble SURREY felt the sacred rage,[10]
SURREY, the GRANVILLE of a former age:
Matchless his pen, victorious was his lance,
Bold in the lists, and graceful in the dance:
In the same shades the Cupids tuned his lyre,   295
To the same notes, of love, and soft desire:
Fair Geraldine, bright object of his vow,
Then filled the groves, as heavenly Mira now.

[9] Mr. Cowley died at Chertsey, on the borders of the Forest, and was
from thence conveyed to Westminster. P.
[10] Henry Howard, Earl of Surrey, one of the first refiners of the English
poetry; who flourished in the time of Henry VIII. P.

Oh wouldst thou sing what Heroes Windsor bore,
What Kings first breathed upon her winding shore,   300
Or raise old warriors, whose adored remains
In weeping vaults her hallowed earth contains!
With Edward's acts adorn the shining page,[11]
Stretch his long triumphs down through every age,
Draw monarchs chained, and Cressy's glorious
field,   305
The lilies blazing on the regal shield:
Then, from her roofs when Verrio's colours fall,
And leave inanimate the naked wall,
Still in thy song should vanquished France appear,
And bleed for ever under Britain's spear.   310
    Let softer strains ill-fated Henry mourn,[12]
And palms eternal flourish round his urn.
Here o'er the Martyr King the marble weeps,
And, fast beside him, once-feared Edward sleeps:[13]
Whom not th' extended Albion could contain,   315
From old Belerium to the northern main,
The grave unites; where e'en the great find rest,
And blended lie th' oppressor and th' opprest!
    Make sacred Charles's tomb for ever known
(Obscure the place, and uninscribed the stone),   320
Oh fact accurst! what tears has Albion shed,
Heavens, what new wounds! and how her old have bled!
She saw her sons with purple deaths expire,
Her sacred domes involved in rolling fire,
A dreadful series of intestine wars,   325
Inglorious triumphs and dishonest scars.
At length great ANNA said—"Let Discord cease!"
She said! the world obeyed, and all was Peace!
    In that blest moment from his oozy bed
Old father Thames advanced his reverend head.   330
His tresses dropped with dews, and o'er the stream

[11] Edward III born here. P.
[12] Henry VI. P.
[13] Edward IV. P.

His shining horns diffused a golden gleam:
Graved on his urn appeared the moon, that guides
His swelling waters, and alternate tides;
The figured streams in waves of silver rolled,   335
And on their banks Augusta rose in gold.
Around his throne the sea-born brothers stood,
Who swell with tributary urns his flood;
First the famed authors of his ancient name,
The winding Isis and the fruitful Thame: 340
The Kennet swift, for silver eels renowned;
The Loddon slow, with verdant alders crowned;
Cole, whose dark streams his flowery islands lave;
And chalky Wey, that rolls a milky wave:
The blue, transparent Vandalis appears;   345
The gulfy Lee his sedgy tresses rears;
And sullen Mole, that hides his diving flood;
And silent Darent, stained with Danish blood.

    High in the midst, upon his urn reclined
(His sea-green mantle waving with the wind),   350
The God appeared: he turned his azure eyes
Where Windsor domes and pompous turrets rise;
Then bowed and spoke; the winds forget to roar,
And the hushed waves glide softly to the shore.

    Hail, sacred Peace! hail, long-expected days,   355
That Thames's glory to the stars shall raise!
Though Tiber's streams immortal Rome behold,
Though foaming Hermus swells with tides of gold,
From heaven itself though sevenfold Nilus flows,
And harvests on a hundred realms bestows;   360
These now no more shall be the Muse's themes,
Lost in my fame, as in the sea their streams.
Let Volga's banks with iron squadrons shine.
And groves of lances glitter on the Rhine,
Let barbarous Ganges arm a servile train;   365
Be mine the blessings of a peaceful reign.
No more my sons shall dye with British blood
Red Iber's sands, or Ister's foaming flood:
Safe on my shore each unmolested swain

Shall tend the flocks, or reap the bearded grain;   370
The shady empire shall retain no trace
Of war or blood, but in the sylvan chase;
The trumpet sleep, while cheerful horns are blown,
And arms employed on birds and beasts alone.
Behold! th' ascending Villas on my side,   375
Project long shadows o'er the crystal tide.
Behold! Augusta's glittering spires increase,
And Temples rise, the beauteous works of Peace.[14]
I see, I see, where two fair cities bend
Their ample bow, a new Whitehall ascend!   380
There mighty Nations shall inquire their doom,
The World's great Oracle in times to come;
There Kings shall sue, and suppliant States be seen
Once more to bend before a BRITISH QUEEN.
          Thy trees, fair Windsor! now shall leave their
woods,   385
And half thy forests rush into thy floods,
Bear Britain's thunder, and her Cross display,
To the bright regions of the rising day;
Tempt icy seas, where scarce the waters roll,
Where clearer flames glow round the frozen Pole;   390
Or under southern skies exalt their sails,
Led by new stars, and borne by spicy gales!
For me the balm shall bleed, and amber flow,
The coral redden, and the ruby glow,
The pearly shell its lucid globe infold,   395
And Phœbus warm the ripening ore to gold.
The time shall come, when free as seas or wind
Unbounded Thames shall flow for all mankind,[15]
Whole nations enter with each swelling tide,
And seas but join the regions they divide;   400
Earth's distant ends our glory shall behold,
And the new world launch forth to seek the old.
Then ships of uncouth form shall stem the tide,

[14] The fifty new Churches. P.
[15] A wish that London may be made a FREE PORT. P.

And feathered people crowd my wealthy side,
And naked youths and painted chiefs admire   405
Our speech, our colour, and our strange attire!
O stretch thy reign, fair Peace! from shore to shore,
Till Conquest cease, and Slavery be no more;
Till the freed Indians in their native groves
Reap their own fruits, and woo their sable loves,   410
Peru once more a race of Kings behold,
And other Mexico's be roofed with gold.
Exiled by thee from earth to deepest hell,
In brazen bonds, shall barbarous Discord dwell;
Gigantic Pride, pale Terror, gloomy Care,   415
And mad Ambition shall attend her there:
There purple Vengeance bathed in gore retires,
Her weapons blunted, and extinct her fires:
There hateful Envy her own snakes shall feel,
And Persecution mourn her broken wheel: 420
There Faction roar, Rebellion bite her chain,
And gasping Furies thirst for blood in vain.
        Here cease thy flight, nor with unhallowed lays
Touch the fair fame of Albion's golden days:
The thoughts of Gods let GRANVILLE's verse recite,   425
And bring the scenes of opening fate to light.
My humble Muse, in unambitious strains,
Paints the green forests and the flowery plains,
Where Peace descending bids her olives spring,
And scatters blessings from her dovelike wing.   430
Even I more sweetly pass my careless days,
Pleased in the silent shade with empty praise;
Enough for me, that to the listening swains
First in these fields I sung the sylvan strains.

SHORTER POEMS

1713

ODE FOR MUSIC

On St. Cecilia's Day [16]

I

DESCEND, ye Nine! descend and sing;
The breathing instruments inspire,
Wake into voice each silent string,
And sweep the sounding lyre!
   In a sadly pleasing strain   5
   Let the warbling lute complain:
      Let the loud trumpet sound,
      Till the roofs all around
      The shrill echoes rebound:
While in more lengthened notes and slow,   10
The deep, majestic, solemn organs blow.
      Hark! the numbers soft and clear,

[16] In the 1736 edition of his *Works* Pope says that this poem was written in 1708. It was first published in July, 1713.

Gently steal upon the ear;
Now louder, and yet louder rise
And fill with spreading sounds the skies;   15
Exulting in triumph now swell the bold notes,
In broken air, trembling, the wild music floats;
    Till, by degrees, remote and small,
        The strains decay,
        And melt away,   20
    In a dying, dying fall.

II

By Music, minds an equal temper know,
    Nor swell too high, nor sink too low.
If in the breast tumultuous joys arise,
Music her soft, assuasive voice applies;   25
    Or when the soul is pressed with cares,
    Exalts her in enlivening airs.
Warriors she fires with animated sounds;
Pours balm into the bleeding lover's wounds:
    Melancholy lifts her head,   30
    Morpheus rouses from his bed,
    Sloth unfolds her arms and wakes,
    Listening Envy drops her snakes;
Intestine war no more our Passions wage,
And giddy Factions hear away their rage.   35

III

But when our Country's cause provokes to Arms,
How martial music every bosom warms!
So when the first bold vessel dared the seas,
High on the stern the Thracian raised his strain,
    While Argo saw her kindred trees   40
    Descend from Pelion to the main.
    Transported demigods stood round,[17]

[17] The Greek poet Apollonius Rhodius in his *Argonautica* (i, 553) tells how the Centaur Chiron and his wife came down to the shore to show the child Achilles to his father Peleus as the latter passed in the *Argo*.

And men grew heroes at the sound,
Enflamed with glory's charms:
Each chief his sevenfold shield displayed,   45
And half unsheathed the shining blade:
And seas, and rocks, and skies rebound
To arms, to arms, to arms!

IV

But when through all th' infernal bounds,
Which flaming Phlegethon surrounds,   50
Love, strong as Death, the Poet led
To the pale nations of the dead,
What sounds were heard,
What scenes appeared,
    O'er all the dreary coasts!   55
        Dreadful gleams,
        Dismal screams,
        Fires that glow,
        Shrieks of woe,
        Sullen moans,   60
        Hollow groans,
    And cries of tortured ghosts!
But hark! he strikes the golden lyre;
And see! the tortured ghosts respire,
      See, shady forms advance!   65
    Thy stone, O Sisyphus, stands still,
    Ixion rests upon his wheel,
      And the pale spectres dance!
    The Furies sink upon their iron beds,
And snakes uncurled hang listening round their
heads.   70

V

By the streams that ever flow,
By the fragrant winds that blow
    O'er th' Elysian flowers;
By those happy souls who dwell

In yellow meads of Asphodel,   75
    Or Amaranthine bowers;
By the heroes' armèd shades,
Glittering through the gloomy glades;
By the youths that died for love,
    Wandering in the myrtle grove,   80
Restore, restore Eurydice to life:
Oh take the husband, or return the wife!
    He sung, and hell consented
        To hear the Poet's prayer:
    Stern Proserpine relented,   85
        And gave him back the fair.
        Thus song could prevail
      O'er death, and o'er hell,
A conquest how hard and how glorious!
    Though fate had fast bound her   90
    With Styx nine times round her,
Yet music and love were victorious.

VI

But soon, too soon, the lover turns his eyes:
Again she falls, again she dies, she dies!
How wilt thou now the fatal sisters move?   95
No crime was thine, if 'tis no crime to love.
    Now under hanging mountains,
    Beside the fall of fountains,
    Or where Hebrus wanders,
    Rolling in Mæanders,   100
        All alone,
        Unheard, unknown,
        He makes his moan;
        And calls her ghost,
        For ever, ever, ever lost!   105
    Now with Furies surrounded,
    Despairing, confounded,
    He trembles, he glows,
    Amidst Rhodope's snows:

See, wild as the winds, o'er the desert he flies;   110
Hark! Hæmus resounds with the Bacchanals' cries—
        Ah see, he dies!
Yet even in death Eurydice he sung,
Eurydice still trembled on his tongue,
      Eurydice the woods,   115
      Eurydice the floods,
Eurydice the rocks, and hollow mountains rung.

VII

    Music the fiercest grief can charm,
    And fate's severest rage disarm:
    Music can soften pain to ease,   120
        And make despair and madness please:
           Our joys below it can improve,
           And antedate the bliss above.
    This the divine Cecilia found,
And to her Maker's praise confined the sound.   125
When the full organ joins the tuneful quire,
    Th' immortal powers incline their ear;
Borne on the swelling notes our souls aspire,
While solemn airs improve the sacred fire;
    And Angels lean from heaven to hear.   130
Of Orpheus now no more let Poets tell,
To bright Cecilia greater power is given;
    His numbers raised a shade from hell,
      Hers lift the soul to heaven.

1717–1736

ODE ON SOLITUDE[18]

HAPPY the man whose wish and care
    A few paternal acres bound,
Content to breathe his native air,
        In his own ground.

Whose herds with milk, whose fields with bread,   5
    Whose flocks supply him with attire,
Whose trees in summer yield him shade,
        In winter fire.

Blest, who can unconcernedly find
    Hours, days, and years slide soft away,   10
In health of body, peace of mind,
        Quiet by day,

[18] This was a very early production of our Author, written at about twelve years old. P. An early version of this poem appears in a letter to Cromwell of July 17, 1709, where Pope calls it an Ode "which I found yesterday by great accident, and which I find by the date was written when I was not twelve years old." "You may perceive how long I have continued in my passion for a rural life, and in the same employments of it." But the manuscript of Pope's letter is said to show that even after he had transcribed the poem he made alterations. The dates which appear above at the head of the poem are that of its first publication, in an intermediate version, and that of the first publication of the final version, here presented.

Sound sleep by night; study and ease,
    Together mixed; sweet recreation;
And Innocence, which most does please   15
        With meditation.

Thus let me live, unseen, unknown,
    Thus unlamented let me die,
Steal from the world, and not a stone
        Tell where I lie.   20

THE DYING CHRISTIAN
TO HIS SOUL [19]

I

Vital spark of heavenly flame!
Quit, oh quit this mortal frame:
Trembling, hoping, lingering, flying,
Oh the pain, the bliss of dying!
Cease, fond Nature, cease thy strife,   5
And let me languish into life.

II

Hark! they whisper; Angels say,
Sister Spirit, come away.
What is this absorbs me quite?
Steals my senses, shuts my sight,   10
Drowns my spirits, draws my breath?
Tell me, my Soul, can this be Death?

III

The world recedes; it disappears!
Heaven opens on my eyes! my ears

[19] This ode was written in imitation of the famous sonnet of Hadrian to his departing soul; but as much superior in sense and sublimity to his original, as the *Christian* Religion is to the *Pagan*. [W.] A first draft of the poem may have been written as early as 1712.

    With sounds seraphic ring: 15
Lend, lend your wings! I mount! I fly!
O Grave! where is thy Victory?
    O Death! where is thy Sting?

AN ESSAY ON CRITICISM

WRITTEN IN THE YEAR MDCCIX

PART I

Introduction. That 'tis as great a fault to judge ill, as to write ill, and a more dangerous one to the public, l. 1.

That a *true Taste* is as rare to be found, as a *true Genius*, ll. 9–18.

That most men are born with some Taste, but spoiled by false *Education*, ll. 19–25.

The multitude of *Critics*, and causes of them, ll. 26–45.

That we are to study our own *Taste*, and know the *Limits* of it, ll. 46–67.

Nature the best guide of Judgment, ll. 68–87.

Improved by *Art* and *Rules*, which are but *methodized Nature*, l. 88

Rules derived from the Practice of the *Ancient Poets*, ll. 88–110.

That therefore the *Ancients* are necessary to be studied by a Critic, particularly *Homer* and *Virgil*, ll. 120–138.

Of *Licences*, and the use of them by the Ancients, ll. 140–180.

Reverence due to the *Ancients*, and praise of them, ll. 181 ff.

'Tis hard to say, if greater want of skill
Appear in writing or in judging ill;
But, of the two, less dangerous is th' offence
To tire our patience, than mislead our sense.

Some few in that, but numbers err in this,   5
Ten censure wrong for one who writes amiss;
A fool might once himself alone expose,
Now one in verse makes many more in prose.
    'Tis with our judgments as our watches, none
Go just alike, yet each believes his own.   10
In Poets as true genius is but rare,
True Taste as seldom is the Critic's share;
Both must alike from Heaven derive their light,
These born to judge, as well as those to write.
Let such teach others who themselves excel,   15
And censure freely who have written well.

Authors are partial to their wit, 'tis true,
But are not Critics to their judgment too?
    Yet if we look more closely, we shall find
Most have the seeds of judgment in their mind: 20
Nature affords at least a glimmering light;
The lines, though touched but faintly, are drawn right.
But as the slightest sketch, if justly traced,
Is by ill colouring but the more disgraced,
So by false learning is good sense defaced: 25
Some are bewildered in the maze of schools,
And some made coxcombs Nature meant but fools.
In search of wit these lose their common sense,
And then turn Critics in their own defence:
Each burns alike, who can, or cannot write,   30
Or with a Rival's, or an Eunuch's spite.
All fools have still an itching to deride,
And fain would be upon the laughing side.
If Mævius scribble in Apollo's spite,
There are who judge still worse than he can write.   35
    Some have at first for Wits, then Poets past,
Turned Critics next, and proved plain fools at last.
Some neither can for Wits nor Critics pass,
As heavy mules are neither horse nor ass.
Those half-learned witlings, numerous in our isle,   40
As half-formed insects on the banks of Nile;

Unfinished things, one knows not what to call,
Their generation's so equivocal:
To tell 'em, would a hundred tongues require,
Or one vain wit's, that might a hundred tire.   45
     But you who seek to give and merit fame,
And justly bear a Critic's noble name,
Be sure yourself and your own reach to know,
How far your genius, taste, and learning go;
Launch not beyond your depth, but be discreet,   50
And mark that point where sense and dulness meet.
     Nature to all things fixed the limits fit,
And wisely curbed proud man's pretending wit.
As on the land while here the ocean gains,
In other parts it leaves wide sandy plains;   55
Thus in the soul while memory prevails,
The solid power of understanding fails;
Where beams of warm imagination play,
The memory's soft figures melt away.
One science only will one genius fit;   60
So vast is art, so narrow human wit:
Not only bounded to peculiar arts,
But oft in those confined to single parts.
Like Kings we lose the conquests gained before,
By vain ambition still to make them more;   65
Each might his several province well command,
Would all but stoop to what they understand.
     First follow Nature, and your judgment frame
By her just standard, which is still the same:
Unerring NATURE, still divinely bright,   70
One clear, unchanged, and universal light,
Life, force, and beauty, must to all impart,
At once the source, and end, and test of Art.
Art from that fund each just supply provides,
Works without show, and without pomp presides: 75
In some fair body thus th' informing soul
With spirits feeds, with vigour fills the whole,
Each motion guides, and every nerve sustains;
Itself unseen, but in the effects, remains.

Some, to whom Heaven in wit has been profuse,   80
Want as much more, to turn it to its use;
For wit and judgment often are at strife,
Though meant each other's aid, like man and wife.
'Tis more to guide, than spur the Muse's steed;
Restrain his fury, than provoke his speed;   85
The wingèd courser, like a generous horse,
Shows most true mettle when you check his course.
    Those RULES of old discovered, not devised,
Are Nature still, but Nature methodized;
Nature, like Liberty, is but restrained   90
By the same Laws which first herself ordained.
    Hear how learned Greece her useful rules indites,
When to repress, and when indulge our flights:
High on Parnassus' top her sons she showed,
And pointed out those arduous paths they trod;   95
Held from afar, aloft, th' immortal prize,
And urged the rest by equal steps to rise.
Just precepts thus from great examples given,
She drew from them what they derived from Heaven.
The generous Critic fanned the Poet's fire,   100
And taught the world with reason to admire.
Then Criticism the Muses' handmaid proved,
To dress her charms, and make her more beloved:
But following wits from that intention strayed,
Who could not win the mistress, wooed the maid;   105
Against the Poets their own arms they turned,
Sure to hate most the men from whom they learned.
So modern 'Pothecaries, taught the art
By Doctor's bills to play the Doctor's part,
Bold in the practice of mistaken rules,   110
Prescribe, apply, and call their masters fools.
Some on the leaves of ancient authors prey,
Nor time nor moths e'er spoiled so much as they.
Some drily plain, without invention's aid,
Write dull receipts how poems may be made.   115
These leave the sense, their learning to display,
And those explain the meaning quite away.

You then whose judgment the right course would
steer,
Know well each ANCIENT's proper character;
His Fable, Subject, scope in every page;   120
Religion, Country, genius of his Age:
Without all these at once before your eyes,
Cavil you may, but never criticize.
Be Homer's works your study and delight,
Read them by day, and meditate by night;   125
Thence form your judgment, thence your maxims bring,
And trace the Muses upward to their spring.
Still with itself compared, his text peruse;
And let your comment be the Mantuan Muse.
        When first young Maro in his boundless mind   130
A work t' outlast immortal Rome designed,
Perhaps he seemed above the Critic's law,
And but from Nature's fountains scorned to draw:
But when t' examine every part he came,
Nature and Homer were, he found, the same.   135
Convinced, amazed, he checks the bold design;
And rules as strict his laboured work confine,
As if the Stagirite o'erlooked each line.
Learn hence for ancient rules a just esteem;
To copy nature is to copy them.   140
        Some beauties yet no Precepts can declare,
For there's a happiness as well as care.
Music resembles Poetry, in each
Are nameless graces which no methods teach,
And which a master hand alone can reach.   145
If, where the rules not far enough extend,
(Since rules were made but to promote their end)
Some lucky Licence answer to the full
Th' intent proposed, that Licence is a rule.
Thus Pegasus, a nearer way to take,   150
May boldly deviate from the common track;
From vulgar bounds with brave disorder part,
And snatch a grace beyond the reach of art,
Which without passing through the judgment, gains

The heart, and all its end at once attains.   155
In prospects thus, some objects please our eyes,
Which out of nature's common order rise,
The shapeless rock, or hanging precipice.
Great Wits sometimes may gloriously offend,
And rise to faults true Critics dare not mend.   160
But though the Ancients thus their rules invade,
(As Kings dispense with laws themselves have made)
Moderns, beware! or if you must offend
Against the precept, ne'er transgress its End;
Let it be seldom, and compelled by need;   165
And have, at least, their precedent to plead.
The Critic else proceeds without remorse,
Seizes your fame, and puts his laws in force.
        I know there are, to whose presumptuous thoughts
Those freer beauties, even in them, seem faults.   170
Some figures monstrous and misshaped appear,
Considered singly, or behold too near,
Which, but proportioned to their light, or place,
Due distance reconciles to form and grace.
A prudent chief not always must display   175
His powers in equal ranks, and fair array,
But with th' occasion and the place comply,
Conceal his force, nay seem sometimes to fly.
Those oft are stratagems which error seem,
Nor is it Homer nods, but we that dream.   180
        Still green with bays each ancient Altar stands,
Above the reach of sacrilegious hands;
Secure from Flames, from Envy's fiercer rage,
Destructive War, and all-involving Age.
See, from each clime the learned their incense bring!   185
Hear, in all tongues consenting Pæans ring!
In praise so just let every voice be joined,
And fill the general chorus of mankind.
Hail, Bards triumphant! born in happier days;
Immortal heirs of universal praise!   190
Whose honours with increase of ages grow,
As streams roll down, enlarging as they flow;

Nations unborn your mighty names shall sound,
And worlds applaud that must not yet be found!
Oh may some spark of your celestial fire,   195
The last, the meanest of your sons inspire,
(That on weak wings, from far, pursues your flights;
Glows while he reads, but trembles as he writes)
To teach vain Wits a science litt'e known,
T' admire superior sense, and doubt their own!   200

PART II

Causes hindering a *true Judgment*. 1. *Pride*, 1. 201. 2. *Imperfect Learning*,
1. 215. 3. Judging by *parts*, and not by the whole, ll. 233–288. Critics in
Wit, Language, Versification, only, ll. 288, 305, 339 ff. 4. Being too hard
to please, or too apt to admire, 1. 384. 5. *Partiality*—too much Love to a
Sect,—to the *Ancients* or *Moderns*, 1. 394. 6. *Prejudice* or *Prevention*,
1. 408. 7. *Singularity*, 1. 424. 8. *Inconstancy*, 1. 430. 9. *Party Spirit*, ll. 452 ff. 10.
Envy, 1. 466. Against Envy, and in praise of Good Nature, ll. 508 ff. When
Severity is chiefly to be used by Critics, ll. 526 ff.

Of all the Causes which conspire to blind
Man's erring judgment, and misguide the mind,
What the weak head with strongest bias rules,
Is *Pride*, the never-failing vice of fools.
Whatever Nature has in worth denied,   205
She gives in large recruits of needful Pride:
For as in bodies, thus in souls, we find
What wants in blood and spirits, swelled with wind:
Pride, where Wit fails, steps in to our defence,
And fills up all the mighty Void of sense.   210
If once right reason drives that cloud away,
Truth breaks upon us with resistless day.
Trust not yourself; but your defects to know,
Make use of every friend—and every foe.
A *little learning* is a dangerous thing;   215

Drink deep, or taste not the Pierian spring:
There shallow draughts intoxicate the brain,
And drinking largely sobers us again.
Fired at first sight with what the Muse imparts,
In fearless youth we tempt the heights of Arts,   220
While from the bounded level of our mind,
Short views we take, nor see the lengths behind;
But more advanced, behold with strange surprise
New distant scenes of endless science rise!
So pleased at first the towering Alps we try,   225
Mount o'er the vales, and seem to tread the sky,
Th' eternal snows appear already past,
And the first clouds and mountains seem the last:
But, those attained, we tremble to survey
The growing labours of the lengthened way,   230
Th' increasing prospect tires our wandering eyes,
Hills peep o'er hills, and Alps on Alps arise!
    A perfect Judge will read each work of Wit
With the same spirit that its author writ:
Survey the WHOLE, nor seek slight faults to find   235
Where nature moves, and rapture warms the mind;
Nor lose, for that malignant dull delight,
The generous pleasure to be charmed with wit.
But in such lays as neither ebb, nor flow,
Correctly cold, and regularly low,   240
That shunning faults, one quiet tenour keep;
We cannot blame indeed——but we may sleep.
In Wit, as Nature, what affects our hearts
Is not th' exactness of peculiar parts;
'Tis not a lip, or eye, we beauty call,   245
But the joint force and full result of all.
Thus when we view some well-proportioned dome,
(The world's just wonder, and even thine, O Rome!)
No single parts unequally surprise,
All comes united to th' admiring eyes;   250
No monstrous height, or breadth, or length appear;
The Whole at once is bold, and regular.
    Whoever thinks a faultless piece to see,

Thinks what ne'er was, nor is, nor e'er shall be.
In every work regard the writer's End,   255
Since none can compass more than they intend;
And if the means be just, the conduct true,
Applause, in spite of trivial faults, is due.
As men of breeding, sometimes men of wit,
T' avoid great errors, must the less commit: 260
Neglect the rules each verbal Critic lays,
For not to know some trifles, is a praise.
Most Critics, fond of some subservient art,
Still make the Whole depend upon a Part:
They talk of principles, but notions prize,   265
And all to one loved Folly sacrifice.

    Once on a time, La Mancha's Knight, they say,[1]
A certain Bard encountering on the way,
Discoursed in terms as just, with looks as sage,
As e'er could Dennis of the Grecian stage;   270
Concluding all were desperate sots and fools,
Who durst depart from Aristotle's rules.
Our Author, happy in a judge so nice,
Produced his Play, and begged the Knight's advice;
Made him observe the subject, and the plot,   275
The manners, passions, unities; what not?
All which, exact to rule, were brought about,
Were but a Combat in the lists left out.
"What! leave the Combat out?" exclaims the Knight;
Yes, or we must renounce the Stagirite.   280
"Not so by Heaven" (he answers in a rage)
"Knights, squires, and steeds, must enter on the stage."
So vast a throng the stage can ne'er contain.
"Then build a new, or act it in a plain."

    Thus Critics, of less judgment than caprice,   285
Curious not knowing, not exact but nice,
Form short Ideas; and offend in arts
(As most in manners) by a love to parts.
    Some to *Conceit* alone their taste confine,

---

[1] A story taken by our Author from the *Spurious Don Quixote*.   [W.]

And glittering thoughts struck out at every line;   290
Pleased with a work where nothing's just or fit;
One glaring Chaos and wild heap of wit.
Poets like painters, thus, unskilled to trace
The naked nature and the living grace,
With gold and jewels cover every part,   295
And hide with ornaments their want of art.
True Wit is Nature to advantage dressed,
What oft was thought, but ne'er so well expressed;
Something, whose truth convinced at sight we find,
That gives us back the image of our mind.   300
As shades more sweetly recommend the light,
So modest plainness sets off sprightly wit.
For works may have more wit than does 'em good,
As bodies perish through excess of blood.
    Others for *Language* all their care express,   305
And value books, as women men, for Dress:
Their praise is still,—the Style is excellent:
The Sense, they humbly take upon content.
Words are like leaves; and where they most abound,
Much fruit of sense beneath is rarely found.   310
False Eloquence, like the prismatic glass,
Its gaudy colours spreads on every place;
The face of Nature we no more survey,
All glares alike, without distinction gay:
But true Expression, like th' unchanging Sun,   315
Clears, and improves whate'er it shines upon,
It gilds all objects, but it alters none.
Expression is the dress of thought, and still
Appears more decent, as more suitable;
A vile conceit in pompous words expressed,   320
Is like a clown in regal purple dressed:
For different styles with different subjects sort,
As several garbs with country, town, and court.
Some by old words to fame have made pretence,
Ancients in phrase, mere moderns in their sense;   325
Such laboured nothings, in so strange a style,
Amaze th' unlearned, and make the learnèd smile.

Unlucky, as Fungoso in the Play,[2]
These sparks with awkward vanity display
What the fine gentleman wore yesterday;   330
And but so mimic ancient wits at best,
As apes our grandsires, in their doublets drest.
In words, as fashions, the same rule will hold;
Alike fantastic, if too new, or old:
Be not the first by whom the new are tried,   335
Nor yet the last to lay the old aside.
    But most by Numbers judge a Poet's song;
And smooth or rough, with them is right or wrong:
In the bright Muse though thousand charms conspire,
Her Voice is all these tuneful fools admire;   340
Who haunt Parnassus but to please their ear,
Not mend their minds; as some to Church repair,
Not for the doctrine, but the music there.
These equal syllables alone require,
Though oft the ear the open vowels tire;   345
While expletives their feeble aid do join;
And ten low words oft creep in one dull line:
While they ring round the same unvaried chimes,
With sure returns of still expected rhymes;
Where'er you find "the cooling western breeze,"   350
In the next line, it "whispers through the trees:"
If crystal streams "with pleasing murmurs creep,"
The reader's threatened (not in vain) with "sleep:"
Then, at the last and only couplet fraught
With some unmeaning thing they call a thought,   355
A needless Alexandrine ends the song,
That, like a wounded snake, drags its slow length along.
Leave such to tune their own dull rhymes, and know
What's roundly smooth, or languishingly slow;
And praise the easy vigour of a line,   360
Where Denham's strength, and Waller's sweetness join.
True ease in writing comes from art, not chance,
As those move easiest who have learned to dance.

[2] See Ben Jonson's *Every Man out of his Humour.* P.

'Tis not enough no harshness gives offence,
The sound must seem an Echo to the sense: 365
Soft is the strain when Zephyr gently blows,
And the smooth stream in smoother numbers flows;
But when loud surges lash the sounding shore,
The hoarse, rough verse should like the torrent roar:
When Ajax strives some rock's vast weight to throw,   370
The line too labours, and the words move slow;
Not so, when swift Camilla scours the plain,
Flies o'er th' unbending corn, and skims along the main.
Hear how Timotheus' varied lays surprise,[3]
And bid alternate passions fall and rise!   375
While, at each change, the son of Libyan Jove
Now burns with glory, and then melts with love;
Now his fierce eyes with sparkling fury glow,
Now sighs steal out, and tears begin to flow:
Persians and Greeks like turns of nature found,   380
And the World's victor stood subdued by Sound!
The power of Music all our hearts allow,
And what Timotheus was, is DRYDEN now.
      Avoid Extremes; and shun the fault of such,
Who still are pleased too little or too much.   385
At every trifle scorn to take offence,
That always shows great pride, or little sense;
Those heads, as stomachs, are not sure the best,
Which nauseate all, and nothing can digest.
Yet let not each gay Turn thy rapture move;   390
For fools admire, but men of sense approve:
As things seem large which we through mists descry,
Dulness is ever apt to magnify.
      Some foreign writers, some our own despise;
The Ancients only, or the Moderns prize.   395
Thus Wit, like Faith, by each man is applied
To one small sect, and all are damned beside.
Meanly they seek the blessing to confine,
And force that sun but on a part to shine,

---

[3] See *Alexander's Feast, or the Power of Music;* an Ode by Mr. Dryden.   P.

Which not alone the southern wit sublimes,   400
But ripens spirits in cold northern climes;
Which from the first has shone on ages past,
Enlights the present, and shall warm the last;
Though each may feel increases and decays,
And see now clearer and now darker days.   405
Regard not then if Wit be old or new,
But blame the false, and value still the true.
      Some ne'er advance a Judgment of their own,
But catch the spreading notion of the Town;
They reason and conclude by precedent,   410
And own stale nonsense which they ne'er invent.
Some judge of authors' names, not works, and then
Nor praise nor blame the writings, but the men.
Of all this servile herd, the worst is he
That in proud dulness joins with Quality.   415
A constant Critic at the great man's board,
To fetch and carry nonsense for my Lord.
What woeful stuff this madrigal would be,
In some starved hackney sonneteer, or me?
But let a Lord once own the happy lines,   420
How the wit brightens! how the style refines!
Before his sacred name flies every fault,
And each exalted stanza teems with thought!
      The Vulgar thus through Imitation err;
As oft the Learned by being singular;   425
So much they scorn the crowd, that if the throng
By chance go right, they purposely go wrong:
So Schismatics the plain believers quit,
And are but damned for having too much wit.
Some praise at morning what they blame at night;   430
But always think the last opinion right.
A Muse by these is like a mistress used,
This hour she's idolized, the next abused;
While their weak heads like towns unfortified,
Twixt sense and nonsense daily change their side.   435
Ask them the cause; they're wiser still, they say;
And still tomorrow's wiser than today.

We think our fathers fools, so wise we grow;
Our wiser sons, no doubt, will think us so.
Once School divines this zealous isle o'erspread;   440
Who knew most Sentences, was deepest read;
Faith, Gospel, all, seemed made to be disputed,
And none had sense enough to be confuted:
Scotists and Thomists, now, in peace remain,
Amidst their kindred cobwebs in Duck Lane.[4]   445
If Faith itself has different dresses worn,
What wonder modes in Wit should take their turn?
Oft, leaving what is natural and fit,
The current folly proves the ready wit;
And authors think their reputation safe,   450
Which lives as long as fools are pleased to laugh.
    Some valuing those of their own side or mind,
Still make themselves the measure of mankind:
Fondly we think we honour merit then,
When we but praise ourselves in other men.   455
Parties in Wit attend on those of State,
And public faction doubles private hate.
Pride, Malice, Folly, against Dryden rose,
In various shapes of Parsons, Critics, Beaus;
But sense survived, when merry jests were past;   460
For rising merit will buoy up at last.
Might he return, and bless once more our eyes,
New Blackmores and new Milbourns must arise:
Nay should great Homer lift his awful head,
Zoilus again would start up from the dead.   465
Envy will merit, as its shade, pursue;
But like a shadow, proves the substance true;
For envied Wit, like Sol eclipsed, makes known
Th' opposing body's grossness, not its own.
When first that sun too powerful beams displays,   470
It draws up vapours which obscure its rays;
But even those clouds at last adorn its way,
Reflect new glories, and augment the day.
    Be thou the first true merit to befriend;

---

[4] A place where old and secondhand books were sold formerly, near Smithfield. P.

His praise is lost, who stays till all commend.   475
Short is the date, alas, of modern rhymes,
And 'tis but just to let them live betimes.
No longer now that golden age appears,
When Patriarch wits survived a thousand years:
Now length of Fame (our second life) is lost,   480
And bare threescore is all even that can boast;
Our sons their fathers' failing language see,
And such as Chaucer is, shall Dryden be.
So when the faithful pencil has designed
Some bright Idea of the master's mind,   485
Where a new world leaps out at his command,
And ready Nature waits upon his hand;
When the ripe colours soften and unite,
And sweetly melt into just shade and light;
When mellowing years their full perfection give,   490
And each bold figure just begins to live,
The treacherous colours the fair art betray,
And all the bright creation fades away!
    Unhappy Wit, like most mistaken things,
Atones not for that envy which it brings.   495
In youth alone its empty praise we boast,
But soon the short-lived vanity is lost:
Like some fair flower the early spring supplies,
That gaily blooms, but even in blooming dies.
What is this Wit, which must our cares employ?   500
The owner's wife, that other men enjoy;
Then most our trouble still when most admired,
And still the more we give, the more required;
Whose fame with pains we guard, but lose with ease,
Sure some to vex, but never all to please;   505
'Tis what the vicious fear, the virtuous shun,
By fools 'tis hated, and by knaves undone!
    If Wit so much from Ignorance undergo,
Ah let not Learning too commence its foe!
Of old, those met rewards who could excel,   510
And such were praised who but endeavoured well:
Though triumphs were to generals only due,
Crowns were reserved to grace the soldiers too.

Now, they who reach Parnassus' lofty crown,
Employ their pains to spurn some others down;   515
And while self-love each jealous writer rules,
Contending wits become the sport of fools:
But still the worst with most regret commend,
For each ill Author is as bad a Friend.
To what base ends, and by what abject ways,   520
Are mortals urged through sacred lust of praise!
Ah ne'er so dire a thirst of glory boast,
Nor in the Critic let the Man be lost.
Good nature and good sense must ever join;
To err is human, to forgive, divine.   525
    But if in noble minds some dregs remain
Not yet purged off, of spleen and sour disdain;
Discharge that rage on more provoking crimes,
Nor fear a dearth in these flagitious times.
No pardon vile Obscenity should find,   530
Though wit and art conspire to move your mind;
But Dulness with Obscenity must prove
As shameful sure as Impotence in love.
In the fat age of pleasure, wealth and ease,
Sprung the rank weed, and thrived with large increase: 535
When love was all an easy Monarch's care;
Seldom at council, never in a war:
Jilts ruled the state, and statesmen farces writ;
Nay wits had pensions, and young Lords had wit:
The Fair sat panting at a Courtier's play,   540
And not a Mask went unimproved away:
The modest fan was lifted up no more,
And Virgins smiled at what they blushed before.
The following licence of a Foreign reign
Did all the dregs of bold Socinus drain;   545
Then unbelieving Priests reformed the nation,
And taught more pleasant methods of salvation;
Where Heaven's free subjects might their rights dispute,
Lest God himself should seem too absolute:
Pulpits their sacred satire learned to spare,   550
And Vice admired to find a flatterer there!

Encouraged thus, Wit's Titans braved the skies,
And the press groaned with licensed blasphemies.
These monsters, Critics! with your darts engage,
Here point your thunder, and exhaust your rage!   555
Yet shun their fault, who, scandalously nice,
Will needs mistake an author into vice;
All seems infected that th' infected spy,
As all looks yellow to the jaundiced eye.

PART III

Rules for the *Conduct* of *Manners* in a Critic. 1. *Candour*, l. 563. *Modesty*, l. 566. *Good Breeding*, l. 572. *Sincerity*, and *Freedom* of advice, l. 578. 2. When one's Counsel is to be restrained, l. 584. Character of an *incorrigible Poet*, l. 600. And of an *impertinent Critic*, ll. 610 ff. Character of a *good Critic*, l. 629. The *History of Criticism*, and Characters of the best Critics: Aristotle, l. 645. *Horace*, l. 653. *Dionysius*, l. 665. *Petronius*, l. 667. *Quintilian*, l. 670. *Longinus*, l. 675. Of the Decay of Criticism, and its Revival. *Erasmus*, l. 693. *Vida*, l. 705. *Boileau*, l. 714. *Lord Roscommon*, etc., l. 725. Conclusion.

LEARN then what MORALS Critics ought to show,   560
For 'tis but half a Judge's task, to know.
'Tis not enough, taste, judgment, learning, join;
In all you speak, let truth and candour shine:
That not alone what to your sense is due
All may allow; but seek your friendship too.   565
   Be silent always when you doubt your sense;
And speak, though sure, with seeming diffidence:
Some positive, persisting fops we know,
Who, if once wrong, will needs be always so;
But you, with pleasure own your errors past,   570
And make each day a Critic on the last.
   'Tis not enough, your counsel still be true;
Blunt truths more mischief than nice falsehoods do;

Men must be taught as if you taught them not,
And things unknown proposed as things forgot.   575
Without Good Breeding, truth is disapproved;
That only makes superior sense beloved.
    Be niggards of advice on no pretence;
For the worst avarice is that of sense.
With mean complacence ne'er betray your trust,   580
Nor be so civil as to prove unjust.
Fear not the anger of the wise to raise;
Those best can bear reproof, who merit praise.
    'Twere well might Critics still this freedom take,
But Appius reddens at each word you speak,   585
And stares, tremendous, with a threatening eye,[5]
Like some fierce Tyrant in old tapestry.
Fear most to tax an Honourable fool,
Whose right it is, uncensured, to be dull;
Such, without wit, are Poets when they please,   590
As without learning they can take Degrees.
Leave dangerous truths to unsuccessful Satires,
And flattery to fulsome Dedicators,
Whom, when they praise, the world believes no more,
Than when they promise to give scribbling o'er.   595
'Tis best sometimes your censure to restrain,
And charitably let the dull be vain:
Your silence there is better than your spite,
For who can rail so long as they can write?
Still humming on, their drowsy course they keep,   600
And lashed so long, like tops, are lashed asleep.
False steps but help them to renew the race,
As, after stumbling, Jades will mend their pace.
What crowds of these, impenitently bold,
In sounds and jingling syllables grown old,   605
Still run on Poets, in a raging vein,

[5] This picture was taken to himself by *John Dennis,* a furious old Critic
by profession, who, upon no other provocation, wrote against this Essay
and its author, in a manner perfectly lunatic: For, as to the mention made
of him in l. 270, he took it as a Compliment, and said it was treacherously
meant to cause him to overlook this *Abuse of his Person.* P.

Even to the dregs and squeezings of the brain,
Strain out the last dull droppings of their sense,
And rhyme with all the rage of Impotence.
    Such shameless Bards we have; and yet 'tis true,   610
There are as mad abandoned Critics too.
The bookful blockhead, ignorantly read,
With loads of learnèd lumber in his head,
With his own tongue still edifies his ears,
And always listening to himself appears.   615
All books he reads, and all he reads assails,
From Dryden's Fables down to Durfey's Tales.
With him, most authors steal their works, or buy;
Garth did not write his own Dispensary.[6]
Name a new Play, and he's the Poet's friend,   620
Nay showed his faults—but when would Poets mend?
No place so sacred from such fops is barred,
Nor is Paul's church more safe than Paul's churchyard:
Nay, fly to Altars; there they'll talk you dead:
For Fools rush in where Angels fear to tread.   625
Distrustful sense with modest caution speaks,
It still looks home, and short excursions makes;
But rattling nonsense in full volleys breaks,
And never shocked, and never turned aside,
Bursts out, resistless, with a thundering tide.   630
    But where's the man, who counsel can bestow,
Still pleased to teach, and yet not proud to know?
Unbiased, or by favour, or by spite;
Not dully prepossessed, nor blindly right;
Though learned, well-bred; and though well-bred, sincere;
Modestly bold, and humanly severe: 636
Who to a friend his faults can freely show,
And gladly praise the merit of a foe?
Blest with a taste exact, yet unconfined;
A knowledge both of books and human kind;   640
Generous converse; a soul exempt from pride;

[6] A common slander at that time in prejudice of that deserving Author. Our Poet did him this justice, when that slander most prevailed; and it is now (perhaps the sooner for this very verse) dead and forgotten. P.

And love to praise, with reason on his side?
     Such once were Critics; such the happy few,
Athens and Rome in better ages knew.
The mighty Stagirite first left the shore,   645
Spread all his sails, and durst the deeps explore;
He steered securely, and discovered far,
Led by the light of the Mæonian Star.
Poets, a race long unconfined, and free,
Still fond and proud of savage liberty,   650
Received his laws; and stood convinced 'twas fit,
Who conquered Nature, should preside o'er Wit.
     Horace still charms with graceful negligence,
And without method talks us into sense,
Will, like a friend, familiarly convey   655
The truest notions in the easiest way.
He, who supreme in judgment, as in wit,
Might boldly censure, as he boldly writ,
Yet judged with coolness, though he sung with fire;
His Precepts teach but what his works inspire.   660
Our Critics take a contrary extreme,
They judge with fury, but they write with fle'me:[7]
Nor suffers Horace more in wrong Translations
By Wits, than Critics in as wrong Quotations.
     See Dionysius Homer's thoughts refine,   665
And call new beauties forth from every line!
     Fancy and art in gay Petronius please,
The scholar's learning, with the courtier's ease.
     In grave Quintilian's copious work, we find
The justest rules, and clearest method joined: 670
Thus useful arms in magazines we place,
All ranged in order, and disposed with grace,
But less to please the eye, than arm the hand,
Still fit for use, and ready at command.
     Thee, bold Longinus! all the Nine inspire,   675
And bless their Critic with a Poet's fire.
An ardent Judge, who zealous in his trust,

---

[7] Phlegm.

With warmth gives sentence, yet is always just;
Whose own example strengthens all his laws;
And is himself that great Sublime he draws.   680
  Thus long succeeding Critics justly reigned,
Licence repressed, and useful laws ordained.
Learning and Rome alike in empire grew;
And Arts still followed where her Eagles flew;
From the same foes, at last, both felt their doom,   685
And the same age saw Learning fall, and Rome.
With Tyranny, then Superstition joined,
As that the body, this enslaved the mind;
Much was believed, but little understood,
And to be dull was construed to be good;   690
A second deluge Learning thus o'errun,
And the Monks finished what the Goths begun.
  At length Erasmus, that great injured name,
(The glory of the Priesthood, and the shame!)
Stemmed the wild torrent of a barbarous age,   695
And drove those holy Vandals off the stage.
  But see! each Muse, in Leo's golden days,
Starts from her trance, and trims her withered bays,
Rome's ancient Genius, o'er its ruins spread,
Shakes off the dust, and rears his reverend head.   700
Then Sculpture and her sister arts revive;
Stones leaped to form, and rocks began to live;
With sweeter notes each rising Temple rung;
A Raphael painted, and a Vida sung.
Immortal Vida: on whose honoured brow   705
The Poet's bays and Critic's ivy grow:
Cremona now shall ever boast thy name,
As next in place to Mantua, next in fame!
  But soon by impious arms from Latium chased,
Their ancient bounds the banished Muses passed;   710
Thence Arts o'er all the northern world advance,
But Critic learning flourished most in France:
The rules a nation, born to serve, obeys;
And Boileau still in right of Horace sways.
But we, brave Britons, foreign laws despised,   715

And kept unconquered, and uncivilized;
Fierce for the liberties of wit, and bold,
We still defied the Romans, as of old.
Yet some there were, among the sounder few
Of those who less presumed, and better knew,   720
Who durst assert the juster ancient cause,
And here restored Wit's fundamental laws.
Such was the Muse, whose rules and practice tell,[8]
"Nature's chief Masterpiece is writing well."
Such was Roscommon, not more learned than good,   725
With manners generous as his noble blood;
To him the wit of Greece and Rome was known,
And every author's merit, but his own.
Such late was Walsh—the Muse's judge and friend,
Who justly knew to blame or to commend;   730
To failings mild, but zealous for desert;
The clearest head, and the sincerest heart.
This humble praise, lamented shade! receive,
This praise at least a grateful Muse may give:
The Muse, whose early voice you taught to sing,   735
Prescribed her heights, and pruned her tender wing,
(Her guide now lost) no more attempts to rise,
But in low numbers short excursions tries:
Content, if hence th' unlearned their wants may view,
The learned reflect on what before they knew: 740
Careless of censure, nor too fond of fame;
Still pleased to praise, yet not afraid to blame;
Averse alike to flatter, or offend;
Not free from faults, nor yet too vain to mend.

[8] *Essay on Poetry* by the Duke of Buckingham. . . . Our Author . . . was honoured very young with his friendship, and it continued till his death in all the circumstances of a familiar esteem. P.

THE RAPE OF THE LOCK

An Heroi-comical Poem

Nolueram, Belinda, tuos violare capillos;
Sed juvat, hoc precibus me tribuisse tuis
MARTIAL [Epigrams xii. 84.][1]

To Mrs. Arabella Fermor

MADAM,

It will be in vain to deny that I have some regard for this piece, since I dedicate it to You. Yet you may bear me witness, it was intended

---

[1] It appears, by this Motto, that the following Poem was written or published at the Lady's request. But there are some further circumstances not unworthy relating. Mr Caryll (a Gentleman* who was Secretary to Queen Mary, wife of James II., whose fortunes he followed into France, Author of the Comedy of *Sir Solomon Single,* and of several translations in Dryden's Miscellanies) originally proposed the subject to him in a view of putting an end, by this piece of ridicule, to a quarrel that was risen between two noble Families, those of Lord Petre and of Mrs. Fermor, on the trifling occasion of his having cut off a lock of her hair. The Author sent it to the Lady, with whom he was acquainted; and she took it so well as to give about copies of it. That first sketch (we learn from one of his Letters) was written in less than a fortnight, in 1711, in two Cantos

only to divert a few young Ladies, who have good sense and good humour enough to laugh not only at their sex's little unguarded follies, but at their own. But as it was communicated with the air of a Secret, it soon found its way into the world. An imperfect copy having been offered to a Bookseller, you had the good nature for my sake to consent to the publication of one more correct: This I was forced to, before I had executed half my design, for the Machinery was entirely wanting to complete it.

The Machinery, Madam, is a term invented by the Critics, to signify that part which the Deities, Angels, or Dæmons are made to act in a Poem: For the ancient Poets are in one respect like many modern Ladies: let an action be never so trivial in itself, they always make it appear of the utmost importance. These Machines I determined to raise on a very new and odd foundation, the Rosicrucian doctrine of Spirits.

I know how disagreeable it is to make use of hard words before a Lady; but 'tis so much the concern of a Poet to have his works understood, and particularly by your Sex, that you must give me leave to explain two or three difficult terms.

The Rosicrucians are a people I must bring you acquainted with. The best account I know of them is in a French book called *Le Comte de Gabalis,* which both in its title and size is so like a Novel, that many of the Fair Sex have read it for one by mistake. According to these Gentlemen, the four Elements are inhabited by Spirits, which they call Sylphs, Gnomes, Nymphs, and Salamanders. The Gnomes or Dæmons of Earth delight in mischief; but the Sylphs, whose habitation is in the Air, are the best-conditioned creatures imaginable. For they say, any mortals may enjoy the most intimate familiarities with these gentle Spirits, upon a condition very easy to all true Adepts, an inviolate preservation of Chastity.

As to the following Cantos, all the passages of them are as fabulous as the Vision at the beginning, or the Transformation at the end; (except the loss of your Hair, which I always mention with rever-

---

only, and it was so printed; first, in a Miscellany of Bernard Lintot's, without the name of the Author. But it was received so well that he made it more considerable the next year by the addition of the machinery of the Sylphs, and extended it to five Cantos. . . . P.   [W.]

This insertion he always esteemed, and justly, the greatest effort of his *skill* and *art* as a Poet.   [W.]

* Pope's friend John Caryll was actually the nephew of the "Gentleman" here described.

ence). The Human persons are as fictitious as the Airy ones; and the character of Belinda, as it is now managed, resembles you in nothing but in Beauty.

If this Poem has as many Graces as there are in your Person, or in your Mind, yet I could never hope it should pass through the world half so Uncensured as You have done. But let its fortune be what it will, mine is happy enough, to have given me this occasion of assuring you that I am, with the truest esteem,

MADAM,

Your most obedient, Humble Servant,

A. POPE.

The Rape of the Lock

CANTO I

WHAT dire offence from amorous causes springs,
What mighty contests rise from trivial things,
I sing—This verse to CARYLL, Muse! is due:
This, even Belinda may vouchsafe to view:
Slight is the subject, but not so the praise,   5
If She inspire, and He approve my lays.
     Say what strange motive, Goddess! could compel
A well-bred Lord t' assault a gentle Belle?
O say what stranger cause, yet unexplored,
Could make a gentle Belle reject a Lord?   10
In tasks so bold, can little men engage,
And in soft bosoms dwells such mighty Rage?
     Sol through white curtains shot a timorous ray,
And oped those eyes that must eclipse the day:
Now lap dogs give themselves the rousing shake,   15
And sleepless lovers, just at twelve, awake:
Thrice rung the bell, the slipper knocked the ground,
And the pressed watch returned a silver sound.
Belinda still her downy pillow prest,
Her guardian SYLPH prolonged the balmy rest: 20
'Twas He had summoned to her silent bed
The morning dream that hovered o'er her head;
A Youth more glittering than a Birth-night Beau,
(That even in slumber caused her cheek to glow)
Seemed to her ear his winning lips to lay,   25

And thus in whispers said, or seemed to say.
    Fairest of mortals, thou distinguished care
Of thousand bright Inhabitants of Air!
If e'er one Vision touched thy infant thought,
Of all the Nurse and all the Priest have taught;   30
Of airy Elves by moonlight shadows seen,
The silver token, and the circled green,
Or virgins visited by Angel powers,
With golden crowns and wreaths of heavenly flowers;
Hear and believe! thy own importance know,   35
Nor bound thy narrow views to things below.
Some secret truths, from learnèd pride concealed,
To Maids alone and Children are revealed:
What though no credit doubting Wits may give?
The Fair and Innocent shall still believe.   40
Know, then, unnumbered Spirits round thee fly,
The light Militia of the lower sky:
These, though unseen, are ever on the wing,
Hang o'er the Box, and hover round the Ring.
Think what an equipage thou hast in Air,   45
And view with scorn two Pages and a Chair.
As now your own, our beings were of old,[2]
And once enclosed in Woman's beauteous mould;
Thence, by a soft transition, we repair
From earthly Vehicles to these of air.   50
Think not, when Woman's transient breath is fled,
That all her vanities at once are dead;
Succeeding vanities she still regards,
And though she plays no more, o'erlooks the cards.
Her joy in gilded Chariots, when alive,[3]   55

[2] He here forsakes the Rosicrucian system; which, in this part, is too
extravagant even for Poetry; and gives a beautiful fiction of his own, on
the Platonic Theology of the continuance of the passions in *another state,*
when the mind, before its leaving *this,* has not been purged and purified
by philosophy; which furnishes an occasion for much useful satire. [W.]
[3]   Quae gratia currûm
Armorumque fuit vivis, quae cura nitentes
Pascere equos, eadem sequitur tellure repostos.
    Virgil *Æneid* vi [653 ff.]. P.

And love of Ombre, after death survive.
For when the Fair in all their pride expire,
To their first Elements their Souls retire:
The Sprites of fiery Termagants in Flame
Mount up, and take a Salamander's name.   60
Soft yielding minds to Water glide away,
And sip, with Nymphs, their elemental Tea.
The graver Prude sinks downward to a Gnome,
In search of mischief still on Earth to roam.
The light Coquettes in Sylphs aloft repair,   65
And sport and flutter in the fields of Air.
    Know further yet; whoever fair and chaste
Rejects mankind, is by some Sylph embraced:
For Spirits, freed from mortal laws, with ease
Assume what sexes and what shapes they please.   70
What guards the purity of melting Maids,
In courtly balls, and midnight masquerades,
Safe from the treacherous friend, the daring spark,
The glance by day, the whisper in the dark,
When kind occasion prompts their warm desires,   75
When music softens, and when dancing fires?
'Tis but their Sylph, the wise Celestials know,
Though Honour is the word with Men below.
    Some nymphs there are, too conscious of their face,
For life predestined to the Gnomes' embrace.   80
These swell their prospects and exalt their pride,
When offers are disdained, and love denied:
Then gay Ideas crowd the vacant brain,
While Peers, and Dukes, and all their sweeping train,
And Garters, Stars, and Coronets appear,   85
And in soft sounds, Your Grace salutes their ear.
'Tis these that early taint the female soul,
Instruct the eyes of young Coquettes to roll,
Teach Infant cheeks a bidden blush to know,
And little hearts to flutter at a Beau.   90
    Oft, when the world imagine women stray,
The Sylphs through mystic mazes guide their way,
Through all the giddy circle they pursue,

And old impertinence expel by new.
What tender maid but must a victim fall   95
To one man's treat, but for another's ball?
When Florio speaks what virgin could withstand,
If gentle Damon did not squeeze her hand?
With varying vanities, from every part,
They shift the moving Toyshop of their heart;   100
Where wigs with wigs, with sword-knots sword-knots strive,
Beaux banish beaux, and coaches coaches drive.
This erring mortals Levity may call;
Oh blind to truth! the Sylphs contrive it all.

    Of these am I, who thy protection claim,   105
A watchful sprite, and Ariel is my name.
Late, as I ranged the crystal wilds of air,
In the clear Mirror of thy ruling Star
I saw, alas! some dread event impend,
Ere to the main this morning sun descend,   110
But heaven reveals not what, or how, or where:
Warned by the Sylph, oh pious maid, beware!
This to disclose is all thy guardian can:
Beware of all, but most beware of Man!

    He said; when Shock, who thought she slept too long,
Leaped up, and waked his mistress with his tongue.   116
'Twas then, Belinda, if report say true,
Thy eyes first opened on a Billet-doux;
Wounds, Charm, and Ardors were no sooner read,
But all the Vision vanished from thy head.   120

    And now, unveiled, the Toilet stands displayed,
Each silver Vase in mystic order laid.
First, robed in white, the Nymph intent adores,
With head uncovered, the Cosmetic powers.
A heavenly image in the glass appears,   125
To that she bends, to that her eyes she rears;
Th' inferior Priestess, at her altar's side,[4]
Trembling, begins the sacred rites of Pride.

[4] There is a small inaccuracy in these lines. He first makes his Heroine the chief Priestess, and then the Goddess herself.   [W.] Is the "inaccuracy" noticed by Warburton a fault in these lines?

Unnumbered treasures ope at once, and here
The various offerings of the world appear;   130
From each she nicely culls with curious toil,
And decks the Goddess with the glittering spoil.
This casket India's glowing gems unlocks,
And all Arabia breathes from yonder box.
The Tortoise here and Elephant unite,   135
Transformed to combs, the speckled, and the white.
Here files of pins extend their shining rows,
Puffs, Powders, Patches, Bibles, Billet-doux.
Now awful Beauty puts on all its arms;
The fair each moment rises in her charms,   140
Repairs her smiles, awakens every grace,
And calls forth all the wonders of her face;
Sees by degrees a purer blush arise,
And keener lightnings quicken in her eyes.
The busy Sylphs surround their darling care,   145
These set the head, and those divide the hair,
Some fold the sleeve, whilst others plait the gown;
And Betty's praised for labours not her own.

CANTO II

NOT with more glories, in th' etherial plain,
The Sun first rises o'er the purpled main,
Than, issuing forth, the rival of his beams
Launched on the bosom of the silver Thames.
Fair Nymphs, and well-dressed Youths around her shone,
But every eye was fixed on her alone.   6
On her white breast a sparkling Cross she wore,
Which Jews might kiss, and Infidels adore.
Her lively looks a sprightly mind disclose,

Quick as her eyes, and as unfixed as those: 10
Favours to none, to all she smiles extends;
Oft she rejects, but never once offends.
Bright as the sun, her eyes the gazers strike,
And, like the sun, they shine on all alike.
Yet graceful ease, and sweetness void of pride,   15
Might hide her faults, if Belles had faults to hide:
If to her share some female errors fall,
Look on her face, and you'll forget 'em all.
     This Nymph, to the destruction of mankind,
Nourished two Locks, which graceful hung behind   20
In equal curls, and well conspired to deck
With shining ringlets the smooth ivory neck.
Love in these labyrinths his slaves detains,
And mighty hearts are held in slender chains.
With hairy springes we the birds betray,   25
Slight lines of hair surprise the finny prey,
Fair tresses man's imperial race ensnare,
And beauty draws us with a single hair.
     Th' adventurous Baron the bright locks admired;
He saw, he wished, and to the prize aspired.   30
Resolved to win, he meditates the way,
By force to ravish, or by fraud betray;
For when success a Lover's toil attends,
Few ask, if fraud or force attained his ends.
     For this, ere Phœbus rose, he had implored   35
Propitious heaven, and every power adored,
But chiefly Love—to Love an Altar built,
Of twelve vast French Romances, neatly gilt.
There lay three garters, half a pair of gloves;
And all the trophies of his former loves;   40
With tender Billets-doux he lights the pyre,
And breathes three amorous sighs to raise the fire.
Then prostrate falls, and begs with ardent eyes
Soon to obtain, and long possess the prize:
The powers gave ear, and granted half his prayer,   45
The rest, the winds dispersed in empty air.
     But now secure the painted vessel glides,

The sunbeams trembling on the floating tides:
While melting music steals upon the sky,
And softened sounds along the waters die;   50
Smooth flow the waves, the Zephyrs gently play,
Belinda smiled, and all the world was gay.
All but the Sylph—with careful thoughts opprest,
Th' impending woe sat heavy on his breast.
He summons strait his Denizens of air;   55
The lucid squadrons round the sails repair:
Soft o'er the shrouds aërial whispers breathe,
That seemed but Zephyrs to the train beneath.
Some to the sun their insect wings unfold,
Waft on the breeze, or sink in clouds of gold;   60
Transparent forms, too fine for mortal sight,
Their fluid bodies half dissolved in light,
Loose to the wind their airy garments flew,
Thin glittering textures of the filmy dew,
Dipped in the richest tincture of the skies,   65
Where light disports in ever-mingling dyes,
While every beam new transient colours flings,
Colours that change whene'er they wave their wings.
Amid the circle, on the gilded mast,
Superior by the head, was Ariel placed;   70
His purple pinions opening to the sun,
He raised his azure wand, and thus begun.
      Ye Sylphs and Sylphids, to your chief give ear!
Fays, Fairies, Genii, Elves, and Dæmons, hear!
Ye know the spheres and various tasks assigned   75
By laws eternal to th' aërial kind.
Some in the fields of purest Æther play,
And bask and whiten in the blaze of day.
Some guide the course of wandering orbs on high,
Or roll the planets through the boundless sky.   80
Some less refined, beneath the moon's pale light
Pursue the stars that shoot athwart the night,
Or suck the mists in grosser air below,
Or dip their pinions in the painted bow,
Or brew fierce tempests on the wintry main,   85

Or o'er the glcbe distil the kindly rain.
Others on earth o'er human race preside,
Watch all their ways, and all their actions guide:
Of these the chief the care of Nations own,
And guard with Arms divine the British Throne.   90
       Our humbler province is to tend the Fair,
Not a less pleasing, though less glorious care;
To save the powder from too rude a gale,
Nor let th' imprisoned essences exhale;
To draw fresh colours from the vernal flowers;   95
To steal from rainbows e'er they drop in showers
A brighter wash; to curl their waving hairs,
Assist their blushes, and inspire their airs;
Nay oft, in dreams, invention we bestow,
To change a Flounce, or add a Furbelow.   100
       This day, black Omens threat the brightest Fair
That e'er deserved a watchful spirit's care;
Some dire disaster, or by force, or slight;
But what, or where, the fates have wrapped in night.
Whether the nymph shall break Diana's law,   105
Or some frail China jar receive a flaw;
Or stain her honour or her new brocade;
Forget her prayers, or miss a masquerade;
Or lose her heart, or necklace, at a ball;
Or whether Heaven has doomed that Shock must fall.
Haste, then, ye spirits! to your charge repair: 111
The fluttering fan be Zephyretta's care;
The drops to thee, Brillante, we consign;
And, Momentilla, let the watch be thine;
Do thou, Crispissa, tend her favorite Lock;   115
Ariel himself shall be the guard of Shock.
       To fifty chosen Sylphs, of special note,
We trust th' important charge, the Petticoat:
Oft have we known that sevenfold fence to fail,
Though stiff with hoops, and armed with ribs of whale;
Form a strong line about the silver bound,   121
And guard the wide circumference around.
       Whatever spirit, careless of his charge,

His post neglects, or leaves the fair at large,
Shall feel sharp vengeance soon o'ertake his sins,   125
Be stopped in vials, or transfixed with pins;
Or plunged in lakes of bitter washes lie,
Or wedged whole ages in a bodkin's eye:
Gums and Pomatums shall his flight restrain,
While clogged he beats his silken wings in vain;   130
Or Alum styptics with contracting power
Shrink his thin essence like a rivelled flower:
Or, as Ixion fixed, the wretch shall feel
The giddy motion of the whirling Mill,
In fumes of burning Chocolate shall glow,   135
And tremble at the sea that froths below!
  He spoke; the spirits from the sails descend;
Some, orb in orb, around the nymph extend;
Some thrid the mazy ringlets of her hair;
Some hang upon the pendants of her ear;   140
With beating hearts the dire event they wait,
Anxious, and trembling for the birth of Fate.

CANTO III

Close by those meads, for ever crowned with flowers,
Where Thames with pride surveys his rising towers,
There stands a structure of majestic frame,
Which from the neighboring Hampton takes its name.
Here Britain's statesmen oft the fall foredoom   5
Of foreign Tyrants, and of Nymphs at home;
Here thou, great Anna! whom three realms obey,
Dost sometimes counsel take—and sometimes Tea.
  Hither the heroes and the nymphs resort,
To taste awhile the pleasures of a Court;   10

In various talk th' instructive hours they past,
Who gave the ball, or paid the visit last;
One speaks the glory of the British Queen,
And one describes a charming Indian screen;
A third interprets motions, looks, and eyes;   15
At every word a reputation dies.
Snuff, or the fan, supply each pause of chat,
With singing, laughing, ogling, *and all that*.
    Meanwhile, declining from the noon of day,
The sun obliquely shoots his burning ray;   20
The hungry Judges soon the sentence sign,
And wretches hang that jurymen may dine;
The merchant from th' Exchange returns in peace,
And the long labours of the Toilet cease.
Belinda now, whom thirst of fame invites,   25
Burns to encounter two adventurous Knights,
At Ombre[5] singly to decide their doom;
And swells her breast with conquests yet to come.
Straight the three bands prepare in arms to join,
Each band the number of the sacred nine.   30
Soon as she spreads her hand, th' aërial guard
Descend, and sit on each important card:
First Ariel perched upon a Matadore,
Then each, according to the rank they bore;
For Sylphs, yet mindful of their ancient race,   35

[5] A card game of Spanish origin, popular in English court circles at this time. It was played with a pack of 40 cards, the 10's, 9's, and 8's being removed from an ordinary pack. The three players each held nine cards, the other 13 lying in a stock. The player who got the bid was called the Ombre. He named trumps and had to win more tricks than his stronger opponent, 5 against 4, or 4 against 3 and 2. The two black Aces were always trumps. In the hand which follows, when Belinda has named Spades, the order of strength is: Ace of Spades (Spadillio), 2 of Spades (Manillio), Ace of Clubs (Basto), King of Spades, Queen, Knave, 7, 6, 5, 4, 3. (See Geoffrey Tillotson, *The Rape of the Lock and Other Poems,* London, 1940, Appendix C.) Note the technical precision of Pope's account, in which each trick and all the significant cards are accounted for. Belinda, triumphant up to the fifth trick, suffers a peripeteia or sudden reversal of fortune, which turns again in her favor only at the last trick. Does she merit the epithet "skilful" bestowed on her in line 45?

Are, as when women, wondrous fond of place.
  Behold, four Kings in majesty revered,
With hoary whiskers and a forky beard;
And four fair Queens whose hands sustain a flower,
Th' expressive emblem of their softer power;   40
Four Knaves in garbs succinct, a trusty band,
Caps on their heads, and halberts in their hand;
And particoloured troops, a shining train,
Draw forth to combat on the velvet plain.
  The skilful Nymph reviews her force with care: 45
Let Spades be trumps! she said, and trumps they were.
  Now move to war her sable Matadores,
In show like leaders of the swarthy Moors.
Spadillio first, unconquerable Lord!
Led off two captive trumps, and swept the board.   50
As many more Manillio forced to yield,
And marched a victor from the verdant field.
Him Basto followed, but his fate more hard
Gained but one trump and one Plebeian card.
With his broad sabre next, a chief in years,   55
The hoary Majesty of Spades appears,
Puts forth one manly leg, to sight revealed,
The rest, his many-coloured robe concealed.
The rebel Knave, who dares his prince engage,
Proves the just victim of his royal rage.   60
Even mighty Pam,[6] that Kings and Queens o'erthrew
And mowed down armies in the fights of Lu,
Sad chance of war! now destitute of aid,
Falls undistinguished by the victor Spade!
  Thus far both armies to Belinda yield;   65
Now to the Baron fate inclines the field.
His warlike Amazon her host invades,
Th' imperial consort of the crown of Spades.
The Club's black Tyrant first her victim died
Spite of his haughty mien, and barbarous pride: 70
What boots the regal circle on his head,

---

[6] The Knave of Clubs, the strongest card in the game of Lu.

His giant limbs, in state unwieldy spread;
That long behind he trails his pompous robe,
And, of all monarchs, only grasps the globe?
    The Baron now his Diamonds pours apace;   75
Th' embroidered King who shows but half his face,
And his refulgent Queen, with powers combined
Of broken troops an easy conquest find.
Clubs, Diamonds, Hearts, in wild disorder seen,
With throngs promiscuous strew the level green.   80
Thus when dispersed a routed army runs,
Of Asia's troops, and Afric's sable sons,
With like confusion different nations fly,
Of various habit, and of various dye,
The pierced battalions disunited fall,   85
In heaps on heaps; one fate o'erwhelms them all.
    The Knave of Diamonds tries his wily arts,
And wins (oh shameful chance!) the Queen of Hearts.
At this, the blood the virgin's cheek forsook,
A livid paleness spreads o'er all her look;   90
She sees, and trembles at th' approaching ill,
Just in the jaws of ruin, and Codille.[7]
And now (as oft in some distempered State)
On one nice Trick depends the general fate.
An Ace of Hearts steps forth: The King unseen   95
Lurked in her hand, and mourned his captive Queen:
He springs to vengeance with an eager pace,
And falls like thunder on the prostrate Ace.
The nymph exulting fills with shouts the sky;
The walls, the woods, and long canals reply.   100
    Oh thoughtless mortals! ever blind to fate,
Too soon dejected, and too soon elate.
Sudden, these honours shall be snatched away,
And cursed for ever this victorious day.
    For lo! the board with cups and spoons is crowned,
The berries crackle, and the mill turns round;   106

---

[7] The "elbow," the defeat which would occur if the Baron gained 5 tricks to Belinda's 4.

On shining Altars of Japan they raise
The silver lamp; the fiery spirits blaze:
From silver spouts the grateful liquors glide,
While China's earth receives the smoking tide: 110
At once they gratify their scent and taste,
And frequent cups prolong the rich repast.
Straight hover round the Fair her airy band;
Some, as she sipped, the fuming liquor fanned,
Some o'er her lap their careful plumes displayed,   115
Trembling, and conscious of the rich brocade.
Coffee, (which makes the politician wise,
And see through all things with his half-shut eyes)
Sent up in vapours to the Baron's brain
New stratagems, the radiant Lock to gain.   120
Ah cease, rash youth! desist ere 'tis too late,
Fear the just Gods, and think of Scylla's Fate![8]
Changed to a bird, and sent to flit in air,
She dearly pays for Nisus' injured hair!
      But when to mischief mortals bend their will,   125
How soon they find fit instruments of ill!
Just then, Clarissa drew with tempting grace
A two-edged weapon from her shining case:
So Ladies in Romance assist their Knight,
Present the spear, and arm him for the fight.   130
He takes the gift with reverence, and extends
The little engine on his fingers' ends;
This just behind Belinda's neck he spread,
As o'er the fragrant steams she bends her head.
Swift to the Lock a thousand Sprites repair,   135
A thousand wings, by turns, blow back the hair;
And thrice they twitched the diamond in her ear;
Thrice she looked back, and thrice the foe drew near.
Just in that instant, anxious Ariel sought
The close recesses of the Virgin's thought;   140
As on the nosegay in her breast reclined,
He watched th' Ideas rising in her mind,

---

[8] *Vide* Ovid *Metamorphoses* viii [1 ff.]. P.

Sudden he viewed, in spite of all her art,
An earthly Lover lurking at her heart.
Amazed, confused, he found his power expired,   145
Resigned to fate, and with a sigh retired.
    The Peer now spreads the glittering Forfex wide,
T' enclose the Lock; now joins it, to divide.
Even then, before the fatal engine closed,
A wretched Sylph too fondly interposed;   150
Fate urged the shears, and cut the Sylph in twain,
(But airy substance soon unites again)[9]
The meeting points the sacred hair dissever
From the fair head, for ever, and for ever!
    Then flashed the living lightning from her eyes,   155
And screams of horror rend th' affrighted skies.
Not louder shrieks to pitying heaven are cast,
When husbands, or when lap dogs breathe their last;
Or when rich China vessels fallen from high,
In glittering dust, and painted fragments lie!   160
    Let wreaths of triumph now my temples twine,
(The Victor cried) the glorious Prize is mine!
While fish in streams, or birds delight in air,
Or in a coach and six the British Fair,
As long as Atalantis shall be read,[10]   165
Or the small pillow grace a Lady's bed,
While visits shall be paid on solemn days,
When numerous wax-lights in bright order blaze,
While nymphs take treats, or assignations give,
So long my honour, name, and praise shall live!   170
What Time would spare, from Steel receives its date,
And monuments, like men, submit to fate!
Steel could the labour of the Gods destroy,
And strike to dust th' imperial towers of Troy;
Steel could the works of mortal pride confound,   175

[9] See Milton, Bk. VI of [*Paradise Lost*], Satan cut asunder by the Angel Michael. P.
[10] A famous book written about that time by a woman: full of Court, and Party scandal, and in a loose effeminacy of style and sentiment, which well suited the debauched taste of the better Vulgar. [W.]

And hew triumphal arches to the ground.
What wonder then, fair nymph! thy hairs should feel,
The conquering force of unresisted steel?

CANTO IV

But anxious cares the pensive nymph oppressed,
And secret passions laboured in her breast.
Not youthful kings in battle seized alive,
Not scornful virgins who their charms survive,
Not ardent lovers robbed of all their bliss,   5
Not ancient ladies when refused a kiss,
Not tyrants fierce that unrepenting die,
Not Cynthia when her manteau's pinned awry,
E'er felt such rage, resentment, and despair,
As thou, sad Virgin! for thy ravished Hair.   10
    For, that sad moment, when the Sylphs withdrew,
And Ariel weeping from Belinda flew,
Umbriel, a dusky, melancholy sprite,
As ever sullied the fair face of light,
Down to the central earth, his proper scene,   15
Repaired to search the gloomy Cave of Spleen.
    Swift on his sooty pinions flits the Gnome,
And in a vapour reached the dismal dome.
No cheerful breeze this sullen region knows,
The dreaded East is all the wind that blows.   20
Here in a grotto, sheltered close from air,
And screened in shades from day's detested glare,
She sighs for ever on her pensive bed,
Pain at her side, and Megrim at her head.
    Two handmaids wait the throne: alike in place,   25
But differing far in figure and in face.

Here stood Ill Nature like an ancient maid,
Her wrinkled form in black and white arrayed;
With store of prayers, for mornings, nights, and noons,
Her hand is filled; her bosom with lampoons.   30
    There Affectation, with a sickly mien,
Shows in her cheek the roses of eighteen,
Practised to lisp, and hang the head aside,
Faints into airs, and languishes with pride,
On the rich quilt sinks with becoming woe,   35
Wrapped in a gown, for sickness, and for show.
The fair ones feel such maladies as these,
When each new nightdress gives a new disease.
    A constant Vapour o'er the palace flies;
Strange phantoms rising as the mists arise;   40
Dreadful, as hermit's dreams in haunted shades,
Or bright, as visions of expiring maids.
Now glaring fiends, and snakes on rolling spires,
Pale spectres, gaping tombs, and purple fires:
Now lakes of liquid gold, Elysian scenes,   45
And crystal domes, and Angels in machines.
    Unnumbered throngs on every side are seen,
Of bodies changed to various forms by Spleen.
Here living Teapots stand, one arm held out,
One bent; the handle this, and that the spout: 50
A Pipkin there, like Homer's Tripod walks;[11]
Here sighs a Jar, and there a Goose Pie[12] talks;
Men prove with child, a powerful fancy works,
And maids turned bottles, call aloud for corks.
    Safe passed the Gnome through this fantastic band,
A branch of healing Spleenwort in his hand.   56
Then thus addressed the power: "Hail, wayward Queen!
Who rule the sex to fifty from fifteen:
Parent of vapours and of female wit,
Who give th' hysteric, or poetic fit,   60
On various tempers act by various ways,

[11] See Homer *Iliad* xviii . . . Vulcan's walking Tripods. [P.]
[12] Alludes to a real fact, a Lady of distinction imagined herself in this condition. P.

Make some take physic, others scribble plays;
Who cause the proud their visits to delay,
And send the godly in a pet to pray.
A nymph there is, that all thy power disdains,   65
And thousands more in equal mirth maintains.
But oh! if e'er thy Gnome could spoil a grace,
Or raise a pimple on a beauteous face,
Like Citron waters matrons cheeks inflame,
Or change complexions at a losing game;   70
If e'er with airy horns I planted heads,
Or rumpled petticoats, or tumbled beds,
Or caused suspicion when no soul was rude,
Or discomposed the headdress of a Prude,
Or e'er to costive lap dog gave disease,   75
Which not the tears of brightest eyes could ease:
Hear me, and touch Belinda with chagrin,
That single act gives half the world the spleen."
     The Goddess with a discontented air
Seems to reject him, though she grants his prayer.   80
A wondrous Bag with both her hands she binds,
Like that where once Ulysses held the winds;
There she collects the force of female lungs,
Sighs, sobs, and passions, and the war of tongues.
A Vial next she fills with fainting fears,   85
Soft sorrows, melting griefs, and flowing tears.
The Gnome rejoicing bears her gifts away,
Spreads his black wings, and slowly mounts to day.
     Sunk in Thalestris' arms the nymph he found,
Her eyes dejected and her hair unbound.   90
Full o'er their heads the swelling bag he rent,
And all the Furies issued at the vent.
Belinda burns with more than mortal ire,
And fierce Thalestris fans the rising fire.
"O wretched maid!" she spread her hands, and cried,   95
(While Hampton's echoes, "Wretched maid!" replied)
"Was it for this you took such constant care
The bodkin, comb, and essence to prepare?
For this your locks in paper durance bound,

For this with torturing irons wreathed around?   100
For this with fillets strained your tender head,
And bravely bore the double loads of lead?
Gods! shall the ravisher display your hair,
While the Fops envy, and the Ladies stare!
Honour forbid! at whose unrivalled shrine   105
Ease, pleasure, virtue, all our sex resign.
Methinks already I your tears survey,
Already hear the horrid things they say,
Already see you a degraded toast,
And all your honour in a whisper lost!   110
How shall I, then, your helpless fame defend?
'Twill then be infamy to seem your friend!
And shall this prize, th' inestimable prize,
Exposed through crystal to the gazing eyes,
And heightened by the diamond's circling rays,   115
On that rapacious hand for ever blaze?
Sooner shall grass in Hyde Park Circus grow,
And wits take lodgings in the sound of Bow;
Sooner let earth, air, sea, to Chaos fall,
Men, monkeys, lap dogs, parrots, perish all!"   120
　　　She said; then raging to Sir Plume repairs,[13]
And bids her Beau demand the precious hairs:
(Sir Plume of amber snuffbox justly vain,
And the nice conduct of a clouded cane)
With earnest eyes, and round unthinking face,   125
He first the snuffbox opened, then the case,
And thus broke out—"My Lord, why, what the devil?
Z—ds! damn the lock! 'fore Gad, you must be civil!
Plague on't! 'tis past a jest—nay prithee, pox!
Give her the hair"—he spoke, and rapped his box.   130
　　　"It grieves me much" (replied the Peer again)
"Who speaks so well should ever speak in vain.
But by this Lock, this sacred Lock I swear,[14]

---

[13] Sir George Brown. He was the only one of the Party who took the thing seriously. He was angry that the Poet should make him talk nothing but nonsense; and, in truth, one could not well blame him.   [W.]
[14] In allusion to Achilles' oath in Homer *Iliad* i [309ff.].   P.

(Which never more shall join its parted hair;
Which never more its honours shall renew,   135
Clipped from the lovely head where late it grew)
That while my nostrils draw the vital air,
This hand, which won it, shall for ever wear."
He spoke, and speaking, in proud triumph spread
The long-contended honours of her head.   140
    But Umbriel, hateful Gnome! forbears not so;
He breaks the Vial whence the sorrows flow.
Then see! the nymph in beauteous grief appears,
Her eyes half languishing, half drowned in tears;
On her heaved bosom hung her drooping head,   145
Which, with a sigh, she raised; and thus she said.
    "For ever cursed be this detested day,
Which snatched my best, my favorite curl away!
Happy! ah ten times happy had I been,
If Hampton Court these eyes had never seen!   150
Yet am not I the first mistaken maid,
By love of Courts to numerous ills betrayed.
Oh had I rather unadmired remained
In some lone isle, or distant Northern land;
Where the gilt Chariot never marks the way,   155
Where none learn Ombre, none e'er taste Bohea!
There kept my charms concealed from mortal eye,
Like roses, that in deserts bloom and die.
What moved my mind with youthful Lords to roam?
O had I stayed, and said my prayers at home!   160
'Twas this, the morning omens seemed to tell,
Thrice from my trembling hand the patch box fell;
The tottering China shook without a wind,
Nay, Poll sat mute, and Shock was most unkind!
A Sylph too warned me of the threats of fate,   165
In mystic visions, now believed too late!
See the poor remnants of these slighted hairs!
My hands shall rend what even thy rapine spares:
These in two sable ringlets taught to break,
Once gave new beauties to the snowy neck;   170
The sister lock now sits uncouth, alone,

And in its fellow's fate foresees its own;
Uncurled it hangs, the fatal shears demands,
And tempts once more, thy sacrilegious hands.
Oh hadst thou, cruel! been content to seize   175
Hairs less in sight, or any hairs but these!"

CANTO V

SHE said: the pitying audience melt in tears.
But Fate and Jove had stopped the Baron's ears.
In vain Thalestris with reproach assails,
For who can move when fair Belinda fails?
Not half so fixed the Trojan could remain,   5
While Anna begged and Dido raged in vain.
Then grave Clarissa graceful waved her fan;[15]
Silence ensued, and thus the nymph began.
    "Say why are Beauties praised and honoured most,
The wise man's passion, and the vain man's toast?   10
Why decked with all that land and sea afford,
Why Angels called, and Angel-like adored?
Why round our coaches crowd the white-gloved Beaux,
Why bows the side-box from its inmost rows;
How vain are all these glories, all our pains,   15
Unless good sense preserve what beauty gains:
That men may say, when we the front-box grace,
'Behold the first in virtue as in face!'
Oh! if to dance all night, and dress all day,
Charmed the smallpox, or chased old age away;   20

[15] A new Character introduced in the subsequent Editions, to open more
clearly the Moral of the Poem, in a parody of the speech of Sarpedon to
Glaucus in Homer. P. See *Iliad* xii. 371 ff. in Pope's version, a passage
which he had published in the *Poetical Miscellanies* for 1709.

Who would not scorn what housewife's cares produce,
Or who would learn one earthly thing of use?
To patch, nay ogle, might become a Saint,
Nor could it sure be such a sin to paint.
But since, alas! frail beauty must decay,   25
Curled or uncurled, since Locks will turn to grey;
Since painted, or not painted, all shall fade,
And she who scorns a man, must die a maid;
What then remains but well our power to use,
And keep good humour still whate'er we lose?   30
And trust me, dear! good humour can prevail,
When airs, and flights, and screams, and scolding fail.
Beauties in vain their pretty eyes may roll;
Charms strike the sight, but merit wins the soul."
    So spoke the Dame, but no applause ensued;[16]   35
Belinda frowned, Thalestris called her Prude.
"To arms, to arms!" the fierce Virago cries,
And swift as lightning to the combat flies.
All side in parties, and begin th' attack;
Fans clap, silks rustle, and tough wholebones crack;   40
Heroes' and Heroines' shouts confusedly rise,
And bass and treble voices strike the skies.
No common weapons in their hands are found,
Like Gods they fight, nor dread a mortal wound.
    So when bold Homer makes the Gods engage,   45
And heavenly breasts with human passions rage;
'Gainst Pallas, Mars; Latona, Hermes arms;
And all Olympus rings with loud alarms:
Jove's thunder roars, heaven trembles all around,
Blue Neptune storms, the bellowing deeps resound: 50
Earth shakes her nodding towers, the ground gives way,
And the pale ghosts start at the flash of day!
    Triumphant Umbriel on a sconce's height[17]
Clapped his glad wings, and sat to view the fight:

[16] It is a verse frequently repeated in Homer after any speech, *So spoke—
and all the Heroes applauded.* P.
[17] Minerva in like manner, during the Battle of Ulysses with the Suitors
in the *Odyssey* perches on a beam of the roof to behold it. P.

Propped on their bodkin spears, the Sprites survey   55
The growing combat, or assist the fray.
   While through the press enraged Thalestris flies,
And scatters death around from both her eyes,
A Beau and Witling perished in the throng,
One died in metaphor, and one in song.   60
"O cruel nymph! a living death I bear,"
Cried Dapperwit, and sunk beside his chair.
A mournful glance Sir Fopling upwards cast,
"Those eyes are made so killing"—was his last.
Thus on Mæander's flowery margin lies[18]   65
Th' expiring Swan, and as he sings he dies.
   When bold Sir Plume had drawn Clarissa down,
Chloe stepped in, and killed him with a frown;
She smiled to see the doughty hero slain,
But, at her smile, the Beau revived again.   70
   Now Jove suspends his golden scales in air,[19]
Weighs the Men's wits against the Lady's hair;
The doubtful beam long nods from side to side;
At length the wits mount up, the hairs subside.
   See, fierce Belinda on the Baron flies,   75
With more than usual lightning in her eyes:
Nor feared the Chief th' unequal fight to try,
Who sought no more than on his foe to die.
But this bold Lord with manly strength endued,
She with one finger and a thumb subdued: 80
Just where the breath of life his nostrils drew,
A charge of Snuff the wily virgin threw;
The Gnomes direct, to every atom just,
The pungent grains of titillating dust.
Sudden with starting tears each eye o'erflows,   85
And the high dome re-echoes to his nose.
   Now meet thy fate, incensed Belinda cried,
And drew a deadly bodkin from her side.

[18] Sic ubi fata vocant, udis abjectus in herbis,
  Ad vada Mæandri concinit albus olor. Ovid *Epistle* [vii. 1–2]. P.
[19] *Vide* Homer *Iliad* viii [87 ff.] and Virgil *Aeneid* xii [725ff.]. P.

(The same, his ancient personage to deck,[20]
Her great great grandsire wore about his neck,   90
In three seal rings; which after, melted down,
Formed a vast buckle for his widow's gown:
Her infant grandame's whistle next it grew,
The bells she jingled, and the whistle blew;
Then in a bodkin graced her mother's hairs,   95
Which long she wore, and now Belinda wears.)
     "Boast not my fall" (he cried) "insulting foe!
Thou by some other shalt be laid as low.
Nor think, to die dejects my lofty mind:
All that I dread is leaving you behind!   100
Rather than so, ah let me still survive,
And burn in Cupid's flames—but burn alive."
     "Restore the Lock!" she cries; and all around
"Restore the Lock!" the vaulted roofs rebound.
Not fierce Othello in so loud a strain   105
Roared for the handkerchief that caused his pain.
But see how oft ambitious aims are crossed,
And chiefs contend till all the prize is lost!
The Lock, obtained with guilt, and kept with pain,
In every place is sought, but sought in vain: 110
With such a prize no mortal must be blest,
So heaven decrees! with heaven who can contest?
     Some thought it mounted to the Lunar sphere,
Since all things lost on earth are treasured there.[21]
There Heroes' wits are kept in ponderous vases,   115
And beaux' in snuffboxes and tweezer cases.
There broken vows and deathbed alms are found,
And lovers' hearts with ends of riband bound,
The courtier's promises, and sick man's prayers,
The smiles of harlots, and the tears of heirs,   120
Cages for gnats, and chains to yoke a flea,
Dried butterflies, and tomes of casuistry.
     But trust the Muse—she saw it upward rise,

[20] In imitation of the progress of Agamemnon's sceptre in Homer *Iliad* i [129 ff.]. P.
[21] *Vide* Ariosto [*Orlando Furioso*], Canto XXXIV [stanzas 68 ff.]. P.

Though marked by none but quick, poetic eyes:
(So Rome's great founder to the heavens withdrew,   125
To Proculus alone confessed in view)
A sudden Star, it shot through liquid air,
And drew behind a radiant trail of hair.
Not Berenice's Locks first rose so bright,
The heavens bespangling with dishevelled light.   130
The Sylphs behold it kindling as it flies,
And pleased pursue its progress through the skies.
      This the Beau monde shall from the Mall survey,
And hail with music its propitious ray.
This the blest Lover shall for Venus take,   135
And send up vows from Rosamonda's lake.
This Partridge soon shall view in cloudless skies,[22]
When next he looks through Galileo's eyes;
And hence th' egregious wizard shall foredoom
The fate of Louis, and the fall of Rome.   140
      Then cease, bright Nymph! to mourn thy ravished hair,
Which adds new glory to the shining sphere!
Not all the tresses that fair head can boast,
Shall draw such envy as the Lock you lost.
For, after all the murders of your eye,   145
When, after millions slain, yourself shall die;
When those fair suns shall set, as set they must,
And all those tresses shall be laid in dust,
This Lock, the Muse shall consecrate to fame,
And midst the stars inscribe Belinda's name.   150

[22]John Partridge was a ridiculous Stargazer, who in his Almanacs every year never failed to predict the downfall of the Pope, and the King of France, then at war with the English. P.

PROLOGUE
To Mr. Addison's
Tragedy of Cato

To WAKE the Soul by tender strokes of art,
To raise the genius, and to mend the heart;
To make mankind in conscious virtue bold,
Live o'er each scene, and be what they behold:
For this the Tragic Muse first trod the stage,   5
Commanding tears to stream throught every age;
Tyrants no more their savage nature kept,
And foes to virtue wondered how they wept.
Our author shuns by vulgar springs to move
The hero's glory, or the virgin's love;   10
In pitying Love, we but our weakness show,
And wild Ambition well deserves its woe.
Here tears shall flow from a more generous cause,
Such Tears as Patriots shed for dying Laws:
He bids your breasts with ancient ardour rise,   15
And calls forth Roman drops from British eyes.
Virtue confessed in human shape he draws,
What Plato thought, and godlike Cato was:
No common object to your sight displays,

But what with pleasure Heaven itself surveys,   20
A brave man struggling in the storms of fate,
And greatly falling, with a falling state.
While Cato gives his little Senate laws,
What bosom beats not in his Country's cause?
Who sees him act, but envies every deed?   25
Who hears him groan, and does not wish to bleed?
Even when proud Cæsar midst triumphal cars,
The spoils of nations, and the pomp of wars,
Ignobly vain and impotently great,
Showed Rome her Cato's figure drawn in state;   30
As her dead Father's reverend image past,
The pomp was darkened, and the day o'ercast;
The Triumph ceased, tears gushed from every eye;
The World's great Victor passed unheeded by;
Her last good man dejected Rome adored,   35
And honoured Cæsar's less than Cato's sword.
      Britons, attend: be worth like this approved,
And show, you have the virtue to be moved.
With honest scorn the first famed Cato viewed
Rome learning arts from Greece, whom she subdued;   40
Your scene precariously subsists too long
On French translation, and Italian song.
Dare to have sense yourselves; assert the stage,
Be justly warmed with your own native rage:
Such Plays alone should win a British ear,   45
As Cato's self had not disdained to hear.

ELEGY
To The Memory of
An Unfortunate Lady[1]

WHAT beckoning ghost, along the moonlight shade
Invites my steps, and points to younder glade?
'Tis she!—but why that bleeding bosom gored,
Why dimly gleams the visionary sword?
Oh ever beauteous, ever friendly! tell,   5
Is it, in heaven, a crime to love too well?
To bear too tender, or too firm a heart,
To act a Lover's or a Roman's part?
Is there no bright reversion in the sky,
For those who greatly think, or bravely die?   10
    Why bade ye else, ye Powers! her soul aspire
Above the vulgar flight of low desire?
Ambition first sprung from your blest abodes;
The glorious fault of Angels and of Gods:
Thence to their images on earth it flows,   15
And in the breasts of Kings and Heroes glows.

[1] The lady has never been identified, and the poem seems hardly to require that she should be.

Most souls, 'tis true, but peep out once an age,
Dull sullen prisoners in the body's cage:
Dim lights of life, that burn a length of years
Useless, unseen, as lamps in sepulchres;   20
Like Eastern Kings a lazy state they keep,
And close confined to their own palace, sleep.

    From these perhaps (ere nature bade her die)
Fate snatched her early to the pitying sky.
As into air the purer spirits flow,   25
And separate from their kindred dregs below;
So flew the soul to its congenial place,
Nor left one virtue to redeem her Race.

    But thou, false guardian of a charge too good,
Thou, mean deserter of thy brother's blood!   30
See on these ruby lips the trembling breath,
These cheeks, now fading at the blast of death;
Cold is that breast which warmed the world before,
And those love-darting eyes must roll no more.
Thus, if Eternal justice rules the ball,   35
Thus shall your wives, and thus your children fall:
On all the line a sudden vengeance waits,
And frequent hearses shall besiege your gates.
There passengers shall stand, and pointing say,
(While the long funerals blacken all the way)   40
Lo these were they, whose souls the Furies steeled,
And cursed with hearts unknowing how to yield.
Thus unlamented pass the proud away,
The gaze of fools, and pageant of a day!
So perish all, whose breast ne'er learned to glow   45
For others' good, or melt at others' woe.

    What can atone (oh ever-injured shade!)
Thy fate unpitied, and thy rites unpaid?
No friend's complaint, no kind domestic tear
Pleased thy pale ghost, or graced thy mournful bier.   50
By foreign hands thy dying eyes were closed,
By foreign hands thy decent limbs composed,
By foreign hands thy humble grave adorned,
By strangers honoured, and by strangers mourned!

What though no friends in sable weeds appear,   55
Grieve for an hour, perhaps, then mourn a year,
And bear about the mockery of woe
To midnight dances, and the public show?
What though no weeping Loves thy ashes grace,
Nor polished marble emulate thy face?   60
What though no sacred earth allow thee room,
Nor hallowed dirge be muttered o'er thy tomb?
Yet shall thy grave with rising flowers be drest,
And the green turf lie lightly on thy breast:
There shall the morn her earliest tears bestow,   65
There the first roses of the year shall blow;
While Angels with their silver wings o'ershade
The ground, now sacred by thy reliques made.

   So peaceful rests, without a stone, a name,
What once had beauty, titles, wealth, and fame.   70
How loved, how honoured once, avails thee not,
To whom related, or by whom begot;
A heap of dust alone remains of thee,
'Tis all thou art, and all the proud shall be!

   Poets themselves must fall, like those they sung,   75
Deaf the praised ear, and mute the tuneful tongue.
Even he, whose soul now melts in mournful lays,
Shall shortly want the generous tear he pays;
Then from his closing eyes thy form shall part,
And the last pang shall tear thee from his heart,   80
Life's idle business at one gasp be o'er,
The Muse forgot, and thou beloved no more!

ELOÏSA TO ABELARD

ARGUMENT

ABELARD and Eloïsa flourished in the twelfth Century; they were two of the most distinguished persons of their age in learning and beauty, but for nothing more famous than for their unfortunate passion. After a long course of calamities, they retired each to a several Convent, and consecrated the remainder of their days to religion. It was many years after this separation, that a letter of Abelard's to a Friend, which contained the history of his misfortune, fell into the hands of Eloïsa. This awakening all her tenderness, occasioned those celebrated letters (out of which the following is partly extracted) which give so lively a picture of the struggles of grace and nature, virtue and passion. P.

IN these deep solitudes and awful cells,
Where heavenly-pensive contemplation dwells,
And ever-musing melancholy reigns;
What means this tumult in a Vestal's veins?
Why rove my thoughts beyond this last retreat?   5
Why feels my heart its long-forgotten heat?
Yet, yet I love!—From Abelard it came,
And Eloïsa yet must kiss the name.

    Dear fatal name! rest ever unrevealed,
Nor pass these lips in holy silence sealed: 10
Hide it, my heart, within that close disguise,
Where mixed with God's, his loved Idea lies:

O write it not my hand—the name appears
Already written—wash it out, my tears!
In vain lost Eloïsa weeps and prays,   15
Her heart still dictates, and her hand obeys.
    Relentless walls! whose darksome round contains
Repentant sighs, and voluntary pains:
Ye rugged rocks! which holy knees have worn;
Ye grots and caverns shagged with horrid thorn![1]   20
Shrines! where their vigils pale-eyed virgins keep,
And pitying saints, whose statutes learn to weep!
Though cold like you, unmoved and silent grown,
I have not yet forgot myself to stone.[2]
All is not Heaven's while Abelard has part,   25
Still rebel nature holds out half my heart;
Nor prayers nor fasts its stubborn pulse restrain,
Nor tears for ages taught to flow in vain.
    Soon as thy letters trembling I unclose,
That well-known name awakens all my woes.   30
Oh name for ever sad! for ever dear!
Still breathed in sighs, still ushered with a tear.
I tremble too, where'er my own I find,
Some dire misfortune follows close behind.
Line after line my gushing eyes o'erflow,   35
Led through a sad variety of woe:
Now warm in love, now withering in thy bloom,
Lost in a convent's solitary gloom!
There stern Religion quenched th' unwilling flame,
There died the best of passions, Love and Fame.   40
    Yet write, oh write me all, that I may join
Griefs to thy griefs, and echo sighs to thine.
Nor foes nor fortune take this power away;
And is my Abelard less kind than they?
Tears still are mine, and those I need not spare,   45
Love but demands what else were shed in prayer;

---

[1] In Milton's *Comus* occurs the line (429): "By grots, and caverns shagged
with horrid shades."
[2] Cf. Milton, *Il Penseroso*, 1. 42: "Forget thy self to marble." Pope's poem
echoes several other melancholy phrases in the minor poems of Milton.

No happier task these faded eyes pursue;
To read and weep is all they now can do.
 Then share thy pain, allow that sad relief;
Ah, more than share it, give me all thy grief.   50
Heaven first taught letters for some wretch's aid,
Some banished lover, or some captive maid;
They live, they speak, they breathe what love inspires,
Warm from the soul, and faithful to its fires,
The virgin's wish without her fears impart,   55
Excuse the blush, and pour out all the heart,
Speed the soft intercourse from soul to soul,
And waft a sigh from Indus to the Pole.
 Thou knowst how guiltless first I met thy flame,
When Love approached me under Friendship's name;   60
My fancy formed thee of angelic kind,
Some emanation of th' all-beauteous Mind.
Those smiling eyes, attempering every ray,
Shone sweetly lambent with celestial day.
Guiltless I gazed; heaven listened while you sung;   65
And truths divine came mended from that tongue.
From lips like those what precept failed to move?
Too soon they taught me 'twas no sin to love:
Back through the paths of pleasing sense I ran,
Nor wished an Angel whom I loved a Man.   70
Dim and remote the joys of saints I see;
Nor envy them that heaven I lose for thee.
 How oft, when pressed to marriage, have I said,
Curse on all laws but those which love has made?
Love, free as air, at sight of human ties,   75
Spreads his light wings, and in a moment flies.
Let wealth, let honour, wait the wedded dame,
August her deed, and sacred be her fame;
Before true passion all those views remove,
Fame, wealth, and honour! what are you to Love?   80
The jealous God, when we profane his fires,
Those restless passions in revenge inspires,
And bids them make mistaken mortals groan,
Who seek in love for aught but love alone.

Should at my feet the world's great master fall,   85
Himself, his throne, his world, I'd scorn 'em all:
Not Cæsar's empress would I deign to prove;
No, make me mistress to the man I love;
If there be yet another name more free,
More fond than mistress, make me that to thee!   90
Oh! happy state! when souls each other draw,
When love is liberty, and nature, law:
All then is full, possessing, and possessed,
No craving void left aching in the breast:
Even thought meets thought, ere from the lips it part,   95
And each warm wish springs mutual from the heart.
This sure is bliss (if bliss on earth there be)
And once the lot of Abelard and me.

    Alas, how changed! what sudden horrors rise!
A naked Lover bound and bleeding lies!   100
Where, where was Eloïse? her voice, her hand,
Her poniard, had opposed the dire command.
Barbarian, stay! that bloody stroke restrain;
The crime was common, common be the pain.
I can no more; by shame, by rage suppressed,   105
Let tears, and burning blushes speak the rest.

    Canst thou forget that sad, that solemn day,
When victims at yon altar's foot we lay?
Canst thou forget what tears that moment fell,
When, warm in youth, I bade the world farewell?   110
As with cold lips I kissed the sacred veil,
The shrines all trembled, and the lamps grew pale:
Heaven scarce believed the Conquest it surveyed,
And Saints with wonder heard the vows I made.
Yet then, to those dread altars as I drew,   115
Not on the Cross my eyes were fixed, but you:
Not grace, or zeal, love only was my call,
And if I lose thy love, I lose my all.
Come! with thy looks, thy words, relieve my woe;
Those still at least are left thee to bestow.   120
Still on that breast enamoured let me lie,
Still drink delicious poison from thy eye,

Pant on thy lip, and to thy heart be pressed;
Give all thou canst—and let me dream the rest.
Ah no! instruct me other joys to prize,   125
With other beauties charm my partial eyes,
Full in my view set all the bright abode,
And make my soul quit Abelard for God.
    Ah, think at least thy flock deserves thy care,
Plants of thy hand, and children of thy prayer.   130
From the false world in early youth they fled,
By thee to mountains, wilds, and deserts led.
You raised these hallowed walls; the desert smiled,[3]
And Paradise was opened in the Wild.
No weeping orphan saw his father's stores   135
Our shrines irradiate, or emblaze the floors;
No silver saints, by dying misers given,
Here bribed the rage of ill-requited heaven:
But such plain roofs as Piety could raise,
And only vocal with the Maker's praise.   140
In these lone walls (their days eternal bound)
These moss-grown domes with spiry turrets crowned,
Where awful arches make a noonday night,
And the dim windows shed a solemn light;
Thy eyes diffused a reconciling ray,   145
And gleams of glory brightened all the day.
But now no face divine contentment wears,
'Tis all blank sadness, or continual tears.
See how the force of others' prayers I try,
(O pious fraud of amorous charity!)   150
But why should I on others' prayers depend?
Come thou, my father, brother, husband, friend!
Ah let thy handmaid, sister, daughter move,
And all those tender names in one, thy love!
The darksome pines that o'er yon rocks reclined   155
Wave high, and murmur to the hollow wind,
The wandering streams that shine between the hills,
The grots that echo to the tinkling rills,

[3] He founded the Monastery. P.

pathetic
Fallacy
projection
of one's own
feeling into
nature

orgasmic

The dying gales that pant upon the trees,
The lakes that quiver to the curling breeze;   160
No more these scenes my meditation aid,
Or lull to rest the visionary maid.
But o'er the twilight groves and dusky caves,
Long-sounding aisles, and intermingled graves,
Black Melancholy sits, and round her throws   165
A deathlike silence, and a dead repose:
Her gloomy presence saddens all the scene,
Shades every flower, and darkens every green,
Deepens the murmur of the falling floods,
And breathes a browner horror on the woods.   170
        Yet here for ever, ever must I stay;
Sad proof how well a lover can obey!
Death, only death, can break the lasting chain;
And here, even then, shall my cold dust remain,
Here all its frailties, all its flames resign,   175
And wait till 'tis no sin to mix with thine.
        Ah wretch! believed the spouse of God in vain,
Confessed within the slave of love and man.
Assist me, heaven! but whence arose that prayer?
Sprung it from piety, or from despair?   180
Even here, where frozen chastity retires,
Love finds an altar for forbidden fires.
I ought to grieve, but cannot what I ought;
I mourn the lover, not lament the fault;
I view my crime, but kindle at the view,   185
Repent old pleasures, and solicit new;
Now turned to heaven, I weep my past offence,
Now think of thee, and curse my innocence.
Of all affliction taught a lover yet,
'Tis sure the hardest science to forget!   190
How shall I lose the sin, yet keep the sense,
And love th' offender, yet detest th' offence?
How the dear object from the crime remove,
Or how distinguish penitence from love?
Unequal task! a passion to resign,   195
For hearts so touched, so pierced, so lost as mine.

Ere such a soul regains its peaceful state,
How often must it love, how often hate!
How often hope, despair, resent, regret,
Conceal, disdain,—do all things but forget.   200
But let heaven seize it, all at once 'tis fired;
Not touched, but rapt; not wakened, but inspired!
On come! oh teach me nature to subdue,
Renounce my love, my life, myself—and you.
Fill my fond heart with God alone, for he   205
Alone can rival, can succeed to thee.
    How happy is the blameless Vestal's lot!
The world forgetting, by the world forgot:
Eternal sunshine of the spotless mind!
Each prayer accepted, and each wish resigned;   210
Labour and rest, that equal periods keep;
"Obedient slumbers that can wake and weep;"[4]
Desires composed, affections ever even;
Tears that delight, and sighs that waft to heaven.
Grace shines around her with serenest beams,   215
And whispering Angels prompt her golden dreams.
For her th' unfading rose of Eden blooms,
And wings of Seraphs shed divine perfumes,
For her the Spouse prepares the bridal ring,
For her white virgins Hymeneals sing,   220
To sounds of heavenly harps she dies away,
And melts in visions of eternal day.
    Far other dreams my erring soul employ,
Far other raptures, of unholy joy:
When at the close of each sad, sorrowing day,   225
Fancy restores what vengeance snatched away,
Then conscience sleeps, and leaving nature free,
All my loose soul unbounded springs to thee.
Oh cursed, dear horrors of all-conscious night!
How glowing guilt exalts the keen delight!   230
Provoking Dæmons all restraint remove,
And stir within me every source of love.

---

[4] Taken from Crashaw [*Description of a Religious House*, l. 16]. P.

I hear thee, view thee, gaze o'er all thy charms,
And round thy phantom glue my clasping arms.
I wake:—no more I hear, no more I view,   235
The phantom flies me, as unkind as you.
I call aloud; it hears not what I say:
I stretch my empty arms; it glides away.
To dream once more I close my willing eyes;
Ye soft illusions, dear deceits, arise!   240
Alas, no more! methinks we wandering go
Through dreary wastes, and weep each other's woe,
Where round some mouldering tower pale ivy creeps,
And low-browed rocks hang nodding o'er the deeps.
Sudden you mount, you beckon from the skies;   245
Clouds interpose, waves roar, and winds arise.
I shriek, start up, the same sad prospect find,
And wake to all the griefs I left behind.
    For thee the fates, severely kind, ordain
A cool suspense from pleasure and from pain;   250
Thy life a long dead calm of fixed repose;
No pulse that riots, and no blood that glows.
Still as the sea, ere winds were taught to blow,
Or moving spirit bade the waters flow;
Soft as the slumbers of a saint forgiven,   255
And mild as opening gleams of promised heaven.
    Come, Abelard! for what hast thou to dread?
The torch of Venus burns not for the dead.
Nature stands checked; Religion disapproves;
Even thou art cold—yet Eloïsa loves.   260
Ah hopeless, lasting flames! like those that burn
To light the dead, and warm th' unfruitful urn.
    What scenes appear where'er I turn my view?
The dear Ideas, where I fly, pursue,
Rise in the grove, before the altar rise,   265
Stain all my soul, and wanton in my eyes.
I waste the Matin lamp in sighs for thee,
Thy image steals between my God and me,
Thy voice I seem in every hymn to hear,
With every bead I drop too soft a tear.   270

When from the censer clouds of fragrance roll,
And swelling organs lift the rising soul,
One thought of thee puts all the pomp to flight,
Priests, tapers, temples, swim before my sight:
In seas of flame my plunging soul is drowned,   275
While Altars blaze, and Angels tremble round.
    While prostrate here in humble grief I lie,
Kind, virtuous drops just gathering in my eye,
While praying, trembling, in the dust I roll,
And dawning grace is opening on my soul: 280
Come, if thou darst, all charming as thou art!
Oppose thyself to heaven; dispute my heart;
Come, with one glance of those deluding eyes
Blot out each bright Idea of the skies;
Take back that grace, those sorrows, and those tears; 285
Take back my fruitless penitence and prayers;
Snatch me, just mounting, from the blest abode; } *like Donne*
Assist the fiends, and tear me from my God!
    No, fly me, fly me, far as Pole from Pole;
Rise Alps between us! and whole oceans roll!   290
Ah, come not, write not, think not once of me,
Nor share one pang of all I felt for thee.
Thy oaths I quit, thy memory resign;
Forget, renounce me, hate whate'er was mine.
Fair eyes, and tempting looks (which yet I view!)   295
Long loved, adored ideas, all adieu!
Oh Grace serene! oh virtue heavenly fair!
Divine oblivion of low-thoughted care![5]
Fresh blooming Hope, gay daughter of the sky!
And Faith, our early immortality!   300
Enter, each mild, each amicable guest;
Receive, and wrap me in eternal rest!
    See in her cell sad Eloïsa spread,
Propped on some tomb, a neighbour of the dead.
In each low wind methinks a Spirit calls,   305
And more than Echoes talk along the walls.

---

[5] Cf. Milton, *Comus*, l. 6.

Here, as I watched the dying lamps around,
From yonder shrine I heard a hollow sound.
"Come, sister, come!" (it said, or seemed to say)
"Thy place is here, sad sister, come away!   310
Once like thyself, I trembled, wept, and prayed,
Love's victim then, though now a sainted maid:
But all is calm in this eternal sleep;
Here grief forgets to groan, and love to weep,
Even superstition loses every fear: 315
For God, not man, absolves our frailties here."

    I come, I come! prepare your roseate bowers,
Celestial palms, and ever-blooming flowers.
Thither, where sinners may have rest, I go,
Where flames refined in breasts seraphic glow: 320
Thou, Abelard! the last sad office pay,
And smooth my passage to the realms of day;
See my lips tremble, and my eyeballs roll,
Suck my last breath, and catch my flying soul!
Ah no—in sacred vestments mayst thou stand,   325
The hallowed taper trembling in thy hand,
Present the Cross before my lifted eye,
Teach me at once, and learn of me to die.
Ah then, thy once-loved Eloïsa see!
It will be then no crime to gaze on me.   330
See from my cheek the transient roses fly!
See the last sparkle languish in my eye!
Till every motion, pulse, and breath be o'er;
And even my Abelard be loved no more.
O Death all-eloquent! you only prove   335
What dust we dote on, when 'tis man we love.

    Then too, when fate shall thy fair frame destroy,
(That cause of all my guilt, and all my joy)
In trance ecstatic may thy pangs be drowned,
Bright clouds descend, and Angels watch thee round, 340
From opening skies may streaming glories shine,
And saints embrace thee with a love like mine.
    May one kind grave unite each hapless name,[6]

---

[6] Abelard and Eloïsa were interred in the same grave, or in monuments

And graft my love immortal on thy fame!
Then, ages hence, when all my woes are o'er,   345
When this rebellious heart shall beat no more;
If ever chance two wandering lovers brings
To Paraclete's white walls and silver springs,
O'er the pale marble shall they join their heads,
And drink the falling tears each other sheds;   350
Then sadly say, with mutual pity moved,
"Oh may we never love as these have loved!"
From the full choir when loud Hosannas rise,
And swell the pomp of dreadful sacrifice,
Amid that scene if some relenting eye   355
Glance on the stone where our cold relics lie,
Devotion's self shall steal a thought from heaven,
One human tear shall drop, and be forgiven.
And sure, if fate some future bard shall join
In sad similitude of griefs to mine,   360
Condemned whole years in absence to deplore,
And image charms he must behold no more;
Such if there be, who loves so long, so well;
Let him our sad, our tender story tell;
The well-sung woes will soothe my pensive ghost;   365
He best can paint 'em who shall feel 'em most.

adjoining, in the Monastery of the Paraclete: he died in the year 1142,
she in 1163.   P.

PREFACE TO HOMER'S ILIAD[1]

Homer is universally allowed to have had the greatest *Invention* of any writer whatever. The praise of Judgment Virgil

[1] For a stretch of about eleven years (See Introduction, p. xvii), embracing the fourth decade of his life, or from the publication of his first collected *Works* (1717) to the first edition of the *Dunciad* (1728), Pope busied himself on major projects of translation and editing:—his *Iliad,* in six volumes (1715–1719), his *Odyssey* in five volumes (1725–1726), and his edition of Shakespeare in six volumes (1725). This activity included the writing of a few substantial prose essays in literary criticism, counterparts and developments of his youthful Horatian verse *Essay on Criticism* and at the same time exercises in scholarship and displays of his historico-critical imagination. The Preface to the *Iliad* appeared with the first four books of the poem, in 1715. A few years earlier, during the winter and spring of 1712, Addison in a series of eighteen Saturday *Spectators* had conducted a prolonged celebration of Milton's *Paradise Lost* according to the Aristotelian dramatic categories of fable, characters, sentiments (or thoughts), and language, and according also to the canonical Augustan concern with beauties and faults. Pope turns to the same classic frame of reference, using nearly the same terms, but ordering the whole (with his own subheadings) under the master idea, announced in his first sentence, of *Invention*. Homer was the chief poetic *Inventor* and hence the master and model of all great poetry in the Western tradition. *Invention!* or as we might say (coming after Kant and Coleridge) *Imagination!*—creation,

132

has justly contested with him, and others may have their pre-
tensions as to particular excellencies; but his Invention remains
yet unrivalled. Nor is it a wonder if he has ever been acknowl-

originality (with truth)—or (if we look back rather to Blake, in the
contemporary line of Yeats and Stevens)—*Vision!* the fire of poetic vision.
There was never a more fiery paean in praise of the poetic faculty than
the first two thirds of Pope's Preface. Another near equivalent, though it
has been more difficult for the recent critical mind to realize this, was for
Pope *Wit,* the central term of his *Essay on Criticism,* meaning the *élan
vital* of poetic creation (again producing *Truth,* or working as the life
and energy of *Nature*), as witnessed in Homer and the other ancient
writers—and not only the epopeists but the epistolary, satiric, and critical
writers, whom Pope himself aspired to emulate in his Horatian verse essay.
In his youth, Horace, under the banner of Wit, and now Homer, under
the banner of Invention, are summoned by Pope and rematerialized for
the English Augustan age as eternal witnesses to the power and wisdom
of poetry—against the reductions so seriously threatened by the ration-
alizing trend of the age. Pope himself, and even in his poetry, could bril-
liantly participate in that trend. But all allowances made, it was the aim
of his career as poet to battle against it. The life of a wit was a warfare on
earth. In his *Essay on Criticism* Pope was the English Horace of the age;
in his two Homer translations, on which he labored so many years, he
became even more the English Homer. He was painted by the leading
portraitist of the age, Sir Godfrey Kneller, both as the English Horace,
in ivy garland and toga, and as the English Homer, with pensive brow
and elbow propped on a folio Homer, or standing in his garden holding
the Greek *Iliad* open to the first page of a book lately translated. In his
Preface to the *Iliad* he invoked the rational scheme of Aristotelian criti-
cism but energized it under the rubric of rapturous poetic creation with
all the enthusiasm of the second greatest of the classical critics, whom at
one point he cites, Aristotle's emotive and romantic counterpart, the
Roman Greek celebrator of poetry Longinus. It is characteristic of Pope's
agility that after having thus enacted an intense moment of English
Longinianism, he could later employ the *Peri Hupsous* (*On the Sublime*)
as the vehicle of a sweeping travesty (*Peri Bathous*) against all the hum-
bug and comically inferior poets of his own day. See below pp. 374–424.
    Moments of Special vigor and insight occur also throughout Pope's
annotations of the *Iliad* and in his extended *Postscript* to the *Odyssey*
(where he debates the Longinian view that the *Odyssey* is a cooler product
of Homer's old age).
    The present annotations to Pope's Preface owe a good deal to the
edition of Pope's *Iliad* by Maynard Mack and his associates in Volume
vii of the *Twickenham Pope.* Some more precise references to this work
are given at a few places below.

edged the greatest of poets, who most excelled in that which is the very foundation of poetry. It is the invention that in different degrees distinguishes all great Geniuses: The utmost stretch of human study, learning, and industry, which master every thing besides, can never attain to this. It furnishes Art with all her materials, and without it, Judgment itself can at best but *steal wisely:* For Art is only like a prudent steward that lives on managing the riches of Nature. Whatever praises may be given to works of Judgment, there is not even a single beauty in them to which the Invention must not contribute. As in the most regular gardens, Art can only reduce the beauties of Nature to more regularity, and such a figure which the common eye may better take in, and is therefore more entertained with. And perhaps the reason why common Critics are inclined to prefer a judicious and methodical genius to a great and fruitful one, is because they find it easier for themselves to pursue their observations through an uniform and bounded walk of Art, than to comprehend the vast and various extent of Nature.

Our author's work is a wild paradise, where if we cannot see all the beauties so distinctly as in an ordered garden, it is only because the number of them is infinitely greater. 'Tis like a copious nursery which contains the seeds and first productions of every kind, out of which those who followed him have but selected some particular plants, each according to his fancy, to cultivate and beautify. If some things are too luxuriant, it is owing to the richness of the soil; and if others are not arrived to perfection or maturity, it is only because they are overrun and oppressed by those of a stronger nature.

It is to the strength of this amazing invention we are to attribute that unequalled fire and rapture, which is so forcible in Homer that no man of a true poetical spirit is master of himself while he reads him. What he writes is of the most animated nature imaginable; every thing moves, every thing lives, and is put in action. If a council be called, or a battle fought, you are not coldly informed of what was said or done as from a third person; the reader is hurried out of himself by the force of the Poet's imagination, and turns in one place to a hearer, in another to a spectator. The course of his verses resembles that of the army he describes, οἱ δ'ἄρ' ἴσαν, ὡς εἴ τε πυρὶ χϑὼν πᾶσα νέμοιτο.[2]

They pour along like a fire that sweeps the whole earth before it. 'Tis however remarkable that his fancy, which is everywhere vigorous, is not discovered immediately at the beginning of his poem in its fullest splendor: It grows in the progress both upon himself and others, and becomes on fire like a chariot wheel, by its own rapidity. Exact disposition, just thought, correct elocution, polished numbers, may have been found in a thousand; but this poetical fire, this *Vivida vis animi,* in a very few. Even in works where all those are imperfect or neglected, this can overpower criticism, and make us admire even while we disapprove. Nay, where this appears, though attended with absurdities, it brightens all the rubbish about it, till we see nothing but its own splendor. This *Fire* is discerned in Virgil, but discerned as through a glass, reflected from Homer, more shining than fierce, but every where equal and constant: In Lucan and Statius,[3] it bursts out in sudden, short, and interrupted flashes: In Milton it glows like a furnace kept up to an uncommon ardor by the force of art: In Shakespeare, it strikes before we are aware, like an accidental fire from heaven: But in Homer, and in him only, it burns everywhere clearly, and everywhere irresistibly.

I shall here endeavor to show, how this vast *Invention* exerts itself in a manner superior to that of any poet, through all the main constituent parts of his work, as it is the great and peculiar characteristic which distinguishes him from all other authors.

This strong and ruling faculty was like a powerful star, which in the violence of its course, drew all things within its *vortex.* It seemed not enough to have taken in the whole circle of arts, and the whole compass of nature to supply his maxims and reflections; all the inward passions and affections of mankind, to furnish his characters; and all the outward forms and images of things for his descriptions; but wanting yet an ampler sphere to expatiate in, he opened a new and boundless walk for

[2] *Iliad* ii. 780
[3] Latin epic authors of the first century A.D.; Lucan's *Pharsalia* is considered the greatest Latin epic after the *Aeneid.* As a youth Pope translated the first book of the *Thebaid* of Statius; it was published in a volume of *Miscellaneous Poems and Translations* by Lintot in 1712.

his imagination, and created a world for himself in the invention of *Fable*. That which Aristotle calls the *Soul of poetry*,[4] was first breathed into it by Homer. I shall begin with considering him in this part, as it is naturally the first, and I speak of it both as it means the design of a poem, and as it is taken for fiction.

Fable may be divided into the *probable,* the *allegorical,* and the *marvelous*. The *probable fable* is the recital of such actions as though they did not happen, yet might, in the common course of nature: Or of such as though they did, become fables by the additional episodes and manner of telling them. Of this sort is the main story of an Epic poem, *the return of* Ulysses, *the settlement of the* Trojans *in* Italy, or the like. That of the *Iliad* is the *anger* of Achilles, the most short and single subject that ever was chosen by any Poet. Yet this he has supplied with a vaster variety of incidents and events, and crowded with a greater number of councils, speeches, battles, and episodes of all kinds, than are to be found even in those poems whose schemes are of the utmost latitude and irregularity. The action is hurried on with the most vehement spirit, and its whole duration employs not so much as fifty days. Virgil, for want of so warm a genius, aided himself by taking in a more extensive subject, as well as a greater length of time, and contracting the design of both Homer's poems into one, which is yet but a fourth part as large as his. The other Epic Poets have used the same practice, but generally carried it so far as to superinduce a multiplicity of fables, destroy the unity of action, and lose their readers in an unreasonable length of time. Nor is it only in the main design that they have been unable to add to his invention, but they have followed him in every episode and part of story. If he has given a regular *catalogue* of an *army,* they all draw up their forces in the same order. If he has funeral games for Patroclus, Virgil has the same for Anchises, and Statius (rather than omit them) destroys the unity of his action for those of Archemorus. If

[4] Aristotle's six elements of tragedy are defined in chapter vi of his *Poetics: muthos* (fable, plot), *ēthos* (character), *dianoia* (thought, "sentiment"), *lexis* (diction), *opsis* (spectacle), *melos* (song). The *muthos* is said to be the *archē kai hoion psuchē* (first principle and, as it were, soul) of the tragic poem.

Ulysses visit the shades, the Aeneas of Virgil and Scipio of Silius[5] are sent after him. If he be detained from his return by the allurements of Calypso, so is Aeneas by Dido, and Rinaldo by Armida.[6] If Achilles be absent from the army on the score of a quarrel through half the poem, Rinaldo must absent himself just as long, on the like account. If he gives his hero a suit of celestial armor, Virgil and Tasso make the same present to theirs. Virgil has not only observed this close imitation of Homer, but where he had not led the way, supplied the want from other Greek authors. Thus the story of Sinon and the taking of Troy was copied (says Macrobius) almost word for word from Peisander,[7] as the Loves of Dido and Aeneas are taken from those of Medea and Jason in Apollonius,[8] and several others in the same manner.

To proceed to the *allegorical fable:* If we reflect upon those innumerable knowledges, those secrets of nature and physical philosophy, which Homer is generally supposed to have wrapped up in his *allegories,* what a new and ample scene of wonder may this consideration afford us? How fertile will that imagination appear, which was able to clothe all the properties of elements, the qualifications of the mind, the virtues and vices, in forms and persons; and to introduce them into actions agreeable to the nature of the things they shadowed? This is a field in which no succeeding poets could dispute with Homer; and whatever commendations have been allowed them on this head, are by no means for their invention in having enlarged his circle, but for their judgment in having contracted it. For when the mode of learning changed in following ages, and science was delivered in

[5] In the *Punica* (Bk. xiii) of Silius Italicus, another Roman author of the first century.

[6] Armida is the Damascene enchantress and Rinaldo one of the Christian heroes in the *Jerusalem Delivered* (1576) of Tasso.

[7] Macrobius, Roman philosopher and grammarian (*fl. c.* A.D. 400); in his dialogue *Saturnalia,* containing an extensive critique of Virgil, tells us (Bk. v) that the episode of the taking of Troy (in Bk. ii of Virgil's *Aeneid*) is derived from Peisander, a Rhodian Greek epic poet of the sixth or seventh century B.C.

[8] Bk. iii of the *Argonautica* of Apollonius Rhodius, Greek poet of the third century B.C.

a plainer manner; it then became as reasonable in the more modern poets to lay it aside, as it was in Homer to make use of it. And perhaps it was no unhappy circumstance for Virgil, that there was not in his time that demand upon him of so great an invention, as might be capable of furnishing all those allegorical parts of a poem.

The *marvelous fable* includes whatever is supernatural, and especially the machines of the Gods. He seems the first who brought them into a system of machinery for poetry, and such a one as makes its greatest importance and dignity. For we find those authors who have been offended at the literal notion of the Gods, constantly laying their accusation against Homer as the chief support of it. But whatever cause there might be to blame his *machines* in a philosophical or religious view, they are so perfect in the poetic, that mankind have been ever since contented to follow them: None have been able to enlarge the sphere of poetry beyond the limits he has set: Every attempt of this nature has proved unsuccessful; and after all the various changes of times and religions, his Gods continue to this day the Gods of poetry.

We come now to the *characters* of his persons: And here we shall find no author has ever drawn so many, with so visible and surprising a variety, or given us such lively and affecting impressions of them. Every one has something so singularly his own, that no painter could have distinguished them more by their features, than the Poet has by their manners. Nothing can be more exact than the distinctions he has observed in the different degrees of virtues and vices. The single quality of *courage* is wonderfully diversified in the several characters of the *Iliad*. That of Achilles is furious and intractable; that of Diomede forward, yet listening to advice and subject to command: That of Ajax is heavy, and self-confiding; of Hector active and vigilant: The courage of Agamemnon is inspirited by love of empire and ambition, that of Menelaus mixed with softness and tenderness for his people: We find in Idomeneus a plain direct soldier, in Sarpedon a gallant and generous one. Nor is this judicious and astonishing diversity to be found only in the principal quality which constitutes the main of each character, but even in the underparts of it, to which he takes care to give a tincture of that principal one. For example, the main characters of Ulysses and Nestor consist in *wisdom*; and they are distinct in this, that the wisdom of one is *artificial* and *various,* of the other *natural, open,* and *regular*. But they have, besides, characters of *courage*; and this quality also takes a different turn in each from the difference of his prudence: for one in the war depends still upon *caution,* the other upon *experience*. It would be endless to produce instances of these kinds. The characters of Virgil are far from striking us in this open manner; they lie in a great degree hidden and undistinguished, and where they are marked most evidently, affect us not in proportion to those of Homer. His characters of valor are much alike; even that of Turnus seems no way peculiar but as it is in a superior degree; and we see nothing that differences the courage of Mnestheus from that of Sergestus, Cloanthus, or the rest. In like manner it may be remarked of Statius' heroes, that an air of impetuosity runs through them all; the same horrid and savage courage appears in his Capaneus, Tydeus, Hippomedon, etc. They have a parity of character, which makes them seem brothers of one family. I believe when the reader is led into this track of reflection, if he will pursue it through the *Epic* and *Tragic* writers, he will be convinced how infinitely superior in this point the invention of Homer was to that of all others.

The speeches are to be considered as they flow from the characters, being perfect or defective as they agree or disagree with the manners of those who utter them. As there is more variety of characters in the *Iliad,* so there is of speeches, than in any other poem. *Everything in it has manners* (as Aristotle expresses it),[9] that is, every thing is acted or spoken. It is hardly credible in a work of such length, how small a number of lines are employed in narration. In Virgil the dramatic part is less in proportion to the narrative; and the speeches often consist of general reflections or thoughts, which might be equally just in any person's mouth upon the same occasion. As many of his persons have no apparent characters, so many of his speeches

[9] *Poetics* ch. xxiv. 14.

escape being applied and judged by the rule of propriety. We oftner think of the author himself when we read Virgil, than when we are engaged in Homer: All which are the effects of a colder invention, that interests us less in the action described: Homer makes us hearers, and Virgil leaves us readers.

If in the next place we take a view of the *sentiments,* the same presiding faculty is eminent in the sublimity and spirit of his thoughts. Longinus has given his opinion, that it was in this part Homer principally excelled.[10] What were alone sufficient to prove the grandeur and excellence of his sentiments in general, is, that they have so remarkable a parity with those of the Scripture: Duport, in his *Gnomologia Homerica,*[11] has collected innumerable instances of this sort. And it is with justice an excellent modern writer allows, that if Virgil has not so many thoughts that are low and vulgar, he has not so many that are sublime and noble; and that the Roman author seldom rises into very astonishing sentiments where he is not fired by the *Iliad*.

If we observe his *descriptions, images,* and *similes,* we shall find the invention still predominant. To what else can we ascribe that vast comprehension of images of every sort, where we see each circumstance of art, and individual of nature summoned together, by the extent and fecundity of his imagination; to which all things, in their various views, presented themselves in an instant, and had their impressions taken off to perfection at a heat? Nay, he not only gives us the full prospects of things, but several unexpected peculiarities and side views, unobserved by any Painter but Homer. Nothing is so surprising as the descriptions of his battles, which take up no less than half the *Iliad,* and are supplied with so vast a variety of incidents, that no one bears a likeness to another; such different kinds of deaths, that no two heroes are wounded in the same manner; and such a profusion of noble ideas, that every battle rises above the last in greatness, horror, and confusion. It is certain there is not near that number of images and descriptions in any Epic Poet; though

[10] *Peri Hupsous* ch. ix.
[11] James Duport (1606–1679), Cambridge professor of Greek and chaplain to Charles II, published his *Gnomologia Homerica* (or Homeric aphorisms) in 1660.

every one has assisted himself with a great quantity out of him: And it is evident of Virgil especially, that he has scarce any comparisons which are not drawn from his master.

If we descend from hence to the *expression,* we see the bright imagination of Homer shining out in the most enlivened forms of it. We acknowledge him the father of poetical diction, the first who taught that *language of the Gods* to men. His expression is like the coloring of some great masters, which discovers itself to be laid on boldly, and executed with rapidity. It is indeed the strongest and most glowing imaginable, and touched with the greatest spirit. Aristotle had reason to say, He was the only poet who had found out *living words*;[12] there are in him more daring figures and metaphors than in any good author whatever. An arrow is *impatient* to be on the wing, a weapon *thirsts* to drink the blood of an enemy, and the like. Yet his expression is never too big for the sense, but justly great in proportion to it. 'Tis the sentiment that swells and fills out the diction, which rises with it, and forms itself about it: And in the same degree that a thought is warmer, an expression will be brighter; as that is more strong, this will become more perspicuous: Like glass in the furnace, which grows to a greater magnitude and refines to a greater clearness, only as the breath within is more powerful, and the heat more intense.

To throw his language more out of prose, Homer seems to have affected the *compound epithets.* This was a sort of composition peculiarly proper to poetry, not only as it heightened the *diction,* but as it assisted and filled the *numbers* with greater sound and pomp, and likewise conduced in some measure to thicken the *images.* On this last consideration I cannot but attribute these also to the fruitfulness of his invention, since (as he has managed them) they are a sort of supernumerary pictures of the persons or things to which they are joined. We see the motion of Hector's plumes in the epithet Κορυθαίολος,[13] the landscape of mount Neritus in that of Εἰνοσίφυλλος,[14] and so of others, which particular images could not have been insisted

[12] *Poetics* ch. xxiv.
[13] *Iliad* ii. 816 and elsewhere: with glancing helm.
[14] *Iliad* ii. 632: with quivering foliage.

upon so long as to express them in a description (though but of a single line) without diverting the reader too much from the principal action or figure. As a Metaphor is a short simile, one of these Epithets is a short description.

Lastly, if we consider his *versification,* we shall be sensible what a share of praise is due to his invention in that. He was not satisfied with his language as he found it settled in any one part of Greece, but searched through its differing *dialects* with this particular view, to beautify and perfect his numbers: He considered these as they had a greater mixture of vowels or consonants, and accordingly employed them as the verse required either a greater smoothness or strength. What he most affected was the *Ionic,* which has a peculiar sweetness from its never using contractions, and from its custom of resolving the diphthongs into two syllables: so as to make the words open themselves with a more spreading and sonorous fluency. With this he mingled the *Attic* contractions, the broader *Doric,* and the feebler *Aeolic,* which often rejects its aspirate, or takes off its accent; and completed this variety by altering some letters with the licence of poetry. Thus his measures, instead of being fetters to his sense, were always in readiness to run along with the warmth of his rapture, and even to give a further representation of his notions, in the correspondence of their sounds to what they signified. Out of all these he has derived that harmony, which makes us confess he had not only the richest head, but the finest ear in the world. This is so great a truth, that whoever will but consult the tune of his verses, even without understanding them (with the same sort of diligence as we daily see practised in the case of Italian Operas) will find more sweetness, variety, and majesty of sound, than in any other language or poetry. The beauty of his numbers is allowed by the critics to be copied but faintly by Virgil himself, though they are so just to ascribe it to the nature of the Latin tongue: Indeed the Greek has some advantages both from the natural *sound* of its *words,* and the turn and *cadence* of its *verse,* which agree with the genius of no other language. Virgil was very sensible of this, and used the utmost diligence in working up a more intractable language to whatsoever graces it was capable of; and in particular never failed to bring the sound of his line to a beautiful agreement with its sense. If the Grecian poet has not been so frequently celebrated on this account as the Roman, the only reason is, that fewer critics have understood one language than the other. Dionysius of Halicarnassus has pointed out many of our author's beauties in this kind, in his treatise of the *Composition of Words*,[15] and others will be taken notice of in the course of my Notes. It suffices at present to observe of his numbers, that they flow with so much ease, as to make one imagine Homer had no other care than to transcribe as fast as the *Muses* dictated; and at the same time with so much force and inspiriting vigor, that they awaken and raise us like the sound of a trumpet. They roll along as a plentiful river, always in motion, and always full; while we are borne away by a tide of verse, the most rapid, and yet the most smooth imaginable.

Thus on whatever side we contemplate Homer, what principally strikes us is his *invention*. It is that which forms the character of each part of his work; and accordingly we find it to have made his fable more *extensive* and *copious* than any other, his manners more *lively* and *strongly marked*, his speeches more *affecting* and *transported*, his sentiments more *warm* and *sublime*, his images and descriptions more *full* and *animated*, his expression more *raised* and *daring*, and his numbers more *rapid* and *various*. I hope, in what has been said of Virgil, with regard to any of these heads, I have no way derogated from his character. Nothing is more absurd or endless, than the common method of comparing eminent writers by an opposition of particular passages in them, and forming a judgment from thence of their merit upon the whole. We ought to have a certain knowledge of the principal character and distinguishing excellence of each: It is in *that* we are to consider him, and in proportion to his degree in *that* we are to admire him. No author or man ever excelled all the world in more than one faculty; and as Homer has done this in *invention*, Virgil has in *judgment*. Not that we are to think Homer wanted judgment, because Virgil had it in a more eminent degree; or that Virgil

[15] A Greek rhetorician living at Rome in the time of Augustus, author of works on the Greek orators and of the treatise *Peri Suntheseōs Onomatōn*.

wanted invention, because Homer possessed a larger share of it: Each of these great authors had more of both than perhaps any man besides, and are only said to have less in comparison with one another. Homer was the greater genius, Virgil the better artist. In one we most admire the man, in the other the work. Homer hurries and transports us with a commanding impetuosity. Virgil leads us with an attractive majesty: Homer scatters with a generous profusion, Virgil bestows with a careful magnificence: Homer, like the Nile, pours out his riches with a boundless overflow; Virgil, like a river in its banks, with a gentle and constant stream. When we behold their battles, methinks the two Poets resemble the Heroes they celebrate: Homer, boundless and irresistible as Achilles, bears all before him, and shines more and more as the tumult increases; Virgil, calmly daring like Aeneas, appears undisturbed in the midst of the action; disposes all about him, and conquers with tranquillity. And when we look upon their machines, Homer seems like his own Jupiter in his terrors, shaking Olympus, scattering the lightnings, and firing the Heavens; Virgil, like the same power in his benevolence, counselling with the Gods, laying plans for empires, and regularly ordering his whole creation.

But after all, it is with great parts as with great virtues, they naturally border on some imperfection; and it is often hard to distinguish exactly where the virtue ends, or the fault begins. As prudence may sometimes sink to suspicion, so may a great judgment decline to coldness; and as magnanimity may run up to profusion or extravagance, so may a great invention to redundancy or wildness. If we look upon Homer in this view, we shall perceive the chief *objections* against him to proceed from so noble a cause as the excess of this faculty.

Among these we may reckon some of his *marvelous fictions,* upon which so much criticism has been spent, as surpassing all the bounds of probability. Perhaps it may be with great and superior souls, as with gigantic bodies, which exerting themselves with unusual strength, exceed what is commonly thought the due proportion of parts, to become miracles in the whole; and like the old heroes of that make, commit something near extravagance, amidst a series of glorious and inimitable performances. Thus Homer has his *speaking horses,* and Virgil his *myrtles distilling blood,*[16] where the latter has not so much as contrived the easy intervention of a Deity to save the probability.

It is owing to the same vast invention, that his *Similes* have been thought too exuberant and full of circumstances. The force of this faculty is seen in nothing more, than in its inability to confine itself to the single circumstance upon which the comparison is grounded: It runs out into embellishments of additional images, which however are so managed as not to overpower the main one. His similes are like pictures, where the principal figure has not only its proportion given agreeable to the original, but is also set off with occasional ornaments and prospects. The same will account for his manner of heaping a number of comparisons together in one breath, when his fancy suggested to him at once so many various and correspondent images. The reader will easily extend this observation to more objections of the same kind.

If there are others which seem rather to charge him with a defect or narrowness of genius, than an excess of it; those seeming defects will be found upon examination to proceed wholly from the nature of the times he lived in. Such are his *grosser representations* of the *Gods,* and the vicious and *imperfect manners* of his *Heroes,* which will be treated of in the following[a] *Essay:* But I must here speak a word of the latter, as it is a point generally carried into extremes, both by the censurers and defenders of Homer. It must be a strange partiality to antiquity, to think with Madam Dacier, "that[b] those times and manners are so much the more excellent, as they are more contrary to ours." Who can be so prejudiced in their favor as to magnify the felicity of those ages, when a spirit of revenge and cruelty, joined

[16] *Iliad* xix. 404–17; *Aeneid* iii. 19–46.
[a] See the Articles of Theology and Morality, in the third part of the Essay. [P.] [*An Essay on the Life, Writings, and Learning of Homer,* drafted by Pope's friend Thomas Parnell, followed the Preface in the volume of 1715.]
[b] Preface to her Homer. [P.] [Her translation of the *Iliad,* Paris, 1711. Anne Dacier (1654–1720) was the wife of another classical scholar, André Dacier, an editor of Aristotle's *Poetics.* Both Daciers are often cited in Pope's annotations of the *Iliad.*]

with the practice of rapine and robbery, reigned through the world; when no mercy was shown but for the sake of lucre, when the greatest Princes were put to the sword, and their wives and daughters made slaves and concubines? On the other side, I would not be so delicate as those modern critics, who are shocked at the *servile offices* and mean employments in which we sometimes see the Heroes of Homer engaged. There is a pleasure in taking a view of that simplicity in opposition to the luxury of succeeding ages, in beholding Monarchs without their guards, Princes tending their flocks, and Princesses drawing water from the springs. When we read Homer, we ought to reflect that we are reading the most ancient author in the heathen world; and those who consider him in this light, will double their pleasure in the perusal of him. Let them think they are growing acquainted with nations and people that are now no more; that they are stepping almost three thousand years back into the remotest Antiquity, and entertaining themselves with a clear and surprising vision of things no where else to be found, the only true mirror of that ancient world. By this means alone their greatest obstacles will vanish; and what usually creates their dislike, will become a satisfaction.

This consideration may further serve to answer for the constant use of the same *epithets* to his Gods and Heroes, such as the *far-darting* Phœbus, the *blue-eyed* Pallas, the *swift-footed* Achilles, etc. which some have censured as impertinent and tediously repeated. Those of the Gods depended upon the powers and offices then believed to belong to them, and had contracted a weight and veneration from the rites and solemn devotions in which they were used: they were a sort of attributes with which it was a matter of religion to salute them on all occasions, and which it was an irreverence to omit. As for the epithets of great men, Mons. Boileau is of opinion,[17] that they were in the nature of *Surnames,* and repeated as such; for the Greeks having no names derived from their fathers, were obliged to add some other

[17] Boileau's translation of Longinus and his Preface (1674) helped to stimulate literary debates, to which he himself contributed further with twelve *Réflexions Critiques sur quelques Passages du Rhéteur Longin* (1694–1713). The opinion cited by Pope occurs in the ninth *Réflexion.*

distinction of each person; either naming his parents expressly, or his place of birth, profession, or the like: As Alexander the son of Philip, Herodotus of Halicarnassus, Diogenes the Cynic, etc.[18] Homer therefore complying with the custom of his country, used such distinctive additions as better agreed with poetry. And indeed we have something parallel to these in modern times, such as the names of Harold Harefoot, Edmund Ironside, Edward Longshanks, Edward the Black Prince,[19] etc. If yet this be thought to account better for the propriety than for the repetition, I shall add add a further conjecture. Hesiod, dividing the world into its different ages, has placed a fourth age between the brazen and the iron one, of *Heroes distinct from other men, a divine race, who fought at* Thebes *and* Troy, are called *Demi-Gods, and live by the care of* Jupiter *in the islands of the blessed.*[c] Now among the divine honors which were paid them, they might have this also in common with the Gods, not to be mentioned without the solemnity of an epithet, and such as might be acceptable to them by its celebrating their families, actions, or qualities.

What other cavils have been raised against Homer, are such as hardly deserve a reply, but will yet be taken notice of as they occur in the course of the work. Many have been occasioned by an injudicious endeavor to exalt Virgil; which is much the same, as if one should think to raise the superstructure by undermining the foundation: One would imagine by the whole course of their parallels, that these Critics never so much as heard of Homer's having written first; a consideration which whoever compares these two Poets, ought to have always in his eye. Some accuse him for the same things which they overlook or praise in the other; as when they prefer the fable and moral of the *Aeneis* to those

---

[18] Alexander the Great; the fifth-century Greek historian; the philosopher who asked Alexander to step out of his sunlight.
[19] Harold I, Harefoot, King of the English (d. 1040); Edmund II, Ironside, King of the English (d. 1016), known for bodily strength; Edward I, Longshanks, King of England (d. 1307); Edward, Prince of Wales (d. 1376), named the Black Prince after his victory, perhaps in black armor, at the battle of Crécy (1346).
[c] Hesiod, Op. et Dier. lib. i. v. 155, etc. [P.] [*Works and Days,* ll. 159–169.]

of the *Iliad,* for the same reasons which might set the *Odyssey* above the *Aeneis*: as that the Hero is a wiser man; and the action of the one more beneficial to his country than that of the other: Or else they blame him for not doing what he never designed; as because Achilles is not as good and perfect a prince as Aeneas, when the very moral of his poem required a contrary character: It is thus that Rapin judges in his comparison of Homer and Virgil.[20] Others select those particular passages of Homer which are not so labored as some that Virgil drew out of them: This is the whole management of Scaliger in his *Poetice*.[21] Others quarrel with what they take for low and mean expressions, sometimes through a false delicacy and refinement, oftener from an ignorance of the graces of the original; and then triumph in the awkwardness of their own translations: This is the conduct of Perrault in his *Parallels*.[22] Lastly, there are others, who, pretending to a fairer proceeding, distinguish between the personal merit of Homer, and that of his *work*; but when they come to assign the causes of the great reputation of the *Iliad,* they found it upon the ignorance of his times, and the prejudice of those that followed: And in pursuance of this principle, they make those accidents (such as the contention of the cities, etc.)[23] to be the causes of his fame, which were in reality the consequences of his merit. The same might as well be said of Virgil, or any great author, whose general character will infallibly raise many casual additions to their reputation. This is the method of Mons. de la Motte;[24] who yet confesses upon the whole, that in

[20] René Rapin, *Comparaison d'Homère et de Virgile,* 1668.

[21] J. C. Scaliger, *Poetices Libri Septem,* Lyons and Geneva, 1561.

[22] Charles Perrault, *Parallèle des Anciens et des Modernes,* 4 volumes, Paris, 1688–1696. Perrault was the leader of the Moderns, and Boileau (Nicolas Boileau-Despréaux) the leader of the Ancients in a debate which generated many volumes of Homeric criticism during the later seventeenth century in France. Pope drew copiously upon the French sources. See the summary by Maynard Mack in the Introduction to his edition of Pope's *Iliad* (*Twickenham Poems of Pope,* Vol. vii, pp. xxxix–xli) and the further account by Norman Callan (pp. lxxi-cvii).

[23] Early allusions to Homer mention more than seven cities as claiming to be his birthplace.

[24] Antoine Houdart de la Motte, *Discours sur Homère,* 1714.

whatever age Homer had lived, he must have been the greatest
poet of his nation, and that he may be said in this sense to be
the master even of those who surpassed him.

In all these objections we see nothing that contradicts his
title to the honor of the chief *Invention*; and as long as this
(which is indeed the characteristic of Poetry itself) remains un-
equalled by his followers, he still continues superior to them.
A cooler judgment may commit fewer faults, and be more ap-
proved in the eyes of *one sort* of Critics: but that warmth of
fancy will carry the loudest and most universal applauses, which
holds the heart of a reader under the strongest enchantment.
Homer not only appears the Inventor of poetry, but excels all
the inventors of other arts in this, that he has swallowed upon
the honor of those who succeeded him. What he has done
admitted no increase, it only left room for contraction or regula-
tion. He showed all the stretch of fancy at once; and if he has
failed in some of his flights, it was but because he attempted
everything. A work of this kind seems like a mighty Tree which
rises from the most vigorous seed, is improved with industry,
flourishes, and produces the finest fruit; nature and art conspire
to raise it; pleasure and profit join to make it valuable: and they
who find the justest faults, have only said, that a few branches
(which run luxuriant through a richness of nature) might be
lopped into form to give it a more regular appearance.

Having now spoken of the beauties and defects of the
original, it remains to treat of the translation, with the same view
to the chief characteristic. As far as *that* is seen in the main
parts of the Poem, such as the fable, manners, and sentiments, no
translator can prejudice it but by willful omissions or contrac-
tions. As it also breaks out in every particular image, description,
and simile; whoever lessens or too much softens those, takes off
from this chief character. It is the first grand duty of an inter-
preter to give his author entire and unmaimed; and for the rest,
the diction and versification only are his proper province; since
these must be his own, but the others he is to take as he finds
them.[25]

[25] Consult Pope's *Iliad* or *Odyssey*, or, for a start, his translation of *Odys-*

It should then be considered what methods may afford some equivalent in our language for the graces of these in the Greek. It is certain no literal translation can be just to an excellent original in a superior language: but it is a great mistake to imagine (as many have done) that a rash paraphrase can make amends for this general defect; which is no less in danger to lose the spirit of an ancient, by deviating into the modern manners of expression. If there be sometimes a darkness, there is often a light in antiquity, which nothing better preserves than a version almost literal. I know no liberties one ought to take, but those which are necessary for transfusing the spirit of the original, and supporting the poetical style of the translation: And I will venture to say, there have not been more men misled in former times by a servile dull adherence to the letter, than have been deluded in ours by a chimerical insolent hope of raising and improving their author. It is not to be doubted that the *fire* of the poem is what a translator should principally regard, as it is most likely to expire in his managing: However, it is his safest way to be content with preserving this to his utmost in the whole, without endeavoring to be more than he finds his author is, in any particular place. 'Tis a great secret in writing to know when to be plain, and when poetical and figurative; and it is what Homer will teach us, if we will but follow modestly in his footstep. Where his diction is bold and lofty, let us raise ours as high as we can; but where his is plain and humble, we ought not to be deterred from imitating him by the fear of incurring the censure of a mere English Critic. Nothing that belongs to Homer seems to have been more commonly mistaken than the just pitch of his style: Some of his translators having swelled into fustian in a proud confidence of the *sublime*; others sunk into flatness in a cold and timorous notion of *simplicity*. Methinks I see these different followers of Homer, some sweating and straining after him by violent leaps and bounds (the certain

sey vii. 112-32 quoted in his *Guardian* No. 173, above pp. 37–38, and his *Episode of Sarpedon,* below pp. 160–170. Is it likely that Pope's version is a literal translation of the Greek of Homer in *all* respects except the diction and the versification? Cf. Maynard Mack, *Twickenham Pope,* Vol. vii, pp.l-lxxi; and Douglas Knight and Robert Fagles, pp. clxiv-ccxxi.

signs of false mettle) others slowly and servilely creeping in his train, while the Poet himself is all the time proceeding with an unaffected and equal majesty before them. However, of the two extremes one could sooner pardon frenzy than frigidity: No author is to be envied for such commendations as he may gain by that character of style, which his friends must agree together to call *simplicity,* and the rest of the world will call *dullness.* There is a graceful and dignified simplicity, as well as a bald and sordid one, which differ as much from each other as the air of a plain man from that of a sloven: 'Tis one thing to be tricked up, and another not to be dressed at all. Simplicity is the mean between ostentation and rusticity.

This pure and noble simplicity is nowhere in such perfection as in the *Scripture* and our Author. One may affirm, with all respect to the inspired writings, that the *divine Spirit* made use of no other words but what were intelligible and common to men at that time, and in that part of the world; and as Homer is the author nearest to those, his style must of course bear a greater resemblance to the sacred books than that of any other writer. This consideration (together with what has been observed of the parity of some of his thoughts) may methinks induce a translator on the one hand, to give in to several of those general phrases and manners of expression, which have attained a veneration even in our language from being used in the Old Testament; as on the other, to avoid those which have been appropriated to the Divinity, and in a manner consigned to mystery and religion.

For a further preservation of this air of simplicity, a particular care should be taken to express with all plainness those *moral sentences* and *proverbial speeches* which are so numerous in this Poet. They have something venerable, and as I may say oracular, in that unadorned gravity and shortness with which they are delivered: a grace which would be utterly lost by endeavoring to give them what we call a more ingenious (that is, a more modern) turn in the paraphrase.

Perhaps the mixture of some Grecisms and old words after the manner of Milton, if done without too much affectation, might not have an ill effect in a version of this particular work, which most of any other seems to require a venerable antique cast. But certainly the use of modern terms of war and government, such as *platoon, campaign, junto,* or the like (into which some of his translators have fallen) cannot be allowable; those only excepted, without which it is impossible to treat the subjects in any living language.

There are two peculiarities in Homer's diction which are a sort of *marks* or *moles,* by which every common eye distinguishes him at first sight: Those who are not his greatest admirers look upon them as defects; and those who are, seem pleased with them as beauties. I speak of his *compound epithets,* and of his *repetitions.* Many of the former cannot be done literally into English without destroying the purity of our language. I believe such should be retained as slide easily of themselves into an English compound, without violence to the ear or to the received rules of composition; as well as those which have received a sanction from the authority of our best Poets, and are become familiar through their use of them; such as the *cloud-compelling* Jove, etc. As for the rest, whenever any can be as fully and significantly expressed in a single word as in a compounded one, the course to be taken is obvious.

Some that cannot be so turned as to preserve their full image by one or two words, may have justice done them by circumlocution; as the epithet εἰνοσίφυλλος to a mountain, would appear little or ridiculous translated literally *leaf-shaking,* but affords a majestic idea in the *periphrasis: The lofty mountain shakes his waving woods.* Others that admit of differing significations, may receive an advantage by a judicious variation, according to the occasions on which they are introduced. For example, the epithet of Apollo, ἑκηβόλος, or *far-shooting,* is capable of two explications; one literal in respect of the darts and bow, the ensign of that God; the other allegorical with regard to the rays of the sun: Therefore in such places where Apollo is represented as a God in person, I would use the former interpretation; and where the effects of the sun are described, I would make choice of the latter. Upon the whole, it will be necessary to avoid that perpetual repetition of the same epithets which we find in Homer, and which, though it might be accommodated (as has been already shown) to the ear of those times, is by no means so to ours: But one may wait for opportunities of placing them, where they derive an additional beauty from the occasions on which they are employed; and in doing this properly, a translator may at once show his fancy and his judgment.

As for Homer's *Repetitions,* we may divide them into three sorts; of whole narrations and speeches, of single sentences, and of one verse or hemistich. I hope it is not impossible to have such a regard to these, as neither to lose so known a mark of the author on the one hand, nor to offend the reader too much on the other. The repetition is not ungraceful in those speeches where the dignity of the speaker renders it a sort of insolence to alter his words; as in the messages from Gods to men, or from higher powers to inferiors in concerns of state, or where the ceremonial religion seems to require it, in the solemn forms of prayers, oaths, or the like. In other cases, I believe the best rule is to be guided by the nearness, or distance, at which the repetitions are placed in the original: When they follow too close, one may vary the expression, but it is a question whether a professed translator be authorized to omit any: If they be tedious, the author is to answer for it.

It only remains to speak of the *Versification.* Homer (as has been said) is perpetually applying the sound to the sense, and varying it on every new subject. This is indeed one of the most exquisite beauties of poetry, and attainable by very few: I know only of Homer eminent for it in the Greek, and Virgil in Latin. I am sensible it is what may sometimes happen by chance, when a writer is warm, and fully possessed of his image: however it may be reasonably believed they designed this, in whose verse it so manifestly appears in a superior degree to all others. Few readers have the ear to be judges of it; but those who have, will see I have endeavored at this beauty.

Upon the whole, I must confess myself utterly incapable of doing justice to Homer. I attempt him in no other hope but that which one may entertain without much vanity, of giving a more tolerable copy of him than any entire translation in verse has yet done. We have only those of Chapman,[26], Hobbes,[27] and Ogilby.[28] Chapman has taken the advantage of an immeasurable length of verse, notwithstanding which, there is scarce any paraphrase more loose and rambling than his. He has frequent interpolations of four or six lines, and I remember one in the thirteenth book of the *Odyssey,* v. 312, where he has spun twenty verses out of two. He is often mistaken in so bold a manner, that one might think he deviated on purpose, if he did not in other places of his notes insist so much upon verbal trifles. He appears to have had a strong affectation of extracting new meanings out of his author, insomuch as to promise in his rhyming preface, a poem of the mysteries he had revealed in Homer: and perhaps he endeavored to strain the obvious sense to this end. His expression is involved in fustian, a fault for which he was remarkable in his original writings, as in the tragedy of *Bussy d'Ambois,* etc. In a word, the nature of the man may account for his whole performance; for he appears from his preface and remarks to have been of an arrogant turn, and an enthusiast in poetry. His own boast of having finished half the *Iliad* in less than fifteen weeks, shows with what negligence his version was performed. But that which is to be allowed him, and which very much contributed to cover his defects, is a daring fiery spirit that animates his translation, which is something like what one might imagine Homer himself would have writ before he arrived at years of discretion.

Hobbes has given us a correct explanation of the sense in general, but for particulars and circumstances he continually lops them, and often omits the most beautiful. As for its being esteemed a close translation, I doubt not many have been led into that error by the shortness of it, which proceeds not from

[26] George Chapman, poet, dramatist, and translator, published *Seven Books of the Iliads of Homer* in English "fourteeners," 1598; *Twelve Books,* 1610; and his complete *Iliads of Homer,* 1611.

[27] The philosopher Thomas Hobbes published his *Homer's Iliad in English* in 1676.

[28] John Ogilby, miscellaneous author and printer, published *Homer, His Iliads Translated,* an illustrated folio, in 1660. As a boy of eight Pope read Ogilby's *Iliad*—"that great edition with pictures"—and he recalled the experience "with a sort of rapture" in the year before his death.

his following the original line by line, but from the contractions above-mentioned. He sometimes omits whole similes and sentences, and is now and then guilty of mistakes, into which no writer of his learning could have fallen, but through carelessness. His poetry, as well as Ogilby's, is too mean for criticism.

It is a great loss to the poetical world that Mr. Dryden did not live to translate the *Iliad*. He has left us only the first book, and a small part of the sixth;[29] in which if he has in some places not truly interpreted the sense, or preserved the antiquities, it ought to be excused on account of the haste he was obliged to write in. He seems to have had too much regard to Chapman, whose words he sometimes copies, and has unhappily followed him in passages where he wanders from the original. However, had he translated the whole work, I would no more have attempted Homer after him than Virgil, his version of whom (notwithstanding some human errors) is the most noble and spirited translation I know in any language. But the fate of great geniuses is like that of great ministers, though they are confessedly the first in the commonwealth of letters, they must be envied and calumniated only for being at the head of it.

That which in my opinion ought to be the endeavor of any one who translates Homer, is above all things to keep alive that spirit and fire which makes his chief character: In particular places, where the sense can bear any doubt, to follow the strongest and most poetical, as most agreeing with that character; to copy him in all the variations of his style, and the different modulations of his numbers; to preserve, in the more active or descriptive parts, a warmth and elevation; in the more sedate or narrative, a plainness and solemnity; in the speeches, a fullness and perspicuity; in the sentences, a shortness and gravity: Not to neglect even the little figures and turns on the words, nor sometimes the very cast of the periods; neither to omit nor confound any rites or customs of antiquity: Perhaps too he ought to include the whole in a shorter compass, than has hitherto been done by any translator who has tolerably preserved

[29] Dryden's translation of *Iliad* i had appeared in his *Fables,* 1700, and his *Last Parting of Hector and Andromache,* from *Iliad* vi, in his *Examen Poeticum,* 1693.

either the sense or poetry. What I would further recommend
to him, is to study his author rather from his own text, than
from any commentaries, how learned soever, or whatever figure
they may make in the estimation of the world; to consider him
attentively in comparison with Virgil above all the ancients, and
with Milton above all the moderns. Next these, the Archbishop
of Cambray's *Telemachus*[30] may give him the truest idea of
the spirit and turn of our author, and Bossu's admirable treatise
of the Epic poem[31] the justest notion of his design and conduct.
But after all, with whatever judgment and study a man may
proceed, or with whatever happiness he may perform such a
work, he must hope to please but a few; those only who have
at once a taste of poetry, and competent learning. For to satisfy
such as want either, is not in the nature of this undertaking;
since a mere modern wit can like nothing that is not *modern,*
and a pedant nothing that is not Greek.

What I have done is submitted to the public, from whose
opinions I am prepared to learn; though I fear no judges so
little as our best poets, who are most sensible of the weight of
this task. As for the worst, whatever they shall please to say,
they may give me some concern as they are unhappy men, but
none as they are malignant writers. I was guided in this transla-
tion by judgments very different from theirs, and by persons
for whom they can have no kindness, if an old observation be
true, that the strongest antipathy in the world is that of fools
to men of wit. Mr. Addison was the first whose advice deter-
mined me to undertake this task, who was pleased to write to
me upon that occasion in such terms, as I cannot repeat without
vanity.[32] I was obliged to Sir Richard Steele for a very early
recommendation of my undertaking to the public. Dr. Swift
promoted my interest with that warmth with which he always

---

[30] François de Salignac de la Mothe-Fénelon, eminent Quietist divine and
tutor to the son of the French Dauphin, wrote his gracefully moralized
prose *Aventures de Télémaque* (1699) for the instruction of his royal
pupil.
[31] René le Bossu was author of a *Traité du Poëme Epique* (Paris, 1675)
—"dried preparation of epic," as George Saintsbury has called it, or, as
we might say, "instant epic."
[32] See Addison to Pope, 26 October 1713, in *The Correspondence of Alex-
ander Pope,* ed. George Sherburn (1956), i 196.

serves his friend.[33] The humanity and frankness of Sir Samuel Garth[34] are what I never knew wanting on any occasion. I must also acknowledge with infinite pleasure, the many friendly offices, as well as sincere criticisms of Mr. Congreve, who had led me the way in translating some parts of Homer.[35] I must add the names of Mr. Rowe[36] and Dr. Parnell,[37] though I shall take a further opportunity of doing justice to the last, whose good-nature (to give it a great panegyric) is no less extensive than his learning. The favor of these gentlemen is not entirely undeserved by one who bears them so true an affection. But what can I say of the honor so many of the *Great* have done me, while the *first names* of the age appear as my subscribers, and the most distinguished patrons and ornaments of learning as my chief encouragers. Among these it is a particular pleasure to me to find, that my highest obligations are to such who have done most honor to the name of Poet: That his Grace the Duke of Buckingham was not displeased I should undertake the author to whom he has given (in his excellent *Essay*) so complete a Praise.

> Read *Homer* once, and you can read no more;
> For all Books else appear so mean, so poor,
> Verse will seem Prose: but still persist to read,
> And *Homer* will be all the Books you need.[38]

---

[33] See *Correspondence* i. 245, Pope to Charles Jervas, 27 August 1714.

[34] Physician, author of a burlesque poem *The Dispensary,* 1699.

[35] The dramatist William Congreve's translations of two passages in *Iliad* xxiv, *Priam's Lamentation and Petition to Achilles* and *The Lamentations of Hecuba, Andromache, and Helen over Hector,* appeared in Dryden's *Examen Poeticum,* 1693. In 1720, at the end of the *Iliad,* Pope dedicated the entire work to Congreve.

[36] Nicholas Rowe, editor of Shakespeare (1709) and poet laureate (1715). Pope wrote an epilogue for his "She Tragedy" *Jane Shore* (1714), used his Shakespeare as his own basic text (1725), and wrote his epitaph in 1718. See below, Pope's Preface to *Shakespeare.*

[37] Thomas Parnell, Irish archdeacon and poet, friend of Pope and Swift, contributed the introductory *Essay on the Life, Writings, and Learning of Homer* to Pope's *Iliad* (above p. 145), and also helped Pope with the Homeric commentators (*Correspondence* i. 225).

[38] John Sheffield, third Earl of Mulgrave, published *An Essay upon Poetry* in 1682; Pope quotes 11. 323–326. He was later first duke of Buckingham.

That the Earl of Halifax[39] was one of the first to favor me, of whom it is hard to say whether the advancement of the polite arts is more owing to his generosity or his example. That such a Genius as my Lord Bolingbroke,[40] not more distinguished in the great scenes of business, than in all the useful and entertaining parts of learning, has not refused to be the critic of these sheets, and the patron of their writer. And that the noble author of the Tragedy of *Heroic Love*,[41] has continued his partiality to me, from my writing *Pastorals*, to my attempting the *Iliad*. I cannot deny myself the pride of confessing, that I have had the advantage not only of their advice for the conduct in general, but their correction of several particulars of this translation.

I could say a great deal of the pleasure of being distinguished by the Earl of Carnarvon,[42] but it is almost absurd to particularize any one generous action in a person whose whole life is a continued series of them. Mr. Stanhope, the present Secretary of State,[43] will pardon my desire of having it known that he was pleased to promote this affair. The particular zeal of Mr. Harcourt (the son of the late Lord Chancellor)[44] gave

He died in 1721, and Pope published an edition of his poetical *Works* in 1723.

[39] Charles Montagu, first Earl of Halifax, politician and patron of poets. Pope would later glance at him satirically in the portrait of Bufo in the *Epistle to Arbuthnot*.

[40] Henry St. John, Viscount Bolingbroke, Tory Secretary of State, dismissed and attainted on the accession of George I. On his return to England from France in 1723, he became a chief philosophical and political influence on Pope's *Essay on Man, Moral Essays,* and *Imitations of Horace.*

[41] George Granville, Lord Lansdowne, poet and Tory statesman, Secretary-at-War, to whom Pope dedicated *Windsor Forest* in 1713.

[42] James Brydges, Whig millionaire, patron of the arts, first Duke of Chandos, Earl of Carnarvon, owner of a magnificent mansion at Cannons, near Edgware. Pope later suffered from whispered libels that he had abused the hospitality of Chandos by satirizing him as the tasteless Timon in the moral *Epistle to Burlington*.

[43] James Stanhope, first Earl Stanhope, Whig statesman and military commander; his acquaintance with Pope is not otherwise known.

[44] Simon Harcourt, M.P., only son of Pope's friend the first Viscount Harcourt, helped in getting subscriptions to the *Iliad*. He died in 1720, and Pope wrote his epitaph for the church at Stanton-Harcourt in Oxfordshire.

me a proof how much I am honored in a share of his friendship. I must attribute to the same motive that of several others of my friends, to whom all acknowledgments are rendered unnecessary by the privileges of a familiar correspondence: And I am satisfied I can no way better oblige men of their turn, than by my silence.

In short, I have found more patrons than ever Homer wanted. He would have thought himself happy to have met the same favor at Athens, that has been shown me by its learned rival, the University of Oxford.[45] And I can hardly envy him those pompous honors he received after death, when I reflect on the enjoyment of so many agreeable obligations, and easy friendships, which make the satisfaction of life. This distinction is the more to be acknowledged, as it is shown to one whose pen has never gratified the prejudices of particular *parties,* or the vanities of particular *men.* Whatever the success may prove, I shall never repent of an undertaking in which I have experienced the candor and friendship of so many persons of merit; and in which I hope to pass some of those years of youth that are generally lost in a circle of follies, after a manner neither wholly unuseful to others, nor disagreeable to myself.

[45] Ten Oxford colleges and a number of individual Fellows appear among the 575 subscribers listed in the first volume of Pope's *Iliad.*

THE EPISODE OF SARPEDON,

Translated from the Twelfth *and* Sixteenth *Books of* Homer's *ILIADS*

[A SPECIMEN OF POPE'S HOMER]

THE ARGUMENT[1]

Sarpedon, the Son of *Jupiter*, commanded the *Lycians* who came to the Aid of *Troy*. In the first Battle when *Diomede* had put the *Trojans* to flight, he encouraged *Hector* to rally, and signalized himself by the Death of *Tlepolemus*. Afterwards when the Greeks had raised a Fortification to cover their Fleet, which the *Trojans* endeavored to overthrow, this Prince was the Occasion of effecting it. He incites *Glaucus* to second him in this Action by an admirable Speech, which has been rendered in English by Sir *John Denham*,[2] after whom the Translator had not the Vanity to attempt it for any other reason, than that the Episode must have been very imperfect without so Noble a part of it.

[1] The *Episode of Sarpedon* was published by Jacob Tonson in *Poetical Miscellanies: The Sixth Part*, on 2 May 1709. In the same volume appeared Pope's *Pastorals* and his *January and May*, from Chaucer. The three pieces were Pope's first publication. The two parts of the *Episode*, with slight alterations, reappear in Volumes iii and iv of Pope's *Iliad*, 1717–1718. The text used here is normalized from that of 1709.

[2] *Sarpedon's Speech to Glaucus in the 12th of Homer*, first printed in Denham's *Poems and Translations*, 1668.

THUS *Hector,* great in Arms, contends in vain
To fix the Fortune of the fatal Plain,
Nor *Troy* could conquer, nor the *Greeks* would yield,
'Till bold *Sarpedon* rushed into the Field;
For Mighty *Jove* inspired with Martial Flame   5
His Godlike Son,[3] and urged him on to Fame.
In Arms he shines, conspicuous from afar,
And bears aloft his ample Shield in Air,
Within whose Orb the thick Bull-hides were rolled,
Ponderous with Brass, and bound with ductile Gold;   10
And while two pointed Javelins arm his Hands,
Majestic moves along, and leads his *Lycian* Bands.
    So pressed with Hunger, from the Mountain's Brow,
Descends a Lion on the Flocks below;
So stalks the Lordly Savage o'er the Plain,   15
In sullen Majesty, and stern Disdain:
In vain loud Mastiffs bay him from afar,
And Shepherds gall him with an Iron War;
Regardless, furious, he pursues his way;
He foams, he roars, he rends the panting Prey.   20
    Resolved alike, Divine *Sarpedon* glows
With generous Rage, that drives him on the Foes.
He views the Towers, and meditates their Fall;
To sure Destruction dooms the *Grecian* Wall;
Then casting on his Friend an ardent Look,   25
Fired with the Thirst of Glory, thus he spoke.
    Why boast we, *Glaucus,* our extended Reign,[4]
Where *Xanthus'* Streams enrich the *Lycian* Plain?
Our numerous Herds that range each fruitful Field,
And Hills where Vines their Purple Harvest yield?   30

[3] His mother was Laodamia, daughter of Bellerophon (rider of the winged horse Pegasus and conqueror of the Amazons), who was grandson of the Corinthian king Sisyphus.

[4] This celebrated epitome (11. 27-52) of the Homeric warrior's Stoic and somber code of glory, becomes the background of one of Pope's most deliberate and effective mock-heroic passages, the speech of Clarissa to Belinda (*Rape of the Lock*, v. 9–34) recommending the virtue of maidenly good humor. See above p. 111. The Glaucus whom Sarpedon addresses is his cousin, another grandson of the hero Bellerophon.

Our foaming Bowls with generous *Nectar* crowned,
Our Feasts enhanced with Music's sprightly Sound?
Why on those Shores are we with Joy surveyed,
Admired as Heroes, and as Gods obeyed?
Unless great Acts superior Merit prove,   35
And Vindicate the bounteous Powers above:
'Tis ours, the Dignity They give, to grace;
The first in Valor, as the first in Place:
That while with wondering Eyes our Martial Bands
Behold our Deeds transcending our Commands,   40
Such, they may cry, deserve the Sovereign State,
Whom those that Envy dare not Imitate!
Could all our Care elude the greedy Grave,
Which claims no less the Fearful than the Brave,
For Lust of Fame I should not vainly dare   45
In fighting Fields, nor urge thy Soul to War.
But since, alas, ignoble Age must come,
Disease, and Death's inexorable Doom;
The Life which others pay, let Us bestow,
And give to Fame what we to Nature owe;   50
Brave, though we fall; and honored, if we live;
Or let us Glory gain, or Glory give!
    He said, his Words the listening Chief inspire
With equal Warmth, and rouse the Warrior's Fire;
The Troops pursue their Leaders with Delight,   55
Rush to the Foe, and claim the promised Fight.
Menestheus from on high the Storm beheld,
Threatening the Fort, and blackening in the Field;
Around the Walls he gazed, to view from far
What Aid appeared t'avert th'approaching War,   60
And saw where *Teucer* with th' *Ajaces*[5] stood,
Insatiate of the Fight, and prodigal of Blood.
In vain he calls, the Din of Helms and Shields
Rings to the Skies, and echoes through the Fields,
The Gates resound, the Brazen Hinges fly,   65

[5] The two Ajaxes: the "Greater Ajax" (son of Telamon), leader of the
Salaminians, a warrior represented as stubborn in bravery to the point
of stupidity; and a lesser Ajax (son of Oïleus), captain of the Locrians.

While each is bent to conquer or to die.
Then thus to *Thoös;*—Hence with speed (he said)
And urge the bold *Ajaces* to our Aid;
Their Strength united best may help to bear
The bloody Labors of the doubtful War: 70
Hither the *Lycian* Princes bend their Course,
The best and bravest of the *Trojan* Force.
But if too fiercely, there, the Foes contend,
Let *Telamon* at least our Towers defend,
And *Teucer* haste, with his unerring Bow,[6]   75
To share the Danger, and repel the Foe.
    Swift as the Word, the Herald speeds along
The lofty Ramparts, through the Warlike Throng,
And finds the Heroes, bathed in Sweat and Gore,
Opposed in Combat on the dusty Shore.   80
Straight to the Fort great *Ajax* turned his Care,
And thus bespoke his Brothers of the War:
Now valiant *Lycomede,* exert your Might,
And brave *Oïleus,* prove your Force in Fight:
To you I trust the Fortune of the Field,   85
'Till by this Arm the Foe shall be repelled;
That done, expect me to complete the Day:
Then, with his Sevenfold Shield, he strode away.
With equal Steps bold *Teucer* pressed the Shore,
Whose fatal Bow the strong *Pandion* bore.   90
High on the Walls appeared the *Lycian* Powers,
Like some black Tempest gathering round the Towers:
The *Greeks* oppressed, their utmost Force unite,
Prepared to labor in th'unequal Fight;
The War begins; mixed Shouts and Groans arise;   95
Tumultuous Clamor mounts, and thickens in the Skies.
Fierce *Ajax* first th'advancing Host invades,
And sends the brave *Epicles* to the Shades,
Sarpedon's Friend; Across the Warrior's Way,
Rent from the Walls, a Rocky Fragment lay;   100
In modern Ages not the strongest Swain

---

[6] Half-brother of Telamonian Ajax, the greatest archer among the Greeks attacking Troy. He sometimes shot from behind the shield of Ajax.

Could heave th'unwieldy Burthen from the Plain:
He poised, and swung it round; then tossed on high,
It flew with Force, and labored up the Sky;
Full on the *Lycian's* Helmet thundering down,   105
The ponderous Ruin crushed his battered Crown.
As skillful Divers from some Airy Steep
Headlong descend, and shoot into the Deep,
So falls *Epicles;* then in Groans expires,
And murmering from the Corpse th'unwilling Soul retires.
  While to the Ramparts daring *Glaucus* drew,   111
From *Teucer's* Hand a wingèd Arrow flew,
The bearded Shaft the destined Passage found,
And on his naked Arm inflicts a Wound.
The Chief who feared some Foe's insulting Boast   115
Might stop the Progress of his warlike Host,
Concealed the Wound, and leaping from his Height,
Retired reluctant from th'unfinished Fight.
Divine *Sarpedon* with Regret beheld
Disabled *Glaucus* slowly quit the Field;   120
His beating Breast with generous Ardor glows,
He springs to Fight, and flies upon the Foes.
Alcmaon first was doomed his Force to feel,
Deep in his Breast he plunged the pointed Steel,
Then from the yawning Wound with Fury tore   125
The Spear, pursued by gushing Streams of Gore;
Down sinks the Warrior, with a thundering Sound,
His Brazen Armor rings against the Ground.
  Swift to the Battlement the Victor flies,
Tugs with full Force, and every Nerve applies;   130
It shakes; the ponderous Stones disjointed yield;
The rolling Ruins smoke along the Field.
A mighty Breach appears, the Walls lie bare,
And like a Deluge rushes in the War.
At once bold *Teucer* draws the twanging Bow,   135
And *Ajax* sends his Javelin at the Foe;
Fixed in his Belt[7] the feathered Weapon stood,
And through his Buckler drove the trembling Wood;

---

[7] Whose belt? Study the context.

But *Jove* was present in the dire Debate,
To shield his Offspring, and avert his Fate.   140
The Prince gave back; not meditating Flight,
But urging Vengeance and severer Fight;
Then raised with Hope, and fired with Glory's Charms,
His fainting Squadrons to new Fury warms.
O where, ye *Lycians,* is the Strength you boast,   145
Your former Fame, and ancient Virtue lost?
The Breach lies open, but your Chief in vain
Attempts alone the guarded Pass to gain:
Unite, and soon that Hostile Fleet shall fall,
The Force of powerful Union conquers All.   150
      This just Rebuke inflamed the *Lycian* Crew,
They join, they thicken, and th'Assault renew;
Unmoved, th'embodied *Greeks* their Fury dare,
And fixed support the Weight of all the War:
Nor could the *Greeks* repel the *Lycian* Powers,   155
Nor the bold *Lycians* force the *Grecian* Towers.
As on the Confines of adjoining Grounds,
Two stubborn Swains with Blows dispute their Bounds;
They tug, they sweat; but neither gain, nor yield,
One Foot, one Inch, of the contended Field: 160
Thus obstinate to Death, they fight, they fall;
Nor these can keep, nor those can win the Wall:
Their Manly Breasts are pierced with many a Wound,
Loud Strokes are heard, and rattling Arms resound,
The copious Slaughter covers all the Shore,   165
And the high Ramparts drop with Human Gore.
      As when two Scales are charged with doubtful Loads,
From side to side the trembling Balance nods,
'Till poised aloft, the resting Beam suspends
Each equal Weight, nor this, nor that descends.   170
So Conquest loth for either to declare,
Levels her Wings, and hovering hangs in Air.
'Till *Hector* came, to whose Superior Might
Jove owed the Glory of the destined Fight.
Fierce as Whirlwind, up the Walls he flies,   175
And fires his Host with loud repeated Cries:
Advance ye *Trojans,* lend your valiant Hands,

Haste to the Fleet, and toss the blazing Brands!
They hear, they run, and gathering at his Call,
Raise scaling Engines, and ascend the Wall: 180
Around the Works a Wood of glittering Spears
Shoots up, and All the rising Host appears.
A ponderous Stone bold *Hector* heaved to throw,
Pointed above, and rough and gross below:
Not two strong Men th'enormous Weight could raise,   185
Such Men as live in these degenerate Days.
Yet this, as easy as a Swain would bear
The snowy Fleece, he tossed, and shook in Air:
For *Jove* upheld, and lightened of its Load
Th'unwieldy Rock, the Labor of a God.   190
Thus armed, before the folded Gates he came,
Of massy Substance and stupendous Frame,
With Iron Bars and brazen Hinges strong,
On lofty Beams of solid Timber hung.
Then thundering through the Planks, with forceful Sway,
Drives the sharp Rock; the solid Beams give way,   196
The Folds are shattered, from the crackling Door
Leap the resounding Bars, the flying Hinges roar.
Now rushing in the furious Chief appears,
Gloomy as Night, and shakes two shining Spears;   200
A dreadful Gleam from his bright Armor came,
And from his Eyeballs flashed the living Flame:
He moves a God, resistless in his Course,
And seems a Match for more than Mortal Force.
Then pouring after, through the gaping Space   205
A Tide of *Trojans* flows, and fills the Place;
The *Greeks* behold, they tremble, and they fly,
The Shore is heaped with Death, and Tumult rends the
Sky.

CONNECTION OF THE FOREGOING
WITH THE FOLLOWING PART

The Wall being forced by *Hector,* an obstinate Battle was fought before
the Ships, one of which was set on fire by the *Trojans. Patroclus* there-

upon obtaining of *Achilles* to lead out the *Myrmidons* to the Assistance of the *Greeks,* made a great Slaughter of the Enemy, 'till he was opposed by *Sarpedon.* The Combat betwixt these Two, and the Death of the latter, with the Grief of *Jupiter* for his Son, are described in the ensuing Translation, from the Sixteenth Book of the *Iliads.*

WHEN now the Chief has valiant Friends beheld
Groveling in Dust, and gasping on the Field,   210
With this Reproach his flying Host he warms,
Oh Stain to Honor! oh Disgrace of Arms!
Forsake, inglorious, the contended Plain;
This Hand unaided shall the War sustain:
The Task be mine the Hero's Strength to try,   215
Who mows whole Troops, and makes whole Armies fly.
  He said, and leaped from off his lofty Car;
Patroclus lights, and sternly waits the War.
As when two Vultures on the Mountain's Height
Stoop with their sounding Pinions to the Fight;   220
They cuff, they tear, they raise a screaming Cry;
The Desert echoes, and the Rocks reply:
The Warriors thus opposed in Arms engage,
With equal Valor, and with equal Rage.
  Jove viewed the Combat, whose Event foreseen,   225
He thus bespoke his Sister and his Queen.[8]
The Hour draws on; the Destinies ordain,
My Godlike Son shall press the *Phrygian* Plain:
Already on the Verge of Death he stands,
His Life is owed to fierce *Patroclus'* Hands.   230
What Passions in a Parent's Breast debate!
Say, shall I snatch him from Impending Fate;
And send him safe to *Lycia,* distant far
From all the Dangers and the Toils of War;
Or to his Doom my bravest Offspring yield,   235
And fatten, with Celestial Blood, the Field?
  Then thus the Goddess with the radiant Eyes:
What Words are these, O Sovereign of the Skies?

[8] Hera.

Short is the Date prescribed to Mortal Man;
Shall *Jove,* for one, extend the narrow Span,   240
Whose Bounds were fixed before his Race began?
How many Sons of Gods, foredoomed to Death,
Before proud *Ilion* must resign their Breath!
Were thine exempt, Debate would rise above,
And murmuring Powers condemn their partial *Jove.*   245
Give the bold Chief a glorious Fate in Fight;
And when th'ascending Soul has winged her Flight,
Let *Sleep* and *Death* convey, by thy Command,
The breathless Body to his Native Land.
His Friends and People, to his future Praise,   250
A Marble Tomb and Pyramid shall raise,
And lasting Honors to his Ashes give;
His Fame ('tis all the Dead can have!) shall live.
    She said; the Cloud-Compeller overcome,
Assents to Fate, and ratifies the Doom.   255
Then, touched with Grief, the weeping Heavens distilled
A Shower of Blood o'er all the fatal Field.
The God, his Eyes averting from the Plain,
Laments his Son, predestined to be slain,
Far from the *Lycian* Shores, his happy Native Reign.   260
    Now met in Arms the Combatants appear,
Each heaved the Shield, and poised the lifted Spear:
From strong *Patroclus'* Hand the Javelin fled,
And passed the Groin of valiant *Thrasymed,*
The Nerves unbraced no more his Bulk sustain,   265
He falls, and falling, bites the bloody Plain.
Two sounding Darts the *Lycian* Leader threw,
The first aloof with erring Fury flew,
The next more fatal pierced *Achilles'* Steed,
The generous *Pedasus,* of *Theban* Breed;   270
Fixed in the Shoulder's Joint, he reeled around;
Rolled in the bloody Dust, and pawed the slippery Ground.
His sudden Fall the entangled Harness broke;
Each Axle groaned; the bounding Chariot shook;
When bold *Automedon,* to disengage   275
The starting Coursers, and restrain their Rage,

Divides the Traces with his Sword, and freed
Th'encumbered Chariot from the dying Steed:
The rest move on, obedient to the Rein;
The Car rolls slowly o'er the dusty Plain.   280
     The towering Chiefs to fiercer Fight advance,
And first *Sarpedon* tossed his weighty Lance,
Which o'er the Warrior's Shoulder took its Course,
And spent, in empty Air, its dying Force.
Not so *Patroclus'* never-erring Dart;   285
Aimed at his Breast, it pierced the mortal Part
Where the strong Fibers bind the solid Heart.
Then as the stately Pine, or Poplar tall,
Hewn for the Mast of some great Admiral,
Nods, groans, and reels, 'till with a crackling Sound   290
It sinks, and spreads its Honors on the Ground;
Thus fell the King; and laid on Earth Supine,
Before his Chariot stretched his Form divine:
He grasped the Dust, distained with streaming Gore,
And, pale in Death, lay groaning on the Shore.   295
So lies a Bull beneath the Lion's Paws,
While the grim Savage grinds with foamy Jaws
The trembling Limbs, and sucks the smoking Blood;
Deep Groans and hollow Roars rebellow through the Wood.
     Then to the Leader of the *Lycian* Band,   300
The dying Chief addressed his last Command.
Glaucus, be bold, Thy Task be first to dare
The glorious Dangers of destructive War,
To lead my Troops, to combat at their Head,
Incite the Living, and supply the Dead.   305
Tell 'em, I charged them with my latest Breath,
Not unrevenged to bear *Sarpedon*'s Death.
What Grief, what Shame must *Glaucus* undergo,
If these spoiled Arms adorn a *Grecian* Foe?
Then as a Friend, and as a Warrior, fight;   310
Defend my Corpse, and conquer in my Right;
That taught by great Examples, All may try
Like thee to vanquish, or like me to die.
     He ceased; the Fates suppressed his laboring Breath,

And his Eyes darkened with the Shades of Death: 315
Th'insulting Victor with Disdain bestrode
The prostrate Prince, and on his Bosom trod;
Then drew the Weapon from his panting Heart,
The reeking Fibers clinging to the Dart;
From the wide Wound gushed out a Stream of Blood,   320
And the Soul issued in the Purple Flood.
    Then thus to *Phoebus,* in the Realms above,
Spoke from his Throne the Cloud-compelling *Jove*:
Descend my *Phoebus,* on the *Phrygian* Plain,
And from the Fight convey *Sarpedon* slain;   325
Then bathe his Body in the crystal Flood,
With Dust dishonored, and deformed with Blood:
O'er all his Limbs *Ambrosial* Odors shed,
And with Celestial Robes adorn the mighty Dead.
Those Honors paid, his sacred Corpse bequeath   330
To the soft Arms of silent *Sleep* and *Death*;
They to his Friends the mournful Charge shall bear;
His Friends a Tomb and Pyramid shall rear;
These unavailing Rites he may receive,
These, after Death, are All a God can give!   335
    Apollo bows, and from Mount *Ida*'s Height
Swift to the Field precipitates his Flight;
Thence, from the War, the breathless Hero bore,
Veiled in a Cloud, to silver *Simois* Shore:
There bathed his honorable Wounds, and dressed   340
His Manly Members in th'Immortal Vest,
And with Perfumes of sweet *Ambrosial* Dews,
Restores his Freshness, and his Form renews.
Then *Sleep* and *Death,* two Twins of wingèd Race,
Of matchless Swiftness, but of silent Pace,   345
Received *Sarpedon,* at the God's Command,
And in a Moment reached the *Lycian* Land;
The Corpse amidst his weeping Friends they laid,
Where endless Honors wait the Sacred Shade.

PREFACE
To The Works
of Shakespeare[1]

It is not my design to enter into a criticism upon this author; though to do it effectually and not superficially, would be the

[1] Pope's edition of Shakespeare and his Preface, though bearing marks of his peculiar genius, are not achievements of the same stature as his *Iliad* and Preface. One reason for this may be seen in the relatively unprepared or unsophisticated state of the materials which he put his hand to—with relatively amateurish enthusiasm. Homer was profoundly difficult; he was also a profoundly cultivated classic subject, upon which a poet endowed with both supreme resolution and some classical learning might perform a very impressive job. Shakespeare was an unworked native wilderness. (The argument here parallels that which we shall find Pope himself using when he invokes certain elements of rudeness in Shakespeare's situation to explain his many imperfections.) Four collected editions of Shakespeare's plays had appeared during the seventeenth century: The First Folio, brought out by the actors John Heminges and Henry Condell, seven years after Shakespeare's death, in 1623, was printed, as Pope would argue, from a collection of plays that included many playhouse copies. It was not an impeccable legacy. The Second, Third, and Fourth Folios, 1632, 1663-1664, and 1685, were a successively compounded corruption. In Pope's day, his friend Nicholas Rowe, the tragic dramatist, brought out the first edited collection of the plays, 1709, in six octavo vol-

best occasion that any just writer could take, to form the judgment and taste of our nation. For of all English poets Shake-

umes, prefaced with the first Life of Shakespeare. Rowe's edition in many ways reflects the mind of a man of the theater. When Pope took up the task next, he approached it, as Nichol Smith has so well said, in the spirit of a friend, or brother poet, and literary executor, one who feels a duty of tidying up the dead author's defective papers and preparing them for the press. He seems to have tackled the job, with the help of a few friends, at the same time as his *Odyssey* translation, during a period of about four years, 1721–1724. He came out in six volumes, quarto, in the spring of 1725. He provoked the publication in the following year by his rival Lewis Theobald (soon to be the hero of *The Dunciad*) of a matching quarto volume: *Shakespeare Restored: or, a Specimen of the Many Errors, as well Committed, as Unamended, by Mr. Pope in his Late Edition of this Poet.* Pope did understand both the unique authority and the limitations of the First Folio and the importance of such quartos as were available to him. But his efforts as a textual scholar were in truth gentlemanly and desultory. His first principle was taste. He has been ranked with the printer's reader of the Second Folio as one of the two greatest corrupters of Shakespeare's text.

Echoing his spirited encomium of Homer's Invention in the *Iliad* Preface, he opens his Preface to Shakespeare with an equally high celebration of the power of Nature in Shakespeare and (what was the same thing) his Originality. Even Homer had looked on a Nature patterned according to certain Egyptian precedents. Shakespeare had no comparable handicap. Living in the dayspring of modern English poesy, he looked on Nature pure and reported it directly. He was not an Imitator, but an Instrument, of Nature. Whence then the glaring improprieties and rank confusions which mark his pages? Much undoubtedly can be blamed on three causes:—the rudeness of the popular audience to which Shakespeare pandered, especially in his earlier career; the lewdness of the players, of whom he was one; the corruptions of the text arising from playhouse practice and early editing. Pope's elaborate defences for the shortcomings of Shakespeare are brimful of Augustan confidence in an era of achieved poetic perfection.

"The players," wrote the classically minded Ben Jonson, "have often mentioned it as an honor to Shakespeare, that in his writing (whatsoever he penned) he never blotted out line. My answer hath been, would he had blotted a thousand." Pope's loyalty to Shakespeare struggled somewhat unconvincingly against the imputation of this kind of artistic carelessness. The poetic occasion for the same materials, as in his *Epistle to Augustus,* could produce a cooler tone.

And fluent Shakespeare scarce effaced a line.
Even copious Dryden wanted, or forgot,

speare must be confessed to be the fairest and fullest subject for criticism, and to afford the most numerous, as well as most conspicuous instances, both of beauties and faults of all sorts. But this far exceeds the bounds of a Preface, the business of which is only to give an account of the fate of his works, and the disadvantages under which they have been transmitted to us. We shall hereby extenuate many faults which are his, and clear him from the imputation of many which are not: A design, which though it can be no guide to future critics to do him justice in one way, will at least be sufficient to prevent their doing him an injustice in the other.

I cannot, however, but mention some of his principal and characteristic excellencies, for which (notwithstanding his defects) he is justly and universally elevated above all other dramatic Writers. Not that this is the proper place of praising him, but because I would not omit any occasion of doing it.

If ever any author deserved the name of an *Original,* it was Shakespeare. Homer himself drew not his art so immediately from the fountains of Nature; it proceeded through Egyptian strainers and channels, and came to him not without some tincture of the learning, or some cast of the models, of those before him. The poetry of Shakespeare was inspiration indeed: he is not so much an Imitator, as an Instrument, of Nature; and 'tis not so just to say that he speaks from her, as that she speaks through him.

His *Characters* are so much Nature herself, that 'tis a sort of injury to call them by so distant a name as copies of her. Those of other Poets have a constant resemblance, which shews

> The last and greatest art, the art to blot.

Or, as in *The Dunciad* (i. 133–34), a satiric sting
> There hapless Shakespeare, yet of Tibbald sore,
> Wished he had blotted for himself before.

The present annotations to Pope's Shakespeare Preface owe a good deal to two books by David Nichol Smith, his edition of *Eighteenth-Century Essays on Shakespeare,* Glasgow, 1903, and his three Birkbeck College lectures, *Shakespeare in the Eighteenth Century,* Oxford, 1928; to Tucker Brooke's *Shakespeare of Stratford, A Handbook for Students,* New Haven, 1926; to several volumes in *The Yale Shakespeare;* and to G. E. Bentley's *Shakespeare, A Biographical Handbook,* New Haven, 1961.

that they received them from one another, and were but multipliers of the same image: each picture like a mock-rainbow is but the reflection of a reflection. But every single character in Shakespeare is as much an individual, as those in life itself; it is as impossible to find any two alike; and such as from their relation or affinity in any respect appear most to be twins, will upon comparison be found remarkably distinct. To this life and variety of character, we must add the wonderful preservation of it; which is such throughout his Plays, that, had all the speeches been printed without the very names of the persons, I believe one might have applied them with certainty to every speaker.

The *Power* over our *Passions* were never possessed in a more eminent degree, or displayed in so different instances. Yet all along, there is seen no labor, no pains to raise them; no preparation to guide our guess to the effect, or be perceived to lead toward it: But the heart swells, and the tears burst out, just at the proper places: We are surprised the moment we weep; and yet upon reflection find the passion so just, that we should be surprised if we had not wept, and wept at that very moment.

How astonishing is it again, that the Passions directly opposite to these, Laughter and Spleen, are no less at his command! that he is not more a master of the *great* than of the *ridiculous* in human nature; of our noblest tendernesses, than of our vainest foibles; of our strongest emotions, than of our idlest sensations!

Nor does he only excel in the Passions: in the coolness of Reflection and Reasoning he is full as admirable. His *Sentiments* are not only in general the most pertinent and judicious upon every subject; but by a talent very peculiar, something between penetration and felicity, he hits upon that particular point on which the bent of each argument turns, or the force of each motive depends. This is perfectly amazing, from a man of no education or experience in those great and public scenes of life which are usually the subject of his thoughts: So that he seems to have known the world by intuition, to have looked through human nature at one glance, and to be the only author that gives ground for a very new opinion, That the philosopher and even the man of the world, may be *born,* as well as the poet.

It must be owned that with all these great excellencies, he

has almost as great defects; and that as he has certainly written better, so he has perhaps written worse, than any other. But I think I can in some measure account for these defects, from several causes and accidents; without which it is hard to imagine that so large and so enlightened a mind could ever have been susceptible of them. That all these contingencies should unite to his disadvantage seems to me almost as singularly unlucky, as that so many various (nay contrary) talents should meet in one man, was happy and extraordinary.

It must be allowed that Stage poetry of all other, is more particularly levelled to please the *populace,* and its success more immediately depending upon the *common suffrage.* One cannot therefore wonder, if Shakespeare, having at his first appearance no other aim in his writings than to procure a subsistence, directed his endeavors solely to hit the taste and humor that then prevailed. The audience was generally composed of the meaner sort of people; and therefore the images of life were to be drawn from those of their own rank: accordingly we find, that not our author's only, but almost all the old comedies have their scene among *Tradesmen* and *Mechanics:* And even their historical plays strictly follow the common *old stories* or *vulgar traditions* of that kind of people. In Tragedy, nothing was so sure to *surprise* and cause *admiration,* as the most strange, unexpected, and consequently most unnatural, events and incidents; the most exaggerated thoughts; the most verbose and bombast expression; the most pompous rhymes, and thundering versification. In Comedy, nothing was so sure to *please,* as mean buffoonery, vile ribaldry, and unmannerly jests of fools and clowns. Yet even in these, our author's wit buoys up, and is born above his subject: his genius in those low parts is like some prince of a romance in the disguise of a shepherd or peasant; a certain greatness and spirit now and then break out, which manifest his higher extraction and qualities.

It may be added, that not only the common audience had no notion of the rules of writing, but few even of the better sort piqued themselves upon any great degree of knowledge or nicety that way; 'till Ben Jonson, getting possession of the stage, brought critical learning into vogue: And that this was not done without difficulty, may appear from those frequent lessons (and indeed almost declamations) which he was forced to prefix to his first plays, and put into the mouth of his actors, the *Grex, Chorus,* etc. to remove the prejudices, and inform the judgment of his hearers.[2] 'Till then, our authors had no thoughts of writing on the model of the ancients: their Tragedies were only histories in dialogue; and their comedies followed the thread of any novel as they found it, no less implicitly than if it had been true history.

To judge therefore of Shakespeare by Aristotle's rules, is like trying a man by the laws of one country, who acted under those of another.[3] He writ to the *people*; and writ at first without patronage from the better sort, and therefore without aims of pleasing them: without assistance or advice from the learned, as without the advantage of education or acquaintance among them: without that knowledge of the best models, the ancients, to inspire him with an emulation of them: in a word, without any views of reputation, and of what poets are pleased to call immortality: Some or all of which have encouraged the vanity, or animated the ambition, of other writers.

Yet it must be observed, that when his performances had merited the protection of his prince, and when the encouragement of the court had succeeded to that of the town;[4] the works of his riper years are manifestly raised above those of his former. The dates of his plays sufficiently evidence that his productions improved, in proportion to the respect he had for his auditors. And I make no doubt this observation would be found true in every instance, were but editions extant from which we might learn the exact time when every piece was composed, and whether writ for the town, or the court.

[2] See, for instance, the Prologue to *Everyman in His Humour,* 1616 (acted 1598); the Induction to *Everyman out of His Humour,* 1600 (acted 1599); the Prologue and Dedicatory Epistle of *Volpone,* 1607 (acted 1606).

[3] An argument which had appeared in the comic dramatist George Farquhar's *Discourse upon Comedy,* 1702, and in Rowe's *Life of Shakespeare,* and would become standard in "preromantic" criticism.

[4] Shakespeare and his colleagues of the Globe Theater became "Servants" of the King ("His Majesty's Players") by a royal patent of James I in the spring of 1603. During 1604-1605 they performed seven of Shakespeare's plays at Court.

Another cause (and no less strong than the former) may be deduced from our Author's being a *player,* and forming himself first upon the judgments of that body of men whereof he was a member. They have ever had a standard to themselves, upon other principles than those of Aristotle. As they live by the majority, they know no rule but that of pleasing the present humor, and complying with the wit in fashion; a consideration which brings all their judgment to a short point. Players are just such judges of what is *right,* as tailors are of what is *graceful.* And in this view it will be but fair to allow, that most of our Author's faults are less to be ascribed to his wrong judgment as a Poet, than to his right judgment as a Player.

By these men it was thought a praise to Shakespeare, that he scarce ever *blotted a line.* This they industriously propagated, as appears from what we are told by Ben Jonson in his *Discoveries,*[5] and from the preface of Heminges and Condell to the first folio edition.[6] But in reality (however it has prevailed) there never was a more groundless report, or to the contrary of which there are more undeniable evidences. As the Comedy of the *Merry Wives of Windsor,* which he entirely new writ; the *History of Henry VI,* which was first published under the title of *The Contention of York and Lancaster;* and that of Henry V extremely improved; that of *Hamlet* enlarged to almost as much again as at first,[7] and many others. I believe the common opinion of his want of learning proceeded from no better ground. This

[5] Jonson's *Timber, or Discoveries Made Upon Men and Matter* was published in the second volume of the posthumous folio edition of his works, 1640–1641. The paragraph *De Shakespeare nostrati* (numbered 64 in modern editions) contains this passage: "I *remember,* the Players have often mentioned it as an honour to *Shakespeare,* that in his writing, (whatsoever he penn'd) hee never blotted out line. My answer hath beene, would he had blotted a thousand."

[6] "His mind and hand went together: And what he thought, he uttered with that easinesse, that wee have scarce received from him a blot in his papers."—John Heminges and Henry Condell's preface "To the great variety of Readers," p. A3 of *Mr. William Shakespeares Comedies, Histories & Tragedies. Published according to the True Originall Copies,* London, 1623.

[7] Pope seems to refer to imperfect or pirated editions of the *Merry Wives* (1602), *Henry V* (1600, 1602, 1608), and *Hamlet* (1603), and to a play about King Henry VI which was not by Shakespeare.

too might be thought a praise by some, and to this his errors have as injudiciously been ascribed by others. For 'tis certain, were it true, it could concern but a small part of them; the most are such as are not properly defects, but superfetations; and arise not from want of learning or reading, but from want of thinking or judging: or rather (to be more just to our Author) from a compliance to those wants in others. As to a wrong choice of the subject, a wrong conduct of the incidents, false thoughts, forced expressions, etc. if these are not to be ascribed to the foresaid accidental reasons, they must be charged upon the poet himself, and there is no help for it. But I think the two disadvantages which I have mentioned (to be obliged to please the lowest of people, and to keep the worst of company) if the consideration be extended as far as it reasonably may, will appear sufficient to mislead and depress the greatest Genius upon earth. Nay the more modestly with which such a one is endued, the more he is in danger of submitting and conforming to others, against his own better judgment.

But as to his *want of learning,* it may be necessary to say something more: There is certainly a vast difference between *learning* and *languages.* How far he was ignorant of the latter, I cannot determine; but 'tis plain he had much reading at least, if they will not call it learning, Nor is it any great matter, if a man has knowledge, whether he has it from one language or from another. Nothing is more evident than that he had a taste of natural philosophy, mechanics, ancient and modern history, poetical learning and mythology: We find him very knowing in the customs, rites, and manners of antiquity. In *Coriolanus* and *Julius Caesar,* not only the spirit, but manners, of the Romans are exactly drawn; and still a nicer distinction is shown, between the manners of the Romans in the time of the former, and of the latter. His reading in the ancient historians is no less conspicuous, in many references to particular passages: and the speeches copied from Plutarch[8] in *Coriolanus* may, I think, as

---

[8] The *Parallel Lives* of Greeks and Romans, written in Greek by Plutarch of Chaeronea in the first century A.D., were translated into English by Sir Thomas North, 1579, from the French of Jacques Amyot, and in this form were a principal source for Shakespeare's Roman history plays.

well be made an instance of his learning, as those copied from Cicero in *Catiline,* of Ben Jonson's. The manners of other nations in general, the Egyptians, Venetians, French, etc. are drawn with equal propriety. Whatever object of nature, or branch of science, he either speaks of or describes; it is always with competent, if not extensive knowledge: his descriptions are still exact; all his metaphors appropriated, and remarkably drawn from the true nature and inherent qualities of each subject. When he treats of ethic or politic, we may constantly observe a wonderful justness of distinction, as well as extent of comprehension. No one is more a master of the poetical story, or has more frequent allusions to the various parts of it: Mr. Waller[9] (who has been celebrated for this last particular) has not shown more learning this way than Shakespeare. We have translations from Ovid published in his name, among those poems which pass for his, and for some of which we have undoubted authority (being published by himself, and dedicated to his noble patron the Earl of Southampton:)[10] He appears also to have been conversant in Plautus, from whom he has taken the plot of one of his plays:[11] he follows the Greek authors, and particularly Dares Phrygius, in another:[12] (although I will not pretend to say in what language

[9] Edmund Waller (1606–1687), lyric and amatory poet, an early perfector of the heroic couplet. The meaning of "allusions to the various parts" of "the poetical story" and the relation of this to Waller escape the present editor.

[10] To Rowe's six-volume edition of Shakespeare's *Works* (1709) Edmund Curll had added in 1710 a *Volume the Seventh. Containing, Venus & Adonis, Tarquin & Lucrece* [both dedicated to Southampton] *and his Miscellany Poems.* The latter included translations of Ovid by Thomas Heywood and some poems by Marlowe. (A doubtful relation may be discerned between several parts of Ovid's *Metamorphoses* and Shakespeare's *Venus and Adonis.*) The volume would be reprinted in 1725 and added to Pope's own edition by other editors.

[11] Shakespeare's *Comedy of Errors* is taken partly from the *Menaechmi* of Plautus—as had been argued by Charles Gildon in an *Essay on the Stage,* 1710, and grudgingly admitted by Rowe, who urged Shakespeare's ignorance of ancient languages.

[12] Dares Phrygius, a Trojan priest in Homer's *Iliad* v. 9. A Latin account of the destruction of Troy (*De Excidio Troiae*), popular in the Middle Ages, claimed to be a translation of a work of Dares. It contributed to

he read them.) The modern Italian writers of novels he was manifestly acquainted with;[13] and we may conclude him to be no less conversant with the ancients of his own country, from the use he has made of Chaucer in *Troilus and Cressida*,[14] and in the *Two Noble Kinsmen*, if that Play be his, as there goes a tradition it was (and indeed it has little resemblance of Fletcher, and more of our Author than some of those which have been received as genuine.)[15]

I am inclined to think, this opinion proceeded originally from the zeal of the Partisans of our Author and Ben Jonson;[16] as they endeavored to exalt the one at the expense of the other. It is ever the nature of Parties to be in extremes; and nothing is so probable, as that because Ben Jonson had much the more learning, it was said on the one hand that Shakespeare had none at all; and because Shakespeare had much the most wit and fancy, it was retorted on the other, that Jonson wanted both. Because Shakespeare borrowed nothing, it was said that Ben Jonson borrowed everything. Because Jonson did not write extempore, he was reproached with being a year about every piece; and because Shakespeare wrote with ease and rapidity, they cried, he never once made a blot. Nay the spirit of opposition ran so high, that whatever those of the one side objected to the other,

the tradition which produced Boccaccio's *Filostrato* and Chaucer's *Troilus and Criseyde*, the main source of the story of *Troilus and Cressida* in the satirical play of that title by Shakespeare.

[13] *The Merchant of Venice, The Taming of the Shrew, The Merry Wives of Windsor, Much Ado about Nothing, Twelfth Night, Measure for Measure, All's Well That Ends Well, Othello*, and *Cymbeline* are plays that owe more or less, directly or indirectly, to Italian *novelle*.

[14] See note 12 above.

[15] John Fletcher's play *The Two Noble Kinsmen*, written probably with the collaboration of Shakespeare, and printed in 1634, follows the story of Palamon and Arcite as told in Chaucer's *Knight's Tale*.

[16] Pope here seems to repeat an account of Shakespeare-Jonson partisanship which, according to Joseph Spence (*Anecdotes,* ed. Osborn, 1966, No. 54), he had heard from the veteran Shakespearian actor Thomas Betterton. G. E. Bentley, *Shakespeare and Jonson,* 2 vols. (Chicago, 1945), tells us, on the evidence of several types of "allusions" to the two writers, that the "learned Jonson" enjoyed a higher reputation than Shakespeare almost to the end of the seventeenth century.

was taken at the rebound, and turned into praises; as injudiciously, as their antagonists before had made them objections.

Poets are always afraid of envy; but sure they have as much reason to be afraid of admiration. They are the Scylla and Charybdis of Authors; those who escape one, often fall by the other. *Pessimum genus inimicorum laudantes,* says Tacitus:[17] and Virgil desires to wear a charm against those who praise a poet without rule or reason.

> Si ultra placitum laudarit, baccare frontem Cingito, ne vati noceat.[18]

But however this contention might be carried on by the Partisans on either side, I cannot help thinking these two great poets were good friends, and lived on amicable terms, and in offices of society with each other. It is an acknowledged fact, that Ben Jonson was introduced upon the stage, and his first works encouraged, by Shakespeare.[19] And after his death, that Author writes *To the Memory of His Beloved Mr. William Shakespeare,*[20] which shows as if the friendship had continued through life. I cannot for my own part find any thing *invidious* or *sparing* in those verses, but wonder Mr. Dryden was of that opinion.[21] He exalts him not only above all his contemporaries, but above Chaucer and Spenser, whom he will not allow to be great enough

[17] In his *Agricola* (sec. 41), an encomiastic monograph on his father-in-law, military governor of Britain c. 78 A.D.
[18] "If he praise excessively, bind my brows with foxglove, lest he harm the bard."—*Eclogue* vii. 27–28.
[19] Jonson's Folio of 1616 says that Shakespeare was a "principal Comedian" when *Every Man in His Humour* was put on by the Lord Chamberlain's Servants at the Curtain Theater in 1598. He acted also in Jonson's *Sejanus,* 1603. Rowe in his *Life of Shakespeare,* 1709, records a tradition that it was Shakespeare's influence which persuaded the Chamberlain's company to produce *Every Man in His Humour.*
[20] Jonson's poem *To the Memory of my Beloved, the Author, Mr. William Shakespeare, and What He Hath Left Us,* eighty pentameters in couplets, appears in the first Folio.
[21] Dryden's somewhat perverse phrase ("an insolent, sparing, and invidious panegyric"—*A Discourse Concerning . . . Satire,* 1693, *Essays,* ed. Ker. ii. 18) is an *obiter dictum* incidental to a passage in praise of his patron the Earl of Dorset and Middlesex.

to be ranked with him; and challenges the names of Sophocles, Euripides, and Aeschylus, nay all Greece and Rome at once, to equal him; and (which is very particular) expressly vindicates him from the imputation of wanting *art,* not enduring that all his excellencies should be attributed to *nature.* It is remarkable too, that the praise he gives him in his *Discoveries* seems to proceed from a *personal kindness*; he tells us that he loved the man, as well as honored his memory;[22] celebrates the honesty, openness, and frankness of his temper; and only distinguishes, as he reasonably ought, between the real merit of the Author, and the silly and derogatory applauses of the Players. Ben Jonson might indeed be sparing in his commendations, (though certainly he is not so in this instance) partly from his own nature, and partly from judgment. For men of judgment think they do any man more service in praising him justly, than lavishly. I say, I would fain believe they were friends, though the violence and ill breeding of their followers and flatterers were enough to give rise to the contrary report. I would hope that it may be with *parties,* both in wit and state, as with those monsters described by the poets; and that their heads at least may have something human, though their *bodies* and *tails* are wild beasts and serpents.

As I believe that what I have mentioned gave rise to the opinion of Shakespeare's want of learning; so what has continued it down to us may have been the many blunders and illiteracies of the first publishers of his works. In these editions their ignorance shines in almost every page; nothing is more common than *Actus tertia. Exit omnes. Enter three witches solus.*[23] Their French is as bad as their Latin, both in construction and spelling: Their very Welsh is false.[24] Nothing is more likely than that those palpable blunders of Hector's quoting Aristotle,[25] with

---

[22] "I loved the man and do honor his memory (on this side idolatry) as much as any." See above note 5.

[23] Pope seems to have invented this blunder. The folio texts of *Macbeth* do not supply it; there is no quarto.

[24] See Captain Fluellen in *Henry V* (e.g., III.vi-IVi) and Sir Hugh Evans in *The Merry Wives of Windsor.*

[25] Hector commits the anachronism of citing Aristotle (*Nicomachean Ethics*) in *Troilus and Cressida,* II. ii. 166–167.

others of that gross kind, sprung from the same root: it not being at all credible that these could be the errors of any man who had the least tincture of a school, or the least conversation with such as had. Ben Jonson (whom they will not think partial to him) allows him at least to have had *some* Latin; which is utterly inconsistent with mistakes like these. Nay the constant blunders in proper names of persons and places, are such as must have proceeded from a man, who had not so much as read any history, in any language: so could not be Shakespeare's.

I shall now lay before the reader some of those almost innumerable errors, which have risen from one source, the ignorance of the players, both as his actors, and as his editors. When the nature and kinds of these are enumerated and considered, I dare to say that not Shakespeare only, but Aristotle or Cicero, had their works undergone the same fate, might have appeared to want sense as well as learning.

It is not certain that any one of his plays was published by himself. During the time of his employment in the Theater, several of his pieces were printed separately in quarto. What makes me think that most of these were not published by him, is the excessive carelessness of the press: every page is so scandalously false spelled, and almost all the learned or unusual words so intolerably mangled, that it's plain there either was no corrector to the press at all, or one totally illiterate. If any were supervised by himself, I should fancy the two parts of *Henry IV* and *Midsummer Night's Dream* might have been so:[26] because I find no other printed with any exactness; and (contrary to the rest) there is very little variation in all the subsequent editions of them. There are extant two prefaces, to the first quarto edition of *Troilus and Cressida* in 1609, and to that of *Othello;* by which it appears, that the first was published without his knowledge or consent, and even before it was acted, so late as seven or eight years before he died; and that the latter was not printed till after his death. The whole number of genuine plays which we have

---

[26] Modern scholarship views the First Quarto of *1 Henry IV* (1598), the first known quarto of *Love's Labor's Lost* (1598), the Second of *Romeo and Juliet* (1599), and the Second of *Hamlet* (1604) as good quartos.

been able to find printed in his lifetime amounts but to eleven.[27] And of some of these, we meet with two or more editions[28] by different printers, each of which has whole heaps of trash different from the other: which I should fancy was occasioned by their being taken from different copies, belonging to different Playhouses.

The folio edition (in which all the plays we now receive as his were first collected) was published by two Players, Heminges and Condell, in 1623, seven years after his decease.[29] They declare, that all the other editions were stolen and surreptitious, and affirm theirs to be purged from the errors of the former. This is true as to the literal errors, and no other; for in all respects else it is far worse than the quartos.

First, because the additions of trifling and bombast passages are in this edition far more numerous. For whatever had been added, since those quartos by the actors, or had stolen from their mouths into the written parts, were from thence conveyed into the printed text, and all stand charged upon the Author. He himself complained of this usage in *Hamlet,* where he wishes that *those who play the Clowns would speak no more than is set down for them.* (Act. iii. Sc. iv.)[30] But as a proof that he could not escape it, in the old editions of *Romeo and Juliet* there is no hint of a great number of the mean conceits and ribaldries now to be found there.[31] In others, the low scenes of Mobs, Plebeians and Clowns, are vastly shorter than at present: And I have seen one in particular (which seems to have belonged to the playhouse, by having the parts divided with lines, and the

[27] Eighteen plays were published in quarto editions before the date of Shakespeare's retirement, 1611, and one more before the First Folio, *Othello* in 1622.

[28] A list of Shakespeare editions printed at the end of Pope's Volume vi includes twenty-nine quartos, among them all the plays published before the First Folio except *Much Ado* and *Pericles.*

[29] See above note 1. The Folio adds eighteen plays to the nineteen printed already in quarto, but of the latter number it omits *Pericles.*

[30] Scene ii in modern editions.

[31] The first quarto of *Romeo and Juliet* (1597) is notoriously corrupt. The second quarto (1599) is, however, the source from which later quartos and the Folio are derived.

Actors' names in the margin) where several of those very passages were added in a written hand, which are since to be found in the folio.

In the next place, a number of beautiful passages which are extant in the first single editions, are omitted in this: as it seems without any other reason, than their willingness to shorten some scenes: These men (as it was said of Procrustes) either lopping, or stretching an Author, to make him just fit for their stage.

This edition is said to be printed from the *original copies*. I believe they meant those which had lain ever since the author's days in the playhouse, and had from time to time been cut, or added to, arbitrarily. It appears that this edition, as well as the quartos, was printed (at least partly) from no better copies than the *prompter's book*, or *piecemeal parts* written out for the use of the actors: For in some places their very[a] names are through carelessness set down instead of the *personæ dramatis:* And in others the notes of direction to the *property men* for their *movables*, and to the *players* for their *entries*,[*] are inserted into the text, through the ignorance of the transcribers.

The Plays not having been before so much as distinguished by *acts* and *scenes*, they are in this edition divided according as they played them,[32] often where there is no pause in the action, or where they thought fit to make a breach in it, for the sake of music, masques, or monsters.

[a] *Much Ado about Nothing*, Act ii. Enter Prince Leonato, Claudio, and *Jack Wilson*, instead of Balthasar. And in Act iv. *Cowley*, and *Kemp*, constantly through a whole scene. Edit. Fol. of 1623, and 1632. [P.]

[*] *Such as*, "My Queen is murdered! *Ring the little bell.*" "His nose grew as sharp as a pen, and *a table of Greenfield's*," etc. [P. This note is here added to Warburton's text of 1751 from the original of 1725.] The second instance, generally considered not a stage direction but a part of Shakespeare's text (*Henry V*, II.iii.17—the death of Falstaff) would be the occasion for Lewis Theobald's most brilliant aesthetic emendation, which became one of the best-known passages in Shakespeare: "and a babled of green fields."

[32] Showing the mind of a practical dramatist, Nicholas Rowe had supplied lists of *dramatis personae*, indications of place for scenes, and stage directions. Pope multiplied scene divisions manyfold. Where the First Folio, for instance, has 23 scene divisions, internal to acts, for *King Lear*, Rowe has 18, and Pope, 60.

Sometimes the scenes are transposed and shuffled backward and forward; a thing which could no otherwise happen, but by their being taken from separate and piecemeal written parts.

Many verses are omitted entirely, and others transposed; from whence invincible obscurities have arisen, past the guess of any commentator to clear up, but just where the accidental glimpse of an old edition enlightens us.

Some characters were confounded and mixed, or two put into one, for want of a competent number of actors. Thus in the quarto edition of *Midsummer Night's Dream,* Act v, Shakespeare introduces a kind of Master of the revels called Philostrate; all whose part is given to another character (that of Egeus) in the subsequent editions:[33] So also in *Hamlet* and *King Lear*. This too makes it probable that the prompter's books were what they called the original copies.

From liberties of this kind, many speeches also were put into the mouths of wrong persons, where the Author now seems chargeable with making them speak out of character: Or sometimes perhaps for no better reason, than that a governing player, to have the mouthing of some favorite speech himself, would snatch it from the unworthy lips of an underling.

Prose from verse they did not know, and they accordingly printed one for the other throughout the volume.

Having been forced to say so much of the players, I think I ought in justice to remark, that the judgment, as well as condition, of that class of people was then far inferior to what it is in our days. As then the best playhouses were inns and taverns (the Globe, the Hope, the Red Bull, the Fortune, etc.),[34] so the top

---

[33] Pope reports accurately. The text today follows the First Quarto, of 1600.

[34] Pope conflates theatrical history. Within the city "liberties," the only public dramatic performances took place in inn-yards—e.g., the Bell Savage, the Boar's Head, the Cross Keys, the Bell, the Bull. During the 1570s, however, two regular theaters (the Theater and the Curtain) went up north of London Wall, in Finsbury Fields. A little later the Bankside, south of the Thames, became a favorite site. There in 1599 Shakespeare's company built the Globe. Their chief rivals, the Admiral's Men, built the Fortune, north of the Wall, in 1600. The Hope appeared on the Bankside in 1613. The Red Bull, to the north, on St. John's Street, is thought to

of the profession were then mere players, not gentlemen of the stage: They were led into the buttery by the steward,[35] not placed at the lord's table, or lady's toilette: and consequently were entirely deprived of those advantages they now enjoy, in the familiar conversation of our nobility, and an intimacy (not to say dearness) with people of the first condition.

From what has been said, there can be no question but had Shakespeare published his works himself (especially in his latter time, and after his retreat from the stage) we should not only be certain which are genuine; but should find in those that are, the errors lessened by some thousands. If I may judge from all the distinguishing marks of his style, and his manner of thinking and writing, I make no doubt to declare that those wretched plays, *Pericles, Locrine, Sir John Oldcastle, Yorkshire Tragedy, Lord Cromwell, The Puritan,* and *London Prodigal,* cannot be admitted as his.[36] And I should conjecture of some of the others (particularly *Love's Labor's Lost, The Winter's Tale,* and *Titus Andronicus*) that only some characters, single scenes, or perhaps a few particular passages, were of his hand.[37] It is very probable what occasioned some plays to be supposed Shakespeare's was only this; that they were pieces produced by unknown authors, or fitted up for the theater while it was under his administration: and no owner claiming them, they were adjudged to him, as they give strays to the Lord of the manor: a mistake which (one may also observe) it was not for the interest of the house to remove. Yet the players themselves, Heminges and Condell, afterwards did Shakespeare the justice to reject those eight plays

have been converted from an inn-yard to a playhouse late in the reign of Queen Elizabeth.

[35] True for strolling players, such as appear in *Hamlet* or *The Taming of the Shrew,* but hardly for men like Shakespeare and his fellows, who were licensed by the King.

[36] Only *Pericles* (omitted from the First Folio) is now given to Shakespeare (and this with reservations). The other six are plays published during Shakespeare's lifetime, all bearing an attribution to Shakespeare or to "W. S." on the title page. They had crept into the Third and Fourth Folios.

[37] The extent of Shakespeare's part in the tragedy of horrors *Titus Andronicus* is uncertain.

in their edition; though they were then printed in his name,[38] in everybody's hands, and acted with some applause; (as we learn from what Ben Jonson says of *Pericles* in his Ode on the *New Inn*.) That *Titus Andronicus* is one of this class I am the rather induced to believe, by finding the same Author openly express his contempt of it in the *Induction* to *Bartholomew Fair*,[39] in the year 1614, when Shakespeare was yet living. And there is no better authority for these latter sort, than for the former, which were equally published in his lifetime.

If we give in to this opinion, how many low and vicious parts and passages might no longer reflect upon this great genius, but appear unworthily charged upon him? And even in those which are really his, how many faults may have been unjustly laid to his account from arbitrary additions, expunctions, transpositions of scenes and lines, confusion of characters and persons, wrong application of speeches, corruptions of innumerable passages by the ignorance, and wrong corrections of them again by the impertinence of his first editors? From one or other of these considerations, I am verily persuaded, that the greatest and the grossest part of what are thought his errors would vanish, and leave his character in a light very different from that disadvantageous one, in which it now appears to us.

This is the state in which Shakespeare's writings lie at present; for, since the abovementioned folio edition, all the rest have implicitly followed it,[40] without having recourse to any of the former, or ever making the comparison between them. It is impossible to repair the injuries already done him; too much time has elapsed, and the materials are too few. In what I have done I have rather given a proof of my willingness and desire, than of my ability, to do him justice. I have discharged the full duty of an Editor, to my best judgment, with more labor than I expect

[38] See above notes 1, 36. Pope refers in fact to only seven plays.
[39] "He that will swear *Jeronimo* [Kyd's *Spanish Tragedy,* 1592] or *Andronicus* [c. 1593] are the best plays yet shall pass unexcepted at here, as a man whose judgment shows it is constant and hath stood still these five-and-twenty or thirty years. Though it be an ignorance, it is a virtuous and staid ignorance; and, next to truth, a confirm'd error does well."
[40] See above note 1.

thanks, with a religious abhorrence of all innovation, and without any indulgence to my private sense or conjecture. The method taken in this edition will show itself. The various readings are fairly put in the margin, so that every one may compare them; and those I have preferred into the text are constantly *ex fide codicum,* upon authority. The alterations or additions which Shakespeare himself made, are taken notice of as they occur. Some suspected passages which are excessively bad (and which seem interpolations by being so inserted that one can entirely omit them without any chasm, or deficience in the context) are degraded to the bottom of the page; with an asterisk referring to the places of their insertion. The scenes are marked so distinctly that every removal of place is specified; which is more necessary in this Author than any other, since he shifts them more frequently: and sometimes without attending to this particular, the reader would have met with obscurities. The more obsolete or unusual words are explained. Some of the most shining passages are distinguished by commas in the margin: and where the beauty lay not in particulars but in the whole, a star is prefixed to the scene. This seems to me a shorter and less ostentatious method of performing the better half of Criticism (namely the pointing out an Author's excellencies) than to fill a whole paper with citations of fine passages, with *general applauses,* or *empty exclamations* at the tail of them. There is also subjoined a catalogue of those first editions by which the greater part of the various readings and of the corrected passages are authorized (most of which are such as carry their own evidence along with them.) These editions now hold the place of originals, and are the only materials left to repair the deficiencies or restore the corrupted sense of the Author: I can only wish that a greater number of them (if a greater were ever published) may yet be found, by a search more successful than mine, for the better accomplishment of this end.

I will conclude by saying of Shakespeare, that with all his faults, and with all the irregularity of his *drama,* one may look upon his works, in comparison of those that are more finished and regular, as upon an ancient majestic piece of Gothic architecture, compared with a neat modern building: The latter is more elegant and glaring, but the former is more strong and more solemn. It must be allowed, that in one of these there are materials enough to make many of the other. It has much the greater variety, and much the nobler apartments; though we are often conducted to them by dark, odd, and uncouth passages. Nor does the whole fail to strike us with greater reverence, though many of the parts are childish, ill-placed, and unequal to its grandeur.

AN ESSAY ON MAN
In Four Epistles

To Henry St. John, Lord Bolingbroke

THE DESIGN

Having proposed to write some pieces on Human Life and Manners, such as (to use my Lord Bacon's expression) *come home to Men's Business and Bosoms,* I thought it more satisfactory to begin with considering *Man* in the abstract, his *Nature* and his *State;* since, to prove any moral duty, to enforce any moral precept, or to examine the perfection or imperfection of any creature whatsoever, it is necessary first to know what *condition* and *relation* it is placed in, and what is the proper *end* and *purpose* of its *being.*

The science of Human Nature is, like all other sciences, reduced to a *few clear points:* There are not *many certain truths* in this world. It is therefore in the Anatomy of the mind as in that of the Body; more good will accrue to mankind by attending to the large, open, and perceptible parts, than by studying too much such finer nerves and vessels, the conformations and uses of which will for ever escape our observation. The *disputes* are all upon these last, and, I will venture to say, they have less sharpened the *wits* than the *hearts* of men against each other, and have diminished the practice, more than advanced the theory, of Morality. If I could flatter myself that this Essay has any merit, it is in steering betwixt the extremes of doctrines seemingly opposite, in passing over terms utterly unintelligible, and in forming a *temperate* yet not *inconsistent,* and a *short* yet not *imperfect* system of Ethics.

This I might have done in prose; but I chose verse, and even rhyme, for two reasons. The one will appear obvious; that principles, maxims, or precepts so written, both strike the reader more strongly at first, and are more easily retained by him afterwards: The other may seem odd, but is true, I found I could express them more *shortly* this way than in prose itself; and nothing is more certain, than that much of the *force* as well as *grace* of arguments or instructions, depends on their *conciseness.* I was unable to treat this part of my subject more in *detail,* without becoming dry and tedious; or more *poetically,* without sacrificing perspicuity to ornament, without wandering from the precision, or breaking the chain of reasoning: If any man can unite all these without diminution of any of them, I freely confess he will compass a thing above my capacity.

What is now published, is only to be considered as a *general Map* of MAN, marking out no more than the *greater parts,* their *extent,* their *limits,* and their *connection,* and leaving the particular to be more fully delineated in the charts which are to follow. Consequently, these Epistles in their progress (if I have health and leisure to make any progress) will be less dry, and more susceptible of poetical ornament. I am here only opening the *fountains,* and clearing the passage. To deduce the *rivers,* to follow them in their course, and to observe their effects, may be a task more agreeable.

EPISTLE I

ARGUMENT

Of the Nature and State of Man with respect to the UNIVERSE

OF *Man* in the abstract. I. That we can judge only with regard to our *own system,* being ignorant of the *relations* of systems and things. II. That Man is not to be deemed *imperfect,* but a Being suited to his *place* and *rank* in the creation, agreeable to the *general Order* of things, and conformable to *Ends* and *Relations* to him unknown. III. That it is partly upon his *ignorance* of *future* events, and partly upon the *hope* of a *future* state, that all his happiness in the present depends. IV. The *pride* of aiming at more knowledge, and pretending to more Perfection, the cause of Man's error and misery. The *impiety* of putting himself in the place of *God,* and judging of the fitness or unfitness, perfection or imperfection, justice or injustice of his dispensations. V. The *absurdity* of conceiting himself the *final cause* of the creation, or expecting that perfection in the *moral* world, which is not in the *natural.* VI. The *unreasonableness* of his complaints against *Providence,* while on the one hand he demands the Perfections of the Angels, and on the other the bodily qualifications of the Brutes; though, to possess any of the *sensitive faculties* in a higher degree, would render him miserable. VII. That throughout the whole visible world, an universal *order* and *gradation* in the sensual and mental faculties is observed, which causes a *subordination* of creature to creature, and of all creatures to Man. The gradations of *sense, instinct, thought, reflection, reason;* that Reason alone countervails all the other faculties. VIII. How much further this *order* and *subordination* of living creatures may extend, above and below us; were any part of which broken, not that part only, but the whole connected *creation* must be destroyed. IX. The *extravagance, madness,* and *pride* of such a desire. X. The consequence of all, the *absolute submission* due to Providence, both as to our *present* and *future* state.

> AWAKE, my ST. JOHN! leave all meaner things
> To low ambition, and the pride of Kings.
> Let us (since Life can little more supply
> Than just to look about us and to die)

Expatiate free o'er all this scene of Man;   5
A mighty maze! but not without a plan;
A Wild, where weeds and flowers promiscuous shoot;
Or Garden, tempting with forbidden fruit.
Together let us beat this ample field,
Try what the open, what the covert yield;   10
The latent tracts, the giddy heights, explore
Of all who blindly creep, or sightless soar;
Eye Nature's walks, shoot Folly as it flies,
And catch the Manners living as they rise;
Laugh where we must, be candid where we can;   15
But vindicate the ways of God to Man.
    I. Say first, of God above, or Man below,
What can we reason, but from what we know?
Of Man, what see we but his station here,
From which to reason, or to which refer?   20
Through worlds unnumbered though the God be known,
'Tis ours to trace him only in our own.
He, who through vast immensity can pierce,
See worlds on worlds compose one universe,
Observe how system into system runs,   25
What other planets circle other suns,
What varied Being peoples every star,
May tell why Heaven has made us as we are.
But of this frame the bearings, and the ties,
The strong connexions, nice dependencies,   30
Gradations just, has thy pervading soul
Looked through? or can a part contain the whole?
    Is the great chain, that draws all to agree,
And drawn supports, upheld by God, or thee?
    II. Presumptuous Man! the reason wouldst thou find,
Why formed so weak, so little, and so blind?   36
First, if thou canst, the harder reason guess,
Why formed no weaker, blinder, and no less?
Ask of thy mother earth, why oaks are made
Taller or stronger than the weeds they shade?   40
Or ask of yonder argent fields above,
Why Jove's Satellites are less than Jove?
    Of Systems possible, if 'tis confest

That Wisdom infinite must form the best,
Where all must full or not coherent be, ✳   45
And all that rises, rise in due degree;
Then, in the scale of reasoning life, 'tis plain,
There must be, somewhere, such a rank as Man:
And all the question (wrangle e'er so long)
Is only this, if God has placed him wrong?   50
    Respecting Man, whatever wrong we call,
May, must be right, as relative to all.
In human works, though laboured on with pain,
A thousand movements scarce one purpose gain;
In God's, one single can its end produce;   55
Yet serves to second too some other use.
So Man, who here seems principal alone,
Perhaps acts second to some sphere unknown,
Touches some wheel, or verges to some goal;
'Tis but a part we see, and not a whole.   60
    When the proud steed shall know why Man restrains
His fiery course, or drives him o'er the plains;
When the dull Ox, why now he breaks the clod,
Is now a victim, and now Egypt's God:
Then shall Man's pride and dulness comprehend   65
His actions', passions', being's, use and end;
Why doing, suffering, checked, impelled; and why
This hour a slave, the next a deity.
    Then say not Man's imperfect, Heaven in fault;
Say rather, Man's as perfect as he ought: 70
His knowledge measured to his state and place;
His time a moment, and a point his space.
If to be perfect in a certain sphere,
What matter, soon or late, or here or there?
The blest to day is as completely so,   75
As who began a thousand years ago.
    III.   Heaven from all creatures hides the book of Fate,
All but the page prescribed, their present state:
From brutes what men, from men what spirits know:
Or who could suffer Being here below?   80
The lamb thy riot dooms to bleed today,
Had he thy Reason, would he skip and play?

Pleased to the last, he crops the flowery food,
And licks the hand just raised to shed his blood.
Oh blindness to the future! kindly given,   85
That each may fill the circle marked by Heaven:
Who sees with equal eye, as God of all,
A hero perish, or a sparrow fall,
Atoms or systems into ruin hurled,
And now a bubble burst, and now a world.   90
      Hope humbly then; with trembling pinions soar;
Wait the great teacher Death; and God adore.
What future bliss, he gives not thee to know,
But gives that Hope to be thy blessing now.
Hope springs eternal in the human breast: 95
Man never Is, but always To be blest:
The soul, uneasy and confined from home,
Rests and expatiates in a life to come.
      Lo, the poor Indian! whose untutored mind
Sees God in clouds, or hears him in the wind;   100
His soul, proud Science never taught to stray
Far as the solar walk, or milky way;
Yet simple Nature to his hope has given,
Behind the cloud-topped hill, an humbler heaven;
Some safer world in depth of woods embraced,   105
Some happier island in the watery waste,
Where slaves once more their native land behold,
No fiends torment, no Christians thirst for gold.
To Be, contents his natural desire,
He asks no Angel's wing, no Seraph's fire;   110
But thinks, admitted to that equal sky,
His faithful dog shall bear him company.
    IV. Go, wiser thou! and, in thy scale of sense,
Weigh thy Opinion against Providence;
Call imperfection what thou fanciest such,   115
Say, here he gives too little, there too much:
Destroy all creatures for thy sport or gust,
Yet cry, If Man's unhappy, God's unjust;
If Man alone engross not Heaven's high care,
Alone made perfect here, immortal there: 120

Snatch from his hand the balance and the rod,
Re-judge his justice, be the GOD of GOD.
In Pride, in reasoning Pride, our error lies;
All quit their sphere, and rush into the skies.
Pride still is aiming at the blest abodes,   125
Men would be Angels, Angels would be Gods.
Aspiring to be Gods, if Angels fell,
Aspiring to be Angels, Men rebel:
And who but wishes to invert the laws
Of ORDER, sins against th' Eternal Cause.   130
    V. Ask for what end the heavenly bodies shine,
Earth for whose use? Pride answers, " 'Tis for mine:
For me kind Nature wakes her genial power,
Suckles each herb, and spreads out every flower;
Annual for me, the grape, the rose renew   135
The juice nectareous, and the balmy dew;
For me, the mine a thousand treasures brings;
For me, health gushes from a thousand springs;
Seas roll to waft me, suns to light me rise;
My footstool earth, my canopy the skies."   140
    But errs not Nature from this gracious end,
From burning suns when livid deaths descend,
When earthquakes swallow, or when tempests sweep
Towns to one grave, whole nations to the deep?
"No" ('tis replied) "the first Almighty Cause   145
Acts not by partial, but by general laws;
Th' exceptions few; some change since all began:
And what created perfect?"—Why then Man?
If the great end be human Happiness,
Then Nature deviates; and can Man do less?[1]   150
As much that end a constant course requires
Of showers and sunshine, as of Man's desires;

[1] "While comets move in very eccentric orbs, in all manner of positions, blind Fate could never make all the planets move one and the same way in orbs concentric; some inconsiderable irregularities excepted, which may have risen from the mutual actions of comets and planets upon one another, and which will be apt to increase, till this system wants a reformation." Sir Isaac Newton's *Optics,* Quest. ult. [W.]

As much eternal springs and cloudless skies,
As Men for ever temperate, calm, and wise.
If plagues or earthquakes break not Heaven's design,   155
Why then a Borgia, or a Catiline?
Who knows but he, whose hand the lightning forms,
Who heaves old Ocean, and who wings the storms;
Pours fierce Ambition in a Cæsar's mind,
Or turns young Ammon loose to scourge mankind?   160
From pride, from pride, our very reasoning springs;
Account for moral, as for natural things:
Why charge we Heaven in those, in these acquit?
In both, to reason right is to submit.

     Better for Us, perhaps, it might appear,   165
Were there all harmony, all virtue here;
That never air or ocean felt the wind;
That never passion discomposed the mind.
But ALL subsists by elemental strife;
And Passions are the elements of Life.   170
The general ORDER, since the whole began,
Is kept in Nature, and is kept in Man.

     VI.   What would this Man? Now upward will he soar,
And little less than Angel, would be more;
Now looking downwards, just as grieved appears   175
To want the strength of bulls, the fur of bears.
Made for his use all creatures if he call,
Say what their use, had he the powers of all?
Nature to these, without profusion, kind,
The proper organs, proper powers assigned;   180
Each seeming want compensated of course,
Here with degrees of swiftness, there of force;[2]
All in exact proportion to the state;
Nothing to add, and nothing to abate.
Each beast, each insect, happy in its own: 185
Is Heaven unkind to Man, and Man alone?
Shall he alone, whom rational we call,

[2] It is a certain axiom in the anatomy of creatures, that in proportion as they are formed for strength, their swiftness is lessened; or as they are formed for swiftness, their strength is abated. P.

Be pleased with nothing, if not blessed with all?
    The bliss of Man (could Pride that blessing find)
Is not to act or think beyond mankind;   190
No powers of body or of soul to share,
But what his nature and his state can bear.
Why has not Man a microscopic eye?[3]
For this plain reason, Man is not a Fly.
Say what the use, were finer optics given,   195
T' inspect a mite, not comprehend the heaven?
Or touch, if tremblingly alive all o'er,
To smart and agonize at every pore?
Or quick effluvia darting through the brain,
Die of a rose in aromatic pain?   200
If nature thundered in his opening ears,
And stunned him with the music of the spheres,
How would he wish that Heaven had left him still
The whispering Zephyr, and the purling rill?
Who finds not Providence all good and wise,   205
Alike in what it gives, and what it denies?
    VII. Far as Creation's ample range extends,
The scale of sensual, mental powers ascends:
Mark how it mounts, to Man's imperial race,
From the green myriads in the peopled grass: 210
What modes of sight betwixt each wide extreme,
The mole's dim curtain, and the lynx's beam:
Of smell, the headlong lioness between,[4]
And hound sagacious on the tainted green:
Of hearing, from the life that fills the flood,   215
To that which warbles through the vernal wood:
The spider's touch, how exquisitely fine!

[3] A fairly close parallel to Pope's argument appears in Locke's *Essay Concerning Human Understanding* (1690), Bk. II, Chap. xxiii, § 12.

[4] The manner of the Lions hunting their prey in the deserts of Africa is this: At their first going out in the nighttime they set up a loud roar, and then listen to the noise made by the beasts in their flight, pursuing them by the ear, and not by the nostril. It is probable the story of the jackal's hunting for the lion was occasioned by observation of this defect of scent in that terrible animal. P.

Feels at each thread, and lives along the line:
In the nice bee, what sense so subtly true
From poisonous herbs extracts the healing dew?   220
How Instinct varies in the groveling swine,
Compared, half-reasoning elephant, with thine!
Twixt that, and Reason, what a nice barrier,
For ever separate, yet for ever near!
Remembrance and Reflection how allied;   225
What thin partitions Sense from Thought divide:
And Middle natures, how they long to join,
Yet never pass th' insuperable line!
Without this just gradation, could they be
Subjected, these to those, or all to thee?   230
The powers of all subdued by thee alone,
Is not thy Reason all these powers in one?

     VIII.   See, through this air, this ocean, and this earth,
All matter quick, and bursting into birth.
Above, how high, progressive life may go!   235
Around, how wide! how deep extend below!
Vast chain of Being! which from God began,
Natures ethereal, human, angel, man,
Beast, bird, fish, insect, what no eye can see,
No glass can reach; from Infinite to thee,   240
From thee to Nothing.—On superior powers
Were we to press, inferior might on ours:
Or in the full creation leave a void,
Where, one step broken, the great scale's destroyed:
From Nature's chain whatever link you strike,   245
Tenth or ten thousandth, breaks the chain alike.

     And, if each system in gradation roll
Alike essential to th' amazing Whole,
The least confusion but in one, not all
That system only, but the Whole must fall.   250
Let Earth unbalanced from her orbit fly,
Planets and Suns run lawless through the sky;
Let ruling Angels from their spheres be hurled,
Being on Being wrecked, and world on world;
Heaven's whole foundations to their centre nod,   255

And Nature tremble to the throne of God.
All this dread ORDER break—for whom? for thee?
Vile worm!—Oh Madness! Pride! Impiety!
    IX. What if the foot, ordained the dust to tread,
Or hand, to toil, aspired to be the head?   260
What if the head, the eye, or ear repined
To serve mere engines to the ruling Mind?
Just as absurd for any part to claim
To be another, in this general frame:
Just as absurd, to mourn the tasks or pains,   265
The great directing MIND of ALL ordains.
    All are but parts of one stupendous whole,
Whose body Nature is, and God the soul;
That, changed through all, and yet in all the same;
Great in the earth, as in th' ethereal frame;   270
Warms in the sun, refreshes in the breeze,
Glows in the stars, and blossoms in the trees,
Lives through all life, extends through all extent,
Spreads undivided, operates unspent;
Breathes in our soul, informs our mortal part,   275
As full, as perfect, in a hair as heart;
As full, as perfect, in vile Man that mourns,
As the rapt Seraph that adores and burns:[5]
To him no high, no low, no great, no small;
He fills, he bounds, connects, and equals all.   280
    X. Cease then, nor ORDER Imperfection name:
Our proper bliss depends on what we blame.
Know thy own point: This kind, this due degree
Of blindness, weakness, Heaven bestows on thee.
Submit.—In this, or any other sphere,   285
Secure to be as blest as thou canst bear:
Safe in the hand of one disposing Power,
Or in the natal, or the mortal hour.
All Nature is but Art, unknown to thee;
All Chance, Direction, which thou canst not see;   290
All Discord, Harmony not understood;

---

[5] Alluding to the name *Seraphim,* signifying *burners.* [W.]

All partial Evil, universal Good:
And, spite of Pride, in erring Reason's spite,
One truth is clear, WHATEVER IS, IS RIGHT.

EPISTLE II

ARGUMENT

Of the Nature and State of Man *with respect to* Himself, *as an Individual*

I. *The* business of Man not to pry into *God,* but to study *himself.* His *Middle Nature;* his Powers and Frailties. The Limits of his *Capacity.* II. The two Principles of Man, *Self-love* and *Reason,* both necessary. *Self-love* the stronger, and why. Their end the same.   III. The *Passions* and their use. The *predominant Passion,* and its force. Its Necessity, in directing Men to different purposes. Its providential Use, in fixing our Principle, and ascertaining our Virtue. IV. *Virtue* and *Vice* joined in our *mixed Nature;* the limits near, yet the things *separate* and *evident:* What is the Office of *Reason.*   V. How odious *Vice* in itself, and how we deceive ourselves into it.   VI. That, however, the *Ends* of *Providence* and *general Good* are answered in our Passions and Imperfections. How usefully these are distributed to all *Orders of Men.* How useful they are to *Society.* And to the *Individuals.* In every *state,* and every *age* of life.

I.   KNOW then thyself, presume not God to scan;
The proper study of Mankind is Man.
Placed on this isthmus of a middle state,
A Being darkly wise, and rudely great:
With too much knowledge for the Sceptic side,   5
With too much weakness for the Stoic's pride,
He hangs between; in doubt to act, or rest;
In doubt to deem himself a God, or Beast;
In doubt his Mind or Body to prefer;

Born but to die, and reasoning but to err;   10
Alike in ignorance, his reason such,
Whether he thinks too little, or too much:
Chaos of Thought and Passion, all confused;
Still by himself abused, or disabused;
Created half to rise, and half to fall;   15
Great lord of all things, yet a prey to all;
Sole judge of Truth, in endless Error hurled:[6]
The glory, jest, and riddle of the world!

    Go, wondrous creature! mount where Science guides,
Go, measure earth, weigh air, and state the tides;   20
Instruct the planets in what orbs to run,
Correct old Time, and regulate the Sun;[7]
Go, soar with Plato to th' empyreal sphere,
To the first good, first perfect, and first fair;
Or tread the mazy round his followers trod,   25
And quitting sense call imitating God;
As Eastern priests in giddy circles run,
And turn their heads to imitate the Sun.
Go, teach Eternal Wisdom how to rule—
Then drop into thyself, and be a fool!   30

    Superior beings, when of late they saw
A mortal Man unfold all Nature's law,
Admired such wisdom in an earthly shape,
And showed a NEWTON as we show an Ape.[8]

    Could he, whose rules the rapid Comet bind,   35
Describe or fix one movement of his Mind?
Who saw its fires here rise, and there descend,
Explain his own beginning, or his end?

[6] To *hurl* signifies, not simply to *cast,* but to *cast backward and forward,* and is taken from the rural game called *hurling.* [W.]

[7] This alludes to Sir Isaac Newton's Grecian Chronology, which he reformed on those two sublime conceptions, the difference between the reigns of kings and the generations of men; and the position of the colures of the equinoxes and solstices at the time of the Argonautic expedition. [W.]

[8] The point of these lines is sharpened by comparison with Pope's epigram on Sir Isaac Newton: "Nature and Nature's laws lay hid in night: God said, *Let Newton be!* and all was light."

Alas what wonder! Man's superior part
Unchecked may rise, and climb from art to art;   40
But when his own great work is but begun,
What Reason weaves, by Passion is undone.
Trace Science then, with Modesty thy guide;
First strip off all her equipage of Pride;
Deduct what is but Vanity, or Dress,   45
Or Learning's Luxury, or Idleness;
Or tricks to show the stretch of human brain,
Mere curious pleasure, or ingenious pain;
Expunge the whole, or lop th' excrescent parts
Of all our Vices have created Arts;   50
Then see how little the remaining sum,
Which served the past, and must the times to come!
    II. Two Principles in human nature reign;
Self-love, to urge, and Reason, to restrain;
Nor this a good, nor that a bad we call,   55
Each works its end, to move or govern all:
And to their proper operation still,
Ascribe all Good; to their improper, Ill.
    Self-love, the spring of motion, acts the soul;
Reason's comparing balance rules the whole.   60
Man, but for that, no action could attend,
And but for this, were active to no end:
Fixed like a plant on his peculiar spot,
To draw nutrition, propagate, and rot;
Or, meteor-like, flame lawless through the void,   65
Destroying others, by himself destroyed.
    Most strength the moving principle requires;
Active its task, it prompts, impels, inspires.
Sedate and quiet the comparing lies,
Formed but to check, deliberate, and advise.   70
Self-love still stronger, as its objects nigh;
Reason's at distance, and in prospect lie:
That sees immediate good by present sense;
Reason, the future and the consequence.
Thicker than arguments, temptations throng,   75
At best more watchful this, but that more strong.

The action of the stronger to suspend,
Reason still use, to Reason still attend.
Attention, habit and experience gains;
Each strengthens Reason, and Self-love restrains.   80
    Let subtle schoolmen teach these friends to fight,
More studious to divide than to unite;
And Grace and Virtue, Sense and Reason split,
With all the rash dexterity of wit.
Wits, just like Fools, at war about a name,   85
Have full as oft no meaning, or the same.
Self-love and Reason to one end aspire,
Pain their aversion, Pleasure their desire;
But greedy That, its object would devour,
This taste the honey, and not wound the flower: 90
Pleasure, or wrong or rightly understood,
Our greatest evil, or our greatest good.
    III.   Modes of Self-love the Passions we may call:
'Tis real good, or seeming, moves them all:
But since not every good we can divide,   95
And Reason bids us for our own provide;
Passions, though selfish, if their means be fair,
List under Reason, and deserve her care;
Those, that imparted, court a nobler aim,
Exalt their kind, and take some Virtue's name.   100
    In lazy Apathy let Stoics boast
Their Virtue fixed; 'tis fixed as in a frost,
Contracted all, retiring to the breast;
But strength of mind is Exercise, not Rest:
The rising tempest puts in act the soul,   105
Parts it may ravage, but preserves the whole.
On life's vast ocean diversely we sail,
Reason the card, but Passion is the gale;
Nor God alone in the still calm we find,
He mounts the storm, and walks upon the wind.   110
    Passions, like Elements, though born to fight,
Yet, mixed and softened, in his work unite:
These 'tis enough to temper and employ;
But what composes Man, can Man destroy?

Suffice that Reason keep to Nature's road,   115
Subject, compound them, follow her and God.
Love, Hope, and Joy, fair pleasure's smiling train,
Hate, Fear, and Grief, the family of pain,
These mixed with art, and to due bounds confined,
Make and maintain the balance of the mind: 120
The lights and shades, whose well accorded strife
Gives all the strength and colour of our life.

     Pleasures are ever in our hands or eyes;
And when, in act, they cease, in prospect, rise:
Present to grasp, and future still to find,   125
The whole employ of body and of mind.
All spread their charms, but charm not all alike;
On different senses different objects strike;
Hence different Passions more or less inflame,
As strong or weak, the organs of the frame;   130
And hence one MASTER PASSION in the breast,
Like Aaron's serpent, swallows up the rest.

     As Man, perhaps, the moment of his breath,
Receives the lurking principle of death;
The young disease, that must subdue at length,   135
Grows with his growth, and strengthens with his strength:
So, cast and mingled with his very frame,
The Mind's disease, its RULING PASSION came;
Each vital humour which should feed the whole,
Soon flows to this, in body and in soul: 140
Whatever warms the heart, or fills the head,
As the mind opens, and its functions spread,
Imagination plies her dangerous art,
And pours it all upon the peccant part.

     Nature its mother, Habit is its nurse;   145
Wit, Spirit, Faculties, but make it worse;
Reason itself but gives it edge and power;
As Heaven's blest beam turns vinegar more sour.

     We, wretched subjects, though to lawful sway,
In this weak queen some favorite still obey: 150
Ah! if she lend not arms, as well as rules,
What can she more than tell us we are fools?

Teach us to mourn our Nature, not to mend,
A sharp accuser, but a helpless friend!
Or from a judge turn pleader, to persuade   155
The choice we make, or justify it made;
Proud of an easy conquest all along,
She but removes weak passions for the strong:
So, when small humours gather to a gout,
The doctor fancies he has driven them out.   160
      Yes, Nature's road must ever be preferred;
Reason is here no guide, but still a guard:
'Tis hers to rectify, not overthrow,
And treat this passion more as friend than foe:
A mightier Power the strong direction sends,   165
And several Men impels to several ends:
Like varying winds, by other passions tost,
This drives them constant to a certain coast.
Let power or knowledge, gold or glory, please,
Or (oft more strong than all) the love of ease;   170
Through life 'tis followed, even at life's expense;
The merchant's toil, the sage's indolence,
The monk's humility, the hero's pride,
All, all alike, find Reason on their side.
      Th' Eternal Art educing good from ill,   175
Grafts on this Passion our best principle:
'Tis thus the Mercury of Man is fixed,
Strong grows the Virtue with his nature mixed;
The dross cements what else were too refined,
And in one interest body acts with mind.   180
      As fruits, ungrateful to the planter's care,
On savage stocks inserted, learn to bear;
The surest Virtues thus from Passions shoot,
Wild Nature's vigor working at the root.
What crops of wit and honesty appear   185
From spleen, from obstinacy, hate, or fear!
See anger, zeal and fortitude supply;
Even avarice, prudence; sloth, philosophy;
Lust, through some certain strainers well refined,
Is gentle love, and charms all womankind;   190

Envy, to which th' ignoble mind's a slave,
Is emulation in the learned or brave;
Nor Virtue, male or female, can we name,
But what will grow on Pride, or grow on Shame.

    Thus Nature gives us (let it check our pride)   195
The virtue nearest to our vice allied:
Reason the bias turns to good from ill,
And Nero reigns a Titus, if he will.
The fiery soul abhorred in Catiline,
In Decius charms, in Curtius is divine: 200
The same ambition can destroy or save,
And makes a patriot as it makes a knave.

    IV. This light and darkness in our chaos joined,
What shall divide? The God within the mind.

    Extremes in Nature equal ends produce,   205
In Man they join to some mysterious use;
Though each by turns the other's bound invade,
As, in some well-wrought picture, light and shade,
And oft so mix, the difference is too nice
Where ends the Virtue, or begins the Vice.   210

    Fools! who from hence into the notion fall,
That Vice or Virtue there is none at all.
If white and black blend, soften, and unite
A thousand ways, is there no black or white?
Ask your own heart, and nothing is so plain;   215
'Tis to mistake them, costs the time and pain.

    V. Vice is a monster of so frightful mien,
As, to be hated, needs but to be seen;
Yet seen too oft, familiar with her face,
We first endure, then pity, then embrace.   220
But where th' Extreme of Vice, was ne'er agreed:
Ask where's the North? at York, 'tis on the Tweed;
In Scotland, at the Orcades; and there,
At Greenland, Zembla, or the Lord knows where.
No creature owns it in the first degree,   225
But thinks his neighbour further gone than he;
Even those who dwell beneath its very zone,
Or never feel the rage, or never own;
What happier natures shrink at with affright,

The hard inhabitant contends is right.   230
    VI.   Virtuous and vicious every Man must be,
Few in th' extreme, but all in the degree;
The rogue and fool by fits is fair and wise;
And even the best, by fits, what they despise.
'Tis but by parts we follow good or ill;   235
For, Vice or Virtue, Self directs it still;
Each individual seeks a several goal;
But HEAVEN's great view is One, and that the Whole.
That counterworks each folly and caprice;
That disappoints th' effect of every vice;   240
That, happy frailties to all ranks applied;
Shame to the virgin, to the matron pride,
Fear to the statesman, rashness to the chief,
To kings presumption, and to crowds belief:
That, Virtue's ends from Vanity can raise,   245
Which seeks no interest, no reward but praise;
And build on wants, and on defects of mind,
The joy, the peace, the glory of Mankind.
    Heaven forming each on other to depend,
A master, or a servant, or a friend,   250
Bids each on other for assistance call,
Till one Man's weakness grows the strength of all.
Wants, frailties, passions, closer still ally
The common interest, or endear the tie.
To these we owe true friendship, love sincere,   255
Each home-felt joy that life inherits here;
Yet from the same we learn, in its decline,
Those joys, those loves, those interests to resign;
Taught half by Reason, half by mere decay,
To welcome death, and calmly pass away.   260
    Whate'er the Passion, knowledge, fame, or pelf,
Not one will change his neighbour with himself.
The learned is happy nature to explore,
The fool is happy that he knows no more;
The rich is happy in the plenty given,   265
The poor contents him with the care of Heaven.
See the blind beggar dance, the cripple sing,
The sot a hero, lunatic a king;

The starving chemist in his golden views
Supremely blest, the poet in his Muse.   270
        See some strange comfort every state attend,
And Pride bestowed on all, a common friend;
See some fit Passion every age supply,
Hope travels through, nor quits us when we die.
        Behold the child, by Nature's kindly law,   275
Pleased with a rattle, tickled with a straw:
Some livelier plaything gives his youth delight,
A little louder, but as empty quite:
Scarfs, garters, gold, amuse his riper stage,
And beads and prayer books are the toys of age: 280
Pleased with this bauble still, as that before;
Till tired he sleeps, and Life's poor play is o'er.
        Meanwhile Opinion gilds with varying rays
Those painted clouds that beautify our days;
Each want of happiness by hope supplied,   285
And each vacuity of sense by Pride:
These build as fast as knowledge can destroy;
In Folly's cup still laughs the bubble, joy;
One prospect lost, another still we gain;
And not a vanity is given in vain;   290
Even mean Self-love becomes, by force divine,
The scale to measure others' wants by thine.
See! and confess, one comfort still must rise,
'Tis this, Though Man's a fool, yet GOD IS WISE.

EPISTLE III

ARGUMENT

Of the Nature and State of Man *with respect to* Society

    I. The whole Universe one system of Society. Nothing made wholly
for *itself*, nor yet wholly for *another*. The happiness of *Animals* mutual.
II. *Reason* or *Instinct* operate alike to the good of each Individual. *Reason*

or *Instinct* operate also to Society, in all animals. III. How far *Society* carried by Instinct. How much farther by Reason. IV. Of that which is called the *State of Nature*. Reason instructed by Instinct in the invention of *Arts,* and in the Forms of *Society*. V. Origin of Political Societies. Origin of Monarchy. Patriarchal government. VI. Origin of true Religion and Government, from the same principle, of Love. Origin of Superstition and Tyranny, from the same principle, of Fear. The Influence of Self-love operating to the *social* and *public* Good. Restoration of true Religion and Government on their first principle. Mixed Government. Various Forms of each, and the true end of all.

HERE then we rest: "The Universal Cause
Acts to one end, but acts by various laws."
In all the madness of superfluous health,
The trim of pride, the impudence of wealth,
Let this great truth be present night and day;   5
But most be present, if we preach or pray.
    I. Look round our World; behold the chain of Love
Combining all below and all above.
See plastic Nature working to this end,
The single atoms each to other tend,   10
Attract, attracted to, the next in place
Formed and impelled its neighbour to embrace.
See Matter next, with various life endued,
Press to one centre still, the general Good.
See dying vegetables life sustain,   15
See life dissolving vegetate again:
All forms that perish other forms supply,
(By turns we catch the vital breath, and die)
Like bubbles on the sea of Matter born,
They rise, they break, and to that sea return.   20
Nothing is foreign: Parts relate to whole;
One all-extending, all-preserving Soul
Connects each being, greatest with the least;
Made Beast in aid of Man, and Man of Beast;
All served, all serving: nothing stands alone;   25
The chain holds on, and where it ends, unknown.
    Has God, thou fool! worked solely for thy good,
Thy joy, thy pastime, thy attire, thy food?
Who for thy table feeds the wanton fawn,

For him as kindly spread the flowery lawn: 30
Is it for thee the lark ascends and sings?
Joy tunes his voice, joy elevates his wings.
Is it for thee the linnet pours his throat?
Loves of his own and raptures swell the note.
The bounding steed you pompously bestride,   35
Shares with his lord the pleasure and the pride.
Is thine alone the seed that strews the plain?
The birds of heaven shall vindicate their grain.
Thine the full harvest of the golden year?
Part pays, and justly, the deserving steer: 40
The hog, that ploughs not nor obeys thy call,
Lives on the labours of this lord of all.

      Know, Nature's children all divide her care;
The fur that warms a monarch, warmed a bear.
While Man exclaims, "See all things for my use!"   45
"See man for mine!" replies a pampered goose:
And just as short of reason He must fall,
Who thinks all made for one, not one for all.

      Grant that the powerful still the weak control;
Be Man the Wit and Tyrant of the whole: 50
Nature that Tyrant checks; He only knows,
And helps, another creature's wants and woes.
Say, will the falcon, stooping from above,
Smit with her varying plumage, spare the dove?
Admires the jay the insect's gilded wings?   55
Or hears the hawk when Philomela sings?
Man cares for all: to birds he gives his woods,
To beasts his pastures, and to fish his floods;
For some his Interest prompts him to provide,
For more his pleasure, yet for more his pride: 60
All feed on one vain Patron, and enjoy
Th' extensive blessing of his luxury.
That very life his learnèd hunger craves,
He saves from famine, from the savage saves;
Nay, feasts the animal he dooms his feast,   65
And, till he ends the being, makes it blest;
Which sees no more the stroke, or feels the pain,

Than favoured Man by touch ethereal slain.[9]
The creature had his feast of life before;
Thou too must perish, when thy feast is o'er!   70
    To each unthinking being, Heaven a friend,
Gives not the useless knowledge of its end:
To Man imparts it; but with such a view
As, while he dreads it, makes him hope it too:
The hour concealed, and so remote the fear,   75
Death still draws nearer, never seeming near.
Great standing miracle! that Heaven assigned
Its only thinking thing this turn of mind.
    II. Whether with Reason, or with Instinct blest,
Know, all enjoy that power which suits them best;   80
To bliss alike by that direction tend,
And find the means proportioned to their end.
Say, where full Instinct is th' unerring guide,
What Pope or Council can they need beside?
Reason, however able, cool at best,   85
Cares not for service, or but serves when prest,
Stays till we call, and then not often near;
But honest Instinct comes a volunteer,
Sure never to o'ershoot, but just to hit;
While still too wide or short is human Wit;   90
Sure by quick Nature happiness to gain,
Which heavier Reason labours at in vain,
This too serves always, Reason never long;
One must go right, the other may go wrong.
See then the acting and comparing powers   95
One in their nature, which are two in ours;
And Reason raise o'er Instinct as you can,
In this 'tis God directs, in that 'tis Man.
    Who taught the nations of the field and wood
To shun their poison, and to choose their food?   100
Prescient, the tides or tempests to withstand,
Build on the wave, or arch beneath the sand?

[9] Several of the ancients, and many of the Orientals since, esteemed those who were struck by lightning as sacred persons, and the particular favourites of Heaven. P.

Who made the spider parallels design,
Sure as Demoivre, without rule or line?
Who bid the stork, Columbus-like, explore   105
Heavens not his own, and worlds unknown before?
Who calls the council, states the certain day,
Who forms the phalanx, and who points the way?
    III.   God in the nature of each being founds
Its proper bliss, and sets its proper bounds: 110
But as he framed a Whole, the Whole to bless,
On mutual Wants built mutual Happiness:
So from the first, eternal ORDER ran,
And creature linked to creature, man to man.
Whate'er of life all-quickening æther keeps,   115
Or breathes through air, or shoots beneath the deeps,
Or pours profuse on earth, one nature feeds
The vital flame, and swells the genial seeds.
Not Man alone, but all that roam the wood,
Or wing the sky, or roll along the flood,   120
Each loves itself, but not itself alone,
Each sex desires alike, till two are one.
Nor ends the pleasure with the fierce embrace;
They love themselves, a third time, in their race.
Thus beast and bird their common charge attend,   125
The mothers nurse it, and the sires defend;
The young dismissed to wander earth or air,
There stops the Instinct, and there ends the care;
The link dissolves, each seeks a fresh embrace,
Another love succeeds, another race.   130
A longer care Man's helpless kind demands;
That longer care contracts more lasting bands:
Reflection, Reason, still the ties improve,
At once extend the interest, and the love;
With choice we fix, with sympathy we burn;   135
Each Virtue in each Passion takes its turn;
And still new needs, new helps, new habits rise,
That graft benevolence on charities.
Still as one brood, and as another rose,

These natural love maintained, habitual those: 140
The last, scarce ripened into perfect Man,
Saw helpless him from whom their life began:
Memory and forecast just returns engage,
That pointed back to youth, this on to age;
While pleasure, gratitude, and hope, combined,   145
Still spread the interest, and preserved the kind.
    IV. Nor think, in NATURE's STATE they blindly trod;
The state of Nature was the reign of God:
Self-love and Social at her birth began,
Union the bond of all things, and of Man.   150
Pride then was not; nor Arts, that Pride to aid;
Man walked with beast, joint tenant of the shade;
The same his table, and the same his bed;
No murder clothed him, and no murder fed.
In the same temple, the resounding wood,   155
All vocal beings hymned their equal God:
The shrine with gore unstained, with gold undrest,
Unbribed, unbloody, stood the blameless priest:
Heaven's attribute was Universal Care,
And Man's prerogative to rule, but spare.   160
Ah! how unlike the man of times to come!
Of half that live the butcher and the tomb;
Who, foe to Nature, hears the general groan,
Murders their species, and betrays his own.
But just disease to luxury succeeds,   165
And every death its own avenger breeds;
The Fury-passions from that blood began,
And turned on Man a fiercer savage, Man.
    See him from Nature rising slow to Art!
To copy Instinct then was Reason's part;   170
Thus then to Man the voice of Nature spake—
"Go, from the Creatures thy instructions take:
Learn from the birds what food the thickets yield;[10]

---

[10] It is a common practice amongst Navigators, when thrown upon a
desert coast, and in want of refreshments, to observe what fruits have

Learn from the beasts the physic of the field;[11]
Thy arts of building from the bee receive;   175
Learn of the mole to plough, the worm to weave;
Learn of the little Nautilus to sail,[12]
Spread the thin oar, and catch the driving gale.
Here too all forms of social union find,
And hence let Reason, late, instruct Mankind: 180
Here subterranean works and cities see;
There towns aerial on the waving tree.
Learn each small People's genius, policies,
The Ant's republic, and the realm of Bees;
How those in common all their wealth bestow,   185
And Anarchy without confusion know;
And these for ever, though a Monarch reign,
Their separate cells and properties maintain.
Mark what unvaried laws preserve each state,
Laws wise as Nature, and as fixed as Fate.   190
In vain thy Reason finer webs shall draw,
Entangle Justice in her net of Law,
And right, too rigid, harden into wrong;
Still for the strong too weak, the weak too strong.
Yet go! and thus o'er all the creatures sway,   195
Thus let the wiser make the rest obey;
And, for those Arts mere Instinct could afford,
Be crowned as Monarchs, or as Gods adored."
    V.   Great Nature spoke; observant Men obeyed;
Cities were built, Societies were made: 200

been touched by the Birds: and to venture on these without further hesi-
tation. [W.]
[11] See Pliny's *Natural History,* Bk. VIII, Chap 27, where several instances
are given of Animals discovering the medicinal efficacy of herbs by their
own use of them; and pointing out to some operations in the art of
healing, by their own practice. [W.]
[12] Oppian. *Halieut.* Lib. 1. describes this fish in the following manner:
"They swim on the surface of the sea, on the back of their shells, which
exactly resemble the hulk of a ship; they raise two feet like masts, and
extend a membrane between, which serves as a sail; the other two feet
they employ as oars at the side. They are usually seen in the Mediter-
ranean." P.

Here rose one little state; another near
Grew by like means, and joined, through love or fear.
Did here the trees with ruddier burdens bend,
And there the streams in purer rills descend?
What War could ravish, Commerce could bestow,   205
And he returned a friend, who came a foe.
Converse and Love mankind might strongly draw,
When Love was Liberty, and Nature Law.
Thus States were formed; the name of King unknown,
Till common interest placed the sway in one.   210
'Twas VIRTUE ONLY (or in arts or arms,
Diffusing blessings, or averting harms)
The same which in a Sire the Sons obeyed,
A Prince the Father of a People made.
      VI. Till then, by Nature crowned, each Patriarch sate,
King, priest, and parent of his growing state;   216
On him, their second Providence, they hung,
Their law his eye, their oracle his tongue.
He from the wondering furrow called the food,
Taught to command the fire, control the flood,   220
Draw forth the monsters of th' abyss profound,
Or fetch th' aërial eagle to the ground.
Till drooping, sickening, dying they began
Whom they revered as God to mourn as Man:
Then, looking up from sire to sire, explored   225
One great first father, and that first adored.
Or plain tradition that this All begun,
Conveyed unbroken faith from sire to son;
The worker from the work distinct was known,
And simple Reason never sought but one: 230
Ere Wit oblique had broke that steady light,[13]
Man, like his Maker, saw that all was right;
To Virtue, in the paths of Pleasure, trod,
And owned a Father when he owned a God.
LOVE all the faith, and all th' allegiance then;   235

[13] [An] . . . allusion to the effects of the prismatic glass on the rays of
light. [W.]

For Nature knew no right divine in Men,
No ill could fear in God: and understood
A sovereign being but a sovereign good.
True faith, true policy, united ran,
This was but love of God, and this of Man.   240
      Who first taught souls enslaved, and realms undone,
Th' enormous faith of many made for one;[14]
That proud exception to all Nature's laws,
T' invert the world, and counterwork its Cause?
Force first made Conquest, and that conquest, Law;   245
Till Superstition taught the tyrant awe,
Then shared the Tyranny, then lent it aid,
And Gods of Conquerors, Slaves of Subjects made:
She midst the lightning's blaze, and thunder's sound,
When rocked the mountains, and when groaned the ground,
She taught the weak to bend, the proud to pray,   251
To Power unseen, and mightier far than they:
She, from the rending earth and bursting skies,
Saw Gods descend, and fiends infernal rise:
Here fixed the dreadful, there the blest abodes;   255
Fear made her Devils, and weak Hope her Gods;
Gods partial, changeful, passionate, unjust,
Whose attributes were Rage, Revenge, or Lust;
Such as the souls of cowards might conceive,
And, formed like tyrants, tyrants would believe.   260
Zeal then, not charity, became the guide;
And hell was built on spite, and heaven on pride.
Then sacred seemed th' ethereal vault no more;
Altars grew marble then, and reeked with gore:
Then first the Flamen tasted living food;   265
Next his grim idol smeared with human blood;
With Heaven's own thunders shook the world below,
And played the God an engine on his foe.
      So drives Self-love, through just and through unjust,
To one Man's power, ambition, lucre, lust: 270

---

[14] In this Aristotle placeth the difference between a King and a Tyrant, that the first supposeth himself made for the People; the other, that the People are made for him. . . . *Politics,* Bk. V, Chap. 10.   [W.]

The same Self-love, in all, becomes the cause
Of what restrains him, Government and Laws.
For, what one likes if others like as well,
What serves one will, when many wills rebel?
How shall he keep, what, sleeping or awake,   275
A weaker may surprise, a stronger take?
His safety must his liberty restrain:
All join to guard what each desires to gain.
Forced into virtue thus by Self-defence,
Even Kings learned justice and benevolence: 280
Self-love forsook the path it first pursued,
And found the private in the public good.
    'Twas then, the studious head or generous mind,
Follower of God or friend of humankind,
Poet or Patriot, rose but to restore   285
The Faith and Moral, Nature gave before;
Relumed her ancient light, not kindled new;
If not God's image, yet his shadow drew:
Taught Power's due use to People and to Kings,
Taught nor to slack, nor strain its tender strings,   290
The less, or greater, set so justly true,
That touching one must strike the other too;
Till jarring interests, of themselves create
Th' according music of a well-mixed State.
Such is the World's great harmony, that springs   295
From Order, Union, full Consent of things:
Where small and great, where weak and mighty, made
To serve, not suffer, strengthen, not invade;
More powerful each as needful to the rest,
And, in proportion as it blesses, blest;   300
Draw to one point, and to one centre bring
Beast, Man, or Angel, Servant, Lord, or King.
    For Forms of Government let fools contest;[15]

[15] The Reader will not be displeased to see the Poet's own apology, as I find it written in the year 1740, in his own hand, in the margin of a book, where he found these two celebrated lines misapplied. "The author of these lines was far from meaning that no one form of Government is, in itself, better than another . . . but that no form . . . in itself, can be

Whate'er is best administered is best:
For Modes of Faith let graceless zealots fight;   305
His can't be wrong whose life is in the right:
In Faith and Hope the world will disagree,
But all Mankind's concern is Charity:
All must be false that thwart this One great End;
And all of God, that bless Mankind or mend.   310
   Man, like the generous vine, supported lives;
The strength he gains is from th' embrace he gives.
On their own Axis as the Planets run,
Yet make at once their circle round the Sun;
So two consistent motions act the Soul;   315
And one regards Itself, and one the Whole.
   Thus God and Nature linked the general frame,
And bade Self-love and Social be the same.

EPISTLE IV

ARGUMENT

Of the Nature and State of Man *with respect to* Happiness

I. False Notions of Happiness, Philosophical and Popular, answered.
II. It is the End of all Men, and attainable by all. God intends Happiness
to be *equal;* and to be so, it must be *social,* since all particular happiness
depends on general, and since he governs by *general,* not *particular* Laws.
As it is necessary for *Order,* and the peace and welfare of *Society,* that
external goods should be *unequal,* Happiness is not made to consist in
these. But, notwithstanding that inequality, the *balance of Happiness*
among *Mankind* is kept even by Providence, by two Passions of
Hope and *Fear.* III. What the Happiness of *Individuals* is, as far as is
consistent with the constitution of this world; and that the *good Man* has

sufficient to make a people happy, unless it be administered with integ-
rity." [W.]

here the advantage. The error of imputing to *Virtue* what are only the calamities of *Nature,* or of *Fortune.* IV. The folly of expecting that God should alter his general Laws in favour of particulars. V. That we are not judges who are good; but that, whoever they are, they must be happiest. VI. That *external goods* are not the proper rewards, but often inconsistent with, or destructive of Virtue. That even these can make no Man happy without Virtue: Instanced in *Riches; Honours; Nobility; Greatness; Fame; Superior Talents.* With pictures of human Infelicity in Men possessed of them all. VII. That *Virtue* only constitutes a Happiness, whose object is *universal,* and whose prospect *eternal.* That the *perfection* of *Virtue* and *Happiness* consists in a *conformity* to the ORDER of PROVIDENCE here, and a *Resignation* to it here and hereafter.

OH HAPPINESS! our being's end and aim!
Good, Pleasure, Ease, Content! whate'er thy name:
That something still which prompts th' eternal sigh,
For which we bear to live, or dare to die,
Which still so near us, yet beyond us lies,   5
O'erlooked, seen double, by the fool, and wise.
Plant of celestial seed! if dropped below,
Say, in what mortal soil thou deignst to grow?
Fair opening to some Court's propitious shine,
Or deep with diamonds in the flaming mine?   10
Twined with the wreaths Parnassian laurels yield,
Or reaped in iron harvests of the field?
Where grows?—where grows it not? If vain our toil,
We ought to blame the culture, not the soil:
Fixed to no spot is Happiness sincere,   15
'Tis nowhere to be found, or everywhere;
'Tis never to be bought, but always free,
And fled from monarchs, ST. JOHN! dwells with thee.
    I.   Ask of the Learned the way? The Learned are blind;
This bids to serve, and that to shun mankind;   20
Some place the bliss in action, some in ease,
Those call it Pleasure, and Contentment these;
Some sunk to Beasts, find pleasure end in pain;
Some swelled to Gods, confess even Virtue vain;
Or indolent, to each extreme they fall,   25
To trust in every thing, or doubt of all.

Who thus define it, say they more or less
Than this, that Happiness is Happiness?
    II.   Take Nature's path, and mad Opinion's leave;
All states can reach it, and all heads conceive;   30
Obvious her goods, in no extreme they dwell;
There needs but thinking right, and meaning well;
And mourn our various portions as we please,
Equal is Common Sense, and Common Ease.
    Remember, Man, "the Universal Cause   35
Acts not by partial, but by general laws;"
And makes what Happiness we justly call
Subsist not in the good of one, but all.
There's not a blessing Individuals find,
But some way leans and hearkens to the kind: 40
No Bandit fierce, no Tyrant mad with pride,
No caverned Hermit, rests self-satisfied:
Who most to shun or hate Mankind pretend,
Seek an admirer, or would fix a friend:
Abstract what others feel, what others think,   45
All pleasures sicken, and all glories sink:
Each has his share; and who would more obtain,
Shall find, the pleasure pays not half the pain.
    ORDER is Heaven's first law; and this confest,
Some are, and must be, greater than the rest,   50
More rich, more wise; but who infers from hence
That such are happier, shocks all common sense.
Heaven to Mankind impartial we confess,
If all are equal in their Happiness:
But mutual wants this Happiness increase;   55
All Nature's difference keeps all Nature's peace.
Condition, circumstance is not the thing;
Bliss is the same in subject or in king,
In who obtain defence, or who defend,
In him who is, or him who finds a friend: 60
Heaven breathes through every member of the whole
One common blessing, as one common soul.
But Fortune's gifts if each alike possest,

And each were equal, must not all contest?
If then to all Men Happiness was meant,   65
God in Externals could not place Content.
  Fortune her gifts may variously dispose,
And these be happy called, unhappy those;
But Heaven's just balance equal will appear,
While those are placed in Hope, and these in Fear: 70
Nor present good or ill, the joy or curse,
But future views of better, or of worse.
  Oh sons of earth! attempt ye still to rise,
By mountains piled on mountains, to the skies?
Heaven still with laughter the vain toil surveys,   75
And buries madmen in the heaps they raise.
  III. Know, all the good that individuals find,
Or God and Nature meant to mere Mankind,
Reason's whole pleasure, all the joys of Sense,
Lie in three words, Health, Peace, and Competence.   80
But Health consists with Temperance alone;
And Peace, oh Virtue! Peace is all thy own.
The good or bad the gifts of Fortune gain;
But these less taste them, as they worse obtain.
Say, in pursuit of profit or delight,   85
Who risk the most, that take wrong means, or right?
Of Vice or Virtue, whether blest or curst,
Which meets contempt, or which compassion first?
Count all th' advantage prosperous Vice attains,
'Tis but what Virtue flies from and disdains: 90
And grant the bad what happiness they would,
One they must want, which is, to pass for good.
  Oh blind to truth, and God's whole scheme below,
Who fancy Bliss to Vice, to Virtue Woe!
Who sees and follows that great scheme the best,   95
Best knows the blessing, and will most be blest.
But fools the Good alone unhappy call,
For ills or accidents that chance to all.
See FALKLAND dies, the virtuous and the just!
See godlike TURENNE prostrate on the dust!   100

See SIDNEY bleeds amid the martial strife![16]
Was this their Virtue, or Contempt of Life?
Say, was it Virtue, more though Heaven ne'er gave,
Lamented DIGBY![17] sunk thee to the grave?
Tell me, if Virtue made the Son expire,   105
Why, full of days and honour, lives the Sire?
Why drew Marseille's good bishop purer breath,[18]
When Nature sickened, and each gale was death?
Or why so long (in life if long can be)
Lent Heaven a parent to the poor and me?[19]   110
     What makes all physical or moral ill?
There deviates Nature, and here wanders Will.
God sends not ill; if rightly understood,
Or partial Ill is universal Good,
Or Change admits, or Nature lets it fall;   115
Short, and but rare, till Man improved it all.
We just as wisely might of Heaven complain
That righteous Abel was destroyed by Cain,
As that the virtuous son is ill at ease
When his lewd father gave the dire disease.   120
Think we, like some weak Prince, th' Eternal Cause,
Prone for his favorites to reverse his laws?
    IV.   Shall burning Etna, if a sage requires,[20]
Forget to thunder, and recall her fires?
On air or sea new motions be imprest,   125
Oh blameless Bethel![21] to relieve thy breast?
When the loose mountain trembles from on high,

[16] Lord Falkland was killed at the battle of Newbury in 1643; Marshal
Turenne, near Salzbach in 1675; Sir Philip Sidney was mortally wounded
at Zutphen in 1586. Sidney was 32, Falkand 33, and Turenne 64.
[17] Pope's friend the Hon. Robert Digby died at the age of 40 in 1726, and
Pope wrote his Epitaph.
[18] François de Belsunce, Bishop of Marseilles, distinguished himself by his
activity during the plague which visited that city in 1720–1721. He died
in 1755 at an advanced age.
[19] The Mother of the author, a person of great piety and charity, died
the year this poem was finished, viz. 1733.   [W.]
[20] The philosopher Empedocles perished by jumping into Etna.
[21] See *Satire* II, ii, "To Mr. Bethel."

Shall gravitation cease, if you go by?
Or some old temple, nodding to its fall,
For Chartres' head reserve the hanging wall?[22]   130
     V.   But still this world (so fitted for the knave)
Contents us not. A better shall we have?
A kingdom of the Just then let it be:
But first consider how those Just agree.
The good must merit God's peculiar care;   135
But who, but God, can tell us who they are?
One thinks on Calvin Heaven's own spirit fell;
Another deems him instrument of hell;
If Calvin feel Heaven's blessing, or its rod,
This cries there is, and that, there is no God.   140
What shocks one part will edify the rest,
Nor with one system can they all be blest.
The very best will variously incline,
And what rewards your Virtue, punish mine.
WHATEVER IS, IS RIGHT.—This world, 'tis true,   145
Was made for Cæsar—but for Titus too:
And which more blest? who chained his country, say,
Or he whose Virtue sighed to lose a day?
     "But sometimes Virtue starves, while Vice is fed."
What then? Is the reward of Virtue bread?   150
That, Vice may merit, 'tis the price of toil;
The knave deserves it, when he tills the soil,
The knave deserves it, when he tempts the main,
Where Folly fights for kings, or dives for gain.
The good man may be weak, be indolent;   155
Nor is his claim to plenty, but content.
But grant him Riches, your demand is o'er?
"No—shall the good want Health, the good want Power?"
Add Health, and Power, and every earthly thing,
"Why bounded Power? why private? why no king?"   160
Nay, why external for internal given?
Why is not Man a God, and Earth a Heaven?

---

[22] Eusebius, *History of the Christian Church*, Bk. III, Chap. 29, tells how the roof of the building in which Cerinthus the heretic was bathing fell and crushed him to death.

Who ask and reason thus, will scarce conceive
God gives enough, while he has more to give:
Immense the power, immense were the demand;   165
Say, at what part of nature will they stand?
    VI. What nothing earthly gives, or can destroy,
The soul's calm sunshine, and the heartfelt joy,
Is Virtue's prize: A better would you fix?
Then give Humility a coach and six,   170
Justice a Conqueror's sword, or Truth a gown,
Or Public Spirit its great cure, a Crown.
Weak, foolish man! will Heaven reward us there
With the same trash mad mortals wish for here?
The Boy and Man an individual makes,   175
Yet sighst thou now for apples and for cakes?
Go, like the Indian, in another life[23]
Expect thy dog, thy bottle, and thy wife:
As well as dream such trifles are assigned,
As toys and empires, for a godlike mind.   180
Rewards, that either would to Virtue bring
No joy, or be destructive of the thing:
How oft by these at sixty are undone
The Virtues of a saint at twenty-one!
To whom can Riches give Repute, or Trust,   185
Content, or Pleasure, but the Good and Just?
Judges and Senates have been bought for gold,
Esteem and Love were never to be sold.
Oh fool! to think God hates the worthy mind,
The lover and the love of humankind,   190
Whose life is healthful, and whose conscience clear,
Because he wants a thousand pounds a year.
    Honour and shame from no Condition rise;
Act well your part, there all the honour lies.
Fortune in Men has some small difference made,   195
One flaunts in rags, one flutters in brocade;
The cobbler aproned, and the parson gowned,
The friar hooded, and the monarch crowned.

---

[23] Alluding to the example of the Indian in *Epistle* I, 99. [W.]

"What differ more" (you cry) "than crown and cowl?"
I'll tell you, friend! a wise man and a Fool.   200
You'll find, if once the monarch acts the monk,
Or, cobbler-like, the parson will be drunk,
Worth makes the man, and want of it, the fellow;
The rest is all but leather or prunella.[24]

    Stuck o'er with titles and hung round with strings,
That thou mayst be by kings, or whores of kings.   206
Boast the pure blood of an illustrious race,
In quiet flow from Lucrece to Lucrece:
But by your fathers' worth if yours you rate,
Count me those only who were good and great.   210
Go! if your ancient, but ignoble blood
Has crept through scoundrels ever since the flood,
Go! and pretend your family is young;
Nor own, your fathers have been fools so long.
What can ennoble sots, or slaves, or cowards?   215
Alas! not all the blood of all the HOWARDS.

    Look next on Greatness; say where Greatness lies?
"Where, but among the Heroes and the wise?"
Heroes are much the same, the point's agreed,
From Macedonia's madman to the Swede;   220
The whole strange purpose of their lives, to find
Or make, an enemy of all mankind!
Not one looks backward, onward still he goes,
Yet ne'er looks forward farther than his nose.
No less alike the Politic and Wise;   225
All sly slow things, with circumspective eyes:
Men in their loose unguarded hours they take,
Not that themselves are wise, but others weak.
But grant that those can conquer, these can cheat;
'Tis phrase absurd to call a Villain Great: 230
Who wickedly is wise, or madly brave,
Is but the more a fool, the more a knave.
Who noble ends by noble means obtains,
Or failing, smiles in exile or in chains,

---

[24] A worsted cloth of which clergymen's gowns were made.

Like good Aurelius let him reign, or bleed   235
Like Socrates, that Man is great indeed.
        What's Fame? a fancied life in others' breath,
A thing beyond us, even before our death.
Just what you hear, you have, and what's unknown
The same (my Lord) if Tully's, or your own.   240
All that we feel of it begins and ends
In the small circle of our foes or friends;
To all beside as much an empty shade
An Eugene living, as a Cæsar dead;
Alike or when, or where, they shone, or shine,   245
Or on the Rubicon, or on the Rhine.
A Wit's a feather, and a Chief a rod;
An honest Man's the noblest work of God.
Fame but from death a villain's name can save,
As Justice tears his body from the grave;   250
When what t' oblivion better was resigned,
Is hung on high, to poison half mankind.
All fame is foreign, but of true desert;
Plays round the head, but comes not to the heart:
One self-approving hour whole years outweighs   255
Of stupid starers, and of loud huzzas;
And more true joy Marcellus exiled feels,
Than Cæsar with a senate at his heels.
        In Parts superior what advantage lies?
Tell (for You can) what is it to be wise?   260
'Tis but to know how little can be known;
To see all others' faults, and feel our own:
Condemned in business or in arts to drudge,
Without a second, or without a judge:
Truths would you teach, or save a sinking land?   265
All fear, none aid you, and few understand.
Painful pre-eminence! yourself to view
Above life's weakness, and its comforts too.
        Bring then these blessings to a strict account;
Make fair deductions; see to what they mount: 270
How much of other each is sure to cost;
How each for other oft is wholly lost;

How inconsistent greater goods with these;
How sometimes life is risked, and always ease:
Think, and if still the things thy envy call,   275
Say, wouldst thou be the Man to whom they fall?
To sigh for ribbands if thou art so silly,
Mark how they grace Lord Umbra, or Sir Billy:
Is yellow dirt the passion of thy life?
Look but on Gripus, or on Gripus' wife: 280
If Parts allure thee, think how Bacon shined,
The wisest, brightest, meanest of mankind:
Or ravished with the whistling of a Name,
See Cromwell, damned to everlasting fame!
If all, united, thy ambition call,   285
From ancient story learn to scorn them all.
There, in the rich, the honoured, famed, and great,
See the false scale of Happiness complete!
In hearts of Kings, or arms of Queens who lay,
How happy! those to ruin, these betray.   290
Mark by what wretched steps their glory grows,
From dirt and seaweed as proud Venice rose;
In each how guilt and greatness equal rañ,
And all that raised the Hero, sunk the Man:
Now Europe's laurels on their brows behold,   295
But stained with blood, or ill exchanged for gold:
Then see them broke with toils, or sunk in ease,
Or infamous for plundered provinces.
Oh wealth ill-fated! which no act of fame
E'er taught to shine, or sanctified from shame!   300
What greater bliss attends their close of life?
Some greedy minion, or imperious wife.
The trophied arches, storied halls invade
And haunt their slumbers in the pompous shade.
Alas! not dazzled with their noontide ray,   305
Compute the morn and evening to the day;
The whole amount of that enormous fame,
A Tale, that blends their glory with their shame!
    VII.   Know then this truth (enough for Man to know)
"Virtue alone is Happiness below."   310

The only point where human bliss stands still,
And tastes the good without the fall to ill;
Where only Merit constant pay receives,
Is blest in what it takes, and what it gives;
The joy unequalled, if its end it gain,   315
And if it lose, attended with no pain:
Without satiety, though e'er so blessed,
And but more relished as the more distressed:
The broadest mirth unfeeling Folly wears,
Less pleasing far than Virtue's very tears: 320
Good, from each object, from each place acquired,
For ever exercised, yet never tired;
Never elated, while one man's oppressed;
Never dejected, while another's blessed;
And where no wants, no wishes can remain,   325
Since but to wish more Virtue, is to gain.
  See the sole bliss Heaven could on all bestow!
Which who but feels can taste, but thinks can know:
Yet poor with fortune, and with learning blind,
The bad must miss; the good, untaught, will find;   330
Slave to no sect, who takes no private road,
But looks through Nature up to Nature's God;
Pursues that Chain which links the immense design,
Joins heaven and earth, and mortal and divine;
Sees, that no Being any bliss can know,   335
But touches some above, and some below;
Learns, from this union of the rising Whole,
The first, last purpose of the human soul;
And knows, where Faith, Law, Morals, all began,
All end, in LOVE OF GOD, and LOVE OF MAN.   340
  For him alone, Hope leads from goal to goal,
And opens still, and opens on his soul;
Till lengthened on the Faith, and unconfined,
It pours the bliss that fills up all the mind.
He sees, why Nature plants in Man alone   345
Hope of known bliss, and Faith in bliss unknown:
(Nature, whose dictates to no other kind
Are given in vain, but what they seek they find)

Wise is her present; she connects in this
His greatest Virtue with his greatest Bliss;   350
At once his own bright prospect to be blest,
And strongest motive to assist the rest.
      Self-love thus pushed to social, to divine,
Gives thee to make thy neighbour's blessing thine.
Is this too little for the boundless heart?   355
Extend it, let thy enemies have part:
Grasp the whole worlds of Reason, Life, and Sense,
In one close system of Benevolence:
Happier as kinder, in whate'er degree,
And height of Bliss but height of Charity.   360
      God loves from Whole to Parts: But human soul
Must rise from Individual to the Whole.
Self-love but serves the virtuous mind to wake,[25]
As the small pebble stirs the peaceful lake;
The centre moved, a circle straight succeeds,   365
Another still, and still another spreads;
Friend, parent, neighbour, first it will embrace;
His country next; and next all human race;
Wide and more wide, th' o'erflowings of the mind
Take every creature in, of every kind;   370
Earth smiles around, with boundless bounty blest,
And Heaven beholds its image in his breast.
      Come then, my Friend! my Genius! come along;
Oh master of the poet, and the song!
And while the Muse now stoops, or now ascends,   375
To Man's low passions, or their glorious ends,
Teach me, like thee, in various nature wise,
To fall with dignity, with temper rise;
Formed by thy converse, happily to steer
From grave to gay, from lively to severe;   380
Correct with spirit, eloquent with ease,
Intent to reason, or polite to please.

---

[25] Rochefoucault, Esprit, and their wordy disciple Mandeville, had ob-
served that Self-love was the Origin of all those virtues Mankind most
admire; and therefore foolishly supposed it was the End likewise. [W.]

Oh! while along the stream of Time thy name
Expanded flies, and gathers all its fame,
Say, shall my little bark attendant sail,   385
Pursue the triumph, and partake the gale?
When statesmen, heroes, kings, in dust repose,
Whose sons shall blush their fathers were thy foes,
Shall then this verse to future age pretend
Thou wert my guide, philosopher, and friend?   390
That urged by thee, I turned the tuneful art
From sounds to things, from fancy to the heart;
For Wit's false mirror held up Nature's light;
Showed erring Pride, WHATEVER IS, IS RIGHT;
That REASON, PASSION, answer one great aim;   395
That true SELF-LOVE and SOCIAL are the same;
That VIRTUE only makes our Bliss below;
And all our Knowledge is, OURSELVES TO KNOW.

1738

THE UNIVERSAL
PRAYER[1]

FATHER of All! in every Age,
  In every Clime adored,
By Saint, by Savage, and by Sage,
  Jehovah, Jove, or Lord!

Thou Great First Cause, least understood: 5
  Who all my Sense confined
To know but this, that Thou art Good,
  And that myself am blind;

Yet gave me, in this dark Estate,
  To see the Good from Ill;   10
And binding Nature fast in Fate,
  Left free the Human Will.

What Conscience dictates to be done,
  Or warns me not to do,
This, teach me more than Hell to shun,   15
  That, more than Heaven pursue.

What Blessings thy free Bounty gives,
  Let me not cast away;

[1] Concerning this poem, it may be proper to observe that some passages, in the preceding *Essay*, having been unjustly suspected of a tendency towards Fate and *Naturalism*, the author composed this Prayer as the sum of all, to show that his system was founded in *free will*, and terminated in piety: That the first cause was as well the Lord and Governor of the Universe as the Creator of it; and that, by submission to his will (the great principle enforced throughout the *Essay*) was not meant the suffering ourselves to be carried along with a blind determination; but a religious acquiescence, and confidence full of *Hope* and Immortality. To give all this the greater weight and reality, the poet chose for his model the LORD'S PRAYER, which, of all others, best deserves the title prefixed to this Paraphrase. [W.]

For God is paid when Man receives,
    T' enjoy is to obey.
20

Yet not to Earth's contracted Span
    Thy Goodness let me bound,
Or think Thee Lord alone of Man,
    When thousand Worlds are round:

Let not this weak, unknowing hand
25
    Presume thy bolts to throw,
And deal damnation round the land,
    On each I judge thy Foe.

If I am right, thy grace impart,
    Still in the right to stay;
30
If I am wrong, oh teach my heart
    To find that better way.

Save me alike from foolish Pride,
    Or impious Discontent,
At aught thy Wisdom has denied,
35
    Or aught thy Goodness lent.

Teach me to feel another's Woe,
    To hide the Fault I see;
That Mercy I to others show,
    That Mercy show to me.
40

Mean though I am, not wholly so,
    Since quickened by thy Breath;
Oh lead me wheresoe'er I go,
    Through this day's Life or Death.

This day, be Bread and Peace my Lot:
45
    All else beneath the Sun,
Thou knowst if best bestowed or not,
    And let Thy Will be done.

To thee, whose Temple is all Space,
    Whose Altar Earth, Sea, Skies!
50
One Chorus let all Being raise!
    All Nature's Incense rise!

MORAL ESSAYS
In Four Epistles To Several Persons

Est brevitate opus, ut currat sententia, neu se
Impediat verbis lassas onerantibus aures:
Et sermone opus est modo tristi, sæpe jocoso,
Defendente vicem modo Rhetoris atque Poetæ,
Interdum urbani, parcentis viribus, atque
Extenuantis eas consultò.—Horace [*Satire* I. x. 17–22.]

1734

EPISTLE I

To Sir Richard Temple, Lord Cobham

ARGUMENT

Of the Knowledge *and* Characters *of* MEN

That it is not sufficient for this knowledge to consider Man in the
Abstract: Books will not serve the purpose, nor yet our own *Experience*
singly. General maxims, unless they be formed upon *both,* will be but
notional. Some Peculiarity in every man, characteristic to himself, yet
varying from himself. Difficulties arising from our own Passions, Fancies,
Faculties, etc. The shortness of Life, to obesrve in, and the uncertainty
of the *Principles of action* in men, to observe by. Our *own* Principle of

action often hid from ourselves. Some few Characters plain, but in general confounded, dissembled, or inconsistent. The same man utterly different in different places and seasons. Unimaginable weaknesses in the greatest. Nothing constant and certain but *God* and *Nature.* No judging of the *Motives* from the actions; the same actions proceeding from contrary Motives, and the same Motives influencing contrary actions. II. Yet to form *Characters,* we can only take the *strongest actions* of a man's life, and try to make them *agree:* The utter uncertainty of this, from *Nature* itself, and from *Policy. Characters* given according to the *rank* of men of the world. And some reason for it. *Education* alters the *Nature,* or at least *Character* of many. *Actions, Passions, Opinions, Manners, Humours,* or *Principles* all subject to change. No judging by *Nature.* III. It only remains to find (if we can) his RULING PASSION: That will certainly influence all the rest, and can reconcile the seeming or real inconsistency of all his actions. Instanced in the extraordinary character of *Clodio.* A caution against mistaking *second qualities* for *first,* which will destroy all possibility of the knowledge of mankind. Examples of the strength of the *Ruling Passion,* and its continuation to the last breath.

EPISTLE I

I. YES, you despise the man to Books confined,
Who from his study rails at human kind;
Though what he learns he speaks, and may advance
Some general maxims, or be right by chance.
The coxcomb bird, so talkative and grave,   5
That from his cage cries Cuckold, Whore, and Knave,
Though many a passenger he rightly call,
You hold him no Philosopher at all.
    And yet the fate of all extremes is such,
Men may be read as well as Books, too much.   10
To observations which ourselves we make,
We grow more partial for the Observer's sake;
To written Wisdom, as another's, less:
Maxims are drawn from Notions, these from Guess.

There's some Peculiar in each leaf and grain,   15
Some unmarked fibre, or some varying vein:
Shall only Man be taken in the gross?
Grant but as many sorts of Mind as Moss.
        That each from other differs, first confess;
Next, that he varies from himself no less: 20
Add Nature's, Custom's, Reason's, Passion's strife,
And all Opinion's colours cast on life.
        Our depths who fathoms, or our shallows finds,
Quick whirls, and shifting eddies, of our minds?
On human actions reason though you can,   25
It may be Reason, but it is not Man:
His Principle of action once explore,
That instant 'tis his Principle no more.
Like following life through creatures you dissect,
You lose it in the moment you detect.   30
        Yet more; the difference is as great between
The optics seeing, as the object seen.
All Manners take a tincture from our own;
Or come discoloured through our Passions shown.
Or Fancy's beam enlarges, multiplies,   35
Contracts, inverts, and gives ten thousand dyes.
        Nor will Life's stream for Observation stay,
It hurries all too fast to mark their way:
In vain sedate reflections we would make,
When half our knowledge we must snatch, not take.   40
Oft, in the Passions' wild rotation tost,
Our spring of action to ourselves is lost:
Tired, not determined, to the last we yield,
And what comes then is master of the field.
As the last image of that troubled heap,   45
When Sense subsides, and Fancy sports in sleep,
(Though past the recollection of the thought)
Becomes the stuff of which our dream is wrought:
Something as dim to our internal view,
Is thus, perhaps, the cause of most we do.   50
        True, some are open, and to all men known;
Others so very close, they're hid from none;

(So Darkness strikes the sense no less than Light)
Thus gracious CHANDOS[1] is beloved at sight;
And every child hates Shylock, though his soul   55
Still sits at squat, and peeps not from its hole.
At half mankind when generous Manly raves,
All know 'tis Virtue, for he thinks them knaves:
When universal homage Umbra pays,
All see 'tis Vice, and itch of vulgar praise.   60
When Flattery glares, all hate it in a Queen,
While one there is who charms us with his Spleen.
    But these plain Characters we rarely find;
Though strong the bent, yet quick the turns of mind:
Or puzzling Contraries confound the whole;   65
Or Affectations quite reverse the soul.
The Dull, flat Falsehood serves, for policy;
And in the Cunning, Truth itself's a lie:
Unthought-of Frailties cheat us in the Wise;
The Fool lies hid in inconsistencies.   70
    See the same man, in vigour, in the gout;
Alone, in company; in place, or out;
Early at Business, and at Hazard late;
Mad at a Fox Chase, wise at a Debate;
Drunk at a Borough, civil at a Ball;   75
Friendly at Hackney, faithless at Whitehall.
    Catius is ever moral, ever grave,
Thinks who endures a knave, is next a knave,
Save just at dinner—then, prefers, no doubt,
A Rogue with Venison to a Saint without.   80
    Who would not praise Patritio's high desert,
His hand unstained, his uncorrupted heart,
His comprehensive head! all Interests weighed,
All Europe saved, yet Britain not betrayed.
He thanks you not, his pride is in Piquet,   85
Newmarket fame, and judgment at a Bet.

[1] James Brydges, First Duke of Chandos. By this compliment Pope perhaps hoped to offset the impression that the character of Timon in *Moral Essay* IV was modeled on the Duke.

What made (say Montaigne, or more sage Charron!)[2]
Otho a warrior, Cromwell a buffoon?
A perjured Prince a leaden Saint revere,[3]
A godless Regent tremble at a Star?[4]   90
The throne a Bigot keep, a Genius quit,[5]
Faithless through Piety, and duped through Wit?
Europe a Woman, Child, or Dotard rule,
And just her wisest monarch made a fool?

    Know, GOD and NATURE only are the same: 95
In Man, the judgment shoots at flying game,
A bird of passage! gone as soon as found,
Now in the Moon perhaps, now under ground.

    In vain the Sage, with retrospective eye,
Would from th' apparent What conclude the Why,   100
Infer the Motive from the Deed, and show,
That what we chanced was what we meant to do.
Behold! If Fortune or a Mistress frowns,
Some plunge in business, others shave their crowns:
To ease the Soul of one oppressive weight,   105
This quits an Empire, that embroils a State:
The same adust complexion has impelled
Charles to the Convent, Philip to the Field.[6]

[2] Charron . . . an admirer of Montaigne . . . has transferred an infinite number of his thoughts into his famous book *De la Sagesse;* but his moderating everywhere the extravagant Pyrrhonism of his friend, is the reason why the poet calls him *more sage Charron.*   [W.]

[3] Louis XI of France wore in his Hat a leaden image of the Virgin Mary, which when he swore by, he feared to break his oath.   P.

[4] Philip Duke of Orleans, Regent of France in the minority of Louis XV, superstitious in judicial astrology, though an unbeliever in all religion. [P.?]

[5] Philip V of Spain, who, after renouncing the throne for Religion, resumed it to gratify his Queen; and Victor Amadeus II, King of Sardinia, who resigned the crown, and trying to reassume it, was imprisoned till his death.   P.

[6] The atrabilaire complexion of Philip II is well known, but not so well that he derived it from his father Charles V. . . . this humour made both these princes act contrary to their Character; Charles, who was an active

   Not always Actions show the man: we find
Who does a kindness, is not therefore kind;   110
Perhaps Prosperity becalmed his breast,
Perhaps the Wind just shifted from the east:
Not therefore humble he who seeks retreat,
Pride guides his steps, and bids him shun the great:
Who combats bravely is not therefore brave,   115
He dreads a deathbed like the meanest slave:
Who reasons wisely is not therefore wise,
His pride in Reasoning, not in Acting lies.
   II.   But grant that Actions best discover man;
Take the most strong, and sort them as you can.   120
The few that glare each character must mark,
You balance not the many in the dark.
What will you do with such as disagree?
Suppress them, or miscall them Policy?
Must then at once (the character to save)   125
The plain rough Hero turn a crafty Knave?
Alas! in truth the man but changed his mind,
Perhaps was sick, in love, or had not dined.
Ask why from Britain Cæsar would retreat?
Cæsar himself might whisper he was beat.   130
Why risk the world's great empire for a Punk?
Cæsar perhaps might answer he was drunk.
But, sage historians! 'tis your task to prove
One action Conduct; one, heroic Love.
      'Tis from high Life high Characters are drawn;   135
A Saint in Crape is twice a Saint in Lawn;
A Judge is just, a Chancellor juster still;
A Gownman, learned; a Bishop, what you will;
Wise, if a Minister; but, if a King,
More wise, more learned, more just, more everything.   140
Court virtues bear, like Gems, the highest rate,
Born where Heaven's influence scarce can penetrate:
In life's low vale, the soil the Virtues like,

man, when he retired into a Convent; Philip, who was a man of the
Closet, when he gave the battle of St. Quentin.   [W.]

They please as beauties, here as wonders strike.
Though the same Sun with all-diffusive rays   145
Blush in the Rose, and in the Diamond blaze,
We prize the stronger effort of his power,
And justly set the Gem above the Flower.
    'Tis Education forms the common mind,
Just as the Twig is bent, the Tree's inclined.   150
Boastful and rough, your first Son is a Squire;
The next a Tradesman, meek, and much a liar;
Tom struts a Soldier, open, bold, and brave;
Will sneaks a Scrivener, an exceeding knave:
Is he a Churchman? then he's fond of power: 155
A Quaker? sly: A Presbyterian? sour:
A smart Freethinker? all things in an hour.
    Ask men's Opinions: Scoto now shall tell
How Trade increases, and the World goes well;
Strike off his Pension, by the setting sun,   160
And Britain, if not Europe, is undone.
    That gay Freethinker, a fine talker once,
What turns him now a stupid silent dunce?
Some God, or Spirit he has lately found;
Or chanced to meet a Minister that frowned.   165
    Judge we by Nature? Habit can efface,
Interest o'ercome, or Policy take place:
By Actions? those Uncertainty divides:
By Passions? these Dissimulation hides:
Opinions? they still take a wider range: 170
Find, if you can, in what you cannot change.
    Manners with Fortunes, Humours turn with Climes,
Tenets with Books, and Principles with Times.
    III. Search then the RULING PASSION: There, alone,
The Wild are constant, and the Cunning known;   175
The Fool consistent, and the False sincere;
Priests, Princes, Women, no dissemblers here.
This clue once found, unravels all the rest,
The prospect clears, and Wharton stands confest.[7]

[7] Philip, son of the Marquis of Wharton, born in 1698, died in 1731. He

Wharton, the scorn and wonder of our days,   180
Whose ruling Passion was the Lust of Praise:
Born with whate'er could win it from the Wise,
Women and Fools must like him or he dies;
Though wondering Senates hung on all he spoke,
The Club must hail him master of the joke.   185
Shall parts so various aim at nothing new?
He'll shine a Tully and a Wilmot too.[8]
Then turns repentant, and his God adores
With the same spirit that he drinks and whores;
Enough if all around him but admire,   190
And now the Punk applaud, and now the Friar.
Thus with each gift of nature and of art,
And wanting nothing but an honest heart;
Grown all to all, from no one vice exempt;
And most contemptible, to shun contempt;   195
His Passion still, to covet general praise,
His Life, to forfeit it a thousand ways;
A constant Bounty which no friend has made;
An angel Tongue, which no man can persuade;
A Fool, with more of Wit than half mankind,   200
Too rash for Thought, for Action too refined:
A Tyrant to the wife his heart approves;
A Rebel to the very king he loves;
He dies, sad outcast of each church and state,
And, harder still! flagitious, yet not great.   205
Ask you why Wharton broke through every rule?

was created Duke of Wharton before he was twenty-one years of age, as a
reward for his services in debate. He was President of the celebrated Hell
Fire Club, but at one time went into a monastery to prepare for Easter.
He was a liberal patron of literary men. He neglected his first wife, to
whom he was married when he was seventeen, and after her death
married one of the Maids of Honour to the Queen of Spain. A bill of
indictment was preferred against him for appearing in arms before, and
firing off cannon against, his Majesty's Town of Gibraltar. He died, a
member of the Roman Catholic Church, in a Bernardine monastery among
the mountains of Catalonia.
[8] John Wilmot, E. of Rochester, famous for his Wit and Extravagancies
in the time of Charles the Second.   P.

'Twas all for fear the Knaves should call him Fool.
     Nature well known, no prodigies remain,
Comets are regular, and Wharton plain.
     Yet, in this search, the wisest may mistake,   210
If second qualities for first they take.
When Catiline by rapine swelled his store;
When Cæsar made a noble dame a whore;
In this the Lust, in that the Avarice
Were means, not ends; Ambition was the vice.   215
That very Cæsar, born in Scipio's days,
Had aimed, like him, by Chastity at praise.
Lucullus, when Frugality could charm,
Had roasted turnips in the Sabine farm.
In vain th' observer eyes the builder's toil,   220
But quite mistakes the scaffold for the pile.
     In this one Passion man can strength enjoy,
As Fits give vigour, just when they destroy.
Time, that on all things lays his lenient hand,
Yet tames not this, it sticks to our last sand.   225
Consistent in our follies and our sins,
Here honest Nature ends as she begins.
     Old Politicians chew on wisdom past,
And totter on in business to the last;
As weak, as earnest; and as gravely out,   230
As sober Lanesborough dancing in the gout.[9]
     Behold a reverend sire, whom want of grace
Has made the father of a nameless race,
Shoved from the wall perhaps, or rudely pressed
By his own son, that passes by unblessed: 235
Still to his wench he crawls on knocking knees,
And envies every sparrow that he sees.
     A salmon's belly, Helluo, was thy fate;
The doctor called, declares all help too late:
"Mercy!" cries Helluo, "mercy on my soul!   240

---

[9] An ancient Nobleman, who continued this practice long after his legs were disabled by the gout. Upon the death of Prince George of Denmark, he demanded an audience of the Queen, to advise her to preserve her health and dispel her grief by *Dancing*. P.

Is there no hope?—Alas!—then bring the jowl."
    The frugal Crone, whom praying priests attend,
Still tries to save the hallowed taper's end,
Collects her breath, as ebbing life retires,
For one puff more, and in that puff expires.   245
    "Odious! in woollen! 'twould a Saint provoke,"
(Were the last words that poor Narcissa spoke)[10]
"No, let a charming Chintz, and Brussels lace
Wrap my cold limbs, and shade my lifeless face:
One would not, sure, be frightful when one's dead—   250
And—Betty—give this Cheek a little Red."
    The Courtier smooth, who forty years had shined
An humble servant to all human kind,
Just brought out this, when scarce his tongue could stir,
"If—where I'm going—I could serve you, Sir?"   255
    "I give and I devise (old Euclio said,
And sighed) my lands and tenements to Ned."
"Your money, Sir;" "My money, Sir, what all?
Why,—if I must—(then wept) I give it Paul."
"The Manor, Sir?"—"The Manor! hold," he cried,   260
"Not that,—I cannot part with that"—and died.
    And you! brave COBHAM, to the latest breath
Shall feel your ruling passion strong in death:
Such in those moments as in all the past,
"Oh, save my Country, Heaven!" shall be your last.   265

[10] This story, as well as the others, is founded on fact, though the author had the goodness not to mention the names. Several attribute this in particular to a very celebrated Actress, who, in detestation of the thought of being buried in woollen, gave these her last orders with her dying breath. P. The celebrated actress Anne Oldfield had played Narcissa in Colley Cibber's *Love's Last Shift*. The Act requiring the dead to be buried in woollen was passed in 1678, to protect homespun goods against foreign linen. Mrs. Oldfield was buried in Westminister Abbey, in Brussels lace and Holland linen.

EPISTLE II

To a Lady[11]

Of the Characters of Women

NOTHING so true as what you once let fall,
"Most Women have no Characters at all." ✳
Matter too soft a lasting mark to bear,
And best distinguished by black, brown, or fair.
 How many pictures of one Nymph we view, 5
All how unlike each other, all how true!
Arcadia's Countess, here, in ermined pride,
Is, there, Pastora by a fountain side.
Here Fannia, leering on her own good man,
And there, a naked Leda with a Swan. 10
Let then the Fair one beautifully cry,
In Magdalen's loose hair and lifted eye,
Or dressed in smiles of sweet Cecilia shine,[12]
With simpering Angels, Palms, and Harps divine;
Whether the Charmer sinner it, or saint it, 15
If Folly grow romantic, I must paint it.
 Come then, the colours and the ground prepare!
Dip in the Rainbow, trick her off in Air;
Choose a firm Cloud, before it fall, and in it

---

[11] Generally understood to be Martha Blount, Pope's closest female friend during the latter part of his life. Pope wrote to Swift, February 16, 1733: "Your lady-friend is *semper eadem,* and I have written an Epistle to her on that qualification, in a female character, which is thought by my chief critic, in your absence, to be my *chef-d'oeuvre.*"

[12] *Arcadia's Countess—Pastora by a fountain—Leda with a swan—Magdalen—Cecilia.*—Attitudes in which several ladies affected to be drawn, and sometimes one lady in them all. The poet's politeness and complaisance to the sex is observable in this instance, amongst others, that, whereas in the *Characters of Men* he has sometimes made use of real names, in the *Characters of Women* always fictitious. P.

Catch, ere she change, the Cynthia of this minute.   20
     Rufa, whose eye quick-glancing o'er the Park,
Attracts each light gay meteor of a Spark,
Agrees as ill with Rufa studying Locke,
As Sappho's diamonds with her dirty smock;
Or Sappho at her toilet's greasy task,[13]   25
With Sappho fragrant at an evening Masque:
So morning Insects that in muck begun,
Shine, buzz, and flyblow in the setting sun.
     How soft is Silia! fearful to offend;
The Frail one's advocate, the Weak one's friend: 30
To her, Calista proved her conduct nice;
And good Simplicius asks of her advice.
Sudden, she storms! she raves! You tip the wink,
But spare your censure; Silia does not drink.
All eyes may see from what the change arose,   35
All eyes may see—a Pimple on her nose.
     Papillia, wedded to her amorous spark,
Sighs for the shades—"How charming is a Park!"
A Park is purchased, but the Fair he sees
All bathed in tears—"Oh, odious, odious Trees!"   40
     Ladies, like variegated Tulips, show;
'Tis to their Changes half their charms we owe;
Fine by defect, and delicately weak,
Their happy Spots the nice admirer take,
'Twas thus Calypso once each heart alarmed,   45
Awed without Virtue, without Beauty charmed;
Her tongue bewitched as oddly as her Eyes,
Less Wit than Mimic, more a Wit than wise;
Strange graces still, and stranger flights she had,
Was just not ugly, and was just not mad;   50

[13] Lady Mary Wortley Montagu's slovenliness was notorious. Horace Walpole wrote to his friend Conway, September 25, 1740: "Her dress, her avarice, and her impudence must amaze any one that never heard her name. She wears a foul mob that does not cover her greasy black locks, that hang loose, never combed or curled, an old mazarine blue wrapper, that gapes open and discovers a canvas petticoat. Her face swelled violently on one side, partly covered with a plaster, and partly with white paint, which, for cheapness, she has bought coarse."

Yet ne'er so sure our passion to create,
As when she touched the brink of all we hate.
    Narcissa's nature, tolerably mild,
To make a wash, would hardly stew a child;
Has even been proved to grant a Lover's prayer,   55
And paid a Tradesman once to make him stare;
Gave alms at Easter, in a Christian trim,
And made a Widow happy, for a whim.
Why then declare Good nature is her scorn,
When 'tis by that alone she can be borne?   60
Why pique all mortals, yet affect a name?
A fool to Pleasure, yet a slave to Fame:
Now deep in Taylor and the Book of Martyrs,
Now drinking citron with his Grace and Chartres:
Now Conscience chills her, and now Passion burns;   65
And Atheism and Religion take their turns;
A very Heathen in the carnal part,
Yet still a sad, good Christian at her heart.
    See Sin in State, majestically drunk;
Proud as a Peeress, prouder as a Punk;   70
Chaste to her Husband, frank to all beside,
A teeming Mistress, but a barren Bride.
What then? let Blood and Body bear the fault,
Her Head's untouched, that noble Seat of Thought:
Such this day's doctrine—in another fit   75
She sins with Poets through pure Love of Wit.
What has not fired her bosom or her brain?
Cæsar and Tallboy,[14] Charles and Charlemagne.
As Helluo, late Dictator of the Feast,
The Nose of Hautgout, and the Tip of Taste,   80
Critiqued your wine, and analysed your meat,
Yet on plain Pudding deigned at home to eat;
So Philomedé, lecturing all mankind
On the soft Passion, and the Taste refined,
Th' Address, the Delicacy—stoops at once,   85

---

[14] A low comic character appearing in an opera called *The Jovial Crew*, 1731.

And makes her hearty meal upon a Dunce.
    Flavia's a Wit, has too much sense to Pray;
To Toast our wants and wishes, is her way;
Nor asks of God, but of her Stars, to give
The mighty blessing, "while we live, to live."   90
Then all for Death, that Opiate of the soul!
Lucretia's dagger, Rosamonda's bowl.
Say, what can cause such impotence of mind?
A spark too fickle, or a Spouse too kind.
Wise Wretch! with Pleasures too refined to please; 95
With too much Spirit to be e'er at ease;
With too much Quickness ever to be taught;
With too much Thinking to have common Thought:
You purchase Pain with all that Joy can give,
And die of nothing but a Rage to live.   100
    Turn then from Wits; and look on Simo's Mate,
No Ass so meek, no Ass so obstinate.
Or her, that owns her Faults, but never mends,
Because she's honest, and the best of Friends.
Or her, whose life the Church and Scandal share, 105
For ever in a Passion, or a Prayer.
Or her, who laughs at Hell, but (like her Grace)
Cries, "Ah! how charming, if there's no such place!"
Or who in sweet vicissitude appears
Of Mirth and Opium, Ratafie and Tears,   110
The daily Anodyne, and nightly Draught,
To kill those foes to Fair ones, Time and Thought.
Woman and Fool are two hard things to hit;
For true No-meaning puzzles more than Wit.
    But what are these to great Atossa's mind?[15] 115
Scarce once herself, by turns all Womankind!
Who, with herself, or others, from her birth
Finds all her life one warfare upon earth:

[15] The main model for this portrait was Sarah, Duchess of Marlborough. On the other hand, some of the details bear a closer resemblance to Katharine, Duchess of Buckingham, natural daughter of James II and sister of the Pretender. Atossa was the daughter of Cyrus and sister of Cambyses.

Shines, in exposing Knaves, and painting Fools,
Yet is, whate'er she hates and ridicules.   120
No Thought advances, but her Eddy Brain
Whisks it about, and down it goes again.
Full sixty years the World has been her Trade,
The wisest Fool much Time has ever made.
From loveless youth to unrespected age,   125
No passion gratified except her Rage.
So much the Fury still outran the Wit,
The Pleasure missed her, and the Scandal hit.
Who breaks with her, provokes Revenge from Hell,
But he's a bolder man who dares be well.   130
Her every turn with Violence pursued,
Nor more a storm her Hate than Gratitude:
To that each Passion turns, or soon or late;
Love, if it makes her yield, must make her hate:
Superiors? death! and Equals? what a curse!   135
But an Inferior not dependant? worse.
Offend her, and she knows not to forgive;
Oblige her, and she'll hate you while you live:
But die, and she'll adore you—Then the Bust
And Temple rise—then fall again to dust.   140
Last night, her Lord was all that's good and great;
A Knave this morning, and his Will a Cheat.
Strange! by the Means defeated of the Ends,
By Spirit robbed of Power, by Warmth of Friends,
By Wealth of Followers! without one distress   145
Sick of herself through very selfishness!
Atossa, cursed with every granted prayer,
Childless with all her Children, wants an Heir.
To Heirs unknown descends th' unguarded store,
Or wanders, Heaven-directed, to the Poor.   150
        Pictures like these, dear Madam, to design,
Asks no firm hand, and no unerring line;
Some wandering touches, some reflected light,
Some flying stroke alone can hit 'em right:
For how should equal Colours do the knack?   155
Chameleons who can paint in white and black?

"Yet Chloe sure was formed without a spot"—
Nature in her then erred not, but forgot.
"With every pleasing, every prudent part,
Say, what can Chloe want?"—She wants a Heart.   160
She speaks, behaves, and acts just as she ought;
But never, never, reached one generous Thought.
Virtue she finds too painful an endeavour,
Content to dwell in Decencies for ever.
So very reasonable, so unmoved,   165
As never yet to love, or to be loved.
She, while her Lover pants upon her breast,
Can mark the figures on an Indian chest;
And when she sees her Friend in deep despair,
Observes how much a Chintz exceeds Mohair.   170
Forbid it Heaven, a Favour or a Debt
She e'er should cancel—but she may forget.
Safe is your Secret still in Chloe's ear;
But none of Chloe's shall you ever hear.
Of all her Dears she never slandered one,   175
But cares not if a thousand are undone.
Would Chloe know if you're alive or dead?
She bids her Footman put it in her head.
Chloe is prudent—Would you too be wise?
Then never break your heart when Chloe dies.   180
    One certain Portrait may (I grant) be seen,
Which Heaven has varnished out, and made a *Queen*:
THE SAME FOR EVER! and described by all
With Truth and Goodness, as with Crown and Ball.
Poets heap Virtues, Painters Gems at will,   185
And show their zeal, and hide their want of skill.
'Tis well—but, Artists! who can paint or write,
To draw the Naked is your true delight.
That robe of Quality so struts and swells,
None see what Parts of Nature it conceals: 190
Th' exactest traits of Body or of Mind,
We owe to models of an humble kind.
If QUEENSBURY to strip there's no compelling,
'Tis from a Handmaid we must take a Helen.

From Peer or Bishop 'tis no easy thing   195
To draw the man who loves his God, or King:
Alas! I copy (or my draught would fail)
From honest Máhomet,[16] or plain Parson Hale.[17]
    But grant, in Public Men sometimes are shown,
A Woman's seen in Private life alone: 200
Our bolder Talents in full light displayed;
Your Virtues open fairest in the shade.
Bred to disguise, in Public 'tis you hide;
There, none distinguish twixt your Shame or Pride,
Weakness or Delicacy; all so nice,   205
That each may seem a Virtue, or a Vice.
    In Men, we various Ruling Passions find;
In Women, two almost divide the kind;
Those, only fixed, they first or last obey,
The Love of Pleasure, and the Love of Sway.   210
    That, Nature gives; and where the lesson taught
Is but to please, can Pleasure seem a fault?
Experience, this; by Man's oppression curst,
They seek the second not to lose the first.
    Men, some to Business, some to Pleasure take;   215
But every Woman is at heart a Rake:
Men, some to Quiet, some to public Strife;
But every Lady would be Queen for life.
    Yet mark the fate of a whole Sex of Queens!
Power all their end, but Beauty all the means: 220
In Youth they conquer, with so wild a rage,
As leaves them scarce a subject in their Age:
For foreign glory, foreign joy, they roam;
No thought of peace or happiness at home.
But Wisdom's triumph is well-timed Retreat,   225
As hard a science to the Fair as Great!
Beauties, like Tyrants, old and friendless grown,

[16] Servant to the late King, said to be the son of a Turkish Bassa, whom he took at the Siege of Buda, and constantly kept about his person. P.
[17] Dr. Stephen Hales, not more estimable for his useful discoveries as a natural Philosopher, than for his exemplary life and Pastoral Charity as a Parish Priest. [W.]

Yet hate repose, and dread to be alone,
Worn out in public, weary every eye,
Nor leave one sigh behind them when they die.   230
    Pleasures the sex, as children Birds, pursue,
Still out of reach, yet never out of view;
Sure, if they catch, to spoil the Toy at most,
To covet flying, and regret when lost:
At last, to follies Youth could scarce defend,   235
It grows their Age's prudence to pretend;
Ashamed to own they gave delight before,
Reduced to feign it, when they give no more:
As Hags hold Sabbaths, less for joy than spite,
So these their merry, miserable Night;   240
Still round and round the Ghosts of Beauty glide,
And haunt the places where their Honour died.
    See how the World its Veterans rewards!
A Youth of Frolics, an old Age of Cards;
Fair to no purpose, artful to no end,   245
Young without Lovers, old without a Friend;
A Fop their Passion, but their Prize a Sot;
Alive, ridiculous, and dead, forgot!
    Ah! Friend! to dazzle let the Vain design;
To raise the Thought, and touch the Heart be thine!   250
That Charm shall grow, while what fatigues the Ring,[18]
Flaunts and goes down, an unregarded thing:
So when the Sun's broad beam has tired the sight,
All mild ascends the Moon's more sober light,
Serene in Virgin Modesty she shines,   255
And unobserved the glaring Orb declines.
    Oh! blest with Temper, whose unclouded ray
Can make tomorrow cheerful as today;
She, who can love a Sister's charms, or hear
Sighs for a Daughter with unwounded ear;   260
She, who ne'er answers till a Husband cools,
Or, if she rules him, never shows she rules;

---

[18] The Ring was a clump of trees in Hyde Park, round which the carriages of the fashionable used to drive.

Charms by accepting, by submitting sways,
Yet has her humour most, when she obeys;
Let Fops or Fortune fly which way they will;   265
Disdains all loss of Tickets, or Codille;
Spleen, Vapours, or Smallpox, above them all,
And Mistress of herself, though China fall.
      And yet, believe me, good as well as ill,
Woman's at best a Contradiction still.   270
Heaven, when it strives to polish all it can
Its last best work, but forms a softer Man;
Picks from each sex, to make the Favorite blest,
Your love of Pleasure, our desire of Rest:
Blends, in exception to all general rules,   275
Your Taste of Follies, with our Scorn of Fools:
Reserve with Frankness, Art with Truth allied,
Courage with Softness, Modesty with Pride;
Fixed Principles, with Fancy ever new;
Shakes all together, and produces—You.   280
      Be this a Woman's Fame: with this unblest,
Toasts live a scorn, and Queens may die a jest.
This Phœbus promised (I forget the year)
When those blue eyes first opened on the sphere;
Ascendant Phœbus watched that hour with care,   285
Averted half your Parents' simple Prayer;
And gave you Beauty, but denied the Pelf
That buys your sex a Tyrant o'er itself.
The generous God, who Wit and Gold refines,
And ripens Spirits as he ripens Mines,   290
Kept Dross for Duchesses, the world shall know it,
To you gave Sense, Good Humour, and a Poet.

EPISTLE III[19]

To Allen Lord Bathurst

ARGUMENT

Of the Use *of* RICHES

That it is known to few, most falling into one of the extremes, *Avarice* or *Profusion*. The Point discussed, whether the invention of Money has been more commodious, or pernicious to Mankind. That Riches, either to the *Avaricious* or the *Prodigal,* cannot afford Happiness, scarcely Necessaries. That Avarice is an absolute Frenzy, without an End or Purpose. Conjectures about the Motives of Avaricious men. That the conduct of men, with respect to Riches, can only be accounted for by the ORDER OF PROVIDENCE, which works the general Good out of Extremes, and brings all to its great End by perpetual Revolutions. How a *Miser* acts upon Principles which appear to him reasonable. How a *Prodigal* does the same. The due Medium, and true use of Riches. The *Man* of *Ross.* The fate of the *Profuse* and the *Covetous,* in two examples; both miserable in Life and in Death. The story of *Sir Balaam.*

> P. WHO shall decide, when Doctors disagree,
> And soundest Casuists doubt, like you and me?
> You hold the word, from Jove to Momus given,
> That Man was made the standing jest of Heaven;

[19] This Epistle was written after a violent outcry against our Author, on a supposition that he had ridiculed a worthy nobleman merely for his wrong taste. He justified himself upon that article in a letter to the Earl of Burlington; at the end of which are these words. "I have learnt that there are some who would rather be wicked than ridiculous; and therefore it may be safer to attack vices than follies. I will therefore leave my betters in the quiet possession of their idols, their groves, and their high places; and change my subject from their pride to their meanness, from their vanities to their miseries; and as the only certain way to avoid misconstructions, to lessen offence, and not to multiply ill-natured applications, I may probably, in my next, make use of real names instead of fictitious ones." P.

And Gold but sent to keep the fools in play,   5
For some to heap, and some to throw away.

    But I, who think more highly of our kind,
(And surely, Heaven and I are of a mind)
Opine, that Nature, as in duty bound,
Deep hid the shining mischief under ground: 10
But when by Man's audacious labour won,
Flamed forth this rival to its Sire, the Sun,
Then careful Heaven supplied two sorts of Men,
To squander These, and Those to hide again.

    Like Doctors thus, when much dispute has past,   15
We find our tenets just the same at last.
Both fairly owning Riches, in effect,
No grace of Heaven or token of th' Elect;
Given to the Fool, the Mad, the Vain, the Evil,
To Ward,[20] to Waters,[21] Chartres,[22] and the Devil.[23]   20

[20] John Ward, of Hackney, Esq.; Member of Parliament, being prosecuted by the Duchess of Buckingham, and convicted of Forgery, was first expelled the House, and then stood in the Pillory on March 17, 1727. He was suspected of joining in a conveyance with Sir John Blunt, to secrete fifty thousand pounds of that Director's Estate, forfeited to the South Sea Company by Act of Parliament. The company recovered the fifty thousand pounds against Ward; but he set up prior conveyances of his real estate to his brother and son, and concealed all his personal, which was computed to be one hundred and fifty thousand pounds. These conveyances being also set aside by a bill in Chancery, Ward was imprisoned, and hazarded the forfeiture of his life, by not giving in his effects till the last day, which was that of his examination. . . . To sum up the *worth* of this gentleman, at the several eras of his life: At his standing in the Pillory he was *worth above two hundred thousand pounds;* at his commitment to Prison, he was *worth one hundred and fifty thousand;* but has been since so far diminished in his reputation, as to be thought a *worse man* by *fifty or sixty thousand.* P.
[21] This gentleman's history must be deferred till his death, when his *worth* may be known more certainly. P.
[22] A man infamous for all manner of vices. When he was an ensign in the army, he was drummed out of the regiment for a cheat; he was next banished Brussels, and drummed out of Ghent on the same account. After a hundred tricks at the gaming tables, he took to lending of money at exorbitant interest and on great penalties, accumulating premium, interest, and capital into a new capital, and seizing to a minute when the payments

B.   What Nature wants, commodious Gold bestows,
'Tis thus we eat the bread another sows.
P.   But how unequal it bestows, observe,
'Tis thus we riot, while, who sow it, starve:
What Nature wants (a phrase I much distrust)   25
Extends to Luxury, extends to Lust:
Useful, I grant, it serves what life requires,
But, dreadful too, the dark Assassin hires:
B.   Trade it may help, Society extend.
P.   But lures the Pirate, and corrupts the Friend.   30
B.   It raises Armies in a Nation's aid.
P.   But bribes a Senate, and the Land's betrayed.
In vain may Heroes fight, and Patriots rave;
If secret Gold sap on from knave to knave.
Once, we confess, beneath the Patriot's cloak,[24]   35
From the cracked bag the dropping Guinea spoke,
And jingling down the back stairs, told the crew,
"Old Cato is as great a Rogue as you."
Blest paper credit! last and best supply!
That lends Corruption lighter wings to fly!   40
Gold imped by thee, can compass hardest things,
Can pocket States, can fetch or carry Kings;[25]

became due. . . . His house was a perpetual bawdy-house. He was twice
condemned for rapes, and pardoned; but the last time not without im-
prisonment in Newgate, and large confiscations. He died in Scotland in
1731, aged 62. The populace at his funeral raised a great riot, almost tore
the body out of the coffin, and cast dead dogs, etc., into the grave along
with it. . . . This Gentleman was *worth seven thousand pounds a year*
estate in Land, and about *one hundred thousand in Money*. P.
[23] Alluding to the vulgar opinion, that all mines of metal and subter-
raneous treasure are in the guard of the Devil: which seems to have taken
its rise from the pagan fable of Plutus the God of Riches.   [W.]
[24] This is a true story, which happened in the reign of William III to an
unsuspected old Patriot, who coming out at the back door from having
been closeted by the King, where he had received a large bag of Guineas,
the bursting of the bag discovered his business there.   P.
[25] In our author's time, many Princes had been sent about the world, and
great changes of Kings projected in Europe. The partition treaty had dis-
posed of Spain; France had set up a King for England, who was sent
to Scotland, and back again; King Stanislaus was sent to Poland, and

A single leaf shall waft an Army o'er,
Or ship off Senates to a distant Shore;[26]
A leaf, like Sibyl's, scatter to and fro   45
Our fates and fortunes, as the winds shall blow:
Pregnant with thousands flits the Scrap unseen,
And silent sells a King, or buys a Queen.

    Oh! that such bulky Bribes as all might see,
Still, as of old, encumbered Villainy!   50
Could France or Rome divert our brave designs,
With all their brandies or with all their wines?
What could they more than Knights and Squires confound,
Or water all the Quorum ten miles round?
A Statesman's slumbers how this speech would spoil!   55
"Sir, Spain has sent a thousand jars of oil;
Huge bales of British cloth blockade the door;
A hundred oxen at your levee roar."

    Poor Avarice one torment more would find;
Nor could Profusion squander all in kind.   60
Astride his cheese Sir Morgan might we meet;
And Worldly crying coals from street to street,[27]
Whom with a wig so wild, and mien so mazed,
Pity mistakes for some poor tradesman crazed.
Had Colepepper's whole wealth been hops and hogs,[28] 65
Could he himself have sent it to the dogs?

back again; the Duke of Anjou was sent to Spain, and Don Carlos to Italy. P.

[26] Alludes to several Ministers, Counsellors, and Patriots banished in our times to Siberia, and to that MORE GLORIOUS FATE of the PARLIAMENT OF PARIS, banished to Pontoise in the year 1720. P.

[27] Some misers of great wealth, proprietors of the coal-mines, had entered at this time into an association to keep up coals to an extravagant price, whereby the poor were reduced almost to starve, till one of them taking the advantage of underselling the rest, defeated the design. One of these Misers was *worth ten thousand,* another *seven thousand* a year. P.

[28] Sir William Colepepper, Bart., a person of an ancient family, and ample fortune, without one other quality of a Gentleman, who, after ruining himself at the Gaming Table, passed the rest of his days in sitting there to see the ruin of others; preferring to subsist upon borrowing and begging, rather than to enter into any reputable method of life, and refusing a post in the army which was offered him. P.

His Grace will game: to White's a Bull be led,
With spurning heels and with a butting head.
To White's be carried, as to ancient games,
Fair Coursers, Vases, and alluring Dames.   70
Shall then Uxorio, if the stakes he sweep,
Bear home six Whores, and make his Lady weep?
Or soft Adonis, so perfumed and fine,
Drive to St. James's a whole herd of swine?
Oh filthy check on all industrious skill,   75
To spoil the nation's last great trade, Quadrille!
Since then, my Lord, on such a World we fall,
What say you?   B.   Say? Why take it, Gold and all.
P.   What Riches give us let us then enquire:
Meat, Fire, and Clothes. B. What more? P. Meat,
    Clothes, and Fire.   80
Is this too little? would you more than live?
Alas! 'tis more than Turner[29] finds they give.
Alas! 'tis more than (all his Visions past)
Unhappy Wharton,[30] waking, found at last!
What can they give? to dying Hopkins,[31] Heirs;   85

[29] One who, being possessed of three hundred thousand pounds, laid down his Coach, because Interest was reduced from five to four *per cent.,* and then put seventy thousand into the Charitable Corporation for better interest; which sum having lost, he took it so much to heart, that he kept his chamber ever after. It is thought he would not have outlived it, but that he was heir to another considerable estate, which he daily expected, and that by this course of life he saved both clothes and all other expenses. P.

[30] A Nobleman of great qualities, but as unfortunate in the application of them, as if they had been vices and follies. See his Character in the first Epistle. P.

[31] A citizen whose rapacity obtained him the name of *Vulture Hopkins.* He lived worthless, but died *worth three hundred thousand pounds,* which he would give to no person living, but left it so as not to be inherited till after the second generation. His counsel representing to him how many years it must be before this could take effect, and that his money could only lie at interest all that time, he expressed great joy thereat, and said, "They would then be as long in spending as he had been in getting it." But the Chancery afterwards set aside the will, and gave it to the heir-at-law. P.

To Chartres, Vigour; Japhet,[32] Nose and Ears?
Can they, in gems bid pallid Hippia glow,
In Fulvia's buckle ease the throbs below;
Or heal, old Narses, thy obscener ail,
With all th' embroidery plastered at thy tail?   90
They might (were Harpax not too wise to spend)
Give Harpax' self the blessing of a Friend;
Or find some Doctor that would save the life
Of wretched Shylock, spite of Shylock's Wife:
But thousands die, without or this or that,   95
Die, and endow a College, or a Cat.[33]
To some, indeed, Heaven grants the happier fate,
T' enrich a Bastard, or a Son they hate.
      Perhaps you think the Poor might have their part?
Bond damns the Poor, and hates them from his heart:[34]
The grave Sir Gilbert holds it for a rule,   101
That "every man in want is knave or fool:
God cannot love (says Blunt, with tearless eyes)

[32] Japhet Crook, alias Sir *Peter Stranger,* was punished with the loss of those parts, for having forged a conveyance of an Estate to himself, upon which he took up several thousand pounds. He was at the same time sued in Chancery for having fraudulently obtained a Will, by which he possessed another considerable Estate, in wrong of the brother of the deceased. By these means he was *worth* a great sum, which (in reward for the small loss of his ears) he enjoyed in prison till his death, and quietly left to his executor. P.

[33] A famous Duchess of R[ichmond] in her last Will left considerable legacies and annuities to her Cats. P.

[34] This epistle was written in the year 1730, when a corporation was established to lend money to the poor upon pledges, by the name of the *Charitable Corporation;* but the whole was turned only to an iniquitous method of enriching particular people, to the ruin of such numbers, that it became a parliamentary concern to endeavour the relief of those unhappy sufferers, and three of the managers, who were members of the House, were expelled. By the report of the Committee, appointed to inquire into that iniquitous affair, it appears, that when it was objected to the intended removal of the office, that the Poor, for whose use it was erected, would be hurt by it, Bond, one of the Directors, replied, *Damn the Poor.* That "God hates the poor," and, "That every man in want is knave or fool," etc., were the genuine apothegms of some of the persons here mentioned. P.

The wretch he starves"—and piously denies:
But the good Bishop, with a meeker air,   105
Admits, and leaves them, Providence's care.
    Yet, to be just to these poor men of pelf,
Each does but hate his neighbour as himself:
Damned to the Mines, an equal fate betides
The Slave that digs it, and the Slave that hides.   110
B. Who suffer thus, mere Charity should own,
Must act on motives powerful, though unknown.
P. Some War, some Plague, or Famine they foresee,
Some Revelation hid from you and me.
Why Shylock wants a meal, the cause is found,   115
He thinks a Loaf will rise to fifty pound.
What made Directors cheat in South Sea year?
To live on Venison when it sold so dear.[35]
Ask you why Phryne the whole Auction buys?
Phryne foresees a general Excise.[36]   120
Why she and Sappho raise that monstrous sum?
Alas! they fear a man will cost a plum.[37]
    Wise Peter sees the World's respect for Gold,[38]
And therefore hopes this Nation may be sold:
Glorious Ambition! Peter, swell thy store,   125
And be what Rome's great Didius was before.[39]

[35] In the extravagance and luxury of the South Sea year, the price of a haunch of Venison was from three to five pounds. P.
[36] Many people about the year 1733 had a conceit that such a thing was intended, of which it is not improbable this lady might have some intimation. P.
[37] A "plum" was a hundred thousand pounds.
[38] Peter Walter, a person not only eminent in the wisdom of his profession, as a dextrous attorney, but allowed to be a good, if not a safe, conveyancer; extremely respected by the Nobility of this land, though free from all manner of luxury and ostentation: his Wealth was never seen, and his bounty never heard of, except to his own son, for whom he procured an employment of considerable profit, of which he gave him as much as was *necessary*. Therefore the taxing this gentleman with any Ambition is certainly a great wrong to him. P. He was clerk of the Peace for the county of Middlesex, and steward to the Duke of Newcastle, and represented the borough of Bridport in Parliament.
[39] A Roman Lawyer, so rich as to purchase the Empire when it was set to sale upon the death of Pertinax. P.

  The crown of Poland, venal twice an age,[40]
To just three millions stinted modest Gage.
But nobler scenes Maria's dreams unfold,
Hereditary Realms, and worlds of Gold.   130
Congenial souls! whose life one Avarice joins,
And one fate buries in th' Asturian Mines.
  Much injured Blunt! why bears he Britain's hate?[41]
A wizard told him in these words our fate:
"At length Corruption, like a general flood,   135
(So long by watchful Ministers withstood)
Shall deluge all; and Avarice, creeping on,
Spread like a lowborn mist, and blot the Sun;
Statesman and Patriot[42] ply alike the stocks,
Peeress and Butler share alike the Box,   140
And Judges job, and Bishops bite the town,
And mighty Dukes pack cards for half a crown.
See Britain sunk in lucre's sordid charms,
And France revenged of ANNE's and EDWARD's arms?"
'Twas no Court badge, great Scrivener! fired thy brain,
Nor lordly Luxury, nor City Gain: 146
No, 'twas thy righteous end, ashamed to see
Senates degenerate, Patriots disagree,
And, nobly wishing Party rage to cease,

[40] The two persons here mentioned were of Quality, each of whom in the Mississippi despised to realize above *three hundred thousand pounds;* the Gentleman with a view to the purchase of the Crown of Poland, the Lady on a vision of the like royal nature. They since retired into Spain, where they are still in search of gold in the mines of the Asturias.　P.
[41] Sir John Blunt, originally a scrivener, was one of the first projectors of the South Sea Company, and afterwards one of the directors and chief managers of the famous scheme in 1720. He was also one of those who suffered most severely by the bill of pains and penalties on the said directors. He was a Dissenter of a most religious deportment, and professed to be a greater believer. Whether he did really credit the prophecy here mentioned is not certain, but it was constantly in this very style he declaimed against the corruption and luxury of the age, the partiality of Parliaments, and the misery of party spirit. He was particularly eloquent against *Avarice* in great and noble persons, of which he had indeed lived to see many miserable examples. He died in the year 1732.　P.
[42] "Patriot" was the name assumed by the Opposition in order to contrast their own virtue with the corruption of the ministry.

To buy both sides, and give thy Country peace.   150
    "All this is madness," cries a sober sage:
But who, my friend, has reason in his rage?
"The ruling Passion, be it what it will,
The ruling Passion conquers Reason still."
Less mad the wildest whimsy we can frame,   155
Than even that Passion, if it has no Aim;
For though such motives Folly you may call,
The Folly's greater to have none at all.
    Hear then the truth: "'Tis Heaven each Passion sends,
And different men directs to different ends.   160
Extremes in Nature equal good produce,
Extremes in Man concur to general use."
Ask we what makes one keep, and one bestow?
That POWER who bids the Ocean ebb and flow,
Bids seedtime, harvest, equal course maintain,   165
Through reconciled extremes of drought and rain,
Builds Life on Death, on Change Duration founds,
And gives th' eternal wheels to know their rounds.
    Riches, like insects, when concealed they lie,
Wait but for wings, and in their season fly.   170
Who sees pale Mammon pine amidst his store,
Sees but a backward steward for the Poor;
This year a Reservoir, to keep and spare;
The next, a Fountain, spouting through his Heir,
In lavish streams to quench a Country's thirst,   175
And men and dogs shall drink him till they burst.
    Old Cotta shamed his fortune and his birth,
Yet was not Cotta void of wit or worth:
What though (the use of barbarous spits forgot)
His kitchen vied in coolness with his grot?   180
His court with nettles, moats with cresses stored,
With soups unbought and salads blessed his board?
If Cotta lived on pulse, it was no more
Than Brahmins, Saints, and Sages did before;
To cram the Rich was prodigal expense,   185
And who would take the Poor from Providence?
Like some lone Chartreux stands the good old Hall,

Silence without, and Fasts within the wall;
No raftered roofs with dance and tabor sound,
No noontide bell invites the country round: 190
Tenants with sighs the smokeless towers survey,
And turn th' unwilling steeds another way:
Benighted wanderers, the forest o'er,
Curse the saved candle, and unopening door;
While the gaunt mastiff growling at the gate,   195
Affrights the beggar whom he longs to eat.
     Not so his Son; he marked this oversight,
And then mistook reverse of wrong for right.
(For what to shun will not great knowledge need,
But what to follow, is a task indeed.)   200
Yet sure, of qualities deserving praise,
More go to ruin Fortunes, than to raise.
What slaughtered hecatombs, what floods of wine,
Fill the capacious Squire, and deep Divine!
Yet no mean motive this profusion draws,   205
His oxen perish in his country's cause;
'Tis GEORGE and LIBERTY that crowns the cup,
And Zeal for that great House which eats him up.
The Woods recede around the naked seat,
The Sylvans groan—no matter—for the Fleet: 210
Next goes his Wool—to clothe our valiant bands,
Last, for his Country's love, he sells his Lands.
To town he comes, completes the nation's hope,
And heads the bold Trainbands, and burns a Pope.
And shall not Britain now reward his toils,   215
Britain, that pays her Patriots with her Spoils?
In vain at Court the Bankrupt pleads his cause,
His thankless Country leaves him to her Laws.
     The Sense to value Riches, with the Art
T' enjoy them, and the Virtue to impart,   220
Not meanly, nor ambitiously pursued,
Not sunk by sloth, nor raised by servitude;
To balance Fortune by a just expense,
Join with Economy, Magnificence;
With Splendour, Charity; with Plenty, Health;   225

O teach us, BATHURST! yet unspoiled by wealth!
That secret rare, between th' extremes to move
Of mad Good Nature, and of mean Self-love.
    B.   To Worth or Want well weighed, be Bounty given,
And ease, or emulate, the care of Heaven;   230
(Whose measure full o'erflows on human race)
Mend Fortune's fault, and justify her grace.
Wealth in the gross is death, but life diffused;
As Poison heals, in just proportion used:
In heaps, like Ambergris, a stink it lies,   235
But well dispersed, is Incense to the Skies.
    P.   Who starves by Nobles, or with Nobles eats?
The Wretch that trusts them, and the Rogue that cheats.
Is there a Lord, who knows a cheerful noon
Without a Fiddler, Flatterer, or Buffoon?   240
Whose table, Wit, or modest Merit share,
Unelbowed by a Gamester, Pimp, or Player?
Who copies Yours, or OXFORD's better part,[43]
To ease th' oppressed, and raise the sinking heart?
Where'er he shines, O Fortune, gild the scene,   245
And Angels guard him in the golden Mean!
There, English Bounty yet awhile may stand,
And Honour linger ere it leaves the land.
    But all our praises why should Lords engross?
Rise, honest Muse! and sing the MAN of Ross:[44]   250
Pleased Vaga[45] echoes through her winding bounds,
And rapid Severn hoarse applause resounds.
Who hung with woods yon mountain's sultry brow?

[43] Edward Harley, Earl of Oxford. The son of Robert, created Earl of Oxford and Earl Mortimer by Queen Anne. This Nobleman died regretted by all men of letters, great numbers of whom had experienced his benefits. He left behind him one of the most noble Libraries in Europe.   P.
[44] The person here celebrated, who with a small Estate actually performed all these good works, and whose true name was almost lost (partly by the title of the *Man of Ross* given him by way of eminence, and partly by being buried without so much as an inscription) was called Mr. John Kyrle. He died in the year 1724, aged 90, and lies interred in the chancel of the church of Ross in Herefordshire.   P.
[45] The River Wye.

From the dry rock who bade the waters flow?
Not to the skies in useless columns tost,   255
Or in proud falls magnificently lost,
But clear and artless, pouring through the plain
Health to the sick, and solace to the swain.
Whose Causeway parts the vale with shady rows?
Whose Seats the weary Traveller repose?   260
Who taught that heaven-directed spire to rise?
"The MAN of Ross," each lisping babe replies.
Behold the Market place with poor o'erspread!
The MAN of Ross divides the weekly bread:
He feeds yon Almshouse, neat, but void of state,   265
Where Age and Want sit smiling at the gate:
Him portioned maids, apprenticed orphans blest,
The young who labour, and the old who rest.
Is any sick? the MAN of Ross relieves,
Prescribes, attends, the medicine makes, and gives.   270
Is there a variance? enter but his door,
Balked are the Courts, and contest is no more.
Despairing Quacks with curses fled the place,
And vile Attorneys, now an useless race.
       B.   Thrice happy man! enabled to pursue   275
What all so wish, but want the power to do!
Oh say, what sums that generous hand supply?
What mines, to swell that boundless charity?
       P.   Of Debts, and Taxes, Wife and Children clear,
This man possessed—five hundred pounds a year.   280
Blush, Grandeur, blush! proud Courts, withdraw your
    blaze!
Ye little Stars! hide your diminished rays.
       B.   And what? no monument, inscription, stone?
His race, his form, his name almost unknown?
P.   Who builds a Church to God, and not to Fame,   285
Will never mark the marble with his Name:
Go, search it there, where to be born and die,[46]
Of rich and poor makes all the history;

[46] The Parish Register.   [P.]

Enough, that Virtue filled the space between;
Proved, by the ends of being, to have been.   290
When Hopkins dies, a thousand lights attend
The wretch, who living saved a candle's end:
Shouldering God's altar a vile image stands,
Belies his features, nay extends his hands;
That livelong wig which Gorgon's self might own,   295
Eternal buckle takes in Parian stone.[47]
Behold what blessings Wealth to life can lend!
And see, what comfort it affords our end.
  In the worst inn's worst room, with mat half-hung,
The floors of plaster, and the walls of dung,   300
On once a flock-bed, but repaired with straw,
With tape-tied curtains, never meant to draw,
The George and Garter dangling from that bed
Where tawdry yellow strove with dirty red,
Great Villiers lies—alas! how changed from him,[48] 305
That life of pleasure, and that soul of whim!
Gallant and gay, in Cliveden's[49] proud alcove,
The bower of wanton Shrewsbury and love;[50]
Or just as gay, at Council, in a ring
Of mimicked Statesmen, and their merry King.   310
No Wit to flatter, left of all his store!
No Fool to laugh at, which he valued more.
There, Victor of his health, of fortune, friends,
And fame, this lord of useless thousands ends.

[47] The poet ridicules the wretched taste of carving large periwigs on bustos, of which there are several vile examples in the tombs at Westminster and elsewhere. P.

[48] This Lord, yet more famous for his vices than his misfortunes, after having been possessed of about £50,000 a year, and passed through many of the highest posts in the kingdom, died in the year 1687, in a remote inn in Yorkshire, reduced to the utmost misery. P.

[49] A delightful palace, on the banks of the Thames, built by the Duke of Buckingham. P.

[50] The Countess of Shrewsbury, a woman abandoned to gallantries. The Earl her husband was killed by the Duke of Buckingham in a duel; and it has been said that during the combat she held the Duke's horses in the habit of a page. P.

His Grace's fate sage Cutler[51] could foresee,   315
And well (he thought) advised him, "Live like me."
As well his Grace replied, "Like you, Sir John?
That I can do, when all I have is gone."
Resolve me, Reason, which of these is worse,
Want with a full, or with an empty purse?   320
Thy life more wretched, Cutler, was confessed,
Arise, and tell me, was thy death more blessed?
Cutler saw tenants break, and houses fall,
For very want; he could not build a wall.
His only daughter in a stranger's power,   325
For very want; he could not pay a dower.
A few grey hairs his reverend temples crowned,
'Twas very want that sold them for two pound.
What even denied a cordial at his end,
Banished the doctor, and expelled the friend?   330
What but a want, which you perhaps think mad,
Yet numbers feel, the want of what he had!
Cutler and Brutus, dying both exclaim,
"Virtue! and Wealth! what are ye but a name!"
Say, for such worth are other worlds prepared?   335
Or are they both, in this their own reward?
A knotty point! to which we now proceed.
But you are tired—I'll tell a tale—   B.   Agreed.
P.   Where London's column, pointing at the skies,[52]
Like a tall bully, lifts the head, and lies;   340
There dwelt a Citizen of sober fame,
A plain good man, and Balaam was his name;
Religious, punctual, frugal, and so forth;
His word would pass for more than he was worth.
One solid dish his weekday meal affords,   345
An added pudding solemnized the Lord's:
Constant at Church, and Change; his gains were sure,
His givings rare, save farthings to the poor.

[51] Sir John Cutler, Alderman of London, created a Baronet by Charles II, was noted for habits of personal parsimony.
[52] The Monument built in memory of the fire of London, with an inscription, importing that city to have been burnt by the Papists.   P.

The Devil was piqued such saintship to behold,
And longed to tempt him like good Job of old: 350
But Satan now is wiser than of yore,
And tempts by making rich, not making poor.

Roused by the Prince of Air, the whirlwinds sweep
The surge, and plunge his Father in the deep;
Then full against his Cornish lands they roar,[53]   355
And two rich shipwrecks bless the lucky shore.

Sir Balaam now, he lives like other folks,
He takes his chirping pint, and cracks his jokes:
"Live like yourself," was soon my Lady's word;
And lo! two puddings smoked upon the board.   360

Asleep and naked as an Indian lay,
An honest factor stole a Gem away:
He pledged it to the knight; the knight had wit,
So kept the Diamond, and the rogue was bit.[54]
Some scruple rose, but thus he eased his thought,   365
"I'll now give sixpence where I gave a groat;
Where once I went to Church, I'll now go twice—
And am so clear too of all other vice."

The Tempter saw his time; the work he plied;
Stocks and Subscriptions pour on every side,   370
Till all the Demon makes his full descent
In one abundant shower of Cent per Cent,
Sinks deep within him, and possesses whole,

[53] The author has placed the scene of these shipwrecks in Cornwall, not only from their frequency on that coast, but from the inhumanity of the inhabitants to those to whom that misfortune arrives. When a ship happens to be stranded there, they have been known to bore holes in it, to prevent its getting off; to plunder, and sometimes even to massacre the people: Nor has the Parliament of England been yet able wholly to suppress these barbarities. P.

[54] In the Chauncy ms. this line reads: "So robbed the robber, and was rich as P— —." The allusion is to the famous Pitt diamond. An Indian slave found a 410-carat diamond in the Parteal mines on the Kistna and secreted it in a wound in his leg. The diamond was stolen by an English skipper, who sold it to an Indian merchant, who in turn sold it for £20,400 to Thomas Pitt, Governor of Madras, who sent it to England in 1702. It was cut in London and sold to the Regent of France for £135,000.

Then dubs Director, and secures his soul.
    Behold Sir Balaam, now a man of spirit,   375
Ascribes his gettings to his parts and merit;
What late he called a Blessing, now was Wit,
And God's good Providence, a lucky Hit.
Things change their titles, as our manners turn:
His Countinghouse employed the Sunday morn;   380
Seldom at Church ('twas such a busy life)
But duly sent his family and wife.
There (so the Devil ordained) one Christmastide
My good old Lady catched a cold, and died.
    A nymph of Quality admires our Knight;   385
He marries, bows at Court, and grows polite:
Leaves the dull Cits, and joins (to please the fair)
The well-bred cuckolds in St. James's air:
First, for his Son a gay Commission buys,
Who drinks, whores, fights, and in a duel dies: 390
His daughter flaunts a Viscount's tawdry wife;
She bears a Coronet and P—x for life.
In Britain's Senate he a seat obtains,
And one more Pensioner St. Stephen gains.
My Lady falls to play; so bad her chance,   395
He must repair it; takes a bribe from France;
The House impeach him; Coningsby[55] harangues;
The Court forsake him, and Sir Balaam hangs:
Wife, son, and daughter, Satan! are thy own,
His wealth, yet dearer, forfeit to the Crown: 400
The Devil and the King divide the prize,
And sad Sir Balaam curses God and dies.

[55] Thomas, Lord Coningsby, prominent in the impeachment of Lord Oxford and for his speeches against Roman Catholics. He died in 1729. Spence (*Anecdotes,* ed. Singer, 1820, p. 165) records an epitaph composed by Pope:
    Here lies Lord Coningsby; be civil:
    The rest God knows, perhaps the Devil.

EPISTLE IV

To Richard Boyle, Earl of Burlington

ARGUMENT

Of the Use of RICHES

The Vanity of Expense in People of Wealth and Quality. The abuse of the word *Taste*. That the first principle and foundation, in this as in every thing else, is *Good Sense*. The chief proof of it is to *follow Nature*, even in works of mere Luxury and Elegance. Instanced in *Architecture* and *Gardening*, where all must be adapted to the *Genius* and *Use* of the *Place*, and the Beauties not forced into it, but resulting from it. How men are disappointed in their most expensive undertakings, for want of this true Foundation, without which nothing can please *long*, if *at all;* and the best *Examples* and *Rules* will but be perverted into something *burdensome* or ridiculous. A description of the *false Taste* of *Magnificence;* the first grand Error of which is to imagine that *Greatness* consists in the *Size* and *Dimension*, instead of the *Proportion* and *Harmony* of the *whole*, and the second, either in joining together *Parts incoherent*, or too *minutely resembling*, or in the *Repetition* of the *same* too frequently. A word or two of false Taste in *Books*, in *Music*, in *Painting*, even in *Preaching* and *Prayer*, and lastly in *Entertainments*. Yet Providence is justified in giving Wealth to be squandered in this manner, since it is dispersed to the Poor and Laborious part of mankind [recurring to what is laid down in the first book, Ep. ii. and in the Epistle preceding this]. What are the *proper Objects* of Magnificence, and a proper field for the Expense of *Great Men*, and finally, the Great and Public Works which become a *Prince*.

> 'Tis strange, the Miser should his Cares employ
> To gain those Riches he can ne'er enjoy:
> Is it less strange, the Prodigal should waste
> His wealth, to purchase what he ne'er can taste?
> Not for himself he sees, or hears, or eats;   5
> Artists must choose his Pictures, Music, Meats:

He buys for Topham,[56] Drawings and Designs,
For Pembroke, Statues, dirty Gods, and Coins;
Rare monkish Manuscripts for Hearne alone,
And Books for Mead, and Butterflies for Sloane.[57]   10
Think we all these are for himself! no more
Than his fine Wife, alas! or finer Whore.
    For what has Virro painted, built, and planted?
Only to show, how many Tastes he wanted.
What brought Sir Visto's ill got wealth to waste?   15
Some Dæmon whispered, "Visto! have a Taste."
Heaven visits with a Taste the wealthy fool,
And needs no Rod but Ripley[58] with a Rule.
See! sportive fate, to punish awkward pride,
Bids Bubo build, and sends him such a Guide: 20
A standing sermon, at each year's expense,
That never Coxcomb reached Magnificence!
    You show us, Rome was glorious, not profuse,[59]
And pompous buildings once were things of Use.
Yet shall (my Lord) your just, your noble rules   25
Fill half the land with Imitating Fools;
Who random drawings from your sheets shall take,
And of one beauty many blunders make;
Load some vain Church with old Theatric state,
Turns Arcs of triumph to a Garden gate;   30
Reverse your Ornaments, and hang them all
On some patched dog-hole eked with ends of wall;
Then clap four slices of Pilaster on't,
That, laced with bits of rustic, makes a Front.
Shall call the winds through long arcades to roar,   35

[56] A Gentleman famous for a judicious collection of Drawings. P.
[57] Two eminent Physicians; the one had an excellent Library, the other the finest collection in Europe of natural curiosities; both men of great learning and humanity. P.
[58] This man was a carpenter, employed by a first Minister, who raised him to an Architect, without any genius in the art; and after some wretched proofs of his insufficiency in public Buildings, made him Comptroller of the Board of Works. P.
[59] The Earl of Burlington was then publishing the *Designs* of Inigo Jones, and the *Antiquities of Rome* by Palladio. P.

Proud to catch cold at a Venetian door;
Conscious they act a true Palladian part,
And, if they starve, they starve by rules of art.
　　Oft have you hinted to your brother Peer,
A certain truth, which many buy too dear:　　　　40
Something there is more needful than Expense,
And something previous even to Taste—'tis Sense:
Good Sense, which only is the gift of Heaven,
And though no Science, fairly worth the seven:
A Light, which in yourself you must perceive;　　45
Jones and Le Nôtre have it not to give.[60]
　　To build, to plant, whatever you intend,
To rear the Column, or the Arch to bend,
To swell the Terrace, or to sink the Grot;
In all, let Nature never be forgot.　　　　　　50
But treat the Goddess like a modest fair,
Nor overdress, nor leave her wholly bare;
Let not each beauty everywhere be spied,
Where half the skill is decently to hide.
He gains all points, who pleasingly confounds,　55
Surprises, varies, and conceals the Bounds.
　　Consult the Genius of the Place in all;
That tells the Waters or to rise, or fall;
Or helps th' ambitious Hill the heavens to scale,
Or scoops in circling theatres the Vale;　　　60
Calls in the Country, catches opening glades,
Joins willing woods, and varies shades from shades;
Now breaks, or now directs, th' intending Lines;
Paints as you plant, and, as you work, designs.
　　Still follow Sense, of every Art the Soul,　　65
Parts answering parts shall slide into a whole,
Spontaneous beauties all around advance,
Start even from Difficulty, strike from Chance;
Nature shall join you; Time shall make it grow

[60] Inigo Jones, the celebrated Architect, and M. Le Nôtre, the designer of the best gardens of France. P.

A Work to wonder at—perhaps a STOWE.[61]   70
    Without it, proud Versailles! thy glory falls;
And Nero's Terraces desert their walls:
The vast Parterres a thousand hands shall make,
Lo! COBHAM comes, and floats them with a Lake:
Or cut wide views through Mountains to the Plain,[62]   75
You'll wish your hill or sheltered seat again.
Even in an ornament its place remark,
Nor in an Hermitage set Dr. Clarke.[63]
    Behold Villario's ten years' toil complete;
His Quincunx darkens, his Espaliers meet;   80
The Wood supports the Plain, the parts unite,
And strength of Shade contends with strength of Light;
A waving Glow the bloomy beds display,
Blushing in bright diversities of day,
With silver-quivering rills meandered o'er—   85
Enjoy them, you! Villario can no more;
Tired of the scene Parterres and Fountains yield,
He finds at last he better likes a Field.
    Through his young Woods how pleased Sabinus strayed,
Or sat delighted in the thickening shade,   90
With annual joy the reddening shoots to greet,
Or see the stretching branches long to meet!
His Son's fine Taste an opener Vista loves,
Foe to the Dryads of his Father's groves;
One boundless Green, or flourished Carpet views,[64]   95

[61] The seat and gardens of the Lord Viscount Cobham in Buckingham-shire. P.

[62] This was done in Hertfordshire, by a wealthy citizen, at the expense of above £5,000, by which means (merely to overlook a dead plain) he let in the north wind upon his house and parterre, which were before adorned and defended by beautiful woods. P.

[63] Dr. S. Clarke's busto placed by the Queen in the Hermitage, while the Dr. duly frequented the Court. P.

[64] The two extremes in parterres, which are equally faulty; a *boundless Green*, large and naked as a field, or a *flourished Carpet*, where the great-ness and nobleness of the piece is lessened by being divided into too many

With all the mournful family of Yews;[65]
The thriving plants ignoble broomsticks made,
Now sweep those Alleys they were born to shade.
    At Timon's Villa let us pass a day,
Where all cry out, "What sums are thrown away!"   100
So proud, so grand; of that stupendous air,
Soft and Agreeable come never there.
Greatness, with Timon, dwells in such a draught
As brings all Brobdingnag before your thought.
To compass this, his building is a Town,   105
His pond an Ocean, his parterre a Down:
Who but must laugh, the Master when he sees,
A puny insect, shivering at a breeze!
Lo, what huge heaps of littleness around!
The whole, a laboured Quarry above ground.   110
Two Cupids squirt before: a Lake behind
Improves the keenness of the Northern wind.
His Gardens next your admiration call,
On every side you look, behold the Wall!
No pleasing Intricacies intervene,   115
No artful wildness to perplex the scene;
Grove nods at grove, each Alley has a brother,
And half the platform just reflects the other.
The suffering eye inverted Nature sees,
Trees cut to Statues, Statues thick as trees;   120
With here a Fountain, never to be played;
And there a Summerhouse, that knows no shade;
Here Amphitrite sails through myrtle bowers;
There Gladiators fight, or die in flowers;[66]
Unwatered see the drooping sea-horse mourn,   125

parts, with scrolled works and beds, of which the examples are frequent. P.
[65] Touches upon the ill taste of those who are so fond of Evergreens (particularly Yews, which are the most tonsile) as to destroy the nobler Forest trees, to make way for such little ornaments as Pyramids of dark green continually repeated, not unlike a Funeral procession. P.
[66] The two Statues of the *Gladiator pugnans* and *Gladiator moriens*. P.

And swallows roost in Nilus' dusty Urn.
    My Lord advances with majestic mien,
Smit with the mighty pleasure, to be seen:
But soft—by regular approach—not yet—
First through the length of yon hot Terrace sweat;   130
And when up ten steep slopes you've dragged your thighs,
Just at his Study door he'll bless your eyes.
    His Study! with what Authors is it stored?
In Books, not Authors, curious is my Lord;
To all their dated Backs he turns you round: 135
These Aldus printed, those Du Sueil has bound.
Lo, some are Vellum, and the rest as good
For all his Lordship knows, but they are Wood.[67]
For Locke or Milton 'tis in vain to look,
These shelves admit not any modern book.   140
    And now the Chapel's silver bell you hear,
That summons you to all the Pride of Prayer:
Light quirks of Music, broken and uneven,
Make the soul dance upon a Jig to Heaven.
On painted Ceilings you devoutly stare,   145
Where sprawl the Saints of Verrio or Laguerre,[68]
On gilded clouds in fair expansion lie,
And bring all Paradise before your eye.
To rest, the Cushion and soft Dean invite,
Who never mentions Hell to ears polite.[69]   150
    But hark! the chiming Clocks to dinner call;
A hundred footsteps scrape the marble Hall:
The rich Buffet well-coloured Serpents grace,[70]

[67] The false Taste in Books; a satire on the vanity in collecting them, more frequent in men of Fortune than the study to understand them. . . . some have carried it so far, as to cause the upper shelves to be filled with painted books of wood. P.

[68] Verrio (Antonio) painted many ceilings, etc., at Windsor, Hampton Court, etc., and Laguerre at Blenheim Castle, and other places. P.

[69] This is a fact; a reverend Dean, preaching at Court, threatened the sinner with punishment in "a place which he thought it not decent to name in so polite an assembly." P.

[70] Taxes the incongruity of *Ornaments* (though sometimes practised by

And gaping Tritons spew to wash your face.
Is this a dinner? this a Genial room?   155
No, 'tis a Temple, and a Hecatomb.
A solemn Sacrifice, performed in state,
You drink by measure, and to minutes eat.
So quick retires each flying course, you'd swear
Sancho's dread Doctor and his Wand were there.[71]   160
Between each Act the trembling salvers ring,
From soup to sweet wine, and God bless the King.
In plenty starving, tantalized in state,
And complaisantly helped to all I hate,
Treated, caressed, and tired, I take my leave,   165
Sick of his civil Pride from Morn to Eve;
I curse such lavish cost, and little skill,
And swear no Day was ever passed so ill.

    Yet hence the Poor are clothed, the Hungry fed;
Health to himself, and to his Infants bread   170
The Laborer bears: What his hard Heart denies,
His charitable Vanity supplies.

    Another age shall see the golden Ear
Embrown the Slope, and nod on the Parterre,
Deep Harvests bury all his pride has planned,   175
And laughing Ceres reassume the land.

    Who then shall grace, or who improve the Soil?
Who plants like BATHURST, or who builds like BOYLE.
'Tis Use alone that sanctifies Expense,
And Splendour borrows all her rays from Sense.   180

    His Father's Acres who enjoys in peace,
Or makes his Neighbours glad, if he increase:
Whose cheerful Tenants bless their yearly toil,
Yet to their Lord owe more than to the soil;
Whose ample Lawns are not ashamed to feed   185
The milky heifer and deserving steed;
Whose rising Forests, not for pride or show,

the ancients) where an open mouth ejects the water into a fountain, or
where the shocking images of serpents, etc., are introduced in Grottos
or Buffets. P.
[71] See *Don Quixote,* Chap. 47. P.

But future Buildings, future Navies, grow:
Let his plantations stretch from down to down,
First shade a Country, and then raise a Town.   190
  You too proceed! make falling Arts your care,
Erect new wonders, and the old repair;
Jones and Palladio to themselves restore,
And be whate'er Vitruvius was before:
Till Kings call forth th' Ideas of your mind,   195
(Proud to accomplish what such hands designed,)
Bid Harbours open, public Ways extend,[72]
Bid Temples, worthier of the God, ascend;
Bid the broad Arch the dangerous Flood contain,
The Mole projected break the roaring Main;   200
Back to his bounds their subject Sea command,
And roll obedient Rivers through the Land:
These Honours, Peace to happy Britain brings,
These are Imperial Works, and worthy Kings.

[72] This poem was published in the year 1732, when some of the new-built churches, by the act of Queen Anne, were ready to fall, being founded in boggy land (which is satirically alluded to in our author's imitation of Horace, Bk. II, *Satire* ii.
  Shall half the new-built Churches round thee fall);
others were vilely executed, through fraudulent cabals between undertakers, officers, etc. . . . many of the Highways throughout England were hardly passable; and most of those which were repaired by Turnpikes were made jobs for private lucre, and infamously executed, even to the entrances of London itself: The proposal of building a Bridge at Westminister had been petitioned against and rejected. P.

EPISTLE V[73]

To Mr. Addison

Occasioned by his Dialogues on MEDALS

See the wild Waste of all-devouring years!
How Rome her own sad Sepulchre appears,
With nodding arches, broken temples spread!
The very Tombs now vanished like their dead!
Imperial wonders raised on Nations spoiled,   5
Where mixed with slaves the groaning Martyr toiled:
        [see 22nd printing and following]

    Huge Theatres, that now unpeopled Woods,
    Now drained a distant country of her Floods:
    Fanes, which admiring Gods with pride survey,
    Statues of Men, scarce less alive than they!   10
    Some felt the silent stroke of mouldering age,
    Some hostile fury, some religious rage.
    Barbarian blindness, Christian zeal conspire,
    And Papal piety, and Gothic fire.
    Perhaps, by its own ruins from flame,   15
    Some buried marble half preserves a name;
    That Name the learned with fierce disputes pursue

---

[73] This was originally written in the year 1715, when Mr. Addison intended to publish his book of medals; it was sometime before he was Secretary of State; but not published till Mr. Tickell's Edition of his works; at which time the verses on Mr. Craggs, which conclude the poem, were added, viz. in 1720. P. Addison had died in 1719. The publication of Pope's poem in Tickell's edition of Addison's *Works*, 1721, was followed about a year later by the appearance (perhaps to Pope's surprise) of the celebrated "Atticus" portrait in the *St. James's Journal*. See *Epistle to Arbuthnot*, ll. 193–214.

    This *Epistle* was first aligned with the other ethical epistles in the 1735 edition of Pope's *Works*. It appears under the running head "Moral Essays" in Warburton's edition of 1751.

And give to Titus old Vespasian's due.
    Ambition sighed: She found it vain to trust
The faithless Column and the crumbling Bust: 20
Huge moles, whose shadow stretched from shore to shore,
Their ruins perished, and their place no more!
Convinced, she now contracts her vast design,
And all her triumphs shrink into a Coin.
A narrow orb each crowded conquest keeps;   25
Beneath her Palm here sad Judæa weeps.
Now scantier limits the proud Arch confine,
And scarce are seen the prostrate Nile or Rhine;
A small Euphrates through the piece is rolled,
And little Eagles wave their wings in gold.   30
    The Medal, faithful to its charge of fame,
Through climes and ages bears each form and name:
In one short view subjected to our eye
Gods, Emperors, Heroes, Sages, Beauties, lie.
With sharpened sight[74] pale Antiquaries pore,   35
Th' inscription value, but the rust adore.
This the blue varnish, that the green endears,[75]
The sacred rust of twice ten hundred years!
To gain Pescennius one employs his schemes,
One grasps a Cecrops in ecstatic dreams.   40
Poor Vadius, long with learnèd spleen devoured,
Can taste no pleasure since his Shield was scoured:[76]
And Curio, restless by the Fair one's side,
Sighs for an Otho, and neglects his bride.
    Theirs is the Vanity, the Learning thine: 45
Touched by thy hand, again Rome's glories shine;
Her Gods, and godlike Heroes rise to view,
And all her faded garlands bloom anew.
Nor blush, these studies thy regard engage;
These pleased the Fathers of poetic rage;   50
The verse and sculpture bore an equal part,

[74] Microscopic glasses . . . . [W.]
[75] This a collector of silver; that, of brass coins. [W.]
[76] Cf. *Memoirs of Martinus Scriblerus*, Chap. 3. Vadius is the geologist and antiquary John Woodward, a favorite target of Pope and his friends.

And Art reflected images to Art.
  Oh when shall Britain, conscious of her claim,
Stand emulous of Greek and Roman fame?
In living medals see her wars enrolled,   55
And vanquished realms supply recording gold?
Here, rising bold, the Patriot's honest face;
There Warriors frowning in historic brass?
Then future ages with delight shall see
How Plato's, Bacon's, Newton's looks agree;   60
Or in fair series laurelled Bards be shown,
A Virgil there, and here an Addison.
Then shall thy CRAGGS[77] (and let me call him mine)
On the cast ore, another Pollio, shine;
With aspect open, shall erect his head,   65
And round the orb in lasting notes be read,
"Statesman, yet friend to Truth! of soul sincere,
In action faithful, and in honour clear;
Who broke no promise, served no private end,
Who gained no title, and who lost no friend;   70
Ennobled by himself, by all approved,
And praised, unenvied, by the Muse he loved."

[77] James Craggs, Pope's neighbor and friend, was Addison's successor as Secretary of State in 1718 and died in 1721. See Craggs also in *Epistle* I, vi, 45; *Epilogue to the Satires,* II, 69.

1735

EPISTLE
TO DR. ARBUTHNOT
Being The Prologue To The Satires

ADVERTISEMENT

To the First Publication of this Epistle

THIS paper is a sort of bill of complaint, begun many years since, and drawn up by snatches, as the several occasions offered. I had no thoughts of publishing it, till it pleased some Persons of Rank and Fortune (the Authors of *Verses to the Imitator of Horace*,[1] and of an *Epistle to a Doctor of Divinity from a Nobleman at Hampton Court*[2]) to attack, in a very extraordinary manner, not only my Writings (of which, being public, the Public is judge) but my *Person, Morals,* and *Family,* whereof, to those who know me not, a truer information may be requisite.

[1] Attributed to Lady Mary Wortley Montagu, Lord Hervey, and William Windham. See *Epistle to Arbuthnot,* ll. 305–333 and *Satire* II, i, 6, 83.
[2] By Lord Hervey.

Being divided between the necessity to say something of *myself,* and my own laziness to undertake so awkward a task, I thought it the shortest way to put the last hand to this Epistle. If it have anything pleasing, it will be that by which I am most desirous to please, the *Truth* and the *Sentiment;* and if anything offensive, it will be only to those I am least sorry to offend, *the vicious* or *the ungenerous.*

Many will know their own pictures in it, there being not a circumstance but what is true; but I have, for the most part, spared their *Names,* and they may escape being laughed at, if they please.

I would have some of them know, it was owing to the request of the learned and candid Friend to whom it is inscribed, that I make not as free use of theirs as they have done of mine. However, I shall have this advantage, and honour, on my side, that whereas, by their proceeding, any abuse may be directed at any man, no injury can possibly be done by mine, since a nameless Character can never be found out, but by its *truth* and *likeness.* P.

P.   SHUT, shut the door, good John![3] fatigued, I said,
Tie up the knocker, say I'm sick, I'm dead.
The Dog Star rages! nay 'tis past a doubt,
All Bedlam, or Parnassus, is let out:
Fire in each eye, and papers in each hand,   5
They rave, recite, and madden round the land.
       What walls can guard me, or what shades can hide?
They pierce my thickets, through my Grot they glide;
By land, by water, they renew the charge;
They stop the chariot, and they board the barge.   10
No place is sacred, not the Church is free;
Even Sunday shines no Sabbath day to me:
Then from the Mint[4] walks forth the Man of rhyme,

[3] John Searl, his old and faithful servant: whom he has remembered, under that character, in his Will. [W.]
[4] A place to which insolvent debtors retired, to enjoy an illegal protection, which they were there suffered to afford one another, from the persecution of their creditors. [W.]

Happy! to catch me just at Dinner time.
    Is there a Parson, much bemused[5] in beer,   15
A maudlin Poetess, a rhyming Peer,
A Clerk, foredoomed his father's soul to cross,
Who pens a Stanza, when he should *engross*?
Is there, who, locked from ink and paper, scrawls
With desperate charcoal round his darkened walls?   20
All fly to TwItnam, and in humble strain
Apply to me, to keep them mad or vain.
Arthur,[6] whose giddy son neglects the Laws,
Imputes to me and my damned works the cause:
Poor Cornus sees his frantic wife elope,   25
And curses Wit, and Poetry, and Pope.
    Friend to my Life! (which did not you prolong,
The world had wanted many an idle song)
What *Drop* or *Nostrum* can this plague remove?
Or which must end me, a Fool's wrath or love?   30
A dire dilemma! either way I'm sped,
If foes, they write, if friends, they read me dead.
Seized and tied down to judge, how wretched I!
Who can't be silent, and who will not lie:
To laugh, were want of goodness and of grace,   35
And to be grave, exceeds all Power of face.
I sit with sad civility, I read
With honest anguish, and an aching head;
And drop at last, but in unwilling ears,
This saving counsel, "Keep your piece nine years."   40
    "Nine years!" cries he, who high in Drury Lane,
Lulled by soft Zephyrs through the broken pane,
Rhymes ere he wakes, and prints before *Term* ends,
Obliged by hunger, and request of friends:
"The piece, you think, is incorrect? why, take it,   45

---

[5] *Parson . . . bemused.* The sound of the words strongly suggests that the parson is Laurence Eusden, Poet Laureate, 1718–1730, well known for his "Affection to the Perquisite of Sack."
[6] Arthur Moore, a well-known politician of the day. His son James Moore Smythe had become embroiled with Pope through having used some of Pope's verses in a play. See *Dunciad* II, 50.

I'm all submission, what you'd have it, make it."
    Three things another's modest wishes bound,
My Friendship, and a Prologue, and ten pound.
    Pitholeon[7] sends to me: "You know his Grace,
I want a Patron; ask him for a Place."   50
Pitholeon libelled me—"but here's a letter
Informs you, Sir, 'twas when he knew no better.
Dare you refuse him? Curll invites to dine,
He'll write a *Journal,* or he'll turn Divine."
    Bless me! a packet.—" 'Tis a stranger sues, 55
A Virgin Tragedy, an Orphan Muse."
If I dislike it, "Furies, death and rage!"
If I approve, "Commend it to the Stage."
There (thank my stars) my whole commission ends,
The Players and I are, luckily, no friends.   60
Fired that the house reject him, " 'Sdeath I'll print it,
And shame the fools——Your Interest, Sir, with Lintot."
Lintot, dull rogue! will think your price too much:
"Not, Sir, if you revise it, and retouch."
All my demurs but double his attacks;   65
At last he whispers, "Do; and we go snacks."
Glad of a quarrel, straight I clap the door,
"Sir, let me see your works and you no more."
    'Tis sung, when Midas' Ears begun to spring,
(Midas, a sacred person and a King)   70
His very Minister who spied them first,
(Some say his Queen[8]) was forced to speak, or burst.
And is not mine, my friend, a sorer case,
When every coxcomb perks them in my face?
A. Good friend, forbear! you deal in dangerous things.
I'd never name Queens, Ministers, or Kings; 76
Keep close to Ears, and those let asses prick;
'Tis nothing— P. Nothing? if they bite and kick?

[7] The name taken from a foolish Poet of Rhodes, who pretended much to *Greek.* Schol. in Horat. l. i. Dr. Bentley pretends that this Pitholeon libelled Cæsar also. P.
[8] The story is told, by some, of his Barber, but by *Chaucer* of his Queen. See Wife of Bath's Tale in Dryden's *Fables.* P.

Out with it, DUNCIAD! let the secret pass,
That secret to each fool, that he's an Ass: 80
The truth once told (and wherefore should we lie?)
The Queen of Midas slept, and so may I.
    You think this cruel? take it for a rule,
No creature smarts so little as a fool.
Let peals of laughter, Codrus! round thee break,   85
Thou unconcerned canst hear the mighty crack:
Pit, Box, and gallery in convulsions hurled,
Thou standst unshook amidst a bursting world.
Who shames a Scribbler? break one cobweb through,
He spins the slight, self-pleasing thread anew: 90
Destroy his fib or sophistry, in vain,
The creature's at his dirty work again,
Throned in the centre of his thin designs,
Proud of a vast extent of flimsy lines!
Whom have I hurt? has Poet yet, or Peer,   95
Lost the arched eyebrow, or Parnassian sneer?
And has not Colley still his Lord, and whore?
His butchers Henley,[9] his Freemasons Moore?[10]
Does not one table Bavius still admit?
Still to one Bishop[11] Philips seem a wit?   100
Still Sappho— A. Hold! for God's sake—you'll offend,
No Names—be calm—learn prudence of a friend:
I too could write, and I am twice as tall;
But foes like these— P. One Flatterer's worse than all.
Of all mad creatures, if the learned are right,   105
It is the slaver kills, and not the bite.
A fool quite angry is quite innocent:
Alas! 'tis ten times worse when they *repent*.
    One dedicates in high heroic prose,
And ridicules beyond a hundred foes: 110

---

[9] John Henley, called Orator Henley, was an eccentric who delivered
lectures on religious and general cultural topics. He gave his *Butchers
Lecture* at Newport Market on Easter Day 1729. Cf. *Dunciad* III, 199.
[10] He was of this society, and frequently headed their processions. [W.]
[11] Hugh Boulter, friend and patron of Ambrose Philips, became Bishop
of Armagh in 1724. Philips accompanied him to Ireland as his secretary.

One from all Grubstreet will my fame defend,
And, more abusive, calls himself my friend.
This prints my *Letters,* that expects a bribe,
And others roar aloud, "Subscribe, subscribe."
     There are, who to my person pay their court: 115
I cough like *Horace,* and, though lean, am short,
Ammon's great son one shoulder had too high,
Such *Ovid's* nose, and "Sir! you have an Eye"—[12]
Go on, obliging creatures, make me see
All that disgraced my Betters, met in me.   120
Say for my comfort, languishing in bed,
"Just so immortal *Maro* held his head:"
And when I die, be sure you let me know
Great *Homer* died three thousand years ago.
     Why did I write? what sin to me unknown   125
Dipped me in ink, my parents', or my own?
As yet a child, nor yet a fool to fame,
I lisped in numbers, for the numbers came.
I left no calling for this idle trade,
No duty broke, no father disobeyed.[13]   130
The Muse but served to ease some friend, not Wife,
To help me through this long disease, my Life,
To second, ARBUTHNOT! thy Art and Care,
And teach the Being you preserved, to bear.
     But why then publish? *Granville* the polite,   135
And knowing *Walsh,* would tell me I could write;
Well-natured *Garth* inflamed with early praise;
And *Congreve* loved, and *Swift* endured my lays;
The courtly *Talbot, Somers, Sheffield* read,
Even mitred *Rochester* would nod the head,   140

[12] It is remarkable that amongst these compliments on his infirmities and deformities, he mentions his *eye,* which was fine, sharp, and piercing. [W.]

[13] When Mr. Pope was yet a Child, his Father, though no Poet, would set him to make English verses. He was pretty difficult to please, and would often send the boy back to new turn them. When they were to his mind, he took great pleasure in them, and would say, *These are good rhymes.* [W.]

And *St. John's* self (great *Dryden's* friends before)
With open arms received one Poet more.
Happy my studies, when by these approved!
Happier their author, when by these beloved!
From these the world will judge of men and books,   145
Not from the *Burnets, Oldmixons,* and *Cookes*.[14]
   Soft were my numbers; who could take offence
While pure Description held the place of Sense?
Like gentle *Fanny's* was my flowery theme,
A painted mistress, or a purling stream.   150
Yet then did *Gildon* draw his venal quill;
I wished the man a dinner, and sat still.
Yet then did *Dennis* rave in furious fret;
I never answered—I was not in debt.
If want provoked, or madness made them print,   155
I waged no war with *Bedlam* or the *Mint*.
   Did some more sober Critic come abroad;
If wrong, I smiled; if right, I kissed the rod.
Pains, reading, study, are their just pretence,
And all they want is spirit, taste, and sense.   160
Commas and points they set exactly right,
And 'twere a sin to rob them of their mite.
Yet ne'er one sprig of laurel graced these ribalds,
From slashing *Bentley* down to pidling *Tibalds*:
Each wight, who reads not, and but scans and spells,   165
Each Word-catcher, that lives on syllables,
Even such small Critics some regard may claim,
Preserved in *Milton's* or in *Shakespeare's* name.
Pretty! in amber to observe the forms
Of hairs, or straws, or dirt, or grubs, or worms!   170
The things, we know, are neither rich nor rare,
But wonder how the devil they got there.
   Were others angry: I excused them too;
Well might they rage, I gave them but their due.
A man's true merit 'tis not hard to find;   175
But each man's secret standard in his mind,

[14] Authors of secret and scandalous History. P.

That Casting weight pride adds to emptiness,
This, who can gratify? for who can *guess?*
The Bard whom pilfered Pastorals renown,
Who turns a Persian tale[15] for half a Crown,   180
Just writes to make his barrenness appear,
And strains, from hard-bound brains, eight lines a year;
He, who still wanting, though he lives on theft,
Steals much, spends little, yet has nothing left:
And He, who now to sense, now nonsense leaning,   185
Means not, but blunders round about a meaning:
And He, whose fustian's so sublimely bad,
It is not Poetry, but prose run mad:
All these, my modest Satire bade *translate,*
And owned that nine such Poets made a *Tate.*   190
How did they fume, and stamp, and roar, and chafe!
And swear, not ADDISON himself was safe.

    Peace to all such! but were there One whose fires
True Genius kindles, and fair Fame inspires;
Blest with each talent and each art to please,   195
And born to write, converse, and live with ease:
Should such a man, too fond to rule alone,
Bear, like the Turk, no brother near the throne,
View him with scornful, yet with jealous eyes,
And hate for arts that caused himself to rise;   200
Damn with faint praise, assent with civil leer,
And without sneering, teach the rest to sneer;
Willing to wound, and yet afraid to strike,
Just hint a fault, and hesitate dislike;
Alike reserved to blame, or to commend,   205
A timorous foe, and a suspicious friend;
Dreading even fools, by Flatterers besieged,
And so obliging, that he ne'er obliged;
Like *Cato,* give his little Senate laws,[16]
And sit attentive to his own applause;   210
While Wits and Templars every sentence raise,

---

[15] Ambrose Philips translated a Book called the *Persian Tales.*   P.
[16] Cf. Prologue to Addison's *Cato,* l. 23.

And wonder with a foolish face of praise—
Who but must laugh, if such a man there be?
Who would not weep, if ATTICUS were he?
     What though my Name stood rubric on the walls,   215
Or plastered posts, with claps, in capitals?[17]
Or smoking forth, a hundred hawkers' load,
On wings of wind came flying all abroad?
I sought no homage from the Race that write;
I kept, like *Asian* Monarchs, from their sight: 220
Poems I heeded (now berhymed so long)
No more than thou, great GEORGE! a birthday song.
I ne'er with wits or witlings passed my days,
To spread about the itch of verse and praise;
Nor like a puppy, daggled through the town,   225
To fetch and carry singsong up and down;
Nor at Rehearsals sweat, and mouthed, and cried,
With handkerchief and orange at my side;
But sick of fops, and poetry, and prate,
To *Bufo* left the whole *Castalian* state.   230
     Proud as *Apollo* on his forkèd hill,
Sat full-blown *Bufo,* puffed by every quill;
Fed with soft Dedication all day long,
Horace and he went hand in hand in song.
His Library (where busts of Poets dead   235
And a true *Pindar* stood without a head)[18]
Received of wits an undistinguished race,
Who first his judgment asked, and then a place:
Much they extolled his pictures, much his seat,
And flattered every day, and some days eat: 240
Till grown more frugal in his riper days,
He paid some bards with port, and some with praise;
To some a dry rehearsal was assigned,
And others (harder still) he paid in kind.
Dryden alone (what wonder?) came not nigh,   245

[17] The bills of Quack Doctors and Quack Booksellers being usually pasted together on the same posts. [W.]
[18] Ridicules the affectation of Antiquaries, who frequently exhibit the headless *Trunks* and *Terms* of Statues, for Plato, Homer, Pindar, etc. P.

Dryden alone escaped this judging eye:
But still the *Great* have kindness in reserve,
He helped to bury whom he helped to starve.[19]
     May some choice patron bless each grey goose quill!
May every *Bavius* have his *Bufo* still!   250
So, when a Statesman wants a day's defence,
Or Envy holds a whole week's war with Sense,
Or simple pride for flattery makes demands,
May dunce by dunce be whistled off my hands!
Blest be the *Great!* for those they take away,   255
And those they left me; for they left me GAY;
Left me to see neglected Genius bloom,
Neglected die, and tell it on his tomb:
Of all thy blameless life the sole return
My Verse, and QUEENSBURY weeping o'er thy urn!   260
     Oh let me live my own, and die so too!
(To live and die is all I have to:)
Maintain a Poet's dignity and ease,
And see what friends, and read what books I please:
Above a Patron, though I condescend   265
Sometimes to call a Minister my friend.
I was not born for Courts or great affairs;
I pay my debts, believe, and say my prayers;
Can sleep without a Poem in my head,
Nor know, if *Dennis* be alive or dead.   270
     Why am I asked what next shall see the light?
Heavens! was I born for nothing but to write?
Has Life no joys for me? or, (to be grave)
Have I no friend to serve, no soul to save?
"I found him close with *Swift*"—'Indeed? no doubt,'   275
(Cries prating *Balbus*) 'something will come out.'
'Tis all in vain, deny it as I will.
'No, such a Genius never can lie still;'
And then for mine obligingly mistakes
The first Lampoon Sir *Will*. or *Bubo* makes.   280

[19] Mr. Dryden, after having lived in exigencies, had a magnificent Funeral bestowed upon him by the contribution of several persons of quality. P.

Poor guiltless I! and can I choose but smile,
When every Coxcomb knows me by my *Style?*
    Cursed be the verse, how well soe'er it flow,
That tends to make one worthy man my foe,
Give Virtue scandal, Innocence a fear,   285
Or from the soft-eyed Virgin steal a tear!
But he who hurts a harmless neighbour's peace,
Insults fallen worth, or Beauty in distress,
Who loves a Lie, lame slander helps about,
Who writes a Libel, or who copies out: 290
That Fop, whose pride affects a patron's name,
Yet absent, wounds an author's honest fame:
Who can *your* merit *selfishly* approve,
And show the *sense* of it without the *love;*
Who has the vanity to call you friend,   295
Yet wants the honour, injured, to defend;
Who tells whate'er you think, whate'er you say,
And, if he lie not, must at least betray:
Who to the *Dean,* and *silver bell* can swear,[20]
And sees at *Canons* what was never there;   300
Who reads, but with a lust to misapply,
Make Satire a Lampoon, and Fiction, Lie.
A lash like mine no honest man shall dread,
But all such babbling blockheads in his stead.
    Let *Sporus* tremble— A. What? that thing of silk,
Sporus, that mere white curd of Ass's milk?   306
Satire or sense, alas! can *Sporus* feel?
Who breaks a butterfly upon a wheel?
P. Yet let me flap this bug with gilded wings,
This painted child of dirt, that stinks and stings;   310
Whose buzz the witty and the fair annoys,
Yet wit ne'er tastes, and beauty ne'er enjoys:
So well-bred spaniels civilly delight
In mumbling of the game they dare not bite.

---

[20] Meaning the man who would have persuaded the Duke of Chandos
that Mr. P. meant him in those circumstances ridiculed in the Epistle on
Taste. See Mr. Pope's Letter to the Earl of Burlington concerning this
matter. [W.]

Eternal smiles his emptiness betray,   315
As shallow streams run dimpling all the way.
Whether in florid impotence he speaks,
And, as the prompter breathes, the puppet squeaks;
Or at the ear of *Eve,* familiar Toad,[21]
Half froth, half venom, spits himself abroad,   320
In puns, or politics, or tales, or lies,
Or spite, or smut, or rhymes, or blasphemies.
His wit all seesaw, between *that* and *this,*
Now high, now low, now master up, now miss,
And he himself one vile Antithesis.   325
Amphibious thing! that acting either part,
The trifling head, or the corrupted heart,
Fop at the toilet, flatterer at the board,
Now trips a Lady, and now struts a Lord.
Eve's tempter thus the Rabbins have exprest,   330
A Cherub's face, a reptile all the rest;
Beauty that shocks you, parts that none will trust,
Wit that can creep, and pride that licks the dust.

    Not Fortune's worshipper, nor Fashion's fool,
Not Lucre's madman, nor Ambition's tool,   335
Not proud, nor servile; Be one Poet's praise,
That, if he pleased, he pleased by manly ways:
That Flattery, even to Kings, he held a shame,
And thought a Lie in verse or prose the same.
That not in Fancy's maze he wandered long,   340
But stooped to Truth[22] and moralized his song:
That not for Fame, but Virtue's better end,
He stood the furious foe, the timid friend,
The damning critic, half approving wit,
The coxcomb hit, or fearing to be hit;   345
Laughed at the loss of friends he never had,
The dull, the proud, the wicked, and the mad;
The distant threats of vengeance on his head,
The blow unfelt, the tear he never shed;

[21] See Milton [*Paradise Lost*], Bk. IV [1. 800]. P.
[22] The term is from falconry; and the allusion to one of those untamed birds of spirit, which sometimes wantons at large in airy circles before it regards, or *stoops to,* its prey. [W.]

The tale revived, the lie so oft o'erthrown,[23]   350
Th' imputed trash,[24] and dulness not his own;
The morals blackened when the writings 'scape,
The libeled person, and the pictured shape;
Abuse, on all he loved, or loved him, spread,[25]
A friend in exile, or a father, dead;   355
The whisper, that to greatness still too near,
Perhaps, yet vibrates on his SOVEREIGN's ear—
Welcome for thee, fair *Virtue!* all the past:
For thee, fair Virtue! welcome even the *last!*
    A. But why insult the poor, affront the great?   360
P. A knave's a knave, to me, in every state:
Alike my scorn, if he succeed or fail,
Sporus at court, or *Japhet* in a jail,
A hireling scribbler, or a hireling peer,
Knight of the post corrupt, or of the shire;   365
If on a Pillory, or near a Throne,
He gain his Prince's ear, or lose his own.
    Yet soft by nature, more a dupe than wit,
Sappho can tell you how this man was bit:
This dreaded Satirist *Dennis* will confess   370
Foe to his pride, but friend to his distress:
So humble, he has knocked at *Tibbald's* door,
Has drunk with *Cibber,* nay, has rhymed for *Moore.*
Full ten years slandered,[26] did he once reply?
Three thousand suns went down on *Welsted's* lie.[27]   375

---

[23] As, that he received subscriptions for Shakespeare, that he set his name to Mr. Broome's verses, etc., which, though publicly disproved, were nevertheless shamelessly repeated in the Libels, and even in that called *The Nobleman's Epistle.* P.

[24] Such as profane *Psalms, Court Poems,* and other scandalous things, printed in his Name by Curll and others. P.

[25] Namely on the Duke of Buckingham, the Earl of Burlington, Lord Bathurst, Lord Bolingbroke, Bishop Atterbury, Dr. Swift, Dr. Arbuthnot, Mr. Gay, his Friends, his Parents, and his very Nurse, aspersed in printed papers, by James Moore, G. Ducket, L. Welsted, Tho. Bentley, and other obscure persons. P.

[26] It was so long after many libels the Author of the *Dunciad* published that poem, till when, he never writ a word in answer to the many scurrilities and falsehoods concerning him. P.

[27] This man had the impudence to tell in print that Mr. P. had occa-

To please a Mistress one aspersed his life;
He lashed him not, but let her be his wife:
Let *Budgel* charge low *Grubstreet* on his quill,[28]
And write whate'er he pleased, except his Will;[29]
Let the two *Curlls* of Town and Court, abuse   380
His father, mother, body, soul, and muse.[30]

sioned a *Lady's death,* and to name a person he never heard of. He also published that he libelled the Duke of Chandos; with whom (it was added) that he had lived in familiarity, and received from him a present of *five hundred pounds:* the falsehood of both which is known to his Grace. Mr. P. never received any present, farther than the subscription for Homer, from him, or from *Any great Man* whatsoever. P.

[28] *Budgel,* in a weekly pamphlet called the *Bee,* bestowed much abuse on him, in the imagination that he writ some things about the *Last Will* of Dr. *Tindal,* in the *Grubstreet Journal;* a Paper wherein he never had the least hand, direction, or supervisal, nor the least knowledge of its Author. P.

[29] Alluding to Tindal's Will: by which, and other indirect practices, Budgel, to the exclusion of the next heir, a nephew, got to himself almost the whole fortune of a man entirely unrelated to him. [W.]

[30] In some of Curll's and other pamphlets, Mr. Pope's father was said to be a Mechanic, a Hatter, a Farmer, nay a Bankrupt. But, what is stranger, a *Nobleman* (if such a Reflection could be thought to come from a Nobleman) had dropped an allusion to that pitiful untruth, in a paper called an *Epistle to a Doctor of Divinity:* and the following line,
  Hard as thy Heart, and as thy Birth obscure,
had fallen from a like *Courtly* pen, in certain *Verses to the Imitator of Horace.* Mr. Pope's Father was of a Gentleman's Family in Oxfordshire, the head of which was the Earl of Downe, whose sole Heiress married the Earl of Lindsey. His mother was the daughter of William Turner, Esq. of York: She had three brothers, one of whom was killed, another died in the service of King Charles; the eldest following his fortunes, and becoming a general officer in Spain, left her what estate remained after the sequestrations and forfeitures of her family—Mr. Pope died in 1717, aged 75; She in 1733, aged 93, a very few weeks after this poem was finished. The following inscription was placed by their son on their Monument in the parish of Twickenham, in Middlesex.

D. O. M.

ALEXANDRO . POPE . VIRO . INNOCVO . PROBO . PIO .

QVI . VIXIT . ANNOS . LXXV . OB . MDCCXVII .

ET . EDITHAE . CONIVGI . INCVLPABILI .

PIENTISSIMAE . QVAE . VIXIT . ANNOS .

XCIII . OB . MDCCXXXIII .

PARENTIBVS . BENEMERENTIBVS . FILIVS . FECIT .

ET . SIBI .   P.

Yet why? that Father held it for a rule,
It was a sin to call our neighbour fool:
That harmless Mother thought no wife a whore:
Hear this, and spare his family, *James Moore!*   385
Unspotted names, and memorable long!
If there be force in Virtue, or in Song.

    Of gentle blood (part shed in Honour's cause,
While yet in *Britain* Honour had applause)
Each parent sprung— A. What fortune, pray?— P.
Their own,   390
And better got, than *Bestia's* from the throne.
Born to no Pride, inheriting no Strife,
Nor marrying Discord in a noble wife,[31]
Stranger to civil and religious rage,
The good man walked innoxious through his age.   395
No Courts he saw, no suits would ever try,
Nor dared an Oath, nor hazarded a Lie.[32]
Unlearned, he knew no schoolman's subtle art,
No language, but the language of the heart.
By Nature honest, by Experience wise,   400
Healthy by temperance, and by exercise;
His life, though long, to sickness past unknown,
His death was instant, and without a groan.
O grant me, thus to live, and thus to die!
Who sprung from Kings shall know less joy than I.   405

    O Friend! may each domestic bliss be thine!
Be no unpleasing Melancholy mine:
Me, let the tender office long engage,
To rock the cradle of reposing Age,
With lenient arts extend a Mother's breath,   410
Make Langour smile, and smooth the bed of Death,
Explore the thought, explain the asking eye,
And keep a while one parent from the sky!
On cares like these if length of days attend,
May Heaven, to bless those days, preserve my friend,   415

[31] Alluding to the unhappy marriage of Addison with the Countess of Warwick.
[32] He was a nonjuror, and would not take the oath of allegiance or supremacy, or the oath against the Pope.

Preserve him social, cheerful, and serene,
And just as rich as when he served a QUEEN.[33]
A.   Whether that blessing be denied or given,
Thus far was right, the rest belongs to Heaven.

---

[33] An honest compliment to his Friend's real and unaffected disinterestedness, when he was the favourite Physician of Queen Anne.   [W.]

SATIRES and EPISTLES OF HORACE IMITATED

ADVERTISEMENT

THE Occasion of publishing these *Imitations* was the Clamour raised on some of my *Epistles*. An Answer from *Horace* was both more full, and of more Dignity, than any I could have made in my own person; and the Example of much greater Freedom in so eminent a Divine as Dr. *Donne,* seemed a proof with what indignation and contempt a Christian may treat Vice or Folly, in ever so low, or ever so high, a Station. Both these Authors were acceptable to the *Princes* and *Ministers* under whom they lived. The Satires of Dr. *Donne* I versified at the desire of the Earl of *Oxford* while he was Lord Treasurer, and of the Duke of *Shrewsbury,* who had been Secretary of State; neither of whom looked upon a Satire on Vicious Courts as any Reflection on those they served in. And indeed there is not in the world a greater error than that which Fools are so apt to fall into, and Knaves with good reason to encourage, the mistaking a *Satirist* for a *Libeller;* whereas to a *true Satirist* nothing is so odious as a *Libeller,* for the same reason as to a man *truly virtuous* nothing is so hateful as a *Hypocrite.*

Uni æquus Virtuti atque eius Amicis.[1]   P.

[1] Horace *Satire* II. i. 70.

THE FIRST SATIRE
OF THE
SECOND BOOK OF
HORACE

Satire I

To Mr. Fortescue[2]

P.   THERE are (I scarce can think it, but am told),
There are, to whom my Satire seems too bold:
Scarce to wise Peter complaisant enough,
And something said of Chartres much too rough.[3]
The lines are weak, another's pleased to say,   5
Lord Fanny[4] spins a thousand such a day.

---

[2] The eminent barrister William Fortescue, later a Judge of the Exchequer and of the Common Pleas and Master of the Rolls. He was for years the friend of Pope and Gay. Pope appeals to him as Horace does to the celebrated Roman lawyer C. Trebatius Testa, the friend of Julius Caesar and of Cicero.

[3] See *Moral Essay* III, 20, 123.

[4] *Fanny,* which bears a convenient resemblance to the *Fannius* of Horace's *Satire* I. x, was taken by Lord Hervey to refer to himself. (Cf. *Epistle to Arbuthnot,* ll. 305–333.) Hervey counterattacked in August 1733 with *An Epistle to a Doctor of Divinity.* (Cf. Advertisement to *Epistle to Arbuthnot.*) In November Pope wrote a response—not published until 1751—his *Letter to a Noble Lord:* "Fanny (my Lord) is the plain English of *Fannius,* a real person, who was a foolish critic, and an enemy of Horace, perhaps a noble one. . . . This Fannius was, it seems, extremely fond both of his *poetry* and his *person.* . . . He was moreover of a delicate or effeminate complexion, and constant at the assemblies and operas of those days, where he took it into his head to slander poor Horace . . . till it provoked him at last just to name him, give him a lash, and send him whimpering to the ladies." (*Works of Pope,* ed. Elwin and Courthope, v. [1889], 429.)

While Tories call me Whig, and Whigs a Tory.
Satire's my weapon, but I'm too discreet
To run amuck, and tilt at all I meet;   70
I only wear it in a land of Hectors,
Thieves, Supercargoes, Sharpers, and Directors.
Save but our *Army!* and let Jove encrust
Swords, pikes, and guns, with everlasting rust!
Peace is my dear delight—not FLEURY's[10] more: 75
But touch me, and no Minister so sore.
Whoe'er offends, at some unlucky time
Slides into verse, and hitches in a rhyme,
Sacred to Ridicule his whole life long,
And the sad burden of some merry song.   80
        Slander or Poison dread from Delia's rage,
Hard words or hanging, if your Judge be Page.[11]
From furious Sappho[12] scarce a milder fate,
P—xed by her love, or libelled by her hate.
Its proper power to hurt, each creature feels;   85
Bulls aim their horns, and Asses lift their heels;
'Tis a Bear's talent not to kick, but hug;
And no man wonders he's not stung by Pug.
So drink with Walters, or with Chartres eat,
They'll never poison you, they'll only cheat.   90
        Then, learnèd sir! (to cut the matter short)
Whate'er my fate, or well or ill at Court,

[10] Cardinal Fleury, Minister to Louis XV. In concert with Walpole, he worked for peace. Cf. *Epilogue,* I, 51.

[11] Sir Francis Page, a Judge of the Common Pleas, had presided in 1728 at the trial of Pope's protégé Richard Savage for murder. See Johnson's *Life of Savage* and the satire on Page in Fielding's *Tom Jones,* Bk. VIII, Chap. 2.

[12] These lines were applied to Lady Mary Wortley Montagu. She had the imprudence to urge Lord Peterborough to complain of them to Pope and received Pope's reply in a letter from Lord Peterborough: Pope "said to me what I had taken the liberty to say to you, that he wondered how the town would apply these lines to any but some noted common woman; that he would be yet more surprised if you should take them to yourself." (*Works of Pope,* ed. Elwin and Courthope, III [1881], 279). Cf. *Epistle to Arbuthnot,* Advertisement and ll. 101, 369; *Moral Essay* II, 24–26; III, 121; *Satires of Donne,* II, 6.

Whether old age, with faint but cheerful ray,
Attends to gild the Evening of my day,
Or Death's black wing already be displayed,   95
To wrap me in the universal shade;
Whether the darkened room to muse invite,
Or whitened wall provoke the skewer to write:
In durance, exile, Bedlam, or the Mint,
Like Lee or Budgell, I will rhyme and print.   100
      F.   Alas, young man! your days can ne'er be long,
In flower of age you perish for a song!
Plums and directors, Shylock and his Wife,
Will club their Testers, now, to take your life!
      P.   What? armed for Virtue when I point the pen,   105
Brand the bold front of shameless guilty men;
Dash the proud Gamester in his gilded Car;
Bare the mean Heart that lurks beneath a *Star;*
Can there be wanting, to defend Her cause,
Lights of the Church, or Guardians of the Laws?   110
Could pensioned Boileau lash in honest strain
Flatterers and bigots even in Louis' reign?
Could laureate Dryden Pimp and Friar engage,
Yet neither Charles nor James be in a rage?
And I not strip the gilding off a Knave,   115
Unplaced, unpensioned, no man's heir, or slave?
I will, or perish in the generous cause:
Hear this, and tremble! you who 'scape the Laws.
Yes, while I live, no rich or noble knave
Shall walk the World, in credit, to his grave.   120
To Virtue only and her friends a friend,[13]
The World beside may murmur, or commend.
Know, all the distant din that world can keep,
Rolls o'er my Grotto,[14] and but soothes my sleep.

[13] Cf. the Advertisement to the *Satires and Epistles,* the satirist's motto:
Uni aequus virtuti atque ejus amicis.
[14] Pope's grotto consisted of a series of ornamented chambers or caverns
under his house and a passage running under the high road to his garden.
See the ground plan· drawn by Pope's gardener in *Poetical Works of
Pope,* ed. Robert Carruthers (London, 1853), I, 332.

There, my retreat the best Companions grace,   125
Chiefs out of war, and Statesmen out of place.
There St. John mingles with my friendly bowl
The Feast of Reason and the Flow of soul:
And He, whose lightning pierced th' Iberian Lines,[15]
Now forms my Quincunx, and now ranks my Vines,   130
Or tames the Genius of the stubborn plain,
Almost as quickly as he conquered Spain.
      Envy must own, I live among the Great,
No Pimp of pleasure, and no Spy of state,
With eyes that pry not, tongue that ne'er repeats,   135
Fond to spread friendships, but to cover heats;
To help who want, to forward who excel;
This, all who know me, know; who love me, tell;
And who unknown defame me, let them be
Scribblers or Peers, alike are *Mob* to me.   140
This is my plea, on this I rest my cause—
What saith my Counsel, learnèd in the laws?
      F. Your Plea is good; but still I say, beware!
Laws are explained by Men—so have a care.
It stands on record, that in Richard's times   145
A man was hanged for very honest rhymes.[16]
Consult the Statute: *quart.* I think, it is,
Edwardi sext. or *prim. et quint. Eliz.*
See *Libels, Satires*—here you have it—read.
      P. *Libels* and *satires!* lawless things indeed!   150
But grave *Epistles,* bringing Vice to light,
Such as a King might read, a Bishop write,
Such as Sir Robert would approve—

[15] Charles Mordaunt, Earl of Peterborough, who in the year 1705 took Barcelona, and in the winter following, with only 280 horse and 900 foot, enterprised and accomplished the conquest of Valentia. P.
[16] John Ball, one of the leaders of the Peasants' Revolt in 1381, was author of revolutionary rhymes, including the famous couplet:
              When Adam dalf and Eve span,
              Who was then a gentilman?
At the failure of the Revolt, Ball was hanged, drawn, and quartered. See Pope's *Imitations of Horace,* ed. John Butt (London, 1939), p. 406, for a parallel case, that of the poet Collingbourne under Richard III.

F. Indeed?
The case is altered—you may then proceed;
In such a cause the Plaintiff will be hissed, 155
My Lords the Judges laugh, and you're dismissed.

1734

THE SECOND SATIRE
OF THE
SECOND BOOK OF
HORACE

Satire II

To Mr. Bethel[17]

WHAT, and how great, the Virtue and the Art
To live on little with a cheerful heart;
(A doctrine sage, but truly none of mine)
Let's talk, my friends, but talk before we dine.
Not when a gilt Buffet's reflected pride 5
Turns you from sound Philosophy aside;
Not when from plate to plate your eyeballs roll,
And the brain dances to the mantling bowl.
Hear BETHEL's Sermon, one not versed in schools,
But strong in sense, and wise without the rules. 10
Go work, hunt, exercise! (he thus began)
Then scorn a homely dinner, if you can.
Your wine locked up, your Butler strolled abroad,

[17] Hugh Bethel, one of Pope's earliest friends, owned an estate in Yorkshire of £2000 a year. See *Essay on Man,* IV, 126, "blameless Bethel." His name was placed at the head of this satire by Warburton, somewhat ineptly, as he is made to listen to his own sermon.

Or fish denied (the river yet unthawed),
If then plain bread and milk will do the feat,   15
The pleasure lies in you, and not the meat.

      Preach as I please, I doubt our curious men
Will choose a pheasant still before a hen;
Yet hens of Guinea full as good I hold,
Except you eat the feathers green and gold.   20
Of carps and mullets why prefer the great,
(Though cut in pieces ere my Lord can eat)
Yet for small Turbots such esteem profess?
Because God made these large, the other less.

      Oldfield[18] with more than Harpy throat endued,   25
Cries "Send me, Gods! a whole Hog barbecued!"
Oh blast it, South Winds! till a stench exhale
Rank as the ripeness of a rabbit's tail.
By what Criterion do ye eat, d' ye think,
If this is prized for sweetness, that for stink?   30
When the tired glutton labours through a treat,
He finds no relish in the sweetest meat,
He calls for something bitter, something sour,
And the rich feast concludes extremely poor:
Cheap eggs, and herbs, and olives still we see;   35
Thus much is left of old Simplicity!
The Robin redbreast till of late had rest,
And children sacred held a Martin's nest,
Till Beccaficos sold so devilish dear
To one that was, or would have been a Peer.   40
Let me extol a Cat, on oysters fed,
I'll have a party at the Bedford Head;[19]
Or even to crack live Crawfish recommend;
I'd never doubt at Court to make a friend.

      'Tis yet in vain, I own, to make a pother   45
About one vice, and fall into the other:
Between Excess and Famine lies a mean;
Plain, but not sordid; though not splendid, clean.

[18] This eminent Glutton ran through a fortune of fifteen hundred pounds
a year in the simple Luxury of good eating. [W.]
[19] A famous Eating house. P.

Avidien, or his Wife (no matter which,
For him you'll call a dog, and her a bitch)   50
Sell their presented partridges, and fruits,
And humbly live on rabbits and on roots:
One half-pint bottle serves them both to dine,
And is at once their vinegar and wine.
But on some lucky day (as when they found   55
A lost Bank bill, or heard their Son was drowned)
At such a feast, old vinegar to spare,
Is what two souls so generous cannot bear:
Oil, though it stink, they drop by drop impart,
But souse the cabbage with a bounteous heart.   60
    He knows to live, who keeps the middle state,
And neither leans on this side, nor on that;
Nor stops, for one bad cork, his butler's pay,
Swears, like Albutius, a good cook away;
Nor lets, like Nævius, every error pass,   65
The musty wine, foul cloth, or greasy glass.
    Now hear what blessings Temperance can bring:
(Thus said our Friend, and what he said I sing)
First Health: The stomach (crammed from every dish,
A tomb of boiled and roast, and flesh and fish,   70
Where bile, and wind, and phlegm, and acid jar,
And all the man is one intestine war)
Remembers oft the Schoolboy's simple fare,
The temperate sleeps, and spirits light as air.
    How pale, each Worshipful and Reverend guest   75
Rise from a Clergy, or a City feast!
What life in all that ample body, say?
What heavenly particle inspires the clay?
The Soul subsides, and wickedly inclines
To seem but mortal, even in sound Divines.   80
    On morning wings how active springs the Mind
That leaves the load of yesterday behind!
How easy every labour it pursues!
How coming to the Poet every Muse!
Not but we may exceed, some holy time,   85
Or tired in search of Truth, or search of Rhyme;

Ill health some just indulgence may engage,
And more the sickness of long life, Old age;
For fainting Age what cordial drop remains,
If our intemperate Youth the vessel drains?   90
    Our fathers praised rank Venison. You suppose
Perhaps, young men! our fathers had no nose.
Not so: a Buck was then a week's repast,
And 'twas their point, I ween, to make it last;
More pleased to keep it till their friends could come,   95
Than eat the sweetest by themselves at home.
Why had I not in those good times my birth,
Ere coxcomb pies or coxcombs were on earth?
    Unworthy he, the voice of Fame to hear,
That sweetest music to an honest ear;   100
(For 'faith, Lord Fanny! you are in the wrong,
The world's good word is better than a song)
Who has not learned, fresh sturgeon and ham pie
Are no rewards for want, and infamy!
When Luxury has licked up all thy pelf,   105
Cursed by thy neighbours, thy trustees, thyself,
To friends, to fortune, to mankind a shame,
Think how posterity will treat thy name;
And buy a rope, that future times may tell
Thou hast at least bestowed one penny well.   110
    "Right," cries his Lordship, "for a rogue in need
To have a Taste is insolence indeed:
In me 'tis noble, suits my birth and state,
My wealth unwieldy, and my heap too great."
Then, like the Sun, let Bounty spread her ray,   115
And shine that superfluity away.
Oh Impudence of wealth! with all thy store,
How dar'st thou let one worthy man be poor?
Shall half the new-built churches round thee fall?
Make Quays, build Bridges, or repair Whitehall: 120
Or to thy country let that heap be lent,
As M * * o's[20] was, but not at five per cent.

---

[20] The Duchess of Marlborough lent great sums to the Government and

Who thinks that Fortune cannot change her mind,
Prepares a dreadful jest for all mankind.
And who stands safest? tell me, is it he   125
That spreads and swells in puffed Prosperity,
Or blest with little, whose preventing care
In peace provides fit arms against a war?
    Thus BETHEL spoke, who always speaks his thought,
And always thinks the very thing he ought: 130
His equal mind I copy what I can,
And, as I love, would imitate the Man.
In South Sea days not happier,[21] when surmised
The Lord of Thousands, than if now *Excised;*
In forest planted by a Father's hand,   135
Than in five acres now of rented land.
Content with little, I can piddle here
On broccoli and mutton, round the year;
But ancient friends (though poor, or out of play)
That touch my bell, I cannot turn away.   140
'Tis true, no Turbots dignify my boards,
But gudgeons, flounders, what my Thames affords:
To Hounslow Health I point and Bansted Down,
Thence comes your mutton, and these chicks my own:
From yon old walnut tree a shower shall fall;   145
And grapes, long lingering on my only wall,
And figs from standard and espalier join;
The devil is in you if you cannot dine:
Then cheerful healths (your Mistress shall have place),
And, what's more rare, a Poet shall say Grace.
    Fortune not much of humbling me can boast;   150
Though double taxed, how little have I lost?
My Life's amusements have been just the same,
Before, and after, Standing Armies came.
My lands are sold, my father's house is gone;

was once highly offended with Walpole for presuming to raise money at
a lower rate of interest than she had asked.
[21] Mr. Pope had South Sea stock, which he did not sell out. It was valued
at between twenty and thirty thousand pounds when it fell. [W.] The
celebrated South Sea Bubble broke in 1720.

I'll hire another's;   is not that my own,   155
And yours, my friends? through whose free-opening gate
None comes too early, none departs too late;
(For I, who hold sage Homer's rule the best,
Welcome the coming, speed the going guest.)
"Pray heaven it last!" (cries SWIFT!) "as you go on;   160
I wish to God this house had been your own:
Pity! to build, without a son or wife:
Why, you'll enjoy it only all your life."
Well, if the use be mine, can it concern one,
Whether the name belong to Pope or Vernon?[22]   165
What's *Property?* dear Swift! you see it alter
From you to me, from me to Peter Walter;
Or, in a mortgage, prove a Lawyer's share;
Or, in a jointure, vanish from the heir;
Or in pure equity (the case not clear)   170
The Chancery takes your rents for twenty year:
At best, it falls to some ungracious son,
Who cries, "My father's damned, and all's my own."
Shades, that to BACON could retreat afford,
Become the portion of a booby Lord;   175
And Hemsley, once proud Buckingham's delight,
Slides to a Scrivener or a city Knight.
Let lands and houses have what Lords they will,
Let Us be fixed, and our own masters still.

---

[22] In a letter to this Mr. Bethel, of March 20, 1743, he says, "My land-lady, Mrs. *Vernon,* being dead, this Garden and House are offered me in sale; and, I believe . . . will come at about a thousand pounds. If I thought any very particular friend would be pleased to live in it after my death . . . I would purchase it."   [W.]

THE FIRST EPISTLE
OF THE
FIRST BOOK OF
HORACE

Epistle I

To Lord Bolingbroke

St. John, whose love indulged my labours past,
Matures my present, and shall bound my last!
Why will you break the Sabbath of my days?
Now sick alike of Envy and of Praise,
Public too long, ah let me hide my Age!   5
See, Modest Cibber now has left the Stage:
Our Generals now, retired to their Estates,
Hang their old Trophies o'er the Garden gates,
In Life's cool Evening satiate of Applause,
Nor fond of bleeding, even in Brunswick's cause.[23]   10
　　A Voice there is, that whispers in my ear,
('Tis Reason's voice, which sometimes one can hear)
"Friend Pope! be prudent, let your Muse take breath,
And never gallop Pegasus to death;
Lest stiff, and stately, void of fire or force,   15
You limp, like Blackmore on a Lord Mayor's horse."[24]
　　Farewell then Verse, and Love, and every Toy,

[23] In the former Editions it was *Britain's cause*. But the terms are synonymous. [W.]

[24] The fame of this heavy Poet, however problematical elsewhere, was universally received in the City of London. His versification is here exactly described: stiff, and not strong; stately and yet dull, like the sober and slow-paced animal generally employed to mount the Lord Mayor: and therefore here humorously opposed to Pegasus. P.

The Rhymes and Rattles of the Man or Boy;
What right, what true, what fit we justly call,
Let this be all my care—for this is All: 20
To lay this harvest up, and hoard with haste
What every day will want, and most, the last.
      But ask not, to what Doctors I apply?
Sworn to no Master, of no Sect am I:
As drives the storm, at any door I knock: 25
And house with Montaigne now, or now with Locke.
Sometimes a Patriot, active in debate,
Mix with the World, and battle for the State,
Free as young Lyttleton,[25] her Cause pursue,
Still true to Virtue, and as warm as true: 30
Sometimes with Aristippus, or St. Paul,
Indulge my candor, and grow all to all;
Back to my native Moderation slide,
And win my way by yielding to the tide.
      Long, as to him who works for debt, the day,   35
Long as the Night to her whose Love's away,
Long as the Year's dull circle seems to run,
When the brisk Minor pants for twenty-one:
So slow th' unprofitable moments roll,
That lock up all the Functions of my soul;   40
That keep me from myself; and still delay
Life's instant business to a future day:
That task, which as we follow, or despise,
The eldest is a fool, the youngest wise;
Which done, the poorest can no wants endure;[26]   45
And which not done, the richest must be poor.
      Late as it is, I put myself to school,
And feel some comfort, not to be a fool.
Weak though I am of limb, and short of sight,
Far from a Lynx, and not a Giant quite;   50

[25] George, later first Baron Lyttleton, a leader of the Whig Opposition in Parliament, 1735–1756. He was a patron of letters and one of the younger politicians with whom Pope was at this period acquainted. Cf. *Epilogue to the Satires,* I, 47; II, 131.
[26] Can want nothing. Badly expressed. [W.]

I'll do what Mead and Cheselden advise,[27]
To keep these limbs, and to preserve these eyes.
Not to go back, is somewhat to advance,
And men must walk at least before they dance.
    Say, does thy blood rebel, thy bosom move   55
With wretched Avarice, or as wretched Love?
Know, there are Words, and Spells, which can control
Between the Fits this Fever of the soul:
Know, there are Rhymes, which fresh and fresh applied
Will cure the arrantest Puppy of his Pride.   60
Be furious, envious, slothful, mad, or drunk,
Slave to a Wife, or Vassal to a Punk,
A Swiss, a High Dutch, or a Low Dutch Bear;
All that we ask is but a patient Ear.
    'Tis the first Virtue, Vices to abhor;   65
And the first Wisdom, to be Fool no more.
But to the world no bugbear is so great,
As want of figure, and a small Estate.
To either India see the Merchant fly,
Scared at the spectre of pale Poverty!   70
See him, with pains of body, pangs of soul,
Burn through the Tropic, freeze beneath the Pole!
Wilt thou do nothing for a nobler end,
Nothing, to make Philosophy thy friend?
To stop thy foolish views, thy long desires,   75
And ease thy heart of all that it admires?
    Here, Wisdom calls: "Seek Virtue first, be bold!
As Gold to Silver, Virtue is to Gold."
There, London's voice: "Get Money, Money still!
And then let Virtue follow, if she will."   80
This, this the saving doctrine, preached to all,
From low St. James's up to high St. Paul;[28]
From him whose quills stand quivered at his ear,[29]

[27] Richard Mead, the eminent physician, and William Cheselden, the surgeon. The latter, a close friend of Pope's, attended him in his last illness.
[28] I.e., this is a doctrine in which both Whigs and Tories agree. [W.]
[29] Insinuating that the pen of a Scrivener is as ready as the quill of a porcupine, and as fatal as the shafts of a Parthian. [W.]

To him who notches sticks[30] at Westminster.
    Barnard in spirit, sense, and truth abounds;   85
"Pray then, what wants he?" Fourscore thousand pounds;
A pension, or such Harness for a slave
As Bug now has, and Dorimant would have.
Barnard, thou art a Cit,[31] with all thy worth;
But Bug and D*l, their *Honours,* and so forth.   90
    Yet every child another song will sing,
"Virtue, brave boys! 'tis Virtue makes a King."
True, conscious Honour is to feel no sin,
He's armed without that's innocent within;
Be this thy Screen, and this thy wall of Brass;   95
Compared to this, a Minister's an Ass.
    And say, to which shall our applause belong,
This new Court jargon, or the good old song?
The modern language of corrupted Peers,
Or what was spoke at CRESSY and POITIERS?   100
Who counsels best? who whispers, "Be but great,
With Praise or Infamy leave that to fate;
Get Place and Wealth, if possible, with grace;
If not, by any means get Wealth and Place."
For what? to have a Box where Eunuchs sing,   105
And foremost in the Circle eye a King.
Or he, who bids thee face with steady view
Proud Fortune, and look shallow Greatness through:
And, while he bids thee, sets th' Example too?
If such a doctrine, in St. James's air,   110
Should chance to make the well-dressed Rabble stare;
If honest S*z take scandal at a Spark,
That less admires the Palace than the Park:
Faith I shall give the answer Reynard gave:
"I cannot like, dread Sir, your Royal Cave: 115
Because I see, by all the tracks about,
Full many a Beast goes in, but none come out."
Adieu to Virtue, if you're once a Slave:
Send her to Court, you send her to her grave.

[30] Exchequer Tallies.   [W.]
[31] Sir John Barnard, M.P. for London, knighted in 1732, Lord Mayor in
1737, was one of the leaders of the Opposition. Cf. *Epilogue,* II, 99.

Well, if a King's a Lion, at the least   120
The People are a many-headed Beast:
Can they direct what measures to pursue,
Who know themselves so little what to do?
Alike in nothing but one Lust of Gold,
Just half the land would buy, and half be sold: 125
Their Country's wealth our mightier Misers drain,[32]
Or cross, to plunder Provinces, the Main;
The rest, some farm the Poor-box, some the Pews;
Some keep Assemblies, and would keep the Stews;
Some with fat Bucks on childless Dotards fawn;   130
Some win rich Widows by their Chine and Brawn;
While with the silent growth of ten per cent,
In dirt and darkness, hundreds stink content.
    Of all these ways, if each pursues his own,
Satire be kind, and let the wretch alone: 135
But show me one who has it in his power
To act consistent with himself an hour.
Sir Job sailed forth, the evening bright and still,
"No place on earth (he cried) like Greenwich hill!"
Up starts a Palace; lo, th' obedient base   140
Slopes at its foot, the woods its sides embrace,
The silver Thames reflects its marble face.
Now let some whimsy, or that devil within
Which guides all those who know not what they mean,
But give the Knight (or give his Lady) spleen;   145
"Away, away! take all your scaffolds down,
"For Snug's the word: My dear! we'll live in Town."
    At amorous Flavio is the stocking thrown?
That very night he longs to lie alone.
The Fool, whose Wife elopes some thrice a quarter,   150
For matrimonial solace dies a martyr.
Did ever Proteus, Merlin, any witch,
Transform themselves so strangely as the Rich?
Well, but the Poor—The Poor have the same itch;
They change their weekly Barber, weekly News,   155

---

[32] The undertakers for advancing loans to the Public on the Funds. They
have been commonly accused of making it a job. [W.]

Prefer a new Japanner to their shoes,
Discharge their Garrets, move their beds, and run
(They know not whither) in a Chaise and one;
They hire their sculler, and when once abroad,
Grow sick, and damn the climate—like a Lord.   160
   You laugh, half Beau, half Sloven if I stand,
My wig all powder, and all snuff my band;
You laugh, if coat and breeches strangely vary,
White gloves, and linen worthy Lady Mary!
But when no Prelate's Lawn with hair shirt lined,   165
Is half so incoherent as my Mind,
When (each opinion with the next at strife,
One ebb and flow of follies all my life)
I plant, root up; I build, and then confound;
Turn round to square, and square again to round;   170
You never change one muscle of your face,
You think this Madness but a common case,
Nor once to Chancery, nor to Hale apply;
Yet hang your lip, to see a Seam awry!
Careless how ill I with myself agree,   175
Kind to my dress, my figure, not to Me.
Is this my Guide, Philosopher, and Friend?
This, he who loves me, and who ought to mend?
Who ought to make me (what he can, or none,)
That Man divine whom Wisdom calls her own;   180
Great without Title, without Fortune blessed;
Rich even when plundered, honoured while oppressed;
Loved without youth, and followed without power;
At home, though exiled, free, though in the Tower;
In short, that reasoning, high, immortal Thing,   185
Just less than Jove, and much above a King,
Nay, half in heaven—except (what's mighty odd)
A Fit of Vapours clouds this Demigod.

THE SIXTH EPISTLE
OF THE
FIRST BOOK OF
HORACE

Epistle VI

To Mr. Murray[33]

"Not to admire, is all the Art I know,
To make men happy, and to keep them so."
(Plain truth, dear Murray, needs no flowers of speech,
So take it in the very words of Creech.)[34]
    This Vault of Air, this congregated Ball,   5
Self-centered Sun, and Stars that rise and fall,
There are, my Friend! whose philosophic eyes
Look through, and trust the Ruler with his skies,
To him commit the hour, the day, the year,
And view this dreadful All without a fear.   10
    Admire we then what Earth's low entrails hold,
Arabian shores, or Indian seas enfold;
All the mad trade of Fools and Slaves for Gold?
Or Popularity? or Stars and Strings?
The Mob's applauses, or the gifts of Kings?   15
Say with what eyes we ought at Court to gaze,
And pay the Great our homage of Amaze?

---

[33] William Murray, afterwards the famous Earl of Mansfield, Chief Justice of the King's Bench.
[34] From whose translation of Horace the two first lines are taken. P. Thomas Creech's translation of Horace, 1684, was the only complete English translation available in Pope's day. Creech wrote:

> Not to admire, as most are wont to do,
> It is the only method that I know,
> To make Men happy, and to keep 'em so.

If weak the pleasures that from these can spring,
The fear to want them is as weak a thing:
Whether we dread, or whether we desire,   20
In either case, believe me, we admire;
Whether we joy or grieve, the same the curse,
Surprised at better, or surprised at worse.
Thus good or bad, to one extreme betray
Th' unbalanced Mind, and snatch the Man away;   25
For Virtue's self may too much zeal be had;
The worst of Madmen is a Saint run mad.
    Go then, and if you can, admire the state
Of beaming diamonds, and reflected plate;
Procure a Taste to double the surprise,   30
And gaze on Parian Charms with learnèd eyes:
Be struck with bright Brocade, or Tyrian Dye,
Our Birthday Nobles' splendid Livery.
If not so pleased, at Council board rejoice,
To see their Judgments hang upon thy Voice;   35
From morn to night, at Senate, Rolls, and Hall,
Plead much, read more, dine late, or not at all.
But wherefore all this labour, all this strife?
For Fame, for Riches, for a noble Wife?
Shall One whom Nature, Learning, Birth, conspired   40
To form, not to admire but be admired,
Sigh, while his Chloe blind to Wit and Worth
Weds the rich Dulness of some Son of earth?
Yet Time ennobles, or degrades each Line;
It brightened Craggs's,[35] and may darken thine: 45
And what is Fame? the Meanest have their Day,
The Greatest can but blaze, and pass away.
Graced as thou art, with all the Power of Words,
So known, so honoured, at the House of Lords:
Conspicuous Scene! another yet is nigh,   50
(More silent far) where Kings and Poets lie;
Where Murray (long enough his Country's pride)
Shall be no more than Tully, or than Hyde!

[35] Cf. *Moral Essay* V, 63.

Racked with Sciatics, martyred with the Stone,
Will any mortal let himself alone?   55
See Ward[36] by battered Beaux invited over,
And desperate Misery lays hold on Dover.[37]
The case is easier in the Mind's disease;
There all Men may be cured, whene'er they please.
Would ye be blest? despise low Joys, low Gains;   60
Disdain whatever CORNBURY disdains;[38]
Be virtuous, and be happy for your pains.
　　But art thou one, whom new opinions sway,
One who believes as Tindal[39] leads the way,
Who Virtue and a Church alike disowns,   65
Thinks that but words, and this but brick and stones?
Fly then, on all the wings of wild desire,
Admire whate'er the maddest can admire.
Is Wealth thy passion? Hence! from Pole to Pole,
Where winds can carry, or where waves can roll,   70
For Indian spices, for Peruvian Gold,
Prevent the greedy, and outbid the bold:
Advance thy golden Mountain to the skies;
On the broad base of fifty thousand rise,
Add one round hundred, and (if that's not fair)   75
Add fifty more, and bring it to a square.
For, mark th' advantage; just so many score
Will gain a Wife with half as many more,
Procure her Beauty, make that beauty chaste,
And then such Friends—as cannot fail to last.   80
A Man of wealth is dubbed a Man of worth,

[36] Joshua Ward, a quack doctor whose drop and pill were at this time famous in France as well as in England. Cf. *Epistle to Augustus,* 1. 182.
[37] Thomas Dover, known as "the quicksilver doctor."
[38] "On Lord . . . [Cornbury's] return from his travels [in 1732] his brother-in-law, the Lord Essex, told him, with a great deal of pleasure, that he had got a pension for him. It was a very handsome one, and quite equal to his rank. . . . Lord . . . [Cornbury's] answer was: 'How could you tell, my lord, that I was to be sold? or at least, how could you know my price so exactly?' P." Spence's *Anecdotes,* ed. Singer (1820), p. 292.
[39] Matthew Tindal, Fellow of All Souls, author of *The Rights of the Christian Church Asserted against the Romish and All Other Priests,* 1706.

Venus shall give him Form, and Anstis Birth.[40]
(Believe me, many a German Prince is worse,
Who proud of Pedigree, is poor of Purse.)
His wealth brave Timon gloriously confounds;   85
Asked for a groat, he gives a hundred pounds;
Or if three Ladies like a luckless Play,
Takes the whole House upon the Poet's Day.
Now, in such exigencies not to need,
Upon my word, you must be rich indeed;   90
A noble superfluity it craves,
Not for yourself, but for your Fools and Knaves;
Something, which for your Honour they may cheat,
And which it much becomes you to forget.
If Wealth alone then make and keep us blest,   95
Still, still be getting, never, never rest.

      But if to Power and Place your passion lie,
If in the Pomp of Life consist the joy;
Then hire a Slave, or (if you will) a Lord
To do the Honours, and to give the Word;   100
Tell at your Levee, as the Crowds approach,
To whom to nod, whom take into your Coach,
Whom honour with your hand: to make remarks,
Who rules in Cornwall, or who rules in Berks:
"This may be troublesome, is near the Chair;   105
That makes three Members, this can choose a Mayor."
Instructed thus, you bow, embrace, protest,
Adopt him Son, or Cousin at the least,
Then turn about, and laugh at your own Jest.

      Or if your life be one continued Treat,   110
If to live well means nothing but to eat;
Up, up! cries Gluttony, 'tis break of day,
Go drive the Deer, and drag the finny prey;
With hounds and horns go hunt an Appetite—
So Russel[41] did, but could not eat at night,   115
Called happy Dog! the Beggar at his door,

---

[40] *Anstis*, King at Arms. [W.]
[41] Pope told the same story in more detail to Spence. See *Anecdotes*, ed.
Singer (1820), pp. 291–292.

And envied Thirst and Hunger to the Poor.
   Or shall we every Decency confound,
Through Taverns, Stews, and Bagnios take our round,
Go dine with Chartres, in each Vice outdo   120
K—l's lewd Cargo, or Ty—y's Crew,
From Latian Syrens, French Circean Feasts,
Return well travelled, and transformed to Beasts,
Or for a Titled Punk, or foreign Flame,
Renounce our Country, and degrade our Name?   125
   If, after all, we must with Wilmot own,
The Cordial Drop of Life is Love alone,
And SWIFT cry wisely, "Vive la Bagatelle!"
The Man that loves and laughs, must sure do well.
Adieu—if this advice appear the worst,   130
E'en take the Counsel which I gave you first:
Or better Precepts if you can impart,
Why do, I'll follow them with all my heart.

1737

THE FIRST EPISTLE
OF THE
SECOND BOOK OF
HORACE

ADVERTISEMENT

THE Reflections of *Horace,* and the Judgments passed in his
Epistle to *Augustus,* seemed so seasonable to the present Times,
that I could not help applying them to the use of my own
Country. The Author thought them considerable enough to
address them to his Prince; whom he paints with all the great

and good qualities of a Monarch upon whom the Romans depended for the Increase of an *Absolute Empire*. But to make the Poem entirely English, I was willing to add one or two of those which contribute to the Happiness of a *Free People,* and are more consistent with the Welfare of *our Neighbours*.

This Epistle will show the learned World to have fallen into Two mistakes: one, that *Augustus was a Patron of Poets in general;* whereas he not only prohibited all but the Best Writers to name him, but recommended that Care even to the Civil Magistrate: *Admonebat Prætores ne paterentur Nomen suum obsolefieri,* etc. The other, that this Piece was only a *general Discourse of Poetry;* whereas it was an *Apology for the Poets,* in order to render *Augustus* more their Patron. *Horace* here pleads the Cause of his Contemporaries, first against the Taste of the *Town,* whose humour it was to magnify the Authors of the preceding Age; secondly against the *Court* and *Nobility,* who encouraged only the Writers for the Theatre; and lastly against the *Emperor* himself, who had conceived them of little Use to the Government. He shows (by a View of the Progress of Learning, and the Change of Taste among the Romans) that the Introduction of the Polite Arts of *Greece* had given the Writers of his Time great advantages over their Predecessors; that their *Morals* were much improved, and the License of those ancient Poets restrained; that *Satire* and *Comedy* were become more just and useful; that whatever extravagances were left on the Stage, were owing to the *Ill Taste* of the *Nobility;* that Poets, under due Regulations, were in many respects useful to the *State,* and concludes, that it was upon them the *Emperor* himself must depend for his Fame with Posterity.

We may farther learn from this Epistle that *Horace* made his Court to this Great Prince by writing with a decent Freedom toward him, with a just Contempt of his low Flatterers, and with a manly Regard to his own Character.　　　　　　　　　P.

To Augustus

WHILE you, great Patron of Mankind! sustain
The balanced World, and open all the Main;
Your Country, chief, in Arms abroad defend,

At home, with Morals, Arts, and Laws amend;
How shall the Muse, from such a Monarch, steal   5
An hour, and not defraud the Public Weal?
    Edward and Henry, now the Boast of Fame,
And virtuous Alfred, a more sacred Name,
After a Life of generous Toils endured,
The Gaul subdued, or Property secured,   10
Ambition humbled, mighty Cities stormed,
Or Laws established, and the world reformed;
Closed their long Glories with a sigh, to find
Th' unwilling Gratitude of base mankind!
All human Virtue, to its latest breath,   15
Finds Envy never conquered, but by death.
The great Alcides, every Labour past,
Had still this Monster to subdue at last.
Sure fate of all, beneath whose rising ray
Each star of meaner merit fades away!   20
Oppressed we feel the beam directly beat,
Those Suns of Glory please not till they set.
    To thee, the World its present homage pays,
The Harvest early, but mature the praise:
Great Friend of LIBERTY! in *Kings* a Name   25
Above all Greek, above all Roman Fame:
Whose Word is Truth, as sacred and revered,
As Heaven's own Oracles from Altars heard.
Wonder of Kings! like whom, to mortal eyes
None e'er has risen, and none e'er shall rise.   30
    Just in one instance, be it yet confest
Your People, Sir, are partial in the rest:
Foes to all living worth except your own,
And Advocates for folly dead and gone.
Authors, like coins, grow dear as they grow old;   35
It is the rust we value, not the gold.
Chaucer's worst ribaldry is learned by rote,
And beastly Skelton Heads of houses quote:[42]

---

[42] Skelton, Poet Laureate to Henry VIII, a volume of whose verses has been lately reprinted, consisting almost wholly of ribaldry, obscenity, and scurrilous language. P.

One likes no language but the Faery Queen;
A Scot will fight for Christ's Kirk o' the Green;[43]   40
And each true Briton is to Ben so civil,
He swears the Muses met him at the Devil.[44]

  Though justly Greece her eldest sons admires,
Why should not We be wiser than our sires?
In every Public virtue we excel;   45
We build, we paint, we sing, we dance as well,
And learned Athens to our art must stoop,
Could she behold us tumbling through a hoop.

  If Time improve our Wit as well as Wine,
Say at what age a Poet grows divine?   50
Shall we, or shall we not, account him so,
Who died, perhaps, an hundred years ago?
End all dispute; and fix the year precise
When British bards begin t'immortalize?

  "Who lasts a century can have no flaw,   55
I hold that Wit a Classic, good in law."

  Suppose he wants a year, will you compound?
And shall we deem him Ancient, right and sound,
Or damn to all eternity at once,
At ninety-nine, a Modern and a Dunce?   60

  "We shall not quarrel for a year or two;
By courtesy of England, he may do."

  Then by the rule that made the Horsetail bare,
I pluck out year by year, as hair by hair,
And melt down Ancients like a heap of snow: 65
While you, to measure merits, look in Stowe,[45]
And estimating authors by the year,
Bestow a Garland only on a Bier.

  Shakespeare (whom you and every Playhouse bill
Style the divine, the matchless, what you will)   70
For gain, not glory, winged his roving flight,
And grew immortal in his own despite.
Ben, old and poor, as little seemed to heed

[43] A Ballad made by a King of Scotland. P.
[44] The Devil Tavern, where Ben Jonson held his Poetical Club. P.
[45] John Stowe's *Summarie of Englishe Chronicles* appeared in 1565.

324 Satires and Epistles of Horace Imitated

The Life to come, in every Poet's Creed.
Who now reads Cowley? if he pleases yet,   75
His Moral pleases, not his pointed wit;
Forgot his Epic, nay Pindaric Art,
But still I love the language of his heart.
       "Yet surely, surely, these were famous men!
What boy but hears the sayings of old Ben?   80
In all debates where Critics bear a part,
Not one but nods, and talks of Jonson's Art,
Of Shakespeare's Nature, and of Cowley's Wit;
How Beaumont's judgment checked what Fletcher writ;
How Shadwell hasty, Wycherley was slow;[46]   85
But, for the Passions, Southern sure and Rowe.
These, only these, support the crowded stage,
From eldest Heywood down to Cibber's age."
       All this may be; the People's Voice is odd,
It is, and it is not, the voice of God.   90
To *Gammer Gurton*[47] if it give the bays,
And yet deny the *Careless Husband* praise,[48]
Or say our Fathers never broke a rule;
Why then, I say, the Public is a fool.
But let them own, that greater Faults than we   95
They had, and greater virtues, I'll agree.
Spenser himself affects the Obsolete,
And Sidney's verse halts ill on Roman feet:
Milton's strong pinion now not Heaven can bound,
Now Serpent-like, in prose he sweeps the ground,   100
In Quibbles, Angel and Archangel join,
And God the Father turns a School-divine.
Not that I'd lop the Beauties from his book,
Like slashing Bentley[49] with his desperate hook,
Or damn all Shakespeare, like th' affected Fool   105

[46] *Hasty Shadwell and Slow Wycherley,* is a line of Wilmot, Earl of Rochester [*An Allusion to Horace,* 1. 43]. [W.]
[47] A piece of very low humour, one of the first printed Plays in English, and therefore much valued by some Antiquaries. P.
[48] *The Careless Husband,* 1704, was a comedy by Colley Cibber.
[49] Richard Bentley's edition of *Paradise Lost,* 1732, was marked by slashing emendations. Cf. *Epistle to Arbuthnot,* 1. 164.

At court, who hates whate'er he read at school.
    But for the Wits of either Charles's days,
The Mob of Gentlemen who wrote with Ease;
Sprat, Carew, Sedley, and a hundred more,
(Like twinkling stars the Miscellanies o'er)   110
One Simile, that solitary shines
In the dry desert of a thousand lines,
Or lengthened Thought that gleams through many a page,
Has sanctified whole poems for an age.
I lose my patience, and I own it too,   115
When works are censured, not as bad but new;
While if our Elders break all reason's laws,
These fools demand not pardon, but Applause.
    On Avon's bank, where flowers eternal blow,
If I but ask if any weed can grow?   120
One Tragic sentence if I dare deride,
Which Betterton's grave action dignified,
Or well-mouthed Booth with emphasis proclaims
(Though but, perhaps, a muster-roll of Names),
How will our Fathers rise up in a rage,   125
And swear, all shame is lost in George's Age!
You'd think no Fools disgraced the former reign,
Did not some grave Examples yet remain,
Who scorn a Lad should teach his father skill,
And, having once been wrong, will be so still.   130
He who to seem more deep than you or I,
Extols old Bards, or Merlin's Prophecy,
Mistake him not; he envies, not admires,
And to debase the Sons, exalts the Sires.
Had ancient times conspired to disallow   135
What then was new, what had been ancient now?
Or what remained, so worthy to be read
By learned Critics, of the mighty Dead?
    In Days of Ease, when now the weary Sword
Was sheathed, and *Luxury* with *Charles* restored;   140
In every taste of foreign Courts improved,
"All, by the King's Example, lived and loved."[50]

---

[50] A Verse of the Lord Lansdowne [in *The Progress of Beauty*]. P.

Then Peers grew proud in Horsemanship t'excel,
Newmarket's Glory rose, as Britain's fell;
The soldier breathed the Gallantries of France,   145
And every flowery Courtier writ Romance.[51]
Then Marble, softened into life, grew warm,
And yielding Metal flowed to human form:
Lely on animated Canvas stole
The sleepy Eye, that spoke the melting soul.   150
No wonder then, when all was Love and sport,
The willing Muses were debauched at Court:
On each enervate string they taught the note
To pant or tremble through an Eunuch's throat.[52]
     But Britain, changeful as a Child at play,   155
Now calls in Princes, and now turns away.
Now Whig, now Tory, what we loved we hate;
Now all for Pleasure, now for Church and State;
Now for Prerogative, and now for Laws;
Effects unhappy! from a Noble Cause.   160
     Time was, a sober Englishman would knock
His servants up, and rise by five o'clock,
Instruct his Family in every rule,
And send his Wife to church, his Son to school.
To worship like his Fathers was his care;   165
To teach their frugal Virtues to his Heir;
To prove that Luxury could never hold;
And place, on good Security, his Gold.
Now times are changed, and one Poetic Itch
Has seized the Court and City, poor and rich: 170
Sons, Sires, and Grandsires, all will wear the bays,
Our Wives read Milton, and our Daughters Plays,
To Theatres, and to Rehearsals throng,
And all our Grace at table is a Song.
I, who so oft renounce the Muses, lie,   175

---

[51] The Duke of Newcastle's book of Horsemanship: the Romance of
Parthenissa, by the Earl of Orrery, and most of the French Romances
translated by *Persons of Quality.* P.
[52] *The Siege of Rhodes,* by Sir William Davenant, the first Opera sung
in England. P.

Not ———'s self e'er tells more *Fibs* than I;
When sick of Muse, our follies we deplore,
And promise our best Friends to rhyme no more;
We wake next morning in a raging fit,
And call for pen and ink to show our Wit.   180
　　　He served a Prenticeship, who sets up shop;
Ward tried on Puppies, and the Poor, his Drop;[53]
Even Radcliffe's Doctors[54] travel first to France,
Nor dare to practise till they've learned to dance.
Who builds a Bridge that never drove a pile?   185
(Should Ripley venture, all the world would smile)[55]
But those who cannot write, and those who can,
All rhyme, and scrawl, and scribble, to a man.
Yet, Sir, reflect, the mischief is not great;
These Madmen never hurt the Church or State: 190
Sometimes the Folly benefits mankind;
And rarely Avarice taints the tuneful mind.
Allow him but his plaything of a Pen,
He ne'er rebels, or plots, like other men:
Flight of Cashiers, or Mobs, he'll never mind;   195
And knows no losses while the Muse is kind.
To cheat a Friend, or Ward, he leaves to Peter;
The good man heaps up nothing but mere metre,
Enjoys his Garden and his book in quiet;
And then—a perfect Hermit in his diet.   200
　　　Of little use the Man you may suppose,
Who says in verse what others say in prose;
Yet let me show, a Poet's of some weight,
And (though no soldier) useful to the State.

[53] A famous Empiric, whose Pill and Drop had several surprising effects, and were one of the principal subjects of writing and conversation at this time. P.
[54] John Radcliffe was a popular physician who was frequently called to attend royalty and who had prescribed successfully to Pope when the latter was about seventeen (Spence, ed. Singer, 1820, p. 7). Radcliffe died in 1714, leaving a large fortune for the advancement of medicine and science at Oxford. Two medical fellowships were for ten years each, half of which had to be spent abroad.
[55] See *Moral Essay* IV, 18.

What will a Child learn sooner than a song?   205
What better teach a Foreigner the tongue?
What's long or short, each accent where to place,
And speak in public with some sort of grace.
I scarce can think him such a worthless thing,
Unless he praise some Monster of a King;   210
Or Virtue, or Religion turn to sport,
To please a lewd, or unbelieving Court.
Unhappy Dryden!—In all Charles's days,
Roscommon only boasts unspotted bays;
And in our own (excuse some Courtly stains)   215
No whiter page than Addison remains.
He, from the taste obscene reclaims our youth,
And sets the Passions on the side of Truth,
Forms the soft bosom with the gentlest art,
And pours each human Virtue in the heart.   220
Let Ireland tell, how Wit upheld her cause,
Her Trade supported, and supplied her Laws;
And leave on SWIFT this grateful verse engraved,
"The Rights a Court attacked, a Poet saved."
Behold the hand that wrought a Nation's cure,   225
Stretched to relieve the Idiot and the Poor,
Proud Vice to brand, or injured Worth adorn,
And stretch the Ray to Ages yet unborn.
Not but there are, who merit other palms;
Hopkins and Sternhold glad the heart with Psalms: 230
The Boys and Girls whom charity maintains,
Implore your help in these pathetic strains:
How could Devotion touch the country pews,
Unless the Gods bestowed a proper Muse?
Verse cheers their leisure, Verse assists their work,   235
Verse prays for Peace, or sings down Pope and Turk.[56]

[56] The metrical version of the Psalms by Sternhold and Hopkins (1549–
1562), still commonly used in Pope's day, is followed by a prayer which
begins:

> Preserve us, Lord, by Thy dear word,
> From Turk and Pope defend us, Lord.

The silenced Preacher yields to potent strain,
And feels that grace his prayer besought in vain;
The blessing thrills through all the laboring throng,
And Heaven is won by Violence of Song.   240
    Our rural Ancestors, with little blest,
Patient of labour when the end was rest,
Indulged the day that housed their annual grain,
With feasts, and offerings, and a thankful strain:
The joy their wives, their sons, and servants share, 245
Ease of their toil, and partners of their care:
The laugh, the jest, attendants on the bowl,
Smoothed every brow, and opened every soul:
With growing years the pleasing Licence grew,
And Taunts alternate innocently flew.   250
But Times corrupt, and Nature, ill-inclined,
Produced the point that left a sting behind;
Till friend with friend, and families at strife,
Triumphant Malice raged through private life.
Who felt the wrong, or feared it, took th' alarm,   255
Appealed to Law, and Justice lent her arm.
At length, by wholesome dread of statutes bound,
The Poets learned to please, and not to wound:
Most warped to Flattery's side; but some, more nice,
Preserved the freedom, and forbore the vice.   260
Hence Satire rose, that just the medium hit,
And heals with Morals what it hurts with Wit.
    We conquered France, but felt our Captive's charms;
Her Arts victorious triumphed o'er our Arms;
Britain to soft refinement less a foe,   265
Wit grew polite, and Numbers learned to flow.
Waller was smooth;[57] but Dryden taught to join
The varying verse, the full-resounding line,
The long majestic March, and Energy divine.
Though still some traces of our rustic vein   270

---

[57] Mr. Waller, about this time with the Earl of Dorset, Mr. Godolphin, and others, translated the *Pompey* of Corneille; and the more correct French Poets began to be in reputation. P.

And splayfoot verse remained, and will remain.
Late, very late, correctness grew our care,[58]
When the tired Nation breathed from civil war.
Exact Racine, and Corneille's noble fire,
Showed us that France had something to admire.   275
Not but the Tragic spirit was our own,
And full in Shakespeare, fair in Otway shone:
But Otway failed to polish or refine,
And fluent Shakespeare scarce effaced a line.
Even copious Dryden wanted, or forgot,   280
The last and greatest Art, the Art to blot.
Some doubt, if equal pains, or equal fire
The humbler Muse of Comedy require.
But in known Images of life, I guess
The labour greater, as th' indulgence less.   285
Observe how seldom even the best succeed:
Tell me if Congreve's Fools are Fools indeed?
What pert, low Dialogue has Farquhar writ!
How Van[59] wants grace, who never wanted wit!
The stage how loosely does Astræa[60] tread,   290
Who fairly puts all Characters to bed!
And idle Cibber, how he breaks the laws,
To make poor Pinky[61] eat with vast applause!
But fill their purse, our Poet's work is done,
Alike to them, by Pathos or by Pun.   295
    O you! whom Vanity's light bark conveys
On Fame's mad voyage by the wind of praise,
With what a shifting gale your course you ply,
For ever sunk too low, or borne too high!
Who pants for glory finds but short repose,   300

[58] Pope told his friend Spence: "About fifteen, I got acquainted with Mr. [William] Walsh. He used to encourage me much, and used to tell me, that there was one way left of excelling: for though we had several great poets, we never had any one great poet that was correct; and he desired me to make that my study and aim." Spence's *Anecdotes* (1820), p. 280.
[59] Sir John Vanbrugh.
[60] A Name taken by Mrs. Behn, Authoress of several obscene Plays. P.
[61] William Penkethman, a comic actor, whose buffooneries are ridiculed in *Tatler* 188. "Penkethman devours a cold chick with great applause."

A breath revives him, or a breath o'erthrows.
Farewell the stage! if just as thrives the play,
The silly bard grows fat, or falls away.
     There still remains, to mortify a Wit,
The many-headed Monster of the Pit: 305
A senseless, worthless, and unhonoured crowd;
Who, to disturb their betters mighty proud,
Clattering their sticks before ten lines are spoke,
Call for the Farce, the Bear, or the Black Joke.[62]
What dear delight to Britons Farce affords!   310
Ever the taste of Mobs, but now of Lords;
(Taste, that eternal wanderer, which flies
From heads to ears, and now from ears to eyes.)[63]
The Play stands still; damn action and discourse,
Back fly the scenes, and enter foot and horse;   315
Pageants on pageants, in long order drawn,
Peers, Heralds, Bishops, Ermine, Gold, and Lawn;
The Champion too! and, to complete the jest,
Old Edward's Armour beams on Cibber's breast.[64]
With laughter sure Democritus had died,   320
Had he beheld an Audience gape so wide.
Let Bear or Elephant be e'er so white,
The people, sure, the people are the sight!
Ah luckless Poet! stretch thy lungs and roar,
That Bear or Elephant shall heed thee more;   325
While all its throats the Gallery extends,
And all the Thunder of the Pit ascends!
Loud as the Wolves, on Orcas' stormy steep,[65]
Howl to the roarings of the Northern deep.
Such is the shout, the long-applauding note,   330

---

[62] "The Coal-black Joke" was an indecent song.

[63] From Plays to Operas, and from Operas to Pantomines.   [W.]

[64] The Coronation of Henry VIII and Queen Anne Boleyn, in which the Playhouses vied with each other to represent all the pomp of a Coronation. In this noble contention, the Armour of one of the Kings of England was borrowed from the Tower to dress the Champion.   P.

[65] The farthest Northern Promontory of Scotland, opposite to the Orcades.   P.

At Quin's high plume, or Oldfield's[66] petticoat;
Or when from Court a birthday suit bestowed,
Sinks the lost Actor in the tawdry load.
Booth enters—hark! the Universal peal!
"But has he spoken?" Not a syllable.   335
What shook the stage, and made the people stare?
Cato's long wig, flowered gown, and lacquered chair.

     Yet lest you think I rally more than teach,
Or praise malignly Arts I cannot reach,
Let me for once presume t'instruct the times,   340
To know the Poet from the Man of rhymes:
'Tis he, who gives my breast a thousand pains,
Can make me feel each Passion that he feigns;
Enrage, compose, with more than magic Art,
With Pity, and with Terror, tear my heart;   345
And snatch me, o'er the earth, or through the air,
To Thebes, to Athens, when he will, and where.

     But not this part of the Poetic state
Alone, deserves the favour of the Great:
Think of those Authors, Sir, who would rely   350
More on a Reader's sense, than Gazer's eye.
Or who shall wander where the Muses sing?
Who climb their mountain, or who taste their spring?
How shall we fill a Library with Wit,[67]
When Merlin's Cave is half unfurnished yet?[68]   355
My Liege! why Writers little claim your thought,
I guess; and, with their leave, will tell the fault:
We Poets are (upon a Poet's word)
Of all mankind, the creatures most absurd:
The season, when to come, and when to go,   360
To sing, or cease to sing, we never know;
And if we will recite nine hours in ten,
You lose your patience, just like other men.
When too we hurt ourselves, when to defend

[66] Cf. *Moral Essay* I, 247.
[67] *Munus Apolline dignum.* The Palatine Library then building by Augustus. P.
[68] A Building in the Royal Gardens of Richmond, where is a small, but choice Collection of Books. P.

A single verse, we quarrel with a friend;   365
Repeat unasked; lament, the Wit's too fine
For vulgar eyes, and point out every line.
But most, when straining with too weak a wing,
We needs will write Epistles to the King;
And from the moment we oblige the town,   370
Expect a place, or pension from the Crown;
Or dubbed Historians by express command,
T'enroll your triumphs o'er the seas and land,
Be called to Court to plan some work divine,
As once for Louis, Boileau and Racine.   375
　　　Yet think, great Sir! (so many Virtues shown)
Ah think, what Poet best may make them known?
Or choose at least some Minister of Grace,
Fit to bestow the Laureate's weighty place.
　　　Charles, to late times to be transmitted fair,   380
Assigned his figure to Bernini's care;
And great Nassau to Kneller's hand decreed
To fix him graceful on the bounding Steed;
So well in paint and stone they judged of merit:
But Kings in Wit may want discerning Spirit.   385
The Hero William, and the Martyr Charles,
One knighted Blackmore, and one pensioned Quarles;
Which made old Ben, and surly Dennis swear,
"No Lord's anointed, but a Russian bear."
　　　Not with such majesty, such bold relief,   390
The Forms august, of King, or conquering Chief,
E'er swelled on marble; as in verse have shined
(In polished verse) the Manners and the Mind.
Oh! could I mount on the Mæonian wing,
Your Arms, your Actions, your Repose to sing!   395
What seas you traversed, and what fields you fought!
Your Country's Peace, how oft, how dearly bought!
How barbarous rage subsided at your word,
And Nations wondered while they dropped the sword!
How, when you nodded, o'er the land and deep,   400
Peace stole her wing, and wrapped the world in sleep;
Till earth's extremes your mediation own,
And Asia's Tyrants tremble at your Throne—

But Verse, alas! your Majesty disdains;
And I'm not used to Panegyric strains: 405
The Zeal of Fools offends at any time,
But most of all, the Zeal of Fools in rhyme.
Besides, a fate attends on all I write,
That when I aim at praise, they say I bite.
A vile Encomium doubly ridicules: 410
There's nothing blackens like the ink of fools.
If true, a woeful likeness; and if lies,
"Praise undeserved is scandal in disguise:"
Well may he blush, who gives it, or receives;
And when I flatter, let my dirty leaves   415
(Like Journals, Odes, and such forgotten things
As Eusden, Philips, Settle, writ of Kings)
Clothe spice, line trunks, or fluttering in a row,
Befringe the rails of Bedlam and Soho.[69]

1737

THE SECOND EPISTLE
OF THE
SECOND BOOK OF
HORACE

[*To Colonel Anthony Brown*]

Ludentis speciem dabit, et torquebitur.
                           Horace [*Epistle* II. ii. 124.]

DEAR Colonel, COBHAM's and your country's Friend!
You love a Verse, take such as I can send.

[69] Bethlehem Hospital, or Bedlam, and Wardour Street, originally called
"Old Soho," were centers of the old-book trade. Cf. *Essay on Criticism*,
1. 445, "Duck Lane."

A Frenchman comes, presents you with his Boy,
Bows and begins—"This Lad, Sir, is of Blois:[70]
Observe his shape how clean! his locks how curled! 5
My only son, I'd have him see the world:
His French is pure; his Voice too—you shall hear.
Sir, he's your slave, for twenty pound a year.
Mere wax as yet, you fashion him with ease,
Your Barber, Cook, Upholsterer, what you please: 10
A perfect genius at an Opera song—
To say too much, might do my honour wrong.
Take him with all his virtues, on my word;
His whole ambition was to serve a Lord;
But, Sir, to you, with what would I not part? 15
Though fair, I fear, 'twill break his Mother's heart.
Once (and but once) I caught him in a lie,
And then, unwhipped, he had the grace to cry:
The fault he has I fairly shall reveal,
(Could you o'erlook but that) it is to steal." 20
    If, after this, you took the graceless lad,
Could you complain, my Friend, he proved so bad?
Faith, in such case, if you should prosecute,
I think Sir Godfrey[71] should decide the suit;
Who sent the Thief that stole the Cash away, 25
And punished him that put it in his way.
    Consider then, and judge me in this light;
I told you when I went, I could not write;
You said the same, and are you discontent
With Laws, to which you gave your own assent? 30
Nay worse, to ask for Verse at such a time!
D'ye think me good for nothing but to rhyme?
    In ANNA's Wars, a Soldier poor and old
Had dearly earned a little purse of gold:
Tired with a tedious march, one luckless night, 35
He slept, poor dog! and lost it, to a doit.
This put the man in such a desperate mind,

[70] A Town in Beauce, where the French tongue is spoken in great purity. [W.]
[71] An eminent Justice of Peace, who decided much in the manner of Sancho Panza. P. Sir Godfrey Kneller. [W.]

Between revenge, and grief, and hunger joined
Against the foe, himself, and all mankind,
He leaped the trenches, scaled a Castle wall,   40
Tore down a Standard, took the Fort and all.
"Prodigious well;" his great Commander cried,
Gave him much praise, and some reward beside.
Next pleased his Excellence a town to batter;
(Its name I know not, and it's no great matter)   45
"Go on, my friend" (he cried) "see yonder walls!
Advance and conquer! go where glory calls!
More honours, more rewards, attend the brave."
Don't you remember what reply he gave?
"D'ye think me, noble General, such a Sot?   50
Let him take Castles who has ne'er a groat."
        Bred up at home, full early I begun
To read in Greek the wrath of Peleus' son.
Besides, my Father taught me from a lad,
The better art to know the good from bad: 55
(And little sure imported to remove,
To hunt for Truth in Maudlin's learned grove.)
But knottier points we knew not half so well,
Deprived us soon of our paternal Cell;
And certain Laws, by sufferers thought unjust,   60
Denied all posts of profit or of trust:
Hopes after hopes of pious Papists failed,
While mighty WILLIAM's thundering arm prevailed.
For Right Hereditary taxed and fined,
He stuck to poverty with peace of mind;   65
And me, the Muses helped to undergo it;
Convict a Papist he, and I a Poet.
But (thanks to Homer) since I live and thrive,
Indebted to no Prince or Peer alive,
Sure I should want the care to ten Monroes,[72]   70
If I would scribble, rather than repose.
Years following years, steal something every day,
At last they steal us from ourselves away;

---

[72] Dr. Monroe, Physician to Bedlam Hospital. P.

In one our Frolics, one Amusements end,
In one a Mistress drops, in one a Friend: 75
This subtle Thief of life, this paltry Time,
What will it leave me, if it snatch my rhyme?
If every wheel of that unwearied Mill
That turned ten thousand verses, now stands still?
     But after all, what would you have me do?   80
When out of twenty I can please not two;
When this Heroics only deigns to praise,
Sharp Satire that, and that Pindaric lays?
One likes the Pheasant's wing, and one the leg;
The vulgar boil, the learnèd roast an egg;   85
Hark task! to hit the palate of such guests,
When Oldfield loves what Dartineuf detests.[73]
     But grant I may relapse, for want of grace,
Again to rhyme; can London be the place?
Who there his Muse, or self, or soul attends,   90
In crowds, and courts, law, business, feasts, and friends?
My counsel sends to execute a deed;
A Poet begs me, I will hear him read:
'In Palace Yard at nine you'll find me there—'
'At ten for certain, Sir, in Bloomsbury Square—'   95
'Before the Lords at twelve my Cause comes on—'
'There's a Rehearsal, Sir, exact at one.—'
"Oh but a Wit can study in the streets,
And raise his mind above the mob he meets."
Not quite so well however as one ought;   100
A hackney coach may chance to spoil a thought;
And then a nodding beam, or pig of lead,
God knows, may hurt the very ablest head.
Have you not seen, at Guildhall's narrow pass,
Two Aldermen dispute it with an Ass?   105
And Peers give way, exalted as they are,
Even to their own S-r-v—nce in a Car?
     Go, lofty Poet! and in such a crowd,
Sing thy sonorous verse—but not aloud.

---

[73] Two celebrated Gluttons. [W.]

Alas! to Grottos and to Groves we run,   110
To ease and silence, every Muse's son:
Blackmore himself, for any grand effort,
Would drink and doze at Tooting or Earl's Court.[74]
How shall I rhyme in this eternal roar?
How match the bards whom none e'er matched before?
The Man, who, stretched in Isis' calm retreat,   116
To books and study gives seven years complete,
See! strewed with learnèd dust, his nightcap on,
He walks, an object new beneath the sun!
The boys flock round him, and the people stare: 120
So stiff, so mute! some statue you would swear,
Stepped from its pedestal to take the air!
And here, while town, and court, and city roars,
With mobs, and duns, and soldiers, at their doors;
Shall I, in London, act this idle part?   125
Composing songs, for Fools to get by heart?
        The Temple late two brother Sergeants saw,
Who deemed each other Oracles of Law;
With equal talents, these congenial souls,
One lulled th' Exchequer, and one stunned the Rolls;   130
Each had a gravity would make you split,
And shook his head at Murray, as a Wit.
" 'Twas, Sir, your law"—and "Sir, your eloquence—"
"Yours, Cowper's manner"—and "yours, Talbot's sense."
Thus we dispose of all poetic merit,   135
Yours Milton's genius, and mine Homer's spirit.
Call Tibbald Shakespeare, and he'll swear the Nine,
Dear Cibber! never matched one Ode of thine.
Lord! how we strut through Merlin's Cave,[75] to see
No Poets there, but Stephen, you, and me.[76]   140

---

[74] Two villages within a few miles of London. P.
[75] Cf. *Epistle to Augustus*, l. 355.
[76] Mr. *Stephen Duck,* a modest and worthy man, who had the honour (which many, who thought themselves his betters in poetry, had not) of being esteemed by Mr. Pope. [W.] Stephen Duck was a poet who began life as a farm laborer, a notable instance of Nature's Simple Plan. Pope had no great opinion of his work. He won the favor of Queen

Walk with respect behind, while we at ease
Weave laurel Crowns, and take what names we please.
"My dear Tibullus!" if that will not do,
"Let me be Horace, and be Ovid you:
Or, I'm content, allow me Dryden's strains,   145
And you shall rise up Otway for your pains."
Much do I suffer, much, to keep in peace
This jealous, waspish, wronghead, rhyming race;
And much must flatter, if the whim should bite
To court applause by printing what I write: 150
But let the Fit pass o'er, I'm wise enough,
To stop my ears to their confounded stuff.

    In vain bad Rhymers all mankind reject,
They treat themselves with most profound respect;
'Tis to small purpose that you hold your tongue: 155
Each praised within, is happy all day long.
But how severely with themselves proceed
The men, who write such Verse as we can read?
Their own strict Judges, not a word they spare
That wants or force, or light, or weight, or care,   160
Howe'er unwillingly it quits its place,
Nay though at Court (perhaps) it may find grace:
Such they'll degrade; and sometimes, in its stead,
In downright charity revive the dead;
Mark where a bold expressive phrase appears,   165
Bright through the rubbish of some hundred years;
Command old words that long have slept, to wake,
Words, that wise Bacon, or brave Raleigh spake;
Or bid the new be English, ages hence,
(For Use will farther what's begot by Sense)   170
Pour the full tide of eloquence along,
Serenely pure, and yet divinely strong,
Rich with the treasures of each foreign tongue;
Prune the luxuriant, the uncouth refine,
But show no mercy to an empty line: 175

Caroline and was appointed by her Librarian and keeper of Merlin's Cave
in 1735. Cf. *Epistle to Augustus,* l. 355.

Then polish all, with so much life and ease,
You think 'tis Nature, and a knack to please:
"But ease in writing flows from Art, not chance;
As those move easiest who have learned to dance."[77]
    If such the plague and pains to write by rule,   180
Better (say I) be pleased, and play the fool;
Call, if you will, bad rhyming a disease,
It gives men happiness, or leaves them ease.
There lived *in Primo Georgii* (they record)
A worthy member, no small fool, a Lord;   185
Who, though the House was up, delighted sate,
Heard, noted, answered, as in full debate:
In all but this, a man of sober life,
Fond of his Friend, and civil to his Wife;
Not quite a madman, though a pasty fell,   190
And much too wise to walk into a well.
Him, the damned Doctors and his Friends immured,
They bled, they cupped, they purged; in short, they cured:
Whereat the gentleman began to stare—
"My Friends?" he cried, "pox take your for your care!   195
That from a Patriot of distinguished note,
Have bled and purged me to a simple Vote."
    Well, on the whole, plain Prose must be my fate:
Wisdom (curse on it) will come soon or late.
There is a time when Poets will grow dull: 200
I'll e'en leave verses to the boys at school:
To rules of Poetry no more confined,
I learn to smooth and harmonize my Mind,
Teach every thought within its bounds to roll,
And keep the equal measure of the Soul.   205
    Soon as I enter at my country door,
My mind resumes the thread it dropped before;
Thoughts, which at Hyde Park Corner I forgot,
Meet and rejoin me, in the pensive Grot.
There all alone, and compliments apart,   210
I ask these sober questions of my heart.

[77] Cf. *Essay on Criticism*, ll. 362–363.

If, when the more you drink, the more you crave,
You tell the Doctor; when the more you have,
The more you want; why not with equal ease
Confess as well your Folly, as Disease?   215
The heart resolves this matter in a trice,
"Men only feel the Smart, but not the Vice."
    When golden Angels cease to cure the Evil,
You give all royal Witchcraft to the Devil:
When servile Chaplains cry, that birth and place   220
Endue a Peer with honour, truth, and grace,
Look in that breast, most dirty D—! be fair,
Say, can you find out one such lodger there?
Yet still, not heeding what your heart can teach,
You go to church to hear these Flatterers preach.   225
    Indeed, could wealth bestow or wit or merit,
A grain of courage, or a spark of spirit,
The wisest man might blush, I must agree,
If D* * * loved sixpence, more than he.
    If there be truth in Law, and Use can give   230
A Property, that's yours on which you live.
Delightful Abscourt,[78] if its fields afford
Their fruits to you, confesses you its lord:
All Worldly's hens, nay partridge, sold to town,
His Venison too, a guinea makes your own: 235
He bought at thousands, what with better wit
You purchase as you want, and bit by bit;
Now, or long since, what difference will be found?
You pay a penny, and he paid a pound.
    Heathcote himself, and such large-acred men,   240
Lords of fat Esham, or of Lincoln fen,
Buy every stick of wood that lends them heat,
Buy every Pullet they afford to eat.
Yet these are Wights, who fondly call their own
Half that the Devil o'erlooks from Lincoln town.   245
The Laws of God, as well as of the land,
Abhor, a Perpetuity should stand:

[78] A farm over against Hampton Court.   [W.]

Estates have wings, and hang in Fortune's power
Loose on the point of every wavering hour,
Ready, by force, or of your own accord,   250
By sale, at least by death, to change their lord.
Man? and *for ever?* wretch! what wouldst thou have?
Heir urges heir, like wave impelling wave.
All vast possessions (just the same the case
Whether you call them Villa, Park, or Chase)   255
Alas, my BATHURST! what will they avail?
Join Cotswold hills to Saperton's fair dale,
Let rising Granaries and Temples here,
There mingled farms and pyramids appear,
Link towns to towns with avenues of oak,   260
Enclose whole downs in walls, 'tis all a joke!
Inexorable Death shall level all,
And trees, and stones, and farms, and farmer fall.

    Gold, Silver, Ivory, Vases sculptured high,
Paint, Marble, Gems, and robes of Persian dye,   265
There are who have not—and thank heaven there are,
Who, if they have not, think not worth their care.

    Talk what you will of Taste, my friend, you'll find,
Two of a face, as soon as of a mind.
Why, of two brothers, rich and restless one   270
Ploughs, burns, manures, and toils from sun to sun;
The other slights, for women, sports, and wines,
All Townshend's Turnips,[79] and all Grosvenor's mines:
Why one like Bu— with pay and scorn content,
Bows and votes on, in Court and Parliament;   275
One, driven by strong Benevolence of soul,
Shall fly, like Oglethorpe,[80] from pole to pole:
Is known alone to that Directing Power,
Who forms the Genius in the natal hour;
That God of Nature, who, within us still,   280

[79] Lord Townshend, Secretary of State to George the First and Second. —When this great Statesman retired from business, he amused himself in Husbandry; and was particularly fond of that kind of rural improvement which arises from Turnips. [W.]
[80] Employed in settling the Colony of Georgia. [W.]

Inclines our action, not constrains our will;
Various of temper, as of face or frame,
Each individual: His great End the same.
      Yes, Sir, how small soever be my heap,
A part I will enjoy, as well as keep.   285
My heir may sigh, and think it want of grace
A man so poor would live without a place:
But sure no statute in his favour says,[81]
How free, or frugal, I shall pass my days:
I, who at some times spend, at others spare,   290
Divided between carelessness and care.
'Tis one thing madly to disperse my store;
Another, not to heed to treasure more;
Glad, like a Boy, to snatch the first good day,
And pleased, if sordid want be far away.   295
      What is't to me (a passenger, God wot!)
Whether my vessel be first-rate or not?
The Ship itself may make a better figure,
But I that sail, am neither less nor bigger.
I neither strut with every favoring breath,   300
Nor strive with all the tempest in my teeth.
In power, wit, figure, virtue, fortune, placed
Behind the foremost, and before the last.
      "But why all this of Avarice? I have none."
I wish you joy, Sir, of a Tyrant gone;   305
But does no other lord it at this hour,
As wild and mad? the Avarice of power?
Does neither Rage inflame, nor Fear appal?
Not the black fear of death, that saddens all?
With terrors round, can Reason hold her throne,   310
Despise the known, nor tremble at th' unknown?
Survey both worlds, intrepid and entire,
In spite of witches, devils, dreams, and fire?
Pleased to look forward, pleased to look behind,
And count each birthday with a grateful mind?   315

---

[81] Alluding to the statutes made in England and Ireland, to regulate the Succession of Papists.   [W.]

Has life no sourness, drawn so near its end?
Canst thou endure a foe, forgive a friend?
Has age but melted the rough parts away,
As winter fruits grow mild ere they decay?
Or will you think, my friend, your business done,   320
When, of a hundred thorns, you pull out one?
    Learn to live well, or fairly make your will;
You've played, and loved, and eat, and drank your fill:
Walk sober off; before a sprightlier age
Comes tittering on, and shoves you from the stage: 325
Leave such to trifle with more grace and ease,
Whom Folly pleases, and whose Follies please.

THE SATIRES
OF DR. JOHN DONNE,
Dean of St. Paul's,

VERSIFIED

Quid vetat et nosmet *Lucili* scripta legentes
Quærere, num illius, num rerum dura negarit
Versiculos natura magis factos, et euntes
Mollius?

Horace [Satire I. x. 56–59.]

SATIRE II

YES; thank my stars! as early as I knew
This Town, I had the sense to hate it too:
Yet here, as even in Hell, there must be still
One Giant Vice, so excellently ill,
That all beside, one pities, not abhors;   5
As who knows Sappho, smiles at other whores.
    I grant that Poetry's a crying sin;
It brought (no doubt) th' *Excise* and *Army* in:
Catched like the Plague, or Love, the Lord knows how,
But that the cure is starving, all allow.   10
Yet like the Papist's, is the Poet's state,

Poor and disarmed, and hardly worth your hate!
      Here a lean Bard, whose wit could never give
Himself a dinner, makes an Actor live:
The Thief condemned, in law already dead,   15
So prompts, and saves a rogue who cannot read.
Thus, as the pipes of some carved Organ move,
The gilded puppets dance and mount above.
Heaved by the breath th' inspiring bellows blow:
Th' inspiring bellows lie and pant below.   20
      One sings the Fair; but songs no longer move;
No rat is rhymed to death, nor maid to love:
In love's, in nature's spite, the siege they hold,
And scorn the flesh, the devil, and all but gold.
      These write to Lords, some mean reward to get,   25
As needy beggars sing at doors for meat.
Those write because all write, and so have still
Excuse for writing, and for writing ill.
      Wretched indeed! but far more wretched yet
Is he who makes his meal on others' wit: 30
'Tis changed, no doubt, from what it was before;
His rank digestion makes it wit no more:
Sense, passed through him, no longer is the same;
For food digested takes another name.
      I pass o'er all those Confessors and Martyrs,   35
Who live like S—tt—n, or who die like Chartres,
Outcant old Esdras, or outdrink his heir,
Outusure Jews, or Irishmen outswear;
Wicked as Pages, who in early years
Act sins which Prisca's Confessor scarce hears.   40
Even those I pardon, for whose sinful sake
Schoolmen new tenements in hell must make;
Of whose strange crimes no Canonist can tell
In what Commandment's large contents they dwell.
      One, one man only breeds my just offence;   45
Whom crimes gave wealth, and wealth gave Impudence:
Time, that at last matures a clap to pox,
Whose gentle progress makes a calf an ox,
And brings all natural events to pass,

Hath made him an Attorney of an Ass.   50
No young divine, new-beneficed, can be
More pert, more proud, more positive than he.
What further could I wish the fop to do,
But turn a wit, and scribble verses too;
Pierce the soft labyrinth of a Lady's ear   55
With rhymes of this *per cent*. and that *per year*?
Or court a Wife, spread out his wily parts,
Like nets or lime twigs, for rich Widows' hearts;
Call himself Barrister to every wench,
And woo in language of the Pleas and Bench?   60
Language, which Boreas might to Auster hold
More rough than forty Germans when they scold.
     Cursed be the wretch, so venal and so vain:
Paltry and proud, as drabs in Drury Lane.
'Tis such a bounty as was never known,   65
If PETER deigns to help you to your *own:*
What thanks, what praise, if *Peter* but supplies,
And what a solemn face if he denies!
Grave, as when prisoners shake the head and swear
'Twas only Suretyship that brought 'em there.   70
His *Office* keeps your Parchment fates entire,
He starves with cold to save them from the fire;
For you he walks the streets through rain or dust,
For not in Chariots *Peter* puts his trust;
For you he sweats and labours at the laws,   75
Takes God to witness he affects your cause,
And lies to every Lord in everything,
Like a King's Favourite—or like a King.
These are the talents that adorn them all,
From wicked Waters even to godly * *   80
Not more of Simony beneath black gowns,
Not more of bastardy in heirs to Crowns.
In shillings and in pence at first they deal;
And steal so little, few perceive they steal;
Till, like the Sea, they compass all the land,   85
From *Scots* to *Wight,* from *Mount* to *Dover* strand:
And when rank Widows purchase luscious nights,

Or when a Duke to *Jansen* punts at White's,
Or City heir in mortgage melts away;
Satan himself feels far less joy than they.   90
Piecemeal they win this acre first, then that,
Glean on, and gather up the whole estate.
Then strongly fencing ill-got wealth by law,
Indentures, Covenants, Articles they draw,
Large as the fields themselves, and larger far   95
Than Civil Codes, with all their Glosses, are;
So vast, our new Divines, we must confess,
Are Fathers of the Church for writing less.
But let them write for you, each rogue impairs
The deeds, and dextrously omits, *ses heirs:*   100
No Commentator can more slily pass
O'er a learned, unintelligible place;
Or, in quotation, shrewd Divines leave out
Those words, that would against them clear the doubt.
    So Luther thought the Pater Noster long,   105
When doomed to say his beads and Evensong;
But having cast his cowl, and left those laws,
Adds to Christ's prayer, the *Power and Glory* clause.
        The lands are bought; but where are to be found
Those ancient woods, that shaded all the ground?   110
We see no new-built palaces aspire,
No kitchens emulate the vestal fire.
Where are those troops of Poor, that thronged of yore
The good old landlord's hospitable door?
Well, I could wish, that still in lordly domes   115
Some beasts were killed, though not whole hecatombs;
That both extremes were banished from their walls,
Carthusian fasts, and fulsome Bacchanals;
And all mankind might that just Mean observe,
In which none e'er could surfeit, none could starve.   120
These as good works, 'tis true, we all allow;
But oh! these works are not in fashion now:
Like rich old wardrobes, things extremely rare,
Extremely fine, but what no man will wear.
        Thus much I've said, I trust, without offence;   125

Let no Court Sycophant pervert my sense,
Nor sly informer watch these words to draw
Within the reach of Treason, or the Law.

1733–1735

SATIRE IV

WELL, if it be my time to quit the stage,
Adieu to all the follies of the age!
I die in charity with fool and knave,
Secure of peace at least beyond the grave.
I've had my Purgatory here betimes,   5
And paid for all my satires, all my rhymes.
The Poet's hell, its tortures, fiends, and flames,
To this were trifles, toys and empty names.
     With foolish pride my heart was never fired,
Nor the vain itch t'admire, or be admired;   10
I hope for no commission from his Grace;
I bought no benefice, I begged no place;
Had no new verses, nor new suit to show;
Yet went to Court!—the Devil would have it so.
But, as the Fool that in reforming days   15
Would go to Mass in jest (as story says)
Could not but think, to pay his fine was odd,
Since 'twas no formed design of serving God;
So was I punished, as if full as proud,
As prone to ill, as negligent of good,   20
As deep in debt, without a thought to pay,
As vain, as idle, and as false, as they
Who live at Court, for going once that way!
Scarce was I entered, when, behold! there came
A thing which Adam had been posed to name;   25
Noah had refused it lodging in his Ark,

Where all the Race of Reptiles might embark:
A verier monster, than on Afric's shore
The sun e'er got, or slimy Nilus bore,
Or Sloane[1] or Woodward's[2] wondrous shelves contain,   30
Nay, all that lying Travellers can feign.
The watch would hardly let him pass at noon,
At night, would swear him dropped out of the Moon.
One whom the mob, when next we find or make
A popish plot, shall for a Jesuit take,   35
And the wise Justice starting from his chair
Cry: "By your Priesthood tell me what you are?"
    Such was the wight: Th' apparel on his back
Though coarse, was reverend, and though bare, was black:
The suit, if by the fashion one might guess,   40
Was velvet in the youth of good Queen *Bess,*
But mere tuff-taffety what now remained;
So Time, that changes all things, had ordained!
Our sons shall see it leisurely decay,
First turn plain rash, then vanish quite away.   45
    This thing has travelled, speaks each language too,
And knows what's fit for every state to do;
Of whose best phrase and courtly accent joined,
He forms one tongue, exotic and refined.
Talkers I've learned to bear; Motteux[3] I knew,   50
Henley himself I've heard, and Budgel too.
The Doctor's Wormwood style, the Hash of tongues
A Pedant makes, the storm of Gonson's[4] lungs,
The whole Artillery of the terms of War,
And (all those plagues in one) the bawling Bar: 55
These I could bear; but not a rogue so civil,

[1] Sir Hans Sloane, President of the Royal Society, 1727–1741, and President of the College of Physicians, 1719–1735. Cf. *Moral Essay* IV, 10.
[2] John Woodward, physician, fossilist, and antiquary, satirized by Pope, Gay, and Arbuthnot in their comedy *Three Hours after Marriage,* 1717; in the *Memoirs of Martinus Scriblerus,* Chap. 3; and as Vadius in *Moral Essay* V, 41.
[3] Peter Motteux, an inferior dramatist and journalist.
[4] Sir John Gonson, a famous police magistrate. Cf. l. 256.

Whose tongue will compliment you to the devil.
A tongue, that can cheat widows, cancel scores,
Make Scots speak treason, cozen subtlest whores,
With royal Favourites in flattery vie,   60
And Oldmixon and Burnet[5] both outlie.
        He spies me out, I whisper: 'Gracious God!
What sin of mine could merit such a rod?
That all the shot of dulness now must be
From this thy blunderbuss discharged on me!"   65
"Permit" (he cries) "no stranger to your fame
To crave your sentiment, if —'s your name.
What *Speech* esteem you most?" 'The *King's*,' said I.
"But the best *words?*"—'O Sir, the *Dictionary*.'
"You miss my aim; I mean the most acute   70
And perfect *Speaker?*"—'Onslow, past dispute.'
"But, Sir, of writers?" 'Swift, for closer style,
But Ho—y for a period of a mile.'
"Why yes, 'tis granted, these indeed may pass:
Good common linguists, and so Panurge was;   75
Nay troth th' Apostles (though perhaps too rough)
Had once a pretty gift of Tongues enough:
Yet these were all poor Gentlemen! I dare
Affirm, 'twas Travel made them what they were."
        Thus others' talents having nicely shown,   80
He came by sure transition to his own:
Till I cried out: 'You prove yourself so able,
Pity! you was not Druggerman[6] at Babel;
For had they found a linguist half so good,
I make no question but the Tower had stood.'   85
        "Obliging Sir! for Courts you sure were made:
Why then for ever buried in the shade?
Spirits like you, should see and should be seen,
The King would smile on you—at least the Queen."
'Ah gentle Sir! your Courtiers so cajole us—   90
But Tully has it, *Nunquam minus solus:*

[5] See Henley, Budgel, Oldmixon, and Burnet in the *Epistle to Arbuthnot.*
[6] Dragoman, i.e., interpreter.

And as for Courts, forgive me, if I say
No lessons now are taught the Spartan way:
Though in his pictures Lust be full displayed,
Few are the Converts Aretine[7] has made;   95
And though the Court show Vice exceeding clear,
None should, by my advice, learn Virtue there.'
  At this entranced, he lifts his hands and eyes,
Squeaks like a high-stretched lutestring, and replies:
"Oh 'tis the sweetest of all earthly things   100
To gaze on Princes, and to talk of Kings!"
'Then, happy Man who shows the Tombs!' said I,
'He dwells amidst the royal Family:
He every day, from King to King can walk,
Of all our Harrys, all our Edwards talk,   105
And get by speaking truth of monarchs dead,
What few can of the living, Ease and Bread.'
"Lord, Sir, a mere Mechanic! strangely low,
And coarse of phrase,—your English all are so.
How elegant your Frenchmen?" 'Mine, d'ye mean?   110
I have but one, I hope the fellow's clean.'
"Oh! Sir, politely so! nay, let me die,
Your only wearing is your Paduasoy."
'Not, Sir, my only, I have better still,
And this you see is but my dishabille—'   115
Wild to get loose, his Patience I provoke,
Mistake, confound, object at all he spoke.
But as coarse iron, sharpened, mangles more,
And itch most hurts when angered to a sore;
So when you plague a fool, 'tis still the curse,   120
You only make the matter worse and worse.
  He passed it o'er; affects an easy smile
At all my peevishness, and turns his style.
He asks, "What News?" I tell him of new Plays,
New Eunuchs, Harlequins, and Operas.   125
He hears, and as a Still with simples in it

---

[7] Pietro Aretino, an Italian poet of the sixteenth century, who wrote
sonnets to accompany a set of indecent engravings.

Between each drop it gives, stays half a minute,
Loth to enrich me with too quick replies,
By little and by little, drops his lies.
Mere household trash! of birthnights, balls, and shows,   130
More than ten Holinsheds, or Halls, or Stowes.
When the *Queen* frowned, or smiled, he knows; and what
A subtle Minister may make of that:
Who sins with whom: who got his Pension rug,
Or quickened a Reversion by a drug: 135
Whose place is quartered out, three parts in four,
And whether to a Bishop, or a Whore:
Who having lost his credit, pawned his rent,
Is therefore fit to have a Government:
Who in the secret, deals in Stocks secure,   140
And cheats th' unknowing Widow and the Poor:
Who makes a Trust or Charity a Job,
And gets an Act of Parliament to rob:
Why Turnpikes rise, and now no Cit nor clown
Can gratis see the country, or the town: 145
Shortly no lad shall chuck, or lady vole,
But some excising Courtier will have toll.
He tells what strumpet places sells for life,
What Squire his lands, what citizen his Wife:
And last (which proves him wiser still than all)   150
What Lady's face is not a whited wall.
        As one of Woodward's patients, sick, and sore,
I puke, I nauseate,—yet he thrusts in more:
Trims Europe's balance, tops the statesman's part,
And talks Gazettes and Postboys o'er by heart.   155
Like a big wife at sight of loathsome meat
Ready to cast, I yawn, I sigh, and sweat.
Then as a licensed spy, whom nothing can
Silence or hurt, he libels the great Man;
Swears every place entailed for years to come,   160
In sure succession to the day of doom:
He names the price for every office paid,
And says our wars thrive ill, because delayed:
Nay hints, 'tis by connivance of the Court,

That Spain robs on, and Dunkirk's still a Port.   165
Not more amazement seized on Circe's guests,
To see themselves fall endlong into beasts,
Than mine, to find a subject staid and wise
Already half turned traitor by surprise.
I felt th' infection slide from him to me,   170
As in the pox, some give it to get free;
And quick to swallow me, methought I saw
One of our Giant Statutes ope its jaw.
   In that nice moment, as another Lie
Stood just atilt, the Minister came by.   175
To him he flies, and bows, and bows again,
Then, close as Umbra, joins the dirty train,
Not Fannius' self more impudently near,
When half his nose is in his Prince's ear.
I quaked at heart; and still afraid, to see   180
All the Court filled with stranger things than he,
Ran out as fast, as one that pays his bail
And dreads more actions, hurries from a jail.
   Bear me, some God! oh quickly bear me hence
To wholesome Solitude, the nurse of sense: 185
Where Contemplation prunes her ruffled wings,
And the free soul looks down to pity Kings!
There sober thought pursued th' amusing theme,
Till Fancy coloured it, and formed a Dream.
A Vision hermits can to Hell transport,   190
And forced even me to see the damned at Court.
Not Dante dreaming all th' infernal state,
Beheld such scenes of envy, sin, and hate.
Base Fear becomes the guilty, not the free;
Suits Tyrants, Plunderers, but suits not me: 195
Shall I, the Terror of this sinful town,
Care, if a liveried Lord or smile or frown?
Who cannot flatter, and detest who can,
Tremble before a noble Serving man?
O my fair mistress, Truth! shall I quit thee   200
For huffing, braggart, puffed Nobility?
Thou, who since yesterday hast rolled o'er all

The busy, idle blockheads of the ball,
Hast thou, oh Sun! beheld an emptier sort,
Than such as swell this bladder of a court?   205
Now pox on those who show a *Court in wax!*[8]
It ought to bring all courtiers on their backs:
Such painted puppets! such a varnished race
Of hollow gewgaws, only dress and face!
Such waxen noses, stately staring things—   210
No wonder some folks bow, and think them Kings.
      See! where the British youth, engaged no more
At Fig's, at White's, with felons, or a whore,[9]
Pay their last duty to the Court, and come
All fresh and fragrant, to the drawing room;   215
In hues as gay, and odours as divine,
As the fair fields they sold to look so fine.
"That's velvet for a King!" the flatterer swears;
'Tis true, for ten days hence 'twill be King Lear's.
Our Court may justly to our stage give rules,   220
That helps it both to fools-coats and to fools.
And why not players strut in courtiers' clothes?
For these are actors too, as well as those:
Wants reach all states; they beg but better drest,
And all is splendid poverty at best.   225
      Painted for sight, and essenced for the smell,
Like frigates fraught with spice and cochinel,
Sail in the Ladies: how each pirate eyes
So weak a vessel, and so rich a prize!
Topgallant he, and she in all her trim,   230
He boarding her, she striking sail to him:
"Dear Countess! you have charms all hearts to hit!"
And "Sweet Sir Fopling! you have so much wit!"
Such wits and beauties are not praised for nought,
For both the beauty and the wit are bought.   235

[8] A famous show of the Court of France, in Waxwork. P.
[9] White's was a noted gaming-house: Fig's, a Prize fighter's Academy, where the young Nobility received instruction in those days: It was also customary for the nobility and gentry to visit the condemned criminals in Newgate. P.

'Twould burst even Heraclitus with the spleen,
To see those antics, Fopling and Courtine:
The Presence seems, with things so richly odd,
The mosque of Mahound, or some queer Pagod.
See them survey their limbs by Durer's rules,   240
Of all beau-kind the best-proportioned fools!
Adjust their clothes, and to confession draw
Those venial sins, an atom, or a straw;
But oh! what terrors must distract the soul
Convicted of that mortal crime, a hole;   245
Or should one pound of powder less bespread
Those monkey tails that wag behind their head.
Thus finished, and corrected to a hair,
They march, to prate their hour before the Fair.
So first to preach a white-gloved Chaplain goes,   250
With band of Lily, and with cheek of Rose,
Sweeter than Sharon, in immaculate trim,
Neatness itself impertinent in him.
Let but the Ladies smile, and they are blest:
Prodigious! how the things *protest, protest:*   255
Peace, fools, or Gonson will for Papists seize you,
If once he catch you at your *Jesu! Jesu!*
        Nature made every Fop to plague his brother,
Just as one Beauty mortifies another.
But here's the Captain that will plague them both,   260
Whose air cries Arm! whose very look's an oath:
The Captain's honest, Sirs, and that's enough,
Though his soul's bullet, and his body buff.
He spits fore-right; his haughty chest before,
Like battering-rams, beats open every door: 265
And with a face as red, and as awry,
As Herod's hangdogs in Old Tapestry,
Scarecrow to boys, the breeding woman's curse,
Has yet a strange ambition to look worse;
Confounds the civil, keeps the rude in awe,   270
Jests like a licensed fool, commands like law.
        Frighted, I quit the room, but leave it so
As men from Jails to execution go;

For hung with deadly sins I see the wall,[10]
And lined with Giants deadlier than 'em all: 275
Each man an *Askapart,*[11] of strength to toss
For Quoits, both Temple Bar and Charing Cross.
Scared at the grizly forms, I sweat, I fly,
And shake all o'er, like a discovered spy.

    Courts are too much for wits so weak as mine: 280
Charge them with Heaven's Artillery, bold Divine!
From such alone the Great rebukes endure,
Whose Satire's sacred, and whose rage secure:
    'Tis mine to wash a few light stains, but theirs
To deluge sin, and drown a Court in tears.   285
Howe'er what's now *Apocrypha,* my Wit,
In time to come, may pass for holy writ.

[10] The Room hung with old Tapestry, representing the seven deadly
sins. P.
[11] A Giant famous in Romances. P.

EPILOGUE
TO THE SATIRES
In Two Dialogues

Written in MDCCXXXVIII

DIALOGUE I

Fr. Not twice a twelvemonth you appear in Print,
And when it comes, the Court see nothing in't.
You grow correct, that once with Rapture writ,
And are, besides, too *moral* for a Wit.
Decay of Parts, alas! we all must feel—   5
Why now, this moment, don't I see you steal?
'Tis all from Horace; Horace long before ye
Said, "Tories called him Whig, and Whigs a Tory;"[1]
And taught his Romans, in much better metre,
"To laugh at fools who put their trust in Peter."[2]   10
      But Horace, Sir, was delicate, was nice;
Bubo[3] observes, he lashed no sort of *Vice:*

[1] Cf. *Satire* II, i, 68.
[2] Cf. *Satire* II, i, 40; *Moral Essay* III, 123.
[3] Some guilty person very fond of making such an observation. P.

Horace would say, Sir Billy *served the Crown,*
Blunt could *do Business,* H—ggins[4] *knew the Town;*
In Sappho touch the *Failings of the Sex,*   15
In reverend Bishops note some *small Neglects,*
And own, the Spaniard did a *waggish thing,*
Who cropped our Ears, and sent them to the King.[5]
His sly, polite, insinuating style
Could please at Court, and make AUGUSTUS smile: 20
An artful Manager, that crept between
His Friend and Shame, and was a kind of *Screen.*
But 'faith your very Friends will soon be sore;
Patriots[6] there are, who wish you'd jest no more—
And where's the Glory? 'twill be only thought   25
The Great Man[7] never offered you a groat.
Go see Sir ROBERT——

    P.   See Sir ROBERT!—hum—
And never laugh—for all my life to come?
Seen him I have, but in his happier hour
Of Social Pleasure, ill-exchanged for Power;   30
Seen him, uncumbered with the Venal tribe,
Smile without Art, and win without a Bribe.
Would he oblige me? let me only find,
He does not think me what he thinks mankind.[8]
Come, come, at all I laugh he laughs, no doubt;   35
The only difference is, I dare laugh out.

    F.   Why yes: with *Scripture* still you may be free;
A Horselaugh, if you please, at *Honesty;*

[4] [John Huggins.] Formerly Jailer of the Fleet prison, enriched himself
by many exactions, for which he was tried and expelled. P.

[5] Said to be executed by the Captain of a Spanish ship on one Jenkins, a
Captain of an English one. He cut off his ears, and bid him carry them to
the King his master. P.

[6] This appellation was generally given to those in opposition to the Court.
Though some of them (which our author hints at) had views too mean
and interested to deserve that name. P.

[7] A phrase, by common use, appropriated to the first minister. P.

[8] That great minister . . . thought all mankind Rogues; and that every
one had his price. [W.]

A Joke on JEKYL,[9] or some odd *Old Whig*
Who never changed his Principles, or Wig: 40
A Patriot is a Fool in every age,
Whom all Lord Chamberlains allow the Stage:
These nothing hurts; they keep their Fashion still,
And wear their strange old Virtue, as they will.

    If any ask you, "Who's the man, so near   45
His Prince, that writes in Verse, and has his ear?"
Why, answer, LYTTLETON,[10] and I'll engage
The worthy Youth shall ne'er be in a rage:
But were his Verses vile, his Whisper base,
You'd quickly find him in Lord *Fanny's* case.   50
Sejanus,[11] Wolsey,[11] hurt not honest FLEURY,[12]
But well may put some Statesmen in a fury.

    Laugh then at any, but at Fools or Foes;
These you but anger, and you mend not those.
Laugh at your friends, and, if your Friends are sore,   55
So much the better, you may laugh the more;
To Vice and Folly to confine the jest,
Sets half the world, God knows, against the rest;
Did not the Sneer of more impartial men
At Sense and Virtue, balance all again.   60
Judicious Wits spread wide the Ridicule,
And charitably comfort Knave and Fool.

    P.   Dear Sir, forgive the Prejudice of Youth:
Adieu Distinction, Satire, Warmth, and Truth!
Come, harmless Characters that no one hit;   65

---

[9] Sir Joseph Jekyl, master of the Rolls, a true Whig in his principles, and a man of the utmost probity. . . . P.

[10] George Lyttelton, Secretary to the Prince of Wales, distinguished both for his writings and speeches in the spirit of Liberty. P. Cf. *Epistle* I, i, 29; Dialogue II, 131.

[11] The one the wicked minister of Tiberius; the other, of Henry VIII. The writers against the Court usually bestowed these and other odious names on the Minister, without distinction, and in the most injurious manner. See Dialogue II, 137. P.

[12] Cardinal: and minister to Louis XV. It was a Patriot fashion, at that time, to cry up his wisdom and honesty. P. Cf. *Satire* II, i. 75.

Come, Henley's[13] Oratory, Osborn's[13] Wit!
The Honey dropping from Favonio's tongue,
The Flowers of Bubo, and the Flow of Y—ng!
The gracious Dew of Pulpit Eloquence,[14]
And all the well-whipped Cream of Courtly Sense,   70
That First was H—vy's, F—'s next, and then
The S—te's, and then H—vy's once again.[15]
O come, that easy Ciceronian style,
So Latin, yet so English all the while,
As, though the pride of Middleton and Bland,[16]   75
All Boys may read, and Girls may understand!
Then might I sing, without the least offence,
And all I sung should be the *Nation's Sense;*
Or teach the melancholy Muse to mourn,
Hang the sad Verse on CAROLINA's Urn,   80
And hail her passage to the Realms of Rest,
All Parts performed, and *all* her Children blest!
So—Satire is no more—I feel it die—
No *Gazetteer*[17] more innocent than I—
And let, a-God's name, every Fool and Knave   85
Be graced through Life, and flattered in his Grave.
    F.   Why so? If Satire knows its Time and Place,
You still may lash the greatest—in Disgrace:

[13] See them in their places in *The Dunciad* [i.e., *Dunciad* III, 199; II, 167, 312]. P.

[14] Alludes to some court sermons, and florid panegyrical speeches; particularly one very full of puerilities and flatteries; which afterwards got into an address in the same pretty style; and was lastly served up in an Epitaph, between Latin and English, published by its author. P. The subject of the sermons and panegyrics was Queen Caroline, who died in 1737.

[15] Lord Hervey, Henry Fox, and the "Senate," all in one way or another had a hand in the panegyric of the Queen.

[16] Conyers Middleton, Cambridge theologian, wrote a *Life of Cicero*, 1741, in a style which was highly admired. Henry Bland, Provost of Eton, translated into Latin verse a part of Addison's *Cato.* See *Spectator* No. 628.

[17] The Gazetteer is one of the low appendices to the Secretary of State's office, to write the government's newspaper, published by Authority. [W.]

For Merit will by turns forsake them all;
Would you know when? exactly when they fall.   90
But let all Satire in all Changes spare
Immortal S——k,[18] and grave De——re.[19]
Silent and soft, as Saints remove to Heaven,
All Ties dissolved, and every Sin forgiven,
These may some gentle ministerial Wing   95
Receive, and place forever near a King!
There, where no Passion, Pride, or Shame transport,
Lulled with the sweet Nepenthe of a Court;
There, where no Father's, Brother's, Friend's disgrace
Once break their rest, or stir them from their Place: 100
But past the Sense of human Miseries,
All Tears are wiped for ever from all eyes;
No cheek is known to blush, no heart to throb,
Save when they lose a Question, or a Job.
  P. Good Heaven forbid, that I should blast their glory,
Who know how like Whig Ministers to Tory,   106
And when three Sovereigns died, could scarce be vext,
Considering what a *gracious Prince* was next.
Have I, in silent wonder, seen such things
As Pride in Slaves, and Avarice in Kings;   110
And at a Peer, or Peeress, shall I fret,
Who starves a Sister, or forswears a Debt?
Virtue, I grant you, is an empty boast;
But shall the Dignity of *Vice* be lost?
Ye Gods! shall Cibber's Son[20] without rebuke,   115
Swear like a Lord, or Rich[20] outwhore a Duke?
A Favorite's Porter with his Master vie,
Be bribed as often, and as often lie?

---

[18] *Immortal Selkirk.* A title given to that Lord by King James II. He was Lord of the Bedchamber to King William; he was so to King George I; he was so to King George II. P.

[19] [Lord Delaware] . . . was very skilful in all the forms of the House, in which he discharged himself with great gravity. P.

[20] Two Players: look for them in the *Dunciad.* P.

Shall Ward[21] draw Contracts with a Statesman's skill?
Or Japhet[21] pocket, like his Grace, a Will?   120
Is it for Bond,[22] or Peter, (paltry things)
To pay their debts, or keep their Faith, like Kings?
If Blunt[23] dispatched himself, he played the man,
And so mayst thou, illustrious Passeran![24]
But shall a Printer, weary of his life,   125
Learn from their Books, to hang himself and Wife?
This, this, my friend, I cannot, must not bear;
Vice thus abused, demands a Nation's care:
This calls the Church to deprecate our Sin,
And hurls the Thunder of the Laws on *Gin*.[25]   130
     Let modest FOSTER,[26] if he will, excel
Ten Metropolitans in preaching well;
A simple Quaker, or a Quaker's Wife,
Outdo Landaff[27] in doctrine,—yea in Life:
Let humble ALLEN,[28] with an awkward Shame,   135
Do good by stealth, and blush to find it Fame.
Virtue may choose the high or low Degree,
'Tis just alike to Virtue, and to me;
Dwell in a Monk, or light upon a King,
She's still the same, beloved, contented thing.   140

[21] Cf. *Moral Essay* II, 86; *Dunciad* III, 34.
[22] Cf. *Moral Essay* III, 100.
[23] Author of an impious and foolish book called *The Oracles of Reason,* who being in love with a near kinswoman of his, and rejected, gave himself a stab in the arm, as pretending to kill himself, of the consequence of which he really died. P.
[24] Author of another book of the same stamp, called *A Philosophical Discourse on Death,* being a defence of suicide. [W.]
[25] A spirituous liquor, the exorbitant use of which had almost destroyed the lowest rank of the People, till it was restrained by an Act of Parliament in 1736. P.
[26] James Foster, one of the most popular Dissenting preachers of the day.
[27] A Poor Bishopric in Wales, as poorly supplied. P.
[28] Ralph Allen, the philanthropist, of Prior Park, near Bath. He helped to pay for the authorized edition of Pope's *Letters* in 1737, and Pope became his frequent guest. Allen was the model for Squire Allworthy in Fielding's *Tom Jones.*

Vice is undone, if she forgets her Birth,
And stoops from Angels to the Dregs of Earth:
But 'tis the *Fall* degrades her to a Whore;
Let *Greatness* own her, and she's mean no more,
Her Birth, her Beauty, Crowds and Courts confess,   145
Chaste Matrons praise her, and grave Bishops bless;
In golden Chains the willing World she draws,
And hers the Gospel is, and hers the Laws,
Mounts the Tribunal, lifts her scarlet head,
And sees pale Virtue carted in her stead.   150
Lo! at the wheels of her Triumphal Car,
Old England's Genius, rough with many a Scar,
Dragged in the dust! his arms hang idly round,
His Flag inverted trails along the ground!
Our Youth, all liveried o'er with foreign Gold,   155
Before her dance: behind her, crawl the Old!
See thronging Millions to the Pagod run,
And offer Country, Parent, Wife, or Son!
Hear her black Trumpet through the Land proclaim,
That Not to be corrupted is the Shame.   160
In Soldier, Churchman, Patriot, Man in Power,
'Tis Avarice all, Ambition is no more!
See, all our Nobles begging to be Slaves!
See, all our Fools aspiring to be Knaves!
The Wit of Cheats, the Courage of a Whore,   165
Are what ten thousand envy and adore:
All, all look up, with reverential Awe,
At Crimes that scape, or triumph o'er the Law:
While Truth, Worth, Wisdom, daily they decry—
"Nothing is Sacred now but Villainy."   170
    Yet may this Verse (if such a Verse remain)
Show there was one who held it in disdain.

DIALOGUE II

Fr. 'Tis all a libel—Paxton[29] (Sir) will say.
P. Not yet, my Friend! tomorrow faith it may;
And for that very cause I print today.[30]
How should I fret to mangle every line,
In reverence to the Sins of *Thirty-nine!*   5
Vice with such Giant strides comes on amain,
Invention strives to be before in vain;
Feign what I will, and paint it e'er so strong,
Some rising Genius sins up to my Song.
     F. Yet none but you by Name the guilty lash;   10
Even Guthry[31] saves half Newgate by a Dash.
Spare then the Person, and expose the Vice.
     P. How, Sir! not damn the Sharper, but the Dice?
Come on then, Satire! general, unconfined,
Spread thy broad wing, and souse on all the kind.   15
Ye Statesmen, Priests, of one Religion all!
Ye Tradesmen, vile, in Army, Court, or Hall!
Ye Reverend Atheists. F. Scandal! name them, Who?
     P. Why that's the thing you bid me not to do.
Who starved a Sister,[32] who forswore a Debt,   20
I never named; the Town's inquiring yet.
The poisoning Dame— F. You mean— P. I don't.—
     F. You do.
     P. See, now I keep the secret, and not you!
The bribing Statesman— F. Hold, too high you go.
     P. The bribed Elector— F. There you stoop too low.
     P. I fain would please you, if I knew with what;   26

[29] Late solicitor to the Treasury. [W.]
[30] Dialogue I had appeared in May 1738. Dialogue II appeared in July.
[31] The Ordinary of Newgate, who publishes the memoirs of the Malefactor's, and is often prevailed upon to be so tender of their reputation as to set down no more than the initials of their name. P.
[32] Cf. Dialogue I, 112.

Tell me, which Knave is lawful Game, which not?
Must great Offenders, once escaped the Crown,
Like Royal Harts, be never more run down?
Admit your Law to spare the Knight requires,   30
As Beasts of Nature may we hunt the Squires?
Suppose I censure—you know what I mean—
To save a Bishop, may I name a Dean?
    F.   A Dean, Sir? no: his Fortune is not made,
You hurt a man that's rising in the Trade.   35
    P.   If not the Tradesman who set up today,
Much less the Prentice who tomorrow may.
Down, down, proud Satire! though a Realm be spoiled,
Arraign no mightier Thief than wretched *Wild*;[33]
Or, if a Court or Country's made a job,   40
Go drench a Pickpocket, and join the mob.
    But, Sir, I beg you (for the Love of Vice!)
The matter's weighty, pray consider twice;
Have you less pity for the needy Cheat,
The poor and friendless Villain, than the Great?   45
Alas! the small Discredit of a Bribe
Scarce hurts the Lawyer, but undoes the Scribe.
Then better sure it Charity becomes
To tax Directors, who (thank God) have Plums;
Still better, Ministers; or, if the thing   50
May pinch even there—why, lay it on a King.
    F.   Stop! stop!
    P.   Must Satire, then, nor rise nor fall?
Speak out, and bid me blame no Rogues at all.
    F.   Yes, strike that *Wild,* I'll justify the blow.
    P.   Strike? why, the man was hanged ten years ago:
Who now that obsolete Example fears?   56
Even Peter trembles only for his Ears.[34]

---

[33] Jonathan Wild, a famous Thief and Thief-Impeacher, who was at last caught in his own train and hanged.   P.
[34] Peter had, the year before this, narrowly escaped the Pillory for forgery: and got off with a severe rebuke only from the bench. P. Cf. *Moral Essay* III, 123. Peter Walter appears as Peter Pounce in Fielding's *Joseph Andrews,* Bk. III, Chap. 12.

    F. What, always Peter? Peter thinks you mad,
You make men desperate, if they once are bad:
Else might he take to Virtue some years hence—   60
    P. As S——k, if he lives, will love the Prince.
    F. Strange spleen to S——k!
    P.   Do I wrong the Man?
God knows, I praise a Courtier where I can.
When I confess, there is who feels for Fame,
And melts to Goodness, need I SCARBOROUGH[35] name? 65
Pleased let me own, in *Esher's* peaceful Grove[36]
(Where *Kent*[37] and Nature vie for PELHAM's Love)
The Scene, the Master, opening to my view,
I sit and dream I see my CRAGGS anew!
    Even in a Bishop I can spy Desert;   70
Secker is decent, *Rundle* has a Heart,
Manners with Candour are to *Benson* given,
To *Berkeley*,[38] every Virtue under Heaven.
    But does the Court a worthy Man remove?
That instant, I declare, he has my Love: 75
I shun his Zenith, court his mild Decline;
Thus SOMERS[39] once, and HALIFAX,[40] were mine.
Oft, in the clear, still Mirrour of Retreat,

[35] Earl of, and Knight of the Garter, whose personal attachments to the king appeared from his steady adherence to the royal interest, after his resignation of his great employment of Master of the Horse; and whose known honour and virtue made him esteemed of all parties. P.
[36] The house and gardens of Esher, in Surrey, belonging to the Honourable Mr. Pelham, Brother to the Duke of Newcastle. The author could not have given a more amiable idea of his Character, than in comparing him to Mr. Craggs. P.
[37] William Kent, celebrated landscape gardener, a friend of Pope.
[38] George Berkeley (1684–1753), Bishop of Cloyne, the famous philosopher, a friend of Pope.
[39] John Lord Somers died in 1716. He had been Lord Keeper in the reign of William III, who took from him the seals in 1700. The author had the honour of knowing him in 1706. A faithful, able, and incorrupt minister . . . . P.
[40] A peer, no less distinguished by his love of letters than his abilities in Parliament. He was disgraced in 1710, on the Change of Queen Anne's ministry. P.

I studied SHREWSBURY, the wise and great:
CARLETON's calm Sense, and Stanhope's noble Flame,   80
Compared, and knew their generous End the same:
How pleasing ATTERBURY's[41] softer hour!
How shined the Soul, unconquered in the Tower!
How can I PULTENEY, CHESTERFIELD forget,
While Roman Spirit charms, and Attic Wit: 85
ARGYLL, the State's whole Thunder born to wield,
And shake alike the Senate and the Field:
Or WYNDHAM, just to Freedom and the Throne,
The Master of our Passions, and his own.
Names, which I long have loved, nor loved in vain,   90
Ranked with their Friends, not numbered with their Train;
And if yet higher the proud List should end,
Still let me say! No Follower, but a friend.
            Yet think not, Friendship only prompts my lays;
I follow *Virtue;* where she shines, I praise: 95
Point she to Priest or Elder, Whig or Tory,
Or round a Quaker's Beaver, cast a Glory.
I never (to my sorrow I declare)
Dined with the MAN of ROSS, or my LORD MAYOR.[42]
Some, in their choice of Friends (nay, look not grave)   100
Have still a secret Bias to a Knave:
To find an honest man I beat about,
And love him, court him, praise him, in or out.
        F.   Then why so few commended?
        P.   Not so fierce;
Find you the Virtue, and I'll find the Verse.   105
But random Praise—the task can ne'er be done;
Each Mother asks it for her booby Son,
Each Widow asks it for *the Best of Men,*
For him she weeps, and him she weds again.
Praise cannot stoop, like Satire, to the ground;   110
The Number may be hanged, but not be crowned.

[41] Francis Atterbury, Bishop of Rochester, tried for treason in 1723 and exiled.
[42] Sir John Barnard, Lord Mayor in the year of the Poem, 1738. A Citizen eminent for his virtue, public Spirit, and great talents in Parliament. [W.] For the Man of Ross, see *Moral Essay* III, 262 ff.

Enough for half the Greatest of these days,
To scape my Censure, not expect my Praise.
Are they not rich? what more can they pretend?
Dare they to hope a Poet for their Friend?   115
What RICHELIEU wanted, Louis scarce could gain,
And what young AMMON wished,[43] but wished in vain.
No Power the Muse's Friendship can command;
No Power when Virtue claims it, can withstand:
To *Cato, Virgil* paid one honest line;   120
O let my Country's Friends illumine mine!
—What are you thinking?   F.   Faith, the thought's no sin,
I think your Friends are out, and would be in.
      P.   If merely to come in, Sir, they go out,
The way they take is strangely round about.   125
      F.   They too may be corrupted, you'll allow?
      P.   I only call those Knaves who are so now.
    Is that too little? Come then, I'll comply—
Spirit of *Arnall!*[44] aid me while I lie.
COBHAM's[45] a coward, POLWARTH[46] is a Slave,   130
And LYTTLETON[47] a dark, designing Knave,
ST. JOHN has ever been a wealthy Fool—
But let me add, Sir ROBERT's mighty dull,
Has never made a Friend in private life,
And was, besides, a Tyrant to his Wife.   135
    But, pray, when others praise him, do I blame?
Call Verres, Wolsey, any odious name?
Why rail they then, if but a Wreath of mine,
Oh All-accomplished ST. JOHN! deck thy shrine?
    What! shall each spur-galled Hackney of the day,   140
When Paxton gives him double Pots and Pay,

---

[43] Alexander the Great, at the tomb of Achilles, envied the good fortune of that hero on having found such a herald of his fame as Homer. Cf. Cicero *Pro Archia Poeta* x.

[44] Look for him in his place, *Dunciad* II, 315. [W.]

[45] Cf. *Moral Essay* I, 262.

[46] The Hon. Hugh Hume, Son of Alexander, Earl of Marchmont, Grandson of Patrick, Earl of Marchmont, and distinguished, like them, in the cause of Liberty. P.

[47] Cf. Dialogue I, 47.

Or each new-pensioned Sycophant, pretend
To break my Windows[48] if I treat a Friend?
Then wisely plead, to me they meant no hurt,
But 'twas my Guest at whom they threw the dirt?   145
Sure, if I spare the Minister, no rules
Of Honour bind me, not to maul his Tools;
Sure, if they cannot cut, it may be said
His Saws are toothless, and his Hatchet's Lead.

    It angered TURENNE, once upon a day,   150
To see a Footman kicked that took his pay:
But when he heard th' Affront the Fellow gave,
Knew one a Man of honour, one a Knave;
The prudent General turned it to a jest,
And begged, he'd take the pains to kick the rest: 155
Which not at present having time to do—
    F.   Hold, Sir! for God's sake, where's th' Affront to you?
Against your worship when had S———k[49] writ?
Or P—ge poured forth the Torrent of his Wit?
Or grant the Bard whose distich all commend   160
[*In Power a servant, out of Power a friend*][50]
To W—le guilty of some venial sin;
What's that to you who ne'er was out nor in?
    The Priest whose Flattery bedropped the Crown,
How hurt he you? he only stained the Gown.   165
And how did, pray, the florid Youth[51] offend,
Whose Speech you took, and gave it to a Friend?
P.   Faith, it imports not much from whom it came;
Whoever borrowed, could not be to blame,
Since the whole House did afterwards the same.   170
Let Courtly Wits to Wits afford supply,
As Hog to Hog in huts of Westphaly;

---

[48] Which was done when Lord Bolingbroke and Lord Bathurst were one day dining with him at Twickenham. Warton.
[49] For Selkirk and Page see Dialogue I, 92; *Satire* II, i, 82; and *Dunciad* IV, 30.
[50] A verse taken out of a poem to Sir Robert Walpole. P. The poem is George Bubb Dodington's *Epistle to the Right Honourable Sir Robert Walpole,* 1726.
[51] [Henry Fox.] This seems to allude to a complaint made l. 71 of the preceding Dialogue. P.

If one, through Nature's Bounty or his Lord's,
Has what the frugal, dirty soil affords,
From him the next receives it, thick or thin,   175
As pure a mess almost as it came in;
The blessed benefit, not there confined,
Drops to the third, who nuzzles close behind;
From tail to mouth, they feed and they carouse:
The last full fairly gives it to the *House*.   180
  F. This filthy simile, this beastly line
Quite turns my stomach—
  P.   So does Flattery mine;
And all your courtly Civet Cats can vent,
Perfume to you, to me is Excrement.
But hear me further—Japhet,[52] 'tis agreed,   185
Writ not, and Chartres[52] scarce could write or read,
In all the Courts of Pindus guiltless quite;
But Pens can forge, my Friend, that cannot write;
And must no Egg in Japhet's face be thrown,
Because the Deed he forged was not my own?   190
Must never Patriot then declaim at Gin,
Unless, good man! he has been fairly in?
No zealous Pastor blame a failing Spouse,
Without a staring Reason on his brows?
And each Blasphemer quite escape the rod,   195
Because the insult's not on Man, but God?
  Ask you what Provocation I have had?
The strong Antipathy of Good to Bad.
When Truth or Virtue an Affront endures,
Th' affront is mine, my friend, and should be yours.   200
Mine, as a Foe professed to false Pretence,
Who think a Coxcomb's Honour like his Sense;
Mine, as a Friend to every worthy mind;
And mine as Man, who feel for all mankind.[53]   204
  F. You're strangely proud.
  P.   So proud, I am no Slave:
So impudent, I own myself no Knave:
So odd, my Country's Ruin makes me grave.

---

[52] See the Epistle to Lord Bathurst [*Moral Essay* III, 20, 86]. P.
[53] From Terence: "Homo Sum: Humani nihil a me alienum puto." P.

Yes, I am proud; I must be proud to see
Men not afraid of God, afraid of me:
Safe from the Bar, the Pulpit, and the Throne,   210
Yet touched and shamed by Ridicule alone.
    O sacred weapon! left for Truth's defence,
Sole Dread of Folly, Vice, and Insolence!
To all but Heaven-directed hands denied,
The Muse may give thee, but the Gods must guide: 215
Reverent I touch thee! but with honest zeal;
To rouse the Watchmen of the public Weal,
To Virtue's work provoke the tardy Hall,
And goad the Prelate slumbering in his Stall.
Ye tinsel Insects! whom a Court maintains,   220
That counts your Beauties only by your Stains,
Spin all your Cobwebs o'er the Eye of Day!
The Muse's wing shall brush you all away:
All his Grace preaches, all his Lordship sings,
All that makes Saints of Queens, and Gods of Kings,   225
All, all but Truth, drops deadborn from the Press,
Like the last Gazette, or the last Address.
    When black Ambition stains a public Cause,[54]
A Monarch's sword when mad Vainglory draws,
Not Waller's Wreath[55] can hide the Nation's Scar,   230
Nor Boileau turn the Feather to a Star.[56]
Not so, when diademed with rays divine,
Touched with the Flame that breaks from *Virtue's* Shrine,
Her Priestess Muse forbids the Good to die,
And opes the Temple of *Eternity*.   235
There, other Trophies deck the truly brave,
Than such as Anstis[57] casts into the Grave;

[54] The case of Cromwell in the civil war of England, and (l. 229) of Louis XIV in his conquest of the Low Countries. P.
[55] Refers to a poem by Edmund Waller, *Upon the Late Storme, and of the Death of His Highnesse* [Oliver Cromwell] *Ensuing the Same,* 1659.
[56] See his Ode on Namur, where (to use his own words), "il a fait un Astre de la Plume blanche que le Roi porte ordinairement à son Chapeau, et qui est en effet une espèce de Comète, fatale à nos ennemis." P.
[57] The chief Herald at Arms. It is the custom, at the funeral of great peers, to cast into the grave the broken staves and ensigns of honour. P.

Far other Stars than   *   and   *   *   wear,[58]
And may descend to Mordington[59] from Stair:[60]
(Such as on Hough's[61] unsullied Mitre shine,   240
Or beam, good Digby,[61] from a heart like thine).
Let *Envy* howl, while Heaven's whole Chorus sings,
And bark at Honour not conferred by Kings;
Let *Flattery* sickening see the Incense rise,
Sweet to the World, and grateful to the Skies: 245
Truth guards the Poet, sanctifies the line,
And makes immortal, Verse as mean as mine.

    Yes, the last Pen for Freedom let me draw,
When Truth stands trembling on the edge of Law;
Here, Last of Britons! let your Names be read;   250
Are none, none living? let me praise the Dead,
And for that Cause which made your Fathers shine,
Fall by the Votes of their degenerate Line.

    F.   Alas! alas! pray end what you began,
And write next winter more *Essays on Man.*[62]   255

[58] The asterisks may be satisfactorily read as *George* and *Frederick,* the King and the Prince of Wales.

[59] Lord Mordington ran a low gaming house.

[60] John Dalrymple Earl of Stair, Knight of the Thistle; served in all the wars under the Duke of Marlborough; and afterwards as Ambassador in France. P.

[61] Dr. John Hough, Bishop of Worcester, and the Lord [Edward] Digby. The one an assertor of the Church of England in opposition to the false measures of King James II, the other as firmly attached to the cause of that King. Both acting out of principle, and equally men of honour and virtue. P.

[62] This was the last poem of the kind printed by our author, with a resolution to publish no more; but to enter thus, in the most plain and solemn manner he could, a sort of PROTEST against that insuperable corruption and depravity of manners, which he had been so unhappy as to live to see. Could he have hoped to have amended any, he had continued those attacks; but bad men were grown so shameless and so powerful, that Ridicule was become as unsafe as it was ineffectual. The Poem raised him, as he knew it would, some enemies; but he had reason to be satisfied with the approbation of good men, and the testimony of his own conscience. P.

1728

MARTINUS SCRIBLERUS,
ΠΕΡΙ ΒΑΘΟΥΣ : or of the
Art of Sinking in Poetry

Written in the Year 1727

CONTENTS

374

Chapter I

It hath been long (my dear Countrymen) the subject of my concern and surprise, that whereas numberless Poets, Critics, and Orators have compiled and digested the Art of ancient Poesy, there hath not arisen among us one person so public-spirited, as to perform the like for the Modern. Although it is universally known, that our every-way industrious Moderns, both in the Weight of their writings, and in the Velocity of their judgments, do so infinitely excel the said Ancients.

Nevertheless, too true it is, that while a plain and direct road is paved to their 'ύψος, or Sublime; no track has been yet chalked out, to arrive at our βάθος, or Profund. The Latins, as they came between the Greeks and Us, make use of the word *Altitudo,* which implies equally height and depth. Wherefore considering with no small grief, how many promising Geniuses of this age are wandering (as I may say) in the dark without a guide, I have undertaken this arduous but necessary task, to lead them as it were by the hand, and step by step, the gentle downhill way to the Bathos; the bottom, the end, the central point, the *non plus ultra,* of true Modern Poesy!

When I consider (my dear Countrymen) the extent, fertility, and populousness of our Lowlands of Parnassus, the flourishing state of our Trade, and the plenty of our Manufacture; there are two reflections which administer great occasion of surprise: The one, that all dignities and honours should be bestowed upon the exceeding few meager inhabitants of the Top of the mountain; the other, that our own nation should have arrived to that pitch of greatness it now possesses, without any regular System of Laws.

As to the first, it is with great pleasure I have observed of late the gradual decay of Delicacy and Refinement among mankind, who are become too reasonable to require that we should labour with infinite pains to come up to the taste of these Mountaineers, when they without any may condescend to ours. But as we have now an unquestionable Majority on our side, I doubt not but we shall shortly be able to level the Highlanders, and procure a farther vent for our own product, which is already so much relished, encouraged, and rewarded, by the Nobility and Gentry of Great Britain.

Therefore to supply our former defect, I purpose to collect the scattered Rules of our Art into regular Institutes, from the example and practice of the deep Geniuses of our nation; imitating herein my predecessors the Master of Alexander,[1] and the Secretary of the renowned Zenobia.[2] And in this my undertaking I am the more animated, as I expect more success than has attended even those great Critics; since their Laws (though they might be good) have ever been slackly executed, and their Precepts (however strict) obeyed only by fits, and by a very small number.

At the same time I intend to do justice upon our neighbours, inhabitants of the upper Parnassus; who, taking advantage of the rising ground, are perpetually throwing down rubbish, dirt and stones upon us, never suffering us to live in peace. These men, while they enjoy the crystal stream of Helicon, envy us our common water, which (thank our stars) though it is somewhat muddy, flows in much greater abundance. Nor is this the greatest injustice that we have to complain of; for though it is evident that we never made the least attempt or inroad into Their territories, but lived contented in our native fens; they have often not only committed Petty Larcenies upon our borders, but driven the country, and carried off at once whole Cart-loads of our manufacture; to reclaim some of which stolen goods is part of the design of this Treatise.

[1] Aristotle.

[2] Longinus, the Greek philosopher of the third century, who was supposed to be the author of the celebrated rhetorical treatise ΠΕΡΙ ΥΨΟΤΣ, *On the Sublime,* the model for Pope's travesty.

For we shall see in the course of this work, that our greatest Adversaries have sometimes descended towards us; and doubtless might now and then have arrived at the Bathos itself, had it not been for that mistaken opinion they all entertained, that the Rules of the Ancients were equally necessary to the Moderns; than which there cannot be a more grievous Error, as will be amply proved in the following discourse.

And indeed when any of these have gone so far, as by the light of their own Genius to attempt *new* Models, it is wonderful to observe, how nearly they have approached us in those particular pieces; though in their others they differed *toto cœlo* from us.

Chapter II

That the Bathos, or Profund, is the natural Taste of Man, and in particular, of the present Age.

The Taste of the Bathos is implanted by Nature itself in the soul of man; till, perverted by custom or example, he is taught, or rather compelled, to relish the Sublime. Accordingly, we see the unprejudiced minds of Children delight only in such productions, and in such images, as our true modern writers set before them. I have observed how fast the general Taste is returning to this first Simplicity and Innocence: and if the intent of all Poetry be to divert and instruct, certainly that kind which diverts and instructs the *greatest number,* is to be preferred. Let us look round among the Admirers of Poetry, we shall find those who have a taste of the Sublime to be very few; but the Profund strikes universally, and is adapted to every capacity. 'Tis a fruitless undertaking to write for men of a nice and foppish Gusto, whom after all it is almost impossible to please; and 'tis still more chimerical to write for Posterity, of whose Taste we cannot make any judgment, and whose Applause we can never enjoy. It must be confessed our wiser authors have a present end,

> Et prodesse volunt et delectare Poetæ.

Their true design is Profit or Gain; in order to acquire which, 'tis necessary to procure applause by administering pleasure to the reader: From whence it follows demonstrably, that their productions must be suited to the *present* Taste. And I cannot but congratulate our age on this peculiar felicity, that though we have made indeed great progress in all other branches of Luxury, we are not yet debauched with any high Relish in Poetry, but are in this one Taste less nice than our ancestors. If an Art is to be estimated by its success, I appeal to experience whether there have not been, in proportion to their number, as many starving good Poets, as bad ones.

Nevertheless, in making Gain the principal end of our Art, far be it from me to exclude any great Geniuses of *Rank* or *Fortune* from diverting themselves this way. They ought to be praised no less than those Princes, who pass their vacant hours in some ingenious mechanical or manual Art. And to such as these, it would be ingratitude not to own, that our Art has been often infinitely indebted.

Chapter III

The Necessity of the Bathos, physically considered.

Farthermore, it were great cruelty and injustice, if all such Authors as cannot write in the other way, were prohibited from writing at all. Against this I draw an argument from what seems to me an undoubted physical Maxim, That Poetry is a natural or morbid Secretion from the Brain. As I would not suddenly stop a cold in the head, or dry up my neighbour's Issue, I would as little hinder him from necessary writing. It may be affirmed with great truth, that there is hardly any human creature past childhood, but at one time or other has had some Poetical Evacuation, and, no question, was much the better for it in his health; so true is the saying, *Nascimur Poetæ*. Therefore is the Desire of Writing properly termed *Pruritus*, the "Titillation of the Generative Faculty of the Brain," and the Person is said to conceive; now such as conceive must bring forth. I have known a man thoughtful, melancholy and raving for divers days, who forthwith grew wonderfully easy, lightsome, and cheerful, upon a discharge of the peccant humour, in exceeding purulent Metre. Nor can I question, but abundance of untimely deaths are occasioned for want of this laudable vent of unruly passions: yea, perhaps, in poor wretches, (which is very lamentable) for mere want of pen, ink, and paper! From hence it follows, that a suppression of the very worst Poetry is of dangerous consequence to the State. We find by experience, that the same humours which vent themselves in summer in Ballads and Sonnets, are condensed by the winter's cold into Pamphlets and Speeches for and against the Ministry: Nay, I know not but many times a piece of Poetry may be the most innocent composition of a Minister himself.

It is therefore manifest that *Mediocrity* ought to be allowed, yea indulged, to the good Subjects of England. Nor can I conceive how the world has swallowed the contrary as a Maxim, upon the single authority of that[1] Horace? Why should the golden Mean, and quintessence of all Virtues, be deemed so offensive in this Art? or Coolness or Mediocrity be so amiable a quality in a Man, and so detestable in a Poet?

However, far be it from me to compare these Writers with those great Spirits, who are born with a *Vivacité de pesanteur,* or (as an English Author calls it) an "Alacrity of sinking;" and who by strength of Nature alone can excel. All I mean is to evince the Necessity of Rules to these lesser Geniuses, as well as the Usefulness of them to the greater.

Chapter IV

That there is an Art of the Bathos, or Profund.

We come now to prove, that there is an Art of Sinking in Poetry. Is there not an Architecture of Vaults and Cellars, as well as of lofty Domes and Pyramids? Is there not as much skill and labour in making Dikes, as in raising Mounts? Is there not an Art of Diving as well as of Flying? And will any sober practitioner affirm, that a diving Engine is not of singular use in

---

1   Mediocribus esse poetis
Non dii, non homines, etc. Horace [*Ars Poetica.* ll. 372–373.]   P.

making him long-winded, assisting his sight, and furnishing him with other ingenious means of keeping under water?

If we search the Authors of Antiquity, we shall find as few to have been distinguished in the true Profund, as in the true Sublime. And the very same thing (as it appears from Longinus) had been imagined of that, as now of this: namely, that it was entirely the Gift of Nature. I grant that to excel in the Bathos a Genius is requisite; yet the Rules of Art must be allowed so far useful, as to add weight, or, as I may say, hang on lead, to facilitate and enforce our descent, to guide us to the most advantageous declivities, and habituate our imagination to a depth of thinking. Many there are that can fall, but few can arrive at the felicity of falling gracefully; much more for a man who is amongst the lowest of the Creation, at the very bottom of the Atmosphere, to descend beneath himself, is not so easy a task unless he calls in Art to his assistance. It is with the Bathos as with small Beer, which is indeed vapid and insipid, if left at large, and let abroad; but being by our Rules confined and well stopped, nothing grows so frothy, pert, and bouncing.

The Sublime of Nature is the Sky, the Sun, Moon, Stars, etc. The Profund of Nature is Gold, Pearls, precious Stones, and the Treasures of the Deep, which are inestimable as unknown. But all that lies between these, as Corn, Flower, Fruits, Animals, and Things for the mere use of Man, are of mean price, and so common as not to be greatly esteemed by the curious. It being certain that any thing, of which we know the true use, cannot be invaluable: Which affords a solution, why common Sense hath either been totally despised, or held in small repute, by the greatest modern Critics and Authors.

Chapter V

Of the true Genius for the Profund, and by what it is constituted.

And I will venture to lay it down, as the first Maxim and Cornerstone of this our Art; that whoever would excel therein, must studiously avoid, detest, and turn his head from all the ideas, ways, and workings of that pestilent Foe to Wit, and Destroyer of fine Figures, which is known by the Name of *Common Sense*. His business must be to contract the true *Goût de travers;* and to acquire a most happy, uncommon, unaccountable Way of Thinking.

He is to consider himself as a Grotesque painter, whose works would be spoiled by an imitation of nature, or uniformity of design. He is to mingle bits of the most various, or discordant kinds, landscape, history, portraits, animals, and connect them with a great deal of flourishing, by heads or tails, as it shall please his imagination, and contribute to his principal end, which is to glare by strong oppositions of colours, and surprise by contrariety of images.

Serpentes avibus geminentur, tigribus agni.

Horace.

His design ought to be like a labyrinth, out of which nobody can get clear but himself. And since the great Art of all Poetry is to mix Truth with Fiction, in order to join the *Credible* with the *Surprising;* our author shall produce the Credible, by painting nature in her lowest simplicity; and the Surprising, by contradicting common opinion. In the very Manners he will affect the *Marvellous;* he will draw Achilles with the patience of Job; a Prince talking like a Jack-pudding; a Maid of honour selling bargains; a footman speaking like a philosopher; and a fine gentleman like a scholar. Whoever is conversant in modern Plays, may make a most noble collection of this kind, and, at the same time, form a complete body of *modern Ethics and Morality*.

Nothing seemed more plain to our great authors, than that the world had long been weary of *natural things*. How much the contrary are formed to please, is evident from the universal applause daily given to the admirable entertainments of Harlequins and Magicians on our stage. When an audience behold a coach turned into a wheelbarrow, a conjurer into an old woman, or a man's head where his heels should be; how are they struck with transport and delight? Which can only be imputed to this cause, that each object is changed into that which hath been suggested to them by their own low ideas before.

He ought therefore to render himself master of this happy

and *anti-natural* way of thinking to such a degree, as to be able, on the appearance of any object, to furnish his imagination with ideas infinitely *below* it. And his eyes should be like unto the wrong end of a perspective glass, by which all the objects of nature are lessened.

For Example; when a true genius looks upon the Sky, he immediately catches the idea of a piece of blue lutestring, or a child's mantle.

> The Skies, whose spreading volumes scarce have room,
> Spun thin, and wove in nature's finest loom,
> The newborn world in their soft lap embraced,
> And all around their starry mantle cast.[1]

If he looks upon a Tempest, he shall have an image of a tumbled bed, and describe a succeeding calm in this manner:

> The Ocean, joyed to see the tempest fled,
> New lays his waves, and smooths his ruffled bed.[2]

The Triumphs and Acclamations of the Angels, at the Creation of the Universe, present to his imagination "the Rejoicings of the Lord Mayor's Day;" and he beholds those glorious beings celebrating the Creator, by huzzaing, making illuminations, and flinging squibs, crackers and skyrockets.

> Glorious Illuminations, made on high
> By all the stars and planets of the sky,
> In just degrees, and shining order placed,
> Spectators charmed, and the blest dwelling graced.
> Through all th' enlightened air swift fireworks flew,
> Which with repeated shouts glad Cherubs threw.
> Comets ascended with their sweeping train,

---

[1] *Prince Arthur*, pp. 41, 42.
[2] *Idem*, p. 14.

N. B. In order to do Justice to these great Poets, our Citations are taken from the best, the last, and most correct Editions of their Works. That which we use of *Prince Arthur*, is in *Duodecimo*, 1714. The fourth Edition revised.　P. The references which follow are, with some expansion and regularization, those of Warburton, taken from Pope's editions of 1728 and 1742. A few corrections and additions, in brackets, are from *Works of Pope*, ed. Elwin and Courthope, X (1886), 344–409.

Then fell in starry showers and glittering rain.
In air ten thousand meteors blazing hung,
Which from th' eternal battlements were flung.[3]

If a man who is violently fond of *Wit,* will sacrifice to that passion his friend or his God, would it not be a shame, if he who is smit with the love of the *Bathos* should not sacrifice to it all other transitory regards? You shall hear a zealous Protestant Deacon invoke a Saint, and modestly beseech her to do more for us than Providence:

Look down, blest saint, with pity then look down,
Shed on this land thy kinder influence,
And guide us through the mists of providence,
In which we stray.[4]

Neither will he, if a goodly Simile come in his way, scruple to affirm himself an eyewitness of things never yet beheld by man, or never in existence; as thus,

Thus have I seen in Araby the blest,
A Phœnix couched upon her funeral nest.[5]

But to convince you that nothing is so great which a marvellous genius, prompted by this laudable zeal, is not able to lessen; hear how the most sublime of all Beings is represented in the following images:

First he is a PAINTER.

Sometimes the Lord of Nature in the air,
Spreads forth his clouds, his sable canvas, where
His pencil, dipped in heavenly colour bright,
Paints his fair rainbow, charming to the sight.[6]

[3] *Idem,* p. 50.
[4] Ambrose Philips on the Death of Queen Mary.
[5] Anonymous.
[6] Blackmore, *Job, opt. edit.* 12°, 1716, p. 172. P. The volume to which Pope refers is Sir Richard Blackmore's *A Paraphrase on the Book of Job: As Likewise on the Songs of Moses, Deborah, David: on Four Select Psalms, Some Chapters of Isaiah, and the Third Chapter of Habbakuk,* London, 1716. In the notes which follow all page numbers for Blackmore's Bible paraphrases refer to this edition.

Now he is a CHEMIST.

Th' Almightly Chemist does his work prepare,
Pours down his waters on the thirsty plain,
Digests his lightning, and distils his rain.[7]

Now he is a WRESTLER.

Me in his griping arms th' Eternal took,
And with such mighty force my body shook,
That the strong grasp my members sorely bruised,
Broke all my bones, and all my sinews loosed.[8]

Now a RECRUITING OFFICER.

For clouds, the sunbeams levy fresh supplies,
And raise recruits of vapours, which arise
Drawn from the seas, to muster in the skies.[9]

Now a peaceable GUARANTEE.

In leagues of peace the neighbours did agree,
And to maintain them, God was Guarantee.[10]

Then he is an ATTORNEY.

Job, as a vile offender, God indites,
And terrible decrees against me writes.
God will not be my advocate,
My cause to manage or debate.[11]

In the following Lines he is a GOLDBEATER.

Who the rich metal beats, and then, with care,
Unfolds the golden leaves, to gild the fields of air.[12]

Then a FULLER.

. . . th' exhaling reeks that secret rise,
Born on rebounding sunbeams through the skies,
Are thickened, wrought, and whitened, till they grow
A heavenly fleece.[13]

[7] Blackmore, *Psalm* 104, p. 263.
[8] Blackmore, *Job,* p. 75.
[9] *Idem,* p. 170.
[10] *Idem,* p. 70.
[11] *Idem,* p. 61.
[12] *Idem,* p. 181.
[13] *Idem,* p. 180.

A Mercer, or Packer.

Didst thou one end of air's wide curtain hold,
And help the Bales of Æther to unfold;
Say, which cerulean pile was by thy hand unrolled?[14]

A Butler.

He measures all the drops with wondrous skill,
Which the black clouds, his floating Bottles, fill.[15]

And a Baker.

God in the wilderness his table spread,
And in his airy Ovens baked their bread.[16]

Chapter VI

Of the several Kinds of Geniuses in the Profund, and the Marks and Characters of each.

I doubt not but the reader, by this Cloud of examples, begins to be convinced of the truth of our assertion, that the Bathos is an *Art;* and that the Genius of no mortal whatever, following the mere ideas of Nature, and unassisted with an habitual, nay laborious peculiarity of thinking, could arrive at images so wonderfully low and unaccountable. The great author, from whose treasury we have drawn all these instances (the Father of the Bathos, and indeed the Homer of it) has, like that immortal Greek, confined his labours to the greater Poetry, and thereby left room for others to acquire a due share of praise in inferior kinds. Many painters who could never hit a nose or an eye, have with felicity copied a smallpox, or been admirable at a toad or a red herring. And seldom are we without geniuses for *Still Life,* which they can work up and stiffen with incredible accuracy.

An universal Genius rises not in an age; but when he rises, armies rise in him! he pours forth five or six Epic Poems with

[14] *Idem*, p. 174.
[15] *Idem*, p. 131.
[16] Blackmore, *Song of Moses*, p. 218.

greater facility, than five or six pages can be produced by an elaborate and servile copier after Nature or the Ancients. It is affirmed by Quintilian, that the same genius which made Germanicus so great a General, would with equal application have made him an excellent Heroic Poet. In like manner, reasoning from the affinity there appears between Arts and Sciences, I doubt not but an active catcher of butterflies, a careful and fanciful pattern-drawer, an industrious collector of shells, a laborious and tuneful bagpiper, or a diligent breeder of tame rabbits, might severally excel in their respective parts of the Bathos.

I shall range these confined and less copious Geniuses under proper classes, and (the better to give their pictures to the reader) under the names of *Animals* of some sort or other; whereby he will be enabled, at the first sight of such as shall daily come forth, to know to what kind to refer, and with what Authors to compare them.

1. The *Flying Fishes:* These are writers who now and then rise upon their fins, and fly out of the Profund; but their wings are soon dry, and they drop down to the bottom. G. S. A. H. C. G.[1]

2. The *Swallows* are authors that are eternally skimming and fluttering up and down, but all their agility is employed to *catch flies.* L. T. W. P. Lord H.

3. The *Ostriches* are such, whose heaviness rarely permits them to raise themselves from the ground; their wings are of no use to lift them up, and their motion is between flying and walking; but then they *run very fast.* D. F. L. E. The Hon. E. H.

4. The *Parrots* are they that repeat *another's* words, in such a hoarse odd voice, as makes them seem their *own.* W. B. W. H. C. C. The Reverend D. D.

5. The *Didappers* are authors that keep themselves long out

---

[1] The initial letters, said Pope later, were chosen "for the most part at random. But such was the Number of Poets eminent in that art, that some one or other took every letter to himself" (note to the Preface to the first five editions of *The Dunciad, post,* p. 362). Readers of the *Satires* and *Epistles* and the *Dunciad* will readily make their own conjectures. Cf. *Works,* ed. Elwin and Courthope, X, 361–362.

of sight, under water, and come up now and then where you least expected them. L. W. G. D. Esq. The Hon. Sir W. Y.

6. The *Porpoises* are unwieldy and big; they put all their numbers into a great turmoil and tempest, but whenever they appear in plain light (which is seldom) they are only shapeless and ugly monsters. I. D. C. G. I. O.

7. The *Frogs* are such as can neither walk nor fly, but can *leap* and *bound* to admiration: They live generally in the bottom of a ditch, and make a great noise whenever they thrust their heads above water. E. W. I. M. Esq. T. D. Gent.

8. The *Eels* are obscure authors, that wrap themselves up in their own mud, but are mighty nimble and pert. L. W. L. T. P. M. General C.

9. The *Tortoises* are slow and chill, and, like pastoral writers, delight much in gardens: they have for the most part a fine embroidered Shell, and underneath it, a heavy lump. A. P. W. P. L. E. The Right Hon. E. of S.

These are the chief *Characteristics* of the *Bathos,* and in each of these kinds we have the comfort to be blessed with sundry and manifold choice Spirits in this our Island.

Chapter VII

Of the Profund, when it consists in the Thought.

We have already laid down the Principles upon which our author is to proceed, and the manner of forming his Thought by familiarizing his mind to the lowest objects; to which it may be added, that Vulgar Conversation will greatly contribute. There is no question but the Garret or the Printer's boy may often be discerned in the compositions made in such scenes and company; and much of Mr. Curll himself has been insensibly infused into the works of his learned writers.

The Physician, by the study and inspection of urine and ordure, approves himself in the science; and in like sort should our author accustom and exercise his imagination upon the dregs of nature.

This will render his thoughts truly and fundamentally low,

and carry him many fathoms beyond Mediocrity. For, certain
it is (though some lukewarm heads imagine they may be safe
by temporizing between the extremes) that where there is not a
Triticalness or Mediocrity in the Thought, it can never be sunk
into the genuine and perfect Bathos, by the most elaborate low
Expression: It can, at most, be only carefully obscured, or meta-
phorically debased. But 'tis the Thought alone that strikes, and
gives the whole that spirit, which we admire and stare at. For
instance, in that ingenious piece on a lady's drinking the Bath
waters:

> She drinks! She drinks! Behold the matchless dame!
> To her 'tis water, but to us 'tis flame:
> Thus fire is water, water fire by turns,
> And the same stream at once both cools and burns.[1]

What can be more easy and unaffected than the Diction of
these verses? 'Tis the Turn of Thought alone, and the Variety
of Imagination, that charm and surprise us. And when the same
lady goes into the Bath, the Thought (as in justness it ought)
goes still deeper.

> Venus beheld her, midst her crowd of slaves,
> And thought herself just risen from the waves.[2]

How much out of the way of common sense is this reflection
of Venus, not knowing herself from the lady?

Of the same nature is that noble mistake of a frighted stag
in a full chase, who (saith the Poet)

> Hears his own feet, and thinks they sound like more;
> And fears the hind feet will o'ertake the fore.

So astonishing as these are, they yield to the following, which
is Profundity itself,

> None but Himself can be his Parallel.[3]

Unless it may seem borrowed from the Thought of that Master
of a Show in Smithfield, who writ in large letters, over the
picture of his elephant,

[1] Anonymous.
[2] *Idem.*
[3] Theobald, *Double Falsehood.*

This is the greatest Elephant in the world, except Himself.

However our next instance is certainly an original: Speaking of a beautiful infant,

> So fair thou art, that if great Cupid be
> A child, as Poets say, sure thou art he.
> Fair Venus would mistake thee for her own,
> Did not thy eyes proclaim thee not her son.
> There all the lightnings of thy Mother's shine,
> And with a fatal brightness kill in thine.

First he is Cupid, then he is not Cupid; first Venus would mistake him, then she would not mistake him; next his Eyes are his Mother's, and lastly they are not his Mother's but his own.

Another author, describing a Poet that shines forth amidst a circle of Critics,

> Thus Phœbus through the Zodiac takes his way,
> And amid Monsters rises into day.[4]

What a peculiarity is here of invention? The Author's pencil, like the wand of Circe, turns all into monsters at a stroke. A great Genius takes things in the lump, without stopping at minute considerations: In vain might the ram, the bull, the goat, the lion, the crab, the scorpion, the fishes, all stand in his way, as mere natural animals: much more might it be pleaded that a pair of scales, an old man, and two innocent children, were no monsters: There were only the Centaur and the Maid that could be esteemed out of nature. But what of that? with a boldness peculiar to these daring geniuses, what he found not monsters, he made so.

Chapter VIII

Of the Profund, consisting in the Circumstances, and of Amplification and Periphrase in general.

What in a great measure distinguishes other writers from ours, is their choosing and separating such circumstances in a description as ennoble or elevate the subject.

[4] [Broome, *Epistle to Fenton on his Mariamne.*]

The circumstances which are most natural are *obvious,* therefore not *astonishing* or peculiar. But those that are farfetched, or unexpected, or hardly compatible, will surprise prodigiously. These therefore we must principally hunt out; but above all, preserve a laudable *Prolixity;* presenting the whole and every side at once of the image to view. For Choice and Distinction are not only a curb to the spirit, and limit the descriptive faculty, but also lessen the book; which is frequently of the worst consequence of all to our author.

When Job says in short, "He washed his feet in butter," (a circumstance some Poets would have softened, or passed over) now hear how this butter is spread out by the great Genius.

> With teats distended with their milky store,
> Such numerous lowing herds, before my door,
> Their painful burden to unload did meet,
> That we with butter might have washed out feet.[1]

How cautious! and particular! He had (says our author) so many herds, which herds thrived so well, and thriving so well gave so much milk, and that milk produced so much butter, that, if he did not, he might have washed his feet in it.

The ensuing description of Hell is no less remarkable in the circumstances.

> In flaming heaps the raging ocean rolls,
> Whose livid waves involve despairing souls;
> The liquid burnings dreadful colours shew,
> Some *deeply red* and others *faintly blue.*[2]

Could the most minute Dutch painters have been more exact? How inimitably circumstantial is this also of a war horse!

> His eyeballs burn, he wounds the smoking plain,
> And *knots* of *scarlet ribbon* deck his mane.[3]

Of certain Cudgel players:

They brandish high in air their threatening staves,

---

[1] Blackmore, *Job,* p. 133.
[2] *Prince Arthur,* p. 89.
[3] Anonymous.

> Their hands, a *woven guard* of *osier* saves.
> In which they fix their *hazel weapon's end.*[4]

Who would not think the Poet had passed his whole life at Wakes in such laudable diversions? since he teaches us how to hold, nay how to make a Cudgel!

Periphrase is another great aid to *Prolixity;* being a diffused circumlocutory manner of expressing a known idea, which should be so mysteriously couched, as to give the reader the pleasure of guessing what it is that the author can possibly mean, and a strange surprise when he finds it.

The Poet I last mentioned is incomparable in this figure.

> A waving sea of heads was round me spread,
> And still fresh streams the gazing deluge fed.[5]

Here is a waving sea of heads, which by a fresh stream of heads, grows to be a gazing deluge of heads. You come at last to find, it means a *great crowd.*

How pretty and how genteel is the following?

> Nature's Confectioner,
> Whose suckets are moist alchemy:
> The still of his refining mold
> Minting the garden into gold.[6]

What is this but a Bee gathering honey?

> Little Siren of the stage,
> Empty warbler, breathing lyre,
> Wanton gale of fond desire,
> Tuneful mischief, vocal spell.[7]

Who would think, this was only a poor gentlewoman that sung finely?

We may define *Amplification* to be making the most of a Thought; it is the Spinning wheel of the Bathos, which draws out and spreads it in the finest thread. There are Amplifiers who

---

[4] *Prince Arthur,* p. 197.
[5] Blackmore, *Job,* p. 78.
[6] Cleveland.
[7] [Philips to Miss C——.]

can extend half a dozen thin thoughts over a whole Folio; but for which, the tale of many a vast Romance, and the substance of many a fair volume might be reduced into the size of a primer.

In *The Book of Job* are these words, "Hast thou commanded the morning, and caused the dayspring to know his place?" How is this extended by the most celebrated Amplifier of our age?

> Canst thou set forth th' etherial *mines* on high,
> Which the refulgent *ore* of light supply?
> Is the celestial *furnace* to thee known,
> In which I *melt* the golden metal down?
> Treasures, from whence I deal out light as fast,
> As all my stars and lavish suns can waste.[8]

The same author hath amplified a passage in the civ[th] *Psalm;* "He looks on the earth, and it trembles. He touches the hills, and they smoke."

> The hills forget they're fixed, and in their fright
> Cast off their weight, and ease themselves for flight:
> The woods, with terror winged, outfly the wind,
> And leave the heavy, panting hills behind.[9]

You here see the hills not only trembling, but shaking off the woods from their backs, to run the faster: After this you are presented with a foot-race of mountains and woods, where the woods distance the mountains, that, like corpulent pursy fellows, come puffing and panting a vast way behind them.

Chapter IX

Of Imitation, and the Manner of Imitating.

That the true authors of the Profund are to imitate diligently the examples in their *own way,* is not to be questioned, and that divers have by this means attained to a depth whereunto their own weight could never have carried them, is evident by

[8] Blackmore, *Job,* p. 108:
[9] Blackmore, *Psalm* 104. p. 267.

sundry instances. Who sees not that Defoe was the poetical son of Withers, Tate of Ogilby, E. Ward of John Talyor, and E——n of Blackmore? Therefore when we sit down to write, let us bring some great author to our mind, and ask ourselves this question; How would Sir Richard have said this? Do I express myself as simply as Amb. Philips? Or flow my numbers with the quiet thoughtlessness of Mr. Welsted?

But it may seem somewhat strange to assert, that our Proficient should also read the works of those famous Poets who have excelled in the *Sublime:* Yet is not this a paradox? As Virgil is said to have read Ennius, out of his dunghill to draw gold, so may our author read Shakespeare, Milton, and Dryden for the contrary end, to bury their gold in his own dunghill. A true Genius, when he finds anything lofty or shining in them, will have the skill to bring it down, take off the gloss, or quite discharge the colour, by some ingenious Circumstance or Periphrase, some addition or diminution, or by some of those Figures, the use of which we shall show in our next chapter.

The Book of Job is acknowledged to be infinitely sublime, and yet has not the father of the Bathos reduced it in every page? Is there a passage in all Virgil more painted up and laboured than the description of Etna in the third Æneid?

> Horrificis juxta tonat Ætna ruinis,
> Interdumque atram prorumpit ad æthera nubem,
> Turbine fumantem piceo, et candente favilla,
> Attollitque globos flammarum, et sidera lambit.
> Interdum scopulos avulsaque viscera montis
> Erigit eructans, liquefactaque saxa sub auras
> Cum gemitu glomerat, fundoque exæstuat imo.

(I beg pardon of the gentle English reader, and such of our writers as understand not Latin.) Lo! how this is taken down by our British Poet, by the single happy thought of throwing the mountain into a *fit* of the *colic.*

> Etna, and all the burning mountains, find
> Their kindled stores with inbred storms of wind
> Blown up to rage; and, *roaring out,* complain,

> As torn with inward *gripes,* and torturing pain:
> Laboring, they cast their *dreadful vomit* round,
> And with their *melted bowels* spread the ground.[1]

Horace, in search of the Sublime, struck his head against the Stars;[2] but Empedocles, to fathom the Profund, threw himself into Etna. And who but would imagine our excellent Modern had also been there, from this description?

Imitation is of two sorts; the first is when we force to our own purposes the Thoughts of others; the second consists in copying the Imperfections, or Blemishes of celebrated authors. I have seen a Play professedly writ in the style of Shakespeare; wherein the resemblance lay in one single line,

> And so good morrow t'ye, good master Lieutenant.[3]

And sundry poems in imitation of Milton, where with the utmost exactness, and not so much as one exception, nevertheless was constantly *nathless,* embroidered was *broidered,* hermits were *eremites,* disdained was *'sdeigned,* shady *umbrageous,* enterprise *emprize,* pagan *paynim,* pinions *pennons,* sweet *dulcet,* orchards *orchats,* bridgework *pontifical;* nay, her was *hir,* and their was *thir* through the whole poem. And in very deed, there is no other way by which the true modern poet could read, to any purpose, the works of such men as Milton and Shakespeare.

It may be expected, that, like other Critics, I should next speak of the *Passions:* But as the main end and principal effect of the Bathos is to produce *Tranquillity of Mind,* (and sure it is a better design to promote sleep than madness) we have little to say on this subject. Nor will the short bounds of this discourse allow us to treat at large of the *Emollients* and *Opiates* of Poesy, of the Cool, and the manner of producing it, or of the methods used by our authors in managing the Passions. I shall but transiently remark, that nothing contributes so much to the *Cool,* as the use of *Wit* in expressing passion: The true genius rarely fails of points, conceits, and proper *similes* on such occasions:

---

[1] *Prince Arthur,* p. 75.
[2] Sublimi feriam sidera vertice.
[3] [Nicholas Rowe, *Lady Jane Grey,* Act V, Sc. 1.]

This we may term the *Pathetic epigrammatical,* in which even puns are made use of with good success. Hereby our best authors have avoided throwing themselves or their readers into any indecent Transports.

But as it is sometimes needful to excite the *passions* of our antagonist in the polemic way, the true students in the law have constantly taken their methods from low life, where they observed, that, to move Anger, use is made of scolding and railing; to move Love, of bawdry; to beget Favour and Friendship, of gross flattery; and to produce Fear, of calumniating an adversary with crimes obnoxious to the State. As for shame, it is a silly passion, of which as our authors are incapable themselves, so they would not produce it in others.

Chapter X

Of Tropes and Figures: And first of the variegating, confounding, and reversing Figures.

But we proceed to the *Figures.* We cannot too earnestly recommend to our authors the study of the *Abuse of Speech.* They ought to lay it down as a principle, to say nothing in the usual way, but (if possible) in the direct contrary. Therefore the Figures must be so turned, as to manifest that intricate and wonderful Cast of Head which distinguishes all writers of this kind; or (as I may say) to refer exactly the Mold in which they were formed, in all its inequalities, cavities, obliquities, odd crannies, and distortions.

It would be endless, nay impossible to enumerate all such Figures; but we shall content ourselves to range the principal, which most powerfully contribute to the Bathos, under three Classes.

   I. The Variegating, Confounding, or Reversing Tropes and Figures.

  II. The Magnifying, and

 III. The Diminishing.

We cannot avoid giving to these the Greek or Roman Names; but in tenderness to our countrymen and fellow writers, many of whom, however exquisite, are wholly ignorant of those languages, we have also explained them in our mother tongue.

I.   Of the first sort, nothing so much conduces to the Bathos, as the

CATACHRESIS.

A Master of this will say,

> Mow the Beard,
> Shave the Grass,
> Pin the Plank,
> Nail my Sleeve.

From whence results the same kind of pleasure to the mind, as to the eye when we behold Harlequin trimming himself with a hatchet, hewing down a tree with a razor, making his tea in a cauldron, and brewing his ale in a teapot, to the incredible satisfaction of the British spectator. Another source of the Bathos is,

THE METONYMY,

the inversion of Causes for Effects, of Inventors for Inventions, etc.

> Laced in her Cosins[1] new appeared the bride,
> A Bubble-boy[2] and Tompion[3] at her side,
> And with an air divine her Colmar[4] plied:
> Then oh! she cries, what slaves I round me see?
> Here a bright Redcoat, there a smart Toupee.[5]

[1] Stays. [These five lines are quoted from his own youthful poems; as indeed are most of those marked Anonymous.—Warton.]
[2] Tweezer case.
[3] Watch.
[4] Fan.
[5] A sort of Periwig: All words in use in this present Year 1727. P.

THE SYNECHDOCHE,

which consists, in the use of a part for the whole. You may call a young woman sometimes Pretty-*face* and Pigs-*eyes,* and sometimes Snotty-*nose* and Draggle-*tail.* Or of Accidents for Persons; as a Lawyer is called Split-cause, a Taylor Prick-louse, etc. Or of things belonging to a man, for the man himself; as a *Sword*-man, a *Gown*-man, a *T—m-T—d*-man; a White-*Staff,* a Turn-*key,* etc.

THE APOSIOPESIS.

An excellent figure for the Ignorant, as, "What shall I say?" when one has nothing to say: or "I can no more," when one really can no more. Expressions which the gentle reader is so good as never to take in earnest.

THE METAPHOR.

The first rule is to draw it from the *lowest things,* which is a certain way to sink the highest; as when you speak of the Thunder of Heaven, say,

> The *Lords above* are *angry* and *talk big.*[6]

If you would describe a rich man refunding his treasures, express it thus,

> Though he (as said) may Riches *gorge,* the Spoil
> Painful in massy *Vomit* shall *recoil,*
> Soon shall he perish with a swift decay,
> Like his own *Ordure,* cast with scorn away.[7]

The Second, that, whenever you start a Metaphor, you must be sure to *run it down,* and pursue it as far as it can go. If you get the scent of a State negotiation, follow it in this manner.

[6] Nathaniel Lee, *Alexander the Great.*
[7] Blackmore, *Job,* pp. 91, 93.

> The stones and all the elements with thee
> Shall *ratify* a strict *confederacy;*
> Wild beasts their savage temper shall forget,
> And for a firm *alliance* with thee *treat;*
> The finny tyrant of the spacious seas
> Shall send a scaly *embassy* for peace;
> His *plighted faith* the Crocodile shall keep,
> And seeing thee, for joy sincerely weep.[8]

Or if you represent the Creator denouncing war against the wicked, be sure not to omit one circumstance usual in proclaiming and levying war.

> *Envoys* and *Agents,* who by my command
> Reside in Palestina's land,
> To whom *commissions* I have given,
> To manage there the *interests* of heaven:
> Ye *holy heralds,* who *proclaim*
> Or war or peace, in mine your master's name:
> Ye *pioneers* of heaven, prepare a *road,*
> Make it plain, direct and broad;
> For I *in person* will my people *head;*
>   For the divine deliverer
> Will *on his march* in majesty appear,
> And needs the aid of no *confederate power.*[9]

Under the article of the *Confounding,* we rank

1. THE MIXTURE OF FIGURES,

which raises so many images, as to give you no image at all. But its principal beauty is when it gives an idea just *opposite* to what it seemed meant to describe. Thus an ingenious artist painting the Spring, talks of a *Snow of Blossoms,* and thereby raises an unexpected picture of Winter. Of this sort is the following:

> The gaping clouds pour lakes of sulphur down,
> Whose livid flashes sickening sunbeams drown.[10]

[8] *Idem,* p. 22.
[9] Blackmore, *Isaiah,* ch. 40.
[10] *Prince Arthur,* p. 37.

What a noble Confusion! clouds, lakes, brimstone, flames, sunbeams, gaping, pouring, sickening, drowning! all in two lines.

2. THE JARGON.

> Thy head shall rise, though buried in the dust,
> And midst the clouds his glittering turrets thrust.[11]

Quære, What are the glittering turrets of a man's head?

> Upon the shore, as frequent as the sand,
> To meet the Prince, the glad Dimetians stand.[12]

Quære, Where these Dimetians stood? and of what size they were? Add also to the *Jargon* such as the following:

> Destruction's empire shall no longer last,
> And Desolation lie for ever waste.[13]

> Here Niobe, sad mother, makes her moan,
> And seems converted to a stone in stone.[14]

But for Variegation, nothing is more useful than

3. THE PARANOMASIA, OR PUN,

where a Word, like the tongue of a jackdaw, speaks twice as much by being split: As this of Mr. Dennis,

> Bullets that wound, like Parthians, as they fly;[15]

or this excellent one of Mr. Welsted,

> Behold the Virgin lie
> Naked, and only *covered* by the *Sky.*[16]

To which thou mayst add,

> To see her beauties no man needs to stoop,
> She has the whole Horizon for her hoop.

[11] Blackmore, *Job,* p. 107.
[12] *Prince Arthur,* p. 157.
[13] Blackmore, *Job,* p. 89.
[14] T. Cooke, *Poems.*
[15] *Poems,* 1693, p. 13.
[16] Welsted, *Poems, Acon and Lavinia.*

4. THE ANTITHESIS, OR SEESAW,

whereby Contraries and Oppositions are balanced in such a way, as to cause a reader to remain suspended between them, to his exceeding delight and recreation. Such are these, on a lady who made herself appear out of size, by hiding a young princess under her clothes.

> While the kind nymph changing her faultless shape
> Becomes *unhandsome, handsomely* to scape.[17]

On the Maids of Honour in mourning:

> Sadly they charm, and dismally they please.[18]

> His eyes so bright
> Let in the object and let out the light.[19]

> The Gods look pale to see us look so red.[20]

> The Fairies and their Queen
> In mantles blue came tripping o'er the green.[21]

> All nature felt a reverential shock,
> The sea stood still to see the mountains rock.[22]

Chapter XI

The Figures continued: Of the Magnifying and Diminishing Figures.

A Genuine Writer of the Profund will take care never to *magnify* any object without *clouding* it at the same time: His Thought will appear in a true mist, and very unlike what is in nature. It must always be remembered that Darkness is an essential quality of the Profund, or, if there chance to be a glimmering, it must be as Milton expresses it,

> No light, but rather darkness visible.

[17] Waller.
[18] Steele on Queen Mary.
[19] Quarles.
[20] Lee, *Alexander.*
[21] Philips, *Pastorals.*
[22] Blackmore, *Job,* p. 176.

The chief Figure of this sort is,

1. THE HYPERBOLE, or Impossible.

For instance, of a Lion.

He roared so loud, and looked so wondrous grim,
His very shadow durst not follow him.[1]

Of a Lady at Dinner.

The silver whiteness that adorns thy neck,
Sullies the plate, and makes the napkin black.

Of the same.

Th' obscureness of her birth
Cannot eclipse the lustre of her eyes,
Which make her all one light.[2]

Of a Bull-baiting.

Up to the stars the sprawling mastiffs fly,
And add new monsters to the frighted sky.[3]

Of a Scene of Misery

Behold a scene of misery and woe!
Here Argus soon might weep himself quite blind,
Even though he had Briareus' hundred hands
To wipe those hundred eyes.[4]

And that modest request of two absent lovers:

Ye Gods! annihilate but Space and Time,
And make two lovers happy.

2. THE PERIPHRASIS,

which the Moderns call the *Circumbendibus,* whereof we have
given examples in the ninth chapter, and shall again in the
twelfth.

[1] *Vetus Autor.*
[2] Theobald, *Double Falsehood.*
[3] Blackmore.
[4] Anonymous.

To the same class of the *Magnifying* may be referred the following, which are so excellently modern, that we have yet no name for them. In describing a country prospect,

> I'd call them mountains, but can't call them so,
> For fear to wrong them with a name too low;
> While the fair vales beneath so humbly lie,
> That even humble seems a term too high.[5]

III. The third Class remains, of the *Diminishing* Figures: And 1. the ANTICLIMAX, where the second line drops quite short of the first, than which nothing creates greater surprise.

On the extent of the British Arms.

> Under the Tropics is our language spoke,
> And part of Flanders hath received our Yoke.[6]

On a Warrior.

> And thou Dalhousie the great God of War,
> Lieutenant Colonel to the Earl of Mar.[7]

On the Valour of the English.

> Nor *Art* nor *Nature* has the force
> To stop its steady course,
> Nor *Alps* nor *Pyreneans* keep it out,
> Nor fortified Redoubt.[8]

At other times this figure operates in a larger extent, and when the gentle reader is in expectation of some great image, he either finds it surprisingly imperfect, or is presented with something low, or quite ridiculous. A surprise resembling that of a curious person in a cabinet of Antique Statues, who beholds on the pedestal the names of Homer, or Cato; but looking up, finds Homer without a head, and nothing to be seen of Cato but his privy member. Such are these lines of a Leviathan at sea,

[5] Anonymous.
[6] Waller.
[7] Anonymous.
[8] Dennis [*Ode on the Battle of Aghrim*].

His motion works, and beats the oozy mud,
And with its slime incorporates the flood,
Till all th' encumbered, thick, fermenting stream
Does like *one Pot of boiling Ointment seem.*
Where'er he swims, he leaves along the lake
Such frothy furrows, such a foamy track,
That all the waters of the deep appear
Hoary . . . with age, or *grey* with sudden fear.[9]

But perhaps even these are excelled by the ensuing.

Now the resisted flames and fiery store,
By winds assaulted, in wide forges roar,
And raging seas flow down of melted Ore.
Sometimes they bear long *Iron Bars removed,*
And *to* and *fro* huge *Heaps of Cinders shoved.*[10]

2. THE VULGAR,

is also a Species of the *Diminishing:* by this a spear flying into
the air is compared to a boy whistling as he goes on an errand.

The mighty *Stuffa* threw a massy spear,
Which, with its *Errand pleased, sung* through the air.[11]

A Man raging with grief to a Mastiff Dog:

I cannot stifle this gigantic woe,
Nor on my raging grief a *muzzle* throw.[12]

And Clouds big with water to a woman in great necessity:

Distended with the *Waters* in 'em pent,
The clouds *hang deep* in air, but *hang unrent.*

3. THE INFANTINE.

This is when a Poet grows so very simple, as to think and

---

[9] Blackmore, *Job,* p. 197.
[10] *Prince Arthur,* p. 157.
[11] *Prince Arthur.*
[12] Blackmore, *Job,* p. 41.

talk like a child. I shall take my examples from the greatest
Master in this way: Hear how he fondles, like a mere stammerer.

> *Little Charm* of placid mien,
> *Miniature* of beauty's queen,
> Hither, British muse of *mine,*
> Hither, all ye *Grecian Nine,*
> With the lovely Graces *Three,*
> And your *pretty Nurseling* see.
>
> When the meadows next are seen,
> Sweet enamel, white and green.
> When again the *lambkins* play,
> *Pretty Sportlings* full of *May.*
>
> Then the necks so white and round,
> (*Little Neck* with brilliants bound.)
> And thy *Gentleness* of mind,
> (*Gentle* from a *gentle* kind) etc.
> *Happy* thrice, and *thrice agen,*
> *Happiest* he of *happy* men, etc.[13]

and the rest of those excellent Lullabies of his composition.

How prettily he asks the sheep to teach him to bleat?

Teach me to grieve with bleating moan, my sheep.[14]

Hear how a babe would reason on his nurse's death:

> That ever she *could* die! Oh most *unkind!*
> To die, and leave poor *Colinet* behind?
> And yet, . . . Why blame I her?[15]

With no less simplicity does he suppose that shepherdesses
tear their hair and beat their breasts, at their own deaths:

> Ye brighter maids, faint emblems of my fair,
> With looks cast down, and with disheveled hair,

[13] [Ambrose Philips on Miss C——.]
[14] Philips, *Pastorals.*
[15] *Idem.*

In bitter anguish beat your breast, and moan
Her death untimely, *as it were your own.*[16]

4. THE INANITY, OR NOTHINGNESS.

Of this the same author furnishes us with most beautiful instances:

Ah silly I, more silly than my sheep,
(Which on the flowery plain I once did keep.)[17]

To the grave Senate she could counsel give,
(Which with astonishment they did receive.)[18]

He whom loud cannon could not terrify,
Falls (from the grandeur of his Majesty.)[19]

Happy merry as a king,
Sipping dew, you sip, and sing.[20]

The *Noise* returning with returning *Light,*

What did it?

Dispersed the *Silence,* and dispelled the *Night.*[21]

You easily perceive the Nothingness of every second Verse.

The glories of proud *London* to survey,
The Sun himself shall rise . . . by break of day.[22]

5. THE EXPLETIVE,

admirably exemplified in the Epithets of many authors.

Th' umbrageous shadow, and the verdant green,

[16] *Idem.*
[17] *Idem.*
[18] Philips on Queen Mary.
[19] *Idem.*
[20] *Autor Vetus.*
[21] T. Cooke, *On a Grasshopper.*
[22] Anonymous.

The running current, and odorous fragrance,
Cheer my lone solitude, with joyous gladness.

Or in pretty drawling words like these,
All men this tomb, all men his adore,
And his sons' sons, till there shall be no more.[23]

The rising sun our grief did see,
The setting sun did see the same,
While wretched we remembred thee,
O Sion, Sion, lovely name.[24]

6. THE MACROLOGY AND PLEONASM

are as generally coupled, as a lean rabbit with a fat one; nor is it a wonder, the superfluity of words and vacuity of sense, being just the same thing. I am pleased to see one of our greatest adversaries employ this figure.

The growth of meadows, and the pride of fields.
The food of armies and support of wars.
Refuse of swords, and gleanings of a fight.
Lessen his numbers, and contract his host.
Where'er his friends retire, or foes succeed.
Covered with tempests, and in oceans drowned.[25]

Of all which the Perfection is

THE TAUTOLOGY.

Break through the billows, and . . . divide the main.[26]
In smoother numbers, and . . . in softer verse.

Divide—and *part*—the *severed* World—*in two*.[27]

With ten thousand others equally musical, and plentifully flowing through most of our celebrated modern Poems.

[23] T. Cooke, *Poems.*
[24] *Idem.*
[25] Addison, *Campaign,* [ll. 281, 192, 268, 168, 190].
[26] [*Campaign,* l. 199.]
[27] Tonson's *Miscellany,* 12°, Vol. VI, p. 121, 4th ed.

Chapter XII

Of Expression, and the several Sorts of Style of the present Age.

The *Expression* is adequate, when it is proportionably low to the Profundity of the Thought. It must not be always *Grammatical,* lest it appear pedantic and ungentlemanly; nor too clear, for fear it becomes vulgar; for obscurity bestows a cast of the wonderful, and throws an oracular dignity upon a piece which hath no meaning.

For example, sometimes use the wrong Number; *The Sword and Pestilence at once devours,* instead of *devour.* Sometimes the wrong Case; *And who more fit to soothe the God than thee?*[1] instead of *thou:* And rather than say, *Thetis saw Achilles weep,* she *heard* him weep.

We must be exceeding careful in two things; first, in the *Choice* of *low Words:* secondly, in the *sober* and *orderly* way of *ranging* them. Many of our Poets are naturally blessed with this talent, insomuch that they are in the circumstance of that honest Citizen, who had made *Prose* all his life without knowing it. Let verses run in this manner, just to be a vehicle to the words: (I take them from my last cited author, who, though otherwise by no means of our rank, seemed once in his life to have a mind to be simple.)

> If not, a prize I will myself decree,
> From him, or him, or else perhaps from thee.[2]

>   full of Days was he;
> Two ages past, he lived the third to see.[3]

> The king of forty kings, and honoured more
> By mighty Jove than e'er was king before.[4]

> That I may know, if thou my prayer deny,
> The most despised of all the Gods am I.[5]

[1] Tickell, *Homer's Iliad,* i.
[2] P. 11.
[3] P. 17.
[4] P. 19.
[5] P. 34.

Then let my mother once be ruled by me,
Though much more wise than I pretend to be.[6]

Or these of the same hand.

I leave the arts of poetry and verse
To them that practise them with more success:
Of greater truths I now prepare to tell,
And so at once, dear friend and muse, farewell.[7]

Sometimes a single *Word* will vulgarize a poetical idea; as where a Ship set on fire owes all the *Spirit* of the *Bathos* to one choice word that ends the line.

And his scorched ribs the hot Contagion *fried*.[8]

And in that description of a World in ruins,

Should the whole frame of nature round him break,
He unconcerned would hear the mighty *Crack*.[9]

So also in these,

Beasts tame and savage to the river's brink
Come, from the fields and wild abodes—to *drink*.[10]

Frequently two or three words will do it effectually,

He from the clouds does the *sweet liquor squeeze*,
That cheers the *Forest and the Garden* trees.[11]

It is also useful to employ *Technical Terms*, which estrange your style from the great and general ideas of nature: and the higher your subject is, the lower should you search into mechanics for your expression. If you describe the garment of an angel, say that his *Linen* was *finely spun*, and *bleached on the happy Plains*.[11a] Call an army of angels, *Angelic Cuirassiers*,[12] and, if

---

[6] P. 38.
[7] *Tonson's Miscellany*, 12°, Vol. IV, p. 292, 4th ed.
[8] *Prince Arthur*, p. 151.
[9] *Tonson's Miscellany*, Vol. VI, p. 119.
[10] Blackmore, *Psalm* 104, p. 263.
[11] *Idem*, p. 264.
[11a] *Prince Arthur*, p. 19.
[12] P. 339.

you have occasion to mention a number of misfortunes, style them

> Fresh *Troops* of Pains, and *regimented* Woes.[13]

STYLE is divided by the Rhetoricians into the Proper and the Figured. Of the Figured we have already treated, and the Proper is what our authors have nothing to do with. Of Styles we shall mention only the Principal which owe to the moderns either their chief Improvement, or entire Invention.

1. THE FLORID STYLE,

than which none is more proper to the Bathos, as flowers, which are the *Lowest* of vegetables, are most *Gaudy,* and do many times grow in great plenty at the bottom of *Ponds* and *Ditches.*

A fine writer in this kind presents you with the following Posy:

> The groves appear all dressed with wreaths of flowers,
> And from their leaves drop aromatic showers,
> Whose fragrant heads in mystic twines above,
> Exchanged their sweets, and mixed with thousand kisses,
> As if the willing branches strove
> To beautify and shade the grove, . . .[14]

(which indeed most branches do.) But this is still excelled by our Laureate,

> Branches in branches twined compose the grove,
> And shoot and spread, and blossom into love.
> The trembling palms their mutual vows repeat,
> And bending poplars bending poplars meet.
> The distant platanes seem to press more nigh,
> And to the sighing alders, alders sigh.[15]

Hear also our Homer.

---

[13] Blackmore, *Job,* p. 86.
[14] Behn, *Poems,* p. 2.
[15] *Guardian,* 12°, p. 127.

His *Robe of State* is formed of light refined,
An endless *Train* of lustre *spreads behind.*
His throne's of bright *compacted Glory* made,
With *Pearl* celestial, and with Gems *inlaid:*
Whence *Floods* of joy, and *Seas* of splendor flow,
On all th' angelic gazing throng below.[16]

2. THE PERT STYLE.

This does in as peculiar manner become the low in wit, as
a pert air does the low in stature. Mr. *Thomas Brown,* the au-
thor of the *London Spy,* and all the *Spies* and *Trips* in general,
are herein to be diligently studied: In Verse Mr. *Cibber's Pro-
logues.*

But the beauty and energy of it is never so conspicuous, as
when it is employed in *Modernizing* and *Adapting* to the *Taste
of the Times* the works of the *Ancients.* This we rightly phrase
Doing them into English, and *Making* them English; two ex-
pressions of great Propriety, the one denoting our *Neglect* of the
Manner how, the other the *Force* and *Compulsion* with which
it is brought about. It is by virtue of this Style that Tacitus talks
like a Coffeehouse Politician, Josephus like the British Gazetteer,
Tully is as short and smart as Seneca or Mr. Asgill, Marcus
Aurelius is excellent at Snipsnap, and honest Thomas à Kempis
as Prim and Polite as any preacher at court.

3. THE ALAMODE STYLE,

which is fine by being *new,* and has this happiness attending
it, that it is as durable and extensive as the poem itself. Take
some examples of it, in the description of the Sun in a Mourn-
ing coach upon the death of Queen Mary.

See *Phœbus* now, as once for *Phaethon,*
Has masked his face, and put deep *Mourning* on;
Dark clouds his *sable Chariot* do surround,
And the *dull Steeds stalk o'er* the *melancholy round.*[17]

[16] Blackmore, *Psalm* 104, p. 259.
[17] Ambrose Philips.

Of Prince Arthur's Soldiers drinking.

While rich *Burgundian* wine, and bright *Champagne*
Chase from their minds the terrors of the main.[18]

(whence we also learn, that *Burgundy* and *Champagne* make
a man on shore despise a storm at sea.)

Of the Almighty encamping his Regiments.

He sunk a vast capacious deep,
Where he his *liquid Regiments* does keep,
Thither the waves *file off,* and make their way,
To form the *mighty body* of the sea;
Where they *encamp,* and in their *station stand,*
Entrenched in *Works* of *Rock,* and *Lines* of Sand.[19]

Of two Armies on the Point of engaging.

Yon armies are the *Cards* which both must play;
At least come off a *Saver* if you may:
Throw boldly at the *Sum* the Gods have *set;*
These on your side will all their fortunes *bet.*[20]

All perfectly agreeable to the present Customs and best Fashions
of our Metropolis.

But the principal branch of the *Alamode* is the PRURIENT,
a Style greatly advanced and honoured of late by the practice
of persons of the *first Quality;* and by the encouragement of
the *Ladies,* not unsuccessfully introduced even into the Draw-
ing room. Indeed its incredible Progress and Conquests may be
compared to those of the great *Sesostris,* and are everywhere
known by the *same Marks,* the images of the genital parts of
men or women. It consists wholly of metaphors drawn from two
most fruitful sources or springs, the very Bathos of the human
body, that is to say ... and ... *Hiatus magnus lachrymabilis...*

. . . .

And *selling of Bargains,* and *double Entendre,* and

[18] *Prince Arthur,* p. 16.
[19] Blackmore, *Psalm* 104, p. 261.
[20] Lee, *Sophonisba.*

Κιββέρισμος and Ὀλδφιέλδισμος, all derived from the said
sources.

4. THE FINICAL STYLE,

which consists of the most curious, affected, mincing metaphors,
and partakers of the *alamode*.

As this, of a Brook dried by the Sun.

> *Won* by the summer's *importuning* ray,
> Th' *eloping* stream did from her channel stray,
> And with *enticing* sunbeams *stole away*.[21]

Of an easy Death.

> When watchful death shall on his harvest look,
> And see thee ripe with age, *invite* the hook;
> He'll *gently* cut thy *bending* Stalk, and thee
> Lay *kindly* in the *Grave*, his *Granary*.[22]

Of Trees in a Storm

> Oaks whose extended arms the winds defy,
> The tempest *sees* their strength, *and sighs, and passes by*.[23]

Of Water simmering over the Fire.

> The sparkling flames raise water to a *Smile*,
> Yet the *pleased* liquor *pines*, and lessens all the while.[24]

5. Lastly, I shall place THE CUMBROUS,

which moves heavily under a load of metaphors, and draws after
it a long train of words. And the BUSKIN, or *Stately*, frequently
and with great felicity mixed with the former. For as the first
is the proper engine to depress what is high, so is the second
to raise what is base and low to a ridiculous Visibility: When

---

[21] Blackmore, *Job*, p. 26.
[22] *Idem*, p. 23.
[23] Dennis.
[24] Anonymous, Tonson's *Miscellany*, Part VI, p. 224.

both these can be done at once, then is the Bathos in perfection; as when a man is set with his head downward, and his breech upright, his degradation is complete: One end of him is as *high* as ever, only that end is the *wrong one*. Will not every true lover of the Profund be delighted to behold the most vulgar and low actions of life exalted in the following manner?

Who knocks at the Door?

For whom thus rudely pleads my loud-tongued gate,
That he may enter? . . .

See who is there?

Advance the fringed curtains of thy eyes,
And tell me who comes yonder.. . .[25]

Shut the Door.

The wooden guardian of our privacy
Quick on its axle turn. . . .

Bring my Clothes.

Bring me what Nature, tailor to the *Bear*,
To *Man* himself denied: She gave me Cold,
But would not give me Clothes. . . .

Light the Fire.

Bring forth some remnant of *Promethean* theft,
Quick to expand th' inclement air congealed
By *Boreas'* rude breath. . . .

Snuff the Candle.

Yon Luminary amputation needs,
Thus shall you save its half-extinguished life.

Open the Letter.

Wax! render up thy trust. . . .[26]

Uncork the Bottle, and chip the Bread.

[25] *Tempest*.
[26] Theobald, *Double Falsehood*.

> Apply thine engine to the spongy door,
> Set *Bacchus* from his glassy prison free,
> And strip white *Ceres* of her nut-brown coat.

Chapter XIII

A Project for the Advancement of the Bathos.

Thus have I (my dear Countrymen) with incredible pains and diligence, discovered the hidden sources of the *Bathos,* or, as I may say, broke open the Abysses of this *Great Deep.* And having now established good and wholesome Laws, what remains but that all true moderns with their utmost might do proceed to put the same in execution? In order whereto, I think I shall in the second place highly deserve of my Country, by proposing such a *Scheme,* as may facilitate this great end.

As our Number is confessedly far superior to that of the enemy, there seems nothing wanting but Unanimity among ourselves. It is therefore humbly offered, that all and every individual of the Bathos do enter into a firm association, and incorporate into One regular Body, whereof every member, even the meanest, will some way contribute to the support of the whole; in like manner, as the weakest reeds, when joined in one bundle, become infrangible. To which end our Art ought to be put upon the same foot with other Arts of this age. The vast improvement of modern manufactures ariseth from their being divided into several branches, and parcelled out to several trades: For instance, in Clock-making one artist makes the balance, another the spring, another the crown-wheels, a fourth the case, and the principal workman puts all together: To this economy we owe the perfection of our modern watches, and doubtless we also might that of our modern Poetry and Rhetoric, were the several parts branched out in the like manner.

Nothing is more evident than that divers persons, no other way remarkable, have each a strong disposition to the formation of some particular Trope or Figure. Aristotle saith, that the *Hyperbole* is an ornament fit for young Men of Quality; accordingly we find in those Gentlemen a wonderful propensity toward it, which is marvelously improved by Traveling: Soldiers also and Seamen are very happy in the same Figure. The *Periphrasis* or *Circumlocution* is the peculiar talent of Country Farmers; the *Proverb* and *Apologue* of old Men at their clubs; the *Ellipsis* or Speech by half words, of Ministers and Politicians, the *Aposiopesis* of Courtiers, the *Litotes* or Diminution of Ladies, Whisperers and Backbiters, and the *Anadiplosis* of common Cryers and Hawkers, who, by redoubling the same words, persuade people to buy their oysters, green hastings, or new ballads. *Epithets* may be found in great plenty at Billingsgate, *Sarcasm* and *Irony* learned upon the Water, and the *Epiphonema* or *Exclamation* frequently from the Beargarden, and as frequently from the *Hear him* of the House of Commons.

Now each man applying his whole time and genius upon his particular Figure, would doubtless attain to perfection; and when each became incorporated and sworn into the Society (as hath been proposed) a Poet or Orator would have no more to do but to send to the particular Traders in each Kind, to the *Metaphorist* for his *Allegories,* to the *Simile-maker* for his *Comparisons,* to the *Ironist* for his *Sarcasms,* to the *Apothegmatist* for his *Sentences,* etc. whereby a Dedication or Speech would be composed in a moment, the superior artist having nothing to do but to put together all the Materials.

I therefore propose that there be contrived with all convenient dispatch, at the public expense a *Rhetorical Chest of Drawers,* consisting of three Stories, the highest for the *Deliberative,* the middle for the *Demonstrative,* and the lowest for the *Judicial.* These shall be divided into *Loci,* or *Places,* being repositories for Matter and Argument in the several kinds of oration or writing; and every Drawer shall again be subdivided into Cells, resembling those of Cabinets for Rarities. The apartment for *Peace* or *War,* and that of the *Liberty of the Press,* may in a very few days be filled with several arguments perfectly new; and the *Vituperative Partition* will as easily be replenished with a most choice collection, entirely of the growth and manufacture of the present age. Every composer will soon be taught the use of this Cabinet, and how to manage all the Registers of it, which will be drawn out much in the manner of those in an Organ.

The Keys of it must be kept in honest hands, by some Reverend Prelate, or *Valiant Officer,* of unquestioned Loyalty and Affection to every present Establishment in Church and State; which will sufficiently guard against any mischief which might otherwise be apprehended from it.

And being lodged in such hands, it may be at discretion *let out* by the *Day,* to several great Orators in both Houses; from whence it is to be hoped much *Profit* and *Gain* will also accrue to our Society.

Chapter XIV

How to make Dedications, Panegyrics, or Satires, and of the Colours of Honourable and Dishonourable.

Now of what necessity the foregoing Project may prove, will appear from this single consideration, that nothing is of equal consequence to the success of our Works, as *Speed* and *Dispatch*. Great pity it is, that solid brains are not like other solid bodies, constantly endowed with a velocity in sinking, proportioned to their heaviness: For it is with the Flowers of the Bathos as with those of Nature, which if the careful gardener brings not hastily to market in the Morning, must unprofitably perish and wither before Night. And of all our Productions none is so short-lived as the *Dedication* and *Panegyric,* which are often but the *Praise of a Day,* and become by the next, utterly useless, improper, indecent, and false. This is the more to be lamented, inasmuch as these two are the sorts whereon in a manner depends that *Profit,* which must still be remembered to be the main end of our *Writers* and *Speakers*.

We shall therefore employ this chapter in showing the quickest method of composing them; after which we will teach a *short Way to Epic Poetry*. And these being confessedly the works of most Importance and Difficulty, it is presumed we may leave the rest to each author's own learning or practice.

First of *Panegyric:* Every man is *honourable,* who is so

by Law, Custom, or Title. The *Public* are better judges of what
is honourable than private Men. The Virtues of great Men,
like those of Plants, are inherent in them whether they are ex-
erted or not; and the more strongly inherent, the less they are
exerted; as a Man is the more rich, the less he spends. All great
Ministers, without either private or economical Virtue, are *vir-
tuous* by their *Posts;* liberal and generous upon the *Public Money,*
provident upon *Public Supplies,* just by paying *Public Interest,*
courageous and magnanimous by the *Fleets and Armies,* mag-
nificent upon the *Public Expenses,* and prudent by *Public Suc-
cess.* They have by their Office, a right to a share of the *Public
Stock* of Virtues; besides they are by *Prescription immemorial*
invested in all the celebrated virtues of their *Predecessors* in the
same stations, especially those of their own Ancestors.

As to what are commonly called the *Colours* of *Honour-
able* and *Dishonourable,* they are various in different Countries:
In this they are *Blue, Green,* and *Red.*

But forasmuch as the duty we owe to the Public doth
often require that we should put some things in a strong light,
and throw a shade over others, I shall explain the method of
turning a vicious Man into a Hero.

The first and chief rule is the *Golden Rule* of *Transforma-
tion,* which consists in converting Vices into their bordering
Virtues. A Man who is a Spendthrift, and will not pay a just
Debt, may have his Injustice *transformed* into Liberality;
Cowardice may be metamorphosed into Prudence; Intemperance
into good Nature and good Fellowship; Corruption into Pa-
triotism; and Lewdness into Tenderness and Facility.

The second is the *Rule of Contraries:* It is certain, the less
a Man in endued with any Virtue, the more need he has to
have it plentifully bestowed, especially those good qualities of
which the world generally believes he hath none at all: For who
will thank a Man for giving him that which he *has?*

The Reverse of these Precepts will serve for *Satire,* wherein
we are ever to remark, that whoso loseth his place, or becomes
out of favour with the Government, hath forfeited his share in
public Praise and *Honour.* Therefore the truly public-spirited
writer ought in duty to strip him whom the government hath

stripped; which is the real *poetical Justice* of this age. For a full collection of Topics and Epithets to be used in the Praise and Dispraise of Ministerial and Unministerial Persons, I refer to our *Rhetorical Cabinet;* concluding with an earnest exhortation to all my brethren, to observe the Precepts here laid down, the neglect of which hath cost some of them their *Ears* in a *Pillory.*

Chapter XV

A Receipt to make an Epic Poem.

An Epic Poem, the Critics agree, is the greatest work human nature is capable of. They have already laid down many mechanical rules for compositions of this sort, but at the same time they cut off almost all undertakers from the possibility of ever performing them; for the first qualification they unanimously require in a Poet, is a *Genius.* I shall here endeavour (for the benefit of my Countrymen) to make it manifest, that Epic Poems may be made *without a Genius,* nay without Learning or much Reading. This must necessarily be of great use to all those who confess they never *Read,* and of whom the world is convinced they never *Learn.* Molière observes of making a dinner, that any man can do it with *Money,* and if a professed Cook cannot do it without, he has his Art for nothing; the same may be said of making a Poem, 'tis easily brought about by him that has a *Genius,* but the skill lies in doing it without one. In pursuance of this end, I shall present the reader with a plain and certain *Recipe,* by which any author in the Bathos may be qualified for this grand performance.

For the **FABLE.**

Take out of any old Poem, History book, Romance, or Legend (for instance, *Geoffrey of Monmouth,* or *Don Belianis of Greece*) those parts of story which afford most scope for *long Descriptions:* Put these pieces together, and throw all the adventures you fancy into *one Tale.* Then take a Hero, whom you may choose for the sound of his name, and put him into the midst of these adventures: There let him *work* for twelve books; at the end of which you may take him out, ready prepared to *conquer* or to *marry;* it being necessary that the conclusion of an Epic Poem be *fortunate.*

To make an EPISODE.

Take any remaining adventure of your former collection, in which you could no way involve your Hero; or any unfortunate accident that was too good to be thrown away; and it will be of use, applied to any other person, who may be lost and *evaporate* in the course of the work, without the least damage to the composition.

For the MORAL AND ALLEGORY.

These you may extract out of the Fable afterwards, at your leisure: Be sure you *strain* them sufficiently.

For the MANNERS.

For those of the Hero, take all the best qualities you can find in the most celebrated Heroes of antiquity; if they will not be reduced to a *Consistency,* lay them *all on a heap* upon him. But be sure they are qualities which your *Patron* would be thought to have; and to prevent any mistake which the world may be subject to, select from the alphabet those capital letters that compose his name, and set them at the head of a Dedication before your Poem. However, do not absolutely observe the exact quantity of these Virtues, it not being determined whether or no it be necessary for the Hero of a Poem to be an *honest Man.* For the *Under Characters,* gather them from Homer and Virgil, and change the names as occasion serves.

For the MACHINES.

Take of *Deities,* male and female, as many as you can use:

Separate them into two equal parts, and keep Jupiter in the middle; Let Juno put him in a ferment, and Venus mollify him. Remember on all occasions to make use of volatile Mercury. If you have need of *Devils,* draw them out of Milton's Paradise, and extract your *Spirits* from Tasso. The use of these Machines is evident; since no Epic Poem can possibly subsist without them, the wisest way is to reserve them for your greatest necessities: When you cannot extricate your Hero by any human means, or yourself by your own wit, seek relief from Heaven, and the Gods will do your business very readily. This is according to the direct Prescription of Horace in his Art of Poetry,

> Nec Deus intersit, nisi dignus vindice *Nodus*
> Inciderit. . . .

That is to say, A Poet should never call upon the Gods for their Assistance, but when he is in great Perplexity.

For the DESCRIPTIONS.

For a *Tempest.* Take Eurus, Zephyr, Auster, and Boreas, and cast them together in one verse: add to these of Rain, Lightning and Thunder (the loudest you can) *quantum sufficit:* mix your Clouds and Billows well together till they foam, and thicken your Description here and there with a Quicksand. Brew your Tempest well in your head, before you set it a blowing.

For a *Battle.* Pick a large quantity of Images and Descriptions from Homer's *Iliads,* with a spice or two of Virgil, and if there remain any overplus, you may lay them by for a *Skirmish.* Season it well with *Similes,* and it will make an excellent Battle.

For a *Burning Town.* If such a Description be necessary (because it is certain there is one in Virgil) old Troy is ready burnt to your hands. But if you fear that would be thought borrowed, a Chapter or two of the Theory of the *Conflagration,* well circumstanced and done into verse, will be a good *Succedaneum.*

As for *Similes* and *Metaphors,* they may be found all over the Creation; the most ignorant may *gather* them, but the difficulty is in *applying* them. For this advise with your *Bookseller.*

Chapter XVI

A Project for the Advancement of the Stage.

It may be thought that we should not wholly omit the *Drama,* which makes so great and and so lucrative a part of Poetry. But this Province is so well taken care of, by the present *Managers* of the Theatre, that it is perfectly needless to suggest to them any other Methods than they have already practised for the advancement of the Bathos.

Here therefore, in the Name of all our Brethren, let me return our sincere and humble Thanks to the most August Mr. Barton Booth, the most Serene Mr. Robert Wilks, and the most Undaunted Mr. Cooley Cibber; of whom let it be known, *when the People of this Age shall be Ancestors,* and to all *the Succession of our Successors,* that to this present Day they continue to *Outdo* even their *own Outdoings:* And when the inevitable Hand of sweeping Time shall have brushed off all the Works of *Today,* may this Testimony of a *Contemporary Critic* to their Fame, be extended as far as *Tomorrow.*

Yet, if to so wise an Administration it be possible any thing can be added, it is that more ample and comprehensive Scheme which Mr. Dennis and Mr. Gildon (the two greatest Critics and Reformers then living) made public in the year 1720, in a Project signed with their Names, and dated the 2^d of February. I cannot better conclude than by presenting the Reader with the Substance of it.

1. It is proposed, That the two *Theatres* be incorporated into one Company; that the *Royal Academy of Music* be added to them as an *Orchestra;* and that Mr. Figg with his Prize fighters, and Violante with the Ropedancers, be admitted in Partnership.

2. That a spacious Building be erected at the Public expense, capable of containing at least *ten thousand* Spectators, which is become absolutely necessary by the great addition of Children and Nurses to the Audience, since the new Entertainments. That there be a Stage as large as the Athenian, which was near ninety thousand geometrical paces square, and separate divisions for the two Houses of Parliament, my Lords the Judges,

the honourable the Directors of the Academy, and the Court of Aldermen, who shall all have their Places frank.

3. If *Westminster Hall* be not allotted to this service (which by reason of its proximity to the two Chambers of Parliament above-mentioned, seems not altogether improper); it is left to the wisdom of the Nation whether *Somerset House* may not be demolished, and a Theatre built upon that Site, which lies convenient to receive Spectators from the County of *Surrey,* who may be wafted thither by water carriage, esteemed by all Projectors the cheapest whatsoever. To this may be added, that the river *Thames* may in the readiest manner convey those eminent Personages from Courts beyond the seas, who may be drawn either by Curiosity to behold some of our most celebrated Pieces, or by Affection to see their Countrymen, the Harlequins and Eunuchs; of which convenient notice may be given, for two or three months before, in the public Prints.

4. That the *Theatre* abovesaid be environed with a fair Quadrangle of Buildings, fitted for the accommodation of decayed *Critics* and *Poets;* out of whom *Six* of the most aged (their age to be computed from the year wherein their first work was published) shall be elected to manage the affairs of the society, provided nevertheless that the Laureate for the time being, may be always one. The Head or President over all (to prevent disputes, but too frequent among the learned) shall be the most ancient *Poet* and *Critic* to be found in the whole Island.

5. The *Male Players* are to be lodged in the garrets of the said Quadrangle, and to attend the persons of the Poets, dwelling under them, by brushing their apparel, drawing on their shoes, and the like. The *Actresses* are to make their beds, and wash their linen.

6. A large room shall be set apart for a *Library* to consist of all the modern Dramatic Poems, and all the Criticisms extant. In the midst of this room shall be a round table for the *Council of Six* to sit and deliberate on the Merits of *Plays.* The *Majority* shall determine the Dispute; and if it should happen that *three* and *three* should be of each side, the President shall have a *casting Voice,* unless where the Contention may run so high as to require a decision by *Single Combat.*

7. It may be convenient to place the *Council of Six* in some conspicuous situation in the Theatre, where after the manner usually practised by composers in music, they may give *Signs* (before settled and agreed upon) of Dislike or Approbation. In consequence of these Signs the whole audience shall be required to *clap* or *hiss,* that the Town may learn certainly when and how far they ought to be pleased.

8. It is submitted whether it would not be proper to distinguish the *Council of Six* by some particular Habit or Gown of an honourable shape and colour, to which may be added a square Cap and a white Wand.

9. That to prevent unmarried Actresses making away with their Infants, a competent provision be allowed for the nurture of them, who shall for that reason be deemed the *Children of the Society;* and that they may be educated according to the Genius of their parents, the said Actresses shall declare upon Oath (as far as their memory will allow) the true names and qualities of their several fathers. A private Gentleman's Son shall at the public expense be brought up a Page to attend the *Council of Six:* A more ample provision shall be made for the son of a *Poet;* and a greater still for the son of a *Critic*.

10. If it be discovered that any Actress is got with Child, during the Interludes of any Play wherein she hath a Part, it shall be reckoned a neglect of her business, and she shall *forfeit* accordingly. If any Actor for the future shall commit Murder, except upon the stage, he shall be left to the laws of the land; the like is to be understood of *Robbery* and *Theft*. In all other cases, particularly in those for *Debt,* it is proposed that this, like the other Courts of *Whitehall* and *St. James's,* may be held a *Place of Privilege*. And whereas it has been found, that an obligation to satisfy paltry Creditors has been a Discouragement to Men of Letters, if any Person of Quality or others shall send for any *Poet* or *Critic* of this Society to any remote quarter of the town, the said Poet or Critic shall freely pass and repass without being liable to an *Arrest*.

11. The forementioned Scheme in its several regulations may be supported by Profits arising from every Third night throughout the year. And as it would be hard to suppose that

so many persons could live without any food (though from the former course of their lives, *a very little* will be deemed sufficient) the masters of calculation will, we believe, agree, that out of those Profits, the said persons might be subsisted in a sober and decent manner. We will venture to affirm further, that not only the proper magazines of Thunder and Lightning, but *Paint, Diet drinks, Spitting pots,* and all other *Necessaries* of *Life,* may in like manner fairly be provided for.

12. If some of the Articles may at first view seem liable to Objections, particularly those that give so vast a power to the *Council of Six* (which is indeed larger than any entrusted to the great Officers of state) this may be obviated, by swearing those *Six* Persons of his Majesty's Privy Council, and obliging them to pass every thing of moment *previously* at that most honourable Board.

THE DUNCIAD
In Four Books

PREFACE[1]

Prefixed to the five first imperfect Editions of the DUNCIAD, in three
books, printed at DUBLIN and LONDON, in octavo and duodecimo,
1727.[2]

THE PUBLISHER[3] TO THE READER

IT will be found a true observation, though somewhat surprising,
that when any scandal is vented against a man of the highest
distinction and character, either in the state or in literature, the
public in general afford it a most quiet reception; and the larger
part accept it as favourably as if it were some kindness done to
themselves: whereas if a known scoundrel or blockhead but
chance to be touched upon, a whole legion is up in arms, and it
becomes the common cause of all scribblers, booksellers, and
printers whatsoever.

Not to search too deeply into the reason hereof, I will only
observe as a fact, that every week for these two months past, the
town has been persecuted with pamphlets, advertisements, let-

---

[1] Presumably written by Pope himself. The notes beginning with no. 3
on the next page were added by Pope in later editions.
[2] I.e., 1728.

ters, and weekly essays, not only against the wit and writings, but against the character and person of Mr. Pope. And that of all those men who have received pleasure from his works, which by modest computation may be about a hundred thousand in these kingdoms of England and Ireland; (not to mention Jersey, Guernsey, the Orcades, those in the new world, and foreigners who have translated him into their languages) of all this number not a man hath stood up to say one word in his defence.

The only exception is the author[4] of the following poem,

[3] Who he was is uncertain; but Edward Ward tells us, in his preface to *Durgen,* "that most judges are of opinion this preface is not of English extraction, but Hibernian," etc. He means it was written by Dr. Swift, who, whether publisher or not, may be said in a sort to be author of the poem. For when he, together with Mr. Pope (for reasons specified in the preface to their *Miscellanies*) determined to own the most trifling pieces in which they had any hand, and to destroy all that remained in their power; the first sketch of this poem was snatched from the fire by Dr. Swift, who persuaded his friend to proceed in it, and to him it was therefore inscribed. But the occasion of printing it was as follows:

There was published in those *Miscellanies,* a Treatise of the *Bathos, or Art of Sinking in Poetry,* in which was a chapter, where the species of bad writers were ranged in classes, and initial letters of names prefixed, for the most part at random. But such was the Number of Poets eminent in that art, that some one or other took every letter to himself. All fell into so violent a fury, that for half a year, or more, the common Newspapers (in most of which they had some property, as being hired writers) were filled with the most abusive falsehoods and scurrilities they could possibly devise; a liberty no ways to be wondered at in those people, and in those papers, that, for many years, during the uncontrolled Licence of the press, had aspersed almost all the great characters of the age; and this with impunity, their own persons and names being utterly secret and obscure. This gave Mr. Pope the thought, that he had now some opportunity of doing good, by detecting and dragging into light these common Enemies of mankind; since to invalidate this universal slander, it sufficed to show what contemptible men were the authors of it. He was not without hopes, that by manifesting the dulness of those who had only malice to recommend them; either the booksellers would not find their account in employing them, or the men themselves, when discovered, want courage to proceed in so unlawful an occupation. This it was that gave birth to the *Dunciad;* and he thought it an happiness, that by the late flood of slander on himself, he had acquired such a peculiar right over their Names as was necessary to his design. [P.]

[4] A very plain irony, speaking of Mr. Pope himself. [P.]

who doubtless had either a better insight into the grounds of this clamour, or a better opinion of Mr. Pope's integrity, joined with a greater personal love for him, than any other of his numerous friends and admirers.

Farther, that he was in his peculiar intimacy, appears from the knowledge he manifests of the most private authors of all the anonymous pieces against him, and from his having in this poem attacked no man living,[5] who had not before printed, or published, some scandal against this gentleman.

How I came possessed of it, is no concern to the reader; but it would have been a wrong to him had I detained the publication; since those names which are its chief ornaments die off daily so fast, as must render it too soon unintelligible. If it provoke the author to give us a more perfect edition, I have my end.

Who he is I cannot say, and (which is a great pity) there is certainly nothing in his style and manner of writing,[6] which can distinguish or discover him: For if it bears any resemblance to that of Mr. Pope, 'tis not improbable but it might be done on purpose, with a view to have it pass for his. But by the frequency of his allusions to Virgil, and a laboured (not to say affected) *shortness* in imitation of him, I should think him more an admirer of the Roman poet than of the Grecian, and in that not of the same taste with his friend.

I have been well informed, that this work was the labour of full six years of his life,[7] and that he wholly retired himself from all the avocations and pleasures of the world, to attend diligently to its correction and perfection; and six years more he

[5] The publisher in these words went a little too far; but it is certain, whatever names the reader finds that are unknown to him, are of such; and the exception is only of two or three, whose dulness, impudent scurrility, or self-conceit, all mankind agreed to have justly entitled them to a place in the *Dunciad*.   [P.]

[6] This irony had small effect in concealing the author. The *Dunciad*, imperfect as it was, had not been published two days, but the whole Town gave it to Mr. Pope.   [P.]

[7] This was also honestly and seriously believed by divers gentlemen of the *Dunciad*. . . .   [P.]

intended to bestow upon it, as it should seem by this verse of
Statius, which was cited at the head of his manuscript,

> Oh mihi bissenos multum vigilata per annos,
> Duncia![8]

Hence also we learn the true title of the poem; which with
the same certainty as we call that of Homer the *Iliad,* of Virgil
the *Æneid,* of Camoens the *Lusiad,* we may pronounce, could
have been, and can be no other than

THE DUNCIAD.

It is styled *Heroic,* as being *doubly* so; not only with respect
to its nature, which, according to the best rules of the ancients,
and strictest ideas of the moderns, is critically such; but also
with regard to the heroical disposition and high courage of the
writer, who dared to stir up such a formidable, irritable, and
implacable race of mortals.

There may arise some obscurity in chronology from the
Names in the poem, by the inevitable removal of some authors,
and insertion of others, in their niches. For whoever will con-
sider the unity of the whole design will be sensible, that the
*poem was not made for these authors, but these authors for the
poem.* I should judge that they were clapped in as they rose,
fresh and fresh, and changed from day to day; in like manner
as when the old boughs wither, we thrust new ones into a chim-
ney.

I would not have the reader too much troubled or anxious,
if he cannot decipher them; since when he shall have found
them out, he will probably know no more of the persons than
before.

Yet we judged it better to preserve them as they are, than
to change them for fictitious names; by which the satire would
only be multiplied, and applied to many instead of one. Had
the hero, for instance, been called Codrus, how many would

---

[8] The prefacer to Curll's *Key,* p. 3, took this word to be really in Statius.
"By a quibble on the word *Duncia,* the *Dunciad* is formed. . . ."   [P.]

have affirmed him to have been Mr. T., Mr. E., Sir R. B., etc., but now all that unjust scandal is saved by calling him by a name, which by good luck happens to be that of a real person.

ADVERTISEMENT

To the FIRST EDITION *with Notes, in Quarto, 1729*[9]

IT will be sufficient to say of this edition, that the reader has here a much more correct and complete copy of the DUNCIAD, than has hitherto appeared. I cannot answer but some mistakes may have slipped into it, but a vast number of others will be prevented by the names being now not only set at length, but justified by the authorities and reasons given. I make no doubt, the author's own motive to use real rather than feigned names, was his care to preserve the innocent from any false application; whereas in the former editions, which had no more than the initial letters, he was made, by keys printed here, to hurt the inoffensive; and (what was worse) to abuse his friends, by an impression at Dublin.

The commentary which attends this poem was sent me from several hands, and consequently must be unequally written; yet will have one advantage over most commentaries, that it is not made upon conjectures, or at a remote distance of time: And the reader cannot but derive one pleasure from the very *Obscurity* of the persons it treats of, that it partakes of the nature of a *Secret,* which most people love to be let into, though the men or the things be ever so inconsiderable or trivial.

Of the *Persons* it was judged proper to give some account: For since it is only in this monument that they must expect to survive (and here survive they will, as long as the English tongue shall remain such as it was in the reigns of Queen ANNE and King GEORGE) it seemed but humanity to bestow a word or two upon each, just to tell what he was, what he writ, when he lived, and when he died.

[9] I.e., *The Dunciad, Variorum, with the Prolegomena of Scriblerus.* London, Printed for A. Dod[d], 1729.

If a word or two more are added upon the chief offenders, 'tis only as a paper pinned upon the breast, to mark the enormities for which they suffered; lest the correction only should be remembered, and the crime forgotten.

In some articles it was thought sufficient, barely to transcribe from Jacob, Curll, and other writers of their own rank, who were much better acquainted with them than any of the authors of this comment can pretend to be. Most of them had drawn each other's characters on certain occasions; but the few here inserted are all that could be saved from the general destruction of such works.

Of the part of Scriblerus I need say nothing; his manner is well enough known, and approved by all but those who are too much concerned to be judges.

The Imitations of the Ancients are added, to gratify those who either never read, or may have forgotten them; together with some of the parodies and allusions to the most excellent of the Moderns. If, from the frequency of the former, any man think the poem too much a Cento, our Poet will but appear to have done the same thing in jest which Boileau did in earnest; and upon which Vida, Fracastorius, and many of the most eminent Latin poets, professedly valued themselves.

A LETTER TO THE PUBLISHER

Occasioned by the First Correct Edition[10] *of the Dunciad*

IT is with pleasure I hear, that you have procured a correct copy of the DUNCIAD, which the many surreptitious ones have rendered so necessary; and it is yet with more, that I am informed it will be attended with a COMMENTARY: a Work so requisite, that I cannot think the Author himself would have omitted it, had he approved of the first appearance of this Poem.

Such *Notes* as have occurred to me I herewith send you: You will oblige me by inserting them amongst those which are,

[10] *The Dunciad Variorum* of 1729. The Letter was printed in this edition. Despite the signature of William Cleland (p. 373), the letter is commonly considered the work of Pope.

or will be, transmitted to you by others; since not only the Author's friends, but even strangers, appear engaged by humanity, to take some care of an Orphan of so much genius and spirit, which its parent seems to have abandoned from the very beginning, and suffered to step into the world naked, unguarded, and unattended.

It was upon reading some of the abusive papers lately published, that my great regard to a Person, whose Friendship I esteem as one of the chief honours of my life, and a much greater respect to Truth, than to him or any man living, engaged me in inquiries, of which the enclosed *Notes* are the fruit.

I perceived, that most of these Authors had been (doubtless very wisely) the first aggressors. They had tried, till they were weary, what was to be got by railing at each other: Nobody was either concerned or surprised, if this or that scribbler was proved a dunce. But every one was curious to read what could be said to prove Mr. POPE one, and was ready to pay something for such a discovery: A stratagem, which would they fairly own, it might not only reconcile them to me, but screen them from the resentment of their lawful Superiors, whom they daily abuse, only (as I charitably hope) to get that *by* them, which they cannot get *from* them.

I found this was not all: Ill success in that had transported them to Personal abuse, either of himself, or (what I think he could less forgive) of his Friends. They had called Men of virtue and honour bad Men, long before he had either leisure or inclination to call them bad Writers: And some had been such old offenders, that he had quite forgotten their persons as well as their slanders, till they were pleased to revive them.

Now what had Mr. POPE done before, to incense them? He had published those works which are in the hands of everybody, in which not the least mention is made of any of them. And what has he done since? He has laughed, and written the DUNCIAD. What has that said of them? A very serious truth, which the public had said before, that they were dull: And what it had no sooner said, but they themselves were at great pains to procure or even purchase room in the prints, to testify under their hands to the truth of it.

I should still have been silent, if either I had seen any inclination in my friend to be serious with such accusers, or if they had only meddled with his Writings; since whoever publishes, puts himself on his trial by his Country. But when his Moral character was attacked, and in a manner from which neither truth nor virtue can secure the most innocent—in a manner, which, though it annihilates the credit of the accusation with the just and impartial, yet aggravates very much the guilt of the accusers; I mean by Authors *without names*—then I thought, since the danger was common to all, the concern ought to be so; and that it was an act of justice to detect the Authors, not only on this account, but as many of them are the same who for several years past have made free with the greatest names in Church and State, exposed to the world the private misfortunes of Families, abused all, even to Women, and whose prostituted papers (for one or other Party, in the unhappy divisions of their Country) have insulted the Fallen, the Friendless, the Exiled, and the Dead.

Besides this, which I take to be a public concern, I have already confessed I had a private one. I am one of that number who have long loved and esteemed Mr. POPE; and had often declared it was not his capacity or writings (which we ever thought the least valuable part of his character), but the honest, open, and beneficent man, that we most esteemed, and loved in him. Now, if what these people say were believed, I must appear to all my friends either a fool, or a knave; either imposed on myself, or imposing on them; so that I am as much interested in the confutation of these calumnies, as he is himself.

I am no Author, and consequently not to be suspected either of jealousy or resentment against any of the Men, of whom scarce one is known to me by sight; and as for their Writings, I have sought them (on this one occasion) in vain, in the closets and libraries of all my acquaintance. I had still been in the dark, if a Gentleman had not procured me (I suppose from some of themselves, for they are generally much more dangerous friends than enemies) the passages I send you. I solemnly protest I have added nothing to the malice or absurdity of them; which it behoves me to declare, since the vouchers themselves will be so soon and so irrecoverably lost. You may in some measure prevent it, by preserving at least their Titles, and discovering (as far as you can depend on the truth of your information) the Names of the concealed authors.

The first objection I have heard made to the Poem is, that the persons are too *obscure* for satire. The persons themselves, rather than allow the objection, would forgive the satire; and if one could be tempted to afford it a serious answer, were not all assassinates, popular insurrections, the insolence of the rabble without doors, and of domestics within, most wrongfully chastised, if the Meanness of offenders indemnified them from punishment? On the contrary, Obscurity renders them more dangerous, as less thought of: Law can pronounce judgment only on open facts; Morality alone can pass censure on intentions of mischief; so that for secret calumny, or the arrow flying in the dark, there is no public punishment left, but what a good Writer inflicts.

The next objection is, that these sort of authors are *poor*. That might be pleaded as an excuse at the Old Bailey, for lesser crimes than Defamation (for 'tis the case of almost all who are tried there), but sure it can be none: For who will pretend that the robbing another of his Reputation supplies the want of it in himself? I question not but such authors are poor, and heartily wish the objection were removed by any honest livelihood. But Poverty is here the accident, not the subject: He who describes Malice and Villainy to be pale and meagre, expresses not the least anger against Paleness or Leanness, but against Malice and Villainy. The Apothecary in *Romeo and Juliet* is poor; but is he therefore justified in vending poison? Not but Poverty itself becomes a just subject of satire, when it is the consequence of vice, prodigality, or neglect of one's lawful calling; for then it increases the public burden, fills the streets and highways with Robbers, and the garrets with Clippers, Coiners, and Weekly Journalists.

But admitting that two or three of these offend less in their morals, than in their writings; must Poverty make nonsense sacred? If so, the fame of bad authors would be much better consulted than that of all the good ones in the world; and not one of an hundred had ever been called by his right name.

They mistake the whole matter: It is not charity to encourage them in the way they follow, but to get them out of it; for men are not bunglers because they are poor, but they are poor because they are bunglers.

Is it not pleasant enough, to hear our authors crying out on the one hand, as if their persons and characters were too sacred for Satire; and the public objecting on the other, that they are too mean even for Ridicule? But whether Bread or Fame be their end, it must be allowed, our author, by and in this Poem, has mercifully given them a little of both.

There are two or three, who by their rank and fortune have no benefit from the former objections, supposing them good, and these I was sorry to see in such company. But if, without any provocation, two or three Gentlemen will fall upon one, in an affair wherein his interest and reputation are equally embarked; they cannot certainly, after they have been content to print themselves his enemies, complain of being put into the number of them.

Others, I am told, pretend to have been once his Friends. Surely they are their enemies who say so, since nothing can be more odious than to treat a friend as they have done. But of this I cannot persuade myself, when I consider the constant and eternal aversion of all bad writers to a good one.

Such as claim a merit from being his Admirers I would gladly ask, if it lays him under a personal obligation? At that rate he would be the most obliged humble servant in the world. I dare swear for these in particular, he never desired them to be his admirers, nor promised in return to be theirs: That had truly been a sign he was of their acquaintance; but would not the malicious world have suspected such an approbation of some motive worse than ignorance, in the author of the *Essay on Criticism?* Be it as it will, the reasons of their Admiration and of his Contempt are equally subsisting, for his works and theirs are the very same that they were.

One, therefore, of their assertions I believe may be true,

"That he has a contempt for their writings." And there is another, which would probably be sooner allowed by himself than by any good judge beside, "That his own have found too much success with the public." But as it cannot consist with his modesty to claim this as a justice, it lies not on him, but entirely on the public, to defend its own judgment.

There remains what in my opinion might seem a better plea for these people, than any they have made use of. If Obscurity or Poverty were to exempt a man from satire, much more should Folly or Dulness, which are still more involuntary; nay, as much so as personal Deformity. But even this will not help them: Deformity becomes an object of Ridicule when a man sets up for being handsome; and so must Dulness when he sets up for a Wit. They are not ridiculed because Ridicule in itself is, or ought to be, a pleasure; but because it is just to undeceive and vindicate the honest and unpretending part of mankind from imposition, because particular interest ought to yield to general, and a great number who are not naturally Fools, ought never to be made so, in complaisance to a few who are. Accordingly we find that in all ages, all vain pretenders, were they ever so poor or ever so dull, have been constantly the topics of the most candid satirists, from the Codrus of Juvenal to the Damon of Boileau.

Having mentioned Boileau, the greatest Poet and most judicious Critic of his age and country, admirable for his Talents, and yet perhaps more admirable for his Judgment in the proper application of them; I cannot help remarking the resemblance betwixt him and our author, in Qualities, Fame, and Fortune; in the distinctions shown them by their Superiors, in the general esteem of their Equals and in their extended reputation amongst Foreigners; in the latter of which ours has met with the better fate, as he has had for his Translators persons of the most eminent rank and abilities in their respective nations. But the resemblance holds in nothing more, than in their being equally abused by the ignorant pretenders to Poetry of their times; of which not the least memory will remain but in their own Writings, and in the Notes made upon them. What Boileau has done in almost all his poems, our author has only in this:

I dare answer for him he will do it in no more; and on this principle, of attacking few but who had slandered him, he could not have done it at all, had he been confined from censuring obscure and worthless persons, for scarce any other were his enemies. However, as the parity is so remarkable, I hope it will continue to the last; and if ever he shall give us an edition of this Poem himself, I may see some of them treated as gently, on their repentance or better merit, as Perrault and Quinault were at last by BOILEAU.

In one point I must be allowed to think the character of our English Poet the more amiable. He has not been a follower of Fortune or Success; he has lived with the Great without flattery; been a friend to Men in power, without pensions, from whom, as he asked, so he received no favour, but what was done Him in his Friends. As his Satires were the more just for being delayed, so were his Panegyrics; bestowed only on such persons as he had familiarly known, only for such virtues as he had long observed in them, and only at such times as others cease to praise, if not begin to calumniate them, I mean when out of power or out of fashion.[11] A satire, therefore, on writers so notorious for the contrary practice, became no man so well as himself; as none, it is plain, was so little in their friendships, or so much in that of those whom they had most abused, namely the Greatest and Best of all Parties. Let me add a further reason, that, though engaged in their Friendships, he never espoused their Animosities; and can almost singly challenge this honour, not to have written a line of any man, which, through Guilt, through Shame, or through Fear, through variety of Fortune, or change of Interests, he was ever unwilling to own.

I shall conclude with remarking what a pleasure it must be to every reader of Humanity, to see all along, that our Author

[11] As Mr. Wycherley, at the time the Town declaimed against his book of Poems; Mr. Walsh, after his death; Sir William Trumbull, when he had resigned the Office of Secretary of State; Lord Bolingbroke, at his leaving England after the Queen's death; Lord Oxford, in his last decline of life; Mr. Secretary Craggs, at the end of the South Sea year, and after his death: Others only in Epitaphs.   [P.]

in his very laughter is not indulging his own ill-nature, but only punishing that of others. As to his Poem, those alone are capable of doing it justice, who, to use the words of a great writer, know how hard it is (with regard both to his subject and his manner) VETUSTIS DARE NOVITATEM, OBSOLETIS NITOREM, OBSCURIS LUCEM, FASTIDITIS GRATIAM. I am

ST. JAMES'S,   Your most humble servant,
Dec. 22, 1728.   WILLIAM CLELAND.[12]

ADVERTISEMENT

To the First Edition of the FOURTH BOOK *of the DUNCIAD, when printed separately in the Year 1742.*

WE apprehend it can be deemed no injury to the author of the three first books of the *Dunciad,* that we publish this Fourth. It was found merely by accident, in taking a survey of the *Library* of a late eminent nobleman; but in so blotted a condition, and in so many detached pieces, as plainly shewed it not only to be *incorrect,* but *unfinished.* That the author of the three first books had a design to extend and complete his poem in this manner, appears from the dissertation prefixed to it, where it is said, that *the design is more extensive, and that we may expect other episodes to complete it:* And from the declaration in the argument to the third book, that *the accomplishment of the prophecies therein, would be the theme hereafter of a greater Dunciad.* But whether or no he be the author of this, we declare

[12] This Gentleman was of Scotland, and bred at the University of Utrecht, with the Earl of Mar. He served in Spain under Earl Rivers. After the Peace, he was made one of the Commissioners of the Customs in Scotland, and then of Taxes in England, in which having shown himself for twenty years diligent, punctual, and incorruptible, though without any other assistance of Fortune; he was suddenly displaced by the Minister in the sixty-eighth year of his age; and died two months after, in 1741. He was a person of Universal Learning, and an enlarged Conversation; no man had a warmer heart for his Friend, or a sincerer attachment to the Constitution of his Country. [P.] And yet, for all this, the Public will not allow him to be the Author of this Letter. [W.]

ourselves ignorant. If he be, we are no more to be blamed for the publication of it, than Tucca and Varius for that of the last six books of the *Æneid,* though perhaps inferior to the former.

If any person be possessed of a more perfect copy of this work, or of any other fragments of it, and will communicate them to the publisher, we shall make the next edition more complete: In which we also promise to insert any *Criticisms* that shall be published (if at all to the purpose) with the *Names* of the *Authors;* or any letters sent us (though not to the purpose) shall yet be printed under the title of *Epistolæ Obscurorum Virorum;* which, together with some others of the same kind formerly laid by for that end, may make no unpleasant addition to the future impressions of this poem.

MARTINUS SCRIBLERUS OF THE POEM[13]

THIS poem, as it celebrateth the most grave and ancient of things, Chaos, Night, and Dulness; so is it of the most grave and ancient kind. Homer (saith Aristotle) was the first who gave the *Form,* and (saith Horace) who adapted the *Measure,* to heroic poesy. But even before this, may be rationally presumed from what the Ancients have left written, was a piece by Homer composed, of like nature and matter with this of our poet. For of Epic sort it appeareth to have been, yet of matter surely not unpleasant, witness what is reported of it by the learned archbishop Eustathius, *in Odyss.* x. And accordingly Aristotle, in his *Poetic,* chap. iv., doth further set forth, that as the *Iliad* and *Odyssey* gave example to Tragedy, so did this poem to Comedy its first idea.

From these authors also it should seem, that the Hero, or chief personage of it, was no less *obscure,* and his understanding and sentiments no less quaint and strange (if indeed not more so) than any of the actors of our poem. MARGITES was the name of this personage, whom Antiquity recordeth to have been *Dunce the first;* and surely, from what we hear of him, not un-

[13] This appears first in *The Dunciad Variorum* of 1729 and is of course the work of Pope.

worthy to be the root of so spreading a tree, and so numerous a posterity. The poem, therefore, celebrating him was properly and absolutely a *Dunciad;* which though now unhappily lost, yet is its nature sufficiently known by the infallible tokens aforesaid. And thus it doth appear, that the first *Dunciad* was the first Epic poem, written by Homer himself, and anterior ever to the *Iliad* or *Odyssey*.

Now, forasmuch as our poet had translated those two famous works of Homer which are yet left, he did conceive it in some sort his duty to imitate that also which was lost: And was therefore induced to bestow on it the same form which Homer's is reported to have had, namely that of Epic poem; with a title also framed after the ancient Greek manner, to wit, that of *Dunciad*.

Wonderful it is, that so few of the moderns have been stimulated to attempt some Dunciad! since, in the opinion of the multitude, it might cost less pain and oil than an imitation of the greater Epic. But possible it is also, that, on due reflection, the maker might find it easier to paint a Charlemagne, a Brute, or a Godfrey, with just pomp and dignity heroic, than a Margites, a Codrus, or a Flecknoe.

We shall next declare the occasion and the cause which moved our poet to this particular work. He lived in those days, when (after Providence had permitted the invention of Printing as a scourge for the sins of the learned) Paper also became so cheap, and Printers so numerous, that a deluge of Authors covered the land: Whereby not only the peace of the honest unwriting subject was daily molested, but unmerciful demands were made of his applause, yea of his money, by such as would neither earn the one, nor deserve the other. At the same time, the licence of the Press was such, that it grew dangerous to refuse them either: for they would forthwith publish slanders unpunished, the authors being anonymous, and skulking under the wings of Publishers, a set of men who never scrupled to vend either Calumny or Blasphemy, as long as the Town would call for it.

Now our author, living in those times, did conceive it an endeavour well worthy an honest Satirist, to dissuade the dull,

and punish the wicked, *the only way that was left*. In that pub-
lic-spirited view he laid the plan of this Poem, as the greatest
service he was capable (without much hurt, or being slain) to
render his dear country. First, taking things from their orig-
inal, he considereth the causes creative of such Authors, namely
Dulness and *Poverty;* the one born with them, the other con-
tracted by neglect of their proper talents, through self-conceit of
greater abilities. This truth he wrappeth in an *Allegory* (as the
construction of Epic poesy requireth) and feigns that one of
these Goddesses had taken up her abode with the other, and
that they jointly inspired all such writers and such works. He
proceedeth to shew the *qualities* they bestow on these authors,
and the *effects* they produce: then the *materials,* or *stock,* with
which they furnish them; and (above all) that *self-opinion* which
causeth it to seem to themselves vastly greater than it is, and is
the prime motive of their setting up in this sad and sorry mer-
chandise. The great power of these Goddesses acting in alliance
(whereof as the one is the mother of Industry, so is the other
of Plodding) was to be exemplified in some *one, great* and *re-
markable Action:* And none could be more so than that which
our poet hath chosen, *viz.* the restoration of the reign of Chaos
and Night, by the ministry of Dulness their daughter, in the re-
moval of her imperial seat from the City to the polite World;
as the Action of the *Æneid* is the restoration of the empire of
Troy, by the removal of the race from thence to Latium. But
as Homer singing only the *Wrath* of Achilles, yet includes in
his poem the whole history of the Trojan war; in like manner
our author hath drawn into this *single Action* the whole history
of Dulness and her children.

A *Person* must next be fixed upon to support this Action.
This *Phantom* in the poet's mind must have a *Name:* He finds
it to be ———; and he becomes of course the Hero of the Poem.

The *Fable* being thus, according to the best example, one
and entire, as contained in the Proposition; the *Machinery* is
a continued chain of Allegories, setting forth the whole Power,
Ministry, and Empire of Dulness, extended through her sub-
ordinate instruments, in all her various operations.

This is branched into *Episodes,* each of which hath its

Moral apart, though all conductive to the main end. The Crowd assembled in the second book demonstrates the design to be more extensive than to bad poets only, and that we may expect other Episodes of the Patrons, Encouragers, or Paymasters of such authors, as occasion shall bring them forth. And the third book, if well considered, seemeth to embrace the whole World. Each of the Games relateth to some or other vile class of writers: The first concerneth the plagiary, to whom he giveth the name of Moore; the second, the libellous Novelist, whom he styleth Eliza; the third, the flattering Dedicator; the fourth, the bawling Critic, or noisy Poet; the fifth, the dark and dirty Party writer; and so of the rest; assigning to each some *proper name* or other, such as he could find.

As for the *Characters,* the public hath already acknowledged how justly they are drawn: The manners are so depicted, and the sentiments so peculiar to those to whom applied, that surely to transfer them to any other or wiser personages, would be exceeding difficult: And certain it is, that every person concerned, being consulted apart, hath readily owned the resemblance of every portrait, his own excepted. So Mr. Cibber calls them, "a parcel of *poor wretches,* so many *silly flies:* but adds, our Author's Wit is remarkably more bare and barren, whenever it would fall foul on *Cibber,* than upon any other Person whatever."

The *Descriptions* are singular, the *Comparisons* very quaint, the *Narration* various, yet of one colour: The purity and chastity of *Diction* is so preserved, that in the places most suspicious, not the *words* but only the *images* have been censured, and yet are those images no other than have been sanctified by ancient and classical Authority (though, as was the manner of those good times, not so curiously wrapped up), yea, and commented upon by the most grave Doctors, and approved Critics.

As it beareth the name of *Epic,* it is thereby subjected to such severe indispensable rules as are laid on all Neoterics, a strict imitation of the Ancients; insomuch that any deviation, accompanied with whatever poetic beauties, hath always been censured by the sound Critic. How exact that Imitation hath been in this piece, appeareth not only by its general structure, but by particular allusions infinite, many whereof have escaped both the commentator and poet himself; yea divers by his exceeding diligence are so altered and interwoven with the rest, that several have already been, and more will be, by the ignorant abused, as altogether and originally his own.

In a word, the whole poem proveth itself to be the work of our Author, when his faculties were in full vigour and perfection; at that exact time when years have ripened the Judgment, without diminishing the Imagination: which, by good Critics, is held to be punctually at *forty.* For, at that season it was the Virgil finished his *Georgics;* and Sir Richard Blackmore, at the like age composing his *Arthurs,* declared the same to be the very *Acme* and pitch of life for Epic poesy: Though since he hath altered it to *sixty,* the year in which he published his *Alfred.* True it is, that the talents for *Criticism,* namely smartness, quick censure, vivacity of remark, certainty of asseveration, indeed all but acerbity, seem rather the gifts of Youth than of riper Age: But it is far otherwise in *Poetry;* witness the works of Mr. Rymer and Mr. Dennis, who, beginning with Criticism, became afterwards such Poets as no age hath paralleled. With good reason therefore did our author choose to write his Essay on that subject at twenty, and reserve for his maturer years this great and wonderful work of the *Dunciad.* P.

BY AUTHORITY[14]

By virtue of the Authority in Us vested by the Act for subjecting Poets to the power of a Licenser, we have revised this Piece; where finding the style and appellation of KING to have been given to a certain Pretender, Pseudo-Poet, or Phantom, of the name of TIBBALD; and apprehending the same may be deemed in some sort a reflection on Majesty, or at least an insult on that Legal Authority which has bestowed on another Person the Crown of Poesy: We have ordered the said Pretender,

---

[14] This mock proclamation first appears in *The Dunciad in Four Books* of 1743. For the meaning of the signature " ƆC. Ch." see *The Dunciad,* ed. James Sutherland (London, 1943), p. 252.

Pseudo-Poet, or Phantom, utterly to vanish and evaporate out of this work: And do declare the said Throne of Poesy from henceforth to be abdicated and vacant, unless duly and lawfully supplied by the Laureate himself. And it is hereby enacted, that no other Person do presume to fill the same.   ⊃C. Ch.

THE DUNCIAD

To Dr. Jonathan Swift

Book the First

ARGUMENT

The Proposition, the Invocation, and the Inscription. Then the Original of the great Empire of *Dulness,* and cause of the continuance thereof. The College of the *Goddess* in the City, with her private Academy for Poets in particular; the Governors of it, and the four Cardinal Virtues. Then the Poem *hastes into the midst of things,* presenting her, on the evening of a Lord Mayor's day, revolving the long succession of her Sons, and the glories past and to come. She fixes her eye on *Bays* to be the Instrument of that great Event which is the Subject of the Poem. He is described pensive among his Books, giving up the Cause, and apprehending the Period of her Empire: After debating whether to betake himself to the Church, or to Gaming, or to Party writing, he raises an Altar of proper books, and (making first his solemn prayer and declaration) purposes thereon to sacrifice all his unsuccessful writings. As the pile is kindled, the Goddess, beholding the flame from her seat, flies and puts it out by casting upon it the poem of *Thulè.* She forthwith reveals herself to him, transports him to her Temple, unfolds her Arts, and initiates him into her Mysteries; then announcing the death of *Eusden* the Poet Laureate, anoints him, carries him to Court, and proclaims him Successor.

The Mighty Mother, and her Son, who brings
The Smithfield Muses[1] to the ear of Kings,

[1] *Smithfield* is the place where Bartholomew Fair was kept, whose shows,

I sing. Say you, her instruments the Great!
Called to this work by Dulness, Jove, and Fate;[2]
You by whose care, in vain decried and curst,   5
Still Dunce the second reigns like Dunce the first;
Say, how the Goddess bade Britannia sleep,
And poured her Spirit o'er the land and deep.

    In eldest time, ere mortals writ or read,
Ere Pallas issued from the Thunderer's head,   10
Dulness o'er all possessed her ancient right,
Daughter of Chaos and eternal Night:
Fate in their dotage this fair Idiot gave,
Gross as her sire, and as her mother grave,
Laborious, heavy, busy, bold, and blind,   15
She ruled, in native Anarchy, the mind.

    Still her old Empire to restore she tries,
For, born a Goddess, Dulness never dies.

    O Thou! whatever title please thine ear,
Dean, Drapier, Bickerstaff, or Gulliver![3]   20
Whether thou choose Cervantes' serious air,
Or laugh and shake in Rabelais' easy chair,
Or praise the Court, or magnify Mankind,[4]
Or thy grieved Country's copper chains unbind;
From thy Bœotia[5] though her Power retires,   25
Mourn not, my SWIFT, at aught our Realm acquires.
Here pleased behold her mighty wings outspread

machines, and dramatical entertainments, formerly agreeable only to the
taste of the Rabble, were, by the Hero of this poem and others of equal
genius, brought to the Theatres of Covent Garden, Lincoln's Inn Fields,
and the Haymarket, to be the reigning pleasures of the Court and Town.
This happened in the reigns of King George I and II. . . . See Bk. III
[1. 191]. [P.]

[2] By their *Judgments,* their *Interests,* and their *Inclinations.* W.

[3] The several names and characters he assumed in his ludicrous, his
splenetic, or his party writings; which take in all his works. [W.]

[4] *Ironicè,* alluding to *Gulliver's* representations of both.—The next line
relates to the papers of the *Drapier* against the currency of *Wood's* Copper
coin in *Ireland,* which, upon the great discontent of the people, his Majesty
was graciously pleased to recall. [P.]

[5] Cf. III, 50.

To hatch a new Saturnian age of Lead.
   Close to those walls where Folly holds her throne,
And laughs to think Monroe would take her down,   30
Where o'er the gates, by his famed father's hand,[6]
Great Cibber's brazen, brainless brothers stand;
One Cell there is, concealed from vulgar eye,
The Cave of Poverty and Poetry.
Keen, hollow winds howl through the bleak recess,   35
Emblem of Music caused by Emptiness.
Hence Bards, like Proteus long in vain tied down,
Escape in Monsters, and amaze the town.
Hence Miscellanies spring, the weekly boast
Of Curll's chaste press, and Lintot's rubric post:[7]   40
Hence hymning Tyburn's elegiac lines,[8]
Hence Journals, Medleys, Mercuries, MAGAZINES:
Sepulchral Lies,[9] our holy walls to grace,
And New Year Odes,[10] and all the Grubstreet race.
   In clouded Majesty here Dulness shone;   45
Four guardian Virtues, round, support her throne:
Fierce champion Fortitude, that knows no fears
Of hisses, blows, or want, or loss of ears:
Calm Temperance, whose blessings those partake

[6] Mr. Caius Gabriel Cibber, father of the Poet Laureate. The two Statues of the Lunatics over the gates of Bedlam Hospital were done by him, and (as the son justly says of them) are no ill monuments of his fame as an Artist. [P.]

[7] Two Booksellers, of whom see Book II. The former was fined by the Court of King's Bench for publishing obscene books; the latter usually adorned his shop with titles in red letters. [P.]

[8] It is an ancient English custom for the Malefactors to sing a Psalm at their execution at Tyburn; and no less customary to print Elegies on their deaths, at the same time, or before. [P.]

[9] Is a just satire on the Flatteries and Falsehoods admitted to be inscribed on the walls of Churches, in Epitaphs. [P.]

[10] Made by the Poet Laureate for the time being, to be sung at Court on every New Year's day, the words of which are happily drowned in the voices and instruments. The *New Year Odes* of the Hero of this work were of a cast distinguished from all that preceded him, and made a conspicuous part of his character as a writer, which doubtless induced our Author to mention them here so particularly. [P.]

Who hunger, and who thirst for scribbling sake: 50
Prudence, whose glass presents th' approaching jail:
Poetic Justice, with her lifted scale,
Where, in nice balance, truth with gold she weighs,
And solid pudding against empty praise.
    Here she beholds the Chaos dark and deep,   55
Where nameless Somethings in their causes sleep,
Till genial Jacob, or a warm Third day,
Call forth each mass, a Poem, or a Play:
How hints, like spawn, scarce quick in embryo lie,
How newborn nonsense first is taught to cry,   60
Maggots half-formed in rhyme exactly meet,
And learn to crawl upon poetic feet.
Here one poor word an hundred clenches makes,[11]
And ductile Dulness new meanders takes;
There motley Images her fancy strike,   65
Figures ill paired, and Similes unlike.
She sees a Mob of Metaphors advance,
Pleased with the madness of the mazy dance;
How Tragedy and Comedy embrace;
How Farce and Epic get a jumbled race;   70
How Time himself stands still at her command,
Realms shift their place, and Ocean turns to land.
Here gay Description Egypt glads with showers,
Or gives to Zembla fruits, to Barca flowers;
Glittering with ice here hoary hills are seen,   75
There painted valleys of eternal green,
In cold December fragrant chaplets blow,

---

[11] It may not be amiss to give an instance or two of these operations of *Dulness* out of the Works of her Sons, celebrated in the Poem. A great Critic formerly held these clenches in such abhorrence that he declared, "he that would pun, would pick a pocket." Yet Mr. Dennis's works afford us notable examples in this kind: "*Alexander Pope* hath sent abroad into the world as many *Bulls* as his namesake Pope *Alexander.*—Let us take the initial and final letters of his name, viz. *A. P—E,* and they give you the idea of an *Ape.*—*Pope* comes from the Latin word *Popa,* which signifies a little Wart; or from *poppysma,* because he was continually *popping* out squibbs of wit, or rather *Popysmata,* or *Popisms.*"—DENNIS on *Hom.* and *Daily Journal,* June 11, 1728. [P.]

And heavy harvests nod beneath the snow.
    All these, and more, the cloud-compelling Queen
Beholds through fogs, that magnify the scene.   80
She, tinselled o'er in robes of varying hues,
With self-applause her wild creation views;
Sees momentary monsters rise and fall,
And with her own fool's colours gilds them all.
    'Twas on the day when * * rich and grave,[12]   85
Like Cimon, triumphed both on land and wave:
(Pomps without guilt, of bloodless swords and maces,
Glad chains, warm furs, broad banners, and broad faces)
Now Night descending, the proud scene was o'er,
But lived in Settle's numbers one day more.[13]   90
Now Mayors and Shrieves all hushed and satiate lay,
Yet ate, in dreams, the custard of the day;
While pensive Poets painful vigils keep,
Sleepless themselves, to give their readers sleep.
Much to the mindful Queen the feast recalls   95
What City Swans once sung within the walls;
Much she revolves their arts, their ancient praise,
And sure succession down from Heywood's days.[14]
She saw, with joy, the line immortal run,
Each sire impressed and glaring in his son: 100
So watchful Bruin forms, with plastic care,
Each growing lump, and brings it to a Bear.
She saw old Prynne in restless Daniel shine,[15]

[12] The Procession of a Lord Mayor is made partly by land, and partly by water.—Cimon, the famous Athenian General, obtained a victory by sea, and another by land, on the same day, over the Persians and Barbarians. [P.]

[13] Settle was poet to the City of London. His office was to compose yearly panegyrics upon the Lord Mayors, and verses to be spoken in the Pageants: But that part of the shows being at length frugally abolished, the employment of City poet ceased; so that upon Settle's demise there was no successor to that place. [P.]

[14] John Heywood, whose Interludes were printed in the time of Henry VIII. [P.]

[15] Justly is Daniel . . . [Defoe] made successor to W. Prynne, both of whom wrote verses as well as Politics . . . . And both these authors had

And Eusden eke out Blackmore's endless line;[16]
She saw slow Philips creep like Tate's[17] poor page,   105
And all the mighty Mad in Dennis rage.[18]
        In each she marks her Image full exprest.
But chief in BAYS's monster-breeding breast;
Bays, formed by nature Stage and Town to bless,
And act, and be, a Coxcomb with success.   110
Dulness with transport eyes the lively Dunce,
Remembering she herself was Pertness once.
Now (shame to Fortune!) an ill Run at Play
Blanked his bold visage, and a thin Third day:
Swearing and supperless the Hero sate,   115
Blasphemed his Gods, the Dice, and damned his Fate;
Then gnawed his pen, then dashed it on the ground,
Sinking from thought to thought, a vast profound!
Plunged for his sense, but found no bottom there,

a resemblance in their fates as well as writings, having been alike sentenced to the Pillory. [P.]

[16] Laurence Eusden was Poet Laureate from 1718 to 1730, before Colley Cibber. Cf. *Epistle to Arbuthnot,* 1. 15.

[17] Nahum Tate was Poet Laureate, a cold writer, of no invention: but sometimes translated tolerably when befriended by Mr. Dryden. In his second part of *Absalom and Achitophel* are above two hundred admirable lines together of that great hand, which strongly shine through the insipidity of the rest. [P.]

[18] This is by no means to be understood literally, as if Mr. Dennis were really mad, according to the Narrative of Dr. Norris in Swift and Pope's *Miscellanies,* Vol. III. No—it is spoken of that *Excellent* and *Divine Madness,* so often mentioned by Plato; that poetical rage and enthusiasm, with which Mr. D. hath, in his time, been highly possessed. . . . Mr. John Dennis was the son of a Saddler in London born in 1657. He paid court to Mr. Dryden: and having obtained some correspondence with Mr. Wycherley and Mr. Congreve, he immediately obliged the public with their letters. . . . For his character as a writer, it is given us as follows: "Mr. Dennis is *excellent* at Pindaric writings, *perfectly regular* in all his performances, and a person of *sound Learning.* That he is master of a great deal of *Penetration* and *Judgment,* his criticisms (particularly on *Prince Arthur*) do sufficiently demonstrate." From the same account it also appears that he writ Plays "more to get *Reputation* than *Money.*"—DENNIS of himself. [P.]

Yet wrote and floundered on, in mere despair.   120
Round him much Embryo, much Abortion lay,
Much future Ode, and abdicated Play;
Nonsense precipitate, like running Lead,
That slipped through Cracks and Zigzags of the Head;
All that on Folly Frenzy could beget,   125
Fruits of dull Heat, and Sooterkins of Wit.
Next, o'er his Books his eyes began to roll,
In pleasing memory of all he stole,
How here he sipped, how there he plundered snug,
And sucked all o'er, like an industrious Bug.   130
Here lay poor Fletcher's half-eat scenes, and here
The Frippery of crucified Molière;
There hapless Shakespeare, yet of Tibbald sore,[19]
Wished he had blotted for himself before.[20]
The rest on Outside merit but presume,   135
Or serve (like other Fools) to fill a room;
Such with their shelves as due proportion hold,
Or their fond Parents dressed in red and gold;
Or where the pictures for the page atone,
And Quarles is saved by Beauties not his own.   140
Here swells the shelf with Ogilby the great;[21]

[19] This Tibbald, or Theobald, published an edition of Shakespeare, of which he was so proud himself as to say, in one of Mist's Journals, June 8, "That to expose any Errors in it was impracticable." And in another, April 27, "That whatever care might for the future be taken by any other Editor, he would still give about five hundred Emendations, that *shall* escape them all." [P.]

[20] It was a ridiculous praise which the Players gave to Shakespeare, "that he never blotted a line." Ben Jonson honestly wished he had blotted a thousand; and Shakespeare would certainly have wished the same, if he had lived to see those alterations in his works, which, not the Actors only (and especially the daring Hero of this poem) have made on the *Stage,* but the presumptuous Critics of our days in their *Editions.* [P.]

[21] "John Ogilby was one, who, from a late initiation into literature, made such a progress as might well style him the prodigy of his time! sending into the world so many *large Volumes!* His translations of Homer and Virgil *done to the life,* and *with such excellent sculptures:* And (what

There, stamped with arms, Newcastle shines complete:[22]
Here all his suffering brotherhood retire,
And 'scape the martyrdom of jakes and fire:
A Gothic Library! of Greece and Rome   145
Well purged, and worthy Settle, Banks, and Broome.[23]
    But, high above, more solid Learning shone,
The Classics of an Age that heard of none;
There Caxton slept, with Wynkyn at his side,[24]
One clasped in wood, and one in strong cowhide;   150
There saved by spice, like mummies, many a year,
Dry Bodies of Divinity appear:
De Lyra there a dreadful front extends,[25]
And here the groaning shelves Philemon bends.[26]
    Of these twelve volumes, twelve of amplest size,   155

added great grace to his works) he printed all on *special good paper,* and in a *very good letter."*—Winstanley, *Lives of Poets.* [P.]

[22] "The *Duchess of Newcastle* was one who busied herself in the ravishing delights of Poetry; leaving to posterity in print three *ample Volumes* of her studious endeavours."—Winstanley, *ibid.* Langbaine reckons up *eight* Folios of her Grace's; which were usually adorned with gilded covers, and had her coat of arms upon them. [P.]

[23] The Poet has mentioned these three authors in particular, as they are parallel to our Hero in three capacities: 1. Settle was his brother Laureate; only indeed upon half pay, for the City instead of the Court. . . . 2. Banks was his Rival in *Tragedy* (though more successful) in one of his Tragedies, the *Earl of Essex,* which is yet alive: *Anna Boleyn,* the *Queen of Scots,* and *Cyrus the Great,* are dead and gone. . . . 3. Broome was a serving-man of Ben Jonson, who once picked up a *Comedy* from his Betters, or from some cast scenes of his Master, not entirely contemptible. [P.]

[24] A Printer in the time of Edward IV, Richard III, and Henry VII; Wynkyn de Worde, his successor, in that of Henry VII and VIII. The former translated into prose Virgil's *Æneis,* as a history; of which he speaks in his Proeme, in a very singular manner, as of a book hardly known. [P.]

[25] Nich. de Lyra, . . . a very voluminous commentator, wrote works, in five vast folios, were printed in 1472. [P.]

[26] "Philemon Holland, Doctor in Physic. He translated *so many books,* that a man would think he had done *nothing else;* insomuch that he might be called *Translator general of his age.* The books alone of his turning into English are sufficient to make a *Country Gentleman* a *complete Library."*—Winstanley. [P.]

Redeemed from tapers and defrauded pies,
Inspired he seizes: These an altar raise:
An hecatomb of pure unsullied lays
That altar crowns: A folio Commonplace
Founds the whole pile, of all his works the base;   160
Quartos, octavos, shape the lessening pyre;
A twisted Birthday Ode completes the spire.
      Then he: "Great Tamer of all human art!
First in my care, and ever at my heart;
Dulness! whose good old cause I yet defend,   165
With whom my Muse began, with whom shall end,
E'er since Sir Fopling's Periwig was Praise,[27]
To the last honours of the Butt and Bays:
O thou! of Business the directing soul!
To this our head like bias to the bowl,   170
Which, as more ponderous, made its aim more true,
Obliquely waddling to the mark in view:
O! ever gracious to perplexed mankind,
Still spread a healing mist before the mind;
And, lest we err by Wit's wild dancing light,   175
Secure us kindly in our native night.
Or, if to Wit a coxcomb make pretence,
Guard the sure barrier between that and Sense;
Or quite unravel all the reasoning thread,
And hang some curious cobweb in its stead!   180
As, forced from wind-guns, lead itself can fly,
And ponderous slugs cut swiftly through the sky;
As clocks to weight their nimble motion owe,
The wheels above urged by the load below:
Me Emptiness, and Dulness could inspire,   185
And were my Elasticity and Fire.
Some Daemon stole my pen (forgive th' offence)
And once betrayed me into common sense:

[27] The first visible cause of the passion of the Town for our Hero was a
fair flaxen full-bottomed Periwig, which, he tells us, he wore in his first
play of the *Fool in Fashion*. . . . This remarkable Periwig usually made
its entrance upon the stage in a sedan, brought in by two chairmen, with
infinite approbation of the audience. [P.]

Else all my Prose and Verse were much the same;
This, prose on stilts, that, poetry, fallen lame.   190
Did on the stage my Fops appear confined?
My life gave ampler lessons to mankind.
Did the dead Letter unsuccessful prove?
The brisk Example never failed to move.
Yet sure had Heaven decreed to save the State,   195
Heaven had decreed these works a longer date.
Could Troy be saved by any single hand,
This grey-goose weapon must have made her stand.
What can I now? my Fletcher²⁸ cast aside,
Take up the Bible, once my better guide?²⁹   200
Or tread the path by venturous Heroes trod,
This Box my Thunder, this right hand my God?
Or chaired at White's amidst the Doctors sit,³⁰
Teach Oaths to Gamesters, and to Nobles Wit?
Or bidst thou rather Party to embrace?   205
(A friend to Party thou, and all her race;
'Tis the same rope at different ends they twist;
To Dulness Ridpath is as dear as Mist.)³¹
Shall I, like Curtius, desperate in my zeal,
O'er head and ears plunge for the Commonweal?   210
Or rob Rome's ancient geese of all their glories,
And cackling save the Monarchy of Tories?
Hold—to the Minister I more incline;
To serve his cause, O Queen! is serving thine.

²⁸ A familiar manner of speaking, used by modern Critics, of a favourite
author. Bays might as justly speak thus of Fletcher, as a French Wit did
of Tully, seeing his works in his library, "Ah! mon cher Ciceron! je le
connais bien; ces't de même que Marc Tulle." But he had a better title
to call Fletcher *his own*, having made so free with him. [P.]
²⁹ When, according to his Father's intention, he had been a *Clergyman*,
or (as he thinks himself) a *Bishop* of the Church of England. [P.]
³⁰ The Doctors in this place mean no more than *false Dice*, a Cant phrase
used amongst Gamesters. So the meaning of these four sonorous Lines is
only this, "Shall I play fair or foul?" [P.]
³¹ George Ridpath, author of a Whig paper, called the *Flying Post;*
Nathaniel Mist, of a famous Tory Journal. [P.]

And see! thy very Gazetteers[32] give o'er,   215
Even Ralph repents, and Henley writes no more.
What then remains? Ourself. Still, still remain
Cibberian forehead, and Cibberian brain.
This brazen Brightness, to the Squire so dear;
This polished Hardness, that reflects the Peer: 220
This arch Absurd, that wit and fool delights;
This Mess, tossed up of Hockley Hole and White's;
Where Dukes and Butchers join to wreathe my crown,
At once the Bear and Fiddle of the town.
    "O born in sin, and forth in folly brought!   225
Works damned, or to be damned! (your father's fault)
Go, purified by flames ascend the sky,
My better and more Christian progeny![33]
Unstained, untouched, and yet in maiden sheets;
While all your smutty sisters walk the streets.   230
Ye shall not beg, like gratis-given Bland,[34]
Sent with a Pass, and vagrant through the land;
Not sail with Ward, to Ape-and-monkey climes,[35]
Where vile Mundungus trucks for viler rhymes:
Not sulphur-tipped, emblaze and Alehouse fire;   235
Not wrap up Oranges, to pelt your sire!
O! pass more innocent, in infant state,

---

[32] A band of ministerial writers, . . . who, on the very day their Patron quitted his post, laid down their paper, and declared they would never more meddle in Politics. [P.]

[33] "It may be observable, that my muse and my spouse were equally prolific; that the one was seldom the mother of a Child, but in the same year the other made me father of a Play. I think we had a dozen of each sort between us; of both which kinds some *died* in their *Infancy*," etc.— *Life of C.C.*, 8° ed., p. 217   [P.]

[34] It was a practice so to give the Daily Gazetter and ministerial pamphlets (in which this B. was a writer) and to send them *Post-free* to all the Towns in the kingdom.   [P.]

[35] "Edward Ward, a very voluminous Poet in Hudibrastic verse, but best known by *The London Spy*, in prose . . . ."—Jacob, *Lives of the Poets*, Vol. II, p. 225. Great number of his works were yearly sold into the Plantations.   [P.]

To the mild Limbo of our Father Tate:[36]
Or peaceably forgot, at once be blest
In Shadwell's[36] bosom with eternal Rest!   240
Soon to that mass of Nonsense to return,
Where things destroyed are swept to things unborn."
      With that, a Tear (portentous sign of Grace!)
Stole from the Master of the sevenfold Face:
And thrice he lifted high the Birthday brand,   245
And thrice he dropped it from his quivering hand;
Then lights the structure, with averted eyes:
The rolling smoke involves the sacrifice.
The opening clouds disclose each work by turns:
Now flames the Cid, and now Perolla burns;[37]   250
Great Caesar roars, and hisses in the fires;
King John in silence modestly expires;
No merit now the dear Nonjuror claims,[38]
Molière's old stubble in a moment flames.
Tears gushed again, as from pale Priam's eyes   255
When the last blaze sent Ilion to the skies.
      Roused by the light, old Dulness heaved the head,
Then snatched a sheet of Thulè[39] from her bed;
Sudden she flies, and whelms it o'er the pyre;
Down sink the flames, and with a hiss expire.   260

[36] Two of his predecessors in the Laurel. [P.]

[37] In the first notes on the *Dunciad* it was said, that this Author was particularly excellent at Tragedy. "This (says he) is as unjust as to say I could not dance on a Rope." But certain it is that he had attempted to dance on this Rope, and fell most shamefully, having produced no less than four Tragedies (the names of which the Poet preserves in these few lines): the three first of them were fairly printed, acted, and damned; the fourth suppressed, in fear of the like treatment. [P.]

[38] A Comedy threshed out of Molière's *Tartuffe,* and so much the Translator's favourite, that he assures us all our author's dislike to it could only arise from *disaffection to the Government.* [P.]

[39] An unfinished poem of that name, of which one sheet was printed many years ago, by Amb. Philips, a northern author. It is an usual method of putting out a fire, to cast wet sheets upon it. Some critics have been of opinion that this sheet was of the nature of the Asbestos, which cannot be consumed by fire: But I rather think it an allegorical allusion to the coldness and heaviness of the writing. [P.]

Her ample presence fills up all the place;
A veil of fogs dilates her awful face:
Great in her charms! as when on Shrieves and Mayors
She looks, and breathes herself into their airs.
She bids him wait her to her sacred Dome: 265
Well pleased he entered, and confessed his home.
So Spirits ending their terrestrial race,
Ascend, and recognize their Native Place.
This the Great Mother[40] dearer held than all
The clubs of Quidnuncs, or her own Guildhall: 270
Here stood her Opium, here she nursed her Owls,
And here she planned th' Imperial seat of Fools.
     Here to her Chosen all her works she shows;
Prose swelled to verse, verse loitering into prose:
How random thoughts now meaning chance to find, 275
Now leave all memory of sense behind:
How Prologues into Prefaces decay,
And these to Notes are frittered quite away:
How Index learning turns no student pale,
Yet holds the eel of science by the tail: 280
How, with less reading than makes felons 'scape,
Less human genius than God gives an ape,
Small thanks to France, and none to Rome or Greece,
A vast, vamped, future, old, revived, new piece,
'Twixt Plautus, Fletcher, Shakespeare, and Corneille, 285
Can make a Cibber, Tibbald,[41] or Ozell.[42]
     The Goddess then, o'er his anointed head,
With mystic words, the sacred Opium shed.
And lo! her bird (a monster of a fowl,

---

[40] *Magna Mater,* here applied to *Dulness.* The *Quidnuncs,* a name given to the ancient members of certain political clubs, who were constantly inquiring *quid nunc?* what news? [P.]

[41] Lewis Tibbald (as pronounced) or Theobald (as written) was bred an Attorney, and son to an Attorney (says Mr. Jacob) of Sittenburn in Kent. He was Author of some forgotten Plays, Translations, and other pieces. He was concerned in paper called the *Censor,* and a Translation of Ovid. [P.]

[42] "Mr. John Ozell . . . . has obliged the world with many translations of French Plays."—Jacob, *Lives of Dram. Poets,* p. 198. [P.]

Something betwixt a Heidegger[43] and owl)   290
Perched on his crown. "All hail! and hail again,
My son! the promised land expects thy reign.
Know, Eusden thirsts no more for sack or praise;
He sleeps among the dull of ancient days;
Safe, where no Critics damn, no duns molest,   295
Where wretched Withers,[44] Ward, and Gildon[45] rest,
And highborn Howard,[46] more majestic sire,
With Fool of Quality completes the quire.
Thou, Cibber! thou, his Laurel shalt support,
Folly, my son, has still a Friend at Court.   300
Lift up your Gates, ye Princes, see him come!
Sound, sound, ye Viols; be the Catcall dumb!
Bring, bring the madding Bay, the drunken Vine;
The creeping, dirty, courtly Ivy join.
And thou! his Aide-de-camp, lead on my sons,   305
Light-armed with Points, Antitheses, and Puns.
Let Bawdry, Billingsgate, my daughters dear,
Support his front, and Oaths bring up the rear:
And under his, and under Archer's wing,
Gaming[47] and Grubstreet skulk behind the King.   310

[43] A strange bird from Switzerland, and not (as some have supposed)
the name of an eminent person who was a man of parts, and, as was
said of Petronius, *Arbiter Elegantiarum.* [P.] John James Heidegger,
a Swiss, was manager of the opera house in the Haymarket and master
of the Revels under George II. He was noted for his ugliness.
[44] "George Withers was a great pretender to poetical zeal against the vices
of the times, and abused the greatest personages in power, which brought
upon him *frequent Correction.* The Marshalsea and Newgate were no
strangers to him."—Winstanley. [P.]
[45] Charles Gildon, a writer of criticisms and libels of the last age . . . .
He signalized himself as a critic, having written some very bad Plays;
abused Mr. P. very scandalously in an anonymous pamphlet of the *Life
of Mr. Wycherley,* printed by Curll; in another, called the *New Rehearsal,*
printed in 1714; in a third, entitled the *Complete Art of English Poetry,*
in two volumes; and others. [P.]
[46] Hon. Edward Howard, author of the *British Princes,* and a great num-
ber of wonderful pieces, celebrated by the late Earls of Dorset and
Rochester, Duke of Buckingham, Mr. Waller, etc. [P.]
[47] When the Statute against Gaming was drawn up, it was represented,

"O! when shall rise a Monarch all our own,
And I, a Nursing mother, rock the throne;
'Twixt Prince and People close the Curtain draw,
Shade him from Light, and cover him from Law;
Fatten the Courtier, starve the learnèd band,   315
And suckle Armies, and dry-nurse the land:
Till Senates nod to Lullabies divine,
And all be sleep, as at an Ode of thine."
        She ceased. Then swells the Chapel Royal throat:[48]
"God save King Cibber!" mounts in every note.   320
Familiar White's, "God save King Colley!" cries;
"God save King Colley!" Drury Lane replies:
To Needham's quick the voice triumphal rode,
But pious Needham[49] dropped the name of God;
Back to the Devil[50] the last echoes roll,   325
And "Coll!" each Butcher roars at Hockley Hole.
        So when Jove's block descended from on high
(As sings thy great forefather Ogilby)
Loud thunder to its bottom shook the bog,
And the hoarse nation croaked, "God save King Log!"[51]

that the King, by ancient custom, plays at Hazard one night in the year;
and therefore a clause was inserted, with an exception as to that particu-
lar. Under this pretence, the Groom-porter had a room appropriated to
Gaming all the summer the Court was at Kensington, which his Majesty
accidentally being acquainted of, with a just indignation prohibited. It is
reported the same practice is yet continued wherever the Court resides,
and the Hazard Table there open to all the professed Gamesters in town.
[P.]
[48] The Voices and Instruments used in the service of the Chapel Royal
being also employed in the performance of the Birthday and New Year
Odes.   [P.]
[49] A Matron of great fame, and very religious in her way; whose constant
prayer it was, that she might "get enough by her profession to leave it
off in time, and make her peace with God." But her fate was not so
happy; for being convicted, and set in the pillory, she was (to the lasting
shame of all her great Friends and Votaries) so ill used by the populace,
that it put an end to her days.   [P.]
[50] The Devil Tavern in Fleet Street, where these Odes are usually re-
hearsed before they are performed at Court.   [P.]
[51] See Ogilby's *Æsop's Fables,* where in the story of the Frogs and their
King, this excellent hemistitch is to be found.   [P.]

Book the Second

ARGUMENT

The King being proclaimed, the solemnity is graced with public *Games,* and sports of various kinds; not instituted by the Hero, as by Æneas in Virgil, but for greater honour by the *Goddess* in person (in like manner as the games Pythia, Isthmia, etc., were anciently said to be ordained by the Gods, and as Thetis herself appearing, according to Homer *Odyssey* xxiv, proposed the prizes in honour of her son Achilles). Hither flock the Poets and Critics, attended, as it but just, with their Patrons and Booksellers. The Goddess is first pleased, for her disport, to propose games to the *Booksellers,* and setteth up the Phantom of a *Poet,* which they contend to overtake. The Races described with their divers accidents. Next, the game for a *Poetess.* Then follow the Exercises for the *Poets,* of *tickling, vociferating, diving:* The first holds forth the arts and practices of *Dedicators,* the second of *Disputants* and *fustian Poets,* the third of *profound, dark,* and *dirty Party writers.* Lastly, for the *Critics,* the Goddess proposes (with great propriety) an Exercise, not of their parts, but their patience, in hearing the works of two voluminous Authors, one in *verse,* and the other in *prose,* deliberately read, without sleeping: The various effects of which, with the several degrees and manners of their operation, are here set forth; till the whole number, not of Critics only, but of spectators, actors, and all present, fall fast asleep; which naturally and necessarily ends the games.

> HIGH on a gorgeous seat,[1] that far outshone
> Henley's gilt tub,[2] or Flecknoe's Irish throne,[3]
> Or that where on her Curlls the Public pours,[4]

[1] Cf. Milton, *Paradise Lost,* Bk. II, l. 1.
[2] The pulpit of a Dissenter is usually called a Tub; but that of Mr. Orator Henley was covered with velvet, and adorned with gold. . . . See the history of this person, Book III. [P.]
[3] Richard Flecknoe was an Irish priest, but had laid aside (as himself expressed it) the mechanic part of priesthood. He printed some plays, poems, letters, and travels. I doubt not our Author took occasion to mention him in respect to the Poem of Mr. Dryden, to which this bears some resemblance, though of a character more different from it than that of the *Æneid* from the *Iliad,* or the *Lutrin* of Boileau from the *Défaite des Bouts-rimés* of Sarasin. [P.]
[4] Edmund Curll stood in the pillory at Charing Cross, in March 1727–8.

All-bounteous, fragrant Grains and Golden showers,
Great Cibber sat: The proud Parnassian sneer,   5
The conscious simper, and the jealous leer,
Mix on his look: All eyes direct their rays
On him, and crowds turn Coxcombs as they gaze.
His Peers shine round him with reflected grace,
New edge their dulness, and new bronze their face.   10
So from the Sun's broad beam, in shallow urns
Heaven's twinkling Sparks draw light, and point their
     horns.

    Not with more glee, by hands Pontific crowned,
With scarlet hats wide-waving circled round,
Rome in her Capitol saw Querno sit,[5]   15
Throned on seven hills, the Antichrist of wit.

    And now the Queen, to glad her sons, proclaims
By herald Hawkers, high heroic Games.
They summon all her Race: An endless band
Pours forth, and leaves unpeopled half the land.   20
A motley mixture! in long wigs, in bags,
In silks, in crapes, in Garters, and in rags,
From drawing rooms, from colleges, from garrets,
On horse, on foot, in hacks, and gilded chariots:
All who true Dunces in her cause appeared,   25
And all who knew those Dunces to reward.

    Amid that area wide they took their stand,
Where the tall maypole once o'erlooked the Strand,

"This (saith Edmund Curll) is a false assertion———I had indeed the corporal punishment of what the Gentlemen of the long Robe are pleased jocosely to call *mounting the Rostrum* for one hour: but that scene of Action was not in the month of *March,* but in *February.*" [P.]

[5] Camillo Querno was of Apulia, who, hearing the great Encouragement which Leo X gave to poets, travelled to Rome with a harp in his hand, and sung to it twenty thousand verses of a poem called *Alexias.* He was introduced *as a Buffoon* to Leo, and promoted to the honour of the *Laurel;* a jest which the Court of Rome and the Pope himself entered into so far, as to cause him to ride on an elephant to the Capitol, and to hold a solemn festival on his coronation; at which it is recorded the Poet himself was so transported as to *weep for joy. . . .* Paulus Jovius, *Elog. Vir. doct.* Chap. 82. [P.]

But now (so ANNE and Piety ordain)
A Church collects the saints of Drury Lane.   30
        With Authors, Stationers obeyed the call,
(The field of glory is a field for all).
Glory, and gain, th' industrious tribe provoke;
And gentle Dulness ever loves a joke.
A Poet's form she placed before their eyes,   35
And bade the nimblest racer seize the prize;
No meagre, muse-rid mope, adust and thin,
In a dun nightgown of his own loose skin;
But such a bulk as no twelve bards could raise,
Twelve starveling bards of these degenerate days.   40
All as a partridge plump, full-fed, and fair,
She formed this image of well-bodied air,
With pert flat eyes she windowed well its head;
A brain of feathers, and a heart of lead;
And empty words she gave, and sounding strain,   45
But senseless, lifeless! idol void and vain!
Never was dashed out, at one lucky hit,
A fool, so just a copy of a wit;
So like, that critics said, and courtiers swore,
A Wit it was, and called the phantom Moore.[6]   50
        All gaze with ardour: Some a poet's name,
Others a sword-knot and laced suit inflame.
But lofty Lintot in the circle rose:[7]
"This prize is mine; who tempt it are my foes;
With me began this genius, and shall end."   55
He spoke: and who with Lintot shall contend?
        Fear held them mute. Alone, untaught to fear,
Stood dauntless Curll; "Behold that rival here!
The race by vigour, not by vaunts is won;
So take the hindmost, Hell," he said, and run.   60

---

[6] See *Epistle to Arbuthnot,* l. 23.
[7] We enter here upon the episode of the Booksellers: Persons, whose names being more known and famous in the learned world than those of the Authors in this poem, do therefore need less explanation. The action of Mr. [Bernard] Linton here imitates that of Dares in Virgil, rising just in this manner to lay hold on a *Bull*. [P.]

Swift as a bard the bailiff leaves behind,
He left huge Lintot, and outstripped the wind.
As when a dabchick waddles through the copse
On feet and wings, and flies, and wades, and hops;
So laboring on, with shoulders, hands, and head,   65
Wide as a windmill all his figure spread,
With arms expanded Bernard rows his state,
And left-legged Jacob seems to emulate.
Full in the middle way there stood a lake,
Which Curll's Corinna[8] chanced that morn to make: 70
(Such was her wont, at early dawn to drop
Her evening cates before his neighbour's shop,)
Here fortuned Curll to slide; loud shout the band,
And "Bernard! Bernard!" rings through all the Strand.
Obscene with filth the miscreant lies bewrayed,   75
Fallen in the plash his wickedness had laid:
Then first (if Poets aught of truth declare)
The caitiff Vaticide conceived a prayer.
   "Hear, Jove! whose name my bards and I adore,
As much at least as any God's, or more;   80
And him and his, if more devotion warms,
Down with the Bible, up with the Pope's Arms."[9]
   A place there is, betwixt earth, air, and seas,
Where, from Ambrosia, Jove retires for ease.
There in his seat two spacious vents appear,   85
On this he sits, to that he leans his ear,
And hears the various vows of fond mankind;
Some beg an eastern, some a western wind:
All vain petitions, mounting to the sky,
With reams abundant this abode supply;   90

[8] This name, it seems, was taken by one Mrs. [Elizabeth Thomas], who procured some private letters of Mr. Pope, while almost a boy, to Mr. Cromwell, and sold them without the consent of either of those Gentlemen to [Edmund] Curll, who printed them in 12°, 1727. We only take this opportunity of mentioning the manner in which those letters got abroad, which the author was ashamed of as very trivial things, full not only of levities, but of wrong judgments of men and books, and only excusable from the youth and inexperience of the writer. [P.]
[9] The Bible, Curll's sign; the Cross Keys, Lintot's. [P.]

Amused he reads, and then returns the bills
Signed with that Ichor which from Gods distils.
   In office here fair Cloacina[10] stands,
And ministers to Jove with purest hands.
Forth from the heap she picked her Votary's prayer,   95
And placed it next him, a distinction rare!
Oft had the Goddess heard her servants call,
From her black grottos near the Temple Wall,
Listening delighted to the jest unclean
Of linkboys vile, and watermen obscene;   100
Where as he fished her nether realms for Wit,
She oft had favoured him, and favours yet.
Renewed by ordure's sympathetic force,
As oiled with magic juices for the course,[11]
Vigorous he rises; from th' effluvia strong   105
Imbibes new life, and scours and stinks along;
Repasses Lintot, vindicates the race,
Nor heeds the brown dishonours of his face.
   And now the victor stretched his eager hand
Where the tall Nothing stood, or seemed to stand;   110
A shapeles shade, it melted from his sight,
Like forms in clouds or visions of the night.
To seize his papers, Curll, was next thy care;
His papers light fly diverse, tossed in air;
Songs, sonnets, epigrams the winds uplift,   115
And whisk 'em back to Evans, Young, and Swift.
Th' embroidered suit at least he deemed his prey;
That suit an unpaid tailor snatched away.
No rag, no scrap, of all the beau, or wit,
That once so fluttered, and that once so writ.   120
   Heaven rings with laughter: Of the laughter vain,
Dulness, good Queen, repeats the jest again.
Three wicked imps, of her own Grubstreet choir,
She decked like Congreve, Addison, and Prior;

[10] The Roman Goddess of the common sewers. [P.]
[11] Alluding to the opinion that there are ointments used by witches to
enable them to fly in the air, etc. [P.]

Mears, Warner, Wilkins[12] run: delusive thought!   125
Breval, Bond, Besaleel,[13] the varlets caught.
Curll stretches after Gay, but Gay is gone;
He grasps an empty Joseph[14] for a John:
So Proteus, hunted in a nobler shape,
Became, when seized, a puppy, or an ape.   130
      To him the Goddess: "Son! thy grief lay down,
And turn this whole illusion on the town:[15]
As the sage dame, experienced in her trade,
By names of Toasts retails each battered jade;
(Whence hapless Monsieur much complains at Paris   135
Of wrongs from Duchesses and Lady Maries;)
Be thine, my stationer! this magic gift;
Cook[16] shall be Prior, and Concanen, Swift:
So shall each hostile name become our own,
And we too boast our Garth and Addison."   140
      With that she gave him (piteous of his case,
Yet smiling at his rueful length of face)
A shaggy Tapestry,[17] worthy to be spread

[12] Booksellers, and Printers of much anonymous stuff. [P.]

[13] Besaleel Morris was author of some satires on the translators of Homer, with many other things printed in newspapers.—"Bond writ a satire against Mr. P.——Capt. Breval was author of *The Confederates,* an ingenious dramatic performance, to expose Mr. P., Mr. Gay, Dr. Arb., and some ladies of quality," says Curll, *Key,* p. 11. [P.]

[14] *Joseph Gay,* a fictitious name put by Curll before several pamphlets, which made them pass with many for Mr. Gay's. [P.] *Joseph* also means a loose overcoat.

[15] It was a common practice of this bookseller to publish vile pieces of obscure hands under the names of eminent authors. [P.]

[16] The man here specified writ a thing called *The Battle of Poets,* in which Philips and Welsted were the Heroes, and Swift and Pope utterly routed. He also published some malevolent things in the British, London, and Daily Journals; and at the same time wrote letters to Mr. Pope, protesting his innocence. His chief work was a translation of Hesiod, to which Theobald writ notes and half notes, which he carefully owned. [P.]

[17] A sorry kind of Tapestry frequent in old Inns, made of worsted or some coarser stuff . . . . The imagery woven in it alludes to the mantle of Cloanthus, in *Æneid* v [250 ff.]. [P.]

On Codrus' old, or Dunton's modern bed;[18]
Instructive work! whose wry-mouthed portraiture   145
Displayed the fates her confessors endure.
Earless on high, stood unabashed Defoe,
And Tutchin flagrant from the scourge below.[19]
There Ridpath, Roper,[20] cudgelled might ye view;
The very worsted still looked black and blue.   150
Himself among the storied chiefs he spies,
As, from the blanket, high in air he flies,[21]
And "Oh!" (he cried) "what street, what lane but knows
Our purgings, pumpings, blanketings, and blows?
In every loom our labours shall be seen,   155
And the fresh vomit run for ever green!"
     See in the circle next, Eliza[22] placed,
Two babes of love close clinging to her waist;
Fair as before her works she stands confessed,
In flowers and pearls by bounteous Kirkall[23] dressed.   160
The Goddess then: "Who best can send on high

[18] Of Codrus the poet's bed, see Juvenal, describing his *poverty* very copiously, *Satire* iii. 103 ff.

John Dunton was a broken bookseller, and abusive scribbler; he writ *Neck or Nothing,* a violent satire on some ministers of state; a libel on the Duke of Devonshire and the Bishop of Peterborough, etc. [P.]

[19] John Tutchin, author of some vile verses, and of a weekly paper called the *Observator:* He was sentenced to be whipped through several towns in the west of England, upon which he petitioned King James II to be hanged. When that prince died in exile, he wrote an invective against his memory, occasioned by some humane elegies on his death. He lived to the time of Queen Anne. [P.]

[20] Authors of the *Flying Post* and *Postboy,* two scandalous papers on different sides, for which they equally and alternately deserved to be cudgelled, and were so. [P.]

[21] The history of Curll's being tossed in a blanket, and whipped by the scholars of Westminister, is well known. Of his purging and vomiting, see *A full and true account of a horrid Revenge on the body of Edm. Curll,* etc. in Swift and Pope's *Miscellanies.* [P.]

[22] Eliza Haywood; this woman was authoress of those most scandalous books called the *Court of Carimania,* and the *New Utopia.* [P.]

[23] The name of an Engraver. Some of this Lady's works were printed in four volumes in 12°, with her picture thus dressed up before them. [P.]

The salient spout, far-streaming to the sky;
His be yon Juno of majestic size,
With cow-like udders, and with ox-like eyes.
This China Jordan let the chief o'ercome   165
Replenish, not ingloriously, at home."
      Osborne[24] and Curll accept the glorious strife,
(Though this his Son dissuades, and that his Wife).
One on his manly confidence relies,
One on his vigour and superior size.   170
First Osborne leaned against his lettered post;
It rose, and laboured to a curve at most.
So Jove's bright bow displays its watery round,
(Sure sign that no spectator shall be drowned).
A second effort brought but new disgrace: 175
The wild Meander washed the Artist's face:
Thus the small jet, which hasty hands unlock,
Spirts in the gardener's eyes who turns the cock.
Not so from shameless Curll; impetuous spread
The stream, and smoking flourished o'er his head.   180
So (famed like thee for turbulence and horns)
Eridanus his humble fountain scorns;
Through half the heavens he pours th' exalted urn;
His rapid waters in their passage burn.
      Swift as it mounts, all follow with their eyes: 185
Still happy Impudence obtains the prize.
Thou triumphst, Victor of the high-wrought day,
And the pleased dame, soft smiling, leadst away.
Osborne, through perfect modesty o'ercome,
Crowned with the Jordan, walks contented home.   190
      But now for Authors nobler palms remain;
Room for my Lord! three jockeys in his train;

---

[24] Thomas Osborne. A bookseller in Gray's Inn, very well qualified by his impudence to act this part; and therefore placed here instead of a less deserving Predecessor. This man published advertisements for a year together, pretending to sell Mr. Pope's subscription books of Homer's *Iliad* at half the price: Of which books he had none, but cut to the size of them (which was quarto) the common books in folio, without Copperplates, on a worse paper, and never above half the value. [P.]

Six huntsmen with a shout precede his chair:
He grins, and looks broad nonsense with a stare.
His Honour's meaning Dulness thus exprest,   195
"He wins this Patron, who can tickle best."
    He chinks his purse, and takes his seat of state:
With ready quills the Dedicators wait;
Now at his head the dextrous task commence,
And, instant, fancy feels th' imputed sense;   200
Now gentle touches wanton o'er his face,
He struts Adonis, and affects grimace:
Rolli[25] the feather to his ear conveys,
Then his nice taste directs our Operas:
Bentley[26] his mouth with classic flattery opes,   205
And the puffed orator bursts out in tropes.
But Welsted[27] most the Poet's healing balm
Strives to extract from his soft, giving palm;
Unlucky Welsted! thy unfeeling master,
The more thou ticklest, gripes his fist the faster.   210
    While thus each hand promotes the pleasing pain,
And quick sensations skip from vein to vein;
A youth unknown to Phoebus, in despair,
Puts his last refuge all in heaven and prayer.
What force have pious vows! The Queen of Love   215
His sister sends, her votaress, from above.
    As, taught by Venus, Paris learnt the art

[25] Paolo Antonio Rolli, an Italian Poet, and writer of many Operas in that language, which partly by the help of his genius, prevailed in England near twenty years. He taught Italian to some fine Gentlemen, who affected to direct the Operas. [P.]

[26] Not spoken of the famous Dr. Richard Bentley, but of one Tho. Bentley, a small critic, who aped his uncle in a *little Horace*. The great one was intended to be dedicated to the Lord Halifax, but (on a change of the Ministry) was given to the Earl of Oxford; for which reason the little one was dedicated to his son the Lord Harley. [P.]

[27] Leonard Welsted, author of the *Triumvirate,* or a *Letter in Verse from Palæmon to Cælia at Bath,* which was meant for a satire on Mr. P. and some of his friends about the year 1718. He writ other things which we cannot remember. . . . You have him again in Book III, l. 169. [P.]

To touch Achilles' only tender part;
Secure, through her, the noble prize to carry,
He marches off, his Grace's Secretary.   220
    "Now turn to different sports" (the Goddess cries)
"And learn, my sons the wonderous power of Noise.
To move, to raise, to ravish every heart,
With Shakespeare's nature, or with Jonson's art,
Let others aim: 'Tis yours to shake the soul   225
With Thunder rumbling from the mustard bowl,[28]
With horns and trumpets now to madness swell,
Now sink in sorrows with a tolling bell;
Such happy arts attention can command,
When fancy flags, and sense is at a stand.   230
Improve we these. Three Catcalls be the bribe
Of him, whose chattering shames the Monkey tribe:
And his this Drum, whose hoarse heroic bass
Drowns the loud clarion of the braying Ass."
    Now thousand tongues are heard in one loud din: 235
The Monkey mimics rush discordant in;
'Twas chattering, grinning, mouthing, jabbering all,
And Noise and Norton,[29] Brangling and Breval,[30]
Dennis and Dissonance, and captious Art,
And Snip-snap short, and Interruption smart,   240
And Demonstration thin, and Theses thick,
And Major, Minor, and Conclusion quick.
"Hold!" (cried the Queen) "a Catcall each shall win;
Equal your merits! equal is your din!
But that this well-disputed game may end,   245
Sound forth, my Brayers, and the welkin rend."

[28] The old way of making Thunder and Mustard were the same; but since, it is more advantageously performed by troughs of wood with stops in them. Whether Mr. Dennis was the inventor of that improvement, I know not; but it is certain, that being once at a Tragedy of a new author, he fell into a great passion at hearing some, and cried, " 'Sdeath! that is *my* Thunder." [P.]

[29] See l. 417.

[30] J. Durant Breval, Author of a very extraordinary Book of Travels, and some Poems. See before, Note on l. 126. [P.]

As, when the long-eared milky mothers wait
At some sick miser's triple bolted gate,
For their defrauded, absent foals they make
A moan so loud, that all the guild awake;   250
Sore sighs Sir Gilbert, starting at the bray,
From dreams of millions, and three groats to pay.
So swells each windpipe; Ass intones to Ass,
Harmonic twang! of leather, horn, and brass;
Such as from laboring lungs th' Enthusiast blows,   255
High sound, attempered to the vocal nose;
Or such as bellow from the deep Divine;
There, Webster![31] pealed thy voice, and Whitfield![31] thine.
But far o'er all, sonorous Blackmore's strain;
Walls, steeples, skies, bray back to him again.   260
In Tottenham fields, the brethren, with amaze,
Prick all their ears up, and forget to graze;
Long Chancery Lane[32] retentive rolls the sound,
And courts to courts return it round and round;
Thames wafts it thence to Rufus' roaring hall,   265
And Hungerford re-echoes bawl for bawl.
All hail him victor in both gifts of song,
Who sings so loudly, and who sings so long.[33]
    This labour past, by Bridewell all descend,
(As morning prayer and flagellation end)[34]   270

[31] The one the writer of a Newspaper called the *Weekly Miscellany*, the
other a Field Preacher. . . . W.

[32] The place where the offices of Chancery are kept. The long detention
of Clients in that Court, and the difficulty of getting out, is humourously
allegorized in these lines. [P.]

[33] A just character of Sir Richard Blackmore knight, who (as Mr. Dryden
expresseth it)
        Writ to the rumbling of the coach's wheels,
and whose indefatigable Muse produced no less than six Epic poems:
Prince and *King Arthur*, twenty books; *Eliza*, ten; *Alfred*, twelve; the
Redeemer, six; besides *Job*, in folio; the whole *Book of Psalms;* the *Crea-
tion*, seven books; *Nature of Man*, three books; and many more. 'Tis in
this sense he is styled afterwards the *everlasting Blackmore*. Notwith-
standing all which, Mr. Gildon seems assured that "this admirable author
did not think himself upon the *same foot* with *Homer.*" *Comp. Art of
Poetry*, Vol. I, p. 108. [P.]

[34] It is between eleven and twelve in the morning, after church service,

To where Fleetditch with disemboguing streams
Rolls the large tribute of dead dogs to Thames,
The king of dykes! than whom no sluice of mud
With deeper sable blots the silver flood.
"Here strip, my children! here at once leap in,   275
Here prove who best can dash through thick and thin,
And who the most in love of dirt excel,
Or dark dexterity of groping well.
Who flings most filth, and wide pollutes around
The stream, be his the Weekly Journals bound;[35]   280
A pig of lead to him who dives the best;
A peck of coals apiece shall glad the rest."
      In naked majesty Oldmixon stands,[36]
And Milo-like[37] surveys his arms and hands;
Then, sighing, thus, "And am I now threescore?   285
Ah why, ye Gods! should two and two make four?"

that the criminals are whipped in Bridewell.—This is to mark punctually
the *time* of the day: Homer does it by the circumstance of the Judges
rising from court, or of the Labourer's dinner; our author by one very
proper both to the *Persons* and the *Scene* of his poem, which we may
remember commenced in the evening of the Lord Mayor's day: The first
book passed in that *night;* the next *morning* the games begin in the
Strand, thence along Fleet Street (places inhabited by Booksellers); then
they proceed by Bridewell toward Fleetditch, and lastly through Ludgate
to the City and the Temple of the Goddess. [P.]

[35] Papers of news and scandal intermixed, on different sides and parties,
and frequently shifting from one side to the other, called the *London
Journal, British Journal, Daily Journal,* etc., the concealed writers of
which for some time were Oldmixon, Roome, Arnall, Concanen, and
others; persons never seen by our author. [P.]

[36] Mr. JOHN OLDMIXON, next to Mr. Dennis, the most ancient Critic of
our Nation; and unjust censurer of Mr. Addison. . . . In his *Essay on
Criticism,* and the *Arts of Logic and Rhetoric,* he frequently reflects on
our Author. But the top of his character was a Perverter of History, in
that scandalous one of the Stuarts, in folio, and his *Critical History of
England,* two volumes, octavo. Being employed by Bishop Kennet, in
publishing the Historians in his Collection, he falsified Daniel's *Chronicle*
in numberless places. . . . He was all his life a virulent Party writer for
hire, and received his reward in a small place, which he enjoyed to his
death. [P.]

[37] [Cf. Ovid *Metamorphoses* xv. 229–230.] Fletque Milon senior, cum
spectat inanes Herculeis similes, fluidos pendere lacertos. [P.]

He said, and climbed a stranded lighter's height,
Shot to the black abyss, and plunged downright.
The Senior's judgment all the crowd admire,
Who but to sink the deeper, rose the higher.   290

    Next Smedley[38] dived; slow circles dimpled o'er
The quaking mud, that closed, and oped no more.
All look, all sigh, and call on Smedley lost;
"Smedley" in vain resounds through all the coast.

    Then *[39] essayed; scarce vanished out of sight,   295
He buoys up instant, and returns to light:
He bears no token of the sabler streams,
And mounts far off among the Swans of Thames.

    True to the bottom, see Concanen[40] creep,
A cold, long-winded native of the deep: 300
If perseverance gain the Diver's prize,
Not everlasting Blackmore this denies:
No noise, no stir, no motion canst thou make,
Th' unconscious stream sleeps o'er thee like a lake.

    Next plunged a feeble, but a desperate pack,   305
With each a sickly brother at his back:[41]

---

[38] [Jonathan Smedley.] The person here mentioned, an Irishman, was
author and publisher of many scurrilous pieces, a weekly *Whitehall Jour-
nal*, in the year 1722, in the name of Sir James Baker; and particularly
whole volumes of Billingsgate against Dr. Swift and Mr. Pope, called
Gulliveriana and *Alexandriana*, printed in octavo, 1728. [P.]

[39] A Gentleman of genius and spirit, who was secretly dipped in some
papers of this kind, on whom our Poet bestows a panegyric instead of a
satire, as deserving to be better employed than in Party quarrels, and
personal invectives. [P.]

[40] MATTHEW CONCANEN, an Irishman, bred to the law. . . . He was
author of several dull and dead scurrilities in the *British* and *London
Journals,* and in a paper called the *Speculatist*. In a pamphlet, called a
Supplement to the Profound, he dealt very unfairly with out Poet, not
only frequently imputing to him Mr. Broome's verses (for which he
might indeed seem in some degree accountable, having corrected what
that gentleman did) but those of the Duke of Buckingham, and others:
To this rare piece somebody humorously caused him to take for his
motto, *De profundis clamavi.* . . . [P.]

[41] These were daily Papers, a number of which, to lessen the expense,
were printed one on the back of another. [P.]

Sons of a Day! just buoyant on the flood,
Then numbered with the puppies in the mud.
Ask ye their names? I could as soon disclose
The names of these blind puppies as of those.   310
Fast by, like Niobe (her children gone) [42]
Sits Mother Osborne, [43] stupefied to stone!
And Monumental Brass this record bears,
"These are,—ah no! those were, the Gazetteers!"
    Not so bold Arnall; [44] with a weight of skull,   315
Furious he dives, precipitately dull.
Whirlpools and storms his circling arm invest,
With all the might of gravitation blest.
No crab more active in the dirty dance,
Downward to climb, and backward to advance.   320
He brings up half the bottom on his head,
And loudly claims the Journals and the Lead.
    The plunging Prelate, and his ponderous Grace,
With holy envy gave one Layman place.
When lo! a burst of thunder shook the flood;   325
Slow rose a form, in majesty of Mud;
Shaking the horrors of his sable brows,
And each ferocious feature grim with ooze.
Greater he looks, and more than mortal stares:
Then thus the wonders of the deep declares.   330
    First he relates, how sinking to the chin,
Smit with his mien, the Mud Nymphs sucked him in:

---

[42] See the story in Ovid, where the miserable Petrifaction of this old Lady is pathetically described. [P.]

[43] A name assumed by the eldest and gravest of these writers, who at last, being ashamed of his Pupils, gave his paper over, and in his age remained silent. [P.]

[44] WILLIAM ARNALL, bred an Attorney, was a perfect Genius in this sort of work. He began under twenty with furious Party papers; then succeeded Concanen in the *British Journal*. At the first publication of the *Dunciad,* he prevailed on the Author not to give him his due place in it, by a letter professing his detestation of such practices as his Predecessor's. But since, by the most unexampled insolence, and personal abuse of several great men, the Poet's particular friends, he most amply deserved a niche in the Temple of Infamy. [P.]

How young Lutetia, softer than the down,
Nigrina black, and Merdamante brown,
Vied for his love in jetty bowers below,   335
As Hylas[45] fair was ravished long ago.
Then sung, how shown him by the Nut-brown maids
A branch of Styx here rises from the Shades,
That tinctured as it runs with Lethe's streams,
And wafting Vapours from the Land of dreams,   340
(As under seas Alpheus' secret sluice
Bears Pisa's offerings to his Arethuse)[46]
Pours into Thames: and hence the mingled wave
Intoxicates the pert, and lulls the grave:
Here brisker vapours o'er the TEMPLE creep,   345
There, all from Paul's to Aldgate drink and sleep.
Thence to the banks where reverend Bards repose,
They led him soft; each reverend Bard arose;
And Milbourn[47] chief, deputed by the rest,
Gave him the cassock, surcingle, and vest.   350
"Receive" (he said) "these robes which once were mine,
Dulness is sacred in a sound divine."
          He ceased, and spread the robe; the crowd confess
The reverend Flamen in his lengthened dress.
Around him wide a sable Army stand,   355
A lowborn, cell-bred, selfish, servile band,
Prompt or to guard or stab, to saint or damn,
Heaven's Swiss, who fight for any God, or Man.
          Through Lud's famed gates, along the well-known
     Fleet,
Rolls the black troop, and overshades the street,   360
Till showers of Sermons, Characters, Essays,

[45] Who was ravished by the water nymphs and drawn into the river.
. . . See Virgil *Eclogue* vi [43–48].   [P.]
[46] Of Alpheus's waters gliding secretly under the sea of Pisa, to mix with
those of Arethuse in Sicily, see Moschus *Idyll* viii; Virgil *Eclogue* x[3–4];
and again *Æneid* iii [693–695].   [P.]
[47] Luke Milbourn, a Clergyman, the fairest of Critics; who, when he
wrote against Mr. Dryden's Virgil, did him justice in printing at the
same time his own translations of him, which were intolerable. His
manner of writing has a great resemblance with that of the Gentlemen
of the *Dunciad* against our author.   [P.]

In circling fleeces whiten all the ways:
So clouds replenished from some bog below,
Mount in dark volumes, and descend in snow.
Here stopped the Goddess; and in pomp proclaims   365
A gentler exercise to close the games.
    "Ye Critics! in whose heads, as equal scales,
I weigh what author's heaviness prevails;
Which most conduce to soothe the soul in slumbers,
My H—ley's periods, or my Blackmore's numbers;   370
Attend the trial we propose to make:
If there be man, who o'er such works can wake,
Sleep's all-subduing charms who dares defy,
And boasts Ulysses' ear with Argus' eye;
To him we grant our amplest powers to sit   375
Judge of all present, past, and future wit;
To cavil, censure, dictate, right or wrong,
Full and eternal privilege of tongue."
    Three College Sophs, and three pert Templars came,
The same their talents, and their tastes the same;   380
Each prompt to query, answer, and debate,
And smit with love of Poesy and Prate.
The ponderous books two gentle readers bring;
The heroes sit, the vulgar form a ring.
The clamorous crowd is hushed with mugs of Mum,   385
Till all, tuned equal, send a general hum.
Then mount the Clerks, and in one lazy tone
Through the long, heavy, painful page drawl on;
Soft creeping, words on words, the sense compose;
At every line they stretch, they yawn, they doze.   390
As to soft gales top-heavy pines bow low
Their heads, and lift them as they cease to blow:
Thus oft they rear, and oft the head decline,
As breathe, or pause, by fits, the airs divine.
And now to this side, now to that they nod,   395
As verse, or prose, infuse the drowsy God.
Thrice Budgell[48] aimed to speak, but thrice supprest

---

[48] Famous for his speeches on many occasions about the South Sea scheme, etc. "He is a very ingenious gentleman, and hath written some excellent Epilogues to Plays, and *one small* piece on Love, which is very pretty."

By potent Arthur, knocked his chin and breast.
Toland and Tindal,[49] prompt at priests to jeer,
Yet silent bowed to *Christ's No kingdom here.*[50]   400
Who sat the nearest, by the words o'ercome,
Slept first; the distant nodded to the hum.
Then down are rolled the books; stretched o'er 'em lies
Each gentle clerk, and muttering seals his eyes.
As what a Dutchman plumps into the lakes,   405
One circle first, and then a second makes;
What Dulness dropped among her sons imprest
Like motion from one circle to the rest;
So from the midmost the nutation spreads
Round and more round, o'er all the *sea of heads.*   410
At last Centlivre[51] felt her voice to fail,
Motteux[52] himself unfinished left his tale,
Boyer[53] the State, and Law[54] the Stage gave o'er,
Morgan[55] and Mandeville[56] could prate no more;

—Jacob, *Lives of Poets,* Vol. II, p. 289. [P.] Eustace Budgell, a cousin of Addison, contributed essays to the *Spectator,* translated the *Characters* of Theophrastus, and was Under Secretary of State. He lost money in the South Sea Bubble, acquired an increasingly bad reputation, and in 1737 committed suicide by jumping into the Thames.

[49] Two persons, not so happy as to be obscure, who writ against the Religion of their Country. *Toland,* the author of the Atheist's liturgy, called *Pantheisticon,* was a spy, in pay to Lord Oxford. *Tindal* was author of the *Rights of the Christian Church,* and *Christianity as old as the Creation.* [P.]

[50] This is said by Curll, *Key to Dunciad,* to allude to a sermon of a reverend Bishop. [P.]

[51] Mrs. Susanna Centlivre, wife to Mr. Centlivre, Yeoman of the Mouth to his Majesty. She writ many Plays, and a Song (says Mr. Jacob, Vol. I, p. 32) before she was seven years old. She also writ a Ballad against Mr. Pope's Homer, before he began it. [P.]

[52] Peter Anthony Motteux, a French immigrant, dramatist, journalist and translator.

[53] A Boyer, a voluminous compiler of Annals, Political Collections, etc. [P.]

[54] William Law, A. M., wrote with great zeal against the Stage; Mr. Dennis answered with as great: Their books were printed in 1726. [P.]

[55] A writer against Religion . . . . having stolen his Morality from Tindal, and his Philosophy from Spinoza, he calls himself, by the courtesy of England, a *Moral Philosopher.* W.

Norton,[57] from Daniel and Ostrœa sprung,   415
Blessed with his father's front, and mother's tongue,
Hung silent down his never-blushing head;
And all was hushed, as Folly's self lay dead.
    Thus the soft gifts of Sleep conclude the day,
And stretched on bulks, as usual, Poets lay.   420
Why should I sing, what bards the nightly Muse
Did slumbering visit, and convey to stews;
Who prouder marched, with magistrates in state,
To some famed roundhouse, ever open gate!
How Henley lay inspired beside a sink,   425
And to mere mortals seemed a Priest in drink:
While others, timely, to the neighboring Fleet[58]
(Haunt of the Muses) made their safe retreat.

Book the Third

ARGUMENT

After the other persons are disposed in their proper places of rest, the Goddess transports the King to her Temple, and there lays him to slumber with his head on her lap; a position of marvellous virtue, which causes all the Visions of wild enthusiasts, projectors, politicians, inamoratos, castle-builders, chemists, and poets. He is immediately carried on the wings of Fancy, and led by a mad Poetical Sibyl to the *Elysian shade;* where on the banks of *Lethe,* the souls of the dull are dipped by *Bavius,* before their entrance into this world. There he is met by the ghost of *Settle,* and by him made acquainted with the wonders of the place, and with those which he himself is destined to perform. He takes him to a *Mount of Vision,* from whence he shows him the past triumphs of the

[56] [Bernard de Mandeville.] This writer, who prided himself as much in the reputation of an *Immoral Philosopher,* was author of a famous book called *The Fable of the Bees* (1714); written to prove that moral Virtue is the invention of knaves, and Christian Virtue the imposition of fools, and that Vice is necessary, and alone sufficient to render Society flourishing and happy.   W.
[57] Norton Defoe, offspring of the famous Daniel. *Fortes creantur fortibus.* One of the authors of the *Flying Post,* in which well-bred work Mr. P. had sometime the honour to be abused with his betters; and of many hired scurrilities and daily papers, to which he never set his name.   [P.]
[58] A prison for insolvent Debtors on the bank of the Ditch.   [P.]

Empire of Dulness, then the present, and lastly the future: how small a part of the world was ever conquered by Science, how soon those conquests were stopped, and those very nations again reduced to her dominion. Then distinguishing the Island of *Great Britain,* shows by what aids, by what persons, and by what degrees it shall be brought to her Empire. Some of the persons he causes to pass in review before his eyes, describing each by his proper figure, character, and qualifications. On a sudden the Scene shifts, and a vast number of miracles and prodigies appear, utterly surprising and unknown to the King himself, till they are explained to be the wonders of his own reign now commencing. On this subject *Settle* breaks into a congratulation, yet not unmixed with concern, that his own times were but types of these. He prophesies how first the nation shall be overrun with *Farces, Operas,* and *Shows;* how the throne of Dulness shall be advanced over the *Theatres,* and set up even at *Court;* then how her Sons shall preside in the seats of *Arts* and *Sciences:* giving a glimpse or Pisgah sight of the future Fulness of her Glory, the accomplishment whereof is the subject of the fourth and last book.

> But in her Temple's last recess enclosed,
> On Dulness' lap th' Anointed head reposed.
> Him close she curtains round with Vapours blue,
> And soft besprinkles with Cimmerian dew.
> Then raptures high the seat of Sense o'erflow,   5
> Which only heads refined from Reason know.
> Hence, from the straw where Bedlam's Prophet nods,
> He hears loud Oracles, and talks with Gods:
> Hence the Fool's Paradise, the Statesman's Scheme,
> The air-built Castle, and the golden Dream,   10
> The Maid's romantic wish, the Chemist's flame,
> And Poet's vision of eternal Fame.
>   And now, on Fancy's easy wing conveyed,
> The King descending views th' Elysian Shade.
> A slipshod Sibyl led his steps along,   15
> In lofty madness meditating song;
> Her tresses staring from Poetic dreams,
> And never washed, but in Castalia's streams.
> Taylor,[1] their better Charon, leads an oar,

[1] John Taylor the Water Poet, an honest man, who owns he learned not so much as the Accidence: A rare example of modesty in a Poet!
I must confess I do want eloquence,

(One swan of Thames, though now he sings no more.)   20
Benlowes,[2] propitious still to blockheads, bows;
And Shadwell[3] nods the Poppy on his brows.
Here, in a dusky vale where Lethe rolls,
Old Bavius[4] sits, to dip poetic souls,
And blunt the sense, and fit it for a skull   25
Of solid proof, impenetrably dull:
Instant, when dipped, away they wing their flight,
Where Brown and Mears[5] unbar the gates of Light,
Demand new bodies, and in Calf's array
Rush to the world, impatient for the day.   30
Millions and millions on these banks he views,
Thick as the stars of night, or morning dews,
As thick as bees o'er vernal blossoms fly,
As thick as eggs at Ward in Pillory.[6]
    Wondering he gazed: When lo! a Sage appears,   35
By his broad shoulders known, and length of ears,
Known by the band and suit which Settle wore[7]

And never scarce did learn my Accidence;
   For having got from *possum* to *posset,*
   I there was gravelled, could no farther get.
He wrote fourscore books in the reign of James I and Charles I and afterwards (like Edward Ward) kept an Alehouse in Long Acre. He died in 1654. [P.]
[2] A country gentleman, famous for his own bad Poetry, and for patronizing bad Poets, as may be seen from many Dedications of Quarles and others to him. Some of these anagramed his name, *Benlowes* into *Benevolus:* to verify which, he spent his whole estate upon them. [P.]
[3] Shadwell took Opium for many years, and died of too large a dose, in the year 1692. [P.]
[4] Bavius was an ancient Poet, celebrated by Virgil for the like cause as Bays by our author, though not in so Christian-like a manner: For heathenishly it is declared by Virgil of Bavius, that he ought to be *hated* and *detested* for his evil works; *Qui Bavium non* odit; whereas we have often had occasion to observe our Poet's great *Good Nature* and *Mercifulness* through the whole course of this Poem. SCRIBLERUS. [P.]
[5] Booksellers, Printers for anybody. [P.]
[6] John Ward of Hackney, Esq., Member of Parliament, being convicted of forgery, was first expelled the House, and then sentenced to the Pillory on the 17th of February, 1727. [P.]
[7] Elkanah Settle was once a Writer in vogue, as well as Cibber, both for Dramatic Poetry and Politics. . . . He was author or publisher of many

(His only suit) for twice three years before:
All as the vest, appeared the wearer's frame,
Old in new state, another yet the same.   40
Bland and familiar as in life, begun
Thus the great Father to the greater Son.
     "Oh born to see what none can see awake!
Behold the wonders of th' oblivious Lake.
Thou, yet unborn, hast touched this sacred shore;   45
The hand of Bavius drenched thee o'er and o'er.
But blind to former, as to future fate,
What mortal knows his pre-existent state?
Who knows how long thy transmigrating soul
Might from Bœotian to Bœotian roll?[8]   50
How many Dutchmen she vouchsafed to thrid?
How many stages through old Monks she rid?
And all who since, in mild benighted days,
Mixed the Owl's ivy with the Poet's bays?
As man's Mæanders to the vital spring   55
Roll all their tides, then back their circles bring;
Or whirligigs, twirled round by skilful swain,
Suck the thread in, then yield it out again:
All nonsense thus, of old or modern date,
Shall in thee centre, from thee circulate.   60
For this our Queen unfolds to vision true
Thy mental eye, for thou hast much to view:
Old scenes of glory, times long cast behind
Shall, first recalled, rush forward to thy mind:
Then stretch thy sight o'er all her rising reign,   65
And let the past and future fire thy brain.
     "Ascend this hill, whose cloudy point commands
Her boundless empire over seas and lands.

noted pamphlets in the time of King Charles II. He answered all Dryden's
political poems; and, being carried up on *one side,* succeeded not a little
in his Tragedy of the *Empress of Morocco.*   [P.]   Cf. Bk. I, l. 90.
[8] Bœotia lay under the ridicule of the Wits formerly, as Ireland does now;
though it produced one of the greatest Poets and one of the greatest Gen-
erals of Greece.   [P.] Cf. I, 25. Pope refers to Pindar and Epaminondas.

See, round the Poles where keener spangles shine,[9]
Where spices smoke beneath the burning Line,   70
(Earth's wide extremes) her sable flag displayed,
And all the nations covered in her shade!

    "Far eastward cast thine eye, from whence the Sun
And orient Science their bright course begun:
One godlike Monarch[10] all that pride confounds,   75
He, whose long wall the wandering Tartar bounds;
Heavens! what a pile! whole ages perish there,
And one bright blaze turns Learning into air.

    "Thence to the south extend thy gladdened eyes;
There rival flames with equal glory rise,   80
From shelves to shelves see greedy Vulcan roll,[11]
And lick up all the Physic of the Soul.

    "How little, mark! that portion of the ball,
Where, faint at best, the beams of Science fall:
Soon as they dawn, from Hyperborean skies   85
Embodied dark, what clouds of Vandals rise!
Lo! where Mæotis sleeps, and hardly flows
The freezing Tanais through a waste of snows,
The North by myriads pours her mighty sons,
Great nurse of Goths, of Alans, and of Huns!   90
See Alaric's stern port! the marital frame
Of Genseric! and Attila's dread name!
See the bold Ostrogoths on Latium fall;
See the fierce Visigoths on Spain and Gaul!
See, where the morning gilds the palmy shore   95
(The soil that arts and infant letters bore)[12]
His conquering tribes th' Arabian prophet draws,

[9] Almost the whole Southern and Nothern Continent wrapped in ignorance. [P.]

[10] Chi Ho-am-ti, Emperor of China, the same who built the great wall between China and Tartary, destroyed all the books and learned men of that empire. [P.]

[11] The Caliph Omar I, having conquered Egypt, caused his General to burn the Ptolemean library, on the gates of which was this inscription, ΨΥΧΗΣ ΙΑΤΡΕΙΟΝ, the Physic of the Soul. [P.]

[12] Phœnicia, Syria, etc., where Letters are said to have been invented. In these countries Mahomet began his conquests. [P.]

And saving Ignorance enthrones by Laws.
See Christians, Jews, one heavy sabbath keep,
And all the western world believe and sleep.   100
    "Lo! Rome herself, proud mistress now no more
Of arts, but thundering against heathen lore;
Her grey-haired Synods damning books unread,
- And Bacon trembling for his brazen head.
Padua, with sighs, beholds her Livy burn,   105
And even th' Antipodes Virgilius mourn.
See, the Cirque falls, th' unpillared Temple nods,
Streets paved with Heroes, Tiber choked with Gods:
Till Peter's keys some christened Jove adorn,[13]
And Pan to Moses lends his pagan horn;   110
See, graceless Venus to a Virgin turned,
Or Phidias broken, and Apelles burned.
    "Behold yon Isle, by Palmers, Pilgrims trod,
Men bearded, bald, cowled, uncowled, shod, unshod,
Peeled, patched, and piebald, linsey-wolsey brothers,   115
Grave Mummers! sleeveless some, and shirtless others.
That once was Britain—Happy! had she seen
No fiercer sons, had Easter never been.[14]
In peace, great Goddess, ever be adored;
How keen the war, if Dulness draw the sword!   120
Thus visit not thy own! on this blest age
Oh spread thy Influence, but restrain they Rage!
    "And see, my son! the hour is on its way,
That lifts our Goddess to imperial sway;
This favorite Isle, long severed from her reign,   125

---

[13] After the government of Rome devolved to the Popes, their zeal was for some time exerted in demolishing the Heathen Temples and Statues, so that the Goths scarce destroyed more monuments of Antiquity out of rage, than these out of devotion. At length they spared some of the Temples, by converting them to Churches; and some of the Statues, by modifying them into images of Saints. In much later times, it was thought necessary to change the statues of Apollo and Pallas, on the tomb of Sannazarius, into David and Judith; the Lyre easily became a Harp, and the Gorgon's head turned to that of Holofernes. [P.]

[14] Wars in England anciently, about the right time of celebrating Easter. [P.]

Dove-like, she gathers to her wings again.[15]
Now look through Fate! behold the scene she draws!
What aids, what armies to assert her cause!
See all her progeny, illustrious sight!
Behold, and count them, as they rise to light.   130
As Berecynthia, while her offspring vie
In homage to the Mother of the sky,
Surveys around her, in the blest abode,
An hundred sons, and every son a God:
Not with less glory mighty Dulness crowned,   135
Shall take through Grubstreet her triumphant round;
And her Parnassus glancing o'er at once,
Behold an hundred sons, and each a Dunce.

    "Mark first that youth who takes the foremost place,
And thrusts his person full into your face.   140
With all thy Father's virtues blest, be born!
And a new Cibber shall the stage adorn.

    "A second see, by meeker manners known,
And modest as the maid that sips alone;
From the strong fate of drams if thou get free,   145
Another Durfey, Ward! shall sing in thee.
Thee shall each alehouse, thee each gill-house mourn,
And answering gin-shops sourer sights return.

    "Jacob,[16] the scourge of Grammar, mark with awe,
Nor less revere him, blunderbuss of Law.   150
Lo P—p—le's[17] brow, tremendous to the town,

---

[15] This is fulfilled in the fourth book. [P.]

[16] "This *Gentleman* is son of a *considerable Maltster* of Romsey in South-amptonshire, and bred to the Law under a *very eminent Attorney:* Who, between his *more laborious* studies, has *diverted* himself with Poetry. He is a great admirer of Poets and their works, which has occasioned him to try his genius that way.—He has written in prose the *Lives* of the *Poets, Essays,* and a great many Law books, *The Accomplished Conveyancer, Modern Justice, etc.*—GILES JACOB of himeslf, *Lives of Poets,* Vol. I. He very grossly, and unprovoked, abused in that book the Author's Friend, Mr. *Gay.* [P.]

[17] Popple was the author of some vile Plays and Pamphlets. He published abuses on our Author in a paper called the *Prompter.* [P.]

Horneck's[18] fierce eye, and Roome's[18] funereal Frown.
Lo sneering Goode,[19] half malice and half whim,
A Fiend in glee, ridiculously grim.
Each Cygnet sweet, of Bath and Tunbridge race,   155
Whose tuneful whistling makes the waters pass:[20]
Each Songster, Riddler, every nameless name,
All crowd, who foremost shall be damned to Fame.
Some strain in rhyme; the Muses, on their racks,
Scream like the winding of ten thousand jacks;   160
Some free from rhyme or reason, rule or check,
Break Priscian's head, and Pegasus's neck;
Down, down they larum, with impetuous whirl,
The Pindars, and the Miltons of a Curll.

    "Silence, ye Wolves! while Ralph[21] to Cynthia howls,
And makes Night hideous—Answer him, ye Owls!   166
    "Sense, speech, and measure, living tongues and dead,
Let all give way—and Morris may be read.
Flow, Welsted,[22] flow! like thine inspirer, Beer;
Though stale, not ripe; though thin, yet never clear;[23]   170
So sweetly mawkish, and so smoothly dull;
Heady, not strong; o'erflowing, though not full.

[18] These two were virulent Party writers. . . . The first was Philip Horneck, Author of a Billingsgate paper called *The High German Doctor.* Edward Roome was son of an Undertaker for Funerals in Fleet street, and writ some of the papers called *Pasquin,* where by malicious Innuendos he endeavoured to represent our Author guilty of malevolent practices with a great man then under prosecution of Parliament. [P.]

[19] An ill-natured Critic, who writ a satire on our Author, called *The Mock Æsop,* and many anonymous Libels in Newspapers for hire. [P.]

[20] There were several successions of these sort of minor poets, at Tunbridge, Bath, etc., singing the praise of the Annuals flourishing for that season; whose names indeed would be nameless, and therefore the Poet slurs them over with others in general. [P.]

[21] James Ralph, a name inserted after the first editions, not known to our author till he writ a swearing-piece called *Sawney,* very abusive of Dr. Swift, Mr. Gay, and himself. These lines allude to a thing of his entitled *Night, a Poem.* [P.]

[22] Cf. Bk. II, l. 209.

[23] Cf. Denham's famous lines on the Thames in his *Cooper's Hill.*

"Ah Dennis!²⁴ Gildon ah! what ill-starred rage
Divides a friendship long confirmed by age?
Blockheads with reason wicked wits abhor,   175
But fool with fool is barbarous civil war.
Embrace, embrace, my sons! be foes no more!
Nor glad vile Poets with true Critics' gore.
  "Behold yon Pair,²⁵ in strict embraces joined;
How like in manners, and how like in mind!   180
Equal in wit, and equally polite,
Shall this a *Pasquin,* that a *Grumbler* write;
Like are their merits, like rewards they share,
That shines a Consul, this Commissioner.²⁶
  "But who is he, in closet close y-pent,   185
Of sober face, with learnèd dust besprent?
Right well mine eyes arede the myster wight,²⁷
On parchment scraps y-fed, and Wormius²⁸ hight.
To future ages may thy dulness last,
As thou preservst the dulness of the past!   190
  "There, dim in clouds, the poring Scholiasts mark,

²⁴ The reader, who has seen through the course of these notes, what a constant attendance Mr. Dennis paid to our Author and all his works, may perhaps wonder he should be mentioned but twice, and so slightly touched, in this poem. But in truth he looked upon him with some esteem, for having (more generously than all the rest) *set his Name* to such writings. He was also a very old man at this time. By his own account of himself in Mr. *Jacob's Lives,* he must have been above threescore, and happily lived many years after. So that he was senior to Mr. *Durfey,* who hitherto of all our Poets enjoyed the longest bodily life.   [P.]
²⁵ One of these was Author of a weekly paper called *The Grumbler,* as the other was concerned in another called *Pasquin,* in which Mr. *Pope* was abused with the Duke of *Buckingham,* and Bishop of *Rochester.* They also joined in a piece against his first undertaking to translate the *Iliad,* entitled *Homerides,* by Sir *Iliad Doggrel,* printed 1715.   [P.]
²⁶ Such places were given at this time to such sort of Writers.   [P.]
²⁷ *Myster wight.* Uncouth mortal.   [P.] Pope is mistaken about the meaning of the Spenserian word *myster.*
²⁸ Let not this name, purely fictitions, be conceited to mean the learned *Olaus Wormius;* much less (as it was unwarrantably foisted into the surreptitious editions) our own Antiquary Mr. *Thomas Hearne,* who had no way aggrieved our Poet, but on the contrary published many curious tracts which he hath to his great contentment perused.   [P.]

Wits, who, like owls, see only in the dark,
A Lumber house of books in every head,
For ever reading, never to be read!
    "But, where each Science lifts its modern type,   195
History her Pot, Divinity her Pipe,
While proud Philosophy repines to show,
Dishonest sight! his breeches rent below;
Embrowned with native bronze, lo! Henley stands,[29]
Tuning his voice, and balancing his hands.   200
How fluent nonsense trickles from his tongue!
How sweet the periods, neither said, nor sung!
Still break the benches, Henley! with thy strain,
While Sherlock, Hare, and Gibson preach in vain.[30]
Oh great Restorer of the good old Stage,   205
Preacher at once, and Zany of thy age!
Oh worthy thou of Egypt's wise abodes,
A decent priest, where monkeys were the gods!
But fate with butchers placed thy priestly stall,
Meek modern faith to murder, hack, and maul;   210
And bade thee live, to crown Britannia's praise,
In Toland's, Tindal's, and in Woolston's days.[31]
    "Yet oh, my sons, a father's words attend:
(So may the fates preserve the ears you lend)
'Tis yours, a Bacon or a Locke to blame,   215
A Newton's genius, or a Milton's flame:
But oh! with One, immortal One dispense,
The source of Newton's Light, of Bacon's Sense.
Content, each Emanation of his fires

[29] J. Henley the Orator; he preached on the Sundays upon Theological matters, and on the Wednesdays upon all other sciences. Each auditor paid one shilling. He declaimed some years against the greatest persons, and occasionally did our Author that honour. . . . This man had an hundred pounds a year given him for the secret service of a weekly paper of unintelligible nonsense, called the *Hyp-Doctor*. [P.]

[30] Bishops of Salisbury, Chichester, and London; [P.] whose Sermons and Pastoral Letters did honour to their country as well as stations. [W.]

[31] Of *Toland* and *Tindal,* see Bk. II [l. 399]. *Tho. Woolston* was an impious madman, who wrote in a most insolent style against the Miracles of the Gospel, in the years 1726, etc. [P.]

That beams on earth, each Virtue he inspires,   220
Each Art he prompts, each Charm he can create,
Whate'er he gives, are given for you to hate.
Persist, by all divine in Man unawed,
But, 'Learn, ye DUNCES! not to scorn your God.' "[32]

    Thus he, for then a ray of Reason stole   225
Half through the solid darkness of his soul;
But soon the cloud returned—and thus the Sire:
"See now, what Dulness and her sons admire!
See what the charms, that smite the simple heart
Not touched by Nature, and not reached by Art."   230

    His never-blushing head he turned aside,
(Not half so pleased when Goodman prophesied)[33]
And looked, and saw a sable Sorcerer rise,[34]
Swift to whose hand a wingèd volume flies:
All sudden, Gorgons hiss, and Dragons glare,   235
And ten-horned fiends and Giants rush to war.
Hell rises, Heaven descends, and dance on Earth:[35]
Gods, imps, and monsters, music, rage, and mirth,
A fire, a jig, a battle, and a ball,
Till one wide conflagration swallows all.   240

    Thence a new world to Nature's laws unknown,
Breaks out refulgent, with a heaven its own:
Another Cynthia her new journey runs,
And other planets circle other suns.

[32] Cf. Virgil *Æneid* vi. 619.

[33] Mr. Cibber tells us, in his *Life,* p. 149, that Goodman being at the rehearsal of a play, in which he had a part, clapped him on the shoulder and cried, "If he does not make a good actor, I'll be d—d." —"And (says Mr. Cibber) I make it a question, whether Alexander himself, or Charles the Twelfth of Sweden, when at the head of their first victorious armies, could feel a greater transport in their bosoms than I did in mine." [P.]

[34] Dr. Faustus, the subject of a set of Farces, which lasted in vogue two or three seasons, in which both Playhouses strove to outdo each other for some years. All the extravagancies in the sixteen lines following were introduced on the Stage, and frequented by persons of the first quality in England, to the twentieth and thirtieth time. [P.]

[35] This monstrous absurdity was actually represented in Tibbald's *Rape of Proserpine.* [P.]

The forests dance, the rivers upward rise,   245
Whales sport in woods, and dolphins in the skies;
And last, to give the whole creation grace,
Lo! one vast Egg produces human race.[36]
        Joy fills his soul, joy innocent of thought;
'What power,' he cries, 'what power these wonders wrought?'
"Son, what thou seekest is in thee! Look, and find   251
Each Monster meets his likeness in thy mind.
Yet wouldst thou more? In yonder cloud behold,
Whose sarsenet skirts are edged with flamy gold,
A matchless Youth! his nod these worlds controls,   255
Wings the red lightning, and the thunder rolls.
Angel of Dulness, sent to scatter round
Her magic charms o'er all unclassic ground:
Yon stars, yon suns, he rears at pleasure higher,
Illumes their light, and sets their flames on fire.   260
Immortal Rich![37] how calm he sits at ease
Mid snows of paper, and fierce hail of pease;
And proud his Mistress' order to perform,
Rides in the whirlwind, and directs the storm.
        "But lo! to dark encounter in mid air   265
New wizards rise; I see my Cibber there!
Booth[38] in his cloudy tabernacle shrined,
On grinning dragons thou shalt mount the wind.[39]
Dire is the conflict, dismal is the din,
Here shouts all Drury, there all Lincoln's Inn;   270
Contending Theatres our empire raise,
Alike their labours, and alike their praise.
        "And are these wonders, Son, to thee unknown?
Unknown to thee? These wonders are thy own.

[36] In another of these Farces Harlequin is hatched upon the stage, out of
a large Egg. [P.]
[37] Mr. John Rich, Master of the Theatre Royal in Covent Garden, was the
first that excelled this way. [P.]
[38] Booth and Cibber were joint managers of the Theatre in Drury Lane.
[P.]
[39] In his Letter to Mr. P. Mr. C. solemnly declares this not to be *literally
true*. We hope therefore the reader will understand it *allegorically only*.
[P.]

These Fate reserved to grace thy reign divine,   275
Foreseen by me, but ah! withheld from mine.
In Lud's old walls though long I ruled, renowned
Far as loud Bow's stupendous bells resound;
Though my own Aldermen conferred the bays,
To me committing their eternal praise,   280
Their full-fed Heroes, their pacific Mayors,
Their annual trophies, and their monthly wars:[40]
Though long my Party built on me their hopes,
For writing Pamphlets, and for roasting Popes;[41]
Yet lo! in me what authors have to brag on!   285
Reduced at last to hiss in my own dragon.
Avert it, Heaven! that thou, my Cibber, e'er
Shouldst wag a serpent tail in Smithfield fair!
Like the vile straw that's blown about the streets,
The needy Poet sticks to all he meets,   290
Coached, carted, trod upon, now loose, now fast,
And carried off in some Dog's tail at last.
Happier thy fortunes! like a rolling stone,
Thy giddy dulness still shall lumber on,
Safe in its heaviness, shall never stray,   295
But lick up every blockhead in the way.
Thee shall the Patriot, thee the Courtier taste,
And every year be duller than the last.
Till raised from booths, to Theatre, to Court,
Her seat imperial Dulness shall transport.   300
Already Opera prepares the way,
The sure forerunner of her gentle sway:

[40] *Annual trophies,* on the Lord Mayor's day; and *monthly wars* in the Artillery Ground. [P.]
[41] Settle, like most Party writers, was very uncertain in his political principles. He was employed to hold the pen in the *Character* of a *popish successor,* but afterwards printed his *Narrative* on the other side. He had managed the ceremony of a famous Pope-burning on November 17, 1680, then became a trooper in King James's army, at Hounslow Heath. After the Revolution he kept a booth at Bartholomew Fair, where, in the droll called *St. George for England,* he acted in his old age in a Dragon of green leather of his own invention; he was at last taken into the Charter-house, and there died, aged sixty years. [P.] Cf. I, 90.

Let her thy heart, next Drabs and Dice, engage,
The third mad passion of thy doting age.
Teach thou the warbling Polypheme to roar,[42]   305
And scream thyself as none e'er screamed before!
To aid our cause, if Heaven thou canst not bend,
Hell thou shalt move; for Faustus[43] is our friend:
Pluto with Cato thou for this shalt join,
And link the Mourning Bride to Proserpine.   310
Grubstreet! thy fall should men and Gods conspire,
Thy stage shall stand, ensure it but from Fire.[44]
Another Æschylus appears![45] prepare
For new abortions, all ye pregnant fair!
In flames, like Semele's, be brought to bed,   315
While opening Hell spouts wildfire at your head.
  "Now, Bavius, take the poppy from thy brow,
And place it here! here all ye Heroes bow!
This, this is he, foretold by ancient rhymes:
Th' Augustus born to bring Saturnian times.   320
Signs following signs lead on the mighty year!
See! the dull stars roll round and reappear.
See, see, our own true Phœbus wears the bays!
Our Midas sits Lord Chancellor of Plays!
On Poets' Tombs see Benson's titles writ![46]   325
Lo! Ambrose Philips is preferred for Wit!
See under Ripley rise a new Whitehall,
While Jones' and Boyle's united Labours fall:[47]

[42] He translated the Italian Opera of *Polifemo.* [P.]
[43] Names of miserable Farces, which it was the custom to act at the end
of the best Tragedies, to spoil the digestion of the audience. [P.]
[44] In Tibbald's farce of *Proserpine,* a cornfield was set on fire: whereupon
the other playhouse had a barn burnt down for the recreation of the
spectators. They also rivalled each other in showing the burnings of hell-
fire, in *Dr. Faustus.* [P.]
[45] It is reported of Æschylus, that when his tragedy of the *Furies* was
acted, the audience were so terrified that the children fell into fits. [P.]
[46] Cf. IV, 110.
[47] At the time when this poem was written, the banqueting house at
Whitehall, the church and piazza of Covent Garden, and the palace and
chapel of Somerset House, the works of the famous Inigo Jones, had been

While Wren with sorrow to the grave descends,
Gay dies unpensioned with a hundred friends;[48]   330
Hibernian Politics, O Swift! thy fate;
And Pope's, ten years to comment and translate.
    "Proceed, great days! till Learning fly the shore,
Till Birch shall blush with noble blood no more,
Till Thames see Eton's sons for ever play,   335
Till Westminster's whole year be holiday,
Till Isis' Elders reel, their pupils' sport,
And Alma Mater lie dissolved in Port!"
    'Enough! enough!' the raptured Monarch cries;
And through the Ivory Gate the Vision flies.   340

Book the Fourth

ARGUMENT

The poet being, in this Book, to declare the *Completion* of the *Prophecies* mentioned at the end of the former, makes a new *Invocation;* as the greater Poets are wont, when some high and worthy matter is to be sung. He shows the Goddess coming in her Majesty, to destroy *Order* and *Science,* and to substitute the *Kingdom of the Dull* upon earth. How she leads captive the *Sciences,* and silenceth the *Muses,* and *what* they be who succeed in their stead. All her Children, by a wonderful attraction, are drawn about her; and bear along with them divers others, who promote her Empire by connivance, weak resistance, or discouragement of Arts; such as Half-wits, tasteless Admirers, vain Pretenders, the Flatterers of

for many years so neglected, as to be in danger of ruin. The portico of Covent Garden church had been just then restored and beautified at the expense of the Earl of Burlington; who, at the same time, by his publication of the designs of that great Master and Palladio, as well as by many noble buildings of his own, revived the true taste of Architecture in this kingdom. [P.]

[48] Mr. Gay's fable of the *Hare and many Friends.* This gentleman was early in the friendship of our author, which continued to his death. He wrote several works of humour with great success, the *Shepherd's Week,* *Trivia,* the *What-d'ye-call-it, Fables,* and, lastly, the celebrated *Beggar's Opera;* a piece of satire which hit all tastes and degrees of men, from those of the highest quality to the very rabble. [P.]

Dunces, or the Patrons of them. All these crowd round her; one of them offering to approach her is driven back by a Rival, but she commends and encourages both. The first who speak in form are the *Geniuses* of the *Schools,* who assure her of their care to advance her Cause, by confining Youth to *Words,* and keeping them out of the way of real Knowledge. Their Address, and her gracious Answer; with her Charge to them and the Universities. The *Universities* appear by their proper Deputies, and assure her that the same method is observed in the progress of *Education.* The speech of *Aristarchus* on this subject. They are driven off by a band of young Gentlemen returned from *Travel* with their *Tutors;* one of whom delivers to the Goddess, in a polite oration, an account of the whole Conduct and Fruits of their *Travels:* presenting to her at the same time a young Nobleman perfectly accomplished. She receives him graciously, and endues him with the happy quality of *Want of Shame.* She sees loitering about her a number of *Indolent Persons* abandoning all business and duty, and dying with laziness: To these approaches the Antiquary *Annius,* entreating her to make them *Virtuosos,* and assign them over to him: But *Mummius,* another Antiquary, complaining of his fraudulent proceeding, she finds a method to reconcile their difference. Then enter a Troop of people fantastically adorned, offering her strange and exotic presents: Amongst them, one stands forth and demands justice on another, who had deprived him of one of the greatest Curiosities in nature: but he justifies himself so well, that the Goddess gives them both her approbation. She recommends to them to find proper employment for the *Indolents* before-mentioned, in the study of *Butterflies, Shells, Birds' nests, Moss, etc.,* but with particular caution, not to proceed beyond *Trifles,* to any useful or extensive views of Nature, or of the Author of Nature. Against the last of these apprehensions, she is secured by a hearty address from the *Minute Philosophers* and *Freethinkers,* one of whom speaks in the name of the rest. The Youth, thus instructed and principled, are delivered to her in a body, by the hands of *Silenus,* and then admitted to taste the cup of the *Magus,* her High Priest, which causes a total oblivion of all Obligations, divine, civil, moral, or rational. To these her Adepts she sends *Priests, Attendants,* and *Comforters,* of various kinds; confers on them *Orders* and *Degrees;* and then dismissing them with a speech, confirming to each his *Privileges,* and telling what she expects from each, concludes with a *Yawn* of extraordinary virtue: The Progress and Effects whereof on all Orders of men, and the Consummation of all, in the restoration of *Night* and *Chaos,* conclude the Poem.

YET, yet a moment, one dim Ray of light
Indulge, dread Chaos, and eternal Night!

Of darkness visible[1] so much be lent,
As half to show, half veil, the deep Intent.
Ye Powers! whose Mysteries restored I sing,   5
To whom Time bears me on his rapid wing,
Suspend a while your Force inertly strong,[2]
Then take at once the Poet and the Song.

    Now flamed the Dog Star's unpropitious ray,
Smote every Brain, and withered every Bay;   10
Sick was the Sun, the Owl forsook his bower,
The moon-struck Prophet felt the madding hour:
Then rose the Seed of Chaos, and of Night,
To blot out Order, and extinguish Light,
Of dull and venal a new World to mold,[3]   15
And bring Saturnian days of Lead and Gold.

    She mounts the Throne: her head a Cloud concealed,
In broad Effulgence all below revealed;
('Tis thus aspiring Dulness ever shines)
Soft on her lap her Laureate son reclines.   20

    Beneath for footstool, *Science* groans in Chains,
And *Wit* dreads Exile, Penalties, and Pains.
There foamed rebellious *Logic,* gagged and bound,
There, stripped, fair *Rhetoric* languished on the ground;
His blunted Arms by *Sophistry* are borne,   25
And shameless *Billingsgate* her Robes adorn.
Morality, by her false Guardians drawn,
Chicane in Furs, and *Casuistry* in Lawn,
Gasps, as they straiten at each end the cord,
And dies, when Dulness gives her Page[4] the word.   30

---

[1] Cf. Milton, *Paradise Lost,* Bk. I, l. 63; Bk. III, ll. 1 ff.; and Bk. VII, ll. 1 ff.

[2] Alluding to the *Vis inertiæ of Matter,* which, though it really be no Power, is yet the Foundation of all the Qualities and Attributes of that sluggish Substance.   P. W.

[3] In allusion to the Epicurean opinion, that from the Dissolution of the natural World into Night and Chaos a new one should arise; this the Poet alluding to, in the Production of a new moral World, makes it partake of its original Principles.   P. W.

[4] There was a Judge of this name, always ready to hang any man that came before him, of which he was suffered to give a hundred miserable examples during a long life, even to his dotage.   P. W.

! —Mad *Máthesis* alone was unconfined,
   Too mad for mere material chains to bind,
   Now to pure Space lifts her ecstatic stare,
   Now running round the Circle finds it square.
   But held in tenfold bonds the *Muses* lie,   35
   Watched both by Envy's and by Fattery's eye:[5]
   There to her heart sad Tragedy addrest
   The dagger wont to pierce the Tyrant's breast;
   But sober History restrained her rage,
   And promised Vengeance on a barbarous age.   40
   There sunk Thalia, nerveless, cold, and dead,
   Had not her Sister Satire held her head:
   Nor couldst thou, CHESTERFIELD![6] a tear refuse,
   Thou weptst, and with thee wept each gentle Muse.
      When lo! a Harlot form soft sliding by,[7]   45
   With mincing step, small voice, and languid eye:
   Foreign her air, her robe's discordant pride
   In patchwork fluttering, and her head aside:
   By singing Peers upheld on either hand,
   She tripped and laughed, too pretty much to stand;   50
   Cast on the prostrate Nine a scornful look,
   Then thus in quaint Recitativo spoke.
      "O *Cara! Cara!* silence all that train:
   Joy to great Chaos! let Division reign:[8]

[5] One of the misfortunes falling on Authors, from the *Act* for subjecting *Plays* to the power of a *Licenser,* being the false representations to which they were exposed, from such as either gratified their Envy to Merit, or made their Court to Greatness, by perverting general Reflections against Vice into Libels on particular Persons. P. W.

[6] This Noble Person in the year 1737, when the Act aforesaid was brought into the House of Lords, opposed it in an excellent speech . . . . BENTLEY. P. W.

[7] The Attitude given to this Phantom represents the nature and genius of the *Italian* Opera; its affected airs, its effeminate sounds, and the practice of patching up these Operas with favourite Songs, incoherently put together. These things were supported by the subscriptions of the Nobility. This circumstance that OPERA should prepare for the opening of the grand Sessions was prophesied of in Bk. III, l. 304. P. W.

[8] Alluding to the false taste of playing tricks in Music with numberless divisions, to the neglect of that harmony which conforms to the Sense, and applies to the Passions. . . . P. W.

Chromatic tortures soon shall drive them hence,) 55
Break all their nerves, and fritter all their sense;
One Trill shall harmonize joy, grief, and rage,
Wake the dull Church, and lull the ranting Stage;
To the same notes thy sons shall hum, or snore,
And all thy yawning daughters cry, *encore*. 60
Another Phœbus, thy own Phœbus, reigns,
Joys in my jigs, and dances in my chains.
But soon, ah soon, Rebellion will commence,
If Music meanly borrows aid from Sense.
Strong in new Arms, lo! Giant HANDEL stands,[9] 65
Like bold Briareus, with a hundred hands;
To stir, to rouse, to shake the Soul he comes,
And Jove's own Thunders follow Mars's Drums.
Arrest him, Empress; or you sleep no more—"
She heard, and drove him to the' Hibernian shore. 70

And now had Fame's posterior Trumpet blown,
And all the Nations summoned to the Throne.
The young, the old, who feel her inward sway,
One instinct seizes, and transports away.
None need a guide, by sure attraction led, 75
And strong impulsive gravity of Head:
None want a place, for all their Centre found,
Hung to the Goddess, and cohered around.
Not closer, orb in orb, conglobed are seen
The buzzing Bees about their dusky Queen. 80

The gathering number, as it moves along,
Involves a vast involuntary throng,
Who gently drawn, and struggling less and less,
Roll in her Vortex, and her power confess. 85
Not those alone who passive own her laws,
But who, weak rebels, more advance her cause.
Whate'er of dunce in College or in Town
Sneers at another, in toupee or gown;

[9] Mr. *Handel* had introduced a great number of Hands, and more variety
of Instruments into the Orchestra, and employed even Drums and Cannon
to make a fuller Chorus; which proved so much too manly for the fine
Gentlemen of his age, that he was obliged to remove his Music into Ire-
land. P. W.

Whate'er of mongrel no one class admits,
A wit with dunces, and a dunce with wits.   90
    Nor absent they, no members of her state,
Who pay her homage in her sons, the Great;
Who, false to Phœbus, bow the knee to Baal;
Or, impious, preach his Word without a call.
Patrons, who sneak from living worth to dead,   95
Withhold the pension, and set up the head;
Or vest dull Flattery in the sacred Gown;
Or give from fool to fool the Laurel crown.
And (last and worst) with all the cant of wit,
Without the soul, the Muse's Hypcrite.   100
    There marched the bard and blockhead, side by side,
Who rhymed for hire, and patronized for pride.
Narcissus,[10] praised with all a Parson's power,
Looked a white lily sunk beneath a shower.
There moved Montalto[11] with superior air;   105
His stretched-out arm displayed a Volume fair;
Courtiers and Patriots in two ranks divide,
Through both he passed, and bowed from side to side:
But as in graceful act, with awful eye
Composed he stood, bold Benson[12] thrust him by: 110
On two unequal crutches propped he came,
Milton's on this, on that one Johnston's name.
The decent Knight retired with sober rage,
Withdrew his hand, and closed the pompous page.
But (happy for him as the times went then)   115
Appeared Apollo's Mayor and Aldermen,

---

[10] Lord Hervey, who had a very white face (Cf. *Epistle to Arbuthnot*, l. 306) and was epileptic, and to whom Dr. Conyers Middleton dedicated, with fulsome praise, his *Life of Cicero*, 1741.

[11] An eminent person [Sir Thomas Hanmer], who was about to publish a very pompous Edition of a great Author [Shakespeare], *at his own expense*. P. W.

[12] This man endeavoured to raise himself to Fame by erecting monuments, striking coins, setting up heads, and procuring translations, of *Milton;* and afterwards by as great passion for *Arthur Johnston,* a *Scotch* physician's Version of the Psalms, of which he printed many fine Editions. See more of him, Bk. III, l. 325. P. W.

On whom three hundred gold-capped youths await,
To lug the ponderous volume off in state.
     When Dulness, smiling—"Thus revive the Wits!
But murder first, and mince them all to bits;   120
As erst Medea (cruel, so to save!)
A new Edition of old Æson gave;
Let standard Authors, thus, like trophies born,
Appear more glorious as more hacked and torn.
And you, my Critics! in the chequered shade,   125
Admire new light through holes yourselves have made.

    "Leave not a foot of verse, a foot of stone,
A Page, a Grave, that they can call their own;
But spread, my sons, your glory thin or thick,
On passive paper, or on solid brick.   130
So by each Bard an Alderman shall sit,[13]
A heavy Lord shall hang at every Wit,
And while on Fame's triumphal Car they ride,
Some Slave of mine be pinioned to their side."

     Now crowds on crowds around the Goddess press,   135
Each eager to present their first Address.
Dunce scorning Dunce beholds the next advance,
But Fop shows Fop superior complaisance,
When lo! a Spectre rose, whose index hand
Held forth the Virtue of the dreadful wand;   140
His beavered brow a birchen garland wears,
Dropping with Infant's blood, and Mother's tears.
O'er every vein a shuddering horror runs;
Eton and Winton shake through all their Sons.
All Flesh is humbled, Westminister's bold race   145
Shrink, and confess the Genius of the place:
The pale Boy Senator yet tingling stands,
And holds his breeches close with both his hands.
    Then thus. "Since Man from beast by Words is known,
Words are Man's province, Words we teach alone.   150

---

[13] Alluding to the monument erected for Butler by Alderman Barber.
[W.]

When Reason doubtful, like the Samian letter,[14]
Points him two ways, the narrower is the better.
Placed at the door of Learning, youth to guide,
We never suffer it to stand too wide.
To ask, to guess, to know, as they commence,   155
As Fancy opens the quick springs of Sense,
We ply the Memory, we load the brain,
Bind rebel Wit, and double chain on chain;
Confine the thought, to exercise the breath;
And keep them in the pale of Words till death.   160
Whate'er the talents, or howe'er designed,
We hang one jingling padlock on the mind:
A Poet the first day he dips his quill;
And what the last? A very Poet still.
Pity! the charm works only in our wall,   165
Lost, lost too soon in yonder House or Hall.[15]
There truant WYNDHAM every Muse gave o'er,
There TALBOT sunk, and was a Wit no more!
How sweet an Ovid, MURRAY was our boast!
How many Martials were in PULTENEY lost!   170
Else sure some Bard, to our eternal praise,
In twice ten thousand rhyming nights and days,
Had reached the Work, the All that mortal can;
And South beheld that Masterpiece of Man."[16]
          "Oh" (cried the Goddess) "for some pedant Reign! 175
Some gentle JAMES,[17] to bless the land again;

[14] The letter Y, used by Pythagoras as an emblem of the different roads of Virtue and Vice.

          Et tibi quæ Samios diduxit litera ramos.
Persius [*Satire* iii. 56]. P. W.

[15] Westminster Hall and the House of Commons. [P.]

[16] Viz. an *Epigram*. The famous Dr. *South* declared a perfect Epigram to be as difficult a performance as an Epic Poem. And the Critics say, "an Epic Poem is the greatest work human nature is capable of." P. W.

[17] Wilson tells us that this King, *James* the First, took upon himself to teach the Latin tongue to Car, Earl of Somerset; and that Gondomar, the Spanish ambassador, would speak false Latin to him, on purpose to give him the pleasure of correcting it, whereby he wrought himself into his good graces.

          This great Prince was the first who assumed the title of *Sacred Majesty*. P. W.

To stick the Doctor's Chair into the Throne,
Give law to Words, or war with Words alone,
Senates and Courts with Greek and Latin rule
And turn the Council to a Grammar School!   180
For sure, if Dulness sees a grateful Day,
'Tis in the shade of Arbitrary Sway.
O! if my sons may learn one earthly thing,
Teach but that one, sufficient for a King;
That which my Priests, and mine alone, maintain,   185
Which as it dies, or lives, we fall, or reign:
May you, may Cam and Isis, preach it long!
'The RIGHT DIVINE of Kings to govern wrong.'"
        Prompt at the call, around the Goddess roll
Broad hats, and hoods, and caps, a sable shoal: 190
Thick and more thick the black blockade extends,
A hundred head of Aristotle's[18] friends.
Nor wert thou, Isis![19] wanting to the day,
[Though Christ Church long kept prudishly away.][19a]
Each staunch Polemic, stubborn as a rock,   195
Each fierce Logician, still expelling Locke,[20]
Came whip and spur, and dashed through thin and thick
On German Crousaz, and Dutch Burgersdyck.
As many quit the streams[21] that murmuring fall
To lull the sons of Margaret and Clare Hall,   200
Where Bentley late tempestuous wont to sport
In troubled waters, but now sleeps in Port.[22]

[18] This philosopher, in his *Politics,* hath laid it down as a principle, that some Men were, by nature, made to serve, and others to command.   [W.]
[19] Oxford University.
[19a] This line is doubtless spurious and foisted in by the impertinence of the Editor; and accordingly we have put it between Hooks. For I affirm this College came as early as any other, by its *proper Deputies;* nor did any College pay homage to Dulness in its *whole body.* BENTLEY. [P. W.]
[20] In the year 1703 there was a meeting of the heads of the University of Oxford to censure Mr. Locke's *Essay on Human Understanding,* and to forbid the reading it. See his Letters in the last Edition. P. W.
[21] The River Cam, running by the walls of these Colleges, which are particularly famous for their skill in Disputation. P. W.
[22] Viz. "Now retired into harbour, after the tempests that had long agita-

Before them marched that awful Aristarch;
Ploughed was his front with many a deep Remark:
His Hat, which never vailed to human pride,   205
Walker[23] with reverence took, and laid aside.
Low bowed the rest: He, kingly, did but nod;
So upright Quakers please both Man and God.
"Mistress! dismiss that rabble from your throne:
Avaunt——is Aristarchus[24] yet unknown?   210
Thy mighty Scholiast, whose unwearied pains
Made Horace dull, and humbled Milton's strains.
Turn what they will to Verse, their toil is vain,
Critics like me shall make it Prose again.
Roman and Greek Grammarians! know your Better: 215
Author of something yet more great than Letter;[25]
While towering o'er your Alphabet, like Saul,
Stands our Digamma,[26] and o'ertops them all.
'Tis true, on Words is still our whole debate,
Disputes of *Me* or *Te*,[27] of *aut* or *at*,   220
To sound or sink in *cano,* O or A,
Or give up Cicero to C or K.[28]

ted his society." So *Scriblerus*. But the learned *Scipio Maffei* understands
it of a certain Wine called *Port,* from *Oporto,* a city of Portugal, of which
this Professor invited him to drink abundantly. Scip. Maff. *De Com-
potationibus Academicis.* P. W.

[23] Richard Walker was Vice-Master of Trinity College, Cambridge. Bent-
ley was Master. Cf. IV, 273.

[24] A famous Commentator, and Corrector of Homer, whose name has
been frequently used to signify a complete Critic. Scriblerus. P. W.

[25] Alluding to those Grammarians, such as Palamedes and Simonides, who
invented *single letters.* But Aristarchus, who had found out a *double* one,
was therefore worthy of double honour. Scriblerus. W.

[26] Alludes to the boasted restoration of the Æolic Digamma, in his long
projected Edition of Homer. P. W.

[27] It was a serious dispute, about which the learned were much divided,
and some treatises written: Had it been about *Meum* or *Tuum,* it could
not be more contested, than whether at the end of the first Ode of Horace,
to read, Me *doctarum hederæ præmia frontium,* or Te *doctarum hederæ.*
Scriblerus. W.

[28] Grammatical disputes about the manner of pronouncing Cicero's name
in Greek. W.

Let Freind[29] affect to speak as Terence spoke,
And Alsop[29] never but like Horace joke:
For me, what Virgil, Pliny may deny,   225
{ Manilius or Solinus shall supply:
For Attic Phrase in Plato let them seek,
I poach in Suidas[30] for unlicensed Greek.
In ancient Sense if any needs will deal,
Be sure I give them Fragments, not a Meal;   230
What Gellius[30] or Stobæus[30] hashed before,
Or chewed by blind old Scholiasts o'er and o'er.
The critic Eye, that microscope of Wit,
Sees hairs and pores, examines bit by bit:
How parts relate to parts, or they to whole,   235
The body's harmony, the beaming soul,
Are things which Kuster, Burman, Wasse shall see,
When Man's whole frame is obvious to a *Flea*.
    "Ah, think not, Mistress! more true Dulness lies
In Folly's Cap, than Wisdom's grave disguise.   240
Like buoys, that never sink into the flood,
On Learning's surface we but lie and nod.
Thine is the genuine head of many a house,
And much Divinity without a Νοῦς.
Nor could a Barrow[31] work on every block,   245
Nor has one Atterbury[31] spoiled the flock.
See! still thy own, the heavy Canon[32] roll,

[29] Dr. Robert Freind, master of Westminster School, and canon of Christ Church—Dr. Anthony Alsop, a happy imitator of the Horatian style. P. W.

[30] The first a Dictionary writer, a collector of impertinent facts and barbarous words; the second a minute Critic; the third an author, who gave his Commonplace book to the public, where we happen to find much Mincemeat of old books. P. W.

[31] Isaac Barrow, Master of Trinity, Francis Atterbury, Dean of Christ Church, both great Geniuses and eloquent Preachers; one more conversant in the sublime Geometry, the other in classical Learning; but who equally made it their care to advance the polite Arts in their several Societies. P. W.

[32] Canon here, if spoken of *Artillery,* is the plural number; if of the *Canons of the House,* in the singular, and meant only of *one;* in which case I suspect the *Pole* to be a false reading, and that it should be the

And Metaphysic smokes involve the Pole.
For thee we dim the eyes, and stuff the head
With all such reading as was never read: 250
For thee explain a thing till all men doubt it,
And write about it, Goddess, and about it:
So spins the silkworm small its slender store,
And labours till it clouds itself all o'er.

    "What though we let some better sort of fool   255
Thrid every science, run through every school?
Never by tumbler through the hoops was shown
Such skill in passing all, and touching none.
He may indeed (if sober all this time)
Plague with Dispute, or persecute with Rhyme.   260
We only furnish what he cannot use,
Or wed to what he must divorce, a Muse:
Full in the midst of Euclid dip at once,
And petrify a Genius to a Dunce:
Or set on Metaphysic ground to prance,   265
Show all his paces, not a step advance.
With the same CEMENT, ever sure to bind,
We bring to one dead level every mind.
Then take him to develop, if you can,
And hew the Block off,[33] and get out the Man.   270
But wherefore waste I words? I see advance
Whore, Pupil, and laced Governor from France.
Walker! our hat"————nor more he deigned to say,
But, stern as Ajax' spectre, strode away.[34]

    In flowed at once a gay embroidered race,   275
And tittering pushed the Pedants off the place:

Poll, or Head of that Cannon. It may be objected, that this is a mere *Parono-masia,* or *Pun.* But what of that? Is any figure of *Speech* more apposite to our gentle Goddess, or more frequently use by her and her Children, especially of the University?—SCRIBLERUS.   P.   W.

[33] A notion of Aristotle, that there was originally in every block of marble a Statue, which would appear on the removal of the superfluous parts. P. W.

[34] See Homer *Odyssey* xi, where the Ghost of Ajax turns sullenly from Ulysses . . . who had succeeded against him in the dispute for the arms of Achilles. SCRIBLERUS.   W.

Some would have spoken, but the voice was drowned
By the French horn, or by the opening hound.
The first came forwards, with as easy mien,
As if he saw St. James's and the Queen. 280
When thus th' attendant Orator begun,
"Receive, great Empress! thy accomplished Son:
Thine from the birth, and sacred from the rod,
A dauntless infant! never scared with God.
The Sire saw, one by one, his Virtues wake: 285
The Mother begged the blessing of a Rake.
Thou gav'st that Ripeness, which so soon began,
And ceased so soon, he ne'er was Boy, nor Man.
Through School and College, thy kind cloud o'ercast,
Safe and unseen the young Æneas past:[35] 290
Thence bursting glorious, all at once let down,
Stunned with his giddy Larum half the town.
Intrepid then, o'er seas and lands he flew:
Europe he saw, and Europe saw him too.
There all thy gifts and graces we display, 295
Thou, only thou, directing all our way!
To where the Seine, obsequious as she runs,
Pours at great Bourbon's feet her silken sons;
Or Tiber, now no longer Roman, rolls,
Vain of Italian Arts, Italian Souls: 300
To happy Convents, bosomed deep in vines,
Where slumber Abbots, purple as their wines:
To Isles of fragrance, lily-silvered vales,
Diffusing languor in the panting gales:
To lands of singing, or of dancing slaves, 305
Love-whispering woods, and lute-resounding waves.
But chief her shrine where naked Venus keeps,
And Cupids ride the Lion of the Deeps;[36]
Where, eased of Fleets, the Adriatic main
Wafts the smooth Eunuch and enamoured swain. 310

[35] Cf. Virgil *Aenied* i. 411–417.
[36] The winged Lion, the Arms of Venice. This Republic heretofore the most considerable in Europe, for her Naval Force and the extent of her Commerce; now illustrious for her *Carnivals*. P. W.

Led by my hand, he sauntered Europe round,
And gathered every Vice on Christian ground;
Saw every Court, heard every King declare
His royal Sense, of Operas or the Fair;
The Stews and Palace equally explored,   315
Intrigued with glory, and with spirit whored;
Tried all *hors d'œuvres,* all *liqueurs* defined,
Judicious drank, and greatly daring dined;
Dropped the dull lumber of the Latin store,
Spoiled his own language, and acquired no more;   320
All Classic learning lost on Classic ground;
And last turned *Air,* the Echo of a Sound![37]
See now, half-cured, and perfectly well-bred,
With nothing but a Solo in his head;
As much Estate, and Principle, and Wit,   325
As Jansen, Fleetwood, Cibber[38] shall think fit;
Stolen from a Duel, followed by a Nun,
And, if a Borough choose him not, undone;
See, to my country happy I restore
This glorious Youth, and add one Venus more.   330
Her too receive (for her my soul adores)
So may the sons of sons of sons of whores,
Prop thine, O Empress! like each neighbour Throne,
And make a long Posterity thy own."
Pleased, she accepts the Hero, and the Dame   335
Wraps in her Veil, and frees from sense of Shame.
     Then looked, and saw a lazy, lolling sort,
Unseen at Church, at Senate, or at Court,
Of ever-listless Loiterers, that attend
No Cause, no Trust, no Duty, and no Friend.   340

[37] Yet less a Body than Echo itself: for Echo reflects *Sense* or *Words* at least, this Gentleman only *Airs* and *Tunes.* SCRIBLERUS. W.
[38] Three very eminent persons, all Managers of *Plays;* who, though not Governors by profession, had, each in his way, concerned themselves in the Education of Youth: and regulated their Wits, their Morals, or their Finances, at that period of their age which is the most important, their entrance into the polite world. Of the last of these, and his Talents for this end, see Bk. I, ll. 199 ff. P. W.

Thee too, my Paridel![39] she marked thee there,
Stretched on the rack of a too easy chair,
And heard thy everlasting yawn confess
The Pains and Penalties of Idleness.
She pitied! but her Pity only shed   345
Benigner influence on thy nodding head.

　　But Annius,[40] crafty Seer, with ebon wand,
And well-dissembled emerald on his hand,
False as his Gems, and cankered as his Coins,
Came, crammed with capon, from where Pollio dines. 350
Soft, as the wily Fox is seen to creep,
Where bask on sunny banks the simple sheep,
Walk round and round, now prying here, now there,
So he; but pious, whispered first his prayer.

　　"Grant gracious Goddess! grant me still to cheat, 355
O may thy cloud still cover the deceit!
Thy choicer mists on this assembly shed,
But pour them thickest on the noble head.
So shall each youth, assisted by our eyes,
See other Cæsars, other Homers rise;   360
Through twilight ages hunt th' Athenian fowl,[41]
Which Chalcis Gods, and mortals call an Owl,
Now see an Attys,[42] now a Cecrops[42] clear,

[39] The Poet seems to speak of this young gentleman with great affection. The name is taken from Spenser, who gives it to a *wandering Courtly Squire,* that travelled about for the same reason, for which many young Squires are now fond of travelling, and especially to *Paris.* P. W.

[40] The name taken from Annius the Monk of Viterbo, famous for many Impositions and Forgeries of ancient manuscripts and inscriptions, which he was prompted to by mere Vanity, but our Annius had a more substantial motive. P. W.

[41] The Owl stamped on the reverse on the ancient money of Athens.
　　Which *Chalcis* Gods, and mortals call an Owl,
is the verse by which Hobbes renders that of Homer [*Iliad* xiv. 291]. P. W.

[42] The first Kings of Athens, of whom it is hard to suppose any Coins are extant; but not so improbable as what follows, that there should be any of Mahomet, who forbade all Images; and the story of whose Pigeon was a monkish fable. Nevertheless one of these Anniuses made a counterfeit

Nay, Mahomet! the Pigeon at thine ear;
Be rich in ancient brass, though not in gold,   365
And keep his Lares, though his house be sold;
To headless Phœbe his fair bride postpone,
Honour a Syrian Prince above his own;
Lord of an Otho, if I vouch it true;
Blest in one Niger, till he knows of two."   370
    Mummius[43] o'erheard him; Mummius, Fool-re-
nowned,[44]
Who like his Cheops[45] stinks above the ground,
Fierce as a startled Adder, swelled, and said,
Rattling an ancient Sistrum at his head:
    "Speakst thou of Syrian Princes?[46] Traitor base!   375
Mine, Goddess! mine is all the hornèd race.
True, he had wit, to make their value rise;
From foolish Greeks to steal them, was as wise;

medal of that Impostor, now in the collection of a learned Nobleman.
P. W.

[43] This name is not merely an allusion to the Mummies he was so fond
of, but probably referred to the Roman General of that name, who burned
Corinth, and committed the curious Statues to the Captain of a ship, assur-
ing him, "that if any were lost or broken, he should procure others to be
made in their stead:" by which it should seem (whatever may be pre-
tended) that Mummius was no Virtuoso. P. W.

[44] A compound epithet in the Greek manner, *renowned by Fools,* or *re-
nowned for making Fools.* P.

[45] A King of Egypt, whose body was certainly to be known, as being
buried alone in his Pyramid, and is therefore more genuine than any of
the Cleopatras. This Royal Mummy, being stolen by a wild Arab, was
purchased by the Consul of Alexandria, and transmitted to the Museum
of Mummius; for proof of which he brings a passage in Sandy's *Travels,*
where that accurate and learned Voyager assures us that he saw the
Sepulchre empty, which agrees exactly (saith he) with the time of the
theft above-mentioned. But he omits to observe that Herodotus tells the
same thing of it in his time. P. W.

[46] The strange story following, which may be taken for a fiction of the
Poet, is justified by a true relation in Spon's Voyages. Vaillant (who wrote
the History of the Syrian Kings as it is found on medals) coming from
the Levant, where he had been collecting various Coins, and being pur-
sued by a Corsair of Sallee, swallowed down twenty gold medals. . . .
P. W.

More glorious yet, from barbarous hands to keep,
When Sallee Rovers chased him on the deep.   380
Then taught by Hermes, and divinely bold,
Down his own throat he risked the Grecian gold,
Received each Demigod,[47] with pious care,
Deep in his Entrails—I revered them there,
I bought them, shrouded in that living shrine,   385
And, at their second birth, they issue mine."

    "Witness, great Ammon![48] by whose horns I swore,"
(Replied soft Annius) "this our paunch before
Still bears them, faithful; and that thus I eat,
Is to refund the Medals with the meat.   390
To prove me, Goddess! clear of all design,
Bid me with Pollio sup, as well as dine:
There all the Learned shall at the labour stand,
And Douglas[49] lend his soft obstetric hand."

    The Goddess smiling seemed to give consent;   395
So back to Pollio, hand in hand, they went.

    Then thick as Locusts blackening all the ground,
A tribe, with weeds and shells fantastic crowned,
Each with some wondrous gift approached the Power,
A Nest, a Toad, a Fungus, or a Flower.   400
But far the foremost, two, with earnest zeal,
And aspect ardent to the Throne appeal.

    The first thus opened: "Hear thy suppliant's call,
Great Queen, and common Mother of us all!
Fair from its humble bed I reared this Flower,   405
Suckled, and cheered, with air, and sun, and shower.
Soft on the paper ruff its leaves I spread,
Bright with the gilded button tipped its head;
Then throned in glass, and named it CAROLINE:[50]

---

[47] They are called Θεοί on their Coins. P. W.
[48] Jupiter Ammon is called to witness, as the father of Alexander, to whom those Kings succeeded in the division of the Macedonian Empire, and whose *Horns* they wore on their Medals. P. W.
[49] A Physician of great Learning and no less Taste; above all curious in what related to *Horace,* of whom he collected every Edition, Translation, and Comment, to the number of several hundred volumes. P. W.
[50] It is a compliment which the Florists usually pay to Princes and great

Each maid cried, Charming! and each youth, Divine!   410
Did Nature's pencil ever blend such rays,
Such varied light in one promiscuous blaze?
Now prostrate! dead! behold that Caroline:
No maid cries, Charming! and no youth, Divine!
And lo the wretch! whose vile, whose insect lust   415
Laid this gay daughter of the Spring in dust.
Oh punish him, or to th' Elysian shades
Dismiss my soul, where no Carnation fades!"
He ceased, and wept. With innocence of mien,
Th' Accused stood forth, and thus addressed the Queen.

    "Of all th' enamelled race, whose silvery wing   421
Waves to the tepid Zephyrs of the spring,
Or swims along the fluid atmosphere,
Once brightest shined this child of Heat and Air.
I saw, and started from its vernal bower,   425
The rising game, and chased from flower to flower.
It fled, I followed; now in hope, now pain;
It stopped, I stopped; it moved, I moved again.
At last it fixed, 'twas on what plant it pleased,
And where it fixed, the beauteous bird I seized: 430
Rose or Carnation was below my care;
I meddle, Goddess! only in my sphere.
I tell the naked fact without disguise,
And, to excuse it, need but show the prize;
Whose spoils this paper offers to your eye,   435
Fair even in death! this peerless *Butterfly*."

    "My sons!" (she answered) "both have done your parts:
Live happy both, and long promote our arts!
But hear a Mother, when she recommends
To your fraternal care our sleeping friends.   440
The common Soul, of Heaven's more frugal make,
Serves but to keep fools pert, and knaves awake:

persons, to give their names to the most curious Flowers of their raising:
Some have been very jealous of vindicating this honour, but none more
than that ambitious Gardener, at Hammersmith, who caused his Favourite
to be painted on his Sign, with this inscription, *This is* My *Queen Caroline*,
P. W.

A drowsy Watchman, that just gives a knock,
And breaks our rest, to tell us what's a-clock.
Yet by some object every brain is stirred;   445
The dull may waken to a Hummingbird;
The most recluse, discreetly opened, find
Congenial matter in the Cockle kind;
The mind, in Metaphysics at a loss,
May wander in a wilderness of Moss;[51]   450
The head that turns at superlunar things,
Poised with a tail, may steer on Wilkins' wings.[52]
    "O! would the Sons of Men once think their Eyes
And Reason given them but to study *Flies!*
See Nature in some partial narrow shape,   455
And let the Author of the Whole escape:
Learn but to trifle; or, who most observe,
To wonder at their Maker, not to serve!"
    "Be that my task" (replies a gloomy Clerk,
Sworn foe to Mystery, yet divinely dark;   460
Whose pious hope aspires to see the day
When Moral Evidence shall quite decay,[53]
And damns implicit faith, and holy lies,
Prompt to impose, and fond to dogmatize:)
"Let others creep by timid steps, and slow,   465
On plain Experience lay foundations low,

[51] Of which the Naturalists count I can't tell how many hundred species. P. W.

[52] One of the first Projectors of the Royal Society, who, among many enlarged and useful notions, entertained the extravagant hope of a possibility to fly to the Moon; which has put some volatile Geniuses upon making wings for that purpose. P. W.

[53] Alluding to a ridiculous and absurd way of some Mathematicians, in calculating the gradual decay of Moral Evidence by mathematical proportions: according to which calculation, in about fifty years it will be no longer probable that Julius Cæsar was in Gaul, or died in the Senate House. See Craig's *Theologiæ Christianæ Principia Mathematica.* But as it seems evident, that facts of a thousand years old, for instance, are now as probable as they were five hundred years ago; it is plain that if in fifty more they quite disappear, it must be owing, not to their Arguments, but to the extraordinary Power of our Goddess; for whose help therefore they have reason to pray. P. W.

By common sense to common knowledge bred,
And last, to Nature's Cause through Nature led.
All-seeing in thy mists, we want no guide,
Mother of Arrogance, and Source of Pride!   470
We nobly take the high Priori Road,[54]
And reason downward, till we doubt of God:
Make Nature still encroach upon his plan;[55]
And shove him off as far as e'er we can:
Thrust some Mechanic Cause into his place;[56]   475
Or bind in Matter, or diffuse in Space.[56]
Or, at one bound o'erleaping all his laws,
Make God Man's Image, Man the final Cause,
Find Virtue local, all Relation scorn,
See all in *Self,* and but for self be born: 480
Of naught so certain as our *Reason* still,
Of naught so doubtful as of *Soul* and *Will.*
Oh hide the God still more! and make us see
Such as Lucretius drew, a God like Thee:
Wrapped up in Self, a God without a Thought,   485
Regardless of our merit or default.
Or that bright Image[57] to our fancy draw,

[54] Those who, from the effects in this Visible world, deduce the Eternal Power and Godhead of the First Cause, though they cannot attain to an adequate idea of the Deity, yet discover so much of him, as enables them to see the End of their Creation, and the Means of their Happiness: whereas they who take this high Priori Road (such as Hobbes, Spinoza, Descartes, and some better Reasoners) for one that goes right, ten lose themselves in Mists, or ramble after Visions, which deprive them of all sight of their End, and mislead them in the choice of wrong means. P. W.

[55] This relates to such as, being ashamed to assert a mere Mechanic Cause, and yet unwilling to forsake it entirely, have had recourse to a certain *Plastic Nature, Elastic Fluid, Subtile Matter, etc.* P. W.

[56] The first of these Follies is that of Descartes; the second of Hobbes; the third of some succeeding Philosophers. P. W. "Some succeeding Philosophers" include Spinoza no doubt, and perhaps Newton, who spoke of space as the sensorium of the Deity.

[57] *Bright Image* was the Title given by the later Platonists to that Vision of *Nature,* which they had formed out of their own fancy, so bright, that they called it Αὔτοπτον Ἄγαλμα, or the *Self-seen Image*—i.e., seen by its own light. SCRIBLERUS. W.

Which Theocles in raptured vision saw,
While through Poetic scenes the Genius roves,
Or wanders wild in Academic Groves;   490
That Nature our Society adores,[58]
Where Tindal dictates, and Silenus[59] snores."
    Roused at his name, up rose the bousy Sire,
And shook from out his Pipe the seeds of fire;[60]
Then snapped his box, and stroked his belly down: 495
Rosy and reverend, though without a Gown.
Bland and familiar to the throne he came,
Led up the Youth, and called the Goddess *Dame.*
Then thus. "From Priestcraft happily set free,
Lo! every finished Son returns to thee: 500
First slave to Words, then vassal to a Name,
Then dupe to Party; child and man the same;
Bounded by Nature, narrowed still by Art,
A trifling head, and a contracted heart.
Thus bred, thus taught, how many have I seen,   505
Smiling on all, and smiled on by a Queen?[61]
Marked out for Honours, honoured for their Birth,
To thee the most rebellious things on earth:
Now to thy gentle shadow all are shrunk,
All melted down, in Pension, or in Punk!   510
So K—— so B—— sneaked into the grave,
A Monarch's half, and half a Harlot's slave.
Poor W—— nipped in Folly's broadest bloom,
Who praises now? his Chaplain on his Tomb.
Then take them all, oh take them to thy breast!   515
Thy *Magus,* Goddess! shall perform the rest."
    With that, a Wizard old his *Cup* extends;[62]

[58] See the *Pantheisticon,* with its liturgy and rubrics, composed by *Toland.* W.
[59] Silenus was an Epicurean Philosopher, as appears from Virgil *Eclogue* vi, where he sings the principles of that Philosophy in his drink. P. W.
[60] The Epicurean language, *Semina rerum,* or Atoms. Virgil *Eclogue* vi [31 ff.]. *Semina ignis—semina flammæ.* P. W.
[61] I.e., This Queen or Goddess of Dulness. [W.] Perhaps also Queen Caroline, who was known to smile on freethinkers.
[62] *The Cup of Self-love,* which causes a total oblivion of the obligations

Which whoso tastes, forgets his former friends,
Sire, Ancestors, Himself. One casts his eyes
Up to a *Star,* and like Endymion dies: 520
A *Feather,* shooting from another's head,
Extracts his brain; and Principle is fled;
Lost is his God, his Country, everything;
And nothing left but Homage to a King![63]
The vulgar herd turn off to roll with Hogs,   525
To run with Horses, or to hunt with Dogs;
But, sad example! never to escape
Their Infamy, still keep the human shape.
But she, Goddess, sent to every child
Firm Impudence, or Stupefaction mild;   530
And straight succeeded, leaving shame no room,
Cibberian forehead, or Cimmerian gloom.
    Kind Self-conceit to some her glass applies,
Which no one looks in with another's eyes:
But as the Flatterer or Dependant paint,   535
Beholds himself a Patriot, Chief, or Saint.
    On others Interest her gay livery flings,
Interest that waves on Party-coloured wings:
Turned to the Sun, she casts a thousand dyes,
And, as she turns, the colours fall or rise.   540
    Others the Siren Sisters warble round,
And empty heads console with empty sound.
No more, alas! the voice of Fame they hear,
The balm of Dulness trickling in their ear.
Great C——, H——, P——, R——, K——,   545
Why all your Toils? your Sons have learned to sing.
How quick Ambition hastes to ridicule!
The Sire is made a Peer, the Son a Fool.

---

of Friendship, or Honour; and of the Service of God or our Country.
P. W.

[63] So strange as this must seem to a mere English reader, the famous
Mons. de la Bruyère declares it to be the character of every good Subject
in a Monarchy: "Where (says he) *there is no such thing as Love of our
Country,* the Interest, the Glory, and Service of the *Prince,* supply its
place." *De la République,* Chap. 10. P. W.

On some, a Priest succinct in amice white
Attends; all flesh is nothing in his sight!   550
Beeves, at his touch, at once to jelly turn,
And the huge Boar is shrunk into an Urn:
The board with specious miracles he loads,
Turns Hares to Larks, and Pigeons into Toads.[64]
Another (for in all what one can shine?)   555
Explains the *Sève* and *Verdeur*[65] of the Vine.
What cannot copious Sacrifice atone?
Thy Truffles, Perigord! thy Hams, Bayonne!
With French Libation, and Italian Strain,
Wash Bladen[66] white, and expiate Hays's[66] stain.   560
KNIGHT[66] lifts the head, for what are crowds undone,
To three essential Partridges in one?
Gone every blush, and silent all reproach,
Contending Princes mount them in their Coach.

    Next, bidding all draw near on bended knees,   565
The Queen confers her *Titles* and *Degrees*.
Her children first of more distinguished sort,
Who study Shakespeare at the Inns of Court,
Impale a Glowworm, or Vertú profess,
Shine in the dignity of F.R.S.   570
Some, deep Freemasons, join the silent race
Worthy to fill Pythagoras's place:
Some Botanists, or Florists at the least,
Or issue Members of an Annual feast.
Nor passed the meanest unregarded, one   575
Rose a Gregorian, one a Gormogon.[67]
The last, not least in honour or applause,

---

[64] The miracles of *French Cookery*. . . . *Pigeons en crapaud* were a common dish. P. W.

[65] French Terms relating to Wines, which signify their flavour and poignancy. P. W.

[66] Names of Gamesters. Bladen is a black man. ROBERT KNIGHT, Cashier of the South Sea Company, who fled from England in 1720 (afterwards pardoned in 1742).—These lived with the utmost magnificence at Paris, and kept open Tables frequented by persons of the first Quality of England, and even by Princes of the Blood of France. P. W.

[67] A sort of Lay Brothers, *Slips* from the root of the Freemasons. P. W.

Isis and Cam made Doctors of her Laws.
    Then, blessing all, "Go, Children of my care!
To Practice now from Theory repair.   580
All my commands are easy, short, and full:
My Sons! be proud, be selfish, and be dull.
Guard my Prerogative, assert my Throne:
This Nod confirms each Privilege your own.
The Cap and Switch be sacred to his Grace;   585
With Staff and Pumps the Marquis lead the Race;
From Stage to Stage the licensed Earl may run,
Paired with his Fellow Charioteer the Sun;
The learnèd Baron Butterflies design,
Or draw to silk Arachne's subtile line;[68]   590
The Judge to dance his brother Sergeant call;
The Senator at Cricket urge the Ball;
The Bishop stow (Pontific Luxury!)
An hundred Souls of Turkeys in a pie;
The sturdy Squire to Gallic masters stoop,   595
And drown his Lands and Manors in a Soupe.
Others import yet nobler arts from France,
Teach Kings to fiddle, and make Senates dance.
Perhaps more high some daring son may soar,
Proud to my list to add one Monarch more;   600
And nobly conscious, Princes are but things
Born for First Ministers, as Slaves for Kings,
Tyrant supreme! shall three Estates command,
And make one Mighty Dunciad of the Land!"
    More she had spoke, but yawned—All Nature nods:
What Mortal can resist the Yawn of Gods?[69]   606
Churches and Chapels instantly it reached;
(St. James's first, for leaden G—— preached)

[68] This is one of the most ingenious employments assigned, and there-
fore recommended only to Peers of Learning. Of weaving Stockings of
the Webs of Spiders, see the *Philosophical Transactions*. P. W.
[69] This verse is truly Homerical; as is the conclusion of the Action, where
the great Mother composes all, in the same manner as Minerva at the
period of the Odyssey. P. W.

Then catched the Schools; the Hall scarce kept awake;
The Convocation gaped, but could not speak: 610
Lost was the Nation's Sense, nor could be found,
While the long solemn Unison went round:
Wide, and more wide, it spread o'er all the realm;
Even Palinurus nodded at the Helm:
The Vapour mild o'er each Committee crept;   615
Unfinished Treaties in each Office slept;
And Chiefless Armies dozed out the Campaign;
And Navies yawned for Orders on the Main.
　　O Muse! relate (for you can tell alone,
Wits have short Memories,[70] and Dunces none),   620
Relate, who first, who last resigned to rest;
Whose Heads she partly, whose completely blest;
What Charms could Faction, what Ambition lull,
The Venal quiet, and entrance the Dull;
Till drowned was Sense, and Shame, and Right, and
　　　　Wrong—   625
O sing, and hush the Nations with thy Song!
　*　　　*　　　*　　　*　　　*　　　*　　　*　　　*

　　In vain, in vain—the all-composing Hour
Resistless falls: The Muse obeys the Power.
She comes! she comes! the sable Throne behold
Of *Night* Primeval, and of *Chaos* old!   630
Before her, *Fancy's* gilded clouds decay,
And all its varying Rainbows die away.
Wit shoots in vain its momentary fires,
The meteor drops, and in a flash expires.
As one by one, at dread Medea's strain,   635
The sickening stars fade off th' ethereal plain;
As Argus' eyes by Hermes' wand opprest,
Closed one by one to everlasting rest;
Thus at her felt approach, and secret might,

[70] This seems to be the reason why the Poets, whenever they give us a
Catalogue, constantly call for help on the Muses, who, as the Daughters of
Memory, are obliged not to forget anything. So Homer *Iliad* ii [788 ff.].
And Virgil *Æneid* vii [645–646]. Scriblerus. P. W.

Art after *Art* goes out, and all is Night.   640
See skulking *Truth* to her old cavern fled,[71]
Mountains of Casuistry heaped o'er her head!
Philosophy, that leaned on Heaven before,
Shrinks to her second cause, and is no more.
Physic of *Metaphysic* begs defence,   645
And *Metaphysic* calls for aid on *Sense!*
See *Mystery* to *Mathematics* fly!
In vain! they gaze, turn giddy, rave, and die.
Religion blushing veils her sacred fires,
And unawares *Morality* expires.   650
Nor *public* Flame, nor *private,* dares to shine;
Nor *human* Spark is left, nor Glimpse *divine!*
Lo! thy dread Empire, Chaos! is restored;
Light dies before thy uncreating word:
Thy hand, great Anarch! lets the curtain fall;   655
And universal Darkness buries All.

[71] Alluding to the saying of Democritus, That Truth lay at the bottom
of a deep well [P.], from whence he had drawn her: Though Butler says,
He first put her in, before he drew her out. W.

Rinehart Editions